THE CHIEF
C⚒LPRIT

THE CHIEF CLPRIT

Stalin's Grand Design to Start World War II

Viktor Suvorov

NAVAL INSTITUTE PRESS
Annapolis, Maryland

Naval Institute Press
291 Wood Road
Annapolis, MD 21402

Library of Congress Cataloging-in-Publication Data
Suvorov, Viktor.
  The chief culprit : Stalin's grand design to start World War II / Viktor Suvorov.
    p. cm.
  Includes bibliographical references and index.
  ISBN 978-1-59114-838-8 (alk. paper)
  1. World War, 1939–1945—Soviet Union. 2. World War, 1939–1945—Causes. 3. Stalin, Joseph, 1879–1953—Military leadership. I. Title. II. Title: Stalin's grand design to start World War II.
D742.S58S878 2008
940.53'10947—dc22
                                                                2008015592

Printed in the United States of America on acid-free paper

14 13 12 11 10 09 08   9 8 7 6 5 4 3 2
First printing

All photos are from the author's collection.

To Scarlet Alexandra

Contents

Preface

Hitler had a red flag. And Stalin had a red flag. Hitler ruled in the name of the workers' class, his party was called the workers' party. Stalin also ruled in the name of the workers' class; his power system officially bore the title of "dictatorship of the proletariat." Hitler hated democracy and struggled against it. Stalin hated democracy and struggled against it. Hitler was building socialism. And Stalin was building socialism. Under the title of socialism Hitler saw a classless society. And Stalin, under the title of socialism, saw a classless society. In the midst of the classless society built by Hitler, and in that built by Stalin, flourished slavery in the truest sense of the word.

Hitler held his road to socialism as the only correct one, and viewed all other paths as distortions. Stalin also held his road to socialism uniquely correct, and saw all other paths as diversions from the principal line. Hitler mercilessly destroyed all his party comrades, such as Roehm and his followers, when they strayed from the correct path. Stalin also mercilessly destroyed all who strayed from the correct path. Hitler had a Four Year Plan. Stalin had Five Year Plans.

In Hitler's Germany, one party was in power, the others in jail. And in Stalin's Soviet Union, one party was in power, the others in jail. Hitler's party stood above the nation, and its leaders ruled the country. Stalin's party also stood above the nation, and its leaders ruled the country.

The most important holidays in Stalin's empire were May 1 and November 7–8. In Hitler's empire, they were May 1 and November 8–9.

Hitler had the *Hitler Jugend*, young Hitlerists. Stalin had the *Comsomol*, young Stalinists.

Stalin's official title was Fuehrer; Hitler's was leader. Pardon, Stalin's was leader and Hitler's Fuehrer. In translation, they are identical. Stalin declared that Russians were responsible for all outstanding scientific and technological advances: the hot-air balloon, locomotive, airplane, radio, etc. Hitler claimed the same for Germans.

Hitler loved grandiose structures. He laid in Berlin the foundation to the largest building in the world—the House of Assembly. Its dome spanned 250 meters in diameter, by some counts. The main hall was to have the capacity to hold 150,000 people. Stalin also loved grandiose structures. He laid in Moscow the foundation for the largest building in the world—the Palace of Soviets. Stalin's main hall was smaller than Hitler's, but the entire edifice was much higher. The 400-meter-high building resembled a pedestal for the 100-meter-tall statue of Lenin.

Hitler planned to tear down Berlin, and in its place to raise a new city of monstrous structures. Stalin planned to tear down Moscow, and in its place to raise a new city of monstrous structures.

In Germany, Hitler was an outsider. He was born in Austria, and did not have German citizenship almost until the moment he came into power. For Russia, Stalin was an outsider. He was neither Russian, nor even a Slav. He was born in Georgia.

Sometimes, on rare occasions, Stalin invited foreign visitors to his Kremlin apartment. They were shocked by the modesty of the interiors: a plain table, a closet, an iron-post bed, a soldier's bedcover. Hitler ordered the press to run a photograph of his living quarters. The world was shocked by his modesty: a plain table, a closet, an iron-post bed, a soldier's bedcover. Nevertheless, in secluded areas in the midst of magical natural surroundings, Stalin created quite cozy and well-protected residential fortresses, which did not at all resemble an ascetic's cell. Hitler also built impenetrable residence-fortresses in secluded areas in the midst of natural wonders, without frugality in his use of granite and marble.

Hitler's mother dreamed that her son would become a priest. Stalin's mother had the same dream for her son.

Hitler's beloved, Geli Raubal, was more than twenty years his junior. Stalin's beloved, Nadezhda Alliluieva, was more than twenty years his junior. Geli Raubal committed suicide, as did Nadezhda Alliluieva. The circumstances of Raubal's death remain unclear. A theory proposes that Hitler murdered her. The circumstances of Alliluieva's death are mysterious. A theory proposes that Stalin murdered her. The means of suicide (murder) for Geli Raubal was a handgun. It was Hitler's personal handgun. The means of suicide (murder) for Nadezhda Alliluieva was a handgun. It was Stalin's personal handgun.

Hitler said one thing, and did another. So did Stalin. Hitler began his rule under the slogan "Germany Wants Peace." He proceeded to occupy half of Europe. Stalin fought for the "collective security of Europe," without holding back any strength or means. Afterwards, he proceeded to occupy half of Europe.

Hitler had the Gestapo. Stalin had the *Narodnyi Kommissariat Vnutrennikh Del* (NKVD)—the People's Commissariat of Internal Affairs. Hitler had Auschwitz, Buchenwald, and Dachau. Stalin had the *Glavnoe Upravlenie Lagerei* (GULAG)—the Main Prison Camp Directorate.[1]

Hitler had Babyi Yar. Stalin had Katyn. Hitler massacred people by the millions. Stalin also killed people by the millions.

Hitler did not decorate himself with medals of honor, and neither did Stalin. Hitler wore a semi-military uniform without any signs of distinction, and Stalin wore a semi-military uniform without signs of distinction. Some might argue that later on Stalin acquired a taste for military titles, marshal batons, and gilded epaulettes. This is true, but Stalin only named himself Marshal in 1943 after the Stalingrad victory, when it finally became clear that Hitler would lose the war. At the time of receiving this title, Stalin was sixty-three years old. He wore the Marshal's uniform for the first time for the Tehran Conference, while meeting with Churchill and Roosevelt. We cannot in this respect compare Hitler and Stalin simply because Hitler did not live to a comparable age, to see comparable meetings, or comparable victories.

In all other respects, the comparison fits. Stalin did not wear a beard, but had a famous mustache. Hitler had no beard, but a famous mustache. Where does the difference lie? The difference lies in the shapes of the mustaches.

The difference also lies in the fact that Hitler's actions were seen by the world as the greatest of crimes, while Stalin's actions were considered by the world as a struggle for peace and progress.

The world hated Hitler, and commiserated with Stalin. Hitler conquered half of Europe, and the rest of the world declared war against him. Stalin conquered half of Europe, and the world sent him greetings. To ensure that Hitler could not hold on to the conquered European countries, the West sank German ships, bombed German cities, and then landed a massive and powerful army on the European continent. To enable Stalin to conquer and hold on to the other half of Europe, the West gave Stalin hundreds of warships, thousands of war planes and tanks, hundreds of thousands of the world's best war vehicles, and millions of tons of its best fuel, ammunition, and supplies.

This book is about Stalin's aggressive endeavors, about his role in plotting World War II—the bloodiest slaughter in human history. Perhaps one might become suspicious: in exposing Stalin, am I attempting to exonerate Hitler? No, I am not. For me, Hitler remains a heinous criminal. But if Hitler was a criminal it does not at all follow that Stalin was his innocent victim, as Communist propaganda portrayed him before the world.

Acknowledgments

I have planned to write this book since I discovered that the Soviet version of the history of World War II was a lie and concealed the USSR's responsibility for planning the start of the war. The primary reason for my decision to defect to the West in 1978 was to make my discoveries available to the Russian people and the world public. Since then I have been able to publish several books on military topics. All of them received wide acclaim in the West, but that was not the case with the book of my lifework—*The Icebreaker*, published in English in Great Britain in 1990. It quickly sold out, but for reasons never explained to me, the publisher refused to print further editions.

It quickly became apparent that the Western academic community was as reluctant as the Communist propaganda apparatus to accept my new interpretation of the cause of World War II. Instead of confronting my arguments the way the Soviets did, my Western opponents chose a different kind of confrontation—silence.

Meanwhile, communism and the Soviet Union collapsed. In 1990 *The Icebreaker* was published in Russian in Moscow and produced a firestorm. The first edition of *The Icebreaker* totaled 320,000 copies; the second,1,000,000. Hundreds of thousands of copies of my other books on the same topic, including *The Day M*, *The Last Republic*, *The Purification*, and *The Suicide*, quickly sold out. Two television documentaries based on *The Icebreaker* were produced in Russia. Dozens of Russian historians rushed to explore the new horizons opened by my book. Some of them argued and disagreed with my interpretations of specific episodes or details; others raised new questions and suggested new theories.

A similar response to my book was aroused in former Communist coutries. In Poland I became a celebrity overnight. Baltic countries incorporated my findings into their official history and textbooks. More important was the flood of letters I began to receive from 1990 from all over the world, but mostly from the former Soviet Union. People provided me with their unique insights and sent me copies of documents in support of my theory. Many of these details, as well as evidence from newly published materials, are incorporated in *The Chief Culprit*.

However, after encountering a virtual academic boycott in the West, I gave up trying to publish my books in the West. In 1999 I received an inquiry from a man who introduced himself as Alexei Sobchenko, an American of Russian origin, about the English-language version of *The Icebreaker*. I curtly replied that there was no interest in the West for this book. Besides, I was too busy to waste time pursuing an unrealistic goal. "Well, probably, you should write another book, since *The Icebreaker* was written for Russian readers, and hardly can be understood by people who did not live in the Soviet Communist society," replied Sobchenko. "Besides, you wrote four more books after *The Icebreaker* and it would be a good opportunity to update and summarize them, and add your new discoveries."

Alexei was introduced to Jerry and Leona Schecter, who found my ideas challenging, and Leona agreed to become my literary agent for this book. Eventually they became my friends and did much more for this book than a literary agent's job requires. I would also like to thank Dr. Albert Weeks for his longtime support and efforts on my behalf.

Maria Samorodinova-Erb, who at the time was a student at the University of Pennsylvania, volunteered to translate the book into English. Russian Americans Vlad Barash, Leonid Avrashov, and Olga Cherny helped to translate additional chapters. Serghei Kharlamov—a Moscow-based historian, checked the text for factual accuracy. Yuri Felshtinsky, a historian from Boston, worked to tailor the text for Western readers. Misha Shauli, from Israel, skillfully applied his wide knowledge of World War II history to correcting, editing, and retranslating the text as it evolved. Actually, Misha's role in this book was so crucial that, unwillingly, he ended up becoming my editor for *The Chief Culprit*. Copy editor Jehanne Moharram's diligence and concern improved the final editing and proofreading. Nothing, neither the first Russian-language version of *The Icebreaker* nor this new book, would have been possible without the assistance of my devoted wife Tatiana.

I often doubted that this book would be published. It never would have been possible without the dedication of those I have mentioned and those who must remain anonymous, for their safety, who sent me new corroborating archival materials and relevant personal details. Richard Russell, director of the Naval Institute Press, has been instrumental in bringing *The Chief Culprit* to print, and to him and his dedicated colleagues I am deeply grateful. Happily, he proved me wrong in thinking its publication would never happen in the West.

Introduction

Solving puzzles is not for everyone, but for me it is a passion. I feel that I am truly blessed, for fitting pieces together is my job. It is strenuous work that mobilizes your patience and attention; but the benefits are great. You switch off the world of turmoil, you forget about your concerns, debts, and ailments. Hated faces of enemies and opponents dissolve into darkness. Your heart starts beating calmly and steadily. Your brain is cleansed of evil plots, and your soul freed of dirt and soot. No, I am not an archaeologist who, out of clay pieces, assembles an ancient Egyptian pot, and from glass fragments, a precious Roman vase. Neither am I an anthropologist, who out of tiny splinters of bone assembles the skeleton of a mammoth hunter. I am a spy. An intelligence operative of a rare breed, an analyst from the Main Intelligence Directorate of the General Staff of the Soviet Armed Forces (GRU).[1]

For some, intelligence work is violent: kidnapping and killing, or breaking into safes to steal secrets. For others, like myself, it is an office stuffed with books and thick folders piled high to the ceiling with papers that can never be straightened out. It is a green table lamp and a pot of coffee. The puzzles I had to work on were so huge they encompassed more than a hundred thousand pieces. Can you imagine the challenge? Nobody, including me, knew how many puzzles there were in the pile—one, two, or three? All I knew for sure was that some pieces were missing and could never be found. Which pieces belonged to which puzzle? Which ones were complete strays? Then came the most important task—to fill in the blanks. It is essentially the same as restoring a gigantic dinosaur from a fragment of a bone, or predicting the existence of a planet in the darkness of space based on gravitational anomalies. Archaeologists or astronomers can easily be compared to the people who process intelligence information. The difference is that intelligence achievements rarely come out in the open.

You might wonder, how does one become an intelligence operative? I started early. I was eleven years old when I joined the Soviet Army. Seven years of the "Military Boarding School" was a tough school of life. Not everyone who trained there became an intelligence analyst. They taught us situation analysis. They gave us pieces of a puzzle: one, two, three pieces. What did they mean? The answer had to come immediately. For example: the opponent has a tank company here, an artillery battalion there, a bridge here, and there is an ammo dump on the premises. What does he intend to do? What do we have to do if we are stronger at the moment? What if we are weaker? After graduation some of us were chosen for the Frunze High Command Army School in Kiev. That school was training intelligence operatives. Instead of four years it took me three and I graduated with honors.

I started my service duty as an officer in the Carpathian military district. Soon I was transferred to the Volga Military District whose headquarters were in Kuibyshev, the unofficial capital of the Soviet Union that was created when Moscow was threatened by the German invasion in 1941. Stalin and the most important government organizations were in Moscow, but the larger part of the government ministries and all of the foreign embassies and missions were in Kuibyshev. In case of a crisis Stalin was supposed to relocate there. This "spare" capital of the Soviet Union continued to function in the time of peace. All the political, economic, and military data on the United States of America and other countries was processed in Moscow. Simultaneously and independently of Moscow that same data was analyzed in Kuibyshev. That is what I was doing there at the command post.

They had taught us at the Academy to trust no one, to question every fact, to verify every piece of data, to doubt everything. If a hundred secret agents are reporting one way, and one sounds out of place and makes no sense, deal with him. No one will trust him or you, they will laugh at you, and they will not believe you. But this is how great discoveries are made. It is easy to repeat known facts. It is much more difficult to find something that nobody knows. And if you find it, you will be misunderstood and contradicted a lot at first. Then you find proof for it and convince your superiors. I did exactly that, and I was noticed. They sent me to the topmost secret military academy in the Soviet Union. It was called the Soviet Army Academy. It was so secret that no one ever mentioned it in public. It took me three years to complete the course of study there. The curriculum was so intense that it could take fifteen years to complete, but it was compressed for a reason: it was a test. Those who could not handle the stress would not be able to handle intelligence work. The tempo was inhuman. You were flooded with thousands of messages simultaneously: pieces of secret telegrams, secret agents' reports, images from space, photos from passing cars, fragments of taped conversations, wrinkled and dirty topographic maps found at the site of recent maneuvers. All that raw material had to be sorted, analyzed, and evaluated. Everybody knew those who excelled would get the most interesting assignments.

After graduation I was sent to Geneva, the world capital of espionage. My first job was attaché of the USSR Permanent Mission to the United Nations in Geneva. That was my official title, but in reality I spent four years processing intelligence information.

At school they had taught me to ask, "Why?" They had taught me to look for reasons and the internal logic for everything. I believe my instructors overdid it because I started asking too many questions. Why could the Soviet Union launch the first satellite into space, and send up the first dog and human beings, but could not raise enough wheat to feed its own people? Why is America our enemy? Why doesn't the United States like us? What if it is us who do not like them? Why? What do we need Africa for? What are our interests in Vietnam, Cuba, and Chile? Don't we have enough land of our own? Have we resolved our own problems at home, and if not why are we trying to teach everybody else?

The head of my country told Americans: "We will bury you!" That was the essence of the Soviet Union's foreign policy at the time. We were digging a grave for the United States and all the other countries of the world. Our foreign policy was the top priority. We had more nuclear submarines than all of the countries of the world combined. We also had more airborne divisions, tanks, and field artillery. We filled the world with Kalashnikovs. At the same time we could not feed ourselves. So here was the question: Why should we bury America? Are they in our way? If we bury the United States, who is going to feed us?

I became more and more bewildered as I tried to answer my own questions. I had been taught to notice strange occurrences, anomalies, exceptions to the rules. One strange thing that I noticed: No matter what happened in the Soviet Union our leaders always tried to conceal the negative aspects and show the positive. There were no private enterprises in the Soviet Union back then. All the media—and everything else, for that matter—belonged to the government. Our newspapers reported only what was advantageous to the government. For example, the media reported that crime was almost nonexistent and steadily declining. They wrote that everything was fine, culture was flourishing, the quality of life was getting better and better, we would soon surpass the United States. You could not find any negative news.

On the night of October 6, 1948, the city of Ashkhabad was leveled by an earthquake reported to have reached magnitude 10 on the Richter scale, the maximum strength. The epicenter was only twenty kilometers away from downtown. The disaster struck in the middle of the night when all of the people were asleep. The whole city collapsed instantaneously. The only building left standing was the city prison. Everything else turned into broken brick and stone rubble; 110,000 people died under the debris. The facts of this disaster became public only thirty years later. Back in 1948 not a single Soviet newspaper or radio station reported it. Not one government official commented on it. Furthermore, those who spoke about the earthquake were arrested and put in prison for "spreading false rumors." You would ask yourself, why conceal an earthquake? That was the way the Soviet system worked: we are so good that we do not even have earthquakes!

On the same premise no media outlet or official in the Soviet Union mentioned the Chernobyl disaster when it occurred. The Swedes were the first to sound the alarm. The wind had blown the radioactive cloud from the Ukraine through Belarus, Lithuania, Latvia, Poland, and across the Baltic Sea to Sweden where the emergency warning equipment went off at a local nuclear power station. Swedish engineers could not figure out why their equipment was going off; they were looking for problems at their own station. It took them awhile to figure out that the radiation was in the air, carried by the wind from afar. After the international investigation had started the Soviet government admitted that there had been a small accident at the nuclear plant in Chernobyl. Even then the Soviets claimed that the accident was completely insignificant and no one should pay any attention to it.

There were other terrible catastrophes at the Soviet nuclear power stations and nuclear sites prior to Chernobyl, but they were kept under wraps. Soviet television shows relished tragedies elsewhere but nothing was said about our own. On October 24, 1960, the Chief Commander of the Strategic Rocket Forces, Chief Artillery Marshal M. I. Nedelin, was killed as a result of a rocket explosion. His death could not be concealed. The Soviet command announced it, but did not reveal how many people perished with him. Even now, eighteen years after Marshal Nedelin's death, the *Soviet Military Encyclopedia*[2] does not specify where or how he died. The encyclopedia lists dates and places of birth and death for everyone but him.

Modern Russia inherited the tradition of hiding everything negative. When the nuclear submarine *Kursk* sank it was not possible to hush that up. The Russian authorities announced that the submarine was submerged, that communication with the crew was established, there were no victims, and there was a hose pumping air into the vessel. For a week, the Russian government told tall tales about how everything at *Kursk* was going just fine. Later it turned out that there had been no communication with the people on board the *Kursk*, and nobody had pumped air in to them.

I gave you all of those examples to show that these are our traditions and rules. But there is an exception to these rules: June 22, 1941, the day when Germany attacked the Soviet Union. This day is described by Communist propaganda in truly dark colors. Thousands of books, tens of thousands of articles, and radio and TV broadcasts told about the blatant unpreparedness of the Red Army for military action. All of those sources paint a picture of stupid, cowardly Stalin who trusted Hitler. They tell us that after the Germans attacked, Stalin was so scared that he went into hiding and would not show himself. They talk about the army that had no good commanders, about outdated tanks and airplanes that were called "flying coffins," about the terrible ineptitude of the Soviet military leaders, about the absence of war planning.

Hundreds of Western historians fell for those stories: if the Russians themselves were talking about their own stupidity, why not repeat it? Everyone is happy to laugh at someone else's stupidity. As a result the whole world is laughing. I was taught to look for incoherence. There it was, gaping right at me. Why could we not talk about an earthquake, but could speak about bad tanks? Why was it that the Soviets, who thoroughly hid any mistakes, accidents, or catastrophes, made such a tremendous effort to emphasize the mistakes of 1941? Why did we expose the negative developments of 1941, while hiding data about a bad harvest? I took a closer look at the way our history was written and found something even more curious. In 1942 the Red Army suffered a number of monstrous defeats: in the Crimea, near Kharkov, Leningrad, and Rzhev. Our textbooks did not mention those. It struck me as strange that it was acceptable to talk about the defeats of 1941, but not about the defeats of 1942.

Let us look further. In July, August, September, and October of 1941 the Red Army suffered crushing defeats near Smolensk, Kiev, Uman, and Viazma. Our history books did not and still do not mention those either. What could that mean? When, where, and under what kind of circumstances would a person or a nation passionately try to prove that they are stupid and unfit for a fight? I found one example. Imagine a murderer in court trying to convince the jurors that he is not guilty of the crime because he is mentally challenged, completely blind and therefore cannot shoot, and too weak to raise an ax. In addition he says that he has no bullets to shoot, his gun is broken, and his ax is rusty. There is no reason anyone would deem themselves stupid, powerless, and unfit to do anything other than to get out of a situation where they can be accused of a crime.

That is exactly the way Communist propaganda behaved while describing the events of June 1941. Communist historians and propaganda masters went out of their way to hide any details that would enable an outsider to restore the reality of what was happening at the time. They would only show their stupidity and incapacity to the world. For example, Soviet textbooks did not give information about the number of tanks that the Red Army had at that time. The texts just said that the tanks were badly suited for battle. The books did not say anything about the number of planes. They just stated that the planes were outdated. I decided to compose the picture myself, to re-create that reality. I had to find all the shards, all the fragments, all the pieces that were scattered all over. I decided to start from the top. How many field armies were there in the Soviet Union in 1941? I looked through many books on the subject but could not find the answer. Then I started to collect information about every field army individually in order to put the pieces together later. The results were amazing.

In June 1939, when Hitler was the enemy and his name was used to scare children and adults alike, the Soviet Union had two field armies. Neither of them was deployed in the European part of the Soviet Union. In August 1939 Stalin and Hitler, represented by Molotov and Ribbentrop, signed the non-aggression pact. We were told that Stalin decided to believe Hitler. I trusted that information, but here are some statistics: In June 1941 the Soviet Union had thirty-one field armies. Twenty-six of them were deployed in the European part of the country. This surprised me. While Hitler was considered an enemy we did not possess any armies against him, but as soon as the pact between Stalin and Hitler was signed, Stalin increased the number of Soviet armies from zero to twenty-six in a period slightly less than two years. How does that fit with stories of Stalin trusting Hitler?

A corps is the next level within an army. How many of those did we have? The answer is hidden. There are thousands of books about the war, but nobody ever talks about how many corps there were within the Red Army in June 1941. I collected all the data. When I put it together the results were, again, astounding.

How many divisions were there? And most importantly where were they positioned?

If you were analyzing a chess match you would want to know not only the number of pieces on the board but their positions too. The problem was that although there were mountains of books about the war written in the Soviet Union, none of them had a map demonstrating the deployment of the Soviet Forces. In a famous book by Marshal Zhukov, all the maps are colored. The only map that shows the deployment of the armed forces at the moment of Hitler's attack is black and white. It is also very small and shows the span from the Baltic Sea to the Black Sea in six centimeters, less than two and a half inches. You could cover the whole theater of war between the Soviet Union and Germany with the palm of a child's hand. The map says that the 3rd, 4th, and 10th armies were deployed on the German border. It also states that there were other armies. But only nine of the twenty-six are named. The rest are omitted. Most important is that the deployment of the armies is not shown on the map. It is completely unclear where they really were. How can you analyze the beginning of a war if you do not know the number of the armed forces and their positions? I was determined to solve the puzzle. But how does one go about it?

I found a way. I was a student at the Academy at the time. Our professors urged us all to conduct independent scientific research in order to figure out who would make the best intelligence analysts. I took advantage of the situation and chose "The Attack of Germany on the Soviet Union on June 22, 1941" as the title of my paper. I explained my interest in the subject easily. I said that it was a horrible tragedy and I wanted to study how Germany prepared for the attack, in order to make sure that nothing of the kind would ever happen again.

The topic of my research was approved and I was given access to closed archives. The most important things that I needed were the archives of the German army. The Red Army had captured them at the end of the war, transferred them from Berlin to Moscow, and placed them under lock and key. Almost nobody has access to these archives. I was bewildered: If Hitler was the aggressor, why not open the archives for all to see?

There could be only one answer: there was something in those archives that the Soviet leadership did not want to admit. There is an incredible number of German documents in the archives in Podolsk, a small town near Moscow. There are piles and piles of boxes, most packed right after the end of World War II and never opened.

I had to be extra careful not to show my real interest. I asked the archive workers to assist me in my search to find maps of the deployment of the German troops. We found those, but I was looking for something else too and I finally found it. One of the maps showed the deployment of all the German troops just before the invasion. It also showed the positions of all the Red Army divisions the way German military intelligence pictured them just before the beginning of the war. That was exactly what I needed. I made a copy of it and all the other maps.

The map of the German troop deployment gave me quite a shock. The position of the divisions of the Red Army mirrored the position of the German Army. The border between the Soviet Union and Germany went through the territory of Poland which Stalin and Hitler had divided between them. The border was wavy. There was a big foreland of Soviet territory jutting into the German territory, like a Communist cape in the Nazi ocean. Then there was a big foreland of German territory that heavily indented the Soviet land. After that one could see a Soviet landmass going deep into the German territory again, and a German cape in the Soviet territory. The border took the form of two notched wheels. The red notches were cutting into Hitler's brown wheel, and the brown notches were cutting into Stalin's red wheel.

The Soviet forces were concentrated in those two masses of land, two capes that were indenting the German territory. The German divisions, tanks, artillery, and airfields were situated right in front, on the left and on the right of the Soviet troops. Even in peace time, Soviet divisions, corps, and armies were almost encircled by German troops. From a defensive point of view such deployment of the Soviet troops was useless and stupid. The only thing Hitler had to do was to attack the troops at the base of those promontories and the best units of the Red Army would be trapped. The German divisions were also situated in the promontories reaching far into the Soviet territory. They also were almost encircled by Soviet troops in peacetime. Stalin could close the mousetrap just as easily. From the defense point of view this kind of deployment of the German troops was pure suicide. I can only say that the Germans were not preparing for defense. They were getting ready for a sudden strike. For a sudden attack this position was very beneficial.

The Red Army was also preparing for a sudden attack. If you look at the position of the Soviet divisions from the point of view of an offensive, you could not imagine a better deployment. The airfields of the Red Army were moved all the way up to the border. Communist propaganda masters laugh at that. They say: "Look how stupid the Soviet generals were, they situated the airfields in such a fashion that they fell to the enemy in the first hours of the war."

The German airfields were also situated almost on the border itself. Why is it that nobody laughs at them? This way of positioning the troops and logistical forces does not make sense from a defensive point of view. If you look at it from the point of view of offense it makes total sense.

There was no difference between the actions of Stalin and those of Hitler. Hitler just happened to strike first. If Stalin had been the one to attack first, all the advantages of the deployment of the German troops would have turned into disadvantages.

In order to understand what happened I will begin the story from 1917 when the Communists took power in Russia, instead of 1941, when Hitler attacked Stalin.

It is legitimate to wonder if German intelligence made a mistake. What if the Germans were wrong in assessing the situation in the summer of 1941? I had to find an answer to that, and I did. German intelligence saw the situation correctly, but it did not see all of it. The real picture was much graver. The concentration of Soviet troops on the German border was frightful. Anyone can see it for themselves. All you would have to do is open the memoirs of the Soviet generals and put all the data about Soviet divisions, corps, and armies into a computer. Every Soviet general describes his division or corps but also speaks about his neighbors, about superior units, and about subordinates. It takes years to put it all together, but anyone who does that will be convinced that all the data confirm what I said earlier, and the general picture is terrifying.

The following simple fact can serve as additional proof of the aggressive ambition of the Red Army. More than sixty years have passed since the Germans attacked the Soviet Union, but neither the government of modern Russia nor the General Staff ever made public any maps that would demonstrate the deployment of all Soviet divisions on June 21, 1941. All that information remains a state secret. The highest level of secrecy in the Soviet Union is a document labeled "Top Secret: Special Folder." At present the Kremlin archives contain 215,000 "Special Folders." Nobody has access to them. In addition, there are hundreds of thousands of documents labeled "Secret," "Top Secret," and "Top Secret: Of Special Importance."

Sometimes the Kremlin rulers try to show their liberalism and good will. A small number of those secrets come out in the open. They are always heinous secrets. For example, the cooperation agreement between the People's Commissariat for Internal Affairs (NKVD) and the Gestapo became public knowledge. It was signed on November 11, 1938. Beria and Muller signed that document. What areas of cooperation could there be between two of the bloodiest organizations in the world's history? The answer is the following: in their main specialty—suppressing freedom and engaging in the mass elimination of people.

Another document that surfaced recently speaks about secret contacts between Stalin and Hitler. It is dated February 19, 1942. Stalin was an ally to Franklin D. Roosevelt and Winston Churchill. He was trying to strike an agreement with Hitler behind their backs. When papers like these become available to the public one should remember that they are just a drop in a bucket. Those documents are the ones the authorities are not ashamed to show. All the documents that are not accessible to researchers contain secrets that are much scarier and dirtier.

I am not a historian but I believe that there are a lot of similarities between history and intelligence. Both a historian and an intelligence officer have to look for things that nobody knows about. The difference is that a historian would treat the Soviet Union as a regular country, just like any other. That is why he would use traditional methods of historical science. I consider the Soviet Union a criminal conglomerate. The Soviet leaders have committed uncountable acts of atrocity against their own people and against neighboring nations. That is why for me the history of the Soviet Union should be studied using methods of criminology and intelligence rather then classical scientific research. Vladimir Bukovsky was correct in noticing that Western politicians and diplomats just cannot understand the motives of the Soviet leaders. If a policeman from Manhattan were to try to deal with them he would have made sense of their behavior immediately. A policeman would have understood and would have been able to predict all of the moves and actions of the Kremlin rulers. I study the history of the Soviet Union using methods of intelligence. The first rule is: do not believe what is officiously demonstrated to you; seek what is hidden. They are demonstrating the "unpreparedness" of the Soviet Union for the war, but hiding the offensive war plans.

There are documents that point directly to the fact that the Soviet Union was readying itself for an offensive against all of Europe in the summer of 1941. I figured out that one of those documents was kept in the Central Archive of the Russian Ministry of Defense, in holding #16, register #2951, case #241, pages 1 through 16. It is a long story. I would have to write a separate book about how I managed to figure out that this document exists. Juxtaposing facts and evidence, I came to the conclusion that on March 11, 1941, Marshal Timoshenko and Generals Zhukov and Vasilevsky, the heads of the USSR People's Defense Commissariat, forwarded to Stalin the plan of invading Germany. Both generals became marshals two years after that.

While talking on BBC radio on August 17, 1996, I addressed the Russian leaders. I told them: "If you have nothing to hide, publish the document!"

What was left for them to do? They published the document. The book titled *1941* came out a year and a half later, in March 1998. It was a collection of documents. The collection was compiled by A. N. Yakovlev, a former member of the Political Bureau of the Central Committee of the Communist Party of the Soviet Union, E. T. Gaidar, a former head of the Russian Government, E. M. Primakov, a former head of the foreign intelligence service (who later became the head of the Russian government), and many other respectable politicians.

The answer to my public demand to publish the document came almost immediately, although the documents still had to be collected and the book prepared for print. The document I speak about can be found on page 741 of the first volume. I started reading it with excitement. But what was going on? Out of sixteen pages only five were published. The document starts with the description of the German army, and with suppositions about the intentions of the German command. That is all. Once the document goes into describing the Red Army Forces and the plans of the Soviet Union, there is a heavy square bracket, followed by an ellipsis, and another square bracket. After that one can see the signatures of Marshal Timoshenko, and Generals Zhukov and Vasilevsky. The document stops at the most interesting moment.

Two volumes are filled with garbage, documents that are completely insignificant. The leaders of the former Soviet Union ran out of paper before they could publish the war plan. Respectable Russian politicians act as petty crooks. The trick is very old: you take paper and cut it neatly; then you put it in a wad of money to make it seem bigger. That is exactly how they comprised the collection of documents they called *1941*. It looks like a serious publication, it has good solid binding, the paper is high quality, and names of respectable authors are on the cover. There is a lot of unimportant flimflam in order to distract the reader's attention, but no substance, just emptiness.

I want to use this opportunity to repeat my demand: Rulers of Russia, publish document CA MD RF, H. #16, R. #2951, C. #241, pp. 1–16. I will tell you more: open the war archives! Sixty years have passed since the German invasion. It happened in *the first half of the last century.* Why are the archives still closed? What are you hiding from the world?

Until you stop fooling the world with your grifter tricks, I will be forced to use methods of military intelligence to study the history of the twentieth century.

1

The Struggle for Peace, and Its Results

We rely entirely on the hope that our revolution will unleash a European revolution. If the rising people of Europe do not crush capitalism, we will undoubtedly be crushed ourselves. Either the Russian revolution creates a whirlwind of struggle in the West, or the capitalists of all nations will strangle our revolution.

—Leon Trotsky, speech during seizure of power, third speech at the Second All-Russian Conference of Soviets, October 26, 1917

World War I ended on November 11, 1918. Within forty-eight hours, on the morning of November 13, an attempt was made to bring about a second world war. At that time the concepts and names "World War I" and "World War II" did not yet exist. The war of 1914–18, because it was a collision of gigantic empires, was called the Imperialist War. It was also called the Great War, because it surpassed all previously known wars in magnitude, expenditure, and number of participants. No previous wars had known such extended fronts, such intense battles, such massive losses, or such great social and economic consequences. The barbarity of a global slaughterhouse was so obvious that an overwhelming majority of people considered a repeated occurrence of such madness impossible. For this reason, the war of 1914–18 had another name, which is now forever forgotten, the Last War. Many thought that the gory absurdity of the Great War would sober all its participants, and eternally eradicate the desire to fight.

Nevertheless, a small group of people existed in Russia, who dreamed that a second world war would be crueler, that the bloodshed would encompass not only Europe and part of Asia but all the other continents as well. These people called themselves Bolsheviks, or Communists. Vladimir Lenin headed the group, and called their organization a political party. However, the infrastructure, tactics, and strategies of Lenin's group did not resemble those of a political party, but of a small, well-organized, conspiratorial cult. Lenin's party had a perceptible structure, parallel to which ran a secret, invisible organization. Just like a mafia organization, Lenin's party had open and entirely legal associations and undertakings, along with a secret unifying force that always remained in the shadows. On the one hand, representatives from Lenin's party sat in the Russian parliament (the Duma). On the other hand, Lenin and his followers believed the party's funds could be enhanced by any means, including bank robbery. They reasoned there was nothing wrong if occasionally, during the robberies, arbitrary casualties arose, as long as the most important goal of maintaining money in the party cashbox was met. From this point of view, Lenin's cult must be called an organized crime gang, not a political party of a new sort.

The leaders of this cult concealed their real names. Lenin, Trotsky, Stalin, Zinoviev, Kamenev, Molotov, and Kirov: these are all aliases. They all had serious reasons for not revealing their true names. For example, under the alias of "Stalin" hid a bank robber whose real name was Dzhugashvili. He was in charge of filling the party's cashbox.

Lenin and his gang worked hard to draw out World War I as much as possible. As early as September 1916, during the peak of the war, Lenin declared that one world war might be insufficient, and humanity might need another one of the same or even greater destructive scale. He reasoned that war is the mother of revolution, and world war is the mother of world revolution. The longer the war lasts, the more bloodshed and destruction it brings, the sooner revolution takes place. If a world revolution did not arise as a result of the first world war, a second world war becomes necessary.

Lenin's party was not only the most militaristic in the world, but also the most peace-loving. In 1914, almost all political parties of the nations at war voted in unison in the parliaments of their countries to create war credits. Lenin's party counted among the very few exceptions. Together with another branch of Russian Social Democrats, the Mensheviks, Lenin's party voted against increasing military expenditures, despite the obvious understanding that during wartime military expenditures cannot be the same as during peacetime. On July 26, 1914, during an emergency session of the Duma, the Bolsheviks and Mensheviks left the meeting hall "as a protest against the current military insanity."

Lenin's party began an unprecedented campaign for peace. By September–October of 1917, the Bolshevik party had seventy-five newspapers and magazines, with a total daily run esti-mated as high as 600,000 copies. All these publications advocated for immediate peace. The Communists distributed their publications free of charge in city streets, in factories, in military barracks, and in the trenches at the front. On top of the newspapers and magazines, Lenin's party printed millions of books, brochures, pamphlets, and proclamations. Soldiers were told to try to establish friendly relations with the enemy, instead of shooting at them. Communist slogans urged the troops: "Put down your rifles!" "Go home!" "Let's transform the Imperialist War into a Civil War!"

In the fall of 1917, under the leadership of Leon Trotsky and Vladimir Lenin, the Communists carried out a coup and seized control of the capital of the Russian empire, Petrograd (formerly St. Petersburg). For the first time in world history, a group of people living and working under fake names gained control of the capital of such a vast country. Most nations of the world did not recognize the new authorities as legitimate. The only exceptions were countries with which Russia was at war, Germany and Austria-Hungary. Only the enemy recognized Lenin's command. German money was secretly transferred to Lenin's party —both before and after the coup.

Moments after the new power came into being, the first official document—the Peace Decree—was created and signed. The army and navy immediately ceased all military activity.

Every regiment elected committees of soldiers. Delegates from each regiment began conducting their own peace talks with the enemy. They paid no attention to their regimental or division commanders, or higher authorities. At first every regiment, and later on every battalion, independently designed the conditions for peace, without taking into consideration the demands of the other battalions. The Russian army crumbled into hundreds of uncontrollable regiments and thousands of battalions, ceasing to exist as a single unified organism. The front collapsed. Nobody was left to defend Russia. Following the decree to stop fighting, Lenin and his cohorts immediately instituted committees to demobilize and take apart the Russian army.

No major power had ever voluntarily dismantled its army during peacetime. Yet Lenin and Trotsky demolished the Russian army during the peak of World War I, when victory was within their grasp. Germany's position was already completely hopeless during this time. Germany had almost no natural resources. Germany and her allies were blockaded, and had no supply route by sea. Russia's natural resources, in contrast, were limitless. In the fight against Germany, Russia was allied with the mighty French and British colonial empires. In April 1917, the United States of America joined the conflict and declared war on Germany. Against such formidable adversaries, Germany could not have triumphed under any circumstances. All Russia had to do in the given situation was to patiently wait for Germany to beg for peace.

Instead, what happened was something even the German Kaiser could not have dreamed of. The Russian army, acting under Lenin and Trotsky's orders, abandoned its trenches and went home. Thousands of guns, mortars, machine guns, millions of small arms, and huge stores of ammunition, uniforms, and supplies were left behind on the frontlines. Lenin's "Peace Decree" was an act of Russia's utter capitulation before Germany. From this moment the Eastern Front ceased to exist. Germany received the chance to concentrate its efforts on the Western Front against Russia's former allies. In adopting the "Peace Decree" Russia betrayed her allies. Lenin and Trotsky singlehandedly brought Russia out of the war and made their country subject to Germany's mercy.

Despite Russia's withdrawal, the situation in Germany and Austria-Hungary continued to worsen. A general strike broke out in Austria-Hungary in January 1918. During the same month, a general strike was called in Germany. Both countries stood on the verge of chaos. Russian Communists saved their day. To be capable of fighting in the war as long as possible, Germany needed strategic resources in large quantities. Lenin and Trotsky again came to Kaiser Wilhelm's aid. They signed the Brest-Litovsk Treaty in March 1918. The Russian Communists, without battle, handed over approximately a million square kilometers of their territory to the Germans. Fifty-six million people, about a third of the Russian empire's population, inhabited this territory. The occupied area encompassed more than a quarter of the nation's cultivated lands; it housed 26 percent of the railways, and major industrial capabilities. Seventy-three percent of Russia's iron and steel was cast in these territories, and 89 percent of Russia's coal was mined there.

Most important of all, these were Russia's most fertile lands. Mass export of food to Germany began immediately. A financial agreement, signed on August 27, 1918, stated that Russia had to pay Germany war reparations totaling 6 billion marks.[1] Without such a gift, Germany would have been unable to support herself until November of 1918.

Communists are proud of their love of peace. However, the stubbornness with which they fought for peace far surpasses common sense, to the point of suspicion. For the sake of peace, Lenin and Trotsky sacrificed 56 million of their subjects, without considering their wishes and needs. What good was peace for these people, if their homes were taken over by foreign occupants? For the sake of peace, Lenin and Trotsky handed Russia's most fertile lands over to Germany, causing widespread famine in the remaining territories. Without bread, meat, gold, steel, iron, and coal, Russia could not exist. What good is peace if it brings the death of the nation?

It was clear that Germany could not successfully continue to fight on two fronts, but the defeat of Germany would mean the end of the war. Consequently, Lenin's task, to prolong the war, was to create a situation in which Germany fought on only one front. For this purpose, he took Russia out of the war. Lenin's plot was simple: let Germany and Austria-Hungary fight against Great Britain, France, and the United States. Let them wear out each other's strengths. Most importantly, do not allow the flames of war to be extinguished. Russia would remain on the side and add fuel to the fire. While "peace" was being made on Lenin's orders in Brest-Litovsk, intensive preparations for a revolt against the German government were underway in Petrograd. The revolutionaries published half a million copies of a Communist newspaper in German, *Die Fackel* (The Torch). Even before the Brest-Litovsk Treaty was signed, in January 1918 a German Communist organization, *Spartakus*, was formed in Petrograd. The newspapers *Die Weltrevolution* (The World Revolution) and *Die Rote Fahne* (The Red Banner) were also born, not in Germany but in Russia under Lenin's orders, while he made peace with Germany's government. Communism would become deeply rooted in Germany in the 1920s. Part of the credit for this goes to Lenin, who fueled the instability of German politics precisely at the time when he had a peace treaty with the German government. While Germany was conducting a hopeless and devastating military campaign in the West, Lenin was subverting its political system.

Finally, World War I ended. In November 1918 Europe's condition was exactly what the Kremlin leaders had hoped it would be. The economic hardships caused by war had reached their limits in all the nations. Europe was facing an unprecedented crisis that encompassed all spheres of life, including the economy, politics, and ideology. Germany admitted her defeat. The monarchy crumbled. Anarchy and famine ruled the land.

Just then, Lenin and Trotsky's love for peace vanished. The government of Soviet Russia issued, on November 13, 1918, an order for the Red Army to begin offensive operations against Europe.

A review of the protocols of any of the countless meetings and congresses of that period reveals that the only question on the agenda was the World Revolution. The aim of the Soviet advance narrowed down to installing Communism on the European continent. In a few days, the Red Army crossed into the Baltic countries. The Communist government of Estonia was formed on November 29, that of Latvia on December 4. Lithuania followed on December 8, 1918. On December 17, a manifesto published in Riga named Germany as the imminent objective of the offensive. The most important goal of the operation: fuel a new world war.

Lenin's calculations were precise: Worn out by World War I, the German empire is unable to bear the pressures of another war. The war ends with the crushing of the empire and is followed by a revolution. In war-torn Europe, on the remaining fragments of the old empires, Communist countries arise, remarkably similar to Lenin's Bolshevik regime. Lenin was ecstatic: "We are at the doorstep of world revolution!"

2

First Attempts to Unleash a Second World War

The West, full of imperialist cannibals, has turned into the hearth of darkness and slavery. Our task lies in destroying this hearth, and bringing happiness and consolation to all worker nations.

—Joseph Stalin, Moscow, December 15, 1918

As a result of World War I, Europe found itself in a situation which the Communists called revolutionary. In 1918 Communist parties formed in many European countries. In Kiel, German navy seamen called a strike on November 3, 1918. Two days later, the strike spread to all of northern Germany, and on November 7–8 it reached the main industrial regions and the capital city, Berlin. The strikes were suppressed, or subsided on their own. But in January 1919, a Soviet republic was declared in Bremen. The Hungarian Soviet Republic formed in March. In April, the Bavarian Soviet Republic followed. Following the Soviet example, these Communist nations formed Red Armies and secret police squads, which called themselves "extraordinary commissions in the struggle against counterrevolution." These extraordinary commissions immediately instigated a reign of terror against all layers of society, and the Red Armies threw themselves into revolutionary wars to "liberate" the neighboring nations. A part of the Hungarian Red Army marched into Slovakia and, on June 20, 1919, proclaimed the Slovak Soviet Republic. A Communist government formed immediately and declared a policy of nationalization of all private lands and annulment of private property. It nationalized all commercial enterprises, banks, and transportation systems. For silencing the voices of discontent, they formed the Slovak Red Army and Extraordinary Commission. At the same time Soviet Ukraine declared war on Romania, and began preparations to advance west, to connect with Soviet Hungary.

Lenin and Trotsky prepared to establish Communism in Asia as well as in Europe. On August 5, 1919, Trotsky wrote a secret memorandum arguing that "the road to Paris and London lies through the cities of Afghanistan, Punjab, and Bengal." He proposed "preparations for a march on India, to help the Indian revolution." To achieve this goal Trotsky said it was necessary to form "a political and military command center of Asian revolution, and a revolution academy" in the Urals or in Turkestan, to form a special corps of 30,000 to 40,000 horsemen and "unleash them on India" to help the "native revolutionaries."

Civil war raged in Russia and distracted the efforts to ignite a second world war in 1918 and 1919. The main resources of the Red Army were tied up on internal fronts fighting against those who opposed Communism. Lenin and Trotsky were not able to send aid to the Communist nations that sprouted in Central Europe, nor could the Red Army reach Germany.

In 1919 in Moscow, Lenin and Trotsky created the Communist International, abbreviated as Comintern. This organization defined itself as "the Headquarters of World Revolution." The goal of the Comintern was the creation of a "World Soviet Socialist Republic." Thus began the process of creating and strengthening Communist parties on all continents. These parties constituted sections of the Comintern and were subordinate to its leadership.

Allegedly, all Communist parties in the world, including the Russian party, had an equal status. They all contributed to the communal bank of the Comintern. Delegates from all Communist parties of the world held congresses, developed strategies and tactics, and elected a common leadership—the Executive Committee of the Comintern. This organ oversaw all the Communists of the world. The Communist Party of Russia officially was a section of the Comintern, on equal footing with all the other parties, and bound to abide by commonly developed decisions.

In practice, however, the reality was an entirely different story. All the funds in the Comintern budget came from the gold reserves of Soviet Russia. All the Communist parties of the world were paid for by Moscow and existed only through financing from the Kremlin. The Comintern itself was also created with Kremlin funds. The leaders of the Comintern lived and worked in Moscow, under tight control of the Soviet secret police. All their directives came from the Kremlin. Only those who were agreeable to the Kremlin leaders, and who carried out all their orders without dissent, were chosen.

The Comintern was unique. Never before had history seen anything like it. In practically all the nations of the world, from Japan to Uruguay and Chile, Communist parties sprouted and conducted a line of politics that was dictated from Moscow. In many cases, delegates from Communist parties in those countries were members of trade unions, of legislative bodies in their governments, and sometimes even members of governments—but that was only the visible side of Comintern activity.

At the same time, Communists conducted not only an open struggle, but also a secret one. Stated briefly, their ideology narrowed down to advocating:

- The old world must be destroyed, and a new one built in its place.
- To destroy the old world and build a new one, it is necessary to gain political power. Gaining political power requires using all measures, ranging from the most peaceful to the most violent, from the most open to the most secretive.
- The struggle for a new world must unfold not on a national scale, but on a world scale. The interests of the World Revolution are more important than the interests of individual countries.

Every person joining the Communist Party accepted this ideology, meaning he or she agreed to fight against the interests of their own nation, if it became necessary, and to use all methods, including covert and violent action. Suddenly the intelligence services of the Soviet Union received legions of volunteers from practically every nation in the world. All that remained was to select the most competent ones, train them, finance them, and assign them to missions in the fight against their own countries and governments.

In the 1920s Soviet intelligence suddenly became the most powerful intelligence organization in the world. Thousands of Germans, Czechs, Hungarians, Americans, English, Japanese, and French selflessly worked in the name of a bright future for all humanity. In actuality, they worked for the interests of the Kremlin.

On June 28, 1919, the Versailles Treaty was signed, establishing peace between Germany and the allied victors. Victors always come in large numbers. The victors, aside from Great Britain, the United States, and France, also included Bolivia, Guatemala, Haiti, Cuba, Ecuador, Honduras, Liberia, Nicaragua, Panama, Peru, Uruguay, and many others. However, overall the Versailles Treaty was a treaty between vanquished Germany and victorious France and Great Britain, which had the full support of the United States of America.

The conditions dictated by the Allies at Versailles demanded from the vanquished country virtually complete disarmament. All military drafts were abolished in Germany, the number of armed forces fixed at 100,000, the General Staff and all academies disbanded. The treaty forbade the creation of a new General Staff and new academies. Armed forces could only be assembled through voluntary enlistment and used only for maintaining internal order and security. The surface naval fleet was cut drastically; the submarine fleet was abolished completely. The majority of German fortifications were to be blown up. Germany lost the right to have heavy artillery, tanks, submarines, and aviation (including blimps). It was forbidden to have or to design chemical weapons, and all supplies of poisonous gas were destroyed. The treaty also strictly forbade all import into Germany of any weaponry or war material. Arms production in Germany fell under international control.

Germany lost 67,273 square kilometers, one-eighth of its territory, with a population of 5,138,000 people. Germany lost all her colonies. All merchant ships with a capacity over 1,600 tons' displacement were confiscated, as well as one-half of the merchant ships exceeding 1,000 tons' displacement, a quarter of the fishing fleet, and one-fifth of the river fleet. Germany was also required, for the next five years, to build for the Allies merchant ships, totaling 200,000 tons' displacement per year. Germany was obligated to supply France with up to 140 million tons of coal, Belgium 80 million tons, and Italy 77 million tons. Also, it was required to transfer to the winners half of its paints and non-military chemicals and to provide up to a quarter of the future production through 1925.[1] The Allies received the right to use German ports, railroads, and waterways on very beneficial terms. On top of all this, Germany was forced into paying astronomical amounts of retribution.

The Versailles Treaty was not only extremely unfair and degrading to Germany, it was ineffective and did not carry any basis for a lasting peace. The Versailles Treaty only contained the seeds of World War II. Lenin was the first to understand that World War I left a rocky legacy. The victorious allied nations, especially France, were carried away in demanding reparations from Germany. Forced into making huge payments to the victors, Germany faced a sharp economic crisis, and the German people experienced hunger, poverty, and constant misfortune.

Lenin was the first to understand that the Versailles Treaty was a bomb waiting to explode under Europe. Germany would never make peace due to the unfairness of the pact;

there would always be those who opposed the treaty, who would call out for revenge and act to get it. On October 15, 1920, Lenin declared: "The order held by the Versailles peace treaty lies over a volcano, since the seventy percent of the world's people who are enslaved are anxiously awaiting someone to come and start a struggle for their liberation, and to rock the foundation of their countries."[2]

Lenin did not know that this someone had already come. His name was Adolf Hitler. In September 1919 this someone joined the German Workers' Party as number 007, and began the fight against the Versailles Treaty. This fight he called "My Struggle"—*Mein Kampf.*

In 1920 Russian Communists undertook a new attempt to spark a second world war by ripping through Poland into Germany. Although the most favorable conditions for revolution had already lessened, Germany in 1920 was still an acceptable place for class struggles. Germany was ruined and dishonored. All her ideals were besmirched and mocked. The country was enveloped in a harsh economic crisis; in March 1920 Germany experienced a general strike, estimated to have had more than 12 million participants. Germany resembled a powder keg, waiting for just one spark. The Red Army was supposed to bring this spark to Germany. The mood of the Red Army was reflected in its songs and marches. One of the most popular Soviet marches of 1920 included the words: "We're getting Warsaw, Give us Berlin!" The contender for the unofficial march of the Red Army was another song of 1920 called "White Army, Black Baron," which contained the famous verse:

> Fanning the world fire,
> We will level churches and prisons
> Since from the vast taiga to the British seas
> No one is more powerful than the Red Army.

In the summer of 1920, the western front of the Red Army, under the leadership of the ruthless General Mikhail Tukhachevski, began to advance with the objective of crushing Europe. Excerpts from order #1423 given to the western front on July 2, 1920, announced: "Fighters of the Workers' Revolution! The fate of the World Revolution will be decided in the West. The path to the world fire lies over the dead body of White (anti-Communist) Poland. We will carry happiness and peace on our bayonets to the working people of the world. To the West! To decisive battles and thundering victories!"[3]

In the days when the Red Army was advancing toward the Polish cities of Warsaw and Lvov, a second congress of the Comintern was taking place in Russia. The Headquarters of the World Revolution then issued a call:

> Brothers—Red Army Fighters, you should know your fight against the Polish slave drivers is the most just war in history. You are fighting not only for the interests of Soviet Russia, but for the interests of the whole of working mankind, for the interest of the Communist International. . . . Soviet Germany, united with Soviet Russia, will immediately become more powerful than all the capitalist powers combined! The Communist International declared that Soviet Russia's goal is its own goal too. The international proletariat will not sheath its sword until Soviet Russia joins the Federation of the Soviet Republics of the World as an integral link.[4]

On July 23, 1920, directly from the Comintern congress, Lenin telegraphed Stalin at the Polish front: "Situation in Comintern is outstanding. Zinoviev, Bukharin, and I think that it would be proper to encourage a revolution in Italy. My personal opinion is that, to do so, Hungary has to be sovietized, possibly along with Czechoslovakia and Rumania."[5] In a conversation with the French delegates to the congress, Lenin was even blunter: "Yes, the Soviet troops are in Warsaw. Soon, Germany will be ours. We will conquer Hungary again; the Balkans will rise against capitalism. Italy will tremble. Bourgeois Europe is cracking at the seams in the storm."[6]

The Red Army stepped onto Polish territory and immediately in the first occupied city declared the creation of the PSSR—the Polish Soviet Socialist Republic.[7] Felix Dzerzhinski, the head of the Soviet secret police and an ethnic Pole, led the PSSR. By the end of the second congress of the Comintern, Warsaw was half surrounded by the units of the Red Army. Prior to the Polish counterattack, the Red Army crossed the Vistula River in the vicinity of the town of Włocławek—360 kilometers, or ten marching days, from Berlin.[8]

There was no common border between Soviet Russia and Germany. In order to spark the fires of revolution, it was necessary to tear down the dividing barrier—Poland. On September 22, 1920, Lenin spoke to the Ninth Conference of the Russian Communist Party and bluntly described the logic guiding the Bolsheviks in their drive: "The defensive war against capitalism is over, we have won. . . . We are now going to try to attack them, to help the sovietization of Poland. . . . We have set ourselves a task: to seize Warsaw. . . . It turned out that not just the fate of Warsaw is being decided, but the fate of the whole Versailles Treaty."[9]

To the Communists' misfortune, Tukhachevski, who did not understand strategy, was in command of Soviet troops. Tukhachevski's armies were crushed near Warsaw and fled in disgrace. In the critical moment, Tukhachevski lacked strategic reserves, and this decided the outcome of the grandiose battle. This time, Europe was fortunate. The Soviet Communists had to postpone the revolution in Europe until 1923.

3

The First Contact

If a revolutionary shake-up of Europe is to begin, it will be in Germany . . . and a victory
of the revolution in Germany will secure the victory of the international revolution.

—JOSEPH STALIN, *Works*

The crushing of Tukhachevski's army in the summer of 1920 in Poland created unpleasant consequences for Russian Communists. The Russian people, whom the Communists, it seemed, had succeeded in drowning in blood and completely subordinated to their control, suddenly made a last-resort attempt to rid themselves of the Communist dictatorship. At that moment, Lenin and Trotsky were making preparations for a new world war. On December 22, 1920, Lenin advised his fellow party members: "We ended one line of wars, we must prepare ourselves for the second."[1] Lenin was ready for any sacrifice in the name of war: "We are severely lacking in everything, yet we are no poorer than Viennese workers. Viennese workers die, starve—their children also die, starve—but they do not have the most important thing that we possess: hope. They die, oppressed by capitalism, they find themselves in a position to make sacrifices, but their sacrifices are not like ours. We sacrifice for the sake of the war that we are waging against the entire capitalist world."[2]

However, the Russian people demanded peace, not world domination. St. Petersburg, the "cradle of the revolution," experienced one workers' strike after another. The workers demanded bread and freedom. The Bolsheviks crushed the workers' demonstrations, but in March 1921 all of a sudden the Baltic fleet intervened on the workers' behalf. The sailors of the seaport city of Kronstadt (a naval base), the same ones who gave power to Lenin and Trotsky, now sought their freedom from Communist rule. They demanded that the Soviets (the workers' and peasants' councils, the basic organizing units of society created by the Communists) be purged of Communists. In addition, the nation experienced a wave of peasant uprisings. In the forests of the Tambov region, peasants formed an anti-Communist army—well organized, but poorly armed.

The peasants' and sailors' uprisings and the workers' demonstrations were crushed by the same man who lost the Polish war, Mikhail Tukhachevski. He showed inhuman cruelty, and disregarded all international rules of law and human rights. Under his leadership thousands of hostages were executed by firing squad, peasants were shelled with poison gas, and villages were burned. Villagers were drowned in swamps; sailors were drowned, pushed into holes cut in the ice.

Communist leaders were desperately looking for a way out of the crisis. The Comintern, finding itself in this desperate situation, made a decision that the only thing that could save Bolshevism was a revolution in Germany. The head of the Comintern, Grigorii Zinoviev, sent his loyal follower, the Hungarian revolutionary Bela Kun, to Berlin. Kun, who in 1919 had been the actual head of the short-lived Hungarian Soviet Republic, arrived in Berlin in March 1921 with an order from Zinoviev and the Executive Committee of the Comintern to the Central Committee of the German Communist Party to seize power. For this the German Communists had to organize an immediate uprising and abolish the Weimar Republic.

On March 22 a general strike was declared in the industrial regions of central Germany. On March 24 the Communists took control of government buildings in Hamburg. In Leipzig, Dresden, Chemnitz, and other cities of central Germany, the Communists organized a takeover of courts, municipal buildings, banks, and police headquarters. The official organ of German Communists, *Die Rote Fahne*, openly called for revolution."[3]

Walter Krivitsky, one of the most highly positioned chiefs of Soviet intelligence, who took part in the events, wrote: "We were sent to Germany for reconnaissance, mobilization of dissident elements in the Ruhr region, and preparation of workers for an opportune moment to start an uprising. We immediately formed three types of organizations in the German Communist party: an intelligence and reconnaissance service, acting under the supervision of the Fourth Directorate of the Red Army; military formations to serve as the core of the future Red Army of Germany; [and] small fighter squads, whose orders included lowering the morale of the *Reichswehr* (German Army)[4] (The intelligence officers of the German and all other Communist parties worked under the leadership of the Fourth Directorate of the Red Army. The Fourth Directorate, after changing its name several times, subsequently became known as the Main Intelligence Directorate of the General Staff of the Soviet Armed Forces, or GRU.)[5]

Although the attempt to take control of Germany in 1921 suffered defeat, in Moscow preparations immediately began for a new seizure of power in Germany and the world. On December 30, 1922, the Union of Soviet Socialist Republics (USSR) was born. In this name there are no national or geographical limits. According to the plans of the founders of the USSR, the Union was meant to spread throughout the world. The "Declaration of the Founding of the Union of the Soviet Socialist Republics" proclaimed that the USSR is only the first decisive step in a creation of the World Soviet Socialist Republic. The number of republics was planned to expand until the entire world formed one giant Communist state. The Founding Declaration of the USSR was an open and direct declaration of war to the rest of the world. This was an official document that stated the main purpose of the existence of the giant state: to destroy and subordinate all remaining states of the world.

The coat of arms of the USSR contains an image of the globe with symbols of Communism superimposed upon it. On the day of the formation of the USSR, a member of the Central Committee of the Communist Party, Sergei Kirov, proposed to build a "Palace of the Soviets." Kirov explained: "This building must serve as the symbol of future might, the victory of communism not only here, but also there, in the West." He emphasized that the palace must be built for the purpose of holding the ceremony of acceptance for the final republic into the Soviet Union. At that time, nobody could forecast which republic in particular would be the last to come into the Union of Soviets—the Argentine Soviet Republic or the Uruguay Soviet Republic—but the Soviet Communists were certain that this moment would inevitably come.

Attempts to unleash a war and revolution were repeated by the Soviet Communists many times over. There was an attempt to start a "Balkan revolution," and obtain, in Trotsky's words, a direct route from the Balkan region to the ports of France and Britain.[6] An assassination attempt was made against the Bulgarian Tsar Boris, but miraculously he survived. In September 1923 armed uprisings began in Bulgaria, started on the Comintern's orders. On September 27, 1923, the Soviet Politburo ordered ten Bulgarian Communists (officers and pilots) to the navy base in Sevastopol. If a nearby Bulgarian city close to the shore was in rebel hands, the pilots would establish a connection by airplane between the south of Russia and Bulgaria. Then, "upon the establishment of the connection, to send out arms that have been in Sevastopol since last year, prepared for the Bulgarian revolution . . . and . . . send Bulgarian Communists currently in Moscow and other Russian cities to Bulgaria with arms."[7] The leader of the uprisings was Georgy Dimitrov—future head of the Comintern. Attempts were also made to spark revolutions in South America, Estonia, Latvia, Lithuania, China, India, and many other countries.

However, Germany remained the ultimate objective. One of the several attempts to take power in Germany is especially interesting. This attempt was undertaken in the fall of 1923 when Lenin no longer participated in the leadership. The reins of power were almost completely in Stalin's hands, although neither the country, nor the world, not even his rivals within the party, had come to understand this. Stalin's personal secretary, Boris Bazhanov, described the preparations for seizure of power in Germany: "At the end of September an emergency meeting of the Political Bureau of the Central Committee of the Russian Communist Party of Bolsheviks (the former name of the Communist Party of the Soviet Union—the CPSU, as it was renamed in October 1952) was held, so secret that it was attended only by the members of the Politburo and myself. No regular member of the Central Committee was permitted to be present. This meeting was called in order to fix a date for a coup in Germany. It was decided on November 9, 1923."[8]

Bazhanov wrote that the funds earmarked to support the German revolution were tremendous, and a decision was made to support the effort without limits. Inside the Soviet Union, all Communists of German origin and all Communists who knew the German language were mobilized. They were trained and sent to Germany for underground work. Not only regular Soviet Communists were sent to Germany, but leaders of higher rank as well, among them the People's Commissar (member of the cabinet of ministers of the Soviet government) Vasily Schmidt, the members of the Central Committee of the Soviet Communist Party Karl Radek and Grigory Piatakov, the candidate for membership to the Politburo of the Communist party of the USSR Nikolai Bukharin, and many others. In 1923 many others, also under aliases, arrived in Germany: Tukhachevski, Unshlikht, Vatsetis,[9] Menzhinskii,[10]

Trillisser,[11] Yagoda,[12] and many others. The Soviet ambassador to Germany, Nikolai Krestinski, formed a powerful web of secret intelligence. The Soviet embassy transformed itself into the headquarters of the revolution. Through it orders were passed from Moscow, along with a flow of funds, which were immediately transformed into a storm of subversive propaganda, arms, and war supplies.

The Comintern commission dealing with German affairs consisted of the entire Soviet leadership: Stalin, Trotsky, Zinoviev, Bukharin, and Radek. Stalin thought that it was necessary to avoid at all cost anything that might reveal that the revolution was "dictated" or "instigated" by the USSR. The plan was simple: November 7—the anniversary of the Communist takeover in Russia—would be the day for workers' demonstrations of solidarity in Germany. Special units, trained in Moscow by Communist secret police and military intelligence under the supervision of Joseph Unshlikht, would act as *provocateurs* and incite conflicts with police. Their goal was to cause violent clashes and arrests thus inflaming the anger of the workers. On November 8, the clashes were to grow from street fights into more serious threats. On the night of November 9, Unshlikht's units were to seize the most important government establishments, making it appear to be a spontaneous reaction of the masses against police brutality.

The script was simple, yet reliable. The so-called "Great October Socialist Revolution" followed the same script; so did the "proletarian revolutions" in Estonia, Lithuania, and Latvia in 1918 and in 1940. Following this blueprint, Communists took control of many states after World War II: a "spontaneous demonstration" of workers, the wrath of the people—and small units of cunning professionals.

The difference was that in the German revolution of 1923 the Communists had reliable allies: the Nazis. At this point in time, the German Workers' Party already had a new name—it was the National Socialist German Workers' Party (NSDAP was the German acronym)—and it had a new Fuehrer: Adolf Hitler. "A slogan of the Comintern was: 'War on Stresemann [the chancellor and foreign minister of Germany][13] and Poincaré [the prime minister of France]!'[14] A slogan of the Nazis was: 'War on Poincaré and Stresemann!' There had even been talks between Radek and certain leaders of the Nazi party."[15]

Karl Radek was a member of the Executive Committee of the Comintern and a member of the Central Committee of the Communist Party of the USSR. He had been to Germany several times with the goal of triggering a revolution. In 1919 he was arrested by German authorities, but was quickly sent home. In 1923 he once again returned to Germany. Could any of the Nazi party leaders conduct talks with the member of the Executive Committee of the Comintern, Comrade Radek, without having Hitler's express consent for doing so? And could Karl Radek conduct talks with Nazi leaders without a direct order from Stalin? It is remotely possible that Radek acted on his own but, knowing Stalin's obsession with control, it is highly unlikely. Stalin told the Central Committee that "[a] German committee of the Comintern, consisting of Zinoviev, Bukharin, Stalin, Trotsky, Radek, and a number of German comrades, adopted a number of specific decisions dealing with the direct assistance to the German comrades in [the] task of seizing power."[16] Radek expressed an open enthusiasm for Hitler's storm troopers and said: "We can see on the faces of German students wearing brown shirts the same devotion and the same inspiration which shone on [the] faces of Red Army officers."[17] Radek praised the storm troopers as "great guys," adding: "You will see that they will fight for us, lobbing hand grenades."[18]

Let's examine the dates. In August of 1923, Stalin decided that "German Communists, by themselves, will have to seize power in Germany." After this, in October, high-ranking Soviet officials were sent to Germany, and one of Stalin's agents conducted talks with the Nazis and discussed cooperative actions. In other words, the Soviets were saying on the one hand, "Dear Nazis, please help the Communists take power in Germany." On the other hand, they were saying "Let the Communists rule Germany by themselves."

This is a familiar Communist maneuver, and it was Stalin's personal trademark. Communists took power in Russia in alliance with other parties. Then they destroyed their allies after they became useless. Stalin personally acted in the same fashion. He eliminated his political adversaries by using his allies, and then eliminated the allies.

The Communist and Nazi parties did attempt a joint takeover in Germany in 1923. Communist propaganda wants us to believe that in 1923, there was no conspiracy between Communists and Nazis. However, on November 8, 1923, in Munich Hitler and a group of armed followers tried to arrest the government of Bavaria. Hitler declared that the revolution had begun, that the Bavarian and Weimar governments were demolished. A new "government" was formed immediately. On the night of November 8, a group with Ernst Roehm at its head took control of the headquarters of the military district. [19] Attempts to take over other infrastructure and government facilities were put down by the army and the police. On November 9 Hitler proclaimed a demonstration of his supporters. A clash occurred between the demonstrators and the armed police; sixteen of Hitler's supporters and three police officers were killed.

The attempted takeover was crushed by force. Hitler and his closest associates fled, but were soon captured, stood trial, and were sent to serve prison terms in the Landsberg fortress. It was from this prison cell that Hitler wrote *Mein Kampf*. Later, when he came to power, Hitler declared his fallen associates national heroes, and named the dates of the rebellion, November 8–9, as the most important German national holiday. An interesting note: the book *Mein Kampf* is dedicated to Hitler's sixteen fallen comrades, killed on November 9, 1923. But in the huge text (the first volume alone consists of almost six hundred pages in small print) Hitler writes nothing about the events of November 8–9. Hitler wrote the book in a prison cell, but does not mention why and how he came to be behind bars. For some reason, Hitler conceals all that preceded these events. Instead of a detailed explanation, the last page briefly states: "I will not venture here into discussions about events which led us to November 8, 1923." That is all.

This seems strange. The book is titled "My Struggle," and the author describes himself, his party, and his struggle for influence over the masses and for power. The events of November 8–9, 1923, are the culmination point of this struggle, after which Hitler's party was outlawed and he was imprisoned. At the time Hitler wrote his book, nothing more important had happened in his life or in the life of his party than the events of those two days. And yet he omits a description of these most important events.

In fact, he had something to hide. Hitler's failed revolution coincided in a most peculiar fashion with the failed Communist revolution. There are several coincidences, and they are astonishing. The date of the revolution was set in Moscow and kept under the utmost secrecy. But Hitler decided to conduct his coup on the same day, under the same red flag, shouting the same slogans calling for the expropriation of non-workers' income, the nationalization of industrial conglomerates, and the confiscation of German industrialists' war profits. Hitler's tactics completely paralleled the ones Moscow dictated to its agents: conduct demonstrations despite bans on such actions, provoke clashes with police forces, and seize government buildings. There was a total convergence of goals, methods, place, and time down to the hour and minute of the act.

Even stranger, Lenin, Trotsky, and Stalin believed in plots, coups, and the seizure of power by a well-organized minority. This is precisely what they accomplished in Russia, and many times over tried to repeat in other nations of the world. Hitler had a different method. Hitler was a demagogue, an agitator. *Mein Kampf* is a tale of a leader of masses, who knows how to handle the crowds, how to win their trust and affection. *Mein Kampf* is a book about how to obtain power through legal means, but there is not a word in it, not a hint, about underground methods akin to those used by Lenin and Stalin. In the sphere of legal open struggle for power over the masses, Hitler was much stronger than Lenin, Trotsky, and Stalin. But in the sphere of mutiny and plots Hitler was clearly weaker. He was not even prone to think in this direction. Ten years later, he came to power through legal means, through agitation, propaganda, and voting booths. Hitler's way was that of loud speeches and dramatic uplifting parades. He understood his full strength as an orator, and was proud of it.

Then why was Hitler in 1923 drawn to the Lenin-Stalin methods of taking power through armed conflict and at the same time as a coup staged by Moscow? For nearly a century, Soviet and East German historians have been telling us that this was merely a strange chain of coincidences. Sometimes this happened: Communists decided to stage a coup, and Hitler decided the same thing—on the very same day. In fact, Soviet Communists made attempts to use Hitler and his party for destabilizing the political situation in Germany long before Hitler's coming to power.

4

Stalin's Role in the Rebirth of German War Power

Only one country—Soviet Russia—can win in the event of an all encompassing conflict.
—Adolf Hitler, during a meeting with Lord Halifax,
the British foreign minister, November 19, 1937

After World War I, Central and Western Europe were in such a debilitated state that a large war could not arise because no nation was capable of starting one. France was among the main victors. Under the terms of the Versailles Treaty, Germany paid huge reparations to France, and the French had no motive to start a new war in Europe. The main concern of the French government was to maintain the new existing situation in Europe as long as possible. French generals chose strictly defensive strategies. They built the Maginot Line along their border, fashioned after the Great Wall of China.

Great Britain was also among the victors. Great Britain had no claims on any territories in Europe. Therefore, Great Britain had no desire to see a new European war. Great Britain's interests included preserving the newly formed balance of power in Europe. Britain was at the center of the greatest colonial empire in history, and its main interests lay outside of Europe: to preserve its colonies. Great Britain had a powerful navy to defend its colonies and trade routes, and a relatively small army to defend the homeland and maintain order in the colonies. Even if the British government had the desire to start a new war in Europe, its army was insufficiently strong to do so.

Germany, according to the Versailles Treaty, was completely disarmed. The Versailles Treaty not only demanded that Germany pay dues, dues, and more dues to France, but it also forbade Germany to have, buy, construct, test, or produce any offensive arms, and strictly limited defensive arms. The remaining Central and West European nations could not unleash a large war because they did not have sufficient economic or military might to do so and, most importantly, they had no desire to do so.

The Kremlin leaders in this situation could have breathed a sigh of relief and completely devoted themselves to the building of a peacetime economy. In order to avert war in Europe, all that was necessary was to make sure the Versailles Treaty was not breached, that Germany stayed disarmed and weak militarily. Germany was Russia's main opponent in World War I and her most likely opponent in any future conflict. Soviet Russia was not a signatory of the Versailles Treaty, but the pact did give Russia, which turned into the Soviet Union, invaluable advantages. The Soviet Union could produce any model of weapon or military technology. Meanwhile, Germany not only stood still in terms of military progress, it fell far behind.

The Kremlin leaders should have used all the powers of the Soviet diplomacy and intelligence services to uncover and root out all attempts to revive the German military machine. Let Germany stay weak! If Germany does not have tanks, aviation, heavy artillery, poison gases, submarines, if Germany has no trained panzer corps, pilots, navigators, if the German generals are banned from developing new tactics and methods of conducting operations, if German engineers do not have the ability to create new models of weapons, and factories do not produce these weapons—then Germany would never start a new war.

But the Kremlin leaders did not order their intelligence services to undertake a mission for the strict execution of and adherence to the Versailles Treaty. They did the opposite. A secret reorganization of the German army began with the help of the Soviet government. Moscow gave the German commanders all that they were forbidden to possess: tanks, heavy artillery, war planes, training classes, and weapons testing and shooting ranges. Germany was also provided with access to the Soviet factories that produced tanks and airplanes that were the most advanced in the world so the Germans would be able to look, to memorize, to copy. Stalin allowed the German government to create secret design bureaus and training centers on Soviet territory.

On November 26, 1922, an agreement about the production of metal airplanes and plane engines was signed with the German aviation firm Junkers Flugzeugwerke. It was this agreement with Junkers that paved the way for large-scale Soviet-German military cooperation. In July 1923 two new agreements were set out: one was about the production of munitions and military equipment and the other about the construction of a chemical plant. On April 15, 1925, an agreement was signed about the creation of a secret air force center in the Russian city of Lipetsk for training German military pilots. One hundred D-XIII-type military planes were bought by the Soviet government for Germans from the Dutch company Fokker. The preparations for the blossoming of the Third Reich's airpower had begun. Over the years, the German models Heinkel He-45, He-46, He-51, Arado Ar-64 and Ar-65, Junkers K-47, and Dornier Do-11 were successfully developed and tested in the USSR for the Germans. By the end of 1933, the school had prepared 450 fighter pilots, air reconnaissance observers, and members of bomber squads. Many of them later entered the core of *Reischsmarschall* Hermann Goering's command staff. It is safe to say that the Luftwaffe (the German air force) was born in the Soviet town of Lipetsk.

Nobody was supposed to know that Stalin was preparing Germany for a new world war. Planes, designed for training and testing, arrived by non-stop flights at high altitude.

All those Germans who headed to the German aviation school in Lipetsk were formally discharged from the *Reichswehr*. Their names were changed. The return of bodies of those who perished during the frequent training accidents was quite a challenge. They were sent by sea through Leningrad, in containers labeled "Mechanical Parts." Their relatives were not told of the true causes of death.

Stalin understood that the new war would not only be an air war, but a tank war as well. Therefore, he gave particular attention to preparing German Panzer corps. In 1926, near the Soviet city of Kazan, a tank school for the *Reichswehr* was created. German tankers wore Soviet uniforms there. Stalin fully equipped future German Panzer generals: he gave them tanks, fuel, ammunition, transport, housing, repair facilities, and a gigantic well-guarded weapons range—to create, to invent, to test. Kazan became the birthplace and alma mater of German armored divisions. The best Panzer generals of the *Wehrmacht Heer* (the German army) were bred and trained there. In Kazan they mastered the art of modern warfare; later, they led tank units to Warsaw, Paris, Belgrade, and Athens, to the shores of the English Channel, the Adriatic Sea, and the Atlantic Ocean.

It is critically important that engineers constantly work on improving weapons. A break of even ten years carries irreversible consequences. Old engineers and designers either leave for other branches of industry or retire, without passing their experience and knowledge to the new generation. In a few years a twofold problem arises: on the one hand, a technology lapse, on the other hand, the absence of competent and experienced engineers who could bridge this lapse. Fifteen years separate the end of World War I and Hitler's coming to power. Stalin's merit before Hitler's Germany lies in that he did not allow Germany to fall behind its enemies in technological and scientific advancement. Stalin bridged the gap between the retiring generation of engineers from the Kaiser era and the newly ascending generation of the Third Reich. Stalin's efforts secured the transfer of all amassed scientific and technological potential, knowledge, and experience from the retiring designers to the newly starting creators of military equipment and weapons.

The development and production of chemical weapons (poisonous agents such as mustard gas) were set up on the premises of the firm Bersol in Ivashchenko (now Chapaevsk) near the Soviet city of Samara. The daily output of mustard gas, which sadly earned its fame during World War I, reached 3.3 tons, and the daily output of the deadly poisonous gas phosgene was 2.6 tons. That made a total of 5.9 tons per day, which meant over two thousand tons per year. Joint testing of chemical weapons was conducted on two training ranges: one called "Tomka," near the city of Volsk in the Saratov region, and another, "Podosinki," which is today Kuzminki, a district of Moscow. It was there that in 1926–1927 the first joint Soviet-German chemical weapon tests were conducted.

It was not enough to train personnel and perfect models of weapons. One also needs military factories that will produce these weapons. Here as well the Kremlin leaders already, at the end of the 1920s, showed full understanding, and came to the aid of the German war industry. An agreement was worked out about the creation in Russia of production facilities for the German war industry, masked as Soviet-German enterprises. The Junkers deal was the first such enterprise. In 1922 the firm began constructing metal planes and plane motors. Beginning in 1924, the factory already had begun to produce several hundred planes per year. Following Junkers were Friedrich Krupp (cannons, shells, and tanks), BMW (tank motors and plane motors), Bersol (poisonous gases), Karl Walther (rifles), and others.

Stalin prepared Germany for a second world war. Without Stalin's help, Germany could not arm itself and destroy Europe. Obviously, when arming Germany, Stalin was not planning that all this would be used against him.

5

Why Did Stalin Like Hitler's Book So Much?

Germany's most evil enemy is and will always be France.

—Adolf Hitler, *Mein Kampf*

A study of the war between Germany and the Soviet Union should start with the question: Why did Hitler invade? In 1924 Hitler wrote in his book *Mein Kampf*: "We want to return to that point, where our previous development halted six hundred years ago. We want to halt Germany's constant efforts to expand to the south and west, and have our sights set towards the territories situated to the east." This phrase became famous and has been quoted time after time. Politicians, diplomats, generals, historians, and journalists have tirelessly repeated these words. Even in the 1920s this quote was cited in the essays and public speeches of Soviet leaders. Trotsky, Bukharin, Zinoviev, and Kamenev repeated it. In the 1930s, especially after the Nazis came to power, Hitler's frankness resounded with new authority. Any public speaker on the impending war began with this proclamation by Hitler.

After Stalin's death in 1953, hordes of historians quoted Hitler and accused Stalin of short-sightedness. The Fuehrer openly declared his intentions. Stalin should have read *Mein Kampf* and taken appropriate measures. From the moment that *Mein Kampf* first appeared in 1925 until the moment Hitler invaded in 1941, this quote was repeated from every loudspeaker. It was shouted at factory meetings, it was used to scare the people. It was repeated by the Comintern and printed in schoolbooks. After all this, how could the German invasion have been a surprise for Stalin? Did Stalin himself read *Mein Kampf*?

Yes, he read it. Moreover, Stalin was the first foreign reader. He was its greatest scholar and fan. The first translation of *Mein Kampf* was into Russian, under Stalin's personal orders. The book was published for the leadership of the party and the army. Marshal of the Soviet Union Konstantin Konstantinovich Rokossovsky wrote: "In our time we all read Hitler's book *Mein Kampf*."[1] The translation was completed without obtaining the author's permission. But his royalties were paid, though not right away. At the moment *Mein Kampf* was published,

Stalin was not the only leader—there was a whole crowd of leaders in the Kremlin. Not all of them understood the meaning of Hitler's creation. Comrade Stalin, however, immediately grasped, weighed, and evaluated everything. After having strangled his competition, Stalin paid his due to the author of *Mein Kampf.*

The number of copies printed in Russian at that time is unknown to me. One thing is clear: the circulation was minimal. For those few copies of the precious book, Stalin paid generously. How much did he pay? Stalin gave Hitler power over Germany. "Without Stalin, there would have been no Hitler, there would have been no Gestapo"— so said Trotsky in October 1936 as he evaluated Stalin's aid to Hitler.[2] Without Stalin's help, Hitler could not have come to power. Yet even such an incredible fee seemed too little to the generous Stalin. On August 23, 1939, he presented Hitler with Poland, and the rest of Europe. If Stalin had not appreciated *Mein Kampf,* the political career of Adolf Hitler would have ended in 1933 with a crushing defeat in the elections.

Let us clarify the situation in the mid-1920s when Hitler's book first came to light. Stalin sat in the Kremlin; Adolf Hitler sat in the Munich brewery Hoffbrauhaus. Stalin was one of the leaders of the Soviet Union, he was first among equals. But already many people had experienced the stranglehold of Stalin's grasping hands.

Who was Hitler in 1925? He was a failed artist, a wounded soldier returned from the front. Hitler joined a small proletarian party, which marched under the slogan of Gottfried Feder, calling for world revolution with the words "Proletariat of all nations, unite!" This program was adopted by Hitler as the foundation for a movement that he soon came to lead. Hitler's party set before itself Communist goals: banning private ownership of land, putting workers in control of administration in factories, and nationalizing industry.

On November 8, 1923, a socialist revolution hit Germany. The revolution was organized by the Comintern, and carefully directed behind the scenes by Soviet intelligence officers and envoys from Moscow. Although the revolution failed, Hitler's socialist workers' party showed itself as a unified, though small, formation of German workers. Hitler personally led his comrades into police fire. Some of his followers perished; Hitler himself was wounded and landed in jail.

That is where he fell into heresy. Hitler wrote a book, in which he uttered those famous words about lands in the east. Lenin and Trotsky decided that for the sake of the happiness of people everywhere they needed to sacrifice the people of their own country, whereas Hitler decided that the opposite had to be done: for the sake of the happiness of his people, he was willing to sacrifice people of other nations. For example, conquer lands to the east for Germany, regardless of the consequences for the people inhabiting those lands.

Hitlerism could have been eliminated from the moment of its conception. Sending an idealistic murderer to Munich would not have been a difficult feat for Stalin. Nobody would have paid any attention to one socialist breaking the skull of another, a very common occurrence. How many people did Stalin eradicate? Why did he not touch Hitler? He could have easily broken Hitler's neck and burned down his brewery with all his followers inside. Stalin could also have simply not paid any attention to Hitler, and without Stalin's help, Hitlerism would have never blossomed. It would not have yielded bloody fruit. But Stalin chose a third path: multi-faceted aid to Hitler. Stalin paved the way for Hitler to come to power. Hitler's dreams about lands in the east would have remained the pipe-dreams of a Munich dreamer, if not for Stalin's gigantic help.

Stalin read *Mein Kampf* from cover to cover and figured out that the main goal Hitler set for Germany's future was not lands in the east, mentioned in only one phrase in the book, but in liberating Germany from the chains of the Versailles Treaty. Hitler made enemies within and outside Germany. Internal enemies were the Jews. Outside enemies were the French, and the Jews.

Stalin's tactic relied on doing everything with someone else's hands, eliminating one enemy with the hands of the other. "Stalin always found monkeys, who brought him nuts from the hottest fire." This was said by Robert Conquest.[3] "Nobody could make his competitors knock heads like Stalin, always staying on the side and coming out superior to all." This was noted by A. Antonov-Ovseenko.[4] To this, one must add that Stalin was the most ardent perpetrator of Lenin's mission: to "create a Communist society with the hands of our enemies."[5]

Only once we understand Stalin's methods can we understand why Stalin liked the Munich dreamer and his book so much. The answer can be found in Hitler's book, Chapter XIII: "We must take every point of the Versailles Treaty separately, and systematically make it clear to the broadest masses of the population. We must achieve an understanding among 60 million German men, women, and children, and make them feel the shame of this treaty. We must make these 60 million have a deep hatred for this treaty, so that their scorching hatred brings the will of the people together and evokes a cry in unison: GIVE US BACK OUR ARMS!"

That is precisely what Lenin dreamed of: "that someone would emerge, who would raise a struggle against the Versailles Treaty."[6] This someone did emerge. Adolf Hitler raised a struggle against the Versailles Treaty, and against France. He demanded arms. Stalin put a sword in his hands. The link between the contents of *Mein Kampf* and Stalin's support for Hitler becomes clearer. The proclamation about lands in the east did not scare Stalin. *Mein Kampf* is against France, as can be read in Part 2, Chapter XIII: "We must understand the following to the end: Germany's most evil enemy is and will always be France." Also: "The task of the day for us is not the struggle for world hegemony. . . . France systematically tears apart our people and according to her plans strangles our independence. . . . We simultaneously hear protests and slogans against five or even ten different countries, and meanwhile forget that first of all we need to concentrate all our physical strength and mental powers to deliver a blow to the heart of our vilest enemy. . . . France will inevitably strive to make Germany into a weak and crushed nation. . . . At the current moment, our only enemy is France—that nation, which deprives us of our rightful existence."[7] Further in the book, Hitler continues in the same spirit for many pages and chapters.

Lands in the east were not his immediate task, only a perspective for centuries to come. This opinion was adhered to not only by Hitler, but by all his immediate entourage: "Land must be taken not in Africa, but in Europe, before all in the East. This is the natural course for Germany's geopolitical development in the coming centuries."[8] Defeating France, on the other hand, was Hitler's immediate task. Before taking lands in the east, Hitler needed to secure himself from his mortal enemy. Here is the second reason for Stalin's love of *Mein Kampf* and its author. Stalin knew that France was not only Hitler's main enemy, but it was a mortal enemy. Stalin understood that if Hitler tried to free Germany from France's economic slavery and from the Versailles Treaty, Britain would immediately interfere, because France imposed the treaty in alliance with Britain. If Germany entered into war with Britain and France, other countries would be pulled into the conflict as well. This was just what Stalin needed.

It did not at all follow from *Mein Kampf* that Hitler would advance to the east. In *Mein Kampf* there is a mention of lands in the east, but no indication of when Germany needs to conquer those lands. Hitler simply "pointed his finger" in the direction. He even said (in Part 1, Chapter III): "The effort would have to be envisaged in terms of centuries; just as in all problems of colonization, steady perseverance is a far more important element than the output of energetic effort at the moment." Hitler was planning to build a thousand-year Reich. Even in the famous, repeatedly quoted passage, he speaks of centuries: "We want to return to that point, at which our previous development stopped six hundred years ago."

In order to return to that point, the Germans had to, as Hitler instructed, "halt the constant German push to the south and the west of Europe." This, Hitler was unable to do. He was unable to do it because *Mein Kampf* contains an inherent fundamental contradiction. In order to advance east, it was necessary to stop moving west. On the other hand, in order to advance east, it was necessary to secure Germany's safety from the mortal enemy, France, and first go west. One does not need to have Stalin's insight—anyone can clearly understand that Hitler got confused in 1924. He set a trap for himself. He openly declared his intention to go east, making enemies out of all those to the east of him. Any German movement "towards the sun" could only go through Poland. Therefore, Poland automatically became Hitler's enemy. And not only Poland: "lands in the east" is a very foggy concept. This declaration could have applied to anyone. If your neighbor proclaimed that he wants to rob you, would you like him? One phrase in his book transformed Hitler into a source of fear for all his eastern neighbors. This does not at all testify to his elevated mental capabilities.

It is not wise to disclose one's political goals, if they are strictly criminal. It is not prudent to make enemies with one's neighbors. But Hitler not only openly proclaimed his desire to advance eastward, he also declared that France was his mortal enemy. To this list he also added the Jews. Hitler's heavy load of enemies broke the camel's back.

The book *Mein Kampf* clearly demonstrated the arrival of a man who was going to fight against the world, the man whom the world was going to hate, the man against whom all people would rise up, the man the whole world would declare war upon. The entire world's hatred would concentrate against Hitler and his followers. If Hitler unleashed a war, first and foremost this war would be against anyone but the Soviet Union. If Hitler unleashed a war, logic would demand the dissipation of German strength along the entire European continent, and beyond. Those who fought against Hitler would be considered saviors and liberators. This is exactly what Stalin needed. Stalin knew: if Hitler went to war against France and Britain, the question of lands in the east would fade on its own.

6

Industrialization and Collectivization

For us, Germany's "national liberation" lies not in a war with the West, but in a proletarian revolution encompassing both Central and Western Europe and uniting it with Eastern Europe as [the] Soviet United States.

—L. Trotsky, "Against National Communism!"

In 1927, a Five Year Plan for developing industry was adapted in the Soviet Union. This began the industrialization, over-industrialization, super-industrialization. After the first, the second Five Year Plan followed, and then a third one.

We can judge the purpose of the Five Year Plans from the following fact. At the beginning of the first Plan, the Red Army had seventy-nine tanks; at the end it had over 4,538.[1] Nevertheless, the military accent was not so noticeable in the first five years. The main focus then was not on the production of arms, but on the creation of an industrial base, which later was to produce armaments.

The second Five Year Plan was a continuation of the development of the industrial base. This meant the creation of furnaces, giant electricity plants and oxygen plants, and coal ore mines. The production of arms was not yet the main objective although Stalin does not forget about it either; in the first two five-year intervals, 21,573 warplanes were produced.[2]

But it was the third Five Year Plan, which was scheduled to end in 1942, that had as its goal the output of hoped-for military production, in enormous quantities and of very high quality. Under Stalin, the Soviet Union truly attained grandiose achievements.

The first secret of the success: terror. Communists shut down the borders of the country; it was impossible to run away. Secret police unleashed a fight against "saboteurs." Any accident in a production line, any breakage, any lack of success was declared a result of an evil plot. The guilty (and the innocent) were imprisoned; the terms were quite lavish. Those who were named "malevolent saboteurs" were shot.

The terror had a dual effect. On the one hand, discipline improved, and any opposition was crushed. Now there was no need to fear strikes and demands for higher wages. On the other hand, millions of people ended up in the concentration camps. This was a slave work-force. Inmates do not have to be paid at all. They can be sent anywhere. They do not need housing—a torn tent, wooden barrack that they build for themselves, or a hole in the ground that they will dig will suffice. Inmates can be almost never fed or clothed. Their lives cost nothing. They can be forced to work any number of hours in a day, without holidays. They can be executed for unfulfilled production quotas. The development of the remote regions of Siberia and the Far East would have been impossible without the multi-million-strong armies of the inmates (and the "special settlers," in other words, those deported by force and exiled to those remote regions). The government planned in advance the number of prisoners that would be needed for the next year, and would place an advance order for the arrests with the People's Commissariat of Internal Affairs (NKVD).

The second secret of Stalin's industrialization success: vast resources available in the USSR. Over a thousand years of its history, Russia had amassed an enormous treasure. The country had huge gold reserves. In churches, monasteries, museums, tsarist palaces, and the homes of rich people, mind-boggling valuables were collected: icons, paintings, statues, medals, books, antique furniture, furs, and jewelry. All this was mercilessly confiscated and sold abroad. Stalin sold enormous reserves of gold, platinum, and diamonds to the outside world. In just a few years, Stalin sold all that the nation had been gathering for centuries. Stalin robbed churches and monasteries, the imperial vaults, and museums. Icons and precious books, paintings by great Renaissance masters, collections of diamonds, and the treasures of museums and libraries were all exported.

On top of all this, Russia has every sort of natural resource and in almost inexhaustible quantities. Millions of people were cutting down forests and transporting the timber to the northern ports. The timber was the base of exports. Stalin also organized gold mining on a never-before-seen scale. Among others, a group of concentration camps was formed under the name "Dal'stroy" (the Russian abbreviation for "Far Eastern Construction Trust"). Jacques Rossi, a Frenchman, spent almost half of his life in Soviet concentration camps. He wrote a remarkable encyclopedia, now known as *The Gulag Handbook: An Encyclopedia and Dictionary of Soviet Penitentiary Institutions and Terms related to the Forced Labor Camps*. Here is how he described this group of camps:

> Dal'stroy is the most powerful and almost autonomous kingdom in the GULAG Empire. Dal'stroy was founded in 1932–1933 on the shores of the Sea of Okhotsk, [at] the mouth of the river Kolyma. The main task was obtaining gold. Local forests, coal, and other resources were exploited only for the internal needs of Dal'stroy. All work was done by the inmates, including the construction of villages and towns for the freely employed, construction of thousands of kilometers of roads, barracks for inmates, etc. By the early 1940s, Dal'stroy stretched a length of 1,300 km from north to south, and 1,700 km from east to west, encompassing the western part of Kamchatka and eastern Yakutia. Dal'stroy was not subordinate to the local administration.[3]

Starting in the late 1930s and all the way into the beginning of the 1950s, several hundred thousand inmates were mining up to 100 tons of gold a year for Stalin.[4] In 1939, just Dal'stroy by itself mined 66.7 tons of gold on Kolyma. The plan for 1940 was for 80 tons of gold. And the production of gold kept on growing. For comparison's sake: In tsarist Russia, the maximum production of gold was 64 tons, in 1913; average annual gold production in the world in 1930–39 was 803 tons. Therefore, just the Kolyma camps were providing Stalin with 12 percent of the world's gold production.[5]

Siberian and Far East gold was the golden key to the success of industrialization. But Dal'stroy was not the only place where gold was mined. Stalin also paid for foreign technology with coal, nickel, manganese, petroleum, cotton, and also with lumber, caviar, and furs. In 1930, the main Soviet export became grain. They managed to get 883 million gold rubles for the exported grain. The sales of oil and oil products and also timber and timber products produced another 430 million gold rubles. Capitalists paid almost 500 million gold rubles for flax and furs.

Later on, because of grain overproduction in the United States, world grain prices dropped. In 1932–33, the overall revenue from grain sales, at very low "dumping" prices, was only 369 million gold rubles. In 1933, the revenue from grain sales was only 8 percent of overall export revenues. Even half of the grain sold during 1932–33 would have been enough to save all of the country's regions from starvation.[6]

Millions of slaves of communism fulfilled the first Five Year Plan, while at the same time the United States experienced an unprecedented economic crisis, which spread to Europe. The crisis gave additional impulse to Stalin's buildup. Finding themselves in the midst of the Great Depression, inventors and businessmen in America, Germany, Great Britain, and France sold technology at low prices. Fortunately, Stalin had plenty of gold in reserve. Western technology was the main key to success. In the beginning of the 1930s, the USSR became the world's biggest importer of machinery and equipment. The People's Commissar of Heavy Industry, Sergo Ordzhonikidze, declared with satisfaction: "Our plants, our mines, our factories are now equipped with such outstanding technology that no other country has. . . .Where did we get it from? We bought from the Americans, from the Germans, from the French, from the British the most advanced technological achievement and then outfitted our enterprises." And then he added, with a dig: "They, themselves, still have their plants and mines equipped with nineteenth- and early twentieth-century equipment."[7]

American engineers traveled to the Soviet Union and designed factories, while Stalin's slaves dug pits, poured concrete roads, and erected walls. Right away, cranes, tools, and equipment came from abroad, and the foreign engineers mounted, set, and tested all this. In the early 1930s, to the amazement of the entire world, in the city of Nizhny Tagil sprang up the most powerful industrial enterprise in the world—Uralvagonzavod (the Ural Railroad Car Factory).

Americans talk with deserved pride of the giant factory which they designed and built not in America, but in the Soviet Union. During the course of six decades, until the very crumbling of the Soviet Union, Uralvagonzavod remained the largest enterprise in the world (the Guinness book of world records confirms this). Uralvagonzavod was built in such a manner that it could at any moment switch from producing railroad cars to producing tanks. In 1941, an order was issued to produce tanks, and Uralvagonzavod without any delays began mass production. During four years of war, Uralvagonzavod produced 35,000 T-34 tanks. It also produced other weapons.

The Chelyabinsk tractor factory was also built in the Urals at the same time. It also was built according to American designs and fully outfitted with American equipment, and it also was built in such a way that at any moment it could stop producing tractors and instead begin producing tanks. During the course of the war, this factory was called Tankograd. It built not only the medium T-34 tanks, but also the heavy IS and KV classes.

Not far away, in Sverdlovsk, a third gigantic factory was built—Uralmash. This factory is among the top ten engineering factories in the world. In order to supply these giants in the Urals, the net of steel-casting factories was greatly expanded. A city of metallurgists—Magnitogorsk—was built, as well as a huge plant, the main output of which was steel armor.

The Urals were not at all the only center of tank building. In Stalingrad, a tractor factory was built, which also on the surface was designed for producing tractors but in reality was for producing tanks. At the same time, automobile, motor, aviation, and artillery factories were being erected. The most powerful aviation factory in the world was built in the Far East. In order to service the factory, the city Komsomolsk-na-Amure was built. This city was a complement to the factory. Both the factory and the city were built according to American designs and furnished with the most modern American equipment. The scope of construction in Komsomolsk astounded even the American engineers, who were there to install the equipment.

Modern factories were built in the Soviet Union, but the lives of the people were not at all improving as a result. The most ordinary pots and pans, rubber boots, plates, the simplest furniture, cheapest clothing, nails, and matches—all these became scarce. Huge lines formed outside the stores. Stalin was paying for industrialization with his people's standard of living, letting it drop very low.

Stalin had one more ace: spies. The West supplied Stalin with the most contemporary industrial equipment, and sold licenses for production of the newest models of weapons and military technology. But all that could not be obtained by legal means was stolen by Stalin's spies. Stalin was generous with his gold when it came to spying.

In order to raise the productivity of his scientists and engineers, Stalin imprisoned entire collectives of engineers, accusing them of being spies. Prominent aviation, tank, and artillery engineers found themselves behind bars. Among them was S. O. Korolev—the future inventor of the first artificial satellite to orbit Earth, N. N. Polikarpov, A. N. Tupolev, R. L. Bartini, V. M. Myasishev, V. M. Petlyakov, and thousands of others. The task set before them was simple: create the best bomber (tank, cannon, engine, and submarine) in the world and you will receive freedom; fail and you will go to Dal'stroy to extract gold; the inmates there do not live too long. Imprisoned engineers did not have to be paid millions for their work, they did not need good houses or apartments, and there was no need to send them to resorts by the warm sea: without all this, they were still very interested in creating the best weapons in the world on very short deadlines. These were talented people; on top of talent, Stalin's spies supplied everything that was created by the best minds in the world. Every imprisoned engineer had before him the best American, German, British, and other designs in the given field. He could choose the best, and based on it create something even more remarkable.

Immediately after the Communists seized power, the land was divided among the peasants. Land was divided rather fairly—according to the number of mouths to feed, meaning the size of area a family received depended on the number of its members. Millions of Russian peasants dreamed for centuries of receiving land. Now their dreams had finally come true, but resulted in a widespread famine across the land. The cause for this was that the Communists gave people the land, but demanded everything the peasants could grow to be given back to the government. The land is yours, but all that you can grow on it is not yours.

It is understandable that nobody wanted to voluntarily give up the fruits of his labor. In answer to this, Communists created "food regulation" brigades and entire armies—units of armed men who took away from the peasants all their reserves. The peasants answered with armed resistance, but they failed.

In the struggle for bread the Communists won, but they celebrated their victory too soon. It is possible to take away from the peasant all his bread, his potatoes, to lead away his cows and to slaughter his pigs; however, it is impossible to force a man to continue working hard. The Russian peasants stopped growing agricultural products since the Communists were taking away what they produced. This resulted in the horrible famine of 1920–21.

Lenin was forced to retreat from his rigid politics. Free trade of foodstuffs was allowed; the gold ruble was introduced. All this was called by the term NEP— New Economic Policy. There was nothing new in it. It was good old capitalism. The country was revived almost immediately. By 1923, there was so much produce that Russia was once again able to export grain. Then, in 1927, Stalin began his industrialization. This process brought on consequences that were not foreseen by the Communists. The country had huge reserves of produce, but peasants were in no rush to sell them. The reason was simple: over several years, hardworking peasants had hoarded significant reserves of gold rubles. They went to the shops in search of manufactured products, but there was nothing to buy. Practically all industrial production in the Soviet Union focused on the military. There were tanks, airplanes, parachutes, cannons, shells, cartridges, and machine guns, but no home appliances. What does a man need cash for, if there is nothing to buy? The peasants once again either stopped selling products or stopped producing them.

The Communists now faced a dilemma: either direct a part of production to producing goods for the wealthy peasants to consume or get rid of the wealthiest, meaning the most hardworking, the smartest. Rather than return to normal human existence and end communism, Stalin chose to enslave the peasants on collective farms and eliminate private ownership. In 1928, Stalin began the bloody war against peasants, which was called collectivization.

Units of the Red Army encircled entire regions. Those peasants who produced more than others were, in the middle of winter, herded together with their families into railroad cattle cars and transported across thousands of kilometers to Siberia, the Urals, or Kazakhstan, where they were thrown out into the cold on the bare steppes. This grandiose operation was initiated on Stalin's orders and executed by his rising deputy Molotov. Many years later, Molotov was asked how many people were transported to the wild, uninhabited regions during collectivization. He answered: "Stalin said that we relocated ten million. In reality, we relocated twenty million."[8]

Historical literature and documentary sources offer different numbers of the demographic losses resulting from the collectivization and starvation of 1932–33. Presently, the following figures look most justified: 3.5 to 5 million people perished from famine, and about 3 to 4 million people died at the places of exile as a result of intolerable conditions of repression and unbearable life. Cannibalism flourished in the country. Stalin, meanwhile, during these horrible times was selling millions of tons of grain each year to accumulate currency in order to produce weapons in mass quantities.[9]

7

Stalin's Role in Elevating Hitler

If Russia makes peace, this peace will only be temporary. The Socialist Revolution in Russia will only win when it is surrounded by a ring of sister Socialist republics. A peace made with imperialist Germany would only be an episodic phenomenon. It will provide a short break, after which war will boil once again.

—G. ZINOVIEV, *COLLECTED WORKS*

The year 1927 was when Stalin finally secured and firmly established his place atop the power structure. From this moment, Stalin's attention was concentrated not only on fortifying his dictatorship, but on issues of the Communist movement and the World Revolution. Stalin needed victory in Europe, especially in Germany. For this, he needed to eliminate three obstacles that were preventing the German revolution. Stalin had to bring order to the German Communist Party and force it to execute orders coming from Moscow, establish common borders with Germany, and destroy the German Social Democrats.

Stalin understood better than anyone else that revolution comes as a result of war. War heightens tensions, ruins economies, and brings nations closer to the fateful limits, beyond which their ordinary existence ceases to be. In matters of war and peace, he adhered to this principle: if the Social Democrats, with their pacifism, divert the proletariat's attention from revolution and from war that gives birth to revolution, then merciless war must be waged against the Social Democrats. On November 6, 1927, Stalin sounded the slogan: "It is impossible to finish off capitalism without finishing off the Social Democrats."[1] In the following year, Stalin declared war on Social Democrats to be the main task before the Communists: "First of all, a tireless struggle against Social Democrats on all lines . . . including exposure of bourgeois pacifism."[2] Regarding those who wanted war, for example regarding the "German fascists" (Communists did not call them "Nazis" because they did not want their people to know about the "socialist" and "worker" aspects of the name of Hitler's party), Stalin's position was clear and rigid: they must be supported. Let the fascists take care of the pacifists and Social Democrats; let them start a new war. Everyone knows that what follows a big war is revolution.

In 1927 Stalin foresaw the Nazi takeover in Germany, and considered this development desirable: "Precisely the fact that the capitalist government is turning fascist is leading to a heightening of tensions within the capitalist countries, and to revolutionary actions by workers," Stalin told the Central Committee in 1927.[3] Stalin gave Hitler's regime the name "terrorist dictatorship" and stressed that "the revolutionary crisis will increase faster [since] the more the bourgeoisie gets confused in its combinations and tactics, the more it employs terrorist methods." In his report to the Seventeenth Party Congress, he stressed: "I speak not about fascism in general, but about fascism of the German type."

In 1925, Stalin declared that World War II was inevitable, as was the Soviet Union's entrance into that war. "There can be no doubt that a war in Europe will start and they will all fight in it."[4] But Stalin did not want to start the war himself, or to be its participant from the first day: "We will have to enter, but we will enter last, we will enter in order to throw in our weight and tip the scale."[5] The more crimes Hitler committed in Europe, the better for Stalin, the more reasons Stalin had to send the Red Army to liberate Europe.

For Stalin's strategy to be implemented Hitler needed to secure an absolute majority of the votes in the German parliamentary elections. He could not do this alone. On July 31, 1932, Hitler's party amassed 13.7 million votes in the elections to the *Reichstag* (German parliament), 37.3 percent of the total number of votes—the peak for the Nazi party, after which its popularity began to decline. However, this was not enough for an absolute majority. In the following four months, Hitler lost 2 million votes. The decline continued, and gained momentum. The breakdown of the votes for the major German political parties on November 6, 1932, when the emergency *Reichstag* election took place, was as follows:

> Hitler's party (NSDAP)—11,705,000
> Social Democrats—7,231,000
> Communist Party—5,971,000

Hitler's National Socialist Workers' Party faced a crisis. At first glance, Hitler seemed to be the winner and the most popular politician in Germany, and therefore should have taken power. However, he did not have an absolute majority, and could not take power. But combined, the Social Democrats and the Communists had more votes. Hitler's National Socialist Workers' Party was in a deep financial crisis as well, its funds diminishing fast. Goebbels wrote in his diary: "All hope has disappeared. . . . There is not a pfennig in our cash boxes. . . . Nobody gives us any credit. . . . We are on our last breath." Goebbels's entry on December 23, 1932, said: "I am overwhelmed by a terrible feeling of loneliness, which borders on a sense of total loss! The year 1932 was a sequence of one misfortune after another. It should be erased completely. . . . We have no prospects, no hopes left." The terrible position the Nazis found themselves in was no secret to outside observers. By New Year's Eve, the powerful newspaper *Frankfurter Zeitung* was already rejoicing at the "disintegration of the NSDAP myth." Harold Laski, one of the leading intellectuals of the English left, was assured that: "The day when the National Socialists presented a lethal danger has passed. . . . If we discount chance, it is not so improbable that Hitler will finish his career as an old man in some Bavarian village, telling tales to his friends in the evenings in some beer hall, about how he once almost orchestrated a takeover in the German Reich."[6]

Facing bankruptcy, Hitler, as recorded in Goebbels's diary, considered two options: the first was flight, the other was suicide. Ten years after the crisis, Hitler himself told his inner circle: "The situation was at its worst in 1932, when we were forced to sign many debt obligations in order to fund our press and election campaigns, and keep the party running. . . . In the name of the NSDAP, I signed for these obligations, knowing that if the NSDAP stopped functioning, everything was lost."[7] At the end of 1932, Hitler's time would be up, and he would be finished as a politician. For the time being he was still the most popular political figure in Germany, but his party was in deep debt, and running out of money. German National Socialism faced doom until Hitler was saved by Stalin.

Comrade Stalin did not just save Hitler; he handed him the keys to power. Democracy is structured in such a way that, during the turning points of history, minority groups play the key roles. This occurs because history has innumerable possible courses and outcomes. When everything goes well, people agree with the leaders' course of action, but during times of crisis alternative ideas and plans arise. Policy alternatives split the nation almost evenly between two diametrically opposed views. In such a situation, a third party—a minority—becomes the kingmaker, and its role can be decisive.

In 1932 Germany experienced precisely this situation: Hitler was in first place, the Social Democrats second, and the Communists third. But none of the three could control the absolute majority needed to come to power. In this case, Germany's fate, and the fate of Europe, was in the hands of the German Communists. If the Communists sided with the Social Democrats, Nazism would perish and never again resurface. If the Communists turned against the Social Democrats, Social Democracy would crumble.

For the Communists, forming a coalition with the Social Democrats meant defeating Hitler. After this victory, the Communists would automatically rise from third place to second, and share power with the first-place party, the Social Democrats—a very appealing option.

The Communists had a second option: to go against the Social Democrats, thereby opening the way for Hitler to take power. The consequences of such a move were very predictable: Hitler, having come to power, would throw both Social Democrats and Communists into concentration camps. If the German Communists went against the Social Democrats, they would be sentencing to death both themselves and the Social Democrats.

Acting on Stalin's orders, the German Communist leaders chose the second option—they did not wish to form a block with the Social Democrats. Publicly, for regular Communists and workers, the Communist Party policy against the Social Democrats was explained with twisted reasoning: there is no radical difference between a regime of parliamentary democracy and a fascist dictatorship. Both are forms of dictatorship by the bourgeoisie, which was growing more and more reactionary. The German Communist leaders kept repeating, after their Moscow masters, that a fascist-like turn taken by the bourgeois parties and their Social Democrat supporters was even more dangerous than the Nazis because the Social Democrats hid their true motives. German Communist leaders told the workers: We are Communists, struggling against capitalism and fascism, while the Social Democrats are acting as protectors of capitalism, and are becoming de facto allies of the fascists. Therefore, the Social Democrats are really nothing more than a "left wing" of fascism, or they are "social fascists," a party which conducts a policy of "hidden fascism" that is more dangerous than Nazi policy. The peace-loving policy of the Social Democrats prevents war; therefore it prevents revolution and, ultimately, prevents the victory of the Working Class, while the Nazi policy enhances the chances for war and revolution and, ultimately, the victory of the Working Class. From this bizarre dialectic, they concluded that Hitler's party must carry out the main attack on the Social Democrats, since they were the most dangerous enemy, which still retained some influence over the worker class and hindered an effective war on capitalism.

Hitler came to power as a result of this perverted ideological mind game. German Communists, out of instincts for self-preservation, should have joined a coalition with the Social Democrats. But Stalin intervened and opened the way for Hitler. The first time there was open cooperation between the Nazis and Communists was in August 1931 in Eastern Prussia, where the Social Democrats were in power. The Nazis initiated a referendum to oust the Social Democrats. At first the Communists were opposed to the referendum. However, after instructions from Moscow, they changed their minds. The Nazis and Communists joined forces under a common red flag, on which the swastika and the hammer and sickle were intertwined. Despite the Communists' calling the plebiscite a "Red Referendum" and the Nazis "working people's comrades," the referendum failed to gain a majority.

A year later, several days before the November 1932 elections for the *Reichstag*, a public transportation strike began in Berlin. The Communists and Nazis jointly coordinated the strike. Storm troopers and *rotfronters* (Communist paramilitary) paralyzed public transportation for five days, dug up tram tracks, picketed, beat up those who came to work, and used force to stop the cars that the authorities managed to put to work.

Once the Nazis came to power, Stalin used all his might to push them toward war. When Germany attacked Poland, and France and Britain entered the war against Germany, Stalin ordered the Communists of the Western democracies to oppose the war. The Western democracies were branded as capitalist imperialists, and the Comintern ordered its members to weaken the armies of the Western democracies through strikes in armament and airplane factories. The Communist Parties were to demand an end to the "imperialist war." Hitler was portrayed as a fighter for the working classes. But by pushing Hitler into conflict with democratic Europe, Stalin had issued Hitler a death sentence. By offering to divide Poland with Hitler, Stalin had dragged him into a larger scale war with no end in sight. Stalin expected that the Western allies and Germany would exhaust their strength by fighting against each other as they did in World War I. The struggle between Hitler and the Western democracies would create the moment for a "mighty strike" from the East and bring forth world revolution on the bayonets of the Red Army. Five years prior to the Nazis' rise to power in Germany, Stalin had already planned their annihilation: "[We will] crush fascism, destroy capitalism, establish Soviet power, and liberate the colonies from slavery."[8]

8

Stalin and the Destruction of Soviet Strategic Aviation

> Given the existence of a massive invasion army, the main task of the air force is to support the advancement of this army, for which all forces must be concentrated.
>
> —Brigade Commander Alexander Lapchinsky, *The Air Army*

Stalin could have averted World War II with one stroke of his pen. He had many such opportunities. Here is one of them: In 1936, the Soviet Union developed the heavy high-speed, high-altitude bomber TB-7 (later renamed Pe-8). Here are reviews of it:

Air Force Major General P. Stefanovsky, test-pilot of the TB-7: "The multi-ton ship surpassed in its flight capabilities at an altitude of ten kilometers all the best European fighters of its time."[1]

Air Force Major General V. Shumikhin: "At altitudes above 10,000 meters the TB-7 could not be reached by the majority of existing fighters at that time, and the ceiling of 12,000 meters made it untouchable even by anti-aircraft artillery."[2]

Airplane designer V. Shavrov: "A remarkable airplane. It was on the TB-7 that the first five-ton bombs were lifted, earlier than in the United States or in England."[3]

Professor L. Kerber: "This machine had a strong defense system consisting of 20-mm cannons and 12.7-mm heavy machine guns. Bombs of the largest caliber could fit in the large bomb compartment. . . . [It was] unreachable at maximum altitude of its flight by anti-aircraft cannons and fighters of that time. The TB-7 was the most powerful bomber in the world."[4] "A record-setting plane. . . . Now, we have every reason to assert that the TB-7 was more powerful than the American flying fortress B-17."[5]

Historians agree with such appraisals. John V. R. Taylor: "At heights of 26,250 to 29,500 feet its speed surpassed the speed of German Me-109 and He-112 fighters."[6] Vaclav Nemecek: "This machine had an incredibly long life. In the fifties, one could still encounter [some of] these planes on polar routes, where they were used for transporting cargo."[7] There is no need to prove that only good planes live and fly for such a long time.

The remarkable qualities of the TB-7 were demonstrated to Western experts in the spring of 1942, when the arrival of a Soviet delegation headed by Molotov was awaited in the

United States and in Britain. It was thought that the only possible route was through Siberia and Alaska. But Molotov flew on a TB-7 from Moscow to Britain over occupied Europe. One must remember who ruled the skies above Europe in the spring of 1942, in order to appraise the level of trust of Soviet leadership in this airplane. Molotov did not fear landing on the defendant's bench in Nazi court, and Stalin did not fear letting Molotov fly. The TB-7 proved itself. It flew over all of Europe, stopped in Britain, flew to America, and returned by the same route, once again flying over German holdings undisturbed.

After the war, a commission of the Soviet government conducted an analysis of the German anti-aircraft defenses at the time of Molotov's flight. It turned out that, along the flight path, German fighters did not go up to intercept the enemy aircraft, there was no alert sounded at the anti-aircraft batteries, the observation posts did not register the flight of the TB-7 at all. Simply put, the German anti-aircraft defenses not only could not take down the TB-7, they could not detect its presence in their air territory.

Colonel (at that time, Captain) E. Pussep, who flew a TB-7 over Germany many times (not only with Molotov's precious self, but with other cargo), recounted: "The anti-aircraft guns reach at such altitudes with hardly any aim, if at all. A fighter plane at such height can act only like a sleepy fly. Who can do anything to me?"[8]

So, long before the war the Soviet Union had created an untouchable bomber, and a government order was prepared to produce a thousand TB-7s by November 1940. What remained to be done? All that was left to do was to sign the order with seven letters: J. STALIN.[9]

When the first TB-7s flew at unreachable altitudes, engineers in other countries of the world still had problems with the unseen barrier of height: in thin air, engines lost their power from a deficiency of oxygen.[10] They literally suffocated, like mountaineers at the summit of Mount Everest. One possible way of increasing the power of engines existed: to use exhaust gases to rotate a turbo-compressor, which supplies the engine with additional air. This was simple in theory, difficult in practice. In experimental trials, in record-setting airplanes, this was successful. But in series models, it was not.

Components of the turbo-compressor work in a hot stream of corrosive gas at a temperature of over 1000 degrees Celsius when the surrounding air is minus 60 degrees Celsius, and then return to the warm ground. Uneven heating and rapid changes in pressure and temperature ruined the parts, and the sound of the turbo-compressor drowned out the roar of the engines. Protective paints and coatings burned during the first flight and, when back on the ground, moisture settled on cooling engines, and corrosion ate through the mechanisms. The bearings had the worst fate: they melted, like wax candles. On a trial plane, if out of ten attempts one time the turbo-compressor doesn't break, good. But what is one to do with the mass production airplanes?

Everyone searched for the solution, but it was discovered by Vladimir Petliakov, the creator of the TB-7. Petliakov's solution was kept as a top government secret. The TB-7 had four propellers, and from the outside appeared to be a four-engine plane. But inside its body, behind the crew cabin, Petliakov installed an additional fifth engine, which did not rotate any propellers. At low and medium altitudes, the four main engines were engaged, and at high altitudes, the fifth was switched on and brought into action the system of a centralized supply of additional oxygen. Using this oxygen, the fifth engine fed itself and the four others. That is how the TB-7 could climb where no other plane could reach it. With it, one could fly over Europe, bomb any object, and not worry about its own safety.

With a thousand untouchable TB-7s, any invasion could have been averted. All that had to be done was to invite delegations of certain countries and in their presence somewhere in a remote steppe drop at least one thousand tons of bombs from astounding altitudes.[11] Then follow up with an explanation: This has nothing to do with you, this is a surprise we hold for the capital city of that country which ventures to attack ours. Precision? There is no precision. Why would there be? We drop the bombs from incredible heights. The lack of precision will be corrected through repeated drops. Every day several hundred tons will rain on the capital of the aggressor, until we reach the desired outcome, and then other cities will get a taste of this hailstorm as well. Do you understand what will happen to the opponent before he has a chance to reach Moscow? The TB-7 is untouchable when in the air, and cannot be attacked by the opponent on land: our bases are hidden far from the borders, and our probable enemies have no strategic aviation to speak of. . . . And now, gentlemen, let us drink to eternal peace.

Such a speech could have been given by Stalin's diplomats, if the Soviet Union had several hundred or even a thousand TB-7s. But Stalin decided not to build a thousand TB-7s. Is it possible to understand Stalin's motives? Yes, it is possible.

If we compare a thousand TB-7s to a game of chess, this situation is the equivalent of being able to declare checkmate to the opponent's king before the start of the game, and if the partner still ventures to play, one can call checkmate after his first move. If one thousand tons of bombs, which several hundred TB-7s could deliver in one trip, are to be translated into contemporary strategic terms, it is equivalent to one kiloton. This is the language of the nuclear age. If one kiloton is insufficient, in two sorties twice this amount can be delivered. Twenty kilotons equals what (without much precision) was dropped on Hiroshima. A thousand TB-7s is like a nuclear missile, aimed at the enemy's capital. The power is such that, for a potential aggressor, war loses all sense.

Some argue that during the course of the war the British and American strategic aviation dropped many more bombs on Germany, without being able to bomb her into surrender. This is true. However, these were bomb raids during the course of the war, when it was too late for Hitler to ask for mercy. A different story would have been to demonstrate such power to Hitler and his generals before the war, and warn them that if they started a war all this would fall on their heads. In that case, Hitler personally, or those surrounding him, would have thought twice about the consequences of their actions.

In the late 1930s Stalin had the capacity to create an instrument that would serve as a severe warning to Hitler. With one stroke of Stalin's pen on an order to produce a series of TB-7s, the German invasion of Soviet territory could have been averted. Of course, in August 1939 Stalin could not have had a thousand TB-7s. But he could have had two, three, four, or maybe even five hundred. If only Stalin had in due time signed an order for the serial production of the TB-7.

To do him justice, it must be noted that Stalin did sign such an order—but then he canceled it. And signed it again! And repealed it again, and again. Four times the production of TB-7s started, and four times it was canceled.[12] After each order, the industry had time to put out three or four TB-7s, and then the order was reversed. Everything started anew, and once again was interrupted. By June 22, 1941, the TB-7 series was not in production. In the four attempts, the aviation industry had time to issue and give over to the air force not a thousand TB-7s, but only eleven. Moreover, almost all of the eleven planes lacked the most important detail—the fifth additional engine.[13] Without it, the best strategic bomber of the world became an average commodity. After Hitler's invasion, the TB-7 series was resumed in production. But by then it was too late.

A question arises: If Stalin had issued the order to produce a thousand TB-7s and did not cancel it, could the Soviet industry have fulfilled such an order? Could it have put out, by the end of 1940, a thousand such airplanes? The creator of the TB-7, Vladimir Petliakov (after Petliakov's tragic death the TB-7 was renamed Pe-8), did not doubt this for a minute. Alexander Mikulin, creator of the engines for the TB-7, was completely certain that Soviet industry could meet such a demand. Professor L. Kerber, the deputy to the airplane designer A. Tupolev, and experts in the air industry S. Eger, S. Leshchenko, E. Stoman, chief engineer of the factory that produced the TB-7s I. Nezval, head technologist of the factory E. Shekunov, and many others on whom production of the TB-7 depended—all thought the task could be accomplished by the designated deadline. Airplane designers V. Shavrov and A. Tupolev held that one thousand TB-7s could be ready by November 1940.

The confidence of the engineers and leaders of industry is understandable: the TB-7 was not being built just anywhere. Russia is the motherland of strategic bombers. I say this with pride and without irony. At the beginning of the twentieth century, when the entire world was flying on single-engine planes, Russia was the first in the world to start producing twin-engine airplanes. The world did not have the time to fully appreciate this advancement, when the great Russian engineer Igor Ivanovich Sikorsky built the first four-engine heavy bomber Ilya Muromets in 1913. The Muromets was unrivaled in terms of armament, bomb capacity, and range for several years. It had the best navigation system, bomb-aiming sight, and the first electrical bomb release mechanism in the world. For defense, it had eight machine guns, and there had even been an attempt to install a 76-mm cannon on board. In 1914, Russia became the first country in the world to create a unit of heavy bombers—a squadron of air ships.

When the Communists took over the country, Igor Sikorsky found himself among the exiles. However, Russia's technological potential remained large, and development continued. Despite the terror, despite the Communist burden, Russia continued to be the leader in the area of heavy bombers. In 1925, the design bureau of A. Tupolev created the TB-1, the first entirely metal bomber in the world, also the first monoplane with a cantilever wing. The rest of the world at the time still built wooden biplane bombers. The test trials of the TB-1 yielded two world records. In a short time, 216 TB-1s were built—another record.[14] Russia had more heavy bombers than all the other nations combined. As the planes were built, more and more squadrons, regiments, and brigades were formed.

In 1930, Tupolev put out an even more powerful bomber—the TB-3, the first four-engine monoplane with a cantilever wing. The TB-3 was the largest of all airplanes in the world, both military and passenger. Such planes were unseen not only in production, but even in blueprints. Tupolev, in 1933, had already begun experimenting with refueling the TB-3 while in flight. The TB-3 set several world records, including high altitude flights with cargos of 5, 10, and 12 tons. The design of the TB-3 became a basic model for this class of airplane for many decades to come. The plane was assembled with astonishing speed, which reached three TB-3 models per day.[15]

Soviet industry broke its own records—in a short period it put out 819 TB-3s. Air regiments and brigades were no longer enough. On March 23, 1932, the Soviet Union became the first country in the world to create a heavy bomber corps. In January 1936, the first aviation army was created, a second army in March, and a third aviation army a bit later. No other nation at the time had either an aviation army or even a corps of strategic aviation. A fleet of a thousand heavy bombers is a strategist's dream, and this dream materialized first in the Soviet Union. Generals and politicians of all nations disputed the doctrine of the Italian air power theorist General Giulio Douhet, a strong proponent of strategic bombing.[16] Only Stalin did not argue.

But that is not all: the plans were for rearming three aviation armies with the newest bombers and additionally deploying three more armies in the Byelorussia, Kiev, and Leningrad military districts.[17] While the TB-3 was "learning to fly," while it was being "put on its wings," approximately ten design bureaus were already engaged in fierce competition to receive the order for the newest strategic bomber, which would come to replace one thousand of Tupolev's TB-1s and TB-3s. Tupolev himself proposed the eight-engine Maxim Gorky. Only one model was built as a show piece to be flown over parades, awing the crowds with its dimensions. Maxim Gorky crashed in 1935, after a mid-air collision with a small escort plane. Thirty-seven people—the passengers and crew of both aircraft—died. A conspiracy theory has arisen alleging that the pilot of the escort plane deliberately rammed the Maxim Gorky because he believed Stalin was aboard.

Pavel Sukhoi proposed a one-motor long-distance bomber, the DB-1, with an incredibly large wingspan. The DB stands for *Dal'nyi Bombardirovshik*, which means "long-distance bomber." This plane (under a different name) completed several flights across the North Pole to America. America greeted Soviet pilots as heroes, not understanding that they were running tests of an experimental bomber. Sergei Kozlov proposed a twelve-motor "Ghigant" (Giant), capable of lifting several tens of tons of bombs, and of delivering to the enemy's rear paratroop divisions complete with any heavy artillery, including tanks.

Bolkhovitinov proposed a heavy bomber, the DB-A. Though it looked like a new airplane in design and description, it is a remodeling of the TB-3. This is a classic example of how a new airplane can be created with minimal expenditures, at the same factories that produced the old models. The DB-A broke four world records. It was the newest plane, but it could be produced by the same factories that put out the TB-3, without rebuilding the assembly lines, without changing equipment, without disrupting the established production flow, without retraining workers and engineers—in short, without the usual reduction in output and even without the need to retrain pilots, technicians, or engineers. If time was an issue, it was possible to launch a series of DB-As and fully renew the strategic aviation fleet by the start of World War II. But then a new, true miracle appeared—Petliakov's TB-7. The TB-7 eclipsed all other models.

By the time the TB-7 appeared, production of heavy bombers was as perfected in the Soviet Union as Henry Ford's production of automobiles had become in the United States. Changing a model is usually a difficult process, but it is simpler than creating a new model from scratch. During those horrible years, when millions died of hunger, the Soviet Union was first in the world in production of heavy bombers. Then, when the economy had somewhat improved, the country suddenly voluntarily backed away from its first-place position in this field. When no one threatened the nation, it took bread from dying children to continue to build heavy bombers. But when Hitler appeared nearby, and war came within sight, the production of heavy bombers was halted.

The question is not whether or not there would have been enough time to build a thousand TB-7s before the beginning of the war. The question is: why did they not try?

By the time the TB-7 came onto the scene, the Soviet Union had created design bureaus capable of creating airplanes that were ahead of their time, and an industry capable of a mass output that surpassed the demand of peacetime. Air academies, pilot schools, and technical schools were opened, the theory of military use was developed, and combat experience was obtained in local conflicts and grandiose training exercises. Air bases, learning centers, and test sites were built; personnel from command staff to machine-gun operators, from navigation officers to engineers to photo-decipherers were trained. Pilots, meteorologists, aviation medics, and others were all ready. Collectives formed, traditions were born, theorists and practitioners were raised.

After all this, the country that was the leader in the field of strategic aviation entered World War II without strategic aviation. On Stalin's orders, in November 1940, the Soviet air armies were disbanded. On June 22, 1941, Soviet strategic aviation did not have any armies in its ranks. Only five corps and three separate divisions remained. They were mostly equipped with the DB-3f, which is a magnificent bomber, but not a strategic bomber. They also still had TB-3s, which could be used to transport cargo, but as bombers they were obsolete. As we already know, there were only eleven TB-7s, not even enough to outfit one squadron.

It seems that there was no situation in which the TB-7 would become superfluous. If Stalin planned to avert World War II, he needed the TB-7. If Stalin decided to allow Hitler to unleash the world war, and planned to himself remain neutral, the TB-7 would be very needed, as a guarantee of neutrality. If Stalin planned defensive war, troops should have been ordered to dig themselves into the ground, as was done later on near Kursk. He needed to barricade the borders with impassable minefields from sea to sea, and while the enemy would be gnawing through our defenses, let the TB-7 fly at unreachable altitudes and ruin German economic power. In a defensive war, the TB-7s were needed. Stalin's resources were unlimited, while Hitler's were limited. Therefore, if the war started, it was to Stalin's advantage to draw it out: a war of attrition was deadly for Germany. In order to exhaust the enemy's resources more quickly, Stalin needed strategic bombers to weaken the military and economic potential of the enemy. There could be no better instrument for such a task than the TB-7.

The fate of the TB-7 disproves the legend that Stalin feared Hitler. If he was afraid, why not order the TB-7? The more he feared, the more planes he should have ordered. The reader should agree with me that when at night we fear walking across a cemetery, we pick up a stick. The more we fear, the bigger the stick we pick up, and we swing it menacingly. Stalin, on the other hand, had to be coaxed into picking up a stick. His personal advisor, airplane designer Lieutenant Colonel General Alexander Yakovlev, testifies that the chief of an R&D Center of the Air Forces, Major General A. I. Philin, was not afraid to prove to Stalin, in the presence of many, the necessity of producing a series of TB-7s.

Arguing with Stalin was tantamount to suicide. "Philin demanded, a few others supported him. In the end, Stalin conceded, saying: 'OK, let it be your way, though you have not convinced me.'"[18] This is one of those cases when Stalin allowed the issue of TB-7s. Soon after, Stalin changed his mind and repealed his order. Once again, some brave souls began to argue and plead with him. The question is: Why was it necessary to prove to Stalin this plane's usefulness? If we all understand the indisputable advantages of the TB-7 and the need for its production, why could not Stalin understand such simple facts? If everything boils down to

Stalin's stupidity, the TB-7 would have been forbidden with one blow, and Stalin would not have returned again and again to the question. But Stalin changed his mind eight times. Why these doubts?

Exterminate millions of the best peasants, feeders of Russia? Order given—and the murderous collectivization starts. Purge the command staff of the army? No problem. Sign a pact with Hitler? No doubts. Stalin rarely had doubts. Repealing the order to build the TB-7 was the most difficult decision Stalin made in his lifetime.

The TB-7 had powerful enemies, and it is time to name them. The General Staff of the Red Army was formed in 1935. Before the German invasion the post of Commander of the General Staff was occupied in succession by Marshals A. I. Egorov and B. M. Shaposhnikov and Generals of the Army K. A. Meretskov and G. K. Zhukov. All of them were opponents of the TB-7. Other opponents of the TB-7, and of all strategic bombers, included many important aviation generals, including P. V. Rychagov, F. K. Arzhanukhin, and F. P. Polynin. The People's Commissar for Defense Marshal S. K. Timoshenko also opposed the TB-7. Airplane designer A. S. Yakovlev, Stalin's advisor on questions of aviation, was an avid opponent. And, of course, almost all Soviet military theorists, starting with V. K. Triandaphillov, were opposed to strategic bombers.

The best of all arguments against heavy bombers was put forward by a professor, Brigade Commander Alexander Nikolaevich Lapchinsky, the leading Soviet theorist of air warfare. He wrote several brilliant works on the theory of military aviation. His ideas are simple and understandable. Bombing cities, factories, and sources and storages of strategic resources is good. But it is even better to take over all this and use it to enhance one's own might. It is possible to transform the enemy's country into a smoking heap, but is it necessary? Bombing roads and bridges is useful in any situation except one: when we are preparing an invasion into enemy territory. In that case, bridges and roads should not be bombed, but taken over intact, without allowing the retreating enemy to use or to destroy them. Bombing cities drastically lowers the morale of the local population. This is true, who would argue with such a fact? But a forceful advancement of our troops toward enemy cities demoralizes the population more than any bombing. Lapchinsky recommended to Stalin to direct all efforts of the Red Army not toward undermining the military and economic capabilities of the enemy, but toward taking them over. The Red Army's objective was to destroy the opponent's armies. The objective of Soviet aviation was to open the road to our armies and support their rapid advancement.

Lapchinsky recommended not declaring a war, but starting a war with a sudden crushing attack by Soviet aviation on enemy air bases. The suddenness and power of the strike needed to be such that in the first hours it would destroy all of the enemy's aviation, without letting it leave the ground. Having destroyed the enemy's aviation on the ground, we would open the road for tanks, and advancing tanks in their turn would "level the enemy air bases." The target for our aviation should not be city districts, not electric plants and factories, but the enemy airplanes on the ground, the hidden machine gun hindering the advancement of our infantry, the column of trucks with fuel for enemy tanks, the anti-tank cannon hiding in the bushes.

In other words, one should bomb specific targets, many of them mobile. Bombing should take place not in the enemy's rear, but in the closest tactical space, on the front lines. For such work, one needs a light, maneuverable plane, whose pilot can use it to come close to his target, recognize it, and hit the enemy precisely without hitting his own troops. The bomber is not needed. One needs a plane that either dives from heights or comes to the target in a hedgehopping flight, barely missing the treetops.

If we plan to blow up the neighbor's house, we need a crate of dynamite. But if we plan to kill the neighbor, and take over his house, we do not need the dynamite; we need cheaper, lighter, and more precise tools. Lapchinsky recommended to Stalin a different tool: a light bomber or a low-flying attack plane. A strategic bomber flies from faraway stationary bases and covers great distances, while the Soviets needed a plane that would always be nearby, could land on any dirt airfield, could easily change bases following advancing divisions, and could immediately fulfill the requests of tankers. They needed a light plane, whose pilots could themselves see the situation and instantly react to changes, contributing to the successful outcome of a quick and decisive battle.

Vladimir Petliakov, aside from the heavy four-engine (or rather five-engine) TB-7, created another plane—a small, twin engine, fast, maneuverable dive-bomber, the Pe-2. This was exactly what Stalin needed. Stalin decided: "Build two-motor ones, as many as possible."[19] Was it not possible to build heavy and light bombers simultaneously? "No," said Lapchinsky, "impossible." All resources, all efforts had to be concentrated on achieving the central goal: obtaining full air superiority through a sudden attack on enemy air bases. If such a strike was delivered, there would be no need to bomb cities and factories. Stalin allowed the production of both types of airplane for a long time, but then understood that he must choose one or the other. He made his choice.

If we cannot grasp Stalin's iron logic, it is easier to declare Stalin insane. But let us look at Hitler. He is also an aggressor, and that is why he also has no strategic aviation. Hitler prepared a lightning takeover of France, and needed to take over and safeguard bridges rather than bomb them. German tank divisions needed the bridges for quick advancement. Paris also did not need to be bombed. Paris, with all its treasures, would go to the victor. Hitler did not need to destroy the shipyards of Brest, the tank and artillery factories of Cherbourg, Chaumont, and Bourges, the airplane factories of Amsterdam and Toulouse. They would be needed to strengthen the military might of the Third Reich!

For the blitzkrieg, Hitler needed aviation, but the type that would destroy French planes on the ground and paralyze, through sudden strikes, the French system of military command, not the type that destroys cities and factories. He needed aviation that would open the way for tanks and secure the quickness of their thrust toward the ocean. He needed aviation that hovered over the battlefields, fulfilling the requests from the tankers; aviation that struck not on giant areas, but on concrete targets. For the *Blitzkrieg*, he needed a small dive-bomber that carried a light load, but bombs precisely: a single-engine Ju-87, or a dual-engine Ju-88.

Later, the war changed its course and turned from a quick war into a war of attrition. New cities inaccessible to Hitler's tanks became targets—London, Cheliabinsk, Bristol, Kuibyshev, Sheffield, and Magnitogorsk. Here, Hitler would not have minded having strategic aviation, but he did not have any.

Lapchinsky's ideas, written long before Hitler came to power, were used by Stalin. Not in 1941, as was planned, but in 1945. Stalin's Pe-2 dive-bombers and low-flying attack planes Il-2 suddenly attacked Japanese airbases, and Soviet tank units entered Manchuria. It was an easy victory. When Japan was bled to death by fighting in the Pacific, and the first A-bomb was dropped, Stalin conveniently struck from the rear and seized Manchuria, creating the conditions for Mao's victory in 1949. Soviet paratroops landed in Chinese cities not to destroy bridges, roads, and factories, but to prevent their destruction. In such a war there was no work for strategic aviation.

In the 1920s and early 1930s, Stalin needed strategic aviation so that nobody could hinder him from building Soviet military and economic power. In the second half of the 1930s, Stalin more and more leaned toward the scenario of a war that would result not in the destruction of Germany, but in its takeover. In November 1940, Stalin fully decided to accomplish against Germany what he would in August 1945 accomplish against Japan.

9

Stalin's Preparations for War: Tanks

Germans were surprised to discover that it was practically impossible to stop the Red Army's KV tanks.

—Robert Goralski, *World War II Almanac, 1931–1945*

Stalin's goal was to develop and mass-produce the best tanks in the world. Tanks were to be the spearhead for the Soviet offensive against Western Europe, and Stalin set about developing them as he built Soviet industry.

In 1933, the Red Army adopted the T-28 tank. A variation of this model was designed in 1937—the T-28 PKh (*Podvodny Khod*—"underwater traversing" tank). Tests showed that if necessary, all series of T-28s could be converted to cross water barriers underwater, at a depth of up to 4.5 meters and width of up to one kilometer with a stream speed up to one m/s (meter per second).[1] Not a single German, British, American, French, or Japanese tank from the 1930s could compete with the T-28 in terms of weapons, armor, or engine power.[2]

At the end of 1937, the Germans started producing the Pz-IVA, the most powerful German tank of the first half of World War II. It had 15-mm armor.[3] The T-28's armor was of higher quality and twice as thick—30 mm. This most powerful German tank had a 250-horsepower engine. The T-28's was twice as powerful: 500 horsepower. The German tank had two machine guns, while the T-28 had four or five. The gun on the German tank was approximately equal to the Soviet one. The T-28 had a 76-mm KT-28 gun, while the German tank had a gun of slightly smaller caliber—75 mm; therefore, the shells were slightly lighter. The T-28 fired shells with an initial speed of 381 m/s. The German Pz-IVA had a slightly longer barrel (16.5 caliber); therefore the speed of the shells was slightly higher—385 m/s. Thus the muzzle energy of both guns was practically the same. Soviet designers could not reconcile themselves to the fact that the Germans had caught up with them at least in one parameter. In response, starting in 1938, the Soviet T-28 tanks were produced with a new L-10 gun. Its barrel length was 26 calibers. The muzzle velocity of its shells was 555 m/s. The Germans did not catch up with this innovation until 1942. The L-10 Soviet tank gun in 1941 was unrivaled in Germany or anywhere else in the world. "In terms of arms, the T-28 absolutely surpassed all German tanks. The L-10 gun (as well as the KT-28, by the way) could effectively destroy the tanks of the *Wehrmacht Heer* at distances out of range for their weapons."[4]

The Germans installed the HL-120TR 300-horsepower engine on the later models of their most powerful tank, the Pz-IV. But they still did not catch up with the Soviet 500-horsepower engines. The Germans enhanced the armor to 30 mm. The Soviet response was the T-28 E, with a maximum thickness of 80 mm. The T-28 had sufficient allowances in its design to permit the installation of the 85-mm F-39 gun with a 52-caliber length.[5] The tank successfully passed all tests with that gun model. However, at that time, the Soviet tank industry made another breakthrough: it created the T-34. Its classic design became the sire of the future development of tanks worldwide. Further modernization of the T-28 was unnecessary.

After the war, Soviet generals and historians called the T-28 obsolete. But the T-28 was obsolete only by Soviet standards, only compared to the T-34. In comparison with all foreign tanks, the T-28 was still outstanding. If in the summer of 1941 a foreign tank had had a 76-mm gun with muzzle velocity of 555 m/s and four or five machine guns, it would have been the national pride of that country. But nobody had such a tank. If a foreign tank had had a frontal armor of 80 mm, it would have been considered an outstanding design achievement.[6] If anyone in the world in 1941 had had a 500-horsepower tank engine, this would have been a world record. The "obsolete" Soviet T-28 was a combination of three world records, each of which even taken independently would have been the national pride in any other country.

After the war, the Soviet historians excluded all T-28 tanks (and many others) from the statistics, and put them in the "obsolete and worn-out" category. However, the "obsolete" T-28 tanks captured by Finland in 1939 and 1941 were used by the Finnish army, served until the very end of the war, and were successfully used against the Red Army. One of the "worn-out" T-28s was remodeled into an evacuation vehicle and served until 1951. By the way, there were no spare parts for these tank models in Finland. But the T-28 was designed in such a way that even without spare parts it served for several years in a war in terrible climates, almost impassable terrain, against a powerful enemy—the Soviet KV and T-34 tanks. And it even served six years after the war.

On December 19, 1939, the Red Army enlisted in its ranks the T-34. Following are German reviews of its performance. General Field Marshal von Kleist said: "Their T-34 was the best in the world." Major General von Mellentin agreed: "We had nothing equal to the T-34." General Field Marshal von Rundstedt also thought that the T-34 was the best tank in the world. Colonel General Guderian remembered: "A large number of T-34 tanks were used in battle [Guderian is referring to the hostilities in October 1941 near Mtsensk, northeast of Orel], causing significant losses among our tanks. Previously existing hardware superiority of our tank forces was now lost and shifted to the opponent. Therefore, a prospect for rapid and continuous success disappeared."[7] "Our 50-mm and 37-mm anti-tank guns were completely useless against the T-34."[8]

Lieutenant General Westphal admitted: "The arrival of Soviet weapons that surpassed the German ones in quality was a very unpleasant surprise. One such weapon was the T-34 tank, against which the German anti-tank weapons were powerless."[9]

Infantry General Blumentritt agreed with his colleagues: "In 1941, the T-34 was the most powerful of all existing tanks. . . . In the vicinity of Verei, the T-34 without any hesitation penetrated the positions of the 7th Infantry Division, reached the artillery positions and literally squashed the guns. One can imagine what kind of impact it had on the morale of the infantry. The so-called 'tank phobia' started."[10]

I could endlessly quote German soldiers, officers, generals, and even field marshals; entire volumes of rave reviews of the T-34 have been published. Its debut caused a sensation at the beginning of the war. Sixty years after the T-34 first appeared, British professor Richard Ogarkovets, world famous as the leading authority in the field of designing armored technology, believes that the world tank-building industry still remains fully under the influence of ideas incorporated into the design of this remarkable tank. The T-34 was the only tank in the world created before the beginning of World War II that was not obsolete by its end. The T-34 fought for decades after Word War II. Not a single other tank in the world had such a long lifespan.

The arrival of the T-34 surprised both Stalin's enemies and his allies. Leading British historian and military theorist B. H. Liddell Hart said: "None of our tanks could compare with the T-34." French General G. Bouche recounted: "The arrival of the T-34 tank, significantly superior to German tanks, greatly surprised the Germans." German officers demanded the production of exactly the same tank. However, as Guderian explained, Germany, the homeland of Rudolph Diesel, could not design a sufficiently powerful diesel engine for tanks. Moreover, it was impossible to deliver the needed raw materials for the steel-casting industry to Germany and, as a result, during the war Germany was incapable of producing alloyed steel of the same quality as the Soviets.[11] The lack of alloy compounds in Germany resulted from the Molotov-Ribbentrop Pact. Stalin knew what he was doing on August 23, 1939. By supporting German aggression in Poland, Stalin made Germany the enemy of Britain and France. The blockade of Germany by the British fleet and the resulting shortages of many raw materials was an inevitable consequence.

The T-34 was armed with a 76-mm long-barrel gun, designed by Vasily Grabin (the barrel was 41 calibers). It was the most powerful tank gun of its time. If the T-34 had had no distinctions aside from this gun, it would still have been considered the best tank in the world, because it could destroy the most tanks of its kind. But the T-34 had other distinctions. In 1942, American experts conducted full technical tests and analyses of a T-34 given by Stalin, and concluded: "The distinguishing characteristics of the T-34 were: a low, flowing silhouette, simplicity of design, low specific pressure on the ground. The angles of the armor create brilliant possibilities for its protection."[12] The experts thought and continue to think that the shape of the T-34's body was ideal. The T-34 also had a powerful diesel engine, specifically designed for it. In the armies of other countries, such engines did not exist either at the beginning of the war or at the end. Just for that engine alone the T-34 could be considered the best tank in the world.

If the T-34 had neither a powerful gun, nor an ideal body shape, nor a diesel engine, it still could be considered the best tank in the world because of its wide caterpillar tracks, which allowed it to act on any terrain and in any weather. The T-34 surpassed any German tank in all parameters: speed, acceleration ability, cross-country ability, especially when moving on sand, mud, and snow.

The T-34 was famous, because all its innovations were incorporated into one design, and it achieved a harmonic combination of all its remarkable qualities. On top of everything, the T-34, unlike other tanks, was good for mass production. Any large-scale automobile factory could be converted to produce this tank. The production of the T-34 did not demand a highly qualified workforce. It was easy to use and repair. The T-34 had almost inexhaustible reserves for improvement. Its weight could be significantly increased without lowering the quality of its movement characteristics.

The T-34 served not only as a model for many imitations, but was also the prototype for many generations of new tank models. Not a single tank of World War II left behind it a row of descendants. The only exceptions were the T-34 and the KV. The KV was constantly improved upon and became the IS-1, then underwent a long evolution and turned into the IS-4 and the T-10. The lineage of the T-34 continues today, and direct descendants of the T-34 are among the most numerous units in the world.

In June 1941, the Red Army suffered a crushing defeat, which had to be explained. Communist historians acknowledged the remarkable qualities of the T-34, but added that these tanks were very few in number; there were only 967 of them. Many educated and honest historians repeated that on June 21, 1941, Stalin only had 967 T-34s. Even if this had been true, the word "only" was disputable—the rest of the world had none. In the five western border military districts, which constituted the first strategic echelon of the Red Army, there really were 967 T-34 tanks. But the forces of the second strategic echelon were being secretly transferred to the western regions of the country. They also had T-34 tanks. In total, the Red Army had 1,225 of them on May 31, 1941. By June 21, the factories shipped out and unloaded another 138 T-34s. On top of this, another 37 T-34s were produced, tested, but not yet shipped. Overall, at the time of the invasion, the Soviet Union had exactly 1,400 T-34s.[13]

However, even this was not all. The T-34 was produced in series. Meanwhile, the attempts to create an equal or superior tank in Germany began only on November 25, 1941. In June, July, August, September, and October 1941, Germany had not yet begun attempts to create an analogous tank, while the Soviet factories continued producing the T-34. During the second half of 1941, Soviet industry put out another 1,789 T-34s in addition to the 1,400 that existed on June 22. In 1942, the production of T-34s went at a rate of thirty-five a day. In 1942, 12,520 T-34 tanks were produced.[14] Very few, I agree. But in Germany, the production of an analogous tank had not yet begun.

The German equal of the T-34 was the Panther, which first appeared in the summer of 1943 during the great tank battle at Kursk. The Panther was a magnificent tank. Some experts considered it the best tank of World War II, and claimed that the Panther surpassed the T-34 in all aspects. Oddly enough, after the war, practically all designers in the world copied the best aspects of the T-34, while nobody copied the Panther. This tank did not leave any descendants behind, and for a good reason. Let's look at those parameters according to which the Panther did not surpass the T-34.

First, the T-34 had a diesel engine, while the Panther had a carburetor one. A diesel engine was more economical and less susceptible to fire. Second, the Panther had a very irrational design. The designers copied many aspects of the T-34, but not the most important—the rational location of both the engine and the transmission, in the rear of the tank. As a result, the Panther weighed 44.8 tons, even though it was supposed to weigh 30 tons. The Panther was considered a medium tank, but in weight it equaled the Soviet heavy tanks: the most massive version of the Panther weighed 45.5 tons, while the Soviet heavy tank IS-2 weighed 46 tons. In length, width, and height of the body, the Panther surpassed the Soviet heavy KV and IS tanks. This meant that it was easier to hit the Panther. If we have two safes of equal weights, but different sizes, the one that is larger in size has thinner walls. The same thing is true for tanks: larger sizes given equal weights always means weaker armor protection.

With its dimensions and weight, the Panther could not compete with the T-34 in anything related to mobility. The T-34 surpassed the Panther in maneuverability, acceleration, and cross-country mobility, that is, in all parameters needed for offence. No matter how ferocious a tank is in defense, a country cannot win a war through defense. I will reiterate that only mobility can bring victory. The T-34 was good for maneuver warfare, while the Panther was completely unfit for it. There was not a single successful offensive operation in history that was conducted with the participation of Tiger and Panther tanks. German General F. W. von Mellentin described the T-34 as "the best example of an offensive weapon of [World War II]." The heavy Panther could crush anybody in defense, but it could not compete with the T-34 on a raid of many kilometers deep into the enemy rear.

It is simple to create complicated things. It is very difficult to create simple things. The designers of the T-34 tank made it as simple as possible. Therefore, the T-34 was good for mass production. Before the war, tanks in the Soviet Union were produced in three main centers: Leningrad, Stalingrad, and Kharkov. Kharkov was lost during the course of the war. Leningrad was not lost, but the Kirov plant, which prior to the war built tanks, was only seven streetcar stops away from the front line. Leningrad was under siege, and had no metals, no energy, and therefore no mass production of tanks. Stalingrad was not lost, but the events of the war were not beneficial for mass tank production. After the three main centers stopped production, it was organized in new places, and during World War II there were more T-34 tanks produced alone than tanks of all types in Great Britain, Germany, and Japan put together.[15]

The Panther's main flaw was its complex design, which made the tank unfit for mass production. Only 5,976 tanks of this model were produced. Additionally, another 392 self-propelled guns based on the Panther were made.[16] The Soviet Union produced nine T-34s for every Panther.[17] For every self-propelled gun based on the Panther, the Soviet Union produced thirteen Su-85 and Su-100 self-propelled guns based on the T-34. Just of these two types, 5,139 self-propelled guns were produced.[18]

General Heinz Guderian loved the Panther with all his heart, but when Hitler ordered a halt in the production of all earlier models, so that only Panthers and Tigers would be produced, Guderian protested and managed to reverse the order. He was right: if only the most expensive and complex tanks were produced, there would be few of them. After the war Guderian wrote: "Such a path inevitably led to the defeat of Germany in the near future. The Russians would have won the war without help from the West, and occupied all of Europe. No force on earth could have stopped them. Europe's problems would have been simplified and we all would have learned what real 'democracy' means."[19]

The Germans were unable to design a good tank for mass production. Therefore, until almost the very end of the war Germany had to produce obsolete models to supplement the Tigers and Panthers and compensate for the losses incurred in battle. The American tank expert Steven Zaloga went so far as to consider the production of Panthers a mistake: "The decision to enlist among weapons such a large, heavy, and complex tank as the Panther in the category of medium tanks was one of the factors that limited the German tank production to a level much lower than the Soviet."[20]

The Panther and the T-34 should not even be compared. Comparing them is like comparing boxers from different weight classes. If Stalin didn't have any other tanks, then we would be forced to compare the T-34 with the Panther. But Stalin had the IS-2. The IS-2 was adopted in the same year as the Panther, and weighed the same. They should be compared. The Panther resembled the IS-2 tank in another aspect as well: the Panther was a complex, expensive tank for elite formations. The IS-2 was deployed in exactly the same way, to fight in heavy breakthrough tank units and nowhere else. With the same weight and roughly equal mobility characteristics, the IS-2 had a much more powerful armor and surpassed the Panther in fire power.[21]

In 1941, only two armies in the world recognized the necessity of heavy tanks. Obviously, they were the German and the Soviet armies. The order to begin project development of the first German heavy tank was given on May 26, 1941. The project was called MK4501: 45 tons, model one. The project resulted in the Tiger. Once again the German designers were unable to stick to the planned weight. The tank was supposed to be 45 tons, but came out at 57 tons. However, this happened later:: in 1941, obviously, there was no tank yet. By June 22, German designers had only made the first set of sketches. It was still a long time until the test models made of metal, but at least the attempt to create a heavy tank was made on paper.

In contrast, work on creating a heavy tank in the Soviet Union began in 1930. In 1933, the first Soviet heavy tank, the T-35, was produced in series and entered the ranks of the troops. It was a five-turret giant, weighed 45 tons, and was operated by a crew of eleven men. It was the only five-turret tank in the world that was used by troops. It had three guns and six machine guns. Its armor was 30 mm thick. In 1941, not a single German tank, and no other tank in the world, was equal to the Soviet medium T-28 tank. Obviously, none of them could even approximately compare with the heavy T-35. Design of the T-35 was continuously improved. For example, the models from 1938 increased the number of machine guns to seven, and the armor was made 50 mm. The last series of T-35 joined the troops in 1939. But the tank was improved even after the production was completed: after the war in Finland, all T-35s were returned to the factories and their armor was reinforced to 80 mm. The weight of the tanks reached 50 tons.

In 1939, government tests of three of the newest Soviet heavy tanks, the KV-1, SMK, and T-100, were conducted in combat conditions. These tanks were tested in "anti-tank" territory, in conditions in which the use of tanks was theoretically impossible. The Soviet heavy tanks withstood the extreme challenges of the war in Finland: the absence of roads, the obstacles hidden under piles of snow, the impenetrable forests, swamps, deadly fire, vast minefields, anti-tank ditches, steel hedgehogs, scarps and counterscarps, and cold temperatures that caused steel to crumble.

The bloody experiment in Finland proved that Soviet heavy tanks could fight successfully even in those conditions. Out of the three heavy experimental tanks, the KV-1 was recognized as the best. On December 19, 1939, the Red Army enlisted it among its weapons, and the industry received orders to produce it in series. In February 1940, the heavy KV-2 tank was tested in military conditions and also was accepted into the army.

The KV-1 and KV-2 weighed 47 and 52 tons, respectively. The KV was the first tank in the world with a true anti-shell armor: it had a frontal armor of 75 mm, which could be further reinforced. The wide caterpillar tracks of the KV allowed it to fight on almost any terrain in any weather conditions. Imagine the situation of the following year, 1941: German tanks got stuck in the snow and the mud; the crews (and future historians) cursed the weather and lack of roads, while the KV advanced through the mud. Hitler lost the war, but the mud and the cold weather were not to blame—it was the German designers, who counted on easy victories and on operations only during the resort season and only in places that had good roads. They should have designed tanks for war, not for parades. They should have tested them in Finland. They should have given them wider caterpillar tracks. And they should have installed diesel engines. The KV had a 600-horsepower diesel engine. The Soviet tank's diesel engine surpassed all foreign tank engines in power, reliability, and economy. The use of a diesel engine drastically reduced the risk of catching fire. A 76-mm long-barrel F-32 gun was installed on the KV. At that time, this gun was unrivaled in the world. In comparison, Germany had great tanks, which conquered all of Europe, but the most powerful German tank gun at the beginning of World War II was the 75-mm short-barrel gun on the Pz-IV tank. The initial speed of the shells it fired was 385 m/s. This was a very good gun. But the KV-1 had an initial shell speed of 662 m/s. The difference in initial shell speed was a difference both in the energy of the shell and in the precision of firing.

The KV-2 had even more powerful weapons. It had the 152-mm howitzer. The most powerful German tank shell of that time weighed 6.8 kg. It was a very good shell for a very good weapon. But the KV-2 fired concrete-destroying shells that weighed 39.9 kg at an initial speed of 529 m/s, and high-explosive shells that weighed 48.7 kg. There were even reports of a shell that weighed 50.8 kg. The Chief of the General Staff of the German land army Colonel-General Franz Halder simply did not believe the report of a weapon of such caliber on a Soviet tank.[22] At the same time two other heavy tanks, the SMK (55 tons) and the T-100 (58 tons), also passed government tests. If the choice had fallen on any of them they could have been launched into production. Aside from these tanks, the KV-3 and the KV-220 were created and subjected to government tests. Prototypes of the KV-4 (90 tons) and the KV-5 were also designed but never produced because of Hitler's attack.

Germany and the USSR shared the two first places in heavy tank production. There was nobody in third place. Elsewhere around the world, generals and designers did not even think of drafting a heavy tank on paper. The situation was such that while Germany had a heavy tank just on paper, other countries did not have heavy tanks even on their minds, while the Soviet Union was the only country in the world that in 1941 had heavy tanks both in experimental stages and in series production. The Red Army was the only army in the world that had heavy tanks among its units.

Nonetheless, Western and Soviet historians claim that Germany was ready for war, and the Soviet Union was not. They pronounced the T-35 tank obsolete and didn't mention it in statistics, even though the rest of the world had nothing comparable to the T-35 tank. The T-35 surpassed everything other countries had in terms of weapons, armor, and engine power—all the main characteristics. Moreover, the T-35, despite its size and weight, exerted less pressure on the ground than the German tanks, which meant it had much greater mobility, did not sink in snow, mud, and soft ground, where twice- and three-times-lighter tanks of other armies sank. If the T-35 were declared obsolete, all other tanks around the world had to be declared obsolete as well, and excluded from statistics.

As for the KV, the same trick was used. It was described as a great tank, but there were "only" 508 of them. Once again, I will repeat that the rest of the world had none! Besides, 508 KVs were just in the first strategic echelon of the Red Army on May 31, 1941. On the same date, the second strategic echelon had an additional 128 KVs. By June 21, factories unloaded another 41 KVs. Yet another 34 KVs were produced, but not yet shipped.[23] Thus, on June 21, 1941, the Soviet Union had 711 KV tanks, and continued their production through all of 1942, while German designers drafted sketches, made prototypes, and assembled test models.

It is impossible even in theory to compare the KV-1 and KV-2 with the very best German tanks, the Pz-III and Pz-IV: the KV was a heavy tank, while the German army had no tank of this weight class in 1941. The leading German theoretician and practitioner of tank warfare Colonel General Heinz Guderian maintained that "warfare of tank against tank is similar to naval warfare. There, battle is also conducted only by the strongest."[24] When the war began, Stalin put into use the KV-1 (47 tons) and the KV-2 (52 tons), as well as the "obsolete" T-35 (50 tons), while Hitler had nothing similar and was forced to use the best that he had—the obsolete medium Pz-III and Pz-IV tanks, which weighed 20 to 21 tons. I would not compare them at all if the German army had anything more noteworthy, but it did not. During the war, the KV fought against the best that was available in the German army—and the war drew its comparisons.

General of the Army K. N. Galitsky described the battle between one heavy KV and three medium German Pz-IIIs: The KV fired two shots and two of the German tanks were destroyed, while the third German tank decided to leave, but its engine stalled while trying to drive across a ditch. The KV caught up with it and "smashed it with its weight, crushed it like a nut."[25] General Galitsky described another incident: A damaged Soviet KV was found, surrounded by ten destroyed German tanks. The KV was hit by forty-three shells, out of which forty made dents, and only three went through the armor. While the German tanks were destroying one KV, it destroyed ten German tanks.

Colonel General A. I. Rodimtsev remembered: "During the course of eleven months of war, we did not know a single instance in which a German gun pierced the armor of this tank. It had happened that a KV tank had ninety to one hundred dents from enemy shells, but still continued to go into battle."[26] Other Soviet generals had many similar examples. Perhaps Soviet generals were embellishing the situation? No. In German sources of that time there was a subdued panic: German tankers were used to their tanks being the best in the world, and suddenly they came against the KV. They were unprepared. German documents of the time are sufficiently known. I will not repeat them. The general conclusion for the year 1941 was: "The KV is the most frightening weapon that a soldier has ever had to encounter in battle. Anti-tank guns are powerless against it."

The works of contemporary Western historians also confirm the invincibility of the KV. The British military historian R. Goralski described a battle between one KV and a group of German tanks and anti-tank guns: during just this one battle, the KV took seventy direct hits; all the shells left dents in the armor, but not one went through it.[27] American historian Steven Zaloga also provides similar examples. (I recommend his books to everyone for there is no better foreign expert on Soviet tanks.) He wrote of an incident when one KV destroyed eight German tanks, took thirty direct hits from a very close range, and not one shell pierced its armor.[28]

The KV remained the most powerful tank in the world throughout the first half of World War II, right up to the Stalingrad battle. No other country in the world had anything comparable in the same weight class. The KV design had reserves for improvement, which enabled it to undergo several stages of development from the KV-1 to the KV-13. Later, it turned into the IS-1 and then the IS-2, the most powerful tank of World War II.

The evolution yielded stronger armor and increased gun power, and in 1943 the IS-2 was put into use. B. H. Liddell Hart wrote: "These monsters had six-inch [150-mm] armor and were armed with 122-mm guns, while the most powerful German Tiger had just an 88-mm gun and four-inch [100-mm] armor."[29] Steven Zaloga said: "In rare instances, a shell from the IS-2 tank did not pierce the armor of German tanks, but this did not change anything: the energy of the shell was so great that it tore the turret off any German tank."[30] Major General F. W. von Mellentin admitted: "[IS-2s] caused excessive problems for our Tigers."[31]

Designers of the Soviet heavy tank accomplished a technological feat: they almost doubled the thickness of the armor and installed a gun that was three times more powerful, while staying in the same weight class and even reducing the weight of the heavy tank. The KV-1 weighed 47.5 tons, while the IS-2, its direct and several times more powerful descendant, weighed 46 tons.

Stalin had a remarkable pair: the most powerful heavy tank, in terms of fire power and armor, for elite units, and a wonderful, mass-produced, truly medium T-34 for regular units. Stalin understood that the T-34 needed to be improved, but it couldn't be allowed to turn into a heavy, complex, expensive tank for the elite. In that case, the T-34 would stop being a mass-produced tank, and the war would be lost. Soviet designers succeeded in improving the characteristics of the T-34 during the war, but in weight and in simplicity of production and maintenance they kept it in the medium tank class, which could easily be put out by the tens of thousands.

Soviet medium and heavy tanks were an inseparable pair, like two complementary weapon systems. The availability of tens of thousands of relatively inexpensive and simple T-34s allowed them to be used anywhere, thereby conserving the energy of the heavy tanks for secondary objectives. The crews of the T-34s could confidently fight, knowing that they had the support of an almighty KV or IS behind them. The availability of the heavy tank increased the battle capabilities of the medium tanks.

10

On the "Obsolete" Soviet Tanks

If I had known that the Russians really possessed such a number of tanks . . . I think I
would not have started this war.

—Adolf Hitler, August 4, 1941

When Hitler came to power in Germany in 1933, the German armed forces had zero tanks, while the Red Army had 4,000 tanks. In the whole of 1933, not a single tank was produced in Germany; in contrast, 3,819 tanks of all types and modifications were produced in the Soviet Union.[1] The production of tanks in Germany began in 1934: in the next five years, German factories produced 2,683 tanks.[2] Soviet factories in the same time period produced 14,283 tanks.[3] On January 1, 1939, the Red Army was equipped with 21,100 battle-ready tanks.[4] In 1939, Hitler started World War II with 3,195 tanks, the same number that Soviet factories produced per year in peacetime.

In 1941, the German army, by a crushing blow, defeated gigantic gatherings of Soviet troops in the border regions. Thousands of Soviet tanks were destroyed or simply abandoned by the troops. This catastrophe had to be explained somehow. Communist historians explained what happened very simply: the tanks were obsolete, and therefore useless. The whole world laughed at Stalin and at his "obsolete" tanks. But how many of them were there? To this question, an equally simple answer was prepared: why count them if they were obsolete? For the six decades since the disaster of 1941, the number of Soviet tanks has never officially been named. Only after the dismantling of the Soviet Union has the truth slowly started to emerge.

What were these "obsolete" tanks? A few thousand of them had the "BT" marker. Their spiritual father was the great American tank genius George Walter Christie. Soviet commanders and designers were the only ones to see the value of Christie's achievements. Two of Christie's tanks were purchased and shipped to the Soviet Union with fake documents, in which they were listed as agricultural tractors. On December 24, 1930, a ship carrying the "tractors" of Christie's design left New York.

In the Soviet Union, all aspects of Christie's "tractors" were carefully studied. An entire family of tanks was created based on their design—the BT-2, BT-5, BT-7, BT-7A, and BT-7M. BT stood for *bystrokhodnyi* (high-speed) tank. The shape of the BT was simple and rational. Not a single tank in the world during the prewar period and the early period of World War II had an armor of such a shape. The best tank of World War II, the T-34, was a direct descendant of the BT. The shape of its body was a development of the idea of the great American designer. After the T-34, the principle of a sloped location of the frontal armor sheets was used on the German Panther, and later on tanks around the world.

In the 1930s, practically all tanks around the world were produced according to one design: the engine in the rear, the transmission in the front part. The BT was an exception: its engine and transmission were both in the rear. Twenty-five years later, the entire world understood the advantages of the BT design. The BT tanks were heavily armed for their time. The 45-mm cannon could penetrate the armor of any foreign tank. Great Britain and the United States began installing such cannons on their tanks only a decade later, in 1942 and 1943. In addition to thousands of BT tanks, armed with 45-mm cannons, 154 BT-7As were manufactured and armed with 76-mm KT-26 cannons.[5] At the beginning of World War II, no tank in the world outside the borders of the Soviet Union had weaponry of comparable caliber.

What about the armor? The BT had just bullet-proof armor. At that time, most of the world had tanks with the same kind of bullet-proof armor. The engine is the heart of the tank. The BT-2, which was made operational in the Red Army in 1932, had a 400-horsepower M-5 engine. German tanks began having engines of equal power only by the end of 1942. The specific power of the BT was 36.4 horsepower per ton of mass.[6] Not a single tank in the world had such a high specific power, which allowed the tank to do unbelievable things: "BT units could jump over obstacles to a distance of 15 to 20 meters; a few could do it to a distance of 40 meters."[7] The cinematography of those times preserved such incredible stunts of Soviet tank drivers for posterity. Nonetheless, Soviet historians categorized these tanks among the obsolete models, calling them so obsolete that until 1991 they were not included in statistics.

In April 1941, Germany began producing in series the T-IIIJ tank. In the German army it had the highest specific power—13.9 horsepower per ton of mass. How could the BT-2 be obsolete, if its specific power was almost three times higher than that of the best German tank? The first BTs had a speed of 69 mph, that is, over 110 km/h.[8] Seventy years later any tanker would still be envious of such high speed. Soviet sources point to the much lower figures of 86 km/h for BT-7Ms, and 72 km/h for BT-2s and BT-5s, as maximum speeds for BT tanks on paved roads.[9] This discrepancy, between Soviet and foreign sources, is simply explained: on Soviet roads, the engine was too powerful for the transmission, so a speed-limiting device had to be installed. When the tank was used on highways, the device could easily be taken away. But even if we think of the BT speed as being "only" 86 or even just 72 km/h, at that time no other tanks in the world had such statistics.

The BT tanks were constantly improved. In 1936, after a series of experiments, a number of BT crews became capable of crossing rivers underwater. At the beginning of the twenty-first century, still not all the tanks of the most developed countries have such capabilities. In 1939 the Red Army received the BT-7M. It had the following capacities: on tracks over unpaved roads it could run for 520 km; on tracks over paved roads—630 km; on wheels over paved roads—1,250 km.[10] Sixty years later, this is still the dream of any tanker. The BT-7M had a 500-horsepower engine. At that time, the most powerful foreign tank engines were: the 300-horsepower German Meibach HL 120TRM, the 307-horsepower French Renault for the Renault B1bis tank-horsepower.

The "obsolete" BT-7M had an extremely powerful engine—a legendary high-speed B-2 tank diesel. No other country was able to create such an engine before the end of the war; all of Stalin's enemies and allies had to get by with carburetor engines, which made their tanks extremely vulnerable to fires. In some countries, some tank models were equipped with diesel engines, but these were weak automobile engines. The rest of the world learned to use powerful diesel engines, specifically designed for tanks, only after the war, about ten to twenty years after it was done on the BT-7M.

Having said so many positive things about the quantity and quality of Soviet BT tanks, we must be just and note one small disadvantage: these tanks could not be effectively used on Soviet territory.

The main advantage of the BT tank was its speed. This quality dominated all its other qualities to such an extent that it even had a bearing on the tank's name—high-speed tank. The BT tank was a weapon of aggression. All of its characteristics make the BT resemble a small, but extremely mobile, horseback warrior from the undefeatable hordes of Genghis Khan. That great world conqueror vanquished all his enemies through a sudden attack of colossal masses of extremely mobile warriors. He destroyed his enemies mainly not by powerful weapons, but through decisive maneuvers. He did not need heavy, clumsy knights, only light, quick, mobile troops, capable of traversing vast territories, crossing rivers, and going deep into the enemy's rear. The BT tanks were exactly the same. At the beginning of World War II, the Red Army had 6,456 BT tanks—that's as many as all operational tanks of all types in the rest of the world. [11] Soviet commanders clearly understood that BT tanks were not good for conventional warfare, but they were great in situations when the Red Army suddenly broke into enemy territory. "High speed tanks [by] their nature are a weapon of sudden attack. Their full effect (and success in general) can be obtained only if their use is sudden."[12] In other words, if we suddenly attack the enemy, we will have success, but if the element of surprise is not on our side, we will not.

The BT tanks could only be used in aggressive warfare, only in the enemy's rear, and only in a decisive aggressive operation, when hordes of tanks suddenly broke through onto enemy territory and bypassed points of opposition, thrusting deep behind enemy lines, where there were no enemy troops, but where all cities, bridges, factories, airports, ports, storage facilities, command posts, and communication units were located.[13]

The amazing aggressive characteristics of the BT were achieved by using a unique landing gear. On field roads, the BT moved using caterpillar tracks, but when it found itself on good roads, it shed the heavy tracks and sped forward on wheels like a racecar. It is well known that speed and cross-country ability are a trade-off: either we have a racecar that only rides on good roads, or a slow tractor that can ride anywhere. The Soviet marshals chose in favor of the racecar, so the BT tanks were not good for the bad roads of Soviet territory. In the battles fought on Soviet territory, thousands of BT tanks were abandoned. Off the roads, even with the caterpillar tracks they were difficult to use. The great potential of the BT tanks was never realized, because it was impossible to realize it on Soviet territory. To the question of what was most important for the BT tanks, its wheels or its caterpillar tracks, Soviet textbooks give a clear answer—the wheels. The BT's most important characteristic, its speed, was achieved through use of its wheels.

Seventy years ago, there were no highways on Soviet territory. And in 1939, not a single immediate Soviet neighbor had an autobahn either. But in the following year, through the Molotov-Ribbentrop Pact, Stalin divided Poland and established common borders with a nation that had autobahns. This nation was Germany.

They say that Stalin's tanks were not ready for war. This is not true. They were not ready for a defensive war on their own territory. They simply were prepared to fight on different territories.

Here is another family of Soviet tanks: T-37A, T-38, and T-40. The T-37A was received by the Red Army on August 11, 1933. It weighed 3.2 tons, its crew consisted of two men, and it had bullet-proof armor. It was armed with one DT machine gun, had a 40-horsepower engine and a maximum speed of 36 to 40 km/h on paved roads and 6 km/h in the water. The T-37A was a light tank—but light does not mean bad and obsolete. The T-37A was the first amphibious tank in the world to be regularly used by troops.[14] Even if the T-37A really was a bad tank, its inclusion in the armed forces still meant a technological breakthrough of historical importance, because there was nothing comparable or close in the armies of other countries at the time. The Japanese actively pursued amphibious tank warfare in the 1920s and 1930s. They even tested a few prototype models. But not one of the models was massproduced as a part of the Japanese armed forces before 1941.

The German Pz-I was accepted by the army a year later—in 1934. It had almost the same weight—3.5 tons, the same crew—two men, the same bulletproof armor, and the same caliber machine gun. Only it could not float. When the high-minded scholars laugh at the T-37A that could float, I offer to compare the characteristics of the oldest, lightest Soviet amphibious tank with the characteristics of the best, most powerful German amphibious tank. Here, the laughter stops. It turns out that Germany does not have and never had amphibious tanks. Before the war it had none, and during the war none appeared. The great Germany entered the twenty-first century without amphibious tanks. It is unknown when it will begin producing them. Stalin on the other hand had amphibious tanks in the early '30s. In this field Stalin was many decades ahead of Hitler.

France did not have amphibious tanks at that time. Britain also had none before or during the war. The birthday of American tank forces is July 10, 1940. When the *Wehrmacht Heer* crushed with its tanks Poland, Belgium, Holland, France, and the British army on the continent, the Red Army tanks were crushing the Japanese Sixth Army at Khalkhin-Gol and were "liberating" Finland, Estonia, Lithuania, Latvia, Bessarabia, and Bukovina. America at that time had no tank troops at all. After the defeat of French and British troops on the continent, American generals realized that it was time to get off horses and to think of creating tank troops. A year later, in June 1941, the United States had less than four hundred tanks.[15] These were weak, old-fashioned machines, very tall, with very light armor and a multi-tiered distribution of completely obsolete weapons. The most powerful tank weapon of American tanks in 1941 was the 37-mm cannon. Even this was mounted only on some tanks. The majority of American tanks had only machine guns. America had no amphibious tanks at the time. By the end of the war, in 1944, the United States had developed amphibious armored personnel carriers of huge dimensions, and some of them had the turrets of light tanks. These were reliable machines, they had great floating capability. But nonetheless, these were not tanks, and nobody tried to call them such. So, the difference we have is: in America, something resembling an amphibious tank appeared by the end of the war, while in the Soviet Union, amphibious tanks were enlisted in the armed forces long before the war's beginning.

So, what was the nature of the "light and obsolete" T-37A? Here is some information about it. In August 1935 upon orders from Voroshilov, the Commissar of Defense of the USSR, seven T-37As started out from Leningrad, traversed several tens of kilometers on caterpillar tracks, then sailed along the river Luga, through impenetrable weeds, then on to the river Shelon and Lake Ilmen. There was a storm on the lake. The distance across the lake was 55 kilometers. The tanks crossed this distance in 8 hours and 15 minutes. Then they came to the river Volkhov, the Novoladozhsky Canal, and the ferocious, treacherous river Neva. All seven tanks reached the finish line by the Petropavlov fortress. In eleven days they had crossed seven hundred kilometers, six hundred of them by sailing—all this without a single accident or even a breakdown.

Of course, not every single T-37A and not every tank driver was capable of setting such a record. Nonetheless, this is a record that since 1935 has not been successfully repeated by anybody. Nobody has even come close to reproducing it. Until 1941, the position of the rest of the world regarding the creation of amphibious tanks had barely changed. In 1941, no country in Europe and America (other than the Soviet Union) had amphibious tanks as part of its national armament. That year, only in Japan did the emperor's fleet begin implementing the floating Gami tank for amphibious assaults; the Gachi and Togu floating tanks were introduced later on.[16]

The Soviet T-37A was produced from 1933 until 1936. A tank, if there is no war, can serve for ten, fifteen, even twenty years. In theory, the T-37A tanks that were produced in 1933 were scheduled to be replaced between 1943 and 1948, perhaps even later. The last tanks, produced in 1936, did not have to be replaced until 1951 to1955. How could they be too old in 1941? And how did it happen that unique tanks, which by 1941 had only served five to eight years, were completely obliterated from the historical record?

What are they needed for? What use comes from amphibious tanks? If we are defending our own territory, if we are conducting strictly defensive warfare, amphibious tanks are not really needed. We can get by without them. In order to stop the enemy, one wants to have tanks with heavy armor and powerful weapons—the heavier and more powerful, the better.

If we cannot stop the enemy in defensive warfare, we are forced to retreat. We retreat using our own bridges. When threatened with a takeover, we can detonate our bridges and send them up into the sky. There is little use for tanks with light armor and machine guns in a defensive war. Their ability to float also remains completely unused: there is nowhere to sail to in defensive war.

But if we are conducting a crusade for world domination, then in order to herd the population of the planet into concentration camps, labor armies, and barracks, we have different needs. In order to break through the enemy's front, we need heavy tanks, more armor, and more powerful cannon. If a battle occurs, if two waves of tanks collide, once again, we need the most powerful tanks. Once the front line is broken and the enemy's tank waves are deflected and crushed, our task becomes to take advantage of the moment and complete a thrust deep into the enemy's rear, in order to split up his defenses, to have access to his communications and supply lines, to reach the aortas in order to cut them, to cut the enemy off from his supply bases, to reach his capital, his industrial regions, his sources of oil, and his ports. A heavy tank is not very good for such a thrust. Due to its weight, it breaks roads and bridges and gets in the way of all those who are following. A heavy tank consumes a lot of fuel—try to provide fuel to several thousand tanks and artillery tow trucks and tens of thousands of automobiles, which are pushing forward deep into enemy territory. Aside from all this, a heavy tank is also slow and not very agile. It slows down the movement of your columns. Moreover, it quickly wears out and chokes, like a heavyweight in a marathon. For a forward thrust, medium and light tanks are ideal. They have less armor, weaker weapons, but they have much higher speed, maneuverability, and cross-country ability, and they are more economical with their fuel.

Now our armored armada is standing before a water obstacle. Here all heavy and medium tanks, and those light ones that have not been taught how to float, lose all their aggressive options. Their value is zero. They need a bridge. But the enemy protects the bridges, and blows them up when threatened with a takeover. Bridges have to be fought for. And it is better to fight for them not from our side, but from the side of the enemy, from where they are not anticipating it. In this situation, the value of light amphibious tanks grows tremendously. If two, three, five, ten such tanks sail across the river during the night in the direction of the bridge, and with a sudden attack from the rear seize the bridge, this can decide the fate of an entire operation, or even an entire war. Now you can send to the enemy shores, across the newly seized bridge, your heavy and medium tanks, along with artillery, infantry, staff, hospitals, thousands of tons of ammunition, fuel, and spare parts. You can use the seized bridge to send in reserves, and to send the wounded, prisoners, and trophies to the rear, to send damaged machinery back for repair.

If it is impossible to seize the bridge, the amphibious tanks become truly priceless. If there are no enemy bridges, we need to establish our own temporary bridges and means of sending goods across the river. For this we need to establish a bridgehead on the other side. The infantry is sent into battle. On logs, wooden planks, and inflatable rafts, they swim to the other shore. Meanwhile they are being fired upon by machine guns, mortars, and automatic rifles. Here, among the swimming men, imagine having ten or twenty light tanks. Their armor is not harmed by bullets and shell fragments, while their machine guns are capable of firing when none of the swimming men can.

Now we have reached the other shore. The most important thing is to catch hold of something, to dig our forces into the ground during the next twenty minutes or so, so that no counterattacks can hinder us. Then the mortars and machine guns are not so destructive, and the enemy gunners and snipers are not quite so deadly. Our wet, wounded, and exhausted infantry does not carry heavy weapons or ammunition. So, in these very first, most frightening minutes on enemy shores, the presence, help, and support of even one of the lightest tanks with just one machine gun is far more valuable and important than ten more powerful heavy tanks that would be forced to remain on our side of the river.

The number of Soviet amphibious tanks was kept secret for half a century. Later, it slowly began to become clearer. So, how many of them were there? The answer is: there were 2,627 T-37A tanks produced.[17] In local conflicts the T-37A was rarely used, and they were rarely sent abroad. So in 1941, they were almost all fully functioning. In 1936, production of a perfected T-38 amphibious tank began. This tank continued to be produced in series until 1939. Overall, 1,375 tanks of this type were produced.[18] The Kremlin historians called this tank obsolete as well. But we will ask the same question: how could a tank be obsolete, if there were no analogous tanks in the world, and its age was only between two and five years?

December 19, 1939, is the brightest and the most remarkable day in the history of world tank design. On this day the Red Army received and enlisted an entire spectrum of new armor-tank weaponry—the three newest tanks: the light amphibious T-40, the medium T-34, and the heavy breakthrough KV tank. The T-34 is the best tank of all time. The KV was the most powerful tank in the world during the first half of World War II, right up until the Battle of Stalingrad. But the T-40 was no worse than these. In its class, it was also the best in the world and also had no equal.

It is interesting that the Kremlin historians remember the T-34 and the KV, but forget about the T-40. Meanwhile, the T-40 had a new, never-before-seen body shape, weighed 5.5 tons, and was armed with two machine guns: the large-caliber DShK and the regular DT. A variant of this model, the T-40S, was armed with 20-mm automatic cannon instead of the DShK. By June 21, 1941, a total of 277 T-40 tanks were built.[19]

By June 22, 1941, Hitler had on the eastern front 180 tanks in the under-six-ton category.[20] Not one of them was amphibious and not one of them could compete with the Soviet light tanks. Stalin, on the other hand, had more than 4,000 tanks in this weight category. All of them were amphibious. Among them were 277 T-40s, which not only were amphibious, but also were capable of using their large-caliber DShK machine guns (and of course the 20-mm cannons) to pierce the armor of the German Pz-I tanks. Moreover, German Pz-I production was stopped in 1938, and these tanks not only were obsolete but also heavily worn-out, while the T-40 tanks were still in production, the paint not yet dried on many of them.

Foreign experts, those who understand even a little bit about tanks, talk of the T-40 with sighs of high regard. The vast majority of the T-40s were less than a year old. Some had left the factory doors on June 21, and some were still in the factory courtyard. When did they have time to become obsolete? When did they have time to become worn out? On June 22, 1941, on the eastern front, Hitler had 3,350 tanks in total of all types, all of them obsolete and among all of them not a single amphibious one, while Stalin's amphibious tanks alone numbered over 4,000.

By overcoming stormy Lake Ilmen, even the oldest of Soviet amphibious tanks proved the possibility of crossing the English Channel. But these tanks were designed for action on lakes and rivers. For crossing the English Channel, Stalin had other designs in the works for the future—the amphibious tank PT-1 and its variants. It weighed 14 tons, had a 500-horsepower engine, a speed of 6 km/h in the water and could reach 62 km/h on land, and 90 km/h when it shed its caterpillar tracks.[21] This was a hybrid of a highway and an amphibious tank, a cross between a reconnaissance and a lightning battle tank. It was armed with a 45-mm cannon and four machine guns. It had a crew of four men. The PT-1 had a large body and impeccable floatability. This tank was designed and tested, but was not launched into series, for now sailing across the channels was not in the plans. When it would become needed, it could be launched into series.

The fate of Soviet amphibious tanks is a sad one: they were of no use in defensive war. Where would they sail? Upon orders from the People's Commissar for Defense, Marshal of the Soviet Union Timoshenko, and the chief of the general staff, General of the Army Zhukov, tens of thousands of tons of spare parts for the tanks, hundreds of thousands of tons of ammunition and fuel, were brought out to the very borders of the country. In the first hours of the war, all this fell under fire or in the hands of the enemy. Soviet tanks were left without fuel, ammunition, or spare parts. Four thousand light amphibious tanks demanded a large amount of fuel and had little use in defensive war. Therefore, commanders easily parted with them: they ordered what was left of the fuel to be pumped into the medium and heavy tanks. The light ones were blown up, burned, broken, sunk, or just abandoned.

The best (and only) in the world, Soviet amphibious tanks in 1941 became unnecessary and played no role in the war. But why does nobody ask the question: why then were they developed and built? What were they prepared for? Why did Stalin need four thousand amphibious tanks, which he could not use in defensive war? Where was comrade Stalin planning to sail?

11

Winged Genghis Khan

Logic hinted that we should not wait for the enemy to bring all his aviation into action, but instead we should ourselves take initiative in the air and be the first to carry our massive strikes against his air bases.

—CHIEF MARSHAL OF AVIATION A. NOVIKOV,
IN *VOENNO-ISTORICHESKY ZHURNAL*

"Stalin" is not a real name. It is the most famous of many pseudonyms of a man who for thirty years led the most criminal and most bloody empire in human history. But it is not his only pseudonym. Like every big criminal, Stalin had several different names and nicknames: "Vasiliev," "Chizhikov," "Besoshvili" ("son of the devil"), "Ivanovich," and others. His closest comrades had the right to use the nickname "Koba" in their tight circle. Under this name Stalin was known long before he came to power, when he was a simple bank robber.

In extraordinary cases, Stalin used yet another secret pseudonym: "Ivanov." Sometimes a minister, ambassador, general, admiral, or marshal received a cable, which began simply and harshly: "Comrade Ivanov ordered . . ." The highest-ranking leaders of the Soviet Union knew that this order must be obeyed at any cost, quickly, precisely, and within the indicated deadline. There was only one price to pay for an imprecise or untimely fulfillment of "Comrade Ivanov's" orders—one's life. In turn, every high-ranking official—a minister, ambassador, marshal, or other—could at any moment write a letter or telegram and send it simply to the address: "Moscow. Ivanov." Bypassing all steps, the letter or telegram with such an address without any delays was laid directly on Stalin's desk.

And one more fact which seems at first glance to have no ties to anything said above. In the summer of 1941, the Red Army suddenly employed completely unusual weapons: the multiple-launcher rocket weapons BM-8 and BM-13. They entered history under the name "Stalin's Pipe Organs" or "Katyusha." On August 6, 1941, the Red Army was equipped with a multiple-launcher rocket artillery system, the BM-8-36, and in the summer of the subsequent year, 1942, the BM-8-48.[1] A salvo from one BM-13 was sixteen rocket-propelled rounds of 132-mm caliber. A salvo from the BM-8 was thirty-six rocket-propelled rounds of 82-mm caliber (forty-eight rounds starting in 1942). One battery consisted of four to six BM-8s or BM-13s. Usually one target was fired upon not by one battery, but by a group of batteries or even regiments. The advantage lay in the fact that hundreds or even thousands of missiles covered a huge territory almost simultaneously. Fire from a group of batteries was an avalanche of fire, accompanied by wild roar and noise. Many German soldiers, officers, and generals remember that this was a terrible weapon. General Field Marshal Albrecht von Kesselring: "The terrible psychological effect of 'Stalin's Pipe Organs' is a highly unpleasant memory for any German soldier who was on the Eastern front."[2]

The statistics are as follows: on June 1, 1941, the Red Army had seven BM-13 rocket launcher vehicles. One month later, there were seventeen such vehicles. Some were destroyed in battle, but others were produced, and by September 1 there were forty-nine of them. Production of the BM-8 began at the same time. By October 1, 1941, the Red Army, despite its losses, had 406 BM-8s and BM-13s. Later on, the count would mount into the thousands, and soon this weapon became a mass weapon. Despite losses of industrial and raw material bases, the Soviet Union managed to quickly supply its army with a principally new system of weapons.

In 1940 the Red Army's Air Force received into their inventory the newest airplane, the "Ivanov" Su-2. It was created by a group of designers headed by Pavel Osipovich Sukhoy, one of the greatest aviation designers of the twentieth century. Stalin personally issued the order to design the Ivanov. In the history of Soviet aviation, there was only one airplane that was designed under Stalin's secret pseudonym; moreover, the name of the project was not the initiative of devoted low-ranking officials, but given directly by Stalin himself. Aviation designer V. Shavrov testifies: "The codename 'Ivanov' was given according to Stalin's order. It was his telegraph address."[3] There was no airplane yet, the designers had not even picked up their pencils, but Stalin had already given his name to the plane. The eventual production was planned for about 100,000 to 150,000 planes of this type.

The Su-2 had many uses: it could be a light bomber, a tactical reconnaissance plane, and an attack plane. Its design was extremely simple and rational. The Su-2 was better suited for mass production than any other airplane in the world. It possessed great firepower. Under its wings it could carry up to ten rocket-propelled shells of 82-mm or 132-mm caliber. These were eventually installed at the end of 1941 on some of the aircraft; they were the same missiles that were fired by "Stalin's Pipe Organs," the BM-8 and BM-13. The rocket-propelled shells were a ferocious weapon, especially if used suddenly and simultaneously by groups of ten planes from an extremely low altitude. Groups of Su-2 planes were to become "flying batteries." Aside from rocket missiles, the Ivanov Su-2 carried 400 to 600 kilograms of bombs, and five ShKAS machine guns (on the later Su-2 modifications), which at that time held the record in firing rate.

This was a magnificent airplane. The Su-2 had dual controls—one for the pilot and one for the gunner-navigator sitting behind him. Therefore, there was no need to put out a training version of the model: every battle-ready Su-2 could be used for training, and every plane used for training could also be used in battle. This simplified the mass preparation of pilots. The Su-2 could be managed by a pilot of any qualification.

Lieutenant General Anatoly Pushkin (in 1941 he was a major, commander of the 52nd Air Regiment) remembers: "The Su-2 was also great because it did not need airbases. It could take off and land on any even field."

Marshal Ivan Pstygo: "The Su-2 made a strong impression—it was a bomber, but looked like a fighter—small, compact, beautiful."

On top of it all, the Su-2 had remarkable resiliency. Hero of the Soviet Union M. Lashin: "I flew the Su-2. It is a light plane, flies well, maneuverable, extremely durable. It took [a] long time for the Su-2 to burn. It never burst into flames like a torch." Hero of the Soviet Union V. I. Strelchenko: "The Su-2 did not burn even when its fuel tank was damaged—the carbon dioxide defense helped."

On June 22, 1941, the German army delivered a sudden crushing blow to the Red Army. This happened at the point of time when the Su-2s were just beginning to be delivered to the troops en masse. By June 22, 1941, about six hundred Su-2s were produced and delivered to eight air regiments located in the western border military districts. However, many aircraft were still parked at the plant airports and on their way to the places of deployment. On November 19, 1941, a decision was made to stop Su-2 production.[4] An output of 100,000 to 150,000 was planned, but only about eleven hundred were produced. After the war, historians explained this by saying that the Su-2 was obsolete, so production was stopped. This explanation is surprising. How could it be that the outstanding designer Sukhoy created an airplane that became obsolete in the following year? How could a plane become obsolete if there is no other plane in the world that can compare to it in terms of firepower?

Airplane designer V. B. Shavrov wrote the fullest and the most objective history of the development of Soviet aviation. All other designers were his competitors, so Shavrov was not frugal in criticizing them. But he did not criticize the creators of the Su-2: "[I]ts creators cannot be reproached for anything; the plane corresponded to realistic demands that appeared only until the war [started]."[5] In other words, everything was good, there was nothing to reproach the designers, before June 21, 1941, the Su-2 corresponded to demands, but at dawn on June 22 it no longer could satisfy those demands. How are we to understand this?

The tale of the Su-2 began five years before the German invasion. In the summer of 1936 Stalin gathered airplane designers at his dacha, greeted them with hospitality, and then gave them the task to construct an airplane under the codename "Ivanov." Many groups simultaneously worked on Project Ivanov, including some under the command of Tupolev, Neman, Polikarpov, Grigorovich, as well as the design teams of Petlyakov, Sukhoy, Arkhangelsky, Myasishchev, Mikoyan and Gurevich, Lavochkin, and Grushin. In other words, almost all the Soviet airplane designers were concentrated on fulfilling this one single request. And do not think they cooperated. On the contrary: there was harsh competition—only the strongest would win, and all knew "Comrade Ivanov" had plenty of whips and rewards. The Su-2 was the one plane that Stalin placed his stakes on in the upcoming war, which he constantly described as necessary and unavoidable. What did the customer need in his order?

If Stalin had intended to avert World War II, he would have needed a strategic bomber in order to take away the potential aggressor's desire to invade. But Stalin already had a strategic bomber. Remember, this was the same year, 1936, when Petlyakov finished working on the TB-7. If Stalin was intending to avert war, he had no need to gather designers and to put before them the task of creating a new airplane: he simply should have issued an order to start series production of the TB-7. But he did not do this. Stalin did not need an airplane to avert war. So, Stalin was not going to give an order to start producing such a plane in series. Or, actually, he issued such an order four times, and repealed it four times as well.

If Stalin was preparing for a truly defensive war to protect the Motherland, then he should have ordered his designers to create the best fighter in the world, capable of defending the skies over the Soviet Union. But this did not interest Stalin either. Nikolay Polikarpov was among those present at Stalin's dacha. He was a great designer of fighters: he had already created the I-15 and I-16 fighters. The I-15 was unequaled in its horizontal maneuverability. It was this aircraft that pilot Vladimir Kokkinaki used to set a world altitude record of 14,575 meters on November 21, 1935. And the I-16 opened a new page in the world development of aviation: it was the first mass-produced high-speed monoplane in the world. In 1936 Polikarpov was already working on even more powerful machines: he had the lead in the world race for the best fighter. Stalin should have left Polikarpov alone, not bothered him and not distracted him. Polikarpov knew how to make fighters; his pace should not have been interrupted. There was a race on, and every hour, every minute was worth its weight in blood. But no: Stalin ordered Polikarpov to drop all his work on creation of a fighter and start developing a light bomber, the Ivanov. Stalin was not very interested in fighter planes for a defensive war.

So, what was the ideal combat plane that Stalin had in mind, for the development of which he engaged all his best designers, all the creators of fighters as well as bombers? Stalin himself explained the demand thus: "*samolyot chistogo neba* [a clean sky aircraft]"—a light bomber designed to operate free of enemy resistance. From the creators of the Ivanov plane Stalin demanded neither record speed, nor record altitude, nor record range. Stalin was satisfied with the speed of 375 km/h near ground and 460 km/h up in the sky. Record-breaking characteristics were not required. Stalin demanded only simplicity, durability, and firepower. Stalin's plan was to create a plane that could be produced in numbers surpassing all warplanes of all types in all countries of the world combined.

The name of the plane, Ivanov, had one more significant feature. Ivanov was not only Stalin's secret nickname, but also the most common Russian name. "Stalin formulated the task in the following way: the plane must be very simple to produce, so that there could be as many planes as there are people in our country with the name Ivanov."[6] So, Stalin planned to produce the largest series of planes in human history. But this was not a plane for defensive war. This was an aggressor airplane. Stalin planned, literally, to build as many light bombers as there were small but mobile horsemen in the hordes of Genghis Khan.

Pavel Osipovich Sukhoy fulfilled Stalin's demands to the highest level. He won the contest. Sukhoy's Ivanov was launched into production immediately, in two factories. Then it began to be produced at a third factory. Additionally, factories that produced other types of planes were ready upon orders to switch to making the Ivanov. In 1940, after the new indexing system was introduced, Sukhoy's Ivanov was named the Su-2 in honor of its creator.

A question arises: If on Stalin's orders 100,000 to 150,000 light bombers had been built, would not all the neighbors have been frightened? Stalin foresaw such a danger. Therefore, he did not plan the mass production of the Ivanov in peacetime. During the secret mobilization of 1940 through the first half of 1941, a small (in Soviet terms) series was produced—only several hundred of these planes. The objective of this series was to open the production line, gain experience, fly the planes, and test them in small conflicts. These first several hundred were meant to be used in the first strike, especially in secondary locations or combined with other aircraft that had higher speed. After the first sudden strike, it was planned to begin a mass production of the Ivanov, by the thousands. The Ivanov was like an invisible mobilization reserve. It was the same as the situation with the PPSh submachine gun. The PPSh—the Shpagin submachine gun—was created before the war, tested, and approved. The war began and immediately every workshop, every plant that produced hardware, every small-scale factory began producing the most simple, reliable, very powerful weapon in inconceivable quantities. Stalin planned to proceed exactly the same way with the Ivanov airplane. Immediately after carrying out the first strike, Soviet aviation industry was to begin a mass production of the Su-2.

Here the question of defense arises. A relatively slow bomber, acting above the battlefield and adjacent enemy territory must be protected by fighters. If Stalin planned to simultaneously launch production of a corresponding number of fighters for cover, the light Su-2 bombers could have been used in any situation, for example for deflecting aggression. But there was no order for fighter planes in such quantities; therefore there was only one possible way to use the Ivanov Su-2 planes in war: to attack the enemy first and neutralize his aviation. Using large masses of such planes is impossible without crushing the enemy's air bases first. This is why Stalin's plan to produce a minimum of 100,000 light Su-2 bombers was equivalent to a decision to start the war with a sudden strike against the enemy's air bases.

In order to picture Stalin's plan, we must imagine ourselves on the shores of the Hawaiian Islands in December 1941. It is a bright sunny morning. The American fleet is in its harbor. Suddenly, the first wave of Japanese bombers, fighters, and torpedo-planes arrives. The first wave consists of 183 planes. Less than a quarter of these are fighters for cover. A powerful cover is not needed in the given situation. The calculations are based on the premise that American fighters will not have time to get off the ground and deflect the sudden strike. The Japanese air armada consisted mostly of attack planes—the bombers and torpedo-carriers Nakajima B-5N1 and B-5N2. There was nothing remarkable about the design and characteristics of the B-5N aircraft, but in a sudden attack it was awesome. In appearance, size, and flight characteristics, the Nakajima B-5N resembled a fighter more than a bomber. This gave it the ability to fly so low above its target that the faces of the pilots could be seen from the ground and the ships, so low that there were almost no misses when its lethal cargo was dropped. The Nakajima B-5N was a monoplane, with a low wing configuration and one radial two-row engine equipped with an air-cooling system. In some planes the crew consisted of three men: pilot, navigator, and gunner. But in most, it was only two: the planes were used in tight formations, like swarms of enraged bees, so there was no need for every plane to have a navigator. The bomb load of the plane was less than a ton, but each drop was made at point blank range. The B-5N had relatively weak defense weapons—one or two machine guns to defend the hind hemisphere. These planes did not need much defense weaponry. These were planes for sudden attack, "planes of clear sky," a sky in which there are either very few enemy planes or none at all.

The light bomber Nakajima B-5N worked very well at Pearl Harbor, but its heroic days were over after that. The sudden attack was insufficient to take the American fleet and aviation out of the war for long. In consequent battles, when the Americans recovered, when regular war began without stabs in the back, the B-5N did not show any particular usefulness. Production of these planes continued for some time. Overall there were over 1,149 of them produced, and on that their history ended. [7] The B-5N was created for a situation when nothing hampered its work in the sky. The B-5N was frightening to the weak and defenseless, frightening in groups, frightening during a sudden attack. It was frightening like a pack of ferocious, bloodthirsty hyenas that do not have remarkable strength or speed, but have powerful fangs and act in groups against a victim weaker than they are, against him who does not anticipate attack and is not prepared to deflect it.

What does all this have to do with the Soviet plane Ivanov Su-2? The Ivanov was almost an exact copy of the Japanese air aggressor. In the summer of 1936, nobody could have predicted what would happen at Pearl Harbor five years later. In the summer of 1936, the Nakajima B-5N did not yet exist. There were only plans, which the Japanese did not announce. Therefore, it was impossible to suppose that Soviet designers were copying the Japanese. Copying demands time, and even if it had been possible to steal technological documentation (which would have meant mountains of papers), even then the translation (from Japanese!) would have taken several years. The Nakajima B-5N in Japan and the simultaneous varieties of the Ivanov plane in the USSR were created almost in parallel: the first flight of the B-5N was in January 1937, and the first flight of the Ivanov was on August 25 of the same year. Therefore, we are not talking of copying, but of two very similar yet independent processes of development.

On Stalin's orders, several variants of the Ivanov airplane were created. Each designer jealously guarded his secrets from his competitors, but every Soviet designer came up with the same winged hyena: a light bomber, bearing more resemblance to a fighter in appearance, size, and flight characteristics. Every Soviet designer chose the same scheme independently from his competitors: a monoplane with a low wing location, one radial engine in a dual row, with an air-cooling system. This is no miracle. It's just that all the designers were given one task: to create an instrument for doing the same job. Since the job was the same, the instruments created by different designers to perform it were also quite similar.

In the summer of 1936 the Nakajima B-5N had not yet flown once, and there was little information known about it. There was nothing record-breaking about the design of the new Japanese airplane, nothing that could have attracted Stalin's attention. But in 1936 Stalin was already thinking in the same terms as the Japanese admirals. In 1936, Stalin ordered his designers to create the same type of airplane that one beautiful morning would suddenly appear above the enemy, at a moment when the enemy does not anticipate an attack. This was the exact same scenario Stalin planned to use to enter World War II.

A relatively slow-speed plane can be a horrific weapon. Hitler subscribed to the exact same school of thought. He had his own winged jackal—the Ju-87. This was a single-motor plane, which bore more resemblance to a fighter than to a bomber. The crew of the plane was two people. Its defense weapons were weak: one machine gun to defend the rear hemisphere and two wing-mounted machine guns. The bomb load was less than one ton.[8] It was of that generation of airplanes that did not pull up their gear during flight. It had a laughably slow speed. But groups of ten Ju-87 carried out sudden raids against sleeping air bases and with these raids they cleared the skies. After the first strike against the airbase, they flew above the enemy's territory in complete calm and did not need record speed, since there was nobody to chase them. The Ju-87 ruled above Poland, Norway, and France. In Britain it encountered resistance. It was impossible to crush the British air bases with a sudden attack—the conditions were not fit for carrying out surprise raids. After participating in several raids, the losses of Ju-87 were so high that an order was given to stop using them above the British Isles.

In the spring of 1941 came the Yugoslavia and Greece campaigns. The Ju-87 delivered a sudden strike and once again they were successful and loved. In May they carried out a blow to Crete. Here they encountered British troops, but the strike was a surprise, so the Ju-87 once again became the symbol of Blitzkrieg, success, and victory. In June came a sudden attack on Soviet air bases. On a beautiful sunny morning, the German air force secured for itself a clear sky and could use airplanes of any model—there was nobody to be afraid of.

The Ju-87's rule lasted until the time when Soviet aviation gained strength. In the second half of the war, the Ju-87 was being used more and more rarely on the Soviet-German front, until it completely disappeared. "During the course of the eastern campaign, the loss of air superiority during a short time put in question the usefulness of using [the] relatively slow and not maneuverable dive-bombers Ju-87."[9]

The Ivanov was created later than the Ju-87. Therefore, the Ivanov's characteristics were higher, and in terms of designs the two planes had significant differences. But in spirit and general idea, in their assigned roles, the Ju-87 and Ivanov are twins. The plane Nakajima B-5N and the Ivanov are brothers, not just in idea and spirit, but in their main characteristics as well.

The planes for sudden attack did not need record-breaking characteristics. Stalin's logic is clear and simple: if a sudden attack can take care of the enemy's air bases and clear the sky of enemy planes, we will need a simple airplane with powerful weapons that can be mass produced; the most important of its designated uses is to give support to our advancing waves of tanks and paratroops, creating an air terror above defenseless territories. This was exactly the sort of airplane Stalin ordered from his designers.

The Su-2 had a tragic fate. In terms of firepower and speed it surpassed both the German Ju-87 and the Japanese Nakajima. But both the Ju-87 and the Nakajima B-5N got a chance to prove themselves in sudden attacks and gain fame. Hitler did not permit the Ivanov to do the work it was primarily designed to do. Hitler carried out a preemptive strike on Soviet air bases, so the Su-2 was left without the work for which it was created. The Su-2 was not needed in a defensive war. Some factories that were preparing the mass output of Su-2s (for example the Kharkov aviation factory) fell into enemy hands. Although some of the production equipment was evacuated, the production pace was lost. The Su-2s produced earlier suffered great casualties: they had little speed and could not escape the enemy when chased. They had weak defense weapons and could not fight off the fighters. Also, there were no Soviet fighters to give the Su-2 cover.

In a defensive war, fighters are needed first and foremost. Aviation designer S. A. Lavochkin urgently needed a powerful, reliable engine for the modernization of the LaGG-3 fighter, and he needed it in huge quantities. No problems arose—industry was prepared to produce the M-82 engine, which was meant for the Su-2 (as the replacement for the original M-8 and M-88B engines, which did not work as well as expected), in any quantity. Lavochkin installed it, and the renowned fighter La-5, beloved by pilots, was born.

Soviet industry was prepared for the mass production of ShKAS machine guns for many different types of airplanes, but before all for the Su-2. The Su-2 was only produced in limited numbers, but the preparedness of industry was not wasted. These machine guns were simply installed on other types of airplanes. Soviet industry was prepared for the mass production of bombs for the Su-2, and it did produce them. These bombs went to arming different types of airplanes as well. Soviet industry was ready to mass-produce 82-mm- and 132-mm-caliber rocket missiles, and it did produce them. They were used not only in aviation, but in ground artillery as well. In the blink of an eye, the Red Army had thousands of

"Stalin's Pipe Organs." The Communists called this an economic miracle, but there was no miracle. Simply during the period of secret mobilization Soviet industry was prepared to produce rocket missiles for the Su-2.

These weapons were much more effective when they armed the Su-2: artillerists had first to receive information about their targets, while pilots could seek out the targets themselves; artillerists sent their missiles several kilometers away, without seeing the target, while pilots flew hundreds of kilometers, saw their target and the results of their work; the next wave of airplanes always had the opportunity to finish the unfinished mission of the previous one.

Production of the Su-2 was stopped, but industry continued to produce rocket missiles by the millions. They were simply readjusted to be fired from ground installations and other types of airplanes. Production of 100,000 to 150,000 Su-2 planes was planned for conditions in which the Red Army would deliver the first attack, and nobody would hinder the industry's work. Hitler ruined Stalin's plan. But even after losing all the supplies of aluminum, and most of its aircraft and motor factories, the Soviet Union produced 38,729 airplanes, which were incomparably more complex in terms of production—the Il-2 and Il-10. Additionally, tens of thousands of planes of other types, all more complex than the Ivanov, were produced.

One more question: where did Stalin plan to find so many pilots to fly 100,000 to 150,000 Su-2 airplanes? This was not a problem. Stalin prepared an excess of pilots. True, they were trained to fly in clear skies. These pilots were not asked to have high-level pilot skills, to be able to fly at night, or to be able to navigate well in new places and situations. A huge number of Soviet pilots were trained for easy work: take off at dawn, fly in a powerful formation in a straight line, and reach the target. Pilots with this sort of qualification were not needed in defensive war, just like the Su-2 plane they were trained to fly. There were so many trained pilots that in 1942 many of them were given rifles and dropped by the thousands over Stalingrad, to reinforce the infantry.[10]

Hitler destroyed the plans of a Soviet invasion, but he did not even have a hint of Stalin's true might, of the seriousness of his intentions, of how well Stalin was prepared to lead a war of aggression. In March 1939 at the Eighteenth Congress of the Communist Party, Stalin declared: "The aviation arms race in the capitalist countries [has continued] for a number of years and unquestionably presents one of the most characteristic and definitive signs of the inevitable general military conflict." Stalin was right: in the late 1930s, there was a truly mad race in aviation technology. Military aviation forces in some of the largest Western nations reached two to three thousand aircraft and even crossed that threshold. Germany was far in the lead. The German air force reached four thousand warplanes. In March 1939, it was clear to Stalin that such a number of warplanes signaled the inevitability of a war—exactly as it happened. In that same year, 1939, Hitler began his war for global domination.

If we call three or four thousand warplanes by the term "wild arms race of aviation weapons," then what do we call the preparations to produce the Su-2? If four thousand of Hitler's warplanes of all types were enough testimony of the "inevitability of a general military conflict," then what in that case does the preparation for producing 100,000 warplanes of just one type attest to?

12

About "Obsolete" Airplanes

Air force superiority is on the side of the enemy. The number of our units [that are] active on the front has been drastically reduced.

—CHIEF OF GENERAL STAFF OF GERMAN GROUND FORCES,
COLONEL GENERAL FRANZ HALDER, JULY 17, 1941

From the moment that aviation came into being, the problem of acquiring air superiority—and, ideally, complete air domination—presented itself before military strategists. Without air superiority, victory is impossible. Air superiority can be attained through one of two ways: either destruction of the enemy's air force on the ground, or through air battles. Usually both of these methods are used simultaneously. However, a commander of any rank unavoidably has to determine, based on the way the situation develops, which of these two methods is his priority at the given moment, and which is secondary. Before the war starts, the military and political high command of the country should clearly determine its position on the given question: which of these methods will be primary, especially in the early period of the war? If the primary method of attaining air superiority is to be the way of air battles, the attention of all designers should be turned to creating fighter aircraft. Designers of fighter aircraft should be given the best production facilities, the best aircraft engines, the most expensive equipment, and the rarest materials. If it is decided to win air superiority through air battles, the best pilots need to be sent to fighter aviation. These fighter pilots should be given the largest part of training resources and fuel, even if it is done at the expense of training other pilots. If, however, we have decided to win air superiority by destroying the enemy's air force on the ground, then the attention of the designers should be turned to creating planes of an entirely different nature. Low-flying attack planes and light bombers are perfect for carrying out raids on air bases. The low-flying aircraft is not designed for air battle. This plane needs neither record speed, nor altitude, nor maneuverability. This plane has to meet entirely different requirements. It must be well defended from powerful fire from the ground, and must carry its own weapons powerful enough to destroy targets on the ground.

Both methods of attaining air superiority have their advantages and disadvantages. If we decide that the primary method of winning superiority in the air is to be through air battles, then we must be prepared for large losses of planes and pilots, and for prolonged, exhausting battles. The training of fighter pilots is a risky venture that requires a lot of time and huge expenditures. This method of winning superiority in the air has only one advantage: it is universal; it can be used in any situation. If we decide to win air superiority through destruction of the enemy's air force on the ground, the task can be accomplished quickly. During the course of one day or even just a few hours, we can secure not just superiority but total domination. All this can be accomplished with just one sudden, powerful raid, and no exhausting, prolonged air battles would need to follow. And we would not need to spend tremendous resources on training pilots. Even pilots of relatively low qualification are good for this job. They do not need to learn tricks. It is enough to teach them how to take off and land, to follow a route, and to shoot at stationary targets on the ground. This scenario has only one drawback: it can only be used against an enemy who is not awaiting an invasion.

Before and during the war, the Soviet Union designed quite a few remarkable and at the same time very simple airplanes. But the best achievement of the Soviet air force was not in designing airplanes that destroy enemy planes in the air, but in creating airplanes that destroy enemy planes and other targets on the ground. The Il-2 was the highest Soviet achievement in aviation technology during World War II. Air bases were its primary target. The Il-2 was a unique armored low-flying attack plane. We are not talking of armor sheets, which add a shield to a plane, but of a purely armored body up to 12 mm in thickness. The strength of this armor was reinforced by the fact that its details had a rounded shape. The problem of transparent parts was also solved. When bullets hit the front glass of the Il-2, they left only insignificant cracks, even when the fire came from extremely close ranges. The secret was the use of armored glass 63 mm thick.

The Il-2 was the only armored plane in history, a true flying tank. The crew cabin, engine, and fuel tanks were all covered with armor. Only the wings, the tail part of the fuselage, and the tail unit were left unshielded. Aside from the armor protection, a unique survivor rate, and remarkable body characteristics, the Il-2 had extremely powerful weapons: eight rocket missiles, two 23-mm automatic cannon that fired at 550 rounds per minute, two machine guns with a world-record firing rate, and 400 to 600 kilograms of bombs. [1]

When creating this attack airplane the designer, Ilyushin, included a small defensive detail as well. The early model of the Il-2 was a two-seater. Pilot and gunner sat back to back: the pilot flew the plane and destroyed targets on the ground, while the gunner, with a .50-caliber machine gun, covered the hind hemisphere from attacking enemy fighters. Stalin personally called Ilyushin and asked to have the gunner with the machine gun removed, and make the Il-2 a one-seater. Stalin ordered the entire decrease in weight to be used to enlarge the bomb load and the fuel tank. Stalin needed the Il-2 for situations in which not a single enemy fighter would have the time to get off the ground.

The changes in design took several months. The problem was that the technology used in producing the Il-2 was extremely complex. The cabin was assembled from over twenty armored parts, which had a double bend, like fragments of a broken mug. The entire technology for producing the armored fuselage had to be replaced. This delayed the beginning of mass production of the Il-2. By the time of the German invasion, only 249 of them had been produced.

But Hitler did not have a single comparable plane. And the rest of the world had nothing comparable. Not a single nation in the world succeeded by the end of the war in creating anything equal to what the Red Army had at its beginning. Stalin had "only" 249 Il-2 planes, but Soviet industry was ready to produce them in any quantity. Even after the losses in the second half of 1941 of the greater part of aviation and motor factories, after the loss of all factories that produced aluminum, the Il-2 was still produced in the largest-scale series in the history of world aviation. The Il-2 did not become obsolete until the very end of the war, and entered history as the most mass-produced warplane of all time.

The Il-2 carried huge losses. The low-flying attack plane was not designed for air battle, and following Stalin's orders it had no defensive weapons. Several days after the German invasion, Stalin personally called Ilyushin and demanded that the Il-2 be produced again as a two-seater: in defensive war, even an aggressor airplane needs to have defensive weapons. However, it was already impossible to return to the original designs without stopping production. And it was impossible to stop production. Therefore, the plane continued to be made as a one-seater. The Il-2 delivered a huge amount of destruction to the enemy, but it also was quick to perish. If the Il-2 had also had a rear gunner protecting the hind hemisphere, the Red Army in no time would have had thousands of armed airplanes of this type. Each of them could have completed tens and even hundreds of raids. The Il-2 attack-planes alone could have turned the tide of war. But there was no gunner, so in the early period of the war the Il-2 planes perished by the hundreds and thousands. In the years 1941 and 1942, an Il-2 plane in action could reasonably be expected to last only ten or thirteen flights before it was destroyed.[2]

Only by the end of 1942 was there some success in changing the finalized design of the plane. The Il-2 was once again produced as a two-person plane. Now the plane had a gunner with a large-caliber machine gun. However, this was still only a half-valid solution. There was never a return to the original design. The shooter's cabin was added outside the armored compartment.[3] The pilot was safe behind the armor, while the gunner was just covered by plywood. Of course he deflected the attacks of enemy fighters that came up from the tail, but he quickly perished himself, and then the Il-2 once again became defenseless. The best pilots trained before the war perished in the first months of war due to a lack of defensive weaponry on the Il-2. When defensive weaponry was finally installed on the planes, Il-2s were already operated by war-time pilots, trained in very specific ways. One of my mentors at the Military Academy, Air Force Major General Alexander Kuchumov, Hero of the Soviet Union, had arrived at the front in 1942. He had standard war-time training behind him—an hour and a half of flight time on the Il-2. The unique attack plane, the best of its kind, proved to be a particularly effective weapon. But it could have yielded even better results had well-trained pilots flown it. A few of the war-time trainees who survived became masters of their craft, heroes, and generals. And thousands perished after just a few missions.

But the problem was not that there were too few Il-2 planes. And the problem was not that they were bad planes. The problem was that the design of the plane was dictated by strategy, and the strategy was that of a sudden attack against the enemy's air bases, after which the plan was to continue the war without resistance from the enemy's air force. The Il-2 had to be used in a defensive war, when the enemy had air superiority. But this great airplane was created for an entirely different kind of war.

Stalin had a dive-bomber, the Pe-2. Hitler had good airplanes, but the Pe-2 surpassed any of them, in all the major characteristics. For example, the Pe-2 had a top speed of 75 km/h more than the best German bomber, the Ju-88, and 100 km/h more than the He-111. Prior to June 22, 1941, 490 Pe-2 planes had been produced,[4] more than all the Ju-88s positioned on the entire Soviet-German front.

Stalin had three types of new fighters—the MiG-3, the LaGG-3, and the Yak-1. Each of them was equal or superior to the best German models. For example, the MiG-3 had a speed of 628 km/h at an altitude of 7,000 meters. Hitler had nothing similar in 1941. On June 22, 1941, Hitler had 1,129 fighters of all types on the Soviet-German front. Stalin had 1,309 of the newest MiG-3 model fighters alone.[5] On top of this, Stalin also had 399 of the newest Yak-1 models and 322 LaGG-3s.[6]

Germany mastered the following air forces for the purpose of waging war against the USSR: 3,520 war planes of all kinds (bombers, fighters, reconnaissance, transport, and communications aircraft), plus 307 Finnish planes, 393 Romanian, 48 Hungarian—a total of 4,268 planes.[7] The total number of aircraft available to Germany on June 1, 1941, was 6,852, including 823 reconnaissance planes, 2,017 single-engine fighters, 232 double-engine fighters, 2,141 bombers, 501 dive-bombers, 719 transport planes, 133 communications planes, and 286 planes belonging to the Navy.[8] But Germany was simultaneously fighting on many fronts, from the North Atlantic to the Egyptian border.[9] Against Stalin, Hitler could only send 2,510 airplanes, including the Hs-123, which had a speed of only 338 km/h, and assorted types of aircraft used for transport, communications, and medical purposes.[10]

Stalin had 2,769 of the newest models Il-2, Pe-2, MiG-3, Yak-1, and LaGG-3. But that was not all: Stalin did not just have five new types of planes, he had twelve. He also had the Ar-2, Er-2, Su-2, Pe-8, Yak-2, Yak-4, and Il-4. The Er-2 bomber had a range of 4,000 km. Hitler did not have such a bomber until the very end of the war. The Soviet bomber DB-3f (Il-4), released in 1940, had a range of 3,300 km with M-88 motors and a normal bomb cargo, while the Il-4, released in 1941 and equipped with M-88B motors, had a range of 3,380 km. Hitler did not have this kind of aircraft either. On September 7, 1936, Ilyushin's DB-3 bomber raised 2,000 kg to an altitude of 11,005 meters. This record (among others) was officially registered by the FAI (*Fédération Aéronautique Internationale*) and remained a record throughout the entire war. Not a single dual-engine airplane in the world could repeat this performance. This record was beaten only after the war, in 1946, and not by the B-17 "Flying Fortress" but by the four-engine "Super Fortress," the B-29. How many bombers did Stalin have? The DB-3fs alone, on June 22, 1941, numbered 1,846. This is more than the number of all types of bombers used by Hitler to attack the Soviet Union. In other words, Stalin had more of the newest planes than Hitler had new and old ones combined.

Of course, Stalin had obsolete planes as well. Aside from the twelve newest models, Stalin also had the TB-3 and SB bombers, and the I-16 and I-153 fighters. There is something to be said for these airplanes. Stalin had 541 four-engine TB-3 bombers.[11] Historian V. B. Shavrov said: "This airplane of A. N. Tupolev's design belongs to [the] category of the most remarkable planes not just of their own time period. It was the first four-motor cantilever monoplane bomber with engines that were installed inside the wings. Its design became a prototype for all similar airplanes and planes of various designations."[12] The TB-3 became part of the inventory in 1932. It was produced in series until 1938. In total, 819 airplanes of this type were built. Its crew had eight members. It had four motors. The range of its flight, with a normal bomb cargo, was up to 2,250 km. Its defense weapons were eight machine guns. Its bomb load was two to four tons. In 1941, all these characteristics placed the TB-3 among the top class of airplanes in the world. What about speed? One must concede that the speed was not too great. In 1932, when the airplane was being integrated into the army, the speed seemed unthinkable, but by 1941 concepts of speed had changed. The maximum speed of the TB-3 was 288 km/h.

Let's compare Stalin's "obsolete" heavy TB-3 bomber with Hitler's best heavy bomber. Well, Hitler did not have any new heavy bombers. (A heavy-bomber development program was cancelled after the 1936 death of its proponent, Walther Wever.) There is nothing to compare with. Then let us compare the characteristics of the "obsolete" TB-3 with the characteristics of the best, though obsolete, German heavy bombers. But Hitler did not have any obsolete heavy bombers either, not a single one. He had, of course, dreams, ideas. He had sample models. But nothing went past the experimental stage, so in 1941 Hitler did not have a single bomber with four engines. Hitler in 1941 did not have a single bomber with a range of 4,000 kilometers. Hitler in 1941 did not have a single bomber with a bomb-carrying capacity of 4 tons. The TB-3 had little speed. But Hitler's heavy bombers had no speed, because they did not exist.

Stalin had the "obsolete" SB bomber (mid-range). At approximately the same bomb load and range of flight, the SB surpassed the German Ju-87 bomber by about 70 km/h.[13] By June 22, 1941, the Germans had deployed 324 Ju-87s as a part of their assault against the Soviet Union; Stalin had 6,656 SB planes.[14]

On top of the newest fighters, Stalin had the "obsolete" I-16. The situation on June 22, 1941, was that the air force of the western border regions of the USSR alone had at its disposal a total of 4,226 fighters, of which 1,635 were I-16s. Add to that another 344 I-16s in the air forces of the Northern, Baltic, and Black Sea fleets, to a total of 1,979.[15] Here is what British pilot Alfred Price, who in his lifetime flew in over forty types of airplanes and spent over four thousand hours in the air, thought about this airplane. His opinion of the "obsolete" Soviet fighter: "The most powerful weapon among the series of fighters in the world in September 1939 was possessed by the Russian I-16, which twice surpassed the Bf-109e and almost three times the 'Spitfire-1.' Among all prewar fighters in the world, the I-16 was unique in the sense that it alone had an armor protection around the pilot. Those who think that the Russians were backward peasants before the Second World War and only moved forward under the influence of using German expertise need to remember the facts."[16] To this it must be added that by 1941 the I-16 had not and could not have become obsolete.

Starting in 1937, the I-16 was produced with a cannon and machine-gun armament. The legendary British Spitfire in 1940, during the course of the Battle of Britain, had no cannon. The great American Mustang and Thunderbolt fighters even by the end of the war had no cannon. The I-16 had an amazing lifting power of 553 horsepower per ton of weight. This was a record statistic, and not a single warplane in the world had such power. By the end of the war, not a single plane in the world had reached such a result—the Spitfire Mk-IX and Bf-109K came close, but only when the engine was working in an extreme regime that could not be turned on for longer than seven minutes.

The I-16 surpassed any German fighter and most other airplanes of the world in terms of its longevity. All German fighters had an extremely vulnerable coolant system. If just one bullet hit the radiator, pipeline, pump, or any other part of the cooling system, the liquid leaked out and the motor overheated and stopped working. On the other hand, the I-16 had a coolant system that was not vulnerable to such direct hits, because it was air-cooled. That engine was based on the American Wright Cyclone design.

The I-16 was inferior to the German fighter in speed. The I-16 type 28 had a speed near ground of 427 km/h, while the Bf-109 E-1 flew at 464 km/h, and the Bf-109 E-3 flew at 540 km/h. At an altitude of 5 kilometers, the I-16 type 29 flew at 470 km/h,[17] while the Bf-109 E-1 and E-3 flew at 532 and 555 km/h, respectively.[18] But the I-16 surpassed the Bf-109 in vertical maneuvers and greatly surpassed it in horizontal maneuvers. The I-16 could do a turn in 17 seconds, while the Bf-109 took 25 seconds. If the German fighter did not wish to engage the I-16 in battle, it could always evade it. The Bf-109 evaded battle using its speed, while the I-16 used its maneuverability.

It's interesting to point out what Germany's own fighter pilots thought of the I-16's capabilities: "The I-16, with an able pilot inside, was a dangerous enemy. German pilots did not at all consider the I-16 an easy target. Even though they could almost always win the initiative in air combat against the *Ishachok* ("little donkey"—a Russian nickname for the I-16), the pilots tried to avoid maneuver-based combats against Russian veterans. Among themselves, the Germans used to say that one should not corner a rat, referring, of course, to the plane's nickname, *Rata*, earned on the Spanish front. If the Messerschmitt pilots did not follow this principle, the fight could turn out very badly for them indeed."[19] From 1934 to 1942, 10,292 I-16 units were produced. This number includes 3,189 I-16 type 15s (UTI-4), the training versions of the aircraft. So the total of combat ready I-16 units produced was 7,103.[20]

Aside from this plane, Stalin also had the I-153. There were 3,437 of them produced. This plane had lower speed than the I-16, but it had phenomenal maneuverability. It climbed to a height of 5 kilometers in exactly a minute less than the Bf-109. The I-153 did a turn in 12 seconds. It had time to make two full turns faster than the Me-109 did one.

Why then in the first stage of the war did the Soviet air force lose air superiority from day one? Why did the Germans have the advantage in the air, given that their air force lost out to the Soviet air force both in plane quantity and plane quality? The answer is simple: the majority of Soviet pilots, including fighter pilots, were not taught the dogfights. Soviet aviation was oriented to conduct one grandiose, sudden, aggressive operation, in which the Soviet air force in one raid would crush the enemy's air force on the ground and claim air superiority. Already in 1929 in the Soviet journal *Voyna I Revolutsia* (War and Revolution), the fundamental article "The Early Period of the War" made the conclusion that was later repeated by Soviet air force directives, including ones from 1940 and 1941: "It seems to be extremely advantageous to show initiative and be the first to attack the enemy. He who exhibits initiative by attacking his enemy's air bases with his air force can later count on air superiority."[21]

Precisely for this reason Soviet aviation in 1941 was concentrated along the borders. The field air base of the 123rd fighter air force regiment, for example, was located only two kilometers away from the German border. In a war situation, this saves fuel during takeoff in the direction of the enemy. In the 123rd regiment, just like in many others, the majority of altitude gain after takeoff was to be acquired over German territory. Ten years after these events, Major V. Khmelev, then an eyewitness, described them: "The bomber aviation air bases [were] located no further than 80 km from the new German-Soviet border. It was at that time clear to every Soviet soldier and officer that the entire Red Army was feverishly preparing for aggressive operations of unheard-of dimensions."[22] But Hitler attacked first, and from the first day of the German invasion many Soviet air bases found themselves under the tracks of German tanks. Aside from the huge losses in planes, entire air bases—with unbelievable reserves of fuel, ammunition, and other supplies, without which conducting war was impossible—were lost to the enemy.

13

Soviet Airborne Assault Troops
and Their Mission

In the battles to come, we shall operate on the territory of the enemy. That is prescribed by
our rules.

> —COLONEL A. I. RODIMTSEV, SPEECH AT THE EIGHTEENTH
> CONGRESS OF THE COMMUNIST PARTY, 1939

Airborne assault troops are designed for action in sudden, decisive offensive operations. "The use of paratroops is pointless unless they are part of an offensive operation," said one military newspaper in 1940.[1] *The Field Rules of the Red Army for 1936 (PU-36)* states: use of airborne assault troops can only be made in the course of offensive operations and only in conjunction with regular troops advancing against the enemy.[2]

The Soviet Union was the first nation in the world in which airborne assault troops were created. They were created in 1930, before Hitler came to power in Germany. Only two other nations developed airborne troops before World War II: Germany, in 1936, and Italy. By the beginning of the war Hitler had four thousand parachutists and Italy had trained seven hundred parachutists.

Stalin took the lead in developing airborne warfare. "By the end of 1933 the Red Army had one air assault brigade, four mobile paratroops units, twenty-nine separate battalions, and several companies that altogether numbered about ten thousand men."[3]

At the beginning of the war, the Soviet Union had more than one million trained parachutists, according to the official Communist Party newspaper, *Pravda*, on August 18, 1940. In light of declassified documents it is clear that this was a deliberate underestimation of the real number, which arguably was closer to two million parachutists. Never before had the world seen such large-scale preparations for offensive war. To calm fears of Soviet aggression, *Pravda* lowered the number of Russian paratroopers to one million.

In the 1930s, the Soviet Union went through a true parachute craze. In less than two years (from April 1934 until February 1936), 427,000 parachutists were trained in Ukraine alone.[4] Not a single city park was without a parachute tower, and a parachutist's badge became a necessary symbol of manhood for all young men. However, it was not easy to earn it. The badge was awarded for jumping out of an airplane, but only to those who beforehand had completed tests in running, swimming, shooting, throwing hand grenades for long distances and with accuracy, climbing obstacle courses, learning to use gas masks, and other military tests. Jumping from an airplane was the culmination of the training of an airborne soldier.

In the 1930s, western regions of the USSR were shaken up by grandiose military maneuvers. Only one theme was developed in each maneuver—"Deep Penetration"—a sudden attack by gigantic masses of tanks deep into "enemy" territory. The scenario always simple but menacing. In all training exercises, the sudden attack of land troops was always preceded by a surprise attack of Soviet aviation on the "enemy" air bases. This was followed by a drop of the paratroops to take over the air bases. Following the first wave of parachutists, a second wave of assault troops, with heavy weapons, landed on the air bases.

In 1935 at the Kiev military district training maneuvers 1,200 paratroopers were dropped, followed by the landing of 2,500 assault troops with heavy weapons, including artillery, armored cars, and tanks. In 1936, in Byelorussia, the same invasion technique was practiced. A parachute force of 1,800 men was dropped and followed by 5,700 assault troops with heavy weapons. In the same year, during attack maneuvers in the Moscow military district, the 84th Rifle Division was fully deployed by airborne transport. In 1938, six new air assault brigades—the 201st, 202nd, 204th, 211th, 212th, and 214th—were created.[5] In total the six brigades consisted of 18,000 men.[6]

In 1939, Stalin ordered the destruction of guerrilla warfare bases and partisan units that were designed for action on Soviet territory in the event of enemy aggression. Instead, Stalin ordered the formation of new paratroop forces. In the Moscow military district three regiments co sisting of three battalions each and several separate battalions, five hundred to seven hundred parachutists each, were formed.[7] In April 1941 five air assault corps were secretly formed in the Soviet Union.[8] All the corps were stationed in the western regions of the Soviet Union. Each corps included an administration, staff, service formations, three air assault brigades, an artillery battalion, a separate tank battalion (of fifty-four tanks), and other formations. Each corps numbered 10,419 men.[9]

Twice awarded the title of "Hero of the Soviet Union," Colonel General Alexander Rodimtsev, who in May 1941 was commander of the 5th Air Assault Brigade of the 3rd Paratroops Corps, testified about those events in his memoirs. At that time, Rodimtsev was a colonel with combat experience in Spain, where he had received his first Hero of the Soviet Union medal. Rodimtsev recalled:

> I had to serve with excellently trained warriors, the best of our Soviet youth. . . . The officers were mostly experienced parachutists: each of them [had] made from fifty to one hundred jumps. The brigade consisted of four separate paratroops battalions, a separate artillery battalion, a sergeants' school, a separate reconnaissance company, a separate machine gun company, [and] a separate communications company. The brigade was fully equipped with weapons and necessary supplies, as well as parachutes. An excellent collective of officers, disciplined and friendly. Later my first impression was confirmed. Every one of them showed extreme courage and selflessness in battle for the Motherland. The brigade trained according to schedule. . . . I was pleased by the hard-working nature of my parachutists, their courage and their will power, which was easy to feel amongst that confident youth. . . . All the time was used for preparations for jumps and [for the] jumps themselves.

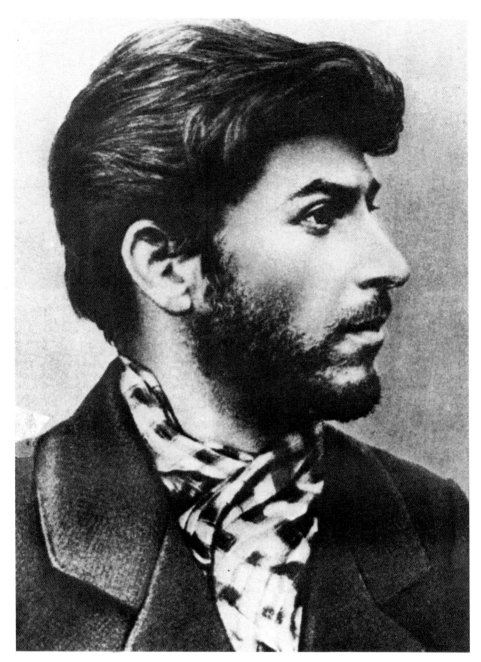

Stalin, a terrorist and robber from the Caucasus also known as Koba, Ivanov, Vassiliev, Chizhikov, Ivanovich, Dzhugashvili, Bessoshvili, Salin.

Государственный герб
Союза Советских Социалистических Республик.

The coat of arms of the Union of the Soviet Socialist Republics. There are no borders on the map because the whole world was to become part of the Soviet Union through wars and revolutions.

The Palace of Soviets was supposed to be the tallest building in the world at five hundred meters high. It was designed for the ceremony of accepting new republics joining the Soviet Union, but in 1941 construction was halted and the frame dismantled. The steel beams were used to construct anti-tank defenses near Moscow.

Joachim von Ribbentrop signs the Molotov-Ribbentrop pact dividing Poland between the Soviet Union and Germany. Hitler was not aware that France and England would declare war against Germany after he attacked Poland. But Stalin knew it. It was part of his plan for the conquest of Europe.

Stalin shakes Ribbentrop's hand. Next to Stalin is Marshal Shaposhnikov, Chief of Staff of the Red Army, who coined the slogan, "Mobilization is war." On August 19, 1939, Stalin ordered secret mobilization.

Ribbentrop brings great news to Hitler: "We can start the war against Poland." They do not realize they have fallen into Stalin's trap.

Soviet and German officers looking at maps dividing Poland after the invasion, September 1939.

NKVD and SS officers, now brothers in arms after the division of Poland.

Traditionally, history presents Stalin as a victim of Hitler's aggression. But at the time of the signing of the pact in August 1939 the world saw them as equal villains. Bulgarian cartoonist Ivan Beshkov saw them with daggers drawn against each other.

German General Hans Guderian exchanges smiles with the Soviet Commander S. Krivosheev at a border meeting dividing Poland. Note how the officers keep their hands behind their backs as in the cartoon. Krivosheev ended the war in 1945 in Berlin as a lieutenant general of Soviet armored forces.

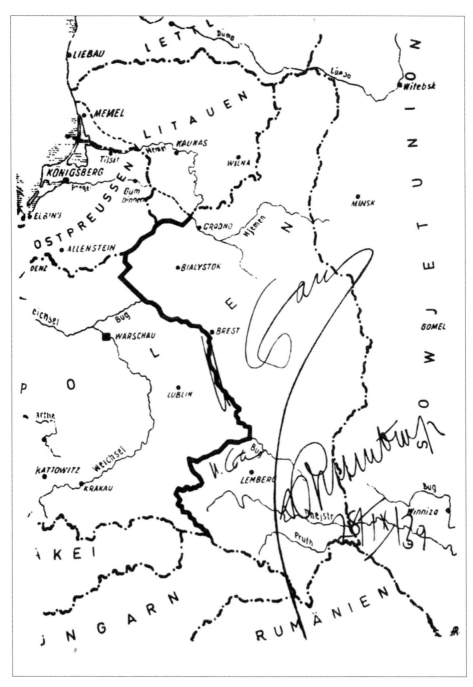

On September 28, 1939, a detailed map of the division of Poland was signed by Stalin and Ribbentrop. Stalin wrote the first letters of his name then stopped and continued again with larger letters, unable to hide his excitement. Stalin, who held no state office at the time, should have let Molotov, the foreign minister, sign.

On September 29, 1939, Nikita Khrushchev, then a Politburo member, inspected the
new border on the river San. General I. Tyulenev, accompanying Khrushchev, wrote
that Khrushchev said, "Let the Germans do their evil crimes and then we will come as
liberators."

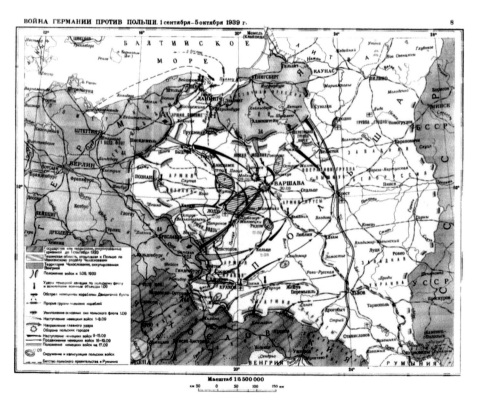

The Soviet official map of the German war against Poland with the territory occupied by the
Soviet Union left unmarked, as if there was no Soviet participation in the war against Poland.

Soviet troops preparing for the "liberation" of Europe. It is difficult to distinguish them from German troops.

Soviet oil delivery to Hitler. Without Soviet supplies of oil, cotton, grain, magnesium, chrome, copper, tin, nickel, vanadium, wolfram, and molybdenum, Hitler would have been unable to conquer Europe.

The Soviet BT tank, with high speed, high maneuverability, and light armor. A new tank for a new kind of warfare: lightning offensive operations. It was of limited use in defensive warfare.

The amphibious T-40 tank. The Soviet Union was the only country in the world which by 1941 had amphibious tanks, which can be used only in an offensive war.

The KV-1 heavy tank. The Soviet Union was the only country in the world which by 1941 had heavy tanks in its arsenal. The Soviet heavy tanks could sustain up to twenty to thirty direct hits from German anti-tank guns. Once these tanks crossed the border nothing could stop them. Hitler was fortunate in attacking at the moment these tanks were still being moved forward on railroad cars.

The KV-2 heavy tank. By the end of June 1941 German frontline officers reported that the Russians had tanks with powerful engines, wide tracks, impenetrable armor, and six-inch guns that used 48-kg (105.6-lb) projectiles. Berlin did not believe these reports.

By 1936 the Soviet Union created the TB-7 strategic bomber, which was capable of reaching altitudes where anti-aircraft fire and enemy interceptors could not reach them. In 1942 the Soviet foreign minister, Vyacheslav Molotov, used a TB-7 to fly over German occupied territories without fear of being attacked while en route to Great Britain and the USA. The TB-7 had the capacity to carry 11,000-pound bombs. Before 1941 Soviet industry had the capacity to produce a thousand of these planes, but Stalin ordered a halt to mass production of the TB-7. By the summer of 1941 only seventeen of these bombers were built. Stalin had decided he did not want to destroy European cities, factories, and ports; he wanted to seize them undamaged and for that purpose he needed different aircraft.

The 212th Air Assault Brigade, secretly transferred from the Far East, trained next to Rodimtsev's brigade in "conditions that were closer to actual battle conditions." Rodimtsev said its soldiers and commanders each had one hundred and sometimes even up to two hundred jumps, while the commander, Colonel I. I. Zatevakhin had at least three hundred jumps.[10]

Rodimtsev's account was mirrored in the memoirs of Colonel I. G. Starchak, titled *Battle from the Sky*, and by General A. S. Zhadov, who in 1941 was a major general in command of the 4th Air Assault Corps.[11] Zhadov attested: "All brigade and corps formations were manned with well-trained personnel, supplies, and weapons."[12] All five corps were in a state of full readiness for deployment.

The air assault corps quickly graduated from general battle preparations to very concrete ones. After June 13, 1941, the appropriate orders were issued and the final preparations for war were completed. Tens of thousands of parachutes were folded for action in the loading areas of the airbases. The air assault corps were issued powerful artillery and even battalions of light amphibious tanks. All paratroop corps were stationed so close to the borders that they could be deployed on enemy territory without additional regrouping. All corps conducted intensive preparations for an impending landing. All corps were concentrated in the forests, away from public view. The 4th and 5th Corps could, without regrouping, be used against Germany, the 3rd against Romania. The 1st and 2nd Corps were to be dropped in Germany, Romania, or in Czechoslovakia or Austria, in order to cut off the petroleum routes that ran through the mountains from Romania to Germany.

On June 12, 1941, the Command Staff for Air Assault Troops was created in the Red Army, with plans for an additional five air assault corps to be formed by August 1941. Their creation was decided upon in May 1941.[13] Aside from the five corps, five separate air assault brigades were also formed. Altogether, in the summer of 1941 Stalin had ten air assault corps (three brigades each), six separate brigades, and several separate regiments.

Aside from the air assault corps, brigades, and regiments, a significant number of parachutist landing battalions were created as units included with the regular Soviet infantry. Marshal Ivan Bagramian relates that in the beginning of 1941 the 55th Rifle Corps, which was located close to the Romanian border, conducted intensive training for several parachutist battalions.

In addition to parachute formations, several regular rifle divisions were also prepared for transfer by air, in those days a radical shift in deployment of troops. On June 21, 1941, the day before Hitler attacked the Soviet Union, the Soviet army was practicing airborne offensive operations, proof of how far they were from any defensive war strategy.

To deliver hundreds of thousands of paratroops the Red Army needed an air armada of transport planes and gliders. Stalin understood this perfectly, which is why the parachute craze of the 1930s was accompanied by a glider craze. Soviet gliders and gliding hobbyists were up to world standards. By the beginning of World War II thirteen of the eighteen world records in gliding were held by the Soviet Union.[14] The best Soviet warplane designers were also busy designing gliders. The future creator of the first satellite, Sergei Korolev, was asked to develop gliders.

The offensive military orientation of Soviet gliding was not disputable. Even before Hitler came to power, the USSR had already created the first cargo glider, the G-63, designed by B. Urlapov. Then the USSR created heavy gliders, capable of carrying trucks. Designer

P. Gorokhovsky created a rubber inflatable glider. After being deployed in the enemy's rear, several of these gliders could be loaded into one transport plane and returned to their own territory for repeated use.

Soviet generals dreamed not only of dropping a multitude of paratroops into Western Europe, but also hundreds, possibly thousands, of tanks. Designers eagerly searched for the most simple and inexpensive ways to realize these dreams. Oleg Antonov, the man who later created the largest cargo warplane in the world, suggested adding wings and empennage (a tail assembly) to a regular tank, using the body of the tank as the fuselage of the hybrid. This system received the name KT—*Krylatyi Tank* ("winged tank"). The gears from the steering were connected to the cannon of the tank. The tank's crew could guide the flight from the tank cabin, by turning the turret and barrel. The KT was amazingly simple. Of course, the flight risk in the tank was, to put it mildly, higher than normal, but human life in the Soviet Union cost less than adding wings to a tank. Before landing, the tank's engine was turned on and the caterpillar tracks launched to maximum speed. The KT landed on its tracks and slowed down. On the ground, the wings and empennage were dropped, and the hybrid once again became a regular tank. Oleg Antonov's winged tank was not ready at the beginning of the war, and since the war did not start the way Stalin had planned, the winged tanks became just as useless as the million silk parachutes folded neatly for an attack against Germany and Romania.[15]

The Soviet Union entered World War II with the highest number of glider pilots in the world. In 1939 alone 30,000 people were simultaneously training to become pilot gliders. The pilots' skills frequently reached the highest levels. For example, in 1940 there was a demonstration of eleven flying gliders towed by just one plane. In the late 1930s, more than ten design bureaus in the Soviet Union were competing fiercely to create the best military cargo glider. O. Antonov, aside from the winged tank, created the large military glider A-7. V. Gribovsky designed the magnificent military glider G-11. D. Kolesnikov created a glider for carrying twenty soldiers—KTs-20, while G. Korbula worked on creating a giant glider.

In January 1940, by a decision of the Central Committee (meaning by Stalin's orders) a directorate for the production of military cargo gliders was created within the structure of the Ministry of Aviation, the People's Commissariat (Russian abbreviation—*Narkomat*) of Aviation Industry. The year 1940 was spent on intensive preparations, and from spring 1941 factories run by this directorate began the mass production of cargo gliders. On April 23, 1941, a decision of the Party Central Committee and the Council of Ministers ordered the Commissariat of Aviation Industry to accelerate the production of an 11-seat glider, with a deadline of May 15, 1941, and of a 20-seat glider by July 1, 1941. Stalin and Molotov personally signed the order.

On June 16, 1941, General Zhukov sent out a "Memorandum from the Chief of Staff of the Red Army to the People's Commissariat of Soviet Aviation Industry," # 567240, which ordered 7,500 gliders to be manufactured in 1941–42.[16]

The gliders that were produced in the spring of 1941 had to be used in the summer of 1941, or, at the latest, in the early fall. Unlike ordinary warplanes, gliders had light and fragile bodies and wings. They could not be parked outdoors, and all available hangars were already full with previously produced gliders. Keeping a huge cargo glider outdoors, during fall winds and rains, and winter cold and snow, would harm it beyond repair. The mass production of cargo gliders in 1941 meant they were intended for use in 1941. If Stalin had intended to drop hundreds of thousands of his airborne troops into Central and Western Europe in 1942, the mass production of gliders should have been scheduled for spring of 1942.

Gliders deliver cargo and groups of assault troops without parachutes, while assault forces with parachutes are delivered to the enemy's rear by cargo warplanes. The best cargo warplane in the world at the beginning of World War II was the legendary American Douglas DC-3. This plane set the record for durability—fifty-five years of use. It was an extraordinary plane for its time.

The American Douglas DC-3, although under a different name (PS-84),[17] formed the core of Soviet war-transport aviation. In 1938, the U.S. government sold to Stalin the production license and the necessary amount of the most complex equipment for its production. Giants like Fokker and Mitsubishi also purchased licenses for the production of Douglas aircraft, but could not produce them in mass without parts from America. Soviet industry, on the other hand, was able to start mass production using Soviet parts—an important step in the field of cargo aircraft. Before the war, the Soviet Union bought twenty Douglas units from the United States, and in 1939 six identical aircraft were produced on Soviet soil. In 1940, fifty-one aircraft were produced; in 1941, 237 aircraft. During the entire war 2,419 DC-3s or Soviet PS-84/Li-2 planes came out of Soviet factories.[18]

Aside from the DC-3, the Soviet Union had several hundred TB-3 strategic bombers, which could also be used as cargo planes.[19] All large-scale drops of paratroops in the 1930s were done from the TB-3. There were enough of them to lift several thousand paratroopers and heavy weapons, including tanks, armored cars, and artillery.

A Soviet air armada of gliders and transport planes would be easy prey for enemy fighters if they did not secure complete air superiority. Soviet generals understood all this perfectly. The most important document that guided the actions of the Red Army in war was the Field Order (*Polevoy Ustav*—PU). At that time, the Field Order of 1939 was in action—PU-39. The order clearly stated that to conduct a "deep penetration" and a mass drop of air assault corps, the Soviet air force must dominate the skies. This field order, as well as air force battle orders and "instruction on independent use of aviation," foresaw the conduct in the beginning of the war of a massive strategic operation that would crush the air force of the enemy. According to the plans of Soviet commanders, the air forces of several fronts, naval aviation, and fighter aviation were to participate in such an operation.

In December 1940 the highest-ranking commanders of the Red Army, at a secret meeting with Stalin and members of the Politburo, discussed these operations in great detail. The euphemism for a Soviet surprise attack on German air forces was "special operations at the initial stage of war." The commander of Soviet aviation, General P. V. Rychagov, stressed the necessity of carefully concealing the preparations of Soviet aviation for carrying out a surprise attack, in order to "find all enemy air forces on their bases."[20] Obviously, it would be impossible in a wartime situation to "find all enemy air forces on their bases." It is only possible during peacetime, when the enemy does not suspect any danger. It is impossible to first start a war and then carry out a surprise attack on the majority of enemy air bases. It is possible to carry out an attack during peacetime, but such an attack will mean war.

Stalin created so many air assault troops that it was possible to use them only in one scenario: an air attack and a massive invasion. The Red Army had to begin the war, suddenly and treacherously, by an attack of its air force against the enemy's air bases. Thousands of paratroops would be dropped to seize and control key bases and strategic sites. Any other scenario was not viable. Instead, it was Hitler who carried out a preemptive strike. The Communists' strategy to strike the first blow was aborted. Stalin's carefully designed plans to mount a massive offensive air assault became irrelevant in the desperate rush to fight a defensive war.

For many years after World War II it was not clear what had happened to the Soviet airborne forces. A Western military historian writing in 1978 noted: "In June 1941, when Germany invaded Russia, the latter had more than one million trained parachutists. It seems extraordinary that the investment this represented was not used constructively during the war."[21] For Soviet paratroopers, it was immediately clear why Stalin's "extraordinary investment" was not used "constructively." In 1941 the chief of staff of the Southwestern front, Lieutenant General M. A. Purkaev, astutely explained the reality created by the German surprise attack. He told Colonel A. I. Rodimtsev: "Yes, the situation now is such, comrade Rodimtsev, that it is easy to find one's way behind the enemy's lines without a paratroop drop. Some of our units and even large formations are already encircled."[22]

In defensive war there is nowhere to jump. One must stop enemy tanks. All five air assault corps of the first wave were sent to stem the German tide. However, everything had already been prepared for the now-useless landing. Parachutes had been delivered to the air base loading areas. Commander of the 4th Air Assault Corps Zhadov recalled how he summoned Captain A. I. Goryachev, the aide to the chief of operations sector of the corps staff: "'Do you know, comrade captain, what is gold?' He was dumbfounded by such an unanticipated question, but nevertheless answered: 'I have an idea, but I never had any gold.' 'Not true,' I said to him. 'A parachute was given to every Red Army soldier and commander. This is our nation's gold. Do you know where there are thousands of parachutes sitting out in the open? In the forest, one kilometer east of the river Berezina. Organize the transportation of this precious material to the rear.'"[23]

Captain Goryachev carried out the order. He found trucks, and under machine-gun fire from the advancing Germans, brought the parachutes to a safe place, for which he was rewarded with a medal. But these parachutes were never used again.

An airborne force is a fine precision tool in war. Using it as a defense force instead of regular infantry is to squander a precious asset. The paratroop units do not have the same heavy and powerful weapons as regular infantry, so their resistance in defense is much lower than that of regular infantry. Using paratroops to fight against tanks is the same as transporting bricks in a Ferrari race car—expensive and ineffective. But it was necessary to fight back, and the air assault corps were sent to the trenches to stop the tanks. Ten air assault corps, 100,000 men—150,000 if we count the separate brigades and reserve regiments. But where were the million paratroopers mentioned by *Pravda*?

In the spring of 1942 the Red Army suffered several crushing defeats at the same time: the 39th Army of Lieutenant General I. I. Maslennikov was surrounded and perished near Rzhev; the 33rd Army of Lieutenant General M. G. Efremov perished after being surrounded near Vyazma; the 2nd Shock Army of Lieutenant General A. A. Vlassov was cut off and encircled. Those who did not follow Vlassov's example and surrender, perished. The Crimean front was broken, during which the 44th, 47th, and 51st armies perished; and in the battle of Kharkov the 6th, 9th, 28th, and 57th armies were destroyed, along with seven separate tank and cavalry corps and a significant number of divisions, brigades, and regiments. Thousands of tanks and weapons and ample strategic resources were lost, and hundreds of thousands of soldiers and officers were killed or taken prisoner. The Soviet strategic front in the south was broken along a vast stretch of territory, and the German troops, not meeting any opposition, made a gigantic thrust forward with two targets at once: the Caucasus and Stalingrad.

The loss of the Caucasus and its oil would have meant defeat for Stalin. The fall of Stalingrad would have meant the same thing: oil was transported through the Caspian Sea up the Volga. The easiest way to cut off the oil artery was to take Stalingrad. All that was needed was to get to the banks of the Volga, to set up a stronghold there, and to sink all incoming petroleum barges. Soviet troops were retreating in a disorganized manner. More simply put, they ran. Stalin issued the threatening order No. 227 that introduced anti-retreat detachments and penal battalions. The detachments were NKVD squads with machine guns, positioned behind the troops, and in the event of unauthorized retreat they fired on their own soldiers. Commanders who did not show enough tenacity in combat had their rank signs torn away and were sent to penal battalions as regular soldiers to expiate their guilt with their blood.

The demoralized Soviet troops could not be stopped by monstrous orders. Fresh reserves were needed. But regular reserves had already been used up during the winter offensive and in unsuccessful attempts to break through the Leningrad blockade and prevent defeat in Kharkov and in the Crimea. The focal point of the eastern front, the small town of Rzhev, was also the scene of heavy casualties.

Stalin could only be saved by a miracle, but a miracle happened. Two fresh and fully manned Guards corps, the 10th and the 11th, arrived and formed a defense wall before the German Fourth Tank Army that advanced in the direction of the Caucasus. Their appearance at the most critical moment precisely where they were badly needed saved the day. The offensive was halted and exhausted troops were able to catch their breath and regroup. Soviet commanders reinstated order and stability, and turned a rout into an organized retreat that soon stabilized the front lines for prolonged battles that led to a counteroffensive.

There were nine Guards rifle corps in the Red Army then, but they had long since been drawn into battle, exhausted and depleted.[24] It was impossible to take those remaining away from the fronts where they were fighting. So, where did the two new and fresh corps come from?

Another miracle occurred in the Stalingrad region. At that moment, the Red Army had the 31st Guards Rifle Division. It was impossible to pull it out of the "slaughterhouses" in which it was trapped and send it to Stalingrad. Yet suddenly near Stalingrad appeared the fresh, new 32nd Guards Rifle Division. Immediately, it was followed by similar divisions— the 33rd, 34th, 35th, and 36th. Both Hitler and Stalin were throwing fresh troops into the battle for Stalingrad. As the stakes rose, Stalin trumped with an ace: he introduced into the battle the 1st Guards Army, under Lieutenant General F. I. Golikov, which had five Guards rifle divisions: the 37th, 38th, 39th, 40th, and 41st. Before, there had been Guards regiments and brigades, divisions and corps. This was the entire 1st Guards Army, and not just any army, but a fresh one, fully staffed and with the best men, and a former GRU chief in command. Was Stalin a magician? No one knew where they were coming from, these Guards armies with serial numbers all in a row, just like brand-new money, crisp bills in a pack.

The war followed its course, and the Guards miracles continued. In the summer of 1943, a violent battle began on the Kursk bulge. The enemy carried out two extremely powerful attacks in converging directions. They were not successful in breaking through the Soviet defenses. There were many reasons, including the brilliant work done by Soviet intelligence, which uncovered the enemy plan, and the Red Army's superiority in terms of quality and quantity of technology. But miracles also played a part. The German attack from the north was met by the 13th Army of the Central front. Among its components appeared the great 18th Guards Rifle Corps, staffed with the best men. And on the southern face of the Kursk bulge, the unbreakable Guards divisions suddenly appeared, as if from under the ground.

After deflecting the enemy's attacks, Soviet troops shifted to a decisive offensive. And once again, miracles occurred. A strategic reserve was introduced into battle on the Steppe front, in which was included the fully manned 4th Guards Army, staffed with the best soldiers and officers, and the top caliber 5th Guards Army fought bravely alongside them. But the war continued to devour lives. Whenever a crisis would arise a miracle occurred. Stalin always had some fresh select Guards division, corps, or even entire army in reserve.

The last Guards miracle occurred in March 1945 in Hungary, during the course of the Battle of Balaton when the Germans mounted their last powerful counterattack.

By the end of the war, Stalin was desperately short of troops. As Joseph Goebbels noted in his diary on March 3, 1945: "Their troops are extremely well armed, but they suffer more and more from lack of people. Their attacking infantry consists mostly of eastern workers and Poles, taken from our eastern regions."

In the beginning of 1945 the Red Army captured the last significant source of oil in Hungary, after which Germany was destined to crumble. Hitler urgently stopped his counteroffensive against American troops in the Ardennes and sent his main attack force, the Sixth Tank Army of the SS, to Hungary. There, in the Lake Balaton region, began his desperate last offensive to regain oil. A critical situation faced the Soviets. At that moment Stalin once again threw his trump ace on the table: he ordered fresh reserves, the 9th Guards Army, consisting of the 37th, 38th, and 39th Guards Rifle Corps, into battle. Each corps had three Guards rifle divisions. The Ninth Guards Army was fully manned by elite soldiers and officers. The Ninth Guards Army delivered a classic attack to the flank and rear of the SS Sixth Tank Army. Then the Ninth Guards Army continued its advance to Vienna, and through Prague to reach the Elbe River in Germany, where they joined forces with the Americans.

Where did Stalin get the reserves? Lieutenant General of the KGB V. A. Kirpichenko, who was a private in the war, recalled: "I served in the air assault troops-elite. We were trained and then practiced continually, but sent into action only in January 1945, not as airborne assault troops but as ordinary infantry. We broke the German blockade around Balaton, and earned Stalin's praise by stopping the last German offensive during the course of the war. To achieve this, we lost half of our troops."[25]

Stalin never had the opportunity to use his paratroopers for his planned sudden attack against Germany to start the war. The Germans' surprise attack established a significant presence in the air, preventing the effective deployment of Soviet paratroops and glider assault troops. Stalin's airborne offensive was doomed. However, Stalin kept the paratroops in reserve. When crisis situations arose, he gave these elite units the honored title of Guards and sent them to fight German tanks as regular infantry soldiers.[26]

That explains the "miracle."

14

About the Brilliant Military
Leader Tukhachevski

After the unheard-of violence conducted by the Bolsheviks against the very people whom
they betrayed and sentenced to starvation and death, there was no way back. The only
thing left was to run fast to their own grave, under the party flag and Stalin's leadership.

—V. RAPOPORT, YU. ALEXEYEV, AND IZMENA RODINE,
BETRAYAL OF THE MOTHERLAND

In 1937, Stalin carried out an assault on the high command of the Red Army. There are
countless legends about this period. This is what they sound like:
Marshal Tukhachevski was a great strategist. Tukhachevski proposed a modernization of
the army and insisted on rearmament, but Stalin foolishly declined Tukha chevski's proposals,
not understanding and not appreciating them. Hitler's intelligence service decided to behead
the Red Army on the eve of the war, to eliminate Tukhachevski and other geniuses. The
Germans fabricated a false document, and paranoid, suspicious Stalin believed it, unleashing
a terror that took on catastrophic dimensions. Stalin destroyed the most talented men. The
total number of exterminated army commanders was 36,761, and another 3,000 men in the
navy. In total, this was 40,000 great troop commanders. The defeat of the Red Army in 1941
was a direct consequence of the terror in 1937 and 1938. In 1941, because of the mass extermination of the command staff, the vast majority of Soviet commanders did not have the
necessary experience, because they had not been in their positions for more than a year.

All these legends fall apart as soon as they are examined. Let us begin with the first
legend about the brilliant troop leader Tukhachevski.

Mikhail Tukhachevski had no higher education. He never went to a university or
to a military academy. He graduated from a military school that trained junior officers.
Tukhachevski never commanded a company, battalion, regiment, brigade, division, or
corps. He was a deputy to a company commander in a Guards corps. His combat experience
in World War I had been six months. In the beginning of 1915, he was taken prisoner. After
his release, Tukhachevski returned to a reserve battalion of his old regiment. This was during

a time of total decay in the old country and army. Commanders for the most part were not appointed, but elected by soldiers. Understandably, the soldiers did not choose those who would demand discipline and order, but those who would not stop them from doing what soldiers like to do. The soldiers quickly ousted the commanders they did not like, and elected new ones. In order to keep one's position, one had to do nothing, and close one's eyes to all the soldiers' crimes and disorderly conduct. The soldiers liked Tukhachevski and elected him to be company commander. He did not "command" for long. An army with such a command system could not last for long. It rotted and fell apart.

The Communists then began to form their armed forces, which they called the Red Army. Junior officer Tukhachevski had a meeting with Lenin and Trotsky. What they talked about is not known, but Tukhachevski was immediately appointed commander of the 1st Army of the Eastern Front. Here, suddenly, surfaced Tukhachevski's ferocious nature. The Civil War in Russia was not only a war, but also a series of punitive expeditions against those who did not want Communism. Tukhachevski declared all those who opposed the illegal Communist leadership to be "bandits," and viciously exterminated not only them but also their relatives, their neighbors, and everyone who happened to come his way. The foundation of Tukhachevski's "strategy" was: the burning of villages, whippings, and mass shootings. Tukhachevski phrased the main objective not only of the Civil War, but of any other war as well, very clearly: "With an iron hand crush the local enemy classes." Many of Tukhachevski's combat orders are not about how to use a clever maneuver to bypass the enemy and hit him in the flank and rear, but about how many hostages are to be taken and when they are to be executed. Here is an example:

ORDER
To the Plenipotentiary Commission of All-Russia
Central Executive Committee, # 16
City of Tambov
June 23, 1921

The experience of the first combat area shows a high predisposition for quick cleansing from banditry through the following measures. Some localities with particularly strong bandit tendencies are noted, and representatives of the region's Political Commission, of a Special Section, Sections of the Military Tribunal and Command, together with units designed to conduct purges, are sent there. Upon their arrival, they surround the area, take hostage 60–100 of the most prominent persons, and introduce a siege. Entering and exiting the area must be forbidden during the course of the operation. After this, the entire population of the area is gathered, and the orders of the Commission of the All-Russia Central Executive Committee #130 and #171 and the signed sentence for this area are read aloud. The residents are given 2 hours to give up the bandits and their weapons, as well as the bandits' families, and the population is told that in the event of refusal the abovementioned hostages will be shot in 2 hours. If the population does not give up the bandits and weapons within the two-hour time limit, they are once again rounded up and the hostages are shot before their eyes, after which new hostages are taken and those gathered are once again told to give up the bandits and their weapons. Those who wish to comply with the demands are separated, divided into groups of a hundred, and each hundred is put through a questioning commission (consisting of representatives of the Special Sector and the Military Tribunal). Each person must give a testimony, and not be allowed to claim ignorance. In the event of stubbornness, new executions are enacted, etc. From the material obtained through the questioning, expeditionary units are formed with the compulsory inclusion of the persons who gave the testimony, and they venture to capture the bandits. Upon the end of the purge, the siege is ended, and a revolutionary committee and militia are established to rule the area.

The current Plenipotentiary Commission of the All-Russia Central Executive Committee orders to execute this order fully.

Chairman of the Commission
Antonov-Ovseenko

Troops Commander
Tukhachevski

Tukhachevski and all other participants of that war against their own people declared themselves heroes of the Civil War.

Pay particular attention to the date of Tukhachevski's order: June 23, 1921. Twenty years later, Russia would be invaded by different occupants, but they would act in almost the same way. The difference was that Hitler herded the enemy's population into a ravine and machine-gunned them, while Tukhachevski, on top of this, besieged the entire population of his own country with a mutual criminal responsibility. Later on this method would be called, in the criminal underworld, "forced snitching." This is precisely what Antonov-Ovseenko, Tukhachevski, his deputy Uborevich, and all other strategists did: they forced all the people to become traitors and rats, forced them to betray their neighbors, relatives, fathers, and brothers, and then go after them in the forests and kill them. Tukhachevski introduced universal betrayal, using fear to crush and destroy the centuries-old Russian village morale. He replaced all moral codes with fear for one's own skin, and made each person accountable for all the others' deeds. Tukhachevski's idea was to crush the people's sense of their own worth. When we speak of the defeats of 1941, we blame Stalin. Let us not forget that the crushing of the people was done under the immediate command and on the initiative of the very same strategists who were later, during the purges, eliminated by Stalin.

In 1941, the masses who were taught by Tukhachevski to value only their own skin a priori could not have exhibited heroism.

Here is the reason for the army purges of 1937: Stalin was preparing for war against Germany. He decided to beat his country, the Army included, into submission. As a by-product of the purges, Stalin got rid of the bloodiest executioners: of Antonov-Ovseenko, Tukhachevski, Yakir, Uborevich, Blukher, and others like them. Such "troop leaders" could not be placed in positions to lead the masses mobilized for war. Soldiers would not follow these commanders into battle and, given the opportunity, would remember and remind these hatchet men of the crimes they committed during the previous two decades against their parents and older brothers.

On the other hand, all these strategists would have been incapable of leading the people into war. It is well known that an army that has sullied its uniforms with the blood of its own people is incapable of fighting against outside enemies. The primary reason for the decay of any army is its use against its own people. Everyone who has actively participated in this could no longer be a troop leader.

Here is another pearl from the treasury of strategist Tukhachevski's combat experience:

TO THE TROOPS' CHIEF OF STAFF
For signature by Kakurin
By the Political Commission of the 1st, 2nd, 3rd, 4th, 5th, and 6th districts
July 8, 1921

Defeated bandits are hiding in the forests and taking out their impotent rage on the local population, burning bridges [and] damaging dams and other government property. In the interest of securing the bridges, the Commission of the All-Russia Central Executive Committee orders:

Immediately take from the population of villages located near important bridges no less than five hostages, who in the event of damage done to the bridge are to be immediately executed.

Under supervision of the Revolutionary Committees, the local residents are to organize the defense of the bridges from bandit attacks; the local residents are also to take on the responsibility of repairing the damaged bridges no later than within a 24-hour deadline.

This order is to be widely distributed among all villages and towns.

Troop commander
Tukhachevski

The great strategist has strange logic: the bandits "are hiding in the forests and taking out their impotent rage on the local population," so Tukhachevski orders execution of hostages taken out of this very same local population.

All of Tukhachevski's experience can be narrowed down to two things: hostages and executions. Meanwhile, the taking of hostages was forbidden by the Hague Convention of 1907. Hostage taking has always been considered the most serious war crime. A troop leader who sullied his name with this sort of maneuver has always been despised. At Nuremberg and all subsequent trials of German Nazis the practice of taking hostages was regarded as a war crime and those guilty of it were sentenced to death by hanging.

So that would have been a proper place for Tukhachevski, Antonov-Ovseenko, and all other war criminals—on the defendants' bench at Nuremberg, in the company of Hermann Goering, Wilhelm Keitell, Alfred Jodl, and others.

Tukhachevski encountered real enemy troops only once. The Western front of the Red Army under Tukhachevski's command headed to the West with the intention of breaking through to Germany and unleashing a Communist revolution. But Tukhachevski did not reach Germany. His hordes were defeated near Warsaw by the Polish army commanded by Pilsudsky.

The defeat was shameful and total. Tukhachevski became enraged. We have been taught that in 1920 Tukhachevski was defeated by the Polish cavalry, but if he had lived until 1941 and met the German tank armadas he undoubtedly would have defeated them. Lenin and Trotsky did not think so. They understood that Tukhachevski was only good for war against his own people. Therefore, he was once again sent to the inside front—to drown under ice the sailors who started the uprising at Kronstadt, to shoot hostages in Tambov county, and to burn villages. Here, Tukhachevski showed a true strategic talent.

Tukhachevski strove to get power in the stupidest way. He made a bigger fool of himself than anyone in the Civil War, and yet he declared himself a winner. He decided to personally edit the three-volume book *Civil War, 1918–1921*, portraying himself as a great strategist and blaming others for his defeats. Here it must be stressed that Tukhachevski strove specifically to edit history, not write it. Everyone who has read Tukhachevski's book, *March beyond Vistula (Pokhod za Vislu)*, would agree that Tukhachevski was incapable of relating his thoughts. Marshal Joseph Pilsudsky crushed Tukhachevski, first on the battlefields and later in the pages of his book *The Year 1920*. Pilsudsky exposed both Tukhachevski's incapability to fight and his incapability to relate past events. Pilsudsky did not leave any part of Tukhachevski's book standing: "The extreme vagueness of the book gives us the image of a man who analyzes only his own brain or his heart, purposefully rejecting or simply not knowing how to tie his own thoughts with the everyday existence of troops, which not always corresponds to the plans and intentions of their commander, but often contradicts them. . . . Many events in the operations of 1920 occurred as they did precisely because [of] Tukhachevski's propensity to command the army with such an abstract method."

Legend number two: Tukhachevski proposed to Stalin a plan for modernizing the army. This legend is also easy to disperse. For this, one only needs to read Tukhachevski's "scientific works." Only someone who himself has not read Tukhachevski's creations can praise his work. Aside from using purposefully incomprehensible terms and long phrases, the meaning of which can be interpreted in any way one wants, Tukhachevski had one more weakness—he did not understand the significance of numbers. He always wanted to astound the reader and listener with unbelievable numbers.

"Multi-million [strong] armies deployed on the fronts stretching hundreds of thousands of kilometers."[1] This is how Tukhachevski describes World War I. Fronts stretching hundreds of thousands of kilometers? Is this not nonsense? France, Britain, their vassals from the colonies, and later the United States fought against Germany. The Western front stretched from the shores of the North Sea to the Swiss border. In a straight line, this does not even make five hundred kilometers. A front is obviously not drawn in a straight line. But even with all possible bends and turns, one cannot scrounge up enough for a thousand kilometers. And all the millions of French, British, Australian, New Zealander, Canadian, and then American troops in World War I were positioned along these kilometers. If the front had stretched hundreds of thousands of kilometers, how many millions of soldiers would be needed to cover it?

The Eastern front in World War I stretched from the Baltic Sea to the Black Sea. This is less than two thousand kilometers. The front was not a straight line, so let us assume three thousand kilometers. Where did fronts stretching hundreds of thousands of kilometers come from? If the northern hemisphere had fought against the southern, and the trenches were dug along the bottom of the seas and oceans, even then we would still only get forty thousand kilometers. Did Tukhachevski know the length of the equator? Where, on this small planet, could one find fronts hundreds of thousands of kilometers in length?

Yet for decades this was published not only in the *Selected Works* of Tukhachevski, but in compilations that demonstrate the best accomplishments of strategic thought.

In 1927, Chief of Staff of the Red Army Tukhachevski wrote a letter to Stalin and proposed a military reform. Marshal of the Soviet Union S. S. Biruzov in his praising essay, as if by the way, notes that: "The addressing of these questions by M. N. Tukhachevski was correct and timely, but as to concrete data, they needed to be made more specific."[2]

Instead of fulfilling his direct duties Tukhachevski, the genius strategist, plunged into the development of some pipe-dream project. And everything he did was correct, timely, and extremely necessary. Only his numbers needed to be more exact. Does one need to pay attention to such minor details?

I think, yes. The General Staff is the brain of the army. A country cannot have a man more cautious than the Chief of General Staff. His accuracy first and foremost needs to be applied to his work with numbers. Thousands of the most highly qualified officers are under the command of the Chief of General Staff. The General Staff exists to think everything through, count and calculate everything, and then, having weighed all the information and taken into account the thousands of contradictory circumstances, report to the head of the country.

What numbers are we talking about? What exactly did Tukhachevski propose to Stalin? For decades, scholars have praised Tukhachevski the innovator, who proposed something very interesting, but for some reason nobody says what exactly it was that he proposed. We shall think about this: could a person who did not understand the significance of numbers have proposed anything of value?

Lieutenant General of the Air Force V. V. Serebrianikov described what sort of reform Tukhachevski proposed to Stalin. It turns out that in December 1927 Tukhachevski, on top of everything else, suggested to Stalin to produce during the course of 1928 alone 50,000 to 100,000 tanks.[3]

Let us compare and evaluate this number.

In 1928, Hitler was not in power in Germany. Nobody could even imagine that he would ever come to power. Germany at that time did not have one single tank. The entire German army consisted of 100,000 soldiers, officers, and generals—all of them infantry and cavalry. Tukhachevski proposed to have one Soviet tank for every German general, officer, and infantry soldier in the ranks, as well as for every German messenger and cook in the field kitchen.

On September 1, 1939, Hitler entered World War II with 2,980 tanks, among which there were no amphibious tanks and no medium or heavy tanks. We are told that it is clear: if Hitler had such a huge number of tanks, it must have meant they were not for defense, they were not for Europe alone. If Hitler had built such a number of tanks, it obviously meant that he planned to conquer the world.

I fully agree with this. But in that case, what did Tukhachevski plan to do with armadas of 50,000 to 100,000 tanks?

The 2,980 German tanks were built not during one year, but during all the prewar years. Tukhachevski, on the other hand, proposed to build 50,000 to 100,000 tanks in just one year.

It is interesting to compare Tukhachevski's plans for 1928 with real production of tanks (not including self-propelled guns—see below) in Germany during the course of World War II:

YEAR	TANKS
1939	743
1940	1,515
1941	3,113
1942	4,276
1943	5,663
1944	7,975
1945	956

In total, during the prewar months of 1939 and all the subsequent years of the war, Germany produced 24,241 tanks. Japan built 5,085 tanks, most of them light.

We have been taught a formulaic phrase: "the German fascists and Japanese militarists." Indeed, if they produced such a large number of tanks, 24,241 and 5,085 respectively, it is clear to everybody that this is fascism and militarism. But the question arises: Who was Tukhachevski, in the context of these fascists and militarists striving for world domination?

After the war the Soviet Union, already a much more powerful industrial giant, had 50,000 tanks, or even slightly more. But these tanks were not produced in one year; they had accumulated for decades.

But even this careful gradual accumulation of tanks did not save the Soviet Union. The great industrial giant crumbled. Its legs folded under its weight. Those very same thousands of tanks played far from a minor role in the crumbling of the Soviet Union.

Meanwhile, the brilliant Tukhachevski proposed that Stalin not gradually, for decades, amass such a might, but that he produce all at once, in one year, 50,000 to 100,000 tanks. The result of such an action is easy to predict: the legs of the Soviet Union would have folded immediately.

The USSR had no tank factories at that time. Even if they had existed, it would still first of all have been necessary to stop production of all heavy machinery—automobiles, ships, locomotives, railroad cars, tractors, and all others—and to remodel these factories to produce tanks.

If one had accepted Tukhachevski's proposal, it would have been necessary to stop all the industry of a gigantic country for a minimum of one year and fully remodel it for producing tanks.

By the standards of any army, two hundred to three hundred tanks are a tank division. In the 1970s, during the peak of the Cold War, the American army, the army of the most powerful nation in the world, had sixteen divisions, among them four tank divisions.

Hitler went after world domination in September 1939 with just six tank divisions. In 1927 neither Germany, nor the United States, nor France, nor Japan had any tank divisions. If Stalin had listened to Tukhachevski and produced 50,000 to 100,000 tanks, the Soviet Union within one year would have had 166 to 500 tank divisions.

At that time the crew of one tank consisted of three men. Crews for 50,000 to 100,000 tanks would have meant that the tank troops would need to number 150,000 to 300,000 soldiers, correct? No, incorrect.

Tank crews make up an insignificant minority of men in a tank division. First of all, tanks must constantly and at the right time be supplied with liquid fuel and lubricants. Tanks also need shells and cartridges. This adds another column of automobiles with ammunition.

Furthermore, tanks need repair, and not only in stationary repair shops but in the field. For this one needs to have mobile tank-repair shops and even mobile tank-repair factories. This again means more men and automobiles.

But in order to repair a tank it must be towed under enemy fire out of the ditch, swamp, or battlefield and taken to the mobile repair shop. For this one needs specialized repair-evacuation units.

In order to repair a tank in field conditions, the necessary spare parts must constantly be supplied to the battle area. So, our column of tanks is followed by a long tail without which the tank units cannot act.

Tanks need to be defended and protected in close battle; the success of tanks needs to be retained. This is done by the motorized infantry. Every tank division needs its own regiment of motorized infantry, and every corps needs its own motorized infantry division. Tank action needs to be supported by artillery fire. For this we have guns and mortars. The action of tanks, infantry, and artillery needs to be protected. For this we have anti-tank cannons. All this needs to be organized and coordinated. Troop command needs to have a flow of information through thousands of different channels. This is provided by communication units. All this means more automobiles and more men.

The Soviet standard for the year 1940 was as follows: for the bare necessities of supplying the operation of 1,000 tanks (one mechanized corps—1,031 tanks), 36,080 soldiers and officers, 358 guns and mortars, 266 armored cars, 352 tractors, and 5,165 automobiles were needed. This is not counting reinforcements, air force, and the rear formation that had to supply this entire mass of troops.

We thought that one tank just needed three men, but in reality it needed thirty-six men. The war later showed that the prewar calculations were too low. In order to maintain the action of each tank on the battlefield one needed seventy to eighty men per tank, twice as many automobiles as supposed before the war, and thrice as much artillery.

But even using the lowered prewar calculations, to fulfill Tukhachevski's program the tank troops would have needed to have 1.8 million to 3.6 million soldiers and officers, 18,000 to 36,000 tractors, as many guns and mortars, 13,000 to 26,000 armored cars, and 250,000 to 500,000 trucks.

The German armed forces at that time counted 100,000 soldiers, officers, and generals. Meanwhile, Tukhachevski envisioned the Red Army having half a million men just to drive the automobiles in the tank divisions. Not counting the drivers of tanks, artillery pulls, and armored cars, plus commanders, communications officers, sappers, intelligence, and all the rest.

Perhaps Tukhachevski thought the tank troops could do without automobiles?

The Soviet Union at that time could not have devoted half a million automobiles to the tank troops. It could not have given a quarter million either. It could not have devoted so many automobiles not just to the tank troops, but to the entire armed force. And if it had, then agriculture, the transportation system, construction, and industry would have been left without automobiles and tractors. If all automobiles were given to the tank troops, then how much fuel, oil, and spare parts would those cars have used up?

And how would such tank troops have been manned? There was no mandatory universal draft in the Soviet Union at that time. Should one have been instituted? This was already beyond the duties of the Chief of Staff of the Red Army.

Let us assume that Tukhachevski decided to keep 1.8 to 3.6 million soldiers in the tank troops alone. Where would they have been trained? Practically everyone who finds himself in tank forces needs special preparations. These soldiers would have needed to learn how to be radio operators, repairmen, gunners, scouts, and commanders. Would everyone have had to go through training divisions? How many training divisions would have been needed?

And what would have been done about officers? Tukhachevski's proposal was to produce the tanks immediately. Even if they had been produced, how many officers would have been needed to staff at least one hundred new tank divisions? The USSR could have opened new military academies. During peacetime, an officer was trained for three years. Tanks would have been arriving from the plants, as Tukhachevski planned, in 1928, but the officers would not have graduated until 1931, and they all would have been young and inexperienced, while what was needed at the time was commanders for battalions, regiments, divisions, and corps.

Where would the officers have lived? Even now Russia is incapable of building housing for all her officers. Back then, where would the officers have lived—in tents? Where would they have found enough tents?

Where were the tanks to be stored? During wartime it is easy: tanks loaded on railway trains travel from the factories directly to the front and go into action, and the life of a tank in the war is short: very soon it has to go into repair or is melted down, and new tanks take its place. Tanks do not need to be stored. They do not accumulate: while tanks are unloaded from one train, the tanks from the previous one are already burning in battle.

But here is the situation: in peacetime, a stream of steel monsters suddenly flows in from the production plants. What are we to do with them? Keep them in the open fields, in the cold and the snow?

In addition, the armed forces of that time could not consist of just tank corps and tank armies. For every tank and motorized division there needed to be a minimum of three to four rifle divisions. Consequently, there would have to be from 847 to 3,000 rifle divisions. At that time, Germany had twelve divisions, in total.

Some think that the army's strength is in its numbers. Tukhachevski was from that breed of strategists who wanted to fight with numbers. But, as we can see, even with numbers he had some difficulties. He never understood the meaning of numbers. He never learned to work with them.

Tukhachevski was incapable of working out the simplest calculation of the consequences of his actions and proposals. We have to marvel at Stalin's patience—how could such a strategist have been kept in high government positions?

If 50,000 to 100,000 tanks are produced in one year, one should simultaneously produce about as many airplanes, because without air force support the tanks become coffins. Fifty to one hundred thousand airplanes? In one year? Where would they have been built? At what factories? Or, perhaps we would not have produced the planes right away, just put out all the tanks and left them without air support? This would have been a crime; it would have been treason. For such actions one should be executed.

So, what kind of army did Tukhachevski want to form? Or did he plan to just have tanks without airplanes or artillery?

Tukhachevski demanded: we need to produce tanks! Here, many questions arise, and quite an important one among them is: What kinds of tanks?

For mass production, one needs not just an industrial base, but also a model of the machine that is to be produced. In 1928, there was no industrial base, and there was also no fitting tank model for production. In 1927, the Red Army enlisted into its armament the MS-1 tank. The power of its engine speaks for everything else: 35 horsepower. The armor of the MS-1 tank was held together with rivets. Its maximum speed was 16 km/h. On Red Square, for the parade, it went up to 19 km/h. This was our best tank. A small (by our standards) series of these tanks was needed for designers to get their first experience in the creation of a tank, and for troops to get the opportunity to use real tanks in training, although they were extremely weak and flawed. This tank was also useful to the troops for small border disputes. When there is nothing better . . . But to make them by the tens of thousands? Who needs them? Perhaps we could have bought a foreign model? There was nothing to buy. In 1928, nobody in the entire world could have offered a model worthy of being mass-produced in a large series.

Arms production demands colossal expenditures. Therefore, intelligent people design weapons, produce them in small series, and have production and mobilization reserves of everything necessary to supply the mass production of the latest models in a period of threat.

In places where not very intelligent leaders rule, the peacetime army is enormous. The country strains itself trying to clothe, feed, and arm such an army. This army demands a huge amount of weapons during peacetime—but weapons age. The time comes when they have to be replaced, and this is a true disaster for the country. Technology development is rapid, and the gigantic arsenals have to constantly be renewed, which turns into a perpetual catastrophe. The result is that we defeat ourselves.

Why did Tukhachevski need so many weapons in 1927? Hundreds of times more than all potential aggressors put together. Who threatened us then? Who could attack us in 1928? Romania? Finland? Estonia in alliance with Latvia, and egged on by Lithuania? Disarmed Germany? Perhaps Japan? But Japan is an island nation, and to fight her, in order to avert the landing and supplying of Japanese troops on the continent, we would have needed to build a strong fleet in the Far East. But Tukhachevski was opposed to the idea of building a strong fleet and spoke against it publicly.

And so, what were the 100,000 tanks for?

Tukhachevski's defenders say that everything in his proposals is correct, only the numbers had to be clarified. But if numbers are clarified nothing remains of Tukhachevski's proposals at all. Aside from insane numbers, they contained nothing.

Meanwhile, Tukhachevski advanced more and more new projects.

"The USSR's industry had to reach by the year 1938 a production capacity that would be capable during the course of one year to put out 53,000 guns, 90,000 tanks, and 60,000 airplanes. The views about the production possibilities were formed under the influence of M. Tukhachevski."[4] This is quoted in a Soviet military textbook!

Inevitably, the question to be asked here is: what is the difference between Stalin and Tukhachevski? Stalin also planned to produce 100,000 to 150,000 airplanes, of the model Ivanov!

There is a difference, and it is tremendous. Tukhachevski planned an incredibly huge military production during peacetime. This would have bankrupted the country. There was nothing to do with and nowhere to store the produced arsenal. If war had not happened in the near future, the mountains of arms would have quickly aged and rusted.

Stalin, on the other hand, proposed an entirely different plan: to create during peacetime an airplane for mass production, but to produce it in a small series. The beginning of the mass production was to happen only after the beginning of a victorious war.

A legend is told around the world that German intelligence supplied Stalin with a false document proving that Tukhachevski was forming a plot. Stalin believed the false document and destroyed the great strategist Tukhachevski.

If this is the truth, the Red Army should be thankful to German intelligence for an invaluable service.

15

The Cleansing

Only one who first conquers his own people can overcome a powerful enemy.

—Shang Yang, fifth century BC

Power struggles never died down in the Communist Party. Party purges followed one after the other. Stalin drove all his opponents out of the party, and then they were arrested, tried, sent to prisons and labor camps, and executed according to court sentences without an appeal. Stalin put those he personally chose and cultivated into the opened positions. An equally continuous process of replacing the personnel in the secret police, and in the fields of science, art, literature, industry, trade, and agriculture went on at the same time as the permanent purges of the party. Arrests and trials of engineers, historians, and members of defunct political parties and organizations were constant. Any dictator acts in this way, and without any hints from outside sources. In order to lead the country to conquering other nations, any dictator begins with terror against his own surroundings. In order to raise many men and lead them to conquer the world, in order to reach "the last sea," Genghis Khan before all had to conquer the most powerful and rich princes. Those who did not want to follow him had their spines broken on his orders.

This is exactly what Stalin did. In order to raise the nation to accomplish great deeds, he first of all had to obtain unquestioning obedience.

But in all the purges, for many years the army was the exception. The purges left the army alone. Stalin for a long time made sure to see that at the very top he had his own man. The army was only purged by Tukhachevski himself, who chased out all those he did not like personally. But Stalin had to reach the army sometime! Didn't he? Could he have possibly, without receiving the German false document, left the army untouched?

The purges were a struggle for fortification of power, for its preservation. This is a struggle for the leader's personal safety. The purges were a means to avert an uprising. Uprisings are always and everywhere started first and foremost by the military.

In his books, Tukhachevski shamelessly praised and lauded himself. For example, he transformed his disgraceful defeat near Warsaw into a brilliant victory. Everyone who has read Tukhachevski's books clearly saw that they were written by a very strange man completely infatuated with himself, a man with impossible ambitions. Such a man is extremely dangerous in a position at the top of the military command.

Stalin for many years conducted preparations for eliminating high-ranking military leaders whom he deemed untrustworthy. Tukhachevski was one of them: the most famous, but certainly not the only one. Following are the most prominent examples.

On the night of July 2, 1935, Corps Commander G. Gay was arrested. The 3rd Cavalry Corps under his command had been the main assault and maneuvering force in the battle near Warsaw fought by Tukhachevski in 1920. In 1935 Gay was the head of the military history department at the Zhukovsky Air Force Academy. In those times the Soviet Union did not have military history other than the Civil War. All that had preceded the Civil War was treated as a foreword and reviewed very superficially and briefly. The history of the Civil War, on the other hand, was learned meticulously. The reason Gay was arrested was that he was not teaching military history "correctly," and the required reading for his students was the history of the Civil War prepared by Tukhachevski.

On April 17, 1936, N. I. Muralov, who had become commander of the Moscow military district back in 1917, was arrested. It was under Muralov's cover that the Lenin-Trotsky government fled from Petrograd to Moscow in 1918. In 1936 Stalin began to put pressure on all those who had been chosen by Lenin and Trotsky and placed in high positions.

On June 9, 1936, division commander D. Shmidt, a friend of Tukhachevski, was arrested. On August 14, 1936, Corps Commander Primakov was arrested. Primakov was connected with Tukhachevski for many years: he had been under Tukhachevski's command back in 1920, in the campaign to occupy Poland. Later Primakov was tried and executed at the same time as Tukhachevski.

On August 15, 1936, Brigade Commander M. O. Zyuk, commander of the 25th Chapaev Division, was arrested.

On August 20, 1936, another future codefendant was arrested—Corps Commander Putna. Two of the eight defendants from Tukhachevski's group were already in prison. The process had begun.

Corps Commander S. A. Turovsky was arrested on September 2, 1936. Division Commander Y. V. Sablin was arrested on September 25. The Byelorussian military district commander, I. P. Uborevich, a friend and follower of Tukhachevski, was arrested on May 29, 1937. Later they were executed together. So, in January 1937 the composition of the group of high commanders who were to fall under suspicion was already becoming clear: as a group, they vocally opposed K. E. Voroshilov, Stalin's perennial favorite, who then was Minister of Defense.

On January 24, 1937, at an open court trial, former member of the Central Committee of the Communist Party Karl Radek, who had been accused of espionage, treason, and preparation of a coup, named Tukhachevski as a collaborator. Anyone who knows anything about Stalin's open trials, and who has thought about the meaning and significance of these trials, will agree that names were never mentioned there by accident. According to Radek, Tukhachevski had sent Corps Commander Putna to Berlin, where he conducted talks with Trotskyites. Tukhachevski personally was not yet being accused of anything: he only sent Putna to Berlin on business, and Putna used the opportunity.

From this moment, Tukhachevski could have blown his brains out—his fate had not only been decided, but publicly declared. Walther Schellenberg, a Nazi foreign intelligence agent, relates that in May 1937 German Intelligence had succeeded in passing to Stalin a forged document which presented Tukhachevski as a head of the Red Army generals' plot to overthrow the Soviet government.[1] As the story goes, Stalin was duped by this forgery and started the purges in the Red Army. The Germans thus had crippled the Red Army with Stalin's hands.

But a simple check of chronology shows that Schellenberg's story is not correct: the above-mentioned purges started in the summer of 1935, long before the forged document was allegedly created by German Intelligence.

There are many tales about 1937. They are surprisingly absurd and just as surprisingly resilient. But it suffices to ask just one question for the picture that has been painted for decades to immediately fall apart.

Here is one more myth: in 1937–38, Stalin executed forty thousand commanders, therefore in 1941 most commanders had not been at their post for more than one year.

But this could not be!

Let us imagine that in 1937 Stalin executed all commanders—every single one, from platoon commanders to marshals. He herded them all into abandoned cellars and machine-gunned them down, and then appointed new commanders to their posts. Let's imagine this complete change of the command staff. Here is what would have happened: by the summer of 1941, all the newly appointed commanders would have had four years of experience. How could it be that the purge occurred in 1937, but by 1941 the majority of commanders had less than a year's experience in their positions? There are objections that the executions happened not only in 1937, but in 1938 as well. Good, we can allow that the commanders appointed in 1937 were in the following year machine-gunned in the cellars. Another, third group of command personnel was appointed. In this case, the third group appointed in 1938 should have had three years of experience by 1941. If a full change of command occurred, the majority of these commanders could not have gone anywhere. Understandably during three years someone drowned, someone became a drunk. One, two, three hundred were executed in 1939, 1940, and the first half of 1941. There could have been some shuffling and reshuffling. But the majority should have stayed in their places. How did it happen that the purges occurred in 1937–38, but in three to four years the new commanders did not have even a full year of experience at their posts?

The answer to the mysterious lack of experience on the job is simple: in the years 1937–41 the Red Army grew five-fold, from 1.1 million to 5.5 million. The commanding positions had to be filled, so the officers were promoted quickly and did not have time to "grow" into their jobs. Similarly quick promotions occurred then in the German army as well, but nobody claims that German commanders were incompetent.

This problem can be examined from another perspective. Stalin's army was large. Forty thousand commanders are not that many. The officer corps of the Red Army in February 1937 is known to have numbered 206,000. The source of this number is the top-secret speech given at the February–March plenary session of the Central Committee by Politburo member and People's Commissar of Defense of the USSR, Marshal of the Soviet Union K. E. Voroshilov.[2]

Let's allow that 40,000 out of 206,000 were executed. This is less than 20 percent. The question is the same, only seen from a different perspective: how did it happen that less than 20 percent were executed, but in 1941 the majority of commanders did not have a year of experience at their occupied post?

We see that the legends about the year 1937 are quite vulnerable. It is enough to ask the simplest questions—and not one Communist historian will be able to give a reasonable answer.

July 29, 1938, was the peak of the terror. After this, the intensity dropped drastically. On September 19, 1938, the chief of the 6th (Manpower) Department of the command staff of the Red Army, Colonel Shiryaev, presented to the Deputy People's Commissar of Defense E. A. Shchyadenko a document that specified the number of commanders dismissed from the ranks of the Red Army during the period starting in 1937 through September 1938. The document is kept in the Russian State Military Archive, fund 37837, index 10, case 142, sheet 93. Here it is—a primary source. The numbers are as follows: in 1937, 20,643 men were dismissed; in 1938, 16,118, for a total of 36,761.

Let's turn our attention to one small detail: in the document, the numbers refer not to "executed" but to "dismissed" men.

For fifty-four years, this document was secret, and only a very limited number of extremely dishonest men had access to it. These men committed a crime against history. They reported the number—36,761. From this everyone made a seemingly logical deduction: if the person was fired, he was arrested, and if he was arrested, he was executed.

But this was not the case. Dismissed did not always mean arrested. And arrested did not always mean executed.

The document gives additional information: out of the number of people dismissed in 1937, 5,811 were arrested, and 5,057 in 1938. In total, 10,868 people were arrested.

We were told of 40,000 *executed*, but in reality there were 10,868 *arrested*, and of them 1,654 were executed or died in prison before their trials started.[3]

There is a difference between arrest and execution. Some of those arrested were executed, but not all of them. I will use an example to explain the difference. In 1937, Commander of the 5th Cavalry Corps Konstantin Konstantinovich Rokossovskii was dismissed from the ranks of the Red Army. He was not just dismissed, but also arrested. But this is not yet an execution. He was imprisoned, and then let out. He fought through the entire war. He finished the war with the rank of Marshal of the Soviet Union and commanded the victory parade at the Red Square. He was not alone among the 10,868 arrested commanders; many of them were set free.

This is an example of Kremlin propaganda. If the document had been published fully at the time, stating that so many people were dismissed, so many out of them arrested, but not all of them executed, this mess would never have arisen. But the people who had access to the documents purposefully published only fragments of information. The explanations were omitted, which created the necessary conditions for rumors and legends.

Later on, when thousands of historians and agitators wrote into their works the information about forty thousand executed troop commanders, when hundreds of millions of people remembered this number, the document was fully published, but by then it could not change anything. Who would pay attention to a small article in a journal for specialists?

But what happened to the rest, who were dismissed but not arrested? Where did they go?

There is no secret here. In every army there is a continuous process of change, replacing the old with the new, rejuvenating the command staff. Every year military academies turn out thousands of new officers. The army never has too many officers. Every year it takes into its ranks new ones, and sends the same number of old ones back into civilian life. The main reason for dismissal is the completion of service. I will not intrude here with my own calculations, but imagine that your army has two hundred thousand officers. Estimate how many years an officer serves, decide how many commanders you must let go every year to their well-earned retirement, and then replace them with the new graduates from the academies, so that you have a constant process of renewing the ranks and so that you do not have stagnation.

The document presented to the Deputy People's Commissar of Defense is titled accordingly: "Document about the number of dismissals from the command staff in 1937–1938." Who would dare suppose that during these years nobody was dismissed from the army upon completing years of service?

It must also be remembered that not every officer reached his retirement age. A second reason for dismissal was state of health. Those who went through two, or even three wars, had all sorts of experiences. One had frostbitten legs, another had damaged hearing, and another one had old wounds that would not heal. People can be dismissed from the army not only for war wounds, but also for a number of other illnesses, from flat feet to cancer.

Aside from all this, there is such a punishment as dismissal from the army. It is no longer the year 1937, but officers are still being dismissed from the army for all kinds of reasons. The main ones are drunkenness, moral degradation, breach of discipline, and disobedience to authority. Who could dare assert that in 1937 nobody was dismissed from the army for drunkenness? This does not at all entail that the drunk was arrested and executed.

Even of those who were arrested, not all were victims of political repressions. There have always been military crimes and property crimes and so on. Among officers there have always been rapists, murderers, thieves, and other criminals. The document speaks of all those arrested without distinguishing between the political and the criminals. Who could dare assert that in 1937 there were no criminals among the command staff of the Red Army?

On May 5, 1940, E. A. Shchyadenko signed the "Report of the chief of the command of the staff personnel of the Red Army of the Defense Commissariat of the USSR." The concluding phrase: "Those unjustly dismissed are returned to the army: in total by May 1, 1940—12,461." It is important to note that the number of those returned to the ranks is higher than the number of those arrested. And this is easy to explain: both those who were arrested and those who were simply dismissed were returned to the ranks. The Kremlin propaganda endlessly repeats the story about the 40,000 executed commanders, but for some reason nobody likes to remember that 12,461 of those "executed" returned to the ranks. And this is only the beginning of the process. It is known that the main mass of those dismissed returned in the second half of 1940, and especially in the first half of 1941—for example, A. V. Gorbatov, a future General of the Red Army. Many such examples can be brought up. A strange story surfaces: Shchyadenko, who wrote the document about the dismissed commanders, is often quoted. But the same Shchyadenko who reports of the return of those who were dismissed is never remembered or quoted.

We have been taught to think that Stalin executed all the intelligent people and left only idiots in command of the army. But here is the opinion of German Major General F. W. von Mellentin, who fought against the Red Army: "The Russian high command knows its job better than the command of any other army."[4] So it seems that Stalin did not execute all the geniuses before the war; some of them were left.

The enemy's opinion cannot always be trusted, so let us see what the Russian historians say about the effect that the purges of 1937–38 had on the Red Army. G. Gerasimov had studied the hard data and compared the characteristics of the commanders on the eve of German invasion in 1941 and in 1936, before the purges started:

> In 1941, 7.1 percent of all commanders had higher education, while in 1936 that figure was only 6.6 percent;
>
> In 1941, 52 percent of the generals had higher education, in 1936 only 29 percent;
>
> In 1941, 29.5 percent of all commanders had combat experience, while in 1934–38 that figure was 23 percent.[5]

Gerasimov had also found that many of the purged commanders were heroes of the Civil War. Treated as such, they were quickly promoted to the political leadership and, though retaining their high ranks, they in fact left active military service. On the other hand, their less illustrious comrades had to plod through the ranks and thus acquired the experience that the political leaders clearly lacked.

With all that said, Gerasimov hints that the purges might have brought fear and uncertainty among the commanders of the Red Army. But he admits that this criterion can hardly be measured, and his final conclusion is that the purges did not weaken the Red Army.

A surprising fact: Stalin's marshals—Rokossovskii, Malinovsky, Govorov, Meretskov, and Vassilevsky—during the course of the war performed true miracles. Goebbels wrote the following about them in his diary on March 15, 1945: "Stalin has all the reasons to honor the Soviet marshals like movie stars, they showed remarkable military talents."[6] But in the summer of 1941 all these men, to put it subtly, did not show remarkable talents. So what happened? They were idiots in the beginning of the war, and then got smarter by the end? That does not happen. A man acquires experience in the war, but an idiot always stays an idiot. The idiots of 1941 could not have turned into outstanding troop leaders.

Only one conclusion follows from all this: Stalin's commanders were not idiots in 1941. The reasons for the defeat of the Red Army in 1941 should be searched for, but not in the stupidity of Stalin's generals.

16

Spain

All the peoples who fall under the "protection" of victorious Germany will also become our allies. We will have a broad field of action for development of the world revolution.
—JOSEPH STALIN, SPEECH AT A MEETING OF THE POLITBURO OF
THE PARTY CENTRAL COMMITTEE, AUGUST 19, 1939

On July 18, 1936, the radio station of the city of Ceuta (then in Spanish Morocco) transmitted several times the code phrase: "The skies above all of Spain are clear." This was the signal to begin the militant uprising against the Spanish Republic. General José Sanjurjo was at the head of the uprising, and after his death the position was taken over by General Francisco Franco. At the beginning, the troops located in the colonies provided support to the uprising. The militants had to transport these troops quickly from North Africa to Spain. Hitler came to General Franco's aid. He allocated twenty Ju-52 military-transport airplanes, which for almost three months made continuous trips from Morocco to Spain and back.[1] "Between July 28, 1936, and the end of August of the same year, the three-engine Junker Ju-52 aircraft transferred a total of 7,350 soldiers and officers, as well as some artillery units and machine guns, from Africa to Spain. The planes made 461 flights, often with over-limit cargo. An additional 5,455 troops were transferred during 324 such flights in September; then 1,157 more troops during 83 flights in October. Later on, Hitler noted that "Franco needs to erect a monument, honoring the Ju-52 as the aircraft, responsible for his victory in Spain."[2] This was the first mass transport of troops by air in history. This air bridge saved the uprising in its most critical early stage. After this, military units of the Spanish army began coming to Franco's side. "Eighty percent of the armed forces—120,000 soldiers and officers and a significant part of the civilian guard—found themselves on the side of the uprising."[3] General Franco was aided by the dictators of Germany, Italy, and Portugal—Hitler, Mussolini, and Salazar. Fifty thousand German, 150,000 Italian, 20,000 Portuguese, and 90,000 Moroccan soldiers and officers fought on General Franco's side. Foreign aid to General Franco amounted to 2,700 guns, 1,150 tanks and armored cars, and 1,650 airplanes.[4]

The People's Army was formed out of the parts of the Spanish army that remained loyal to the Republic. Volunteers from around the world came to the defense of the Spanish republic and formed seven international brigades. According to the figures of one of the brigade leaders, K. Sverchevsky, the total number of international volunteer troops was no less than 42,000.[5] Volunteers from fifty-four nations of the world were enlisted in the Republican army.[6]

The Soviet Union could not remain on the sidelines. V. A. Antonov-Ovseenko arrived in Spain. In 1917 he had been one of the key figures during the Communist takeover in Russia. He had been among the leaders who stormed the Winter Palace, and had personally arrested the provisional government. Having taken down the legal government, Antonov-Ovseenko entered the illegal government that was not recognized by Russia's allies, but was recognized by her enemies with whom Russia was in a state of war. In 1936 Stalin appointed Antonov-Ovseenko general consul of the Soviet Union in Barcelona. He began with recommending to the Spanish Republic's government to hide the gold reserves of the country. Where should they hide it? In Moscow. The Spanish gold reserves were brought out of the country, and never again returned. They say that the anarchists were thieves. That was true. But the gigantic reserves of Spanish gold were taken away not by anarchists, but by the unselfish Communists. The Spanish gold reserves were payment for the supply of weapons. The supply was indeed a large one, but it should openly be declared that the Soviet Union did not support the government of the Spanish Republic out of honorable feelings, but for gold, which Antonov-Ovseenko brought out of the country.[7]

Stalin appointed Jan Karlovich Berzin, commander of the 4th Directorate of the General Staff of the Red Army, to the position of chief military advisor to the Spanish Republican army. Overall, 2,065 commanders of various ranks were sent from the Red Army to Spain: 772 pilots, 351 tankers, 100 artillerists, 222 general military advisors, and 204 interpreters.[8] Additionally, through the NKVD line, the People's Commissariat of Foreign Affairs, and other administrations, several hundred more Soviet diplomats, intelligence and counterintelligence officers, saboteurs, journalists, agitators, party workers, and military industry specialists were sent to Spain. The total number of volunteers, including civilian specialists, was around three thousand.[9]

Stalin sent to Spain 648 warplanes, 347 tanks, 60 armored cars, 1,186 artillery weapons, 20,486 machine guns, and 497,813 rifles.[10] Aside from this, Spain received from the Soviet Union shells, cartridges, bombs, military equipment, food supplies, fuel, lubricants, and medications.[11] These deliveries of arms could have been much larger, but Spain was blockaded. Soviet merchant ships sailed out of Black Sea ports. In the Mediterranean Sea, the Soviet Union had neither a military fleet nor military naval bases. Defenseless merchant ships crossed the entire Mediterranean Sea to reach Spanish shores. From the Black Sea straits to the destination ports, these ships were followed by Italian and German airplanes and warships. And at the end of their destination, near the Spanish coast, they were awaited by General Franco's warships, airplanes, and submarines. Nonetheless, despite the blockade, Stalin managed to transfer to Spain a huge, by any standards, amount of strategic cargo.

In order to understand the seriousness of Stalin's intent, let us assess several of the commanders he sent to Spain. They were then lieutenants, captains, and colonels. However, they were the most promising commanders of the Red Army, and Stalin had noted them for promotion. Spain was their last test. The majority of them quickly rose in rank after their return from Spain. Here are the heights reached by some of these military advisors in just a few years: R. Y. Malinovsky became a marshal and minister of defense of the USSR; K. A. Meretskov became a marshal and chief of the General Staff; G. I. Kulik became a marshal and the Deputy People's Commissar of Defense of the USSR; N. G. Kuznetsov became admiral of the Soviet fleet, minister of the navy, and for the duration of the entire war he was a member of the Supreme High Command.[12]

And in addition to over twenty future Marshals, Generals of the Army, and Colonel Generals, over forty of those who fought in Spain later became lieutenant generals, vice admirals, major generals, and rear admirals.

Despite all the efforts put forth by Stalin, Communist victory in Spain was impossible. There were many reasons for this. First of all, over 80 percent of Spanish soldiers and officers fought on the side of the uprising. Even the Communists acknowledge this. And this speaks to the fact that the uprising was not just purely originating from the generals. Spanish soldiers and generals had a choice, and the majority of them fought against the Republic. This, in turn, signals that not everything was all right in the Spanish Republic. Secondly, Spain is a long way from Russia. Stalin could not send to Spain any of his divisions. Even if he did, it would have been impossible to supply an entire division. The third reason for defeat was that the Communist party in Spain was extremely weak. It was forced to make alliances with other parties. The Communists' main allies were the anarchists. In regions where they managed to take control, they abolished currency and made all private property public. The general secretary of the Communist Party of Spain, Dolores Ibárruri, describes her allies in the war in the following manner: "The anarchists organized something like a reign of thieves."[13] Marshal of the Soviet Union Meretskov, who fought in Spain, calls the anarchists "jolly butchers." Even if Communists themselves had been angels, they were still destined for defeat with such allies.

It is impossible to win without allies, but with allies like those winning was even more impossible. On March 28, 1939, Madrid fell—the last bastion of the Republic.[14] As a result of an almost three-year-long war, General Franco had won. Soviet military advisors were evacuated.

I have always been concerned about the coincidences in timing in this whole history. The war in Spain was a sort of prologue of World War II. The battles in Spain ended, and five months later a new war began, which spread throughout all of Europe and then throughout the world. Was there a link between the war in Spain and World War II? And if yes, what was it?

When I was sixteen years old, studying military history at a military boarding school, we students were urged to read a book by Chief Marshal of Artillery N. N. Voronov. The book is very interesting. Voronov commanded the entire artillery of the Red Army during World War II. He was one of the first to interrogate General Field Marshal F. Paulus in the ruins of Stalingrad. In all of German history, field marshals had never been taken prisoner. Paulus was the first. Even aside from this one episode, there are a lot of interesting moments in Voronov's book. The book is written in a simple and lively fashion. Voronov had fought in Spain as well. Suddenly, one phrase in this book not only touched me, it wounded me: "The events in Spain deeply upset the Soviet people. Very crowded meetings and gatherings of workers took place in Moscow and other cities. [The] Soviet people expressed their brotherly solidarity with the Spanish people, who were fighting against wild bands of fascists. During a short time workers and farmers donated millions of rubles to raise funds for the Spanish fighters."[15]

I was shocked by this. In 1936, the Soviet people watched anxiously events in remote Spain, expressed outrage at the actions of the insurgents, held meetings of workers in factories and peasants in the fields, and gathered their hard-earned kopeks to help the Spanish people. Meanwhile, three years before this, the Soviet Union had been ravaged by a terrible famine, which was accompanied by cannibalism and the eating of cadavers. And this did not cause any anxiety to the Soviet people. They did not hold meetings, nor did they collect aid. Soviet people were not upset by the simple fact that their brothers, sisters, and neighbors were dying of hunger by the millions, while Stalin exported grain abroad by the millions of tons. Our people carry responsibility for all the people in the world, while being completely irresponsible toward their own. In 1936 in Spain there were no concentration camps, hostages were not yet being executed, but still the Soviet people were terribly upset and anxious. Meanwhile, slave labor flourished in the Soviet Union, millions of people were in concentration camps and prisons, and this did not upset the Soviet people or make them anxious in the least. On December 27, 1932, internal passports were introduced in the Soviet Union, without which it was impossible to work, find a place to live, or move about around the country. The passports were introduced in the midst of hunger, in order to more effectively counter the flight of the peasant population from starving regions into cities or into more prosperous parts of the country. These passports were handed out only to city dwellers. But the peasants, who comprised the majority of the population, were not supposed to get a passport. The Soviet peasant was relegated to the position of a slave who could not leave his owner. And Stalin's military advisors, future generals and marshals, instead of fighting for the freedom of their own people, strove to fight for the freedom of Spanish peasants, who unlike the Soviet ones were free and had the right to go anywhere they wanted, including abroad.

Everything I read about the war in Spain surprised me. Here is an example of a fact that at first glance seems of little importance. The most important advisor to the Republican army was Yan Berzin, commander of the 4th Directorate of the General Staff of the Red Army.

What was the 4th Directorate? In the early 1960s the Soviet Union experienced an almost hysterical wave of laudation for the Soviet intelligence agent Richard Sorge. Films and television programs about him were aired, books and articles were published, lectures read, his name was given to streets and places, and projects for monuments were widely discussed. It was declared that Richard Sorge was recruited and trained by Jan Berzin, the chief of the 4th Directorate of the General Staff of the Red Army. Right away, it was explained to the people what the 4th Directorate was. It was the name given to the military intelligence service of the Red Army in the 1920s and 1930s. Now this organization is denoted by three letters—GRU, which in Russian stand for Main Intelligence Directorate of the General Staff of the Soviet Armed Forces. But why was the head of all Soviet advisors in Spain the chief of intelligence and not some experienced field commander?

During the course of the war, several thousand children of Spanish Communists were transported to the Soviet Union. This is a special and tragic story. They were trained to become fighters on secret fronts during the Cold War in Latin America and Africa. They served as secret agents and special forces. One group was assigned to protect and keep a watchful eye on Fidel Castro. The fate of foreign volunteers in Spain is no less interesting.

Immediately upon arrival in the country, their passports and all other documents were taken away from them. Once he had become part of an international brigade, a volunteer ceased to be a volunteer. He turned into an armed slave, for whom escape was virtually impossible. Somehow, for some reason, fires occurred more frequently in buildings in which the volunteers' documents were kept, and the cars that transported these documents were more frequently in the line of fire. As the result, the majority of fighters from international brigades were left without any documents, while the Soviet intelligence network received real passports and other personal documents for thousands of young men from fifty-four countries. These documents were used by the Military Intelligence to provide authentic identity documents for illegal agents and to improve Soviet document falsification techniques.

Antonov-Ovseenko was called back from Spain to Moscow, arrested, and executed. Yan Berzin returned from Spain to his post as head of the Military Intelligence but soon after was also arrested and executed. Meanwhile, the military advisors who really were fighting, not dealing with politics and espionage, rapidly climbed to the peaks of military power. Some of them fell under Stalin's axe but for other mistakes and errors, not for Spain.

Stalin did not count on military victory in Spain, and understood that it was impossible under such conditions. What was he fighting for? This is no riddle. It is enough to look at the actions of Stalin's diplomats and propaganda from that time period. Three countries with totalitarian regimes—Germany, Italy, and Portugal—were helping General Franco. The Spanish Republic, on a state level, was being helped by the Soviet Union alone. Great Britain and France had policies of nonintervention in Spain's affairs. Soviet propaganda screamed in outrage: children are dying in Spain, while France and Britain issue no reaction! Soviet propaganda scorned Britain and France and accused them of heartless indifference to the fates of Spanish children. Many Communist historians in Russia still cannot forgive Britain and France for their policies of nonintervention. How could they calmly have watched the suffering of the Spanish people? How could they have stayed on the sidelines, while Spanish children were dying?

But the issue was not the fate of children. (In the Soviet Union, Stalin enacted a law on April 7, 1935, that made the death penalty applicable to children aged twelve and older.) Stalin's most obvious goal, which was expressed clearly and openly, was to draw Britain and France into the Spanish war. If this plan had been successful, then a great clash between Germany, Italy, and Portugal on one side and France and Britain on the other would have occurred in the far west of the European continent, on Spanish territory. The Soviet Union was far away. Stalin's advisors and "volunteers" would also have fought, but the war would never have touched the territories of the Soviet Union. All Stalin had to do was pour fuel into a war that was heating up. The international volunteers from fifty-four countries were also a part of his plan. Stalin's agents all over the world agitated honest young men to go to Spain. Stalin was generous with money to fund the agitators, paid for the travels and living costs of the volunteers, and armed the international brigades. His plan was simple: to draw citizens of the entire world into war. First separate citizens, then entire groups, and then the governments of the various nations would have been forced to rescue their citizens. This would have meant a conflict, one way or another, with the governments of Franco, Hitler, Mussolini, and Salazar.

But the war in Spain never went beyond its borders. All the efforts of Stalin's political agents, diplomats, and spies were not enough to spread the Spanish fire throughout Europe. Stalin did not blame his generals, because military victory could not be expected. But he did blame his spies and diplomats for not expanding the war in Spain to the rest of Europe. That is why Berzin, Antonov-Ovseenko, and the rest were executed. After this failure, Stalin drastically changed directions. By the end of 1938, when the war in Spain was clearly quieting down, when the defeat of the Communists became obvious, the exiled Trotsky in distant Mexico sensed the change in Stalin's politics. He warned the entire world about this. In November 1938, Trotsky wrote: "Stalin finally untied Hitler's hands, as well as [those of] his enemies, and pushed all of Europe towards war."[16] This was written a month after the British premier, Lord Chamberlain, upon return from Munich, joyfully waved around a piece of paper and declared that he had brought peace. Trotsky wrote these words when Mussolini still considered himself a peacemaker, and Hitler had not yet issued a directive about preparations for the invasion of Poland or France.

In these sweet months, Europe drew a breath of relief and believed that there would be no war, while Trotsky already knew that it would soon come, and knew who would be responsible for it. In order to fully believe Trotsky, let us listen to another one of his prophecies, uttered on June 21, 1939. At that time intense talks between Britain, France, and the USSR against Germany were under way. Nothing hinted at the possibility of any sort of unanticipated event or complication. Trotsky, however, warned: "The USSR will move its entire mass towards the borders of Germany precisely at the moment when the Third Reich will be drawn into a fight for a new division of the world."[17]

Everything happened just as Trotsky had predicted. In the next year, 1940, Germany fought against France, while Stalin "with all his masses" crushed the neutral countries on his western borders, making his way toward Germany. Even now, over sixty years later, having read Trotsky's generalizations and predictions and appraised their accuracy, we have to ask: how could he know all this? Trotsky did not keep any secrets. He was the organizer of the Communist takeover of Petrograd in 1917, he was the creator of and a former commander of the Red Army, the Soviet representative at Brest-Litovsk, the first leader of Soviet diplomacy, a former leader of the USSR, and a former helmsman of the World Revolution. He knew better than anyone the nature of Communism, of the Red Army, and of Stalin. Trotsky said that all his predictions were based on open Soviet publications. Trotsky was the very first in the world to understand Stalin's game, which was not understood by the Western leaders, and which at first was not understood by Hitler.

Stalin's game, however, was very simple. Trotsky himself was the victim of such a game, which is why he understood it. Stalin, in alliance with Zinovyev and Kamenev, removed Trotsky from power in the Soviet Union. Then, in alliance with Bukharin, he removed Zinovyev and Kamenev. Then he removed Bukharin as well. Stalin removed generations of Dzerzhinsky's secret police henchmen through the hands of Genrikh Yagoda. Then Yagoda and his generation were removed through the hands of Nikolai Ezhov. Then Stalin removed Ezhov and his generation through the hands of Lavrenti Beria, and on and on it went.

Stalin continued his game on the international arena as well, and Trotsky could see this. German Nazism for Stalin was an instrument that could be used to crush the democratic regimes in Europe through Hitler's hands, and then finish Hitler off.

German Nazism could start a war, and the war could grow into a revolution. For Stalin, Hitler was a purifying storm over Europe. Hitler could do that which was inconvenient for Stalin to do himself. Stalin's politics were extremely simple. In Spain, he was unsuccessful in bringing Germany to a clash with Great Britain and France. But the hope was not lost, because they could be brought to a clash in Poland. So in the end of 1938 Stalin drastically changed all his propaganda. All anti-Hitler propaganda in the Soviet Union was brought to an abrupt stop. Now Stalin's priority was to calm Hitler: go to Poland, I will not be in your way.

When I was very young, I was surprised by an image: two generals are standing and smiling. One is Hitler's general, the other Stalin's. This photo was taken in September 1939, during the joint Soviet-Nazi parade commemorating the bloody division of Poland between Stalin and Hitler. I was drawn to this shot like a magnet. The German general was the famous tanker Guderian. He has a friendly smile. But this does not mean anything. Behind the friendly smile, he obviously hides cruel intentions. But who is this naïve Soviet commander? Why is he smiling? Obviously, he was fooled by the Nazis. The naïve Soviet commander was Brigade Commander S. Krivoshein. And if Krivoshein had pleasant conversations with a Nazi, this does not at all mean that Stalin's commander was fooled by the German. In his memoirs, he told of the mood among his subordinates: "We made a pact with the Germans, but this does not mean anything. . . . Now is the best time for a final and constructive resolution of all world problems."[18]

The joint Soviet-Nazi military parade was such an unexpected and unusual event that no Soviet commander would take the challenge of developing specific details of such a parade. Before making any decision any military officer would make sure that his superior officer approved and supported it, and the superior would do the same with his higher command. In any case all the details were supposed to be immediately reported to and vetted by Stalin. In this particular case we shouldn't blame Soviet military officers for lack of initiative or for being incapable of making decisions on their own. After all, the joint military parade is a political military manifestation of the intentions of both nations to the rest of the world. No one can do this without the clearance of every single detail at the highest political level. This is why we have every reason to believe that from the Soviet side the chief stage director of this show was Stalin; nobody else would ever dare to take such responsibility.

At that point Stalin was not afraid of Hitler. In August 1939 Stalin cheated him, and in September Stalin was openly making Hitler look ridiculous. The German side was represented by Panzer general Heinz Guderian. His rank was equal to lieutenant-general, and at the time he was a corps commander. According to military-diplomatic etiquette and traditions, the Soviet side was supposed to be represented by a commander of equal rank. But Stalin sent Semion Krivoshein, who was a brigade commander and whose rank was *Combrig*—two ranks beneath Guderian. There were plenty of senior Soviet military officers in Brest at this moment whose rank equaled that of Guderian, including the 4th Army commander, *Comcor* Vassiliy Chuykov. But Stalin decided to send a low-ranking *Combrig* for the joint parade.

Stalin's message to Hitler was simple: you sent a corps commander to greet me, but you were only worthy of being greeted by a simple *Combrig*.

And that was not all. Stalin opted to send a brigade commander who several months prior was in Spain, where he bravely fought against German Panzers. To rub it in, Stalin decided to humiliate Hitler further—Semion Krivoshein, the commanding Soviet officer of the joint Soviet-Nazi military parade in Brest, was Jewish.

The majority of contemporary historians believe that Stalin was afraid of Hitler and was trying to avoid giving him any reason for attack. Stalin's attitude in September 1939 proves the opposite.

17

Stalin's Trap for Hitler

According to this agreement, it turned out that Hitler started the war. This was beneficial for us from the military and from the moral standpoint. With his actions, he would provoke war with France and England, by going against Poland. We could remain neutral.

—N. Khrushchev

Stalin turned out to be a rare strategist who planned history, a phenomenal tactician who organized victories under a foreign flag and with foreign hands.

—A. Avtorkhanov, *Origins of Partocracy*

In the beginning of May 1939, on the border between Mongolia and China near the river Khalkhin-Gol, an armed conflict occurred between Soviet and Japanese troops. Mongolia was under Soviet control. The adjoining Chinese territory was occupied by Japan. The clash of Soviet and Japanese troops turned into battles, fought with the use of aviation, artillery, and tanks. Nobody declared war, but the intensity of armed operations grew. On June 1, 1939, the government of the Soviet Union officially declared: "We will defend the borders of the Mongolian People's Republic as we defend our own."[1]

Actions went according to those words. Precisely on that day, June 1, 1939, the deputy commander of the Byelorussia military district G. K. Zhukov was summoned from Minsk to appear in Moscow. On the following day, Zhukov flew out of Moscow to Mongolia. There, he took command of the Soviet and Mongolian troops and defended Mongolia from Japanese aggression just as he would have defended the territory of his own country.

Stalin ordered Soviet troops in Mongolia to be armed with the most modern weapons. Upon a direct order from Stalin, a group of the best Soviet pilots, who had battle experience in Spain and China, was sent to Mongolia. Each pilot had in previous battles shot down at least ten enemy planes. The Soviet pilots managed to turn the situation to their advantage and established air superiority above the theater of operations. On August 20, 1939, in the Mongolian sky, five Soviet I-16 fighters for the first time successfully used air-to-air RS-82 rocket missiles, equipped with remote detonators.[2]

Each side increased its power. Soviet troops under Zhukov's command were united into the First Army group. The Japanese forces formed the Sixth Army. During the course of endless exhausting battles, Zhukov prepared a radical solution to the problem—a sudden, crushing defeat of the Japanese Sixth Army.

Meanwhile, the tensions in Europe rose. Hitler demanded a review of the Versailles Treaty. In accordance with this treaty, Eastern Prussia was separated from the main part of Germany, and the city of Danzig was declared a free city. Hitler demanded to be given a corridor through Polish territory to build a highway and a railroad between Eastern Prussia and mainland Germany. Additionally, the city of Danzig was to become a part of Germany. The Polish government refused to satisfy Hitler's demands. Great Britain guaranteed Poland's safety. Treaties guaranteeing mutual aid were signed between Great Britain, France, and Poland. The governments of Great Britain and France decided to attract the Soviet Union to their side. This was a monstrous and fatal mistake.

If the USSR had been interested in safeguarding peace in Europe, it would not have needed agreements with Great Britain and France. Stalin could have solved the problems of Europe's safety on his own. He only had to make his position clear to Hitler: If Hitler were to begin a war against Poland, then he would not receive Soviet oil, grain, cotton, iron ore, magnesium, chrome, zinc, nickel, and tin. Without these things, Hitler could not have fought. It was possible to give an even harsher ultimatum: to declare independently of Britain, France, and Poland that the Soviet Union would defend Polish territory from German aggression as if it was its own, as it defended Mongolian territory from Japanese aggression. It would not matter that the Polish government might not wish to have Soviet troops on Polish territory. When Germany crushed the Polish army and dismantled the Polish government, the Red Army would step into Poland and fight Germany. An invasion of Poland by the Germans would be a signal for the Red Army to get ready for action. After the fall of the Polish state, the Polish people would continue resistance, and would accept any help which the Soviet Union would be willing to give in unlimited quantities.

In the summer of 1939 Hitler should have been reminded that Soviet pilots, sappers, tankers, artillerists, and saboteurs fought in Spain against German military specialists. There the war lasted almost three years. Sending soldiers and arms to Spain was difficult. Poland was not Spain. Poland was much nearer. The Soviet Union could send any number of "volunteers" to Poland—5 or 10 million, plus any number of tanks, airplanes, and artillery. Hitler should have been told that in the event of aggression against Poland, the Soviet Union would give asylum to Polish refugees, would take in any number of Polish children, would offer training to Polish partisans and supply them with necessary equipment. In this case, war against Poland could not be a lightning war. It would be a war of attrition, and Germany did not have the resources for such a war. That is how Stalin should have behaved. But he, for some reason, insisted on having talks with Great Britain and France.

If a novice player sits down to play cards with a pro, he usually makes only one mistake: he picks up his cards. . . . On August 11, 1939, British and French delegations arrived in Moscow for talks about joint action against Germany. The governments of Great Britain and France repeated the mistake of novice card-players. They sat down at the table with Stalin's pros, and lost the talks. Neither the British nor the French envoys understood Stalin's intentions. Stalin's plan, in fact, was very simple: force France and Britain to declare war on

Germany, or push Hitler to actions that would prompt France and Britain to declare war on Germany.

Having received approval from the British and French governments for talks, Stalin immediately found himself in a situation in which he could not lose. For Stalin, two options were open: either the Soviet delegation would set new demands and force Britain and France to start a war against Germany; or Britain and France would refuse to invade Germany, the talks would fail, and it would be possible to accuse Britain and France of being too lax on the aggressor, while Stalin himself could sign a pact with Hitler.

The Soviet delegation set forth insatiable demands: We have no common border with Germany, so our troops need corridors through Poland!

This demand was unacceptable for Poland, and unnecessary for the Soviet Union. It was unacceptable because the Polish government and people knew the nature of the Red Army and the Soviet secret police. In 1920, the Polish people saw the Red Army on their land, and understood that a new arrival of "liberators" would turn into occupation, mass shootings, and terror against all layers of society. Several months after these talks, Estonia, Latvia, and Lithuania allowed the placing of Soviet garrisons on their territories—and fell into Communist slavery, which lasted half a century. If Stalin wanted peace, why did he need corridors in Poland? K. E. Voroshilov, then a member of the Politburo, the People's Commissar for Defense, and a Marshal of the Soviet Union, declared at the talks: "Since the Soviet Union has no common border with Germany . . . there are no roads for engaging the aggressor."[3]

The absence of common borders with Hitler's Germany was a great asset for the Soviet Union. If the Soviet Union was thinking in terms of defense or neutrality in case of war, the Red Army needed no corridors to pass through Polish territory. But Stalin was not planning on defense, and certainly not planning on staying out of the war. He needed corridors through Polish territory on one hand in order to establish a Communist regime in Poland, and on the other hand because the corridors enabled him to deliver a surprise attack to Germany from the rear, in case it became engaged in a war against France and Britain. No other use for passages through Poland can be thought of.

There were other proposals from the Soviet side: Let France and Britain start a war against Germany not only in the case of direct German aggression, but in case of "indirect aggression."[4] What "indirect aggression" meant only Stalin and his diplomats knew. If the proposals of the Soviet delegation had been accepted, Stalin (justifiably) could have demanded that France and Britain start a war against Germany in response to any action by the German government. The wording was very loose, and anything can be labeled "indirect aggression." The scenario of war in this case was simplified: in answer to an action by Germany, France and Britain, according to Stalin's demands, were forced to act against her. The Soviet Union would act against her as well, but on Polish territory not on its own—very convenient and safe.

In any event, the main theater of operations would unfold between France and Germany, and then fresh Soviet troops would carry out decisive strikes into the rear of German forces through the Polish territories.

During the course of the talks, the French and British delegations, wishing to prove the seriousness of their intents, gave the Soviet side very important information that should not have come into Stalin's possession.

Stalin knew that Great Britain and France had given their guarantees to Poland. But how serious was their word? The French and British delegations let him know that it was serious! If Hitler started a war against Poland, Great Britain and France would declare war against Germany. This was exactly the information Stalin was waiting for. Hitler thought that his invasion of Poland would go unpunished, like the entrance of German troops into the Rhineland demilitarized zone, like the *Anschluss* (union) of Austria and Germany, like the taking of Czechoslovakia. Stalin now knew that Hitler would be punished for invading Poland. The key to the ignition of World War II fell into Stalin's hands. It remained for Stalin only to give Hitler the green light: Attack Poland, I will not act against you (but France and England will declare war on you).

Half a century later, Soviet generals slowly started to admit that Stalin and the Red Army opened the way for Hitler to invade Poland. Army General A. Mayorov: "In planning the invasion of Poland, Germany feared most of all the Soviet Union, not England and not France. That is precisely why fascist leaders hurried to conclude a pact about [the] invasion with the USSR."[5]

The head of the GRU, Army General P. I. Ivashutin, expressed this sentiment more clearly: "With this pact, Hitler untied his hands for aggression."[6] Simply stated, if Stalin had not signed a pact with Hitler, there would have been no invasion of Poland, and there would have been no World War II.

If Stalin had wanted peace, in August 1939 he had many opportunities to avert war. One of them was to follow the example of Britain and France and give a guarantee of safety to Poland. Or, he could simply have drawn out his talks with Britain and France, which would have served as a warning to Hitler: Invade Poland, but keep in mind that all of Europe is against you, we are gathered here in Moscow talking about something, and all we have to do is blockade Germany. But Stalin chose his own way. On August 12, 1939, the military delegations of the USSR, Great Britain, and France began talks in Moscow. Stalin's Marshal Voroshilov openly conducted with France and Britain the talks on "containing Hitler's aggression in Europe." Behind the scenes, however, things happened very differently: On August 11—even before the talks got started—Stalin made a decision to start negotiating with Germany for the partition of Poland.[7] Stalin showed the world his willingness to stop Hitler's aggression, but simultaneously (and even beforehand) offered the German dictator a friendly and helping hand. Thus, Stalin safeguarded himself from failure, no matter what happened. Britain, France, and Germany were clearly about to engage in a massive struggle. Stalin kept up, openly or secretly, friendly relations with all the participants in this struggle and at the same time incited them to act more and more aggressively.

On August 19, 1939, Stalin made a series of extremely important decisions, which had consequences for the course of world history. On that day, Stalin decided to stop the talks with Britain and France. On that same day, the German ambassador to Moscow, Friedrich von der Schulenburg, received Stalin's draft of the impending mutual agreement with the directions that "the agreement will be in force only given the simultaneous signing of the special protocol on points of interest to the Agreeing Parties, regarding foreign policy."[8] Hitler didn't know that signing this agreement signified the start of World War II. Stalin did.

On that same day, August 19, according to Stalin's orders the Soviet Union began a mobilization of the Red Army. Earlier, Stalin had given firm approval of conducting a sudden crushing operation to defeat the Japanese Sixth Army in Mongolia. On August 19, 1939, a coded cable from Zhukov informed Stalin that the main goal had been reached, that is, that the Japanese did not suspect the impending attack. Stalin gave his final approval, and Zhukov crushed the Japanese Sixth Army. Zhukov conducted a brilliantly sudden, quick, and audacious operation. The lightning-speed defeat of the Japanese Sixth Army was a prelude to World War II.

On that same day, August 19, 1939, a secret meeting of the Politburo took place, at which Stalin gave a speech. This meeting of the Politburo has never been reported. On the contrary, a lot of efforts were made to convince the whole world that such a meeting never took place. Stalin himself told the newspaper *Pravda* on November 30, 1939, that any report of a meeting of the Politburo on August 19, 1939, "is a sheer invention and lie."

Years went by. The Soviet Union rotted and fell apart. Archives opened slightly. The advisor to the Russian president, Colonel General D. A. Volkogonov, published an article in the newspaper *Izvestia* on January 16, 1993: There was a meeting of the Politburo on August 19, 1939. The general had [the] protocols in his hands. General Volkogonov says that only secondary questions that were discussed at that meeting are preserved in the archives. But even this revelation meant an end to public lies. With one line in a newspaper article, general Volkogonov disclosed the lies of all Soviet leaders, including Stalin.

In the meantime, more brave and more truthful scientists continued the search. And the document was found. It was kept in the Special Archives of the USSR, fund 7, index 1, document 1223. Tatyana Semenovna Bushueva, a talented Russian historian, found it. The document was first published in the December 1994 issue of *Novyi Mir*. This document finally proved that there was a meeting of the Politburo on that date. It turned out that Stalin did indeed speak on that date, and not about secondary problems, but about most vital ones. The document reveals that Stalin spoke of matters of primary, not secondary, importance.

The Russian historical community still denies the validity of this document, claiming it is unclear how and when the document was made. On the other hand, many recently declassified documents support the validity of this account. Let's look at, for instance, a record in the diary of the general secretary of the Comintern, Georgi Dimitrov, made on September 7, 1939. In the company of Molotov and Zhdanov, Stalin explained his new line of foreign policy to the leader of the Comintern: "The war is between two groups of capitalist nations . . . but we are not against it, if they fight a bit and weaken each other. It would be good if Germany could destabilize the positions of the wealthiest capitalist nations (of England especially). Hitler, without knowing it, is weakening the foundations of the capitalist system. . . . We, in the meantime, are able to maneuver, to nudge one country on against the other, so that the fight will be more intense."[9]

Below, as a source of comparison, are several excerpts from Stalin's speech at the Politburo session from August 19, 1939: "If we accept Germany's proposal about the conclusion of a pact regarding invasion, she will of course attack Poland, and France and England's involvement in this war will be inevitable. Western Europe will be subjected to serious disorders and disturbances. Under these conditions, we will have many chances to stay on the sidelines of the conflict, and we will be able to count on our advantageous entrance into the war. . . . It is in the interest of the USSR—the motherland of workers— that the war unfolds between the Reich and the capitalist Anglo-French block. It is necessary to do everything within our powers to make this war last as long as possible, in order to exhaust the two sides. It is precisely for this reason that we must agree to signing the pact, proposed by Germany, and work on making this war, once declared, last a maximum amount of time."

In 1924, Hitler wrote in his book *Mein Kampf* (Chapter XIV): "Already the one fact of concluding an alliance between Germany and Russia would mean [the] inevitability of a future war, the outcome of which would be predetermined. Such a war could only mean the end for Germany."[10] Fifteen years went by, and on August 19, 1939, Prime Minister and People's Commissar for Foreign Affairs of the USSR Vyacheslav Molotov, on Stalin's orders, handed to the German ambassador in Moscow von Schulenburg a plan for the nonaggression pact. Stalin's proposals were so attractive that Hitler accepted. Hitler correctly predicted his fate. As he foretold, the alliance with Moscow meant inevitable war, the outcome of which was predetermined. This war meant the end for Hitler's Germany.

18

Results of the Moscow Pact

Stalin was craftier then Hitler. Craftier and more sly.

—A. Antonov-Ovseenko

On August 23, 1939, Germany and the Soviet Union signed an agreement in Moscow about the destruction of the Polish state and the division of the Polish territories. Poland had mutual assistance agreements with France and the United Kingdom and, therefore, the attack by the Soviet Union and Germany automatically led to a European—and hence world—war. Indeed, in eight days, on September 1, 1939, World War II broke out. It was a direct and unavoidable result of the agreement reached in Moscow.

The USSR-Germany agreement is traditionally called the Molotov-Ribbentrop Pact. This moniker misleads and does not truly reflect the essence of what happened. The pact that was signed in Moscow was a plot between Hitler and Stalin to conduct an aggressive war in Europe together. Therefore, that agreement in effect was a Stalin-Hitler pact. Furthermore, in international practice it is much more common to use not the names of the statesmen that concluded the agreement, but the place where the documents were signed: the Munich Agreements, the Warsaw Pact, the Baghdad Pact, and the Geneva Agreement. Therefore, in accordance with common diplomatic practice, the more precise name of the pact would be the 1939 Moscow Agreement on the Start of World War II. Both parties received approximately equivalent shares—part of Poland went to Hitler, the other part went to Stalin. However, just eight days after signing the Moscow pact, Stalin violated it. Hitler started a war of aggression against Poland with hope that his ally Stalin would do the same. But Stalin cheated Hitler. On September 1 and in the subsequent two weeks the Soviet troops stood next to the Polish borders without conducting warfare and crossing the borders. The explanation of the Soviet government to the German counterpart was: the time has not come yet for action by the Red Army. As a result, the entire fault for the beginning of the war fell upon Germany, upon Hitler and his entourage. They entered world history as the chief and only cause of World War II. Poland was divided not in the Imperial Chancellery, but in the Kremlin. Hitler was not present, Stalin was. But Hitler is at fault for the starting of the war, while Stalin is not. Stalin entered history as an innocent victim and the liberator of Europe.

The invasion of the German troops into Poland had other consequences too: on September 3, 1939, Great Britain and France declared war on Germany. Already on the third day Germany was involved in a two-front war; that is, it wound up in an unwinnable situation. Since Germany practically lacked strategic raw materials, the two-front war was fatal for Germany.

Lack of raw materials not only prohibited Germany from conducting a two-front war, but also a prolonged single-front war. The only hope was for blitzkrieg—instant defeat of the opponent. France could be defeated in a lightning war, but Great Britain is an island nation. To defeat Britain, long and serious preparation is needed, as well as a powerful navy that is equal to or exceeds the British navy, and air dominance is needed too. The German navy lagged significantly behind the British navy. German air power was insufficient to crush British industry and achieve air superiority. Therefore, on the third day the war already looked long and unpromising for Germany.

Furthermore, Britain had a special relationship with the United States. The United States could side with Britain at any moment that was convenient. Germany did not have such allies. Only while he was in a position of power could Hitler rely on Stalin's friendship. In a prolonged war against Britain and her allies, Hitler would inevitably exhaust his resources. In September 1939, the German government repeatedly reminded the government of the USSR about their obligation and demanded the Red Army's invasion of Poland according to the agreement. The Soviet government would refuse—not right away, but with a two- to three-day delay. For example, in response to the German demarche of September 3, the head of the Soviet government and its foreign minister, Vyacheslav Molotov, responded on September 5: "We agree with you that concrete action has to be taken at an appropriate time. However, we consider that such [a] time has not come yet. It is possible that we are mistaken, but it appears to us that excessive haste could cause us harm and facilitate unification among our enemies."[1]

The German government kept repeating its demands and kept getting refused. Red Army units started military action in Poland only after two and a half weeks—September 17. Stalin's troops committed similar, or maybe even worse, atrocities in Poland, but Great Britain and France did not declare war on the Soviet Union. Great Britain, France, and their allies were interested in preventing Germany from using Soviet strategic resources. To do so, it was necessary to keep Stalin at their side at any cost and, in case of war between Germany and the Soviet Union, to keep the Red Army from being defeated.

As a result of the pact signed in Moscow in 1939 Stalin achieved a war, one which he desired and for which he had planned and prepared for a long time: The nations of Western Europe were mired in a destructive war, but the Soviet Union remained neutral. Now Stalin could wait for the total exhaustion and self-destruction of Central and Western Europe. Hitler guessed Stalin's intentions and in 1941 suddenly and almost fatally struck the Soviet Union. In this critical situation, Stalin received free aid from the United States and Great Britain, which in volume and quality did not have a historical precedent. At the same time, the Soviet role in unleashing World War II was quickly and thoroughly forgotten. In the final count, Poland, for whose freedom the Western European states had entered World War II, did not gain its freedom, but was given, along with all of Central Europe and part of Germany, into Stalin's control.

It is customary to consider Britain and France among the victors. However, this is clearly a mistake. The purpose for which Great Britain and France entered World War II was ensuring Poland's independence. This aim was not achieved as a result of the war; therefore, there is no cause to celebrate victory.

As a final result of the Moscow pact, Hitler committed suicide and Stalin became the unbound Red ruler of a huge anti-Western empire, created with the West's help. At the same time, Stalin managed to keep his reputation of a naïve, trustful simpleton, and Hitler entered history as a duplicitous villain. It is accepted that Stalin was not ready for war, but Hitler was ready. But the one who wins the war is the one who prepares for war by dividing his enemies and making them fight each other, not the one who makes loud pronouncements.

19

Blitzkrieg in Poland and Mongolia

It was the Russians who first put forward the idea of amassing mobile units.
—Colonel General F. Halder, Chief of General Staff of
German Land Armies

In August 1939, on the river Khalkhin-Gol in Mongolia, aside from a crushing blow there were other possible choices for action. Soviet troops could have, for example, taken defensive positions and postponed the prepared attack. Aggression is always risky. In the event of Soviet success, Japan would receive a lesson to last for years to come. In the event of failure, the entire world would talk of Stalin's army purges and accuse him of making the army unfit for fighting. In the event of failure, Zhukov could be executed, but his blood would not wash away the military's disgrace.

On Saturday, August 19, 1939, Stalin sent to Zhukov only one code word: "Good." A few hours later, Zhukov delivered the blow. In Moscow, that historical day, August 19, had just ended, but in Mongolia the sun was already rising over a new day. At 5:45 AM, 153 Soviet bombers, under the cover of a corresponding number of fighters, carried out a surprise raid over Japanese air bases and command posts. Artillery joined in immediately. The artillery softening-up was short (2 hours, 45 minutes), but unbelievably intense and powerful. During the course of the artillery action, Soviet aviation carried out a second raid, and at 9:00 AM tank units broke through Japanese defenses. Zhukov's plan was simple. He conducted a classic operation of encirclement. Zhukov had a relatively weak center and two powerful flank groups. The center only holds the enemy, while the strike groups at the flanks do not enter into prolonged battles but go around the main centers of resistance, and determinedly head forward. On August 23, the fourth day of the attack, the circle drawn around Japanese troops was tightened, and the rout began.[1]

The operation on the Khalkhin-Gol was brilliant in planning and in execution. Zhukov took a lot of risks, but they were justified. Zhukov ordered the air bases moved as close to the front lines as possible. This allowed airplanes to carry less fuel and more bombs. The intensity of the use of aviation grew sharply: planes took off, and before they even reached cruising altitude, unloaded their bombs, quickly returned, took more bombs, and repeated the process. When Soviet tanks went far ahead, aviation could support them without relocating the bases. Zhukov moved hospitals and supply bases to the front lines as well—supplying ammunition, fuel, and everything necessary for battle was carried out quickly and efficiently, and evacuation of the wounded did not demand excessive time, so after a short time the soldier found himself on the operating table. Zhukov moved his and all other command posts to the front lines, so he was personally able to see the battlefield panorama, and when the troops moved forward, it was no effort for him to move his command post after them. During the preparations for this offensive, Zhukov forbade almost all use of radio communication. Communication was conducted mainly through wires with short sentences, which were understood only by the two people speaking. The operation was prepared in complete secrecy. Each officer received directions only within the frames of his duties and had no concept of the overall plan, the scope, or the dates of the offensive. Actually, many people did not know about the offensive at all. Zhukov fooled not only the Japanese spies but, before all, his own soldiers and officers. Until the last moment, they thought that they were preparing defenses for a prolonged period. If his own soldiers and officers believed this, the enemy surely did as well.

Disinformation gave the desired results: there had never been such a crushing defeat in all of Japanese history. The defeat of the Japanese Sixth Army on the Khalkhin-Gol had strategic consequences. Japanese aggression in the direction of Mongolia and of the Soviet Union was thwarted. Japanese generals decided to not take any more risks. Their efforts from then on were aimed in a different direction—against the United States and the British colonies. In the fall of 1941, during months critical for the Soviet Union, Japanese generals still heeded the memory of Khalkhin-Gol and did not dare attack.

Khalkhin-Gol was the first lighting war of the twentieth century; it was blitzkrieg in the purest form. It was the first time in history that large masses of tanks were used correctly: to strike in depth. This was the prime example of unseen concentration of artillery in tight areas of the front. It was an example of absolute surprise attacks—during the first hour and a half of battle, the Japanese artillery did not fire a single shot and not a single Japanese plane rose into the air.

At the time that the Soviet army was conducting its operation at Khalkhin-Gol, the German army had no experience of conducting lightning-speed offensive operations and was not even conducting any large-scale training operations using tank masses for sudden breakthrough into the depth of the enemy's defenses. The German command planned to conduct the first of such training exercises in the fall of 1939.[2] Due to Germany's invasion of Poland and the beginning of World War II, these training exercises were never conducted.

On August 29, 1939, Stalin gave Zhukov the title of Hero of the Soviet Union for his lightning defeat of the Japanese Sixth Army. On September 1, Germany attacked Poland. It is interesting to compare the two lightning operations: the Soviet one in Mongolia, and the German in Poland. The difference lay in the fact that the whole world witnessed the German actions in Poland. Embassies from all over the world were located in Warsaw; there were many foreigners in Warsaw and other Polish cities, many journalists in particular. They all witnessed the war and described it in their newspapers and magazines. Hitler's propaganda demonstrated to the entire world the amazing successes of German troops. The whole world saw the menacing footage on their screens: dive-bombers roaring wildly as they flew toward the ground, dropping their deadly loads, and soaring back into the clouds, tanks breaking Polish barricades, letting through hordes of cheerful motorcyclists.

The Red Army's operation in Mongolia, on the other hand, was carried out on hot desert steppes, where there were no international observers and journalists. Few people knew about the operation at the time. For obvious reasons, the Japanese government did not rush to tell the world about the defeat of the Sixth Army in Mongolia. Surprisingly, the Soviet propaganda also did not rush to announce its victory.

During World War II, Major General D. Ortenberg was the editor-in-chief of the central military newspaper *Krasnaya Zvezda* (Red Star). He was directly subordinate to Stalin and had many meetings with him. Before the war, he was the editor-in-chief of the *1st Army Group* newspaper at Khalkhin-Gol. Major General D. Ortenberg testifies that Stalin personally forbade publishing materials concerning the defeat of the Japanese Sixth Army. "In central newspapers all materials about Khalkhin-Gol effectively went to the trash bin: there was a strict order from Stalin to not print anything about the Khalkhin-Gol events."[3] We can check Ortenberg's statement ourselves. It suffices to leaf through *Pravda, Izvestia,* and *Krasnaya Zvezda* from those days—there is not a word about the brilliant lightning-speed defeat of an entire Japanese army!

All Soviet propaganda was extremely and severely centralized. Stalin's empire ran the most powerful and perfected system of censorship. In Stalin's empire, any printed product could be published only after a censor gave permission. Without the permission, even bus tickets could not be printed. The principle of selection of information was extremely simple: hide any defects, catastrophes, and mistakes and praise any accomplishments. The farms produced slightly more milk, dug slightly more potatoes, a new factory was built—those were the reported news. But here we have a true accomplishment: the defeat of an entire Japanese army. This was an unprecedented historical event. Nobody had ever beaten the Japanese. During the Russo-Japanese war of 1904–5 Russians had especially suffered from the hands of the Japanese. Here came a remarkable revenge, huge trophies! The Red Army opened a new chapter in the art of war. The defeat was achieved by a new, previously unseen method.

Yet, Stalin ordered silence. Why? Because he was preparing the same sort of defeat, only on a much grander scale, for all of Europe. Stalin's interest lay in concealing the might of the Red Army, keeping silent its capability for delivering crushing surprise attacks. Stalin's interest lay in letting the whole world believe in the backwardness of the Red Army and its inability to conduct modern warfare. Stalin's interest lay in catching Hitler off-guard, in not scaring him.

At first glance, the Red Army's lightning operation in Mongolia and the German blitz-krieg in Poland are not comparable in scale. The German troops participating in the invasion of Poland numbered 1.6 million soldiers and officers. The Soviet group in Mongolia numbered only 57,000 men. In numbers of people, the German operation surpassed the Soviet one twenty-eight times. However, if one looks at the number of tanks and airplanes, the numbers are comparable. The German operation against Poland had the participation of four times more airplanes, and six times more tanks, than the Soviet operation in Mongolia. The numbers are quite on the same scale.

An analysis of the quality of weapons is even more interesting. The Red Army used long-range bombers in Mongolia; Germany had no such planes.[4] If one examines the quality of tanks, the picture also favors the Red Army. The Pz-I was the most prevalent German tank that participated in the blitzkrieg in Poland. There were 1,445 of them. This tank had a 100-horsepower engine. Earlier models of it had 57-horsepower engines. The second in numbers was the German Pz-II. There were 1,226. The earlier models of it had 130-horsepower engines, the later models, 140-horsepower. Germany had only 98 Pz-IIIs, and 211 Pz-IVs. The first models of these tanks had 250-horsepower engines, the later ones, 300-horsepower.

In contrast, Soviet troops in Mongolia used the BT-5 tanks, with 400-horsepower engines, and the BT-7 with 500-horsepower. The sum power of tank engines used in Mongolia constituted more than half of the sum power of tank engines used by Germany in Poland. In the area of tank armament, the Red Army clearly surpassed the Germans. At Khalkhin-Gol, practically all Soviet tanks were armed with the most powerful tank cannon of that time, with 45-mm .46-caliber barrels. In addition, Soviet armored automobiles were armed with the same cannon. The German army, or any other army in the world, had nothing comparable at the time. The majority of German tanks during the blitzkrieg in Poland had no cannon at all. The Pz-I only had machine guns. The Pz-II had 20-mm cannon. The Pz-III had weak 37-mm cannon, and there were less than a hundred tanks of this model. The Pz-IV had 75-mm cannon with a very short barrel, which was not meant for and not fit for battle against enemy tanks.

In 1939, the same arms gap could be seen between the Red Army and the *Wehrmacht* in terms of artillery. Germany entered World War II with field artillery developed in the time of World War I, while the Red Army had the best cannons, howitzers, and mortars in the world, developed right on the eve of World War II. For every thousand German soldiers during the blitzkrieg in Poland there were less than two tanks. For every thousand Soviet soldiers in Mongolia there were almost nine much more powerful tanks. In other words, Soviet troops at Khalkhin-Gol formed a relatively small army, but were equipped to the limit with the most modern and sophisticated weapons.

There was also a big difference in the conditions under which the operations were conducted. In September 1939, the conditions for conducting a lightning war in Poland were superb. A continuous defense by the Polish army along the perimeter of the country was impossible. Poland, to its misfortune, was an ideal location for the demonstration of tank capabilities. Western Poland formed a wide protrusion, surrounded on three sides by German territory. Its border with Germany stretched two thousand kilometers; after German occupation of Czechoslovakia, the German-Polish border increased by another eight hundred kilometers.[5]

The German army did not have to break through defenses. Ahead of it lay flat terrain, ideal for advance and totally unfit for defense. The river Vistula flows through Poland, but there was no need to cross it. Hitler's troops were located on both sides of the Vistula. There were no other serious water barriers. An attack on Warsaw could be carried out from any direction. The distance from mainland Germany to Warsaw was 230 kilometers, and from the border of Eastern Prussia to Warsaw was 110 kilometers. This meant that there was no need to relocate supply bases—troops could be supplied from stationary bases built during peacetime. There was no need to transfer thousands of tons of ammunition, fuel, and other equipment. In theory, a thrust on Warsaw could be carried out without refueling tanks. Fill up the tanks in Germany, and go! There were no defenses ahead, since they were impossible. There was no need to set up field hospitals, because the wounded could be taken to stationary peacetime hospitals. Aviation bases also did not need to be moved—the air force could conduct its missions from permanent air bases. Command posts with communication lines also stayed in place in underground bunkers. Only small mobile groups of commanders needed to be sent forward.

However, not everything in Poland went as smoothly as shown in Goebbels's propaganda and as described by some modern followers of Hitler. For some reason it is not popular to speak of this, but the German blitzkrieg in Poland failed. On September 15, 1939, two weeks after the start of World War II, the activity of the German air force substantially dropped; the German army was almost completely out of fuel. This was the level of Hitler's and his generals' understanding of modern warfare.

Forget all the tales by Soviet marshals and academics that the Red Army entered Poland in 1939 out of fear that the Germans might go straight for Moscow. Hitler did not have such strength. Even if he headed for Moscow in October 1939, the same exact thing would have happened to his valiant army that happened in October 1941: it would have sunk in the mud. The *Wehrmacht* lacked the fuel, bombs, and ammunition necessary to wage war against the Soviet Union. In 1939 the Red Army entered Poland for different reasons. Most importantly, there was the fear that Hitler's blitzkrieg would stop. It was already slowing down. Stalin's offensive in Poland allowed Hitler to transfer his forces from the eastern to the western front with maximum efficiency. Imagine the situation: all German tanks and cars are stopped, airplanes do not fly. The German army has many horses, though they are load-bearing horses, not cavalry. In this situation, the Polish cavalry could have shown what it means to have superiority in strategic mobility . . . but once again, Stalin saved Hitler.

From the standpoint of grand strategy the operation in Poland was a total failure for Hitler and his generals. It was the first suicidal act of Hitler's Germany: they entered a war having one enemy—Poland, and in two months brilliantly ended that war having Britain, France, India, Australia, New Zealand, Canada, and potentially the United States as enemies. A blitzkrieg cannot be used to win a war against all these nations, and Hitler had no other options. As a result of the blitzkrieg in Poland, Hitler obtained a common border with the "neutral" Soviet Union. Being at war with everyone, Hitler would have been better off having a border with Poland than with the Soviet Union—anything could be expected of comrade Stalin.

One more thing: Poland was not at all crushed by the blitzkrieg.

Immediately after the fall of the government in Warsaw, the Polish government in London was created, and it was acknowledged by most nations of the world and by the League of Nations. According to Polish tradition, underground local governments and an underground state formed on occupied territory. Armed forces were revived. Using the most cautious methods, the Polish Army counted 350,000 soldiers and officers, well trained, organized, and armed. Moreover, Poles fought against Hitler on all fronts: in Britain, France, Italy, Africa, Holland, and the Soviet Union. Starting in 1939, the number of Polish formations fighting Hitler constantly was around one million people. The blitzkrieg started in 1939 in Poland, and ended in 1945 with the storming of Berlin, in which the Polish First and Second armies took part.

We are told that Stalin purged his army, and after 1937–38 it was good for nothing. For some reason, Khalkhin-Gol and the year 1939 are forgotten.

In 1939, the Red Army received a unique and invaluable experience in breaking through powerful field defenses of the Japanese army in Mongolia. At that time not a single army in the world had such experience. From this experience, the right conclusions were drawn: even more attention needed to be given to the issue of breaking through defenses, and even more sophisticated weapons, designed specifically for this purpose, had to be developed. The experience of Khalkhin-Gol showed: if the enemy has dug himself firmly into the ground, aviation is incapable of breaking through such defenses, even if the bombing concentration is 80 tons per square kilometer. Artillery is needed. Soviet artillery was already the most powerful in the world, but from September 1939 began the unfolding of new artillery formations and the construction of new ammunition factories.

The Red Army command not only understood the extreme importance of supplying troops, but had the unique experience of doing it in the extreme conditions at Khalkhin-Gol. The Soviet troops counted 57,000 soldiers, 498 tanks, 500 guns, 385 armored cars, 515 airplanes, artillery transport, automobiles, etc. If everything necessary for life and battle was to be brought to Mongolia from the supply bases in the Baikal military district, the distance to be covered was roughly 1,500 kilometers. But not everything was in storage in the Baikal region. If supplies were to be brought from factories and central storages the distance to be covered was seven to eight thousand kilometers. The last stretch of railroad had very limited load-bearing capacity and ended in a deserted steppe. For the next 650 to 700 kilometers trucks were needed. The most common truck of that period could cover the round-trip of 1,300 to 1,400 kilometers, in good conditions, in roughly five days. The conditions were: heat, dust, no water. People might get by in these conditions, but automobile radiators need water. The troops needed to be supplied with everything. For example, wood to burn in field kitchens. Technology wear and tear was tremendous, as was fuel expenditure. Cars needed to be refueled several times along the way. Once the car had dropped off its cargo at Khalkhin-Gol, it needed to make its way back—and once again, it had to be refueled, so it turned out that the cars had to take away what they had just brought.

To this desert location the Soviets needed to supply by truck 25,000 tons of ammunition, 15,000 tons of fuel and lubricants, 4,000 tons of foodstuffs, 7,000 tons of fuel, and a lot of other cargo. All this was supplied in such a fashion that the enemy did not even suspect preparations for a sudden crushing attack. After such an operation, Soviet command quite clearly understood the meaning of supplies in war.

Nevertheless, Khalkhin-Gol played a mean joke on Stalin and the entire Red Army. In May 1940, Stalin introduced the titles of "general" and "admiral" into the Red Army. Approximately one thousand top Red Army commanders became generals. But only three of them received at that moment the top general rank—General of the Army. At that time, this meant five-star lapels. The first of these men was Zhukov. Zhukov became the first of all Soviet generals. Upon Zhukov's return from Mongolia, Stalin entrusted Zhukov with the most powerful of his military districts—the Kiev district. In February 1941 he appointed Zhukov to the position of Chief of General Staff. In this position Zhukov prepared for the war against Germany. On the German border (only on a much grander scale) he was to repeat everything he had implemented against the Japanese army. Zhukov created two mighty mobile flank attack groups at the L'vov and Belostok bulges, and one group for an attack in Romania.

Zhukov moved air bases to the very borders, with one hundred—sometimes two hundred—planes in each location. Zhukov moved hospitals, supply bases, command posts to the borders. Zhukov moved to the border thousands of tons of ammunition, fuel, and spare parts for tanks and planes.

Zhukov forbade almost all use of radio communication. Zhukov kept his plans in complete secrecy, and very few people in the Red Army knew what was to be done. Upon the surprise enemy attack, all this had catastrophic consequences. All of Zhukov's activity in 1941 has been attributed to a series of mistakes and miscalculations. But these were not mistakes. In 1941, he was preparing against Germany exactly what he had prepared in August 1939 against the Japanese army at Khalkhin-Gol.

20

Mobilization

Mobilization is war, in our minds there is no other meaning for it.
—MARSHALL Y. N. SHAPOSHNIKOV, CHIEF OF THE
GENERAL STAFF OF THE RED ARMY

From time to time we find a lot of interesting materials in the archives, but we will not find what is most important. Here is why: "How many times have I told you—do whatever you want, but do not leave behind any documents, do not leave any traces." These are the words of Stalin himself. He uttered them publicly at the Sixteenth Congress of the Communist Party. The records here note the "Homeric laughter of the entire audience." The congress laughed heartily—comrade Stalin had made a joke. Understandably, Stalin was not talking of himself, but of his opponents, who apparently were guided by the principle of leaving behind no traces or documents. But the congress laughed in vain. Stalin always ascribed his own intentions, principles, and methods to his enemies. Soon after, Stalin executed all his enemies, as well as almost all the delegates present at the Sixteenth Congress who had laughed so heartily. He left a very minimal number of documents about these executions.

Not a single dictator can match Stalin in his ability to cover up the traces of his personal involvement in crimes. Anastas Mikoyan, who beat all records of political survival, tells us how well Stalin kept secrets. Mikoyan was a member of the Central Committee of the Communist Party from 1923 until 1976—that is, for fifty-three years, for forty years of which he was a candidate or member of the Politburo, the most important power organ of the country, which governed the entire Soviet Union and its satellites. Mikoyan describes a meeting held by Stalin: "Most often there were five people. We met late in the evening or at night, rarely in the afternoon, usually without preliminary notice. There were no protocols or records kept during the course of such meetings."[1]

Air Force Colonel General A. S. Yakovlev: "During the meetings of Stalin's inner circle there were no stenographers, no secretaries present, no records or protocols were kept."[2] Marshal of the Soviet Union D. F. Ustinov was the People's Commissar of Arms during the course of the war: "During the meetings and conferences conducted by Stalin, discussions of problems and the making of decisions frequently occurred without records, and often without the corresponding paperwork marking the decision made."[3] In other words, decisions were made but were not fixed on paper, just like in the Mafia.

Marshal of the Soviet Union G. K. Zhukov during the course of the war was deputy to the Commander in Chief, that is, to Stalin: "Many political, military, and general government questions were discussed and solved not only at the official meetings of the Politburo and in the Central Committee Secretariat, but also in the evening at dinner in Stalin's apartment or at his dacha, where the Politburo members closest to him were usually present."[4]

Colonel General B. Vannikov was the People's Commissar of Ammunition: "At the meetings and conferences Stalin had a habit of discussing questions and making decisions without protocols or records. . . . From this it is clear that the understanding of many events just based on documents is incomplete and unclear, and in many cases incorrect."[5]

Hitler's meetings were known for being held in the presence of large crowds. Everything said by Hitler was fixed for history by three stenographers and a personal historian. Stalin's meetings on the other hand were simply secret gatherings of plotters and conspirators, in spirit and in essence. No documents and no traces were left of these meetings. Therefore, as Stalin taught us, we will look not at the words, which are hidden from us, but at the actions, which are in the open.

It is possible that World War II could have not occurred. The choice was up to Stalin. He himself told this to his colleagues at the Politburo meeting on August 19, 1939: "If we make a pact of mutual aid with Great Britain and France, Germany will give up Poland and . . . the War will be averted." Stalin did not make a pact with Great Britain and France; thereby he did not try to avert a war. This day—August 19, 1939—was a long, difficult day. This was a day filled with hopes and worries. This was the day when Stalin cast his fishing rod into the brown swamp that was Hitler's Germany. His hook had bait for Hitler: Danzig and half of Poland. Take it! And as a free gift Germany got war against Great Britain and France.

This was the day when doubts crawled into the hearts of Stalin's colleagues. Stalin had decided to trick Hitler. Would Hitler believe him? Stalin could not possibly always win. Vyacheslav Molotov worked on the scene as the head of the Soviet government and the People's Commissar of Foreign Affairs. When Molotov received the German ambassador von der Schulenburg in his cabinet in the Kremlin, Stalin, Shaposhnikov, Beria, and Malenkov did not show themselves—they were behind the curtains, in Stalin's cabinet. Molotov's conversation with the German ambassador was transmitted to Stalin's office. Molotov worked brilliantly. The most important thing was not to let the ambassador see Stalin's interest in the issue of German-Polish relations. Molotov did not reveal this interest; his attitude to the ambassador was: "All right, let Ribbentrop come, perhaps we will agree on something, perhaps we will find a solution to the question of Danzig and Poland."

After the meeting, Schulenburg went to the German embassy to write a report, while a heated discussion of the outcomes of the meeting was underway in Stalin's cabinet. The German ambassador had barely reached the embassy when he received a call from the Kremlin: Molotov awaits you for a new meeting. This was a difficult day. And it ended in Stalin's victory.

At dawn on September 1, 1939, the German army began war against Poland. But in the twentieth century, a war in Europe automatically meant a world war. The war quickly engulfed all of Europe and practically the entire world.

In a strange coincidence of events, it was precisely on this day—September 1, 1939—that the fourth emergency session of the Supreme Soviet of the USSR ratified the universal military draft. There had been no such law in the history of the USSR. A surprising thing: while children and adults were taught to fear Hitler, while Hitler was considered to be a tyrant and monster, the country could do without a draft. But as soon as a non-aggression pact was signed, a universal mandatory draft all of a sudden became necessary.

Why did the Soviet Union need it? Soviet historians stated that the USSR took measures of precaution. Marshal of the Soviet Union K. A. Meretskov is one of the many of those who assert that the law had a huge significance and was adopted "in the conditions when World War II had already begun."[6]

Let us imagine the Polish-German border on that tragic morning: darkness, fog, fire, motors roaring. Very few people in Poland understood what was happening, whether this was a provocation or an unsanctioned border conflict that arose on its own. But the representatives at the USSR Supreme Soviet already knew that this was no provocation, no conflict, and no German-Polish or even European war—this was the beginning of a world war. They knew that they, the representatives, must meet in Moscow and take the corresponding measures. Why did these representatives not act so efficiently when a similar thing happened on the Soviet-German border in 1941?

On the morning of September 1, 1939, it was not only the Polish government and the governments of the Western countries that did not know that World War II had started. Hitler himself did not know it either. He started the war against Poland hoping that it would be a local fight, like the taking of Czechoslovakia. As Colonel General of the Air Force A. S. Yakovlev (at that time an aircraft designer, deputy people's commissar of aviation industry, and personal advisor to Stalin) concluded: "Hitler was sure that England and France [would] not fight for Poland."[7] When, on September 3, Great Britain and France declared war on Germany, this was an extremely shocking and unpleasant surprise for Hitler. He had not anticipated this. For him, a "strange" war against Great Britain and France began on September 3. In the same month, an equally strange peace began in the East.

Any attempt to establish the exact date of the beginning of World War II and the time that the USSR entered into it brings us to the date of August 19, 1939: Stalin stretched a hand of friendship out to Hitler and signed the non-aggression pact, while on the same day he issued an order to gather the representatives of the Supreme Soviet, so that at the time World War II began they were already sitting in the Kremlin and unanimously voting in favor of everything put before them. What a strange coincidence: the road to Moscow is long—for some it takes ten to twelve days. In order to adopt the law on September 1, 1939, the order to gather the representatives was issued on August 19, meaning that on August 19, 1939, someone in Moscow already knew that in a couple of weeks World War II would begin and a new draft law would be needed.

Chief of General Staff and Marshal of the Soviet Union B. M. Shaposhnikov created the theory of mobilization. He authored the book *Brain of the Army*. The third and final volume was published in 1929, and while the Soviet Army existed, this book served as a manual for every Soviet officer and general. On Lenin's desk, a copy of the book *Mob Psychology* by Gustav le Bon had always been present, and on Stalin's desk it was Shaposhnikov's *Brain of the Army*. The key to the success of Shaposhnikov's book was in the simplicity with which the material was presented, in the crystal-clear argumentation, and in the ability to explain the most complex problems in terms understandable by anybody. The third, concluding part of the book is the most powerful. In the third volume Shaposhnikov examines the questions of mobilization.

The theory was simple, understandable, logical, and unquestionably correct. Stalin understood it, appraised its worth, and added it to the base of his own strategy. This is why reading Shaposhnikov's works (as well as those of his supporters and opponents) and understanding the course of their thought helps us understand Stalin's actions, which at first glance seem illogical and unexplainable. The theory of mobilization, condensed and explained in layman's terms, consists of the following.

1. To achieve victory in a war, not only efforts of the entire army but full efforts by the entire nation, the people, industry, transport, agriculture, etc., are necessary.

2. The nation cannot exist in a constant state of preparedness for war, just as a man cannot constantly hold a gun in each hand. If he is always holding two guns, he cannot do anything else. Similarly a nation cannot constantly expend all its resources on preparations for war. Constant concentration of forces and expenditure of social resources on war preparations ruin the nation. Therefore, during peacetime the army and the military industry must operate at a minimal level. However, the nation, its people, government apparatus, industry, transport, agriculture, communication channels, ideological apparatus, and so forth must be prepared for a maximally quick and full transition from a peacetime to a wartime regime.

3. Mobilization is the transition of the entire country from a peacetime to a wartime regime. Mobilization cannot be curbed or turned back. Metaphorically speaking, mobilization is similar to thrusting one's arm down, unlatching a holster, and aiming the gun at the enemy with one's finger already on the trigger.

4. Mobilization and war are inseparable. If you take out a gun and aim it at the enemy with your finger on the trigger, you have to shoot. As soon as you begin to mobilize, the enemy will mobilize as well. You take aim, and the enemy does the same, trying to be faster than you by at least a fraction of a second. If you are a tiny bit of a second late, he will kill you.

5. You cannot play games with mobilization: if you often brandish guns and aim them at your neighbors with your fingers on the trigger, the outcome will not be a good one for you.

6. Once the path of mobilization has been chosen, you have to follow it up to the end—start a war.

7. Mobilization cannot be partial. Mobilization is a process similar to pregnancy. A woman cannot be a little bit pregnant—the answer is always "yes" or "no." The same is true for mobilization in a country: either the entire government apparatus, industry, transport, armed forces, population, and all the national resources are mobilized toward war, or not.

These ideas, in various orders and manners, are voiced by many different authors. B. M. Shaposhnikov differed from his predecessors only in that he expressed the ideas clearly, briefly, and concisely: "Mobilization is not only a symptom of war, it is war itself. An order by the government to declare mobilization constitutes a de facto declaration of war. . . . In modern conditions, a mobilizing country must make a firm decision ahead of time to conduct war. . . . In a general mobilization, it is understood that there can be no more return to peacetime positions. . . . We maintain that only a general mobilization has value, the concentration of all resources and forces necessary for achieving victory." The book ends with a decisive declaration: "Mobilization is war, and we cannot understand it in any other way."

Stalin not only shared Shaposhnikov's views, but he had the same beliefs. Stalin did not make any distinctions between the process of taking power in his country or in the neighboring ones. He knew how to take power in his own country, and he planned to do the same in the neighboring ones. Stalin did not keep his art a secret. On the contrary, he made it into a display for the masses. In his book *On the Foundations of Leninism*, Stalin proved that games are not permissible in the quest for power. We either take control or we do not. Once the task is attempted, it must be carried out to the end. This goes along with the teachings of Niccolo Machiavelli: either you deliver a lethal blow or you do not attack at all; no in-between decisions can exist in politics or in strategy. This also goes along with Shaposhnikov's ideas: we can either not mobilize at all or we can conduct a full mobilization and enter the war—no partial, in-between positions can be adopted.

There was another problem: mobilization had to be concealed. Long before World War II, Stalin and Shaposhnikov worked out a way to conceal mobilization. For this reason, there was no universal military draft in the Soviet Union until 1939. The army was very selective and did not take in just anybody. This was to show what a peace-loving people we were. The age requirement for entering the armed services was twenty-one. This is strange. Why not draft at eighteen or nineteen, right out of school—let the boy serve his term and be free? By age twenty-one a man could have found a job and started a family, while his future remained uncertain: would they draft him or not? Nobody could really explain why the army had to take men at age twenty-one and not younger.

There was, however, a lot of thought put into this system. It was like a dam on a river: not everyone was let through (that is, drafted), only some, while the rest amassed on the other side. At the necessary moment a universal draft could be instituted (only the pretext had to be invented), and all those who did not earlier serve in the army could be called in. During the intervening years, there were many of them saved up.

The moment came—September 1, 1939. On this day, a universal military draft was instituted, and all those who had not served earlier began to be taken in. In every separate case the calling of a mature man to the army did not raise suspicion that a big war was looming: every man must serve his country, so this or that Ivan had to do now what his friends did before.

Stalin had another tactic in reserve: according to the new law, the draft age was reduced from twenty-one to nineteen, and in some categories to eighteen.[8] My own father was among this group—he had just turned eighteen at the time.

The simultaneous draft of three age groups (never seen before), and the draft of all those who had not served earlier, placed a double burden on the shoulders of the nation. On the one hand, the economy was deprived of all these workers; on the other hand, they all had to be clothed, fed, equipped, and housed somewhere (try to find a place for at least one million new soldiers!). This was an explosive development of military might.

After 173,000 reservists were drafted in the second half of July 1939 to support the troops of the Trans-Baikal military district and the 1st Army Group in Mongolia, the Red

Army (without the navy interior troops or border guards) numbered 1,871,600 men. By June 22, 1941, the Red Army (again without the navy, interior troops, or border guards) numbered 5,081,000 men.[9]

The law adopted on September 1, 1939, allowed for an increase in the ranks of the Red Army from 1.5 million men in the spring of 1939 to 5.7 million in the spring of 1941 without declaring mobilization and alarming the neighbors.[10] Additionally, this law allowed for the preparation of 18 million reservists, so that at any moment they could fill the ranks with the desired number of soldiers.

This army development had a time limit, because Stalin called several age groups into the Red Army at the same time—in essence, all the young men in the country. The duration of army service for the majority of the population—privates in ground forces and NKVD (Political Police) forces—was two years, so the country had to enter a major war before September 1, 1941. If not, all the young people would go home on September 1, 1941, and then there would be almost nobody left to draft. All these new armies—assault and mechanized corps, tanks, air force, and all other divisions—would have to be disbanded. It is impossible to maintain an armed force of this size without a war: it does not produce anything and it consumes everything produced by the country. The creation of such an army could only lead to war. The modern Russian ministry of defense acknowledges this. "No nation can maintain a mobilized army with any intent other than war: the economy cannot stand the strain, and the mobilized but unused army begins to decay."[11] This was said about the mobilization conducted by Stalin starting on August 19, 1939.

When he made the decision to launch a secret mobilization, Stalin firmly knew that in two years, in the summer of 1941, the Soviet Union must enter into a large war. Without war, no terror could suffice to keep five million soldiers, who have already served their two required years, in their barracks. It would be impossible to retain them in the army after their terms in the army expired. To put it more simply, the decision to enter a large war was made in the Kremlin in August 1939 and the deadline for entering the war was set—the summer of 1941.

21

Mobilization of the Economy

A doctrine about war fought on enemy territory took hold during the prewar years, which was of a clearly aggressive nature.

—Colonel S. Vaupshassov, Hero of the Soviet Union

For many years, the People's Commissariat of Defense Industry was in charge of arms production in the USSR. On January 11, 1939, it was dismantled, and four new People's Commissariats were created instead: one for the shipbuilding industry, one for weapons, one for the aviation industry, and one for ammunition.

The Shipbuilding Commissariat was unofficially called the Submarines *Narkomat* (short for People's Commissariat). In theory, this commissariat produced both civilian and military ships. But in practice, the facts were such that "by 1935 all major shipyards were redesigned for production of military ships."[1] In 1939, Germany entered into World War II with fifty-seven submarines. We are assured that the Soviet Union had no intentions of entering into the war, but in September 1939 it possessed 165 submarines. The submarines matched up to the best world standards.[2] Some of the submarine designs were developed in Nazi Germany on Soviet orders by the company Deschimag AG Wesser. They say that Stalin trusted Hitler. They should look more carefully into who trusted whom.

In the Soviet Union, the most modern American technology and renowned American engineers were used in the process of submarine production. They say that Stalin was too trustful, but I think Roosevelt possessed more of that particular quality. Aside from American, German, British, Italian, and French accomplishments, the Soviet shipbuilding industry also made its own technological advances. We also had some talented engineers.

From the moment of its founding, the Shipbuilding Narkomat undertook strictly military projects. Moreover, many ships that had earlier been built for civilian needs were now armed and given over to the navy. With just one directive by the Soviet government, on May 25, 1940, the following numbers of civilian ships were handed over to the military: 74 to the Baltic fleet, 76 to the Black Sea fleet, 65 to the North fleet, and 101 to the Pacific fleet. At the same time, the shipyards of the Narkomat all began to operate on two extended shifts, which practically meant a regime of wartime production. The result of this was that by June 22, 1941, the Soviet Union possessed 218 submarines in its ranks and 91 more in shipyards.

Surface warships were also being built, as well as bought from abroad. For example, right before the war a ship of amazing gracefulness of form and an unusual coloring appeared on the Black Sea. People who did not know what type of ship this beauty was nicknamed it the "blue cruiser." In fact, the ship was a destroyer leader, not a cruiser. It was called the *Tashkent*. The *Soviet Military Encyclopedia* says of most noteworthy ships that they were "built at one of the domestic shipyards." However, this is not said about the *Tashkent*; only the year it was accepted into the fleet is mentioned—1940. The usual words are absent because the pride and beauty of the Black Sea fleet, the leader *Tashkent*, was built in fascist Italy and sold to Stalin.[3]

The *Tashkent* was purchased without weapons. Mussolini would have sold Stalin the weapons as well, but at that time there was nothing in the world that came remotely close to the Soviet 130-mm ship cannon. Therefore, the *Tashkent* was armed with Soviet cannon in the shipyards of Nikolaev.

Italy was not the only country that sold warships to Stalin. On May 31, 1940, the unfinished German cruiser *Lutsow*, renamed the *Petropavlovsk*, arrived in Leningrad and was delivered to the shipyard of shipbuilding plant #189. A cruiser is a huge and complex structure, the building of which would have taken several years to complete, and there was not enough time to introduce changes into its design and to equip it with Soviet weapons. It was decided to build it completely according to German designs and equip it with German weapons, and Germany supplied the weapons.

All this seems unbelievable: May 1940, the heat of the German blitzkrieg in Western Europe, the British fleet blockading the German navy. Hitler had only two options left— either to fight against Britain, for which he needed a powerful fleet, or to seek peace with Britain, for which he also needed a powerful fleet: an enraged Britain would obviously not negotiate with a weak Germany, but instead would demand its immediate withdrawal from all occupied territories. Hitler lagged far behind Britain in the number of above-water ships, and in this critical time he was selling his unfinished, most modern ship to Stalin!

Stalin's behavior is also surprising: he declared neutrality, but continued to build a gigantic fleet and, moreover, bought warships from countries already at war. The answer to this riddle is simple: in 1940 Germany was already suffering from a terrible deficit of raw materials because her naval routes were blockaded, so Hitler could only buy large enough quantities and assortments of materials from Stalin. In exchange for this, Hitler was forced to sell his technology and weaponry, including his newest planes, cannon, ships, communications devices, firearms, and so forth.

Stalin knew that the German economy was facing a crisis, and he could have chosen not to sell raw materials to Hitler. In that case, the war in Europe would have quickly died down. But Stalin wanted the war to gain strength, so that France, Britain, Germany, and all the other countries would expend themselves. Stalin planned to use their weakened position and establish his own regime in Europe. For this Stalin was building up his fleet, buying military technology from everywhere possible, and feeding Hitler the raw materials he needed.

Some might ask why Stalin's two hundred submarines and the rest of his navy could not give the kind of resistance that was to be expected from the most powerful underwater fleet in the world. The answer is simple—this was an attack fleet. It was an instrument created for aggressive warfare. It was very difficult, nearly impossible, to use it in defensive war. "During the course of the war the fleet had to solve problems that were completely unforeseen during its construction. Instead of coordinating their actions with the deep offensive operations of the ground forces, acting near the shores, as the military doctrine dictated, the fleet was forced to secure the naval bases under enemy attack from land and sea and to evacuate troops, population, and property from shoreline cities."[4]

In March 1939, at the Seventeenth Congress of the Communist Party, the commander of the Pacific fleet, 2nd Rank Flagman N. G. Kuznetsov declared: "The fleet must transform itself, and it will, just like the entire Worker-Peasant Red Army, into the most powerful attack fleet." Stalin rewarded him for such words by promoting him to People's Commissar of the Navy. Kuznetsov kept his word—he did his best in order to prepare the Soviet fleet to launch surprise attacks. But entirely different ships with entirely different characteristics are needed for defense: submarine hunters, picket boats, minesweepers, and net-layers. According to Kuznetsov's orders, all reserves of shells, mines, torpedoes, and ship fuel were transported to the German borders in Liepaja and to the Romanian borders in the river ports of the Danube. There, these reserves were quickly seized by the Germans. The port of Liepaja was located so close to the German border that the battles for the city had already begun on June 23, 1941.[5] Nobody had prepared to defend Liepaja from a land attack. Aside from everything else, in Liepaja were concentrated (and lost) three quarters of the Baltic fleet's fuel reserves.

Not only was the basing system of the Soviet navy geared toward aggressive warfare, and its personnel trained to attack, but the armament of the ships was designed exclusively for participation in a war of aggression. Soviet ships, while armed with powerful artillery, mine, and torpedo equipment, had quite weak anti-aircraft armament. The Soviet ships did not have powerful anti-aircraft defenses because Soviet generals had planned to begin the war with a crushing surprise air attack against the enemy's air bases and the annihilation of his aviation. Contrary to the plans, the war turned out to be of a defensive character, and the Soviet armies and fleets were not the ones to carry out the first attacks. The enemy had air superiority, and the Soviet troops and ships had very weak anti-aircraft defenses. The Shipbuilding Narkomat had been building ships with maximal attacking power and minimal defenses, in order to make the Soviet navy the most aggressive in the world.

The Aviation Narkomat also theoretically produced both military and civilian airplanes. But while it is possible to remember a dozen models of magnificent fighters, bombers, and assault planes, all produced in the tens of thousands, it is not so easy to think of the name of a single civilian aircraft. There was one airplane that, at some level, could be classified as a civilian model, but it was purchased from America, not created in the Soviet Union. This was the S-47, the best transport plane in the world. It was built according to the license to serve both as a passenger and as a paratroop-transporting aircraft. It was used in both the military and for civilian purposes, but for the sake of convenience—right at the factories during production—it was painted a camouflage green, so that it would not have to be repainted later.

The third organization in this family—the Weapons Narkomat—does not need to be explained, while the Ammunition Narkomat was something truly original that deserves some commentary. It was original because even during the course of the war all the countries that we are used to thinking of as most aggressive did not have a separate ministry in charge of ammunition. For example, in Germany even after the beginning of World War II only one minister was in charge of the production of weapons and ammunition, not two. The Soviet Union, in peacetime, had created a separate ministry to take care exclusively of the production of ammunition. Stalin's Ammunition Narkomat began to function immediately and fully.

Right from the start there was a problem to be solved: where to locate all the new factories that would be producing shells, gunpowder, cartridges, and so on. The issue of finding locations for the new ammunition industry entailed the issue of the character of the next war.

If Stalin had planned to carry out a sacred defensive war, if he planned to hold down his borders, the new ammunition factories should have been built behind the Volga River. There they would have been fully secure—the enemy tanks and airplanes could not reach so far inland. If Stalin was not sure of his strength, if, as we have been told, Stalin was afraid of Hitler and had reservations about the Red Army's ability to hold the borders, if there had been a belief that it might be forced to retreat—in that case the new factories should have been built not behind the Volga but even farther inland, in the Ural Mountains, where there are raw materials, a sufficient industry and energy base, and where the factories would have been completely secure. Let the enemy take huge territories, but our industrial base would remain whole—then Hitler would have a taste of what a wounded bear is like.

But neither the first nor the second option was even briefly discussed; there was no need for them. The Red Army had no plans to retreat, just as it had no plans of holding down the borders of its country. According to Stalin's plans, the Red Army had to advance forward into a war-devastated and weakened Europe. If the Red Army crossed the borders and advanced, the ammunition factories along with all the other ones (tank, artillery, etc.) would be left behind farther and farther in the rear. Let us imagine that the Red Army needs to be supplied with a small quantity of ammunition, for example 100,000 tons, or 200,000 tons. How could they be transported from the Urals to the western borders? A standard military train could carry nine hundred tons. Imagine how many trains would be needed, how many railroad cars, how many locomotives. Estimate how many workdays would be spent by all the railroad personnel, how much coal would be burned, how many train guards would be needed for how many days.

Aside from all this, it is important to remember that shells were not the only things that would have to be transported along the railroad lines. The railroads during war are crowded with troops, repair crews, hospitals, cisterns, and so on. In other words, if we prepare an attack, the transfer of hundreds of thousands of tons of ammunition and all other equipment has to be done in secret, and secrecy is best achieved by shortening the distance to be covered during the transfer. In an ideal situation, all factories would be located right at the borders. Then the trains would need to travel only a couple of hours, not days across the entire country. In that case, the demand for transportation decreases, and one train can be reused for several trips. This frees up the internal railroad lines for other military needs. So, it was decided to build the new ammunition factories closer to the borders, as close as the metal-forging bases permitted, and not behind the Volga or in the Urals. The locations chosen were Zaporozhie, Dnyepropetrovsk, Dnyeprodzerzhinsk, Kharkov, Krivoy Rog, and Leningrad.

The ammunition factories put out more and more production, while the voracious Ammunition Narkomat consumed the nation's metal resources, including copper, nickel, chromium, lead, tin, and mercury. The more nonferrous metals went to producing ammunition, the less there was left for all the other areas of industry. The question arose as to how long this could be expected to last.

There was another question: what to do with all the ammunition that was produced? All of us have had to solve math problems in school that began with something like: "Water pours from a pipe into a certain container, and simultaneously pours out through another pipe." Such problems can be found in mathematics textbooks from centuries ago as well, even in the famous math book written by Magnitsky that was used to teach children during the reign of Catherine the Second. Stalin and all the military leaders, politicians, and economists also were at some point schoolboys and solved problems that asked about the water running in through one pipe and out the other. In 1939 that was precisely the case that came about: the Red Army consumed a certain amount of ammunition for its military training, for the "wars of liberation," and for "international aid" to Mongolia and China. If the amounts of ammunition coming in and being spent were equal, there would be no problem. But if the supplies coming in were greater than the amount that was being used, then soon there would be no more room to hold all the supplies.

The holding capacity of the artillery storages was known, as was the amount of ammunition used by the army. Through a simple arithmetic calculation it would be easy to determine when there would be no more space to hold all that was produced. What could be done then? Should new storage facilities be created? That is not quite so simple. Imagine that you have been given the task to build storage facilities that are to hold one million tons of ammunition. If the humidity levels at the facility rise above the norm, the metals will be corroded and the gunpowder will become wet. What would comrade Stalin and his loyal disciple comrade Beria do to you in that case? And if the temperature rises slightly above the norm or if the air is slightly too dry . . . . The storages cannot be close together or close to cities and factories—they must be far away from everything that could be harmed by their explosion. To make it short, additional storage facilities are not a valid solution. No matter how many are built, they will become too full if more ammunition pours in than pours out—and more and more was pouring in every day.

Aside from the undertakings of the Ammunition Narkomat, 235 factories under the jurisdiction of other Narkomats were also used to produce various types of ammunition during peacetime.[6] And on top of all this, aside from the Ammunition Narkomat (which itself was huge) the chief directorate for construction of gunpowder, shell, cartridge, and missile factories was created in January 1941. This monster united under its control twenty-three construction areas. Note that all this was geared not toward building storage facilities but toward building new factories. The new directorate put up new factories with astonishing speed and gave them over to the Ammunition Narkomat. They now had to think of how to put to use all that they produced. In April 1941, an order came from the chief artillery directorate of the Red Army to transport the output of the Ammunition Narkomat to the western state borders and lay it on the ground. Ask anyone who has fought on the front what this means.

In the border regions of the Soviet Union the Red Army lost an unthinkable amount of artillery shells that were laid out on the ground. An equally unthinkable amount of shells was lost in railroad trains. In Byelorussia alone 4,216 railroad cars full of artillery shells were left at the border stations.[7] Why were shells kept in railroad cars? Where were they going to be taken? If defense was being prepared, the shells should have been issued to the troops. If retreat was prepared, there would have been no need to concentrate the shells in the border regions.

But this is not what is most important. The most important is the fact that at the very beginning of the war almost all industry capable of producing new ammunition was lost. "From August to November 1941, the German troops took 303 Soviet gunpowder, shell, and missile factories, which had a production capability of supplying 101 million artillery shells, 32 million mines, 24 million air bombs, [and] 3,600 tons of TNT. This constituted 85 percent of all output from the Ammunition Narkomat."[8] In addition to all this, the mobilization reserves of the most valuable raw materials were concentrated in those factories, including lead, forged steel, and tin. All this went to Germany and was used against the Red Army. But Stalin's prewar potential was so great that he was able to rebuild his industries during the course of the war behind the Volga River and in the Urals, and produce all that later was used to defeat the German army.

When the Ammunition Narkomat was created, nobody was posing a threat to the Soviet Union. Japan had a powerful air force and navy, but its land army was relatively small, and it was engaged in a rather unpromising war in China. Japan had limited reserves of raw materials. Soviet intelligence reported to the government that Japan could possibly decide to wage a large war in order to seize raw material sources, but the Japanese were primarily interested in those regions where the mining and purification of the materials was already set up, because Japan needed those resources immediately. In other words, Japan would fight to control the southern territories, and it would not venture into Siberia, where resources were unlimited but where their mining and purification would take several years and huge expenditures.

The Soviet General Staff, the government, and Stalin himself were not very afraid of German aggression in early 1939. There was no common border with Germany back then, so Germany could not attack suddenly. The creation of the Ammunition Narkomat in January 1939 could not be a response to German war preparations. Soviet intelligence knew that at that moment German industry was operating on a peacetime regime. In June 1939 the chief of the GRU, Ivan Proskurov, reported to Stalin that Germany was unprepared for a large-scale war: if Germany invaded Poland, it would use up its air-bomb supplies within ten days. Germany had no reserves.

After the war, the book *Results of World War II* came out in Germany. Field Marshal K. Kesselring, Colonel General H. Guderian, Colonel General L. Rendulic, Lieutenant General E. Schneider, Admiral E. Godt, and others were among the authors of the book. When comparing the analysis made by Soviet intelligence and the actual events, we must acknowledge that Soviet military intelligence was mistaken. The German supply of bombs ran out not after ten days of war, but on the fourteenth day after the attack against Poland.

Apparently the best studies of the development of the German army during the reign of the Third Reich were done by Major General B. Muller-Gillebrand.[9] The general said that in 1939 the German High Command of the land troops demanded that a reserve of ammunition be created that could last for four months of war. However, such reserves were never created. If a four-month supply is taken as 100 percent, then there was in actuality only 30 percent of pistol cartridge reserves, enough for 36 days of war; 15 percent of ammunition for mountain guns; 12 percent of mortar shells for light mortars, and 10 percent for heavy ones. The best supplies were for the heavy field howitzers—there were enough shells to last for two months of war. The worst case was with the tank shells. In September 1939 the main tank of the German *Wehrmacht* was the Pz-II, equipped with 20-mm cannon. There was only 5 percent of the needed supply of shells required for four months of war, meaning only enough for six days of combat.[10]

Despite all this, Hitler was not eager to mobilize the country's industry toward war. The German army waged a war, which began as a European conflict and turned global, but German industry remained operating on a peacetime regime.

For fifty years the Soviet government has been persuading us that in 1939 war was unavoidable, the world was headed for war, and Stalin could do nothing but sign a non-aggression pact with Germany. An analysis of the conditions of German industry in general, and in the area of ammunition production in particular, allows us to assert that the situation was not at all so critical. The world was not headed for inevitable war, and a war could have been averted, if Stalin had wanted to avert it. And what is more, if in September 1939 the Red Army had intervened on the side of Poland, Stalin would not have lost anything, while Hitler could have suffered a devastating defeat simply because he did not have enough ammunition. But Stalin did not capitalize on the German weakness.

When the war began, the German situation regarding ammunition did not improve, but in May 1940 Hitler delivered a fatal blow to France. There were enough shells and missiles to carry out the attack, but if Stalin had attacked Germany in 1940, there would have been nothing left for Germany to use in fending off his attack, because her industries had still not been mobilized. After this followed the Battle of Britain, and once again the German air force was engaged in a war but German industry was not. Then Hitler invaded the Soviet Union. Here, he had tremendous luck—at the very border he was able to take huge quantities of Soviet supplies. Without these supplies he would not have been able to reach Moscow.

The seizure of Stalin's supplies was a tremendous achievement for Hitler, but he had to also think of shifting his own industry to a wartime regime. Hitler, however, was in no hurry to do this. The war in Russia was serious business, and the German army had to spend more shells than ever before. The production of ammunition did not in any way correspond to the expenditures required by the army. Major General B. Muller-Hillebrand cites entire pages of clear-cut statistics. Here are some figures randomly chosen from many thousands like them. In October 1941, the German army engaged in ferocious battles with the Red Army and used 561,000 75-mm shells, while the industry during that period produced only 75,000 of those shells. In December, 494,000 were used and 18,000 received from the factories.[11]

This could not have lasted for very long. But Hitler was in no hurry.

In December 1941, Stalin carried out powerful attacks against the German army near Moscow. In December, Hitler declared war on the United States of America. It would seem to be the perfect time to shift industry from a peacetime to a wartime regime. But Hitler still waited. Only in January 1942 did he make the decision to gradually begin the shift of German industry to fulfill wartime needs. The difference between Stalin and Hitler was that Hitler first waged a war against the entire world, fought for over two years—and only then began to mobilize his industries. Stalin, on the other hand, acted in the exact opposite manner. Stalin tried with all his powers to delay the moment when the Soviet Union would have to enter into the war, but he began mobilizing the industries and setting them on a wartime regime back in January 1939.

During the course of World War II, the Red Army had the most powerful artillery in the world. The artillery was used correctly, meaning that it was secretly concentrated in masses on narrow strips of territory and used in sudden, intense strikes. In the Stalingrad operation, the Don front under Lieutenant General K. K. Rokossovsky broke through defenses on a narrow strip of land—only twelve kilometers. Here, besides the tanks, twenty-four rifle regiments supported by thirty-six artillery regiments led the breakthrough. Rokossovsky concentrated 135 guns on every kilometer, and 167 weapons per kilometer in the primary locations. During the course of the war, the concentration of artillery, tanks, infantry, and aviation constantly increased. By the end of the war, the Soviet staffs began to use kilotons as units of measurement for calculating the power of artillery attacks. Soviet artillery began to speak the language of the atomic age.

In the Vistula-Oder operation, the Soviet command used 34,500 guns and mortars. They were not evenly distributed throughout the force, but rather concentrated on the strips where the breakthrough was to occur. In the strip covered by the 3rd Guards Army, the concentration reached 420 weapons per kilometer. During the course of the war, the duration of artillery softening-up constantly shrank, while artillery power grew. In the same operation, in the area covered by the 5th Shock Army, the duration of softening-up was planned to be reduced to 55 minutes.[12] It began well, but after 25 minutes it was ended. Twenty-three thousand tons of ammunition was used during the 25 minutes, and 15,200 shells of medium and large caliber were used on each kilometer of that front. Penal battalions marched through the breakthrough and did not meet any opposition. Their actions confirmed that additional softening-up was not necessary, nobody would offer any opposition. This saved thirty minutes of time (very significant in war) and thirty thousand tons of ammunition.

Even more artillery was used in the Berlin operation—over 42,000 guns and mortars. Along the breakthrough areas, huge quantities of ammunition were concentrated, as well as huge quantities of weapons. Marshal Ivan Konev broke through thirty-six kilometers of front line, and used 8,626 weapons to do it. Marshal Zhukov concentrated fewer arms—7,318 guns and mortars—but broke through thirty kilometers of front line, so he actually had higher concentrations of artillery. The main forces of the tank and air force armies were also gathered in these areas, as well as corresponding amounts of infantry.

The record was set in the area occupied by the 381st Rifle Division of the 2nd Shock Army, during the course of the East Prussian operation: 468 guns and mortars on one kilometer of front line, not counting the Katyusha salvo-fire installations. During the course of the war the Red Army used 427 million shells and artillery mines and 17 billion cartridges. Just divide this by the number of German soldiers and determine how many shells that makes per soldier. To this you can add the number of hand grenades, land mines, and air bombs. Who could resist such a mighty army?

Here we must also remember that in the war the Soviet Union used only 15 percent of the prewar potential of the Ammunition Narkomat; all the rest was lost during the early periods of the war. Hitler's surprise attack not only annihilated tens of divisions of the Red Army and destroyed the strategic reserves; he also occupied the territories where the newest ammunition factories were located. The Red Army destroyed its own factories or simply abandoned them as it retreated. Some machines were evacuated, but try to move at least one furnace for thousands of kilometers. . . . Try to transport even one thousand tons of ammunition from the border forests to the railroad stations, load them into trains, and evacuate them under enemy fire.

Hitler delivered a surprise blow to Stalin. Stalin lost almost all his ammunition factories. He had to fight back using only 15 percent of the might of the Ammunition Narkomat.[13] The results of the war are well known. Try to imagine what could have happened if Hitler had stalled with his attack and would have, instead, himself been attacked by Stalin. In that case, Stalin would have been using not 15 percent of his ammunition, but the full 100 percent. What would the outcome of World War II have been then?

22

The Winter War: Finland

The Red Army will consider its Bolshevik mission complete when it achieves control of the entire globe.

—Jan Gamarnik, Chief of the Political Directorate of the Red Army, in a speech given at a meeting of the National Committee for Defense of the USSR on March 15, 1937

In October of 1939, immediately after the division of Poland between Germany and the Soviet Union, Stalin's diplomats addressed the government of Finland, demanding the cession of the Karelian Isthmus.[1] In exchange, they offered the Finns a piece of territory twice the size of the isthmus. Upon first glance, the proposition seems alluring—Finland sacrifices 2,761 square kilometers, and receives 5,528 square kilometers in return. However, the proposition was not alluring, but rather contemptuous. The Karelian Isthmus is a direct gateway to the capital of Finland, the largest ports and most populated regions. The geographical disposition of Finland is such that any aggression could come only from the Soviet Union, and only through the Karelian Isthmus. Precisely for this reason, the Finnish army, starting in 1918 (after winning its independence fighting against Russian and local Bolshevik troops during the Russian civil war), began an extensive buildup of defenses on the Karelian Isthmus. Starting in 1929, the scope of the buildup expanded significantly. On the Karelian Isthmus emerged a solid strip of fortifications and obstructions, which became known as the Mannerheim Line, named for the country's commander-in-chief, who had won the war of independence in 1918. Finland spent practically all of her military budget for the ten years preceding the war on the creation of this line of fortifications. Military experts from all countries of the world unanimously agreed that no army, taking any amount of time, could break through the Mannerheim Line. Nevertheless, Stalin's envoys demanded from Finland the cession of her main and only defense structure, meaning they wanted the Finns to put down their arms and hand over to the Red Army, without a fight, the road to their country's unprotected internal regions—well developed and heavily populated. In exchange, they were offering a huge piece of swampland and marshy woods, in which no one lived and which no one needed.

The "exchange" of territories was the first step in the plan. Stalin had prepared a second step as well—a revolution in Finland and takeover by the Communists. Already in October 1939 the 106th Rifle Division of the Red Army was supplemented with Finnish Communists who lived in the Soviet Union.[2] When necessary, this division could be declared the "national army of Finland" and used as a weapon against the legal government. Stalin had prepared a new Communist "government" as well, which was strengthened with officers from the NKVD and the military intelligence. This "government" could at any moment, in accordance with "the will of the Finnish people," be sent to Helsinki. Stalin had started the formation of this "government" already in June 1939. He decided to appoint Division Commander A. Anttila of the Red Army to the position of "minister of defense." Down the road, the same man became a major general in the Soviet army. In the plans, the future "minister of the interior" of Finland was an operator of the NKVD, T. Lekhen. At the head of the "government," Stalin had put the Soviet intelligence officer Otto Kuusinen. Conveniently, Kuusinen was also appointed as "minister of foreign affairs."

Kuusinen had already once been the member of a Communist government in Finland. In 1918, he had created the Communist party of Finland using Soviet money, and had tried to stage a coup. After his plans for a government turnover failed, he spent over a year in the country underground and conducted intensive terrorist activity against Finland in the interests of the World Revolution. After his cover was blown, he fled to the Soviet Union. In 1921 Kuusinen entered the ranks of the highest officials of the Comintern and became one of the leaders of the World Revolution. In 1937 Stalin mercilessly cleansed the Comintern, and a large majority of the leaders were executed. Kuusinen, for some particularly useful service, escaped execution and in 1941 he became a member of the Central Committee of the Communist Party of the Soviet Union (CPSU). In 1952 he became a member of the Presidium of the Central Committee of the CPSU, meaning he entered the most elite group of leaders of the Soviet Union.

Kuusinen's wife, Aino, was an intelligence agent for the General Staff of the Red Army. From 1931 to 1933 she was in the United States illegally, and from 1934 was in Japan working with Richard Sorge. In 1938 Stalin ordered her to return to the Soviet Union and threw her in jail.[3] And so, this Communist Otto Kuusinen made preparations for delivering freedom and happiness to the Finns, while his own wife roted in Stalin's jail, and Stalin could at any moment either raise him to the highest leadership position in the USSR or place him before a firing squad.

Three months before the start of the war in Finland, in August of 1939, the Red Army in a surprise attack obliterated the Japanese Sixth Army in Mongolia. Logic would lead us to the conclusion that if the Red Army had the capacity to destroy an entire Japanese field army, Finland could not possibly present any difficulties. Stalin knew the strength of the Red Army, and was certain that Finland would accede without a fight to all his demands. For this reason he did not conduct any serious preparations for war. However, the people and the government of Finland turned out to be unwilling to bend to Stalin's requests.

Stalin issued an order to crush Finland. For an attack, the Soviets needed a pretext. As if on demand, on November 26, 1939, seven artillery shells allegedly flew in from the Finnish side and exploded on the Soviet side, killing three privates and one junior officer.[4] Finland's government declared that no shell could have come from Finnish territory, because Finland had no artillery near the border. Finland furthermore declared immediate willingness to invite experts from neutral countries or to create a joint committee of Finnish and Soviet experts for further investigation of the incident. But Stalin did not need any investigation. Since Finland "attacked" the Soviet Union, the Red Army must "strike in retaliation."

On November 30, 1939, after a brief but intense artillery softening-up, the Red Army crossed the Finnish border, having as its objective taking Helsinki by December 21, 1939—Stalin's sixtieth birthday. The main strike was carried out on the Karelian Isthmus; secondary strikes were carried out along the entire Finnish-Soviet border, from the Baltic Sea to the Barents Sea. Radio Moscow declared that the Finnish people rose up against capitalists and the Red Army was heading forward to assist the uprising. Units of the Red Army occupied the small village of Terioki. Immediately, Kuusinen's "government" arrived from Moscow to this village and went to work. All the "ministers" of the new Communist Finland for some reason spoke Russian. Kuusinen's son kept the records and protocols, also in Russian. The "government" established diplomatic ties with the USSR on December 1, and on December 2 it signed an "agreement on mutual help and friendship between the Soviet Union and the Finnish Democratic Republic." The agreement was signed by comrades Molotov and Kuusinen and printed in two copies, but in only one language—Russian. Comrade Kuusinen also signed in Russian, using the Cyrillic alphabet.

However, a victory march on Helsinki did not happen. The Mannerheim Line was not located on the immediate border, but deeper in the territory behind the "security pale." This pale was a strip of land that started at the border and stretched from twenty-five to sixty-five kilometers deep into Finnish territory.[5] The security pale was a strip of land full of traps, barricades, obstacles, and minefields. The entire space was filled with granite boulders and concrete blocks, forest blockages, scarps and counterscarps, and anti-tank trenches. In this strip for many years, on purpose, there had been no industrial or transportation buildup. Finland did not keep any large military formations or any large amounts of supplies here. All existing bridges on this strip were wired with explosives and ready to be blown up or burned, along with everything else in sight, by the Finnish border patrol in the event of retreat.

The security pale is a kind of shield used by the defending side against the aggressor. When trapped in this line, the aggressor loses speed of movement, and his troops sustain casualties even before encountering the main forces of the enemy. In this territory the defending side employs only small but very mobile units. The units burst out from under cover, carry out sudden attacks, and quickly retreat to new positions, which were prepared beforehand. These light squads try to pass themselves off as the main forces of their army. The aggressor is forced to stop, turn his troops, and spend shells on empty spaces, while these light squads of the enemy have already quickly and covertly retreated and are preparing ambushes in new positions.

Upon finding himself in the security line, the aggressor loses his most significant advantage—surprise. While the aggressor carries out an exhausting struggle against the light defense squads, the main forces of the defending side have time to achieve full readiness and meet the aggressor in convenient positions. Finland's army acted exactly in this manner. The deeper the security pale stretches, the better for the defense. There can never be too much of a good thing. While breaking through a deep security pale, the aggressor involuntarily shows the main thrust and direction of his movements. Losing the element of surprise, the aggressor himself becomes its victim—the depth of the security pale is unknown to him, so the encounter with the main forces of the defenders occurs at a moment previously unknown to the aggressor, but well planned by the defense.

On the Karelian Isthmus and on other sections of the security pale, Finnish snipers and light mobile squads were fully active and operating to the best of their capacity. Here is a standard situation: a column of Soviet tanks, motorized infantry, and artillery is moving along a forest road. To their left and to their right there is nowhere to go—impassable woods, packed with land mines. Ahead of them is a bridge. The Soviet demolition experts check for mines and come back reporting that the way is clear. The first tanks begin to crawl onto the bridge—and together with the bridge they fly up into the air: packs of dynamite had been inserted into the supporting beams of the bridge during its construction; they are undetectable, and even if they had been discovered, any attempt to diffuse them would have triggered an explosion. Thus, the Soviet column, many kilometers in length, like a giant snake, is stopped in its path. Now, the Finnish snipers spring into action. They take their time. Bang, bang, bang, and once again the forest is silent. And again, bang, bang. The snipers strike from somewhere far away. They hit only Red Army officers and tow-truck drivers. A diversion through the forest is not an option—keep in mind that on both sides of the road lie impenetrable minefields. Any attempt by the Soviet demolition experts to approach the destroyed bridge or to defuse the mines is met by a prompt and accurate response by the Finnish snipers.

The 44th Rifle Division of the Soviet Red Army, which had been advancing four hundred kilometers north of the Karelian Isthmus, was locked in place on three parallel roads which led to three blown-up bridges. In one day of fighting, the division lost practically its entire commanding staff. The same was true in other divisions—the columns became immobile, and could not take a step back or a step forward. At night, the columns suffered brief surprise attacks from somewhere far away in the woods. At night, the Finns fired out a couple of rounds of shells at a time from their concealed positions in the bushes, hitting the defenseless ranks. Then again all became quiet, until the next round.

It is said that the Red Army did not show its best side in Finland. This is true. But let us imagine in place of the Soviets a division from any other army. What can they do in such a situation? Pull back their columns? Heavy artillery and tractors with huge howitzers in tow cannot pull back. Finnish snipers hit tractor drivers, one by one. With tremendous difficulty, inch by inch, the column manages to crawl backwards; meanwhile, behind them another bridge explodes. The column is locked in. All the paths that lead to that other bridge are also blocked by mines, and the snipers there are also taking their time and hitting, one by one, commanders, sappers who try to disarm land mines, and drivers. Far ahead is the practically impenetrable line of concrete fortifications—the Mannerheim Line. To break through this line without artillery and thousands of tons of ammunition is impossible. . . . Soviet troops reached the Finnish fortifications, but their heavy artillery was far behind, bogged down between minefields and blown-up bridges, and under fire. In total, during their retreat on the Karelian Isthmus the subdivisions of the Finnish army destroyed 143 bridges and viaducts.

As a result of these actions, it took the Red Army two weeks to pass through the security pale. After this, the divisions of the Red Army reached the main line of defense, having already suffered heavy losses, with a broken morale and without ammunition, fuel, or supplies.

Their maneuvering capability was strictly limited: any step off the main path could become the last step. The rear had lagged behind and was constantly under threat of repeated attack by the light squads of Finnish soldiers, who had flawlessly memorized the area and knew secret safe passages through all the minefields.

Having overcome the security pale, the Red Army found itself halted by the fortifications of the Mannerheim Line. The line was in fact a brilliantly camouflaged defense structure, well integrated into the surroundings, and stretching 135 km in width and up to 30 km in depth. Its right flank met the shore of the Baltic Sea; its left flank bordered Lake Ladoga. All in all, the Mannerheim Line counted 2,311 concrete, ironclad, and wooden defense structures. The fighting on the Mannerheim Line was especially tenacious. The Red Army succeeded in breaking through the Mannerheim Line only on March 12, 1940, in the process sustaining colossal casualties, in both men and arms: 126,875 soldiers and officers were either killed in action, or disappeared without a trace, or died from wounds and disease. Additionally, the army counted 188,671 wounded, 58,370 ill, and 17,867 frostbitten.[6]

On March 13, 1940, the war between Finland and the Soviet Union was ended. The war lasted 105 days and became known as the Winter War. The Soviet Union received the Karelian Isthmus, but Finland kept her independence.

The whole world was shocked by the unbelievable weakness of the Red Army. The giant Soviet Union could not take care of Finland, whose population was only slightly more than 3.5 million. All around the world, newspapers were filled with caricatures and reports of the Soviet Union's utter lack of readiness for any war, no matter how small.

A conviction arose among military men, writers, historians, and politicians that the Red Army had demonstrated in Finland complete and utter lack of capacity to wage war. For many decades this idea has been taught in military academies, schools, and universities. However, the actions of the Red Army during the Winter War do not demonstrate weakness. They exhibit tremendous strength. First of all, it is necessary to keep in mind that the Red Army acted in conditions that no army had previously faced. It was conducting an attack in an average temperature of 21 to 24 degrees Celsius below zero. Sometimes it was warmer, but frequently it was colder. On the very first night of the war, the temperature was registered at minus 39 degrees Celsius. Some nights had been even colder. Action was taking place not only on the Karelian Isthmus, but also a thousand kilometers to the north, up to the Arctic Circle and even farther. The cold there was even more severe. Not a single army in the world had conducted an offensive operation, even a failed one, under a temperature of minus 20 degrees Celsius. In such temperatures, no one had even attempted to conduct massive attacks, because it is impossible. Nevertheless, the Red Army conducted successful offensive operations in temperatures of minus 30 degrees Celsius and colder. Stalin ordered the army to act in impossible conditions, and the Red Army did the impossible.

How did the Finns defend themselves in those conditions?

Defense is a whole different story. For twenty years, practically Finland's entire military budget went to funding the creation of fortifications on the Karelian Isthmus. Beyond the infinite minefields, the anti-tank trenches and granite obstacles, the concrete tetrahedrons, and the wire obstacles that stretched in rows of ten, twenty, and thirty, there was a place marked on the map as "hill 65.5," protected by forty-seven rows of thick barbwire on metal stakes, connected to mines. In the last rows of barbwire, instead of stakes railroad tracks had been driven into the ground. Behind these rows of barricades were concrete casemates. Each major defensive construction stored ammunition and fuel, contained warm sleeping quarters, a restroom, a kitchen, a dining room, and had running water and electricity. Communication lines, command posts, hospitals—all were below ground, under concrete, in the woods, hidden in the snow, all in warmth. The snipers who spent days waiting for their victims, and the soldiers of the light ski squads which raided the rear of the Red Army, were warmly clad and well equipped. Finnish soldiers are born, raised, and trained to act in these conditions. They know that, after several days of active patrol or ski raids, they will return to their comfortable bunkers, where a bowl of hot soup waits for them and where they can rest before their next assignment. They know that in the event that they are wounded, an operating table well below the ground awaits them, along with a clean, dry, and warm hospital bed.

But try attacking under these conditions. Try to amputate a leg when beyond the thin cloth wall of the hospital tent the temperature is minus 40, and inside it is minus 30.

In addition to the cold, there was the snow. The depth of the snow cover was up to 1.5 meters. Even if the temperature had been warmer, but the snow cover the same, conducting offensive operations would still have been impossible. Under the snow were the swamps. Deep snow acts as insulation, so the swamps do not freeze. Furthermore, chemical reactions take place in the swamps and radiate heat. As a result, even in the most severe cold, people, cars, and tanks fall under the snow and drown in the marshes. But even this is not all. There are not only swamps, but also lakes. Many of them also do not freeze, and for the same reason: where there is no snow, the water freezes to the bottom, but where there is a thick snow cover, the ice is very thin, and can perhaps support a person, but not a tank. Finland is a land of a thousand lakes, but how can you tell what is a lake and what is a field? Everything around was white, fluffy, sparkling. "The theater of operations consisted of 50 percent woodlands, 25 percent water, some swampland, and only about 10 percent of the total surface could be crossed by tanks."[7]

On top of everything, under the snow were granite boulders. To the eye, the fields looked even under the snow. But as soon as the tanks tried to cross them, they ripped their tracks and broke their rollers. This happened even before they reached the minefields. The whole environment in Finland is one big anti-tank measure. Tanks cannot do anything here. Everywhere is either a field full of boulders, or a lake, or an impassible thicket of a forest. And all this is laced with millions of mines. A mistake can be made, but only once.

During the 105 days of the war, there were twenty-five days of flying weather. The rest of the time, blizzards or snowfall impeded flight. In December, there are very few daylight hours. Complete darkness falls at four o'clock. And farther north the day is even shorter, if there is any daytime at all. Any place where trees can grow, there is impenetrable forest. Tanks cannot do anything in the woods; artillery fire cannot be aimed in such thicket. There is no visible horizon. The observer cannot see where his shells go—he can hear them fly above his head, but he cannot see where they land. From the battery he hears yells: Too close? Too far? Who can tell? The only view of where the shells land is from the very field these shells land on. On the other hand, the Finnish artillery had always fought in these regions. Every battery had during years of peace drilled in these areas, and the aimers, observers, and commanders knew by heart the data for precision shelling.

And so, the Soviet artillery was pretty useless, the tanks were useless, for this environment is not for tanks. The air force also could not help, for it could not see anything. A tactics manual teaches: "From above, the forest resembles an even surface, and to locate troops in a forest is a rare occurrence." Under normal conditions, it is difficult to pick out enemy troops in a thick forest. But here, there was nothing to pick out—the Finns were under the snow, underground. In the daylight, the smoke from their stoves could be observed only where they wanted it to be seen, in decoy locations. But where is this daylight anyway?

The advancing armies could not go underground, because in December in Finland the frozen ground is little different from granite. And the wounded did not need to be dragged to the hospital, because in such extreme cold the wounded froze to death even with relatively light blood loss. In 1944 the German Colonel General L. Rendulic fought in the same regions:

> In this forested and rocky zone the trees grow on disorderly piles of rock, which often reach as high as the average person, and even higher. During the first reconnaissance ventures, I sometimes attempted to stray from the path and penetrate the forest, but was rarely successful. Most often this was possible only in a crawling fashion, on all fours. . . . Movement through the rocks and between them is an extremely exhausting occupation. Only on rare occasions was it possible to go around the rocks. Any movement by car, even after the forest had been cleared, was out of the question. Even pack animals cannot pass through. . . . Movement of troops and conduction of warfare in formations, applied in the usual settings, are completely inappropriate here. The region of marshlands and swampy forests is equally covered with trees. Movement through those areas is even more difficult than through the rocky-forested area.[8]

This impenetrable region was further fortified by obstacles, and anti-infantry and anti-tank devices. Manmade obstacles were worked into the natural surroundings with great skill. Streams and small rivers crisscrossed the region and had high cliffs for shores. The shores were scarped. All bridges were blown up. All paths leading to the bridges were mined and under constant fire by the snipers. Behind all this was the main defense line, seven to twelve kilometers in depth.

But we know all this only now. Back then, the Soviet command knew none of this. Behind the main line they once again found fortifications and another security pale, and again minefields, barricades, and another fortified line.

The walls of the defense structures were concrete, one and a half to two meters thick. The above-ground walls were covered by armored plates, and all this was buried under multi-ton granite boulders and covered with soil. All was camouflaged and hidden. Above these casemates rose tall, thick pine forests, which in turn were covered with snow. Machine gunners, riflemen, and artillerymen were sitting behind the steel and concrete fortifications. Deep embrasures dimmed the flashes of fire and dulled the bangs. The Finns fired at point-blank range, while the advancing troops thought they were under long-range fire.

The Finns used cement of the brand "600" in the construction of their fortifications. For every cubic meter of concrete, they used 95 kilograms of steel armature. Here are the results: Soviet 280-mm mortar guns and 203-mm howitzers fired directly on the Finnish strongpoint named "pillbox #0031." They used specially designed ammunition for firing on concrete. A 203-mm shell for the B-4 howitzer weighs 100 kg.[9] The 280-mm shell for the B-5 mortar weighs 246 kg. There were 1,043 of the 203-mm shells and 116 of the 280-mm ones fired at the pillbox #0031. Only after this did the pillbox cease to resist attack. One hundred and thirty-two tons of shells for one pillbox!

Let us imagine preparations for the shelling of this pillbox. First of all, it must be located—this costs many human lives. Then one has to approach the pillbox through mine-fields and other obstacles. This also costs many human lives. Then, under constant fire from the pillbox, one must calculate and prepare positions for one's arms, and then secure them in these positions. The 203-mm howitzer weighs 17.7 tons in battle-ready position, and 19 tons in travel-ready position. The 280-mm mortar gun weighs 18.4 tons and 19.7 tons, respectively. They must be taken apart and towed by tractors on the small country roads and roadless terrain, since the pillbox is never located on a major road. During the transportation, the assembly process, and the positioning, these giants are extremely vulnerable. Then it is necessary to bring in the shells. The net weight of the ammunition used to shell one pillbox #0031 was 132,836 kilograms. But the shells are stored in secure wooden crates, which create additional weight. Boxes weighing 200 to 300 kg must be loaded onto trucks and brought to the firing positions on narrow dirt roads. Here, they must be unloaded. And this is only the shells. There are also the charges. Several tens of kilograms of gunpowder are needed in order to push a shell of such mass from the barrel. In a weapon of such caliber the charges are separate, and instead of cartridges one must use powder bags—silk sacks full of gunpowder that catch flame when used. Several tens of tons of gunpowder in silk bags constitute a very capricious and extremely dangerous cargo. Transportation and storage of this cargo is a very delicate, labor-intensive, and risky occupation.

If during the shelling of the pillbox #0031 the 203-mm howitzer fired one shot every two minutes,[10] then for 1,043 shots they needed 2,086 minutes, or almost thirty-five hours. But firing constantly without breaks is impossible. One can only shoot during daylight, or it is impossible to correctly direct the fire. But perhaps the pillbox #0031 was under fire from an entire battery, not just a lonely howitzer? These weapons are so huge and cumbersome that one battery only has two of them. One battalion has three batteries—six howitzers. If the shelling comes indeed from a battery or from an entire artillery battalion the time needed to take down the pillbox diminishes. But then other difficulties appear: it is one thing to set up one howitzer in a good firing position, a whole different story if one needs to set up two, or six. Plus, the 280-mm mortar guns are nearby and firing away. It becomes very simple for the enemy to detect the firing positions of these giant weapons. These monsters, when in firing position, are extremely vulnerable to all fire.

Furthermore, the barrel of the 203-mm howitzer weighs five tons. At the moment it fires, a giant shell instantly accelerates to a speed of 607 meters per second. The barrel undergoes tremendous heat and dynamic stress. It can quickly overheat, to the point that all firing needs to be stopped. Additionally, the barrel wears out quickly and often needs to be replaced. All this is involved in shelling just one pill-box #0031.

The shelling of Finnish pillboxes was not always as successful as the case described here. Against the pillbox #0011, the Soviets unleashed 1,322 shells from 203-mm howitzers and 280-mm mortars—almost two hundred tons. The pillbox was partially damaged, but even after this it continued to resist. Sometimes, at the cost of much blood, Soviet combat engineers crawling under crossfire made their way to the Finnish pillboxes and attempted to blow them up. They discovered that a charge carrying 5,500 kg of explosives was not sufficient for blowing up a pillbox.[11]

From April 14 to April 17, 1940, in Stalin's presence, the Kremlin assembled a council of the supreme command staff to discuss the events of the Winter War and share opinions. It

was decided that the 203-mm howitzer did not have enough power to destroy such constructions as the pillboxes. To solve this kind of problem a 305-mm howitzer was needed.[12] For the
record: the 1939 model of the Soviet 305-mm howitzer B-18 weighed 45.7 tons, and a shell
for it weighed 330 kg. The initial speed of the shell was 530 m/s. The maximum distance the
shells could be fired was 16.6 km. Only such "monster-weapons" were suited for the destruction of the Finnish defenses.

The military experts of the West should have recognized the amazing warfare capabilities of the Red Army and the fallacy of their assumptions. From the actions in Finland,
there could be only one logical conclusion: nothing is impossible for the Red Army. If it
was capable of advancing in such conditions, then it was capable of advancing in any other
conditions—there could be no worse conditions than those in Finland in the winter. If the
Red Army had broken through the Mannerheim Line, then it was ready to crush Europe and
whoever got in the way. In Finland the Red Army proved that it could accomplish any task,
even an "impossible" one. The victorious Red Army accomplished what the strategists of the
West had deemed unfeasible. But the strategists did not accept the fallacy of their predictions.
Instead they declared the Red Army to be unfit and unprepared for war.

However, all who had followed the developments of the Winter War did not pay attention to certain inconsistencies. The first strange thing happened on March 12, 1940, after the
Red Army broke through the Mannerheim Line. After this, a completely defenseless Finland
spread out before it. Finland could now be taken by bare hands, like a turtle whose shell has
been ruptured. But the Red Army, having broken through the impenetrable defense system
of the Finns, stopped its advance. Why? In December 1939, already having premonitions of
the strength of the Mannerheim Line, the Red Army should have stopped its advance and
not gone to storm it. But if the Red Army did storm the line and, at the cost of unimaginable
casualties, managed to break through it, it should have used what it gained. Stalin broke into
the safe, but then did not take anything from it. Where was Stalin's logic?

The second inconsistency: all leading military experts before the Winter War declared
that breaking through the Mannerheim Line could not be done by any army. The Red Army
did the impossible. Furthermore, it broke through the line impromptu, for it had not prepared for such limiting conditions. The Red Army broke through the line in only three
months, when all the military experts of the West had maintained that it could not be done in
any time frame. And now, all of a sudden these same experts began talking of the Red Army
being completely unfit for war.

The third inconsistency: the first and loudest reports of the Red Army's poor performance in Finland came in newspapers funded by Stalin. Stalin's court poet, Alexander
Tvardovsky, suddenly began speaking of the "infamous war." For some reason he was not
executed. For some reason, he was awarded Stalin's praises. Stalin was wise enough to end his
"liberation crusade" after the Mannerheim Line was broken and Finland was deprived of her
security barrier.

Military operations in Finland were ended on March 13, 1940, and only three months
later the three Baltic states, Estonia, Lithuania, and Latvia, surrendered to Stalin without a
fight and became republics of the Soviet Union. The governments and military leadership of
these countries had carefully watched the war in Finland and drew from their observations
a frightening, but correct conclusion: the Red Army was capable of carrying out impossible
orders, and it would not be stopped by any number of casualties. If Stalin commanded the

Red Army to annihilate somebody, it would sustain whatever losses it took to accomplish the order. Therefore, the three states surrendered without firing a single shot. They understood that resistance was futile. Meanwhile, Stalin issued an ultimatum to the leadership of Romania: give up Bessarabia. Remembering the experience of Finland, the Romanian government did not even organize lengthy talks: it handed over Bessarabia, and on top of it Northern Bukovina.

The Red Army conducted in Finland a unique and unparalleled operation. The Red Army performed in a fashion unrivaled and unrepeated by any army in history, but for some reason Hitler concluded that it had performed poorly. German generals were watching wonders unfold before their eyes, but did not understand the significance of what they were seeing. German generals were unable to appreciate what they observed. Thus, the people surrounding and counseling Hitler made strange deductions concerning Stalin's readiness for war. Goebbels's diary from those days is full of remarks of this sort: "November 11, 1939: The Russian army presents no value. The army is poorly commanded, and it is even more poorly armed. . . . December 4, 1939: The Russian Army is of little value. . . . January 23, 1940: The military strength of Moscow is almost insignificant."[13] Goebbels wrote down not only his own opinion, but also Hitler's: "He once again notes the catastrophic state of the Russian army. It can hardly be used for military action."[14]

For the Red Army, the war in Finland was a vaccine against hubris, boastful dispositions, and underestimating the enemy. The war in Finland taught the Red Army a lot: in 1941 near Moscow and in 1942 near Stalingrad, German troops met the Red Army, which by then knew how to fight in the winter. The German army, however, was not at all taught by the war in Finland. This war played a dirty trick on Hitler. He did not understand this war, did not correctly assess its hardships, and therefore made disastrous miscalculations. He suddenly decided that the Red Army was not ready for war and was unfit for any kind of action. Hitler turned out to be wrong. No conclusion about the strength of the Soviets follows out of the fact that the Red Army did not reach Helsinki. On the contrary, it follows that the Red Army was capable of reaching Berlin.

Many German generals realized that the Red Army, according to the results of the fighting in Finland, was assessed incorrectly. During the Battle of Stalingrad, Goering had publicly declared that the war the Soviet Union had launched against Finland was "perhaps one of the biggest cover-ups in world history." Goering believed that Stalin deliberately "sent to Finland a few divisions, equipped with obsolete weaponry, in order to hide the creation by the Soviet Union of an unprecedented war machine."[15] In closed circles, Hitler himself admitted the mistake. This occurred on April 12, 1942. Hitler said the following: "The entire war with Finland in 1940, just as the Russian advance into Poland with obsolete tanks and weapons and poorly clothed soldiers, was nothing other than a grandiose disinformation campaign, because Russia at that time controlled arms which made it, in comparison with Germany and Japan, a world power." He also said, on June 22, 1942: "Back home in Russia, they created an extremely powerful military industry . . . and the more we find out what goes on in Russia, the more we rejoice that we delivered the decisive blow in time. The Red Army's weaponry is the best proof that they succeeded in reaching extremely high achievements."[16]

23

Germany's Strategic Resources and Stalin's Plans

The Fuehrer noted that the objective of gaining control of the Finnish Gulf is paramount, because free navigation in the Baltic Sea and direct delivery of ore from Lulea becomes possible immediately after the liquidation of the Russian fleet. Taking over Russian ports from the mainland will require three to four weeks. Only then can the enemy's submarines be paralyzed. Four weeks of fighting means 2 million tons of iron ore.

—COLONEL GENERAL F. HALDER, *WAR DIARY*

War is gluttonous, that is why every strategist constructs maps of supply routes that enable key raw materials to reach his country and the country of his opponent. His goals are to defend his supply lines and cut those of the opponent. If one draws a map of supply sources and supply routes, it becomes clear that Germany's position in 1939 was particularly difficult. After 1939 the position did not improve; it actually worsened. On the grand scale, Germany has no raw materials. Germany is tied by thousands of fragile strings to the rest of the world. Taking over Czechoslovakia, Poland, Denmark, Norway, Belgium, Holland, Luxembourg, France, Yugoslavia, and Greece, and conducting the *Anschluss* of Austria and Germany did not solve Germany's supply problem. Gaining control over millions of people and huge territories that did not contain raw materials only led Germany to spread herself thin, and did not bring any advantages.

Here is another aspect of the problem: Germany, France, Belgium—all have powerful steel-casting industries, but they do not have much iron ore. Too many things on the front and in the rear, from the soles of soldiers' boots to battleships, are made of steel. Due to steel shortages, German leaders—as high-ranking as Goering—seriously considered the possibility of building locomotives of concrete instead of steel.[1] Due to steel shortages, damaged bridges were repaired using wooden logs instead of steel beams. Due to steel shortages, railroad rails from spare tracks were used to repair the damaged sectors of primary tracks. Railroad tracks with two-way traffic were transformed into one-track roads. This slowed the entire rhythm of production in Germany and in the countries Germany occupied.

In any case, Hitler could not have counted on a quick victory—he had too many enemies. A long war was a path to suicide for Hitler, in the most literal sense of the word. In order to maintain for just a few years what he wanted to establish, he needed to gain iron ore supply. The richest ore mines in Europe, with high iron readings of up to 60 to 65 percent, were located in the area of Kiruna-Ellivare in the very north of Sweden, and arrived at German ports through the Baltic Sea. [2]

One of the weakest links of the German economy was the loading of iron ore in the Swedish port of Lulea, followed by the long trip along Finland's coast through the Gulf of Bothnia, past the Åland Islands, past the islands Gotland, Oland, Bornholm, and then the unloading in the German ports. The iron ore was loaded almost at the Arctic Circle and was transported across the entire Baltic Sea from the northernmost to the southernmost ports. Neither the British, nor the French, nor any other fleets posed any threat to the transport of iron ore across the Baltic. For a foreign fleet, breaking into the Baltic Sea was like breaking into a mousetrap and staying trapped there. But the Soviet Navy did not need to break into anything. It was already there, in its bases, peacefully awaiting the right opportunity.

For defending the Soviet Union a fleet in the Baltic Sea is not needed at all. Prior to 1940, the Soviet Union held a very small piece of seashore there. For more than two hundred years St. Petersburg (known as Leningrad in the Soviet era) was the capital of the empire, and for that reason along this stretch of shoreline all the Russian tsars, beginning with Peter the Great, had erected fortifications. The entire shoreline was transformed into a chain of sea fortresses, fortified regions, and coastal artillery batteries.

A coastal battery is something more impressive than a field artillery battery. A coastal battery can be compared to the artillery turret of battleships and cruisers. Under these turrets there are labyrinths of concrete casemates. A battleship turret weighs several hundred tons, sometimes even several thousand. Unlike the one on the ship, the same gun turret mounted on land can be defended by armored plates of any weight. Under the turret it is possible to erect casemates from fortified concrete with walls of any thickness. And it must be said that the Russian tsars put down enough concrete and steel in St. Petersburg's surroundings, and the Bolsheviks added even more.

The coastline defenses of the Soviet Union's Baltic fleet on June 21, 1941, had 124 coastal batteries armed with 253 weapons from 100 to 406 mm in caliber and 60 weapons that were 45 and 76 mm in caliber. [3]

The statistics of the coastline defense weapons are impressive. For example, a 305-mm cannon could launch shells weighing 470 kg to a distance of 43.9 km. One of the turrets had the capacity to fire six rounds a minute, almost three tons of metal. A 406-mm weapon launched a shell weighing 1,108 kg to a distance of 45.5 km. This weapon was capable of firing the next round only twenty-four seconds after the preceding one. [4]

Aside from coastline batteries and forts, the Leningrad region had a rather impressive concentration of naval cannons on railroad platforms. These long-range weapons were parked in concrete hideaways. There is a web of railroads around Leningrad, so the long-range weapons on railroad platforms could be maneuvered quickly and fired from prearranged and well-concealed firing positions, and then quickly moved away. The most important weapon of railroad artillery was the 180-mm cannon with shells of 97.5 kg. It could fire five rounds a minute, and its range was 37.8 km. There were also even more powerful cannons: the 203-, 254-, and 356-mm. The 356-mm cannons on railroad transports shot shells weighing 747.8 kg and had a firing range of 44.6 km.

Three naval fortified regions protected the direct gateways to Leningrad: the Kronstadt, Izhorsk, and Luzhsk, so the routes to the city could be shelled by powerful crossfire from all directions. Each battery, each fort, each fortified region, and each naval base had ammunition and supplies enough to last them for the entire four years of the war. No one would have the idea of launching an amphibious assault here or storming the city. Besides, Leningrad had ninety-one anti-aircraft batteries with a total of 352 anti-aircraft cannons. Why on earth would the Baltic region need a fleet on top of all this?

If the Soviet Union meant to defend itself, it did not need battleships in the Baltic Sea. In case of need, even without battleships, it was possible to quickly unload barges full of mines at the mouth of the Gulf of Finland and thus to cut off the approach to Leningrad. In defensive warfare a Soviet Baltic fleet was unnecessary. In fact, that is what happened—the Soviet Baltic fleet stayed without action for the entire duration of the war. In the event of attack by an aggressor, the Soviet Baltic fleet was extremely vulnerable. The aggressor could simply block the Soviet fleet by laying a couple of hundred mines on the shallow accesses to the naval bases. Indeed, that was done by the German fleet in June 1941. In a defensive war, ships, especially large ones, are forced to sideswipe in a shallow and narrow gulf, trapped in a blind alley.

In 1939 Hitler launched World War II against the rest of the world, having in his possession only fifty-seven submarines. His opponents were the almighty British and French fleets and, potentially, the U.S. navy. Hitler's navy had to lead an uneven battle in the Atlantic and the Mediterranean. In the Baltic, Hitler had almost nothing left. In the summer of 1941 in the Baltic Sea, the German navy had only five training submarines and twenty-eight torpedo motorboats, some of which were also used for training. The rest were secondary forces: mine blockers, various motorboats, and minesweepers.[5] But peace-loving comrade Stalin watched the struggle between Germany, France, and Britain and beefed up the might of his Baltic fleet. What for?

In 1933 Stalin had already said: "The Baltic Sea is a sealed bottle, and we can't open it."[6] Nevertheless, out of every three battleships, Stalin kept two in the Baltic, as if in a corked bottle. In 1941 on the Baltic Sea alone Stalin had sixty-nine submarines.[7] No one in the world had such a number of submarines collected in one place. What task could Stalin set before his battleships and submarines in the closed aquarium of the Baltic Sea? Only one: to sink German transports of iron ore. There was no other work there for them.

Aside from submarines and battleships, Stalin had two cruisers, twenty-one destroyers, forty-eight torpedo motorboats, and other forces. On the Baltic Sea, the German navy did not even have its own air force.[8] The Soviet Baltic fleet had 656 war planes, mostly bombers and torpedo carriers.[9] Once again we ask: what was this all for? Why such a huge quantity of torpedo carriers and bombers, if Hitler had no large ships in the Baltic? The answer is always the same: the targets were not his warships, but his transports of ore. At any moment, the Soviet fleet could have raised anchor, reached the German and Swedish ports, blocked them with thousands of mines, and sunk the defenseless transports. This would have ended the war for Germany, and this must have been known and understood in Berlin from the start. Hitler fought against Britain and France, while behind his back Stalin held up high a glittering ax.

At the end of November 1939, Stalin made a huge mistake—he launched a war against Finland. The victory in Finland was a second warning to Hitler that Stalin was approaching the Swedish sources of ore. The Red Army, acting on Stalin's orders, got through the Finnish fortifications and halted its advance. Finland without the fortifications was defenseless. At any moment, Stalin could have given another order and renewed the advance of the Red Army. From Finnish territory it could have bombed Swedish ore mines and railroads unhindered. No one could have impeded this. The seizure of the Åland Islands alone would have been enough to close off the mouth of the Gulf of Bothnia, which would have meant an end to World War II with a Soviet victory.

And that was not all. In the part of Europe that was occupied by Hitler there are no forests. The forests are in Finland and Sweden. Any possible cessation of the shipment of lumber across the Baltic Sea carried with it a multitude of consequences, and all were negative. The wood was needed for building and restoring railroad ties and for mining coal, which was needed for forging steel. No wood meant no transport along the railroads. During peacetime in Germany there was already a yearly timber shortage of about 6 million tons. Instead of wood pulp they had to use potato foliage. The Fuehrer himself attests to that.[10]

But that was just during peacetime, when no one hindered the transport of timber across the Baltic Sea. As soon as Stalin's submarines struck German timber carriers, Germany would have wound up without wood at all. Potato stalks would not have sufficed to make up the shortage, because they cannot replace good wood in all its uses. It is possible to make poor quality paper out of them, but impossible to make railroad ties, impossible to timber coal mines.

On top of everything else, Germany had no nickel. It was impossible to fight without nickel—but the nickel supplies were in Finland. At the beginning of 1940, during the course of the war against Finland, the Red Army had seized control of the nickel mines in Petsamo, and then in the spring of 1940, according to the peace treaty, returned them. But now nickel was obtained according to joint Soviet-Finnish shareholding companies with the participation of Soviet engineers and workers. The Soviet government insisted that the director of the entire operation be a Soviet man. Nickel from Petsamo went to both Germany and the Soviet Union. Germany was receiving 70,000 tons from this area, or 70 percent of Germany's annual demand of this strategic mineral.[11] However, the nickel supply could be stopped at any moment. The Soviet 104th Rifle Division, under Major General Morozov (of the 42nd Rifle Corps of the 14th Army) stood right outside the nickel mines.

German strategists did not fear a new Soviet invasion of Finland in vain. On November 25, 1940, the People's Commissar of Defense of the USSR, Marshal of the Soviet Union S. K. Timoshenko, and Chief of General Staff of the Red Army General K. A. Meretskov signed a directive to the staff of the Leningrad military district. Only one copy of the document was produced, and it was labeled top secret and especially important. Let's remember the date—November 25, 1940—we will return to it later on.

The document begins by saying:

> In the conditions of war only against Finland, the USSR establishes, for convenience of control and material supply, two fronts: the Northern front for action on the shoreline of the Barents Sea and in the direction of Rovaniemi, Kemi and Oulu; the Northwestern front for actions directed toward Kuopio, Mikkeli and Helsinki. The leadership of the Northwestern front falls on the shoulders of the command and staff of the Leningrad military district. It is ordered to start the development of plans for operations opening up the Northwestern front. . . . The main objectives of the

Northwestern front are set: destruction of Finland's armed forces, gaining control of her territories within the boundaries, and gaining access to the Gulf of Bothnia by the forty-fifth day of the operation. . . . On the right, the Northern front (its staff in Kandalaksha) on the fortieth day of mobilization moves to assault, and on the thirtieth day of the operation gains control of the regions of Kemi and Oulu. . . . The Red-Flag Baltic fleet, subordinate in all operations to the Military Council of the Northwestern front, is issued the following tasks: Working jointly with the air force, destroy the active navy of Finland and Sweden (in case of involvement by the latter). Assist the ground forces, acting on the Finland Gulf shore and from the Hanko peninsula, by supplying their flanks and destroying the coastal defenses of the Finns. Provide the transfer of two rifle divisions during the first few days of the war from the northern shore of the Estonian SSR to the Hanko peninsula, as well as transporting and launching an amphibious assault on the Åland Islands. Through cruiser operations of submarines and air forces, interrupt Finnish-Swedish naval communications (in the event of the latter's interference against the USSR) in the Gulf of Bothnia and the Baltic Sea.

This plan of action was given the name "S.3-20." The plan was to be put into action at the moment of receipt of a coded telegram with the signature of the chie of the general staff and the following contents: "Commence execution of plan 'S.3-20'."[12]

In this plan there was no mention of the fact that the Soviet Union would fight for the "guarantee of safety to the city of Lenin," that is, Leningrad. And there were no hints that military actions must be initiated only in response to enemy aggression. The usual words "if the enemy wages war upon us . . ." were absent. Here, it was much simpler: at any moment, the Leningrad staff would receive a telegram from Moscow, and Soviet armies would advance to the Gulf of Bothnia, to the Swedish border, to the Åland Islands! The trusted comrades at the right moment would set up a new "provocation of the Finnish war machine on our frontier," and those whose job it was to do so would explain to the workers of the world the meaning of the "peace-loving global politics of the USSR" and the necessity of our "counterblows to the Finnish aggressors."

The plan "S.3-20" could have been a stand-alone one, but it could also have been part of a much broader scheme. The plan "S.3-20" allowed the armies of the Leningrad and Arkhangelsk districts, together with the Baltic fleet, to deliver blows to Finland before the Red Army hit Germany, simultaneously, or slightly later. But in any case, the blow to Finland was also a blow to Germany. In the event of putting plan "S.3-20" into action, Soviet troops were to seize the nickel mines in Petsamo and the Åland Islands, and make their way to the city of Kemi. It was not a coincidence that in 1940, on the Baltic Sea, the first marine infantry brigade was formed under the leadership of the Soviet saboteur Colonel Parafilo. It remained only to send to the Leningrad headquarters the coded message: "Bring plan into execution." There is no need to search for a plan for war against Germany. If plan "S.3-20" had been realized, it meant a deadly blow not only to Finland, but to Germany as well.

In the summer of 1940, Stalin committed another error: he brought Estonia, Latvia, and Lithuania into the Soviet Union, organized on their territory the Baltic special military district, and concentrated all the forces of that region on the border of Eastern Prussia. This was completely unnecessary, and even harmful, for defense. Some say that Stalin moved his border to the West and thus strengthened the safety of the USSR. But in fact the situation was exactly the opposite. Before the occupation of the Baltic states, the Red Army had a divisive barrier in this region. Consequently, in the event of aggression Hitler's armies had to crush the armed forces of three independent states before meeting the Red Army. Even if he had to spend only a few days in order to crush the armies of Latvia, Lithuania, and Estonia, a surprise attack on Soviet airbases in this direction would have been out of the question. The Red Army would have had the chance to put its forces on high alert and take its positions. After the destruction of the three states' armies Hitler's forces would have approached Lake Chudskoe, which is impossible to cross. If they had tried to go around the lake, Hitler's armies would have come straight into Soviet fortified areas.

But everything unfolded according to a different scenario. The Red Army came out of its fortified areas to the front lines in Lithuania, right up to the German border, and transferred there its air bases, staff headquarters, communication centers, and strategic supply resources. For the people of the three Baltic states, Stalin's army became the aggressor and occupant, and Germany, if it decided to attack the USSR, would have become the liberator.

On June 22, 1941, the Red Army suffered a surprise attack from the German armies along the entire stretch of the border, including the Baltic states. The command centers were disrupted and Soviet aviation suffered significant losses on border air bases. Moreover, a widespread popular uprising in the Baltic states flared up against the Red Army. The Soviet "liberators" were shot at from every rooftop. The Red Army was left in the Baltic region without any fortified regions, and behind their backs, on Russian territory, remained empty fortified areas without any troops. German troops led by General Field Marshal von Manstein seized them immediately.

Skeptics disagree: if Stalin had not occupied the Baltic states, Hitler could have seized them without war, by simply moving his troops there as he did in Czechoslovakia. To this theory, there is a rebuttal. It should have been explained to Hitler clearly that if German troops attempted to enter the Baltic states area, the Soviet Union, without warning, would begin sinking German transports of ore and wood in the Baltic Sea, setting up mines in the entryways of German ports, and bombing Berlin. The Soviet Union would form international brigades and launch them into the Baltic states' territory together with millions of Soviet volunteers. And when Hitler's forces grew weak in the war with the USSR, Britain and France would use the opportunity and strangle Germany according to their best interests, eliminating it as a dangerous adversary and once again imposing retributions.

Such a declaration would have been correctly understood around the world. In such an event the people of the Baltic states would not have been enemies of the Soviets, but their allies. In such an event, the "forest brothers" (the Baltic states' partisans) would have been shooting the backs of German soldiers, not the Soviets. In such an event, international brigades would have been fighting on the side of the Baltic states. There were always enough volunteers to be found around the world.

In August 1939 the Soviet Union's position was announced loud and clear: Mongolian territory will be defended from Japanese aggression as if it was our own. And that was done! This position was correctly understood in the entire world, including Japan. As a result of this decisiveness and strictness, Japanese aggression against the Soviet Union was averted. Why did the Soviet Union, in 1939, not take the same position regarding the Baltic states?

The occupation of those states by the Red Army made sense only if there were plans for an aggressive war against Germany. The Red Army came right up to the German border and transferred its air bases to the very front edge of that border. From the bases in Lithuania it could support the advance of Soviet troops right up to Berlin. Additionally, the Soviet navy received naval bases in Tallinn, Riga, and Liepāja. The primary forces of the navy and reserves were immediately transferred there. From Liepāja to the routes taken by caravans carrying ore, nickel, and wood to Germany, there was a very small distance. A strike from this area could be sudden and crippling.

For Hitler, this would have been the curtain call. Hitler understood that at any moment the Soviet fleet could cut the only tie binding the faraway Swedish ports with the metal-forging bases in Germany.

24

The Carving Up of Romania, and its Consequences

Had we not succeeded in halting Russian troops during their entrance into Romania and forcing them to be content with obtaining only Bessarabia, they would have taken the Romanian oil fields, and no later than that same spring they would have crushed us, for we would have lost all sources of fuel.

—Adolf Hitler, May 18, 1942

Stalin strove to persuade Hitler that he wanted peace. At the same time, Stalin very persistently crawled toward the vital life-sustaining resources of Germany. For Stalin, it was not enough that the Red Army and fleet had under their control all the routes through which Germany got her iron ore, timber, and nickel. Stalin decided to move his divisions right up to the regions from which Germany received its petroleum supplies.

In August 1939, Stalin (with Molotov's hand) signed a pact, according to which Hitler got a war on two fronts, and according to which the British fleet blocked Germany and did not allow petroleum shipments to come in by sea. Germany had only one possible source of oil significant enough to be noted—Ploiești in Romania. The loss of this source of oil would have put a complete stop to German production, army, aviation, and navy. On June 9, 1940, the People's Commissar for Defense, Marshal of the Soviet Union S. K. Timoshenko, signed a directive about the creation of the southern front. General G. K. Zhukov was nominated to command that front. The front consisted of the 5th, 9th, and 12th armies. Overall, the southern front consisted of thirteen corps: ten rifle corps and three mounted corps. Together there were forty divisions: thirty-two rifle divisions, two motorized rifle divisions, and six mounted divisions. There were fourteen separate brigades: eleven tank brigades and three paratroop brigades. Reinforcements consisted of sixteen heavy artillery regiments and four artillery battalions of high power. The Southern front's aviation consisted of twenty-one fighter and twenty-four bomber regiments. The total number of troops was 460,000 soldiers and officers, using twelve thousand guns, three thousand tanks, and two thousand planes.

Having concentrated such might on the Romanian border, Stalin ordered Zhukov to use threats or battle to obtain Bessarabia and Northern Bukovina from Romania, and to secure arm's-length access to Romania's undefended oil fields, which were two hundred kilometers from the border.

Zhukov's Southern front was ready to crush Romania, but in the sumer of 1940 he did not have to fight. Romania's leaders had witnessed the brilliant victories sustained by the Red Army in Finland and had a clear understanding that it was better to accede to Stalin's wishes without battle. The sides agreed to a peaceful resolution of the conflict. At the end of June 1940 Romanian troops retreated from and Soviet troops entered Bessarabia and Northern Bukovina. These territories were added to the constituency of the Soviet Union.

In June 1940 three paths were open before the Southern front commanded by General Zhukov: two were correct, one was deadly. The first correct path: deliver a blow to Bessarabia and continue to advance toward the oil fields of Ploiești. Three thousand Soviet tanks and two thousand airplanes were more than enough to reach the oil fields and ignite a fire. This would have meant the end for Germany. If the Southern front in June 1940 had dealt a blow to Romania, World War II would have ended in 1940 with a victory by the Soviet Union and an establishment of Communist regimes over the entire European continent. If the events had unfolded in such a manner, giant colonies of the French, Belgian, and Dutch empires would have been transferred to Stalin's control.

The second path was more risky, but promised even more victories: in June 1940 Stalin could have simply done nothing. He could have waited. He would not have had to wait much longer. After defeating France, Hitler could have delivered a blow to Britain. The risk for Stalin lay only in the fact that after the defeat of France, Britain and Germany could have concluded peace. In that case, Stalin would have been left one-on-one against Germany. However, if Hitler, as he planned, landed his troops in Britain, the task of "liberating" Europe became much simpler: Zhukov would have struck the Romanian oil fields, then the Red Army would have begun its "liberating operations" in Europe, all while the best German troops were off the continent, in Britain, from where they could return immediately.

The third path was deadly. In June 1940 Zhukov's Southern front took over Bessarabia and Northern Bukovina—then halted halfway to the oilfields of Ploiești.

Hitler said in 1942 that he was able to force Stalin to be satisfied in 1940 with Bessarabia alone. This was not so. Firstly, in the summer of 1940 Stalin had not yet set for Zhukov the objective of crushing Romania. Secondly, in 1940, in the heat of the fighting in France, Hitler had no means of exerting influence over Stalin. If Stalin had ordered his troops to crush Romania in the summer of 1940, nobody would have been capable of stopping the advance of Zhukov's Southern front.

As a result of the "liberation crusades" the distance from the new Soviet frontier to the oil fields of Ploiești was now just 180 km. This was a clear, open area. Troops from the Odessa military district were concentrated at the very border, ready as soon as they got the first order to continue the "liberation" right up to the oil wells. Soviet tanks numbered over three thousand; the Romanians had sixty tanks. The Soviet "obsolete" BT-7M tank even officially had a speed of 86 km/h (in reality it was faster). The Romanian tanks opposing it were FT-17s, and had a maximum speed of 9 km/h. Therefore, the Soviet tanks could just disregard their Romanian opponents, ignore them and bypass them at their will. Even if one were to set one thousand Soviet tanks against sixty Romanian ones, even then the remaining two thousand could advance to Ploiești unhindered, without leaving the main road and without maneuvers. Even if they were to advance at only 25 km/h, they would have needed only seven to eight hours—one night! Moreover, Stalin did not just have simple tanks, but fast-moving ones, made especially for such advances. The area ahead of them was even and flat, the ground was hard, and the roads were in good condition. The BT tanks could easily reach a speed of 40 to 50 km/h here, and without their tracks that would rise to 70 to 80 km/h. That would have come to only three hours of plain driving time. And it was not at all necessary for all the tanks to reach the oil wells. If only ten tanks had reached them that would have sufficed. Oil fields can be ignited with incendiary shells, or even with a simple soldier's lighter. Without oil, one cannot fight. Oil is not only fuel; it is also a raw resource for the chemical industry, without which one cannot get by. If only one Soviet tank company of ten tanks had wound up in the Ploiești vicinity, and if each driver had had a box of matches, the war in Europe would have ended with the early defeat of the Third Reich.

A seizure of Ploiești by Soviet troops, or just a fire in the oil production areas, would have meant paralysis for Germany. In the event of Ploiești falling to the Soviets, all German tanks, automobiles, cruisers, battleships, submarines, and airplanes would have been stopped in their tracks. Who cares that you have talented generals, officers, soldiers, pilots, and artillerists? Without fuel all their talents would be completely useless. A freeze on oil supply to the German war machine opened up the way for thousands of other Soviet tanks. From Brest and Lvov, from Belostok and Grodno, the road to Berlin was now very short. If the German army and aviation were paralyzed, and no one offered resistance, then on good roads the tank units could reach not only Berlin and Munich, but Paris and Marseille as well.

In May and June of 1940 Hitler was crushing the armies of Britain, Belgium, Holland, and France. German tank units headed for the Atlantic Ocean, making a huge detour around Paris. Practically the entire Germany army fought in the West. Hitler victoriously crushed France and British troops on the continent. Against France and Britain, Hitler threw his entire naval fleet, air force, all his tanks, and all his heavy artillery. The best German generals fought there. And in the rear, on the borders of the Soviet Union, Hitler left only ten weak infantry divisions. Here, there was not a single tank, a single airplane, a single heavy artillery weapon. Most importantly, the ten infantry divisions were all in Poland and Slovakia. In Romania, there were no German troops.

In June 1940 neither Hitler nor his generals had any intentions or plans to attack the Soviet Union. The *Oberkommando des Heeres* (OKH—German Army High Command) and the *Oberkommando der Wehrmacht* (OKW—Supreme Command of the Armed Forces) had neither rough drafts nor preliminary designs for a war against the USSR. They had no orders from Hitler in this regard. Not a word was said about war against the USSR.

After the defeat of France, Hitler ordered a drastic reduction in German armed forces. This reduction was widespread and intense, for there were no plans, hints, or foresight indicating that a war against the Soviet Union might be approaching. And all at once came the Soviet strike against Romania. Oil is the blood of war. Without oil, fighting becomes impossible. Stalin's axe was raised over the oil production in Romania.

In Berlin, it was finally recognized that the Soviet threat to Germany was lethal. Soviet tanks advanced to Romania, causing chaos in German headquarters: if the tanks did not stop, if they advanced another 180 km, then Germany would capitulate within the next few months. Romanian troops made no resistance and put up no obstacles to the Soviet advance. There were no German troops in Romania. It was impossible to quickly transfer troops from France. Even if it had been possible, a large number of German troops in Romania could not have received adequate supplies. Even if it had been possible to provide supplies, then Germany would have been forced to have fewer troops in Poland, meaning an even more direct road to Berlin would have been laid open to Stalin's tanks.

Soviet troops occupied Bessarabia and Northern Bukovina and stopped. Berlin breathed a sigh of relief. However, what would have happened if, the next day, Stalin had ordered the advance to continue? A solution was found: in case of an emergency, it would be necessary to deliver a warning blow to the Soviet Union, using ten divisions in another location, thereby creating for the Red Army a diversion from Romania. After conducting the battles on maps, the German high command understood that ten divisions would be insufficient. They decided to use twenty, and saw the same result. They increased the number of divisions, again and again. In the end, it was decided: in order to not allow Stalin to seize or destroy the oil industry in Romania, it was necessary to deliver a blow to the Soviet Union with the might of the entire German armed forces.

On July 21, 1940, Hitler for the first time in a very tight circle uttered the idea of the "Russian problem." On July 21 the head of ground forces, General Field Marshal W. Brauchitsch, received an order from Hitler to begin developing a specific plan for war in the East. The next day, Brauchitsch entrusted Halder, the head of general staff for ground forces, with fully evaluating all the different potentialities "in a military operation against Russia." Major General Erich Marcks was then appointed to Halder's staff as an aide for developing the specifics of the eastern campaign. On July 29 Marcks began planning a military campaign against Russia.[1]

For the Soviet Union, the consequences of a bloodless victory in Romania were catastrophic. First of all, neutral Romania was faced with a terrible choice: whose side should it take? Europe was being torn into pieces by two monsters, Hitler and Stalin. Stalin had suddenly demanded Bessarabia and Northern Bukovina, and Romania was forced to give them up. What would Stalin demand tomorrow? Hitler, on the other hand, did not demand anything. The choice was simple, and Romania got Hitler's protection. The result: the Soviet Union obtained another hostile country along its border; the front, that was supposed to protect the USSR in case of war, stretched for almost another eight hundred kilometers; and Hitler received an ally that held oil. Without oil, Germany could not fight. In other words, having Romania in his arms, Hitler could attack the Soviet Union. Without this new alliance the attack would have been impossible. But the most important effect lay in something else. Stalin frightened Hitler. It was precisely the "liberation" of Bessarabia and Northern Bukovina that acted as the last warning for Hitler. A direct Soviet threat arose over the oil fields of Romania, and precisely because of this threat Hitler ordered his commanders to prepare a strike against the Soviet Union.

In Stalin's career there were few errors. One of the few, but the most significant one, was the occupation of Bessarabia in 1940. He could have taken Bessarabia and continued on to Ploieşti, which would have meant the destruction of Germany. Or, he could have waited until Hitler landed troops in Britain, and after that he could have taken over all of Romania. This too would have ended the "thousand-year Reich." Stalin, however, made one step in the direction of oil, took over the launching ground for the next attack—and stopped to wait. Through these actions, he showed interest in Romanian oil and alarmed Hitler, who before this had concentrated on the West, North, and South, without paying much attention to "neutral" Stalin in the East.

On July 16, 1940, Hitler signed the directive No.16 concerning preparations for landing troops in Great Britain. The operation was given the code name *Zeeloewe* (Sea Lion); the plan was for the operation to be completed by August 15. But the annexation of Bessarabia, Northern Bukovina, Estonia, Latvia, and Lithuania into the Soviet Union forced Hitler to make a sharp U-turn and look at what was happening behind his back.

Why did Stalin need Bessarabia and Northern Bukovina? Here is the official answer of the Soviet historians to that question: "From the Bessarabian territory, the Soviet air force could keep Romanian oil industry, which was the main supplier of oil to Germany, under constant threat. Northern Bukovina was needed because through its territory went a railroad of strategic importance, which stretched from Odessa through Kishinev, Chernovtsi, to Lvov, and which had a European track which enabled it to allow usage by railroad cars from all over Europe."[2]

Here is what Hitler had said regarding the same matter, but half a century earlier:

It is absolutely obvious that the Soviets were determined to direct the unfolding of events in the Balkans in the direction necessary to them, and in that manner to transform the area into launching grounds for an attack on us and the remaining countries of Europe. And, doing everything possible to achieve this goal, they simultaneously declared readiness to sign trade agreements with us, which would seem to be favorable to us but would in fact cut us off from our oil sources as soon as their preparations for the decisive coup were finished. In the summer of 1941 they intended to deliver a crushing defeat to Romania, for it was the only country, except Russia, that delivered us oil.[3]

Soviet historiography advanced Hitler's argument. It talks not only of a real Soviet threat to the only German oil source, but also about a segment of railway for European cars. In the Soviet Union, the railways use a broad gauge. Central and Western Europe use a narrow gauge. In September 1939, during the partition of Poland, the Red Army seized half of Poland's locomotives and railroad cars. They were useless in the territory of the Soviet Union, because the gauge on the "liberated" territories was quickly changed to fit the broad Soviet standard. But Stalin prepared for the "liberation" of Germany and the rest of Europe. During the course of the first future operations, before the German gauge was amended to fit the Soviet standard, Stalin would need many locomotives and trains with a narrow gauge to supply his troops that were quickly moving westward. The Polish locomotives and trains clearly did not suffice to supply millions of tons of ammunition, arms, liquid fuel, and spare parts. That is why Stalin took Bessarabia and Northern Bukovina —to expand the number of trains for railways with a narrow gauge. In the course of the Bessarabian campaign, Soviet forces captured 141 locomotives, 1,866 covered train cars, 325 half-covered train cars, 45 platforms, 19 cisterns, 31 passenger cars, and 2 luggage cars.[4] But even that was not enough for Stalin. At the Soviet-Romanian talks in July 1940, regarding the settlement of contested issues, the Soviet representatives demanded that Romania return all captured mobile railroad units. On July 31, 1940, the two sides signed an agreement on the transfer of 175 locomotives and 4,375 cars to the USSR by August 25.[5]

In a defensive war, trains seized in Poland, Bessarabia, and Northern Bukovina would not have been needed. Thus, Stalin needed Bessarabia and Northern Bukovina not for defense, not in order to "bring the people happiness." Stalin's plot was much broader and deeper: to take Hitler by the throat and to bring "happiness" to all of Europe.

A question arises: are we not giving too much importance to the role played by Romanian oil? Did not Germany establish her own production of synthetic fuel? Such an industry did indeed exist, but the problem of fuel was still not resolved. First of all, it is important to keep in mind that synthetic fuel can never compete in quality with fuel made from petroleum. The use of synthetic fuel significantly lowers the tactical and technical characteristics of weaponry, most of all airplanes, tanks, and ships. Your designers can create a wonderful aircraft, your factories can have the best technological capabilities in the world, your workers and engineers can put into the building process of the plane all their talent and effort, but with low-quality fuel the plane will still be slow, weak, and clumsy.

On top of all this, synthetic fuel is also expensive. With timber, if there was a shortage, Hitler's Germany used potato stalks. Even though they were lower in quality than wood, at least they were cheap. But the production of synthetic fuel costs seven to twelve times as much as the production of fuel from petroleum. Hitler's decision to use synthetic fuel was not born out of good fortunes. Very few would be willing to repeat his experiences. The following facts enable us to judge the quality and costs of synthetic fuel. In the second half of the twentieth century the world suffered from an oil crisis more than once. At the beginning of the new millennium, the global chemical industry is far more powerful than the chemical industry of Germany in 1941. And still, for some reason there is no rush to produce synthetic fuels today.

Now, let us talk about quantity. Germany's minimum requirements for oil in 1941 were estimated at around 20 million tons.[6] Hitler had allies who had armies, navies, and air forces, but they too did not have petroleum. They too had to be supplied by German fuel. Germany in 1941 was producing 4.1 million tons of synthetic fuel—one-fifth of the bare minimum. If one keeps in mind the allies, with whom Germany had to share, then the percentage of synthetic fuel in the overall balance of 1941 is completely insignificant. Aside from synthetic fuel, real petroleum came to Germany from Austria, Czechoslovakia, France, Hungary, and Poland. Altogether, in 1941 that made 1.3 million tons. So for 1941 Germany made synthetic fuel and received real petroleum from occupied countries—together, this makes 5.4 million tons of fuel. Without the Romanian oil, with the remaining amount of fuel the German armies, navies, air forces, transport, and industry would have been able to fight for only three months out of the year and would have had to spend the remaining nine months shivering—until the next year.

Hitler thought that if the Red Army defeated Romania in 1940 or 1941, without Romanian oil Germany could hold on until the spring of 1942. This optimism cannot hold up when checked with arithmetic. Without Romanian oil only a quarter of the needs of the German economy and armed forces would have been met, and with poor and very expensive fuel at that. A taking of Romania by the Red Army in 1940 or 1941 would have turned into a catastrophe for Germany within two to three months.

How much oil was coming from Romania? In 1941, 5 million tons came in. This was not enough. But without it living and fighting were made impossible. While receiving oil from Romania, Germany could balance on a tightrope, somehow making do with an amount about half of its minimum needs. The petroleum situation in the invading army (which, clearly, was in a privileged position relative to all other consumers) on the eve of the war against the Soviet Union was the following: aircraft fuel was more or less in good supply; car and diesel fuel, on the other hand, was predicted to be at a 10 percent deficit even in July, and by August, the army on the Eastern front was going to have to be fueled, for the most part, by supplies directly out of Romania. By fall, the German petroleum reserves were predicted to be completely exhausted, with aircraft fuel only at 50 percent of the required amount, car fuel at 25 percent, and diesel fuel at 50 percent.[7] Thus, the German high command depended heavily on the brevity of the Russian campaign, on shipments from Romania, and on plundered reserves.

During the course of the entire war, Germany's problem with petroleum was never resolved. On June 6, 1942, the OKW evaluated the situation: "The supply of fuel and oil materials in the current year will be one of the weaknesses of our military potential. The shortage of oil materials of all sorts is so great that freedom of operations will be threatened in all three branches of the armed forces, and will have a negative effect on military industry as well. . . . A small improvement can be anticipated toward the end of the year, when new factories for the production of synthetic fuel will be launched, but this will not bring a drastic improvement in the supply of Germany."[8] Germany's supply worsened as the war progressed. Toward the end of the war, Germany was the first in the world to start producing jet-engine planes. The Me-262 fighter surpassed all other planes in speed and weapons. Germany produced 1,433 of them. However, there was not enough kerosene, and without kerosene the best fighter in the world could not fly. Out of almost 1,500 planes of this type built, only slightly more than two hundred took part in battles. The rest remained on the ground.

In the summer of 1940 Stalin made a fateful mistake. Already in 1939 Hitler had found himself in a strategic dead end, without an exit. In 1940 Stalin raised axes over Hitler's head from two sides: over iron ore, timber, and nickel in the north, and over oil in the south. Stalin stalled, waiting for Hitler to attack Britain. But in 1941 Britain was not dangerous to Hitler. The danger came from Stalin. Hitler had no other choice. So, he jumped on Stalin. On June 21, 1941, Hitler wrote a letter to Mussolini: "Russia is trying to destroy the Romanian oil fields. . . . The task for our armies is eliminating this threat as soon as possible." Herein lies the cause of Hitler's attack. This was not at all a struggle for *Lebensraum* (living space).

The strategic miscalculations of 1940 were so rough, deep, and frightening that their catastrophic consequences for the fate of the Soviet Union could not later be resolved by any genius decisions and brilliant victories. Because of Stalin's and Zhukov's mistakes, Hitler attacked the Soviet Union, destroyed its army, and crushed a large part of Soviet industry. In the end, the Soviet Union was unable to conquer Europe. Stalin lost the war for Europe and global domination. The free world survived, and it could not coexist with the Soviet Union. Therefore, the crumbling of the Soviet Union became inevitable. The roots of that crumbling lie in Zhukov's victorious venture into Bessarabia and Northern Bukovina in the summer of 1940. The Soviet Union won World War II, but for some reason disappeared from the globe after this distinguishing victory. When Communists celebrate the so-called "victory day," I ask: Where is this great victorious country? Where did it disappear? Germany lost the war, but we see her, one of the mightiest powers of contemporary Europe, at whose feet we now beg. So where is the great, mighty, uncrushable Soviet Union? Germany lost, but it is still here. The Soviet Union won, but it no longer exists. Who needs such a victory?

25

Destruction of the Buffer States between Germany and the Soviet Union

We are doing a deed that, if it succeeds, will turn the whole world upside down and will free the entire workers' class.

—J. STALIN, IN *PRAVDA*, FEBRUARY 5, 1931

It is a fact of history that on June 22, 1941, Germany attacked the Soviet Union, suddenly and treacherously. However, it is a very strange fact. Before World War II, Germany had no common border with the Soviet Union and therefore could not attack it, especially in a sudden fashion. Germany and the Soviet Union were separated by a solid barrier of neutral countries. In order for the Soviet-German war to take place, it was necessary to create the right conditions: to destroy the barrier of neutral countries and establish common Soviet-German borders.

Everyone interested in the date June 22, 1941, before cursing Hitler and accusing him of treachery, has to answer at least two questions: who destroyed the buffer row of neutral countries between Germany and the Soviet Union and what for? The barrier between Germany and the USSR was double-layered, and only in one place single-layered. Poland was the only country that had at once a border with both Germany and the Soviet Union. Poland is the shortest, most direct, most convenient route between the USSR and Germany. Poland is the thinnest part of the dividing wall between the two countries. Obviously, the potential aggressor, wishing for a Soviet-German war to take place, would try to cut a corridor precisely in this location. Contrarily, the country not wishing for a war should, with all its might, all its wisdom, all the force of its international authority, not allow its adversary to penetrate Polish territory. Or, as a last resort, begin fighting that opponent on Polish soil, without letting him on its territory.

Hitler wrote in *Mein Kampf*: "We want to return to that point, at which our previous development six hundred years ago was halted. We want to halt Germany's constant advance to the south and the west of Europe and decisively point our finger in the direction of territories located in the east." In the 1930s, especially after the Nazis came to power, Hitler's frankness sounded with a new power. But Hitler could not attack Stalin, because they did not share any borders.

Hitler began his movement to the east by turning to Stalin with a proposal for joint efforts in making a hole in the dividing wall between them. Stalin, with pleasure, accepted and enthusiastically tore down the Polish wall, hacking a corridor to meet Hitler. Hitler's motives were understandable. But how does one explain Stalin's actions?

Communist historians invented explanations for the deeds of the Soviet Union. The first explanation: having bloodied and ripped apart Poland, the Soviet Union moved its frontiers to the west, and thus fortified its security. What a strange explanation. Soviet frontiers were indeed moved two to three hundred kilometers, but at the same time Germany moved its frontiers two to three hundred kilometers to the east. This move decreased, rather than increased, the Soviet Union's security. Furthermore, the completely new factor of a common Soviet-German border arose, which carried as a consequence the possibility of sudden war between Germany and the Soviet Union. Explanation number two: having axed Poland in the back at the moment of her desperate fight against the Nazis, Stalin attempted to delay the moment the Soviet-German war would start. This explanation stems from the old pretext: we started a fire in the neighbor's house, hoping that the fire will reach and destroy our house later than it destroys his. The third explanation: France and Great Britain did not want to make a deal with the Soviet Union. It is a blatant lie. France and Great Britain did want an anti-Hitler treaty with the USSR and started negotiations in Moscow. The negotiations were suddenly stopped by the Soviets who immediately signed the Molotov-Ribbentrop Pact with Germany.

Poland, Estonia, Lithuania, Latvia, Finland, and Romania were natural allies of the USSR. Unlike France and Britain, these countries were potential victims of Hitler's *Drang Nach Ost* (Drive towards the East). With them, the USSR should have sought an alliance against Hitler. But Stalin was not seeking such an alliance, and in the cases where pacts did exist, the Soviet Union did not act in accordance with them. Stalin could have remained neutral, but instead he stabbed in the back those who fought against Hitler.

Having crushed Poland, Hitler broke a corridor through the dividing wall. Now, he had a common border with the Soviet Union that was 570 km in length. Hitler calculated this to be sufficient and went back to his affairs in the west, in Africa, in the Mediterranean, and in the Atlantic. What should Stalin have done, when presented with a corridor 570 km in length and with some time to spare? He should have hurriedly fortified his defenses precisely in this area. Along the old borders, there was a powerful row of fortified regions. It should have immediately been reinforced and improved. And it should have been complemented by a second line of defense, and a third, fourth, and fifth line. He should have urgently begun to lay mines under roads, bridges, fields, begun to dig anti-tank trenches and cover them with anti-tank artillery.

Sometime later, in 1943 in Kursk, the Red Army prepared to push back the advance of the Germans. During a short period of time Soviet troops created on the huge front six continuous lines of defense, each one hundreds of kilometers in length. The lines were situated one behind the other, so the total depth of defense was 250 to 300 km. Each kilometer was saturated with trenches, communication tunnels, covers, and firing positions. The average concentration of mines in a given area was brought to seven thousand anti-tank and anti-personnel mines per kilometer of front line. The concentration of anti-tank weapons was brought to a mind-blowing level: forty-one cannons per kilometer, not counting field and anti-aircraft artillery and dug-in tanks. In no time an empty field was transformed into a truly impenetrable defense.

In 1939 conditions for defense were much more favorable: forests, rivers, swamps, few roads, and lots of time. Soviet troops could have created a powerful barrier on the new Soviet-German border, especially since the opening was not wide. But at that moment the Soviet Union stopped producing anti-tank and anti-aircraft cannon. Instead of making the area impassable, it was quickly made more penetrable. The Red Army built bridges and roads, expanded and improved the railroads. Previously existing fortifications were torn down and buried under mounds of ground. One participant of those events, professor and Colonel I. G. Starinov of the GRU, candidly described what went on: "A stupid situation arose. When we faced weak armies of small countries, our borders were truly locked. But when Nazi Germany became our neighbor, the defense structures along the former border were abandoned and even partly dismantled."[1] And: "Engineering command of the Red Army sent a request for 120,000 railroad mines of delayed action. In the event of an invasion, this amount would have sufficed to paralyze the German army's supply routes from the rear, on which it entirely depended. But instead of the requested amount, they sent . . . 120 mines."[2] By the way, a mine is the most simple, most inexpensive, and highly effective weapon. The Soviet Union had huge land mine production, but after the new borders with Germany were established this production was curbed.

What did Stalin do aside from dismantling his own defenses? He also tore to pieces the barrier of neutral countries. For Hitler, one hole in the wall was enough. For Stalin, it was not. Hitler (with Stalin's help) demolished the leadership of only one country in the dividing barrier—Poland. Stalin (without outside help) did the same in three countries (Estonia, Latvia, and Lithuania), tried to do it in a fourth country (Finland), and actively prepared for doing it in a fifth country (Romania), having first ripped from it a huge chunk of land. Hitler strove to force only one opening in the wall, Stalin tried to demolish the entire wall.[3] And Stalin accomplished his goal. Only ten months after the signing of the non-aggression pact the dividing barrier was completely destroyed, from the Arctic Ocean to the Black Sea, by Stalin's efforts. There remained no neutral countries between Stalin and Hitler, and thus the conditions for attack were set.

During this short time all of Stalin's neighbors to the west became his victims. Aside from nations sharing borders with the Soviet Union, Lithuania, which did not have any common borders with the USSR at all, also fell under Stalin's domination. The appearance of Soviet troops in Lithuania meant that they had truly reached Germany's real borders: from September 1939 the Soviet-German border passed through the conquered Polish territories, and from the summer of 1940, Soviet troops came to the border of Eastern Prussia. Here it cannot at all be said that the monstrous Hitler was hacking corridors to the east, and the stupid Stalin was assisting him. No, Stalin hacked corridors to the west without any outside help.

Did the Red Army plan to stop at the borders it attained? The answer was given by the People's Commissar of Defense of the USSR, Marshal of the Soviet Union S. K. Timoshenko: "In Lithuania, Latvia, Estonia we destroyed a power of landowners and capitalists hateful to the workers. The Soviet Union grew significantly and advanced its borders to the west. The capitalist world was forced to tremble and cede to our will. We, the fighters of the Red Army, should not be content and stop at what has been attained!"[4] This was not the speech of a politician and not the announcement of a journalist. It was an official decree for the Red Army. But to the west of Soviet borders there was only Germany, or her allies; and a pact had been signed with Germany

Stalin made no secret of how a true Communist should view promises and pacts: "The question of struggle . . . needs to be examined not from the standpoint of fairness, but from the standpoint of demands of the political moment, from the standpoint of the political demands of the [Communist] Party at each given moment."[5] "A war can turn upside down each and every pact."[6] Here are the "political demands": "History says that when any country wants to fight against another country, even one that it does not neighbor, it begins to seek out borders, through which it could reach the borders of the country it wants to attack,"[7] Stalin wrote.

Stalin needed a situation in which "capitalists gnaw at each other like dogs."[8] The Molotov-Ribbentrop Pact created precisely that situation. *Pravda*'s tone was excited: "Each war like this one brings us closer to that happy period, when there will be no more killings among people."[9] Lieutenant General S. M. Krivoshein describes a conversation with his deputy, P. M. Latyshev (at that time Krivoshein commanded the 25th Motorized Corps): "We made a deal with the Germans, but this does not mean anything. . . . Now is the best time for a final and constructive resolution to all of the world's problems."[10]

Before the war, the main Communist Party newspaper, *Pravda*, did not call upon the Soviet people to build defenses. *Pravda*'s tone was different: soon the entire world will belong to us. "Our country is great. The globe itself needs to rotate nine hours in order for our huge Soviet country to enter the new year of its victories. There will be a time when it will need for this not nine hours, but a whole twenty-four. . . . And who knows where we will be greeting the New Year in five or ten years: along what time belt, on what new Soviet meridian?"[11] With the date of the Soviet break-in into Europe approaching, *Pravda* became more and more straightforward: "Divide your enemies, temporarily satisfy the demands of each of them, and then crush them one by one, without giving them an opportunity to unite."[12]

Hitler decided that he should wait no longer. He made the first move without waiting for the blow in the back from the liberating axe. But even having started the war in the most favorable circumstances that had ever existed for an assailant, he was unable to win. Even in the most unfavorable of circumstances, the Red Army managed to "liberate" half of Europe and dominate Eastern Europe for half a century. One wonders what the outcome would have been if the best German forces had left the European continent to go to Africa and the British Isles, and, behind their back, the Red Army had destroyed the only German oil source in Romania?

26

Destruction of the Security Pale
on the Eve of the War

Mines are powerful stuff, but they are a means for the weak, for those defending themselves. We are strong. We need mine-clearing measures rather than mines.

—G. I. KULIK, MARSHAL OF THE SOVIET UNION

To prevent a sudden enemy attack, a country preparing for defense deploys its troops not on the very border, but deeper in its territory. Between the border and the main line of defense, it creates a continuous zone of obstacles and barriers. This zone is called the security pale. Its purpose is to wear down the aggressor before he meets the main forces of the defense.

In the 1920s, during their attempt to occupy Poland, commanders of the Red Army saw the effectiveness of the Polish security pales for the defense of Poland and had the bitter experiences of advancing through such pales. That is why after the Polish war the special Soviet government commissions studied the western regions of their country and determined the most and the least penetrable zones. All bridges in the western regions of the country were prepared for explosion. Bridge patrols were ready to blow up the bridges at any moment. Aside from bridges, large pipelines, depots, water pumps, water towers, high mounds, and low gullies were all wired for explosion.[1] At the end of 1929, in the Kiev military district alone, sixty demolition squads, numbering 1,400 people, were trained and ready. They had at their disposal "1,640 fully ready charges and tens of thousands of incendiary pipes that could be put into action almost instantly!"[2] Such work was conducted in other military districts as well.

In addition to demolition experts' squads, railroad-blocking battalions were formed in the western regions of the country. Their task included completely demolishing major railroad centers in the event of retreat, blocking the main routes, and installing powerful charges with delayed-action detonators in the event that the enemy attempted to restore the roads. Ukraine had four such battalions by 1932.[3] On top of that, railroad switch transfers, communication equipment, telegraph systems, and in some cases railroad tracks, were all prepared for evacuation. The Soviet security pale was constantly improving. The list of objects prepared for explosion or evacuation became longer. New obstacles and barricades were erected, new forest abatises were prepared, and artificial reservoirs were dug in front of defensive structures; areas of the region could be turned into swamps if necessary.

In September 1939 the border of the USSR was moved 200 to 300 km to the west. The depth of the security pale increased greatly. Moreover, the railroad system on the territories acquired after the division of Poland was poorly developed. Out of 6,696 km of tracks, only 2,008 were two-way, and even they had a low capacity. In case of emergency, it was very easy to make them completely unusable.

In November 1939, the Red Army in Finland learned the hard way that a security pale could ease the position of the defense and complicate the position of the aggressor. Crossing the Finnish security pale required a huge expenditure of time, strength, resources, and blood.

All Soviet commanders expressed their awe at the Finnish line of defense, and among them was K. A. Meretskov, Commander of the 7th Army during the war against Finland.[4] After having surmounted the Finnish defense line and evaluated its qualities, Meretskov was appointed Chief of the General Staff. In accordance with his newly acquired experience, he should have reinforced the Soviet security pale. But he did exactly the opposite. Meretskov ordered the destruction of the security pale created earlier on the old western borders, the disbanding of the demolition experts' squads, the dismantling of the charges, the disarming of the mines, and the flattening out of all barricades. He also ordered his troops not to create a security pale on the Polish territory annexed to the Soviet Union in 1939; to lead the main forces of the Red Army to the edge of the borders (without protecting those forces with any kind of security pale); to move the bulk of the strategic supplies of the Red Army from the depths of the country to the western regions; to build air bases and roads in Western Belorussia and Western Ukraine; to transform one-track railroads into two-track ones (to raise their cargo-carrying capacity); and to build new roads leading straight to the German border.

Here are the results of that policy. In 1939, Poland was divided between Germany and the Soviet Union. Some rivers became borders. Bridges on those rivers that were not used were still kept intact. In the line held by the 4th Army alone, there were six such bridges.

The former Chief of Staff of the 4th Army, Colonel General L. M. Sandalov, asked: "Why, to ask frankly, were so many bridges across the Bug [river] kept intact in the line of the 4th Army?"[5] The German command hoped to use the bridges in an aggressive war, and thus did not ask for their destruction. But what did the Soviet command hope for?

At the beginning of the war, a huge number of German troops went across those bridges, crushing the Soviet 4th Army in a surprise attack. The defeat of the 4th Army opened the way to the rear of the really powerful 10th Army, which also suffered unimaginable devastation. Without encountering any more barriers, Guderian's tanks headed straight for Minsk in Belarus. The German troops advanced without complications, taking bridges on the rivers Daugava, Berezina, Nieman, Pripiat, and Dnepr.

In January 1941, Stalin replaced Chief of General Staff K. A. Meretskov for not being sufficiently active in the construction of new roads, bridges, and air bases in the new regions. On February 1, 1941, General of the Army G. K. Zhukov replaced Meretskov as Chief of the General Staff. The work began at a truly Zhukov speed. Before 1941, the Red

Army had five railroad brigades. Zhukov immediately increased this number to thirteen, ten of them in the west of the country. Each brigade consisted of one regiment, two separate battalions, and supply units. Almost all railroad troops were concentrated in the western border regions and worked intensively to modernize old railroads and build new ones right up to the border.[6] Some of the new railroad lines were: Proskurov—Ternopol—Lvov; Lvov—Iavorov—state border; Lvov—Peremyshl—state border; Timkovichi—Baranovichi; Belovezha—Oranchitsa—state border. The names of some of these stations demonstrated that the Soviet leadership regarded the border area as its own rear zone, where in the event of a quick advance to the west the Soviet army would have to deliver millions of men, millions of tons of ammunition, fuel, and other supplies.

Simultaneously with the construction of railroads, automobile roads were built in the western regions (for example, Orsha—Lepel, Lvov—Peremyshl, Belaya Tserkov—Kazatin, Minsk—Brest). What were those roads built for?

During preparations for a defensive war, roads parallel to the front line are laid down, so that reserves could be moved from passive areas of defense to dangerous areas. Those roads must not be near the border, but much deeper in the country, leaving the border regions as clear of roads and bridges as possible. But the Red Army was building roads and railroads from east to west, which was usually done when preparing for advance, for a quick transfer of reserves from the depths of the country to the borders, and for further supplying the troops after they crossed the borders. New roads led to border towns: Peremyshl, Brest, Iavorov. Zhukov remembered: "The web of automobile roads in Western Belorussia and Western Ukraine was in poor condition. Many bridges could not hold the weight of the medium tanks and artillery."[7] Zhukov should have rejoiced at that fact. He should have commanded his men to covertly weaken the support beams on those bridges and thus lure the attacking enemy to send his tanks to those weakened bridges, to their sure demise. Instead, he built roads and replaced old bridges with new ones, so that any tank and any artillery could pass through.

The official *History of the Kiev Military District* stated: "In early 1941, Hitler's forces began to build bridges, railroads, and field air bases."[8] Obviously, these were signs of preparations for attack. The Soviet railroad forces were doing exactly the same: "Railroad troops in Western Ukraine worked to develop and strengthen the railroads."[9] Railroad brigades, created by Zhukov's order, completed a tremendous amount of work on the Soviet territory, but their main job was planned to be on enemy territory: they had to follow the advancing army and quickly get through the enemy's security pale, repair enemy roads and bridges, and change the European narrow gauge to the broad Soviet standard one. Right on the borders, they piled huge reserves of railroad tracks, demountable bridges, construction materials, and coal.

In addition to the ten railroad brigades in the western regions, almost all the Soviet engineering troops were concentrated along the western borders. Various construction units and squads were active before the war in the border strip. The task was to prepare the "initial points for attack, [the] foundation of passageways for columns, . . . operational and tactical camouflage, organization of joint action in the storming groups with infantry and tanks; [and] to provide the equipment for crossing rivers."[10]

On the eve of the war, the USSR launched a gigantic campaign to modernize and widen its road network in the western regions. All that work harmed the USSR very soon.

Hitler used the roads, bridges, stocks of coal, rails, and the sectional bridges that the Soviet leadership prepared in the western regions of its country.

As we know, all that did not help the invading German army: its advance was not as fast as planned. But even this advance could have been stopped if Zhukov had not built roads on the eve of the war, had not created huge reserves of railroad tracks, bridges, and construction materials. He should have introduced an effective system of defense: all bridges should have been blown up, all materiel reserves liquidated, railroads and trains evacuated, roads destroyed, drowned, turned into swamps and saturated with mines.

On Soviet territory, all mines were disarmed and the barriers taken down. On the eve of the German invasion, General of the Army D. Pavlov, a commander of the Western Special Military District (then already secretly transformed into the Western Front), said that the Soviet sappers were not paying enough attention to preparing themselves properly for removing mines and other obstacles on enemy territory.

If the Soviet marshals had known better, they would have started their war on June 21: then they would not have needed to take down German obstacles, because the German army was doing on the German territory exactly what the Red Army was doing on Soviet territory. In early June, German troops were disarming mines, evening out barricades, and concentrating troops right on the border, without keeping in front of them any security pale.

Soviet Marshal K. S. Moskalenko, who in 1941 commanded the First Artillery Anti-Tank Brigade, counted those German actions as an unquestionable piece of evidence that the Germans would attack soon.[11] At the same time, the NKVD border troops were dismantling their own barbwire on the very border to clear the way into enemy territory for the "liberation" army. They had cut barbwire in exactly the same way before the "liberation" of Poland, Finland, Estonia, Latvia, Bessarabia, and Northern Bukovina. Now it was Germany's turn.

27

Partisans or Saboteurs?

Leninism dictates that a socialist country, using the favorable world situation, must take on the initiative of making military advances against the capitalist surroundings with the purpose of widening the socialist front. . . . Leninism's motto, "defend your land on foreign soil," can at any moment turn into practical action."

—DIRECTIVE OF THE MAIN POLITICAL DIRECTORATE OF THE
RED ARMY, JUNE 3, 1941.

Through partisan actions, one can fight against even the strongest enemy. The aggressor can take over the country in a matter of days, but then for years wage an exhausting war against partisan groups. History abounds with examples of small and poorly armed partisan units eventually defeating powerful armies.

The Red Army had a vast experience fighting against partisans. Commanders of the Red Army knew how difficult and costly partisan warfare could be. During the Russian civil war, the population of the former Russian Empire resisted the Communists mostly through partisan methods. An entire partisan army under the leadership of Nestor Makhno was active in southern Ukraine. In the Tambov province, after the civil war, the Communists waged a real war against the partisan army of Alexander Antonov. In Siberia and in the northern Caucasus, war against partisans continued until the mid-1920s and in Central Asia until the beginning of the 1930s.

Soviet leaders knew that partisan tactics would win the war against any aggressor. The Soviet Union has the largest territory of any country in the world. That territory naturally facilitated partisan warfare. Did Stalin create light mobile units and station them in the woods in the event of a German attack? Yes, Stalin created such units. They were created back in the 1920s. In Belorussia alone, during peacetime there were six partisan units, numbering three hundred to five hundred men each. One should not be confused by the seemingly small numbers. The units were comprised only of commanders, organizers, and specialists. Each peacetime partisan unit was a nucleus, around which at the very beginning of the war developed a powerful formation numbering in the thousands.

Secret bases for peacetime partisan groups were created in impenetrable forests and islets amid the swamps. During peacetime, subterranean shelters, hospitals, storages, and workshops for the production of weapons and ammunition were built. In peacetime, only Belorussian secret subterranean storages held ammunition, weapons, and supplies for fifty thousand partisans. Secret schools were formed for preparing partisan leaders, organizers, and instructors. Secret research and development centers worked on creating special means of warfare, arms, communication channels, and equipment. Partisans were often subjected to training and tests, with divisions of the NKVD often playing the role of the enemy. In addition, small groups were prepared for undercover activities. These groups, in case of aggression, did not retreat to the forests, but stayed in the cities and towns, with the task of "gaining the trust of the enemy" and "offering him assistance."

That sort of work was conducted not only in Belorussia, but also in Ukraine, in the Crimea, in the Leningrad region, and other areas. The same duties were simultaneously, but totally independently from the NKVD, performed by the Soviet Military Intelligence: it set up secret bases, apartments, and hiding places, and prepared lines of communication for conspirators. Soviet Military Intelligence had its own secret schools, its own organizers, and its own instructors. Aside from the NKVD and the military intelligence, the Communist Party prepared some of its leaders in the western regions of the country for transfer to an underground position in the event of a territory takeover by the enemy.

The partisan units were formed in the so-called "death zone"—the Soviet security pale, where during retreat of Soviet troops all bridges should be blown up, tunnels buried, railroads destroyed, and telephone cables and other communication channels evacuated. The partisans had to prevent the enemy from restoring the destroyed infrastructure. The partisans were almost undefeatable—their leaders knew safe passages, which the enemy did not know, through the giant minefields; in an emergency, the partisans could easily disappear from any pursuers into the mined forests and swamps, which were impassable to the enemy.

The security pale and partisan groups, ready at any minute to act in a zone of destruction, were the great defenses of the Soviet Union. However, in the second half of the 1930s, as the country's industrial and military might grew, the Soviet Union tended to fight enemies on their soil rather than protect Soviet land. From that period, defense systems became unnecessary. "Whole caches of weaponry, ammunition, [and] explosives, intended for partisan forces and kept hidden, were liquidated. The network of partisan training schools, along with their very competent leaders, was eliminated. Partisan battle groups were disbanded. Only the few partisan leaders who confronted the fascists in Spain kept their places. Among them were A. K. Sprogis, S. A. Vaupshassov, N. A. Prokopyuk, I. G. Starinov, and others."[1]

On November 30, 1939, the Red Army began the "liberation" of Finland, and hit up against the same elements of self-defense that had earlier existed in the Soviet Union: a line of concrete fortifications, a security pale before it, and light squads of partisan fighters within. The light ski units of Finnish partisans carried out sudden strikes and then immediately disappeared into the forests. The Red Army suffered tremendous casualties from those strikes, and all its modern technology was useless in the fight against an enemy that evaded open battle. Perhaps, having learned a cruel lesson in Finland, Stalin changed his mind and once again created partisan formations in the western regions of the Soviet Union? No, he did not.

One of the fathers of Soviet military terrorism, GRU colonel and professor I. G. Starinov, between 1930 and 1933 headed the secret school that prepared partisan groups which were subordinate to the Soviet Military Intelligence. The colonel wrote in his memoirs: "Safely hidden underground, the weapons and explosives awaited their hour. But before this hour could come, the covert partisan bases were emptied, unquestionably with the knowledge of, and, probably, under direct orders from Stalin."[2]

During the war, P. K. Ponomarenko was Chief of the Main Staff of the Partisan Movement. After the war, he voiced his anguish and frustration: "Stalin's incorrectly aimed statements that, if attacked, we would fight only on enemy territory led to the complete dismantling of all efforts to harness the experience from previous partisan wars and to develop corresponding mobilization directions. As a result, the initial phase of the war was marked by a particularly difficult effort to organize the partisan movement. The Party had to pay dearly for Stalin's mistakes."[3]

Colonel of the KGB S. A. Vaushpass[4] spent the 1930s training Soviet partisans in case of enemy aggression and occupation. He explained the reason for the disbanding of the partisan formations on Soviet territory: "During those threatening pre-war years, a doctrine arose about war on foreign soil . . . it had [a] very clearly expressed aggressive character."[5]

We can agree with these statements or we can dispute them. But so far, no other reason for the destruction of the partisan movement has been put forward.

28

Destruction of the Stalin Line

Only naïve people think that defense is the main task of fortified regions. No, fortified regions are built for a more reliable preparation for advance. They must reliably cover the reserves of attacking groups, deflect any enemy attempt to curb the unfolding of attack, and with the transition of our troops to advance, offer them full fire cover.

—Major General P. G. Grigorenko,
You Only Meet Rats in the Underground

From 1926 to 1937, thirteen fortified regions were constructed along the western borders of the USSR. That chain of fortifications was unofficially known as "the Stalin Line."

A fortified region (FR) was an area prepared for defense; at the same time, it was also a military formation, equal to a regiment or a brigade in number but equal to a corps in firepower. Each FR had a command and staff, from two to eight machine-gun and artillery battalions, an artillery regiment, several separate heavy artillery batteries, a tank battalion, a communications battalion, an engineering-sapper battalion and other formations. Each FR occupied an area from 100 to 180 km long and 30 to 50 km deep. The region was equipped with a complex system of concrete and armored military and supply buildings, mostly subterranean. Within the FR, there were underground concrete storage units, electricity stations, hospitals, command centers, and communication quarters. The underground constructions were connected through a sophisticated system of tunnels, galleries, and covered passageways. There was also an intricate web of railroads for bringing in materials, maneuvering armored trains, and quickly transferring reserves to the troops. Each FR could independently conduct military operations during a long period of time and in isolated conditions.

The fortified regions were built by the distinguished fortification expert of the twentieth century, Professor Dmitryi Karbyshev. In 1940, he was awarded the rank of lieutenant general of engineering troops. Simultaneously with the developments on the western frontiers, Karbyshev's projects also encompassed construction of fortified regions in the Far East and in the Trans-Baikal region. Those field strongholds are still in use today, in the twenty-first century. In 1990, the Soviet military newspaper *Krasnaya Zvezda* described one of the active military buildings: "This is mono-concrete. Solid cast. The depth of the walls is up to one and a half meters. For half a century, they have been there, but even today not a single shell could take them. . . . Roofs of casemates have a low-profile. Ammunition. Command. Diesel engines. Batteries. Filters. An automatic heating system. . . . In this shell, filled with instruments and arms, one feels as if [one is] in a giant buried tank or a submarine hidden underground."[1]

Each FR consisted of "pillboxes," each equipped with its own defenses and each capable of independently defending itself if fully encircled by the enemy, diverting to itself significant enemy forces and attention. The main fighting unit of the fortified region was the LFP—long-duration firing point. *Krasnaya Zvezda* described one of the standard LFPs from the Stalin Line, the LFP #112 of the Mogilyov-Podolsk FR, as follows: "This was a complicated fortified underground structure, consisting of communication passages, caponiers, and compartments. In there, one could find arms, ammunition, foodstuffs, a mess hall, running water (by the way, still in working condition), a 'red corner,' [and] observation and command posts.[2] The LFPs are armed with a machine-gun post of three embrasures in which, on stationary rollers, were three 'Maxim' machine guns and two half-canopies with 76-mm cannon in each."[3] Such an LFP can be considered average. There were also thousands of small, armed constructions with one or two machine guns, as well as giant fortified ensembles.

Major General P. G. Grigorenko, a participant in the construction of the Stalin Line, described in his memoirs one of the field strongholds built in the similar Mogilyov-Podolsk FR: "Nine firing points, connected by underground passageways, were on the high shores of the Dnestr and kept the river and the opposite shore under dense gun and machine-gun fire."[4] Another participant in the construction of the Stalin Line, Colonel R. G. Umanskyi, wrote of multi-kilometer underground structures in the Kiev fortified region.[5] Yet another participant, Colonel General A. I. Shebunin, said that many concrete defensive structures in the Proskurov fortified region were protected by artificial water barriers. In this FR was raised "a mighty line of defense, which counted more than a thousand various military field strongholds. Many objects were so thoroughly masked that even from close up it was difficult to guess their real designation."[6]

Construction of the Stalin Line was not publicized like the construction of the French Maginot Line. The Stalin Line was built in secrecy. During the construction of each field stronghold, NKVD units put cordons around several areas. The construction went on simultaneously in all areas, but it was the real thing only in one—the rest were decoys. Not only the local population but also the construction workers had a very vague understanding of what was being built and where.

There were many differences between the Soviet Stalin Line and the French Maginot Line. The Stalin Line could not be bypassed: its flanks went right to the Baltic Sea in the north and the Black Sea in the south. The Stalin Line was built not only to stop infantry, but mostly to stop tanks. The Stalin Line was much deeper. Aside from concrete, the Soviets also used huge quantities of steel, and granite boulders.

Unlike the Maginot Line, the Stalin Line wasn't built at the very border, but deeper into Soviet territory. A line of fortified regions in the depth of the country means that the first enemy artillery strike will be carried out against an empty space rather than the defending army. Therefore, during a surprise attack, defending garrisons have a minimum of several days to take their places in the casemates and prepare their arms and defense. If the fortified regions are in the depth of the country, the enemy, before beginning the storming, must cover from 20 or 30 to 100 or 150 km of territory saturated with minefields and other unpleasant surprises. The aggressor will have to cross many rivers and streams whose bridges have been destroyed. Before the storming, enemy troops will already have suffered significant casualties in the hundreds of ambushes along the way.

The security pale before the Stalin Line not only reduced the speed of the enemy and wore out his strength, but it also served as a fog over the sea, behind which hid a row of icebergs. Not knowing the exact location of the field strongholds of the Stalin Line, the enemy could unexpectedly find himself right in front of Soviet armed structures and in the midst of their deadly fire. The location of the Stalin Line deep in Soviet territory, behind the security pale, produced the opportunity to counter the surprise element of attack with a surprise element of defense. The fortified regions were masked and hidden in such a way that in most cases a clash between the aggressor and Stalin's army would be unexpected for the aggressor.

Unlike the Maginot Line, the Stalin Line was not continuous. Rather wide passageways were left between the fortified regions. In an emergency, the passages could quickly be closed with land mines, barricades, or field defense by regular troops. Or the passages could stay open, offering the aggressor the option to not storm the fortifications head on, but to squeeze between them instead. If the enemy attempted the latter, most of his advancing troops would be crushed in several isolated columns. Each column had to advance through a corridor shelled from all sides, with its flanks, rear, and communication lines under constant and serious threat.

The thirteen fortified regions on the Stalin Line came at a tremendous cost in effort and money. In 1938 it was decided to strengthen all thirteen regions by building within them heavy artillery installations. The construction of eight more regions started. In one year, the new fortified regions counted 1,028 armed field strongholds.

Then, the Molotov-Ribbentrop Pact was signed. The pact created a common border between Germany and the USSR. In such a threatening atmosphere, Stalin could have done any number of things to increase the safety of the western Soviet borders and guarantee the USSR's neutrality in the war. Instead, in the fall of 1939, at the beginning of World War II, he ordered further construction of fortified regions to stop.[7] Garrisons in fortified regions on the Stalin Line were the first to be cut back in numbers, and then completely disbanded. Soviet factories lowered the output of arms and special materials for field stronghold structures. The existing fortified regions were disarmed; their ammunition, weapons, observation instruments, and communication lines were put in storage.[8] Some buildings were given to the farming associations for use as crop silos. Most were just buried in soil.

In addition to lowering the production of arms for fortified regions, Soviet industry, after the start of World War II, stopped producing other defense weapons. For example, the production of anti-tank cannon stopped completely, as well as the 76-mm division cannon, which could be used against tanks.[9] Anti-tank rifles were taken out of production and out of the supply of the Red Army. They were taken away from all formations and put in storage.[10] Everything connected with defense was mercilessly dismantled and destroyed. At the same time, the Red Army was fighting in Finland, where Stalin and his marshals saw that fortified regions and security pales had tremendous value for defense.

To be fair, during the summer of 1940, the construction of a line of fortified regions began right on the new Soviet-German border. However, the new line was never finished. In the General Staff of the Red Army, these regions were unofficially (and with a dose of irony) referred to as the Molotov Line. It had the same "father": Professor Karbyshev. The decision to construct it came on June 26, 1940.[11] But the defense buildup on the new borders proceeded very slowly, while the destruction on the old borders was surprisingly fast. In the summer of 1941, the tragedy of the Stalin Line reached its climax. Wrote General Grigorenko:

> I do not know how future historians will explain this crime against our people. . . . The present ones bypass this occurrence with complete silence, and I myself do not know how to explain it. Many billions of rubles (according to my calculations, more than 120) were taken by the Soviet government from the people to build impassable barriers on the border, from sea to sea, from the grey Baltic to the blue Black Sea. And on the eve of the war, the spring of 1941, loud explosions boomed across the 1,200 km of fortifications. The formidable concrete structures, triple, double, and single embrasure firing points, command and observation points—tens of thousands of long-term defense structures were blown up according to a personal order from Stalin.[12]

The Stalin Line on the old border was already destroyed, while the Molotov Line on the new border was not yet built. Soviet generals and marshals, after Stalin's death, unanimously expressed their anger. Here are the words of Chief Marshal of Artillery N. N. Voronov: "How could our leadership, without building the necessary defenses on the new western borders of 1939, decide to liquidate and disarm the fortified regions on the old borders?"[13] In addition, as Marshal M. V. Zakharov declared, it was decided to severely limit or even stop the production of all FR-type weaponry.[14]

This is a "red herring" argument used by pro-Communist historians to distract us. They want us to bemoan the folly of breaking the old fortifications line before the new one was ready. But the relevant question is: why break the old one at all? Two lines surely provide better defense than one.

Another pretext is that old fortifications were destroyed in order to move their weapons to the new ones. This is just another set of fallacies. Firstly, the weapons could have been left in the old line, and there had been enough time to order the Soviet industry to supply FR-type weaponry for the new line. But we know that the production of this type of weaponry was reduced immensely in favor of offensive-type arms.

Secondly, one does not demolish his old house just to move the furniture to the new one, unless the old house is not needed. With weapons in the fortifications it is exactly the same.

Thirdly, pro-Communist historians hope that we do not remember the chronology of the events: Stalin started to demolish the old line in September 1939, and decided to build the new one only on June 26, 1940. They want us to believe that the cause came after its consequence.

The dates demonstrate that there was no connection between those two events, except for the fact that the Stalin Line was built for a defensive war and the Molotov Line was built for an aggressive war against Germany, as we shall show further on.

In comparison with the Stalin Line, the Molotov Line was a thin chain of rather light field strongholds that did not require much armament. For example, in the western special military district in Belorussia, there were 193 field strongholds built near the new border. The old one had 876 much more powerful ones. In other military districts, the ratios between the newly built constructions and those destroyed earlier were even more astonishing.

The Molotov Line drastically differed from the Stalin Line in design and in detail. There were four main differences between the field strongholds torn down near the old borders and those created near the new ones: the Molotov Line was built so that the enemy could see it; it was built on secondary locations; it was not covered by a security pale, minefields, or other engineered obstacles; and the builders did not use many opportunities available to them to fortify the line, and did not rush to complete their work.

For example, such a secondary location was in the Brest area. There the border river was crossed at once by six railroad and automotive bridges. The main strategic direction of attack of the Germans was Warsaw-Brest-Minsk-Smolensk-Moscow. That's why the bridges of Brest had huge strategic value. But the new fortified region was built 27 km north of Brest where there were no bridges! The fortified regions of the Molotov Line were pushed to the very edge of the border. They were not covered by a security pale, and in case of sudden attack, the garrisons had no time to take firing positions and prepare their arms.[15]

Unlike the Stalin Line, the fortified regions of the Molotov Line had very little depth. All that could be built on the very edge of the border was built there. According to Lieutenant General V. F. Zotov, rear defenses were neither built nor planned.[16] New fortifications weren't built on locations tactically valuable for defense, but along the state border, following its twists and bends. New military buildings were not defended by barbwire fences, mines, trenches, or tetrahedrons. There were no engineered obstacles in the construction area. The new constructions were not camouflaged.[17]

At the same time, the German generals were doing the same. Between 1932 and 1937, mighty field strongholds were built on the shores of the Oder River, shielding Germany from strikes from the east. These were first-rate military structures, blended with the landscape and brilliantly camouflaged. I will not describe them in detail, but they are a formidable example of the German preciseness, accuracy, and industriousness. Fortified regions in the area between the Oder and the Warta rivers could serve as examples of the highest achievement of military engineering of the early twentieth century.

As soon as the Molotov-Ribbentrop Pact was signed in Moscow and the German army invaded Poland, the magnificent field strongholds near the old German border were abandoned and never again occupied by armies. Many field constructions were used for other purposes. For example, in the Hochwald region there was a powerful fortification ensemble, which included twenty-three four-story military constructions, connected by 30 km of underground tunnels. It was transformed into a factory for airplane motors. Having advanced and met with the Red Army in mid-Poland, the German troops began constructing a new line of fortified regions. They were built on secondary locations and pushed right up to the Soviet borders. In front of the new fortified regions, there were no minefields and no obstacles. The Germans worked night and day, and the Soviet border patrol saw that very clearly.[18]

German construction continued until May 1941, after which, to use Soviet language, "construction was rated as a second-class priority." Out of eighty military constructions planned to be built on the border river San, only seventeen were completed. They were all insufficiently camouflaged. Each of these constructions could be described as light compared to those on the old German-Polish border: relatively thin walls, and steel armor plates of just 100 mm. On the old borders, along the Oder line, they had used much stronger armor plates of up to 350 mm. Soviet officers later saw both German and Soviet LFPs on both sides of the same river. If one showed photos of the LFPs to an expert and asked him to distinguish the German from the Soviet, he would be stumped. They were identical twins: when building the Molotov Line on the shores of the same river San, Soviet engineers also used relatively thin armor plates of 100 mm.

While their neighbor was weak Poland, German troops erected on their borders powerful fortifications; as soon as they crushed Poland and established a common border with the Soviet Union, the Germans abandoned the old fortifications, and built along the new borders, very slowly, only light defense structures. Just like the Red Army! That was because both sides did not plan to defend their new borders for long.

Fortification can be both defensive and offensive. If you are planning to attack, then you follow these rules during the construction of fortified regions:

- Gather attack groups of troops in the primary locations, leave secondary locations almost without troops and protect them with real fortified regions.
- In the primary locations, do not try to camouflage your fortifications; let the enemy think that you are preparing for defense.
- Everything that can be located right on the shores of border rivers should be located there: during your troops' advance across the river, these fortifications, placed right on the border, will support your advance with fire.
- Do not protect frontline fortifications with minefields and barbwire—they would hinder your own advancing troops.
- Do not waste a lot of cement and steel for frontline fortifications—you are not planning to sit in defensive positions for long.
- Do not build fortifications deep in your territory—they will be unnecessary.

These rules governed the actions of the Soviet and German generals from 1939. In August 1939, Zhukov brilliantly used these rules in Khalkhin-Gol: "With these actions, we strove to make the enemy believe in the absence of any sort of preparations for advance from our side, and to show that we [were] conducting widespread defensive works, and only for defense."[19] The Japanese believed in Zhukov's "defensive" works and paid dearly for their folly. Later, on a much grander scale, Zhukov staged the same deception on the German border.

However, he did not fool the German generals. They had their own identical experience with Poland. On August 22, 1939, during the negotiations of the Molotov-Ribbentrop Pact and preparations of the German army to invade Poland, General Guderian received an order to command the "fortification team of Pomerania." The goal was to calm the Poles by showing them strictly defensive preparations, while raising, with minimal effort, light fortifications.

In the spring and summer of 1941, Guderian again was building defenses, this time on the Soviet border. If Guderian built light concrete boxes near the border, it did not at all follow that he intended to defend himself. It meant exactly the opposite. And if Zhukov built identical boxes along the same borders, what did that mean?

The Stalin Line was universal: it could be used either for defense or for attack—the wide passages between the fortified regions were left intact to let through masses of troops advancing west. When the border was moved a few hundred kilometers west, the Stalin Line completely lost its use as a fortified launching ground for attack, and Stalin did not need it for defense after he signed the Molotov-Ribbentrop Pact. As a result, the Stalin Line was disarmed and then dismantled: Stalin was not planning to fight on his territory. After Germany got bogged down in a war against Great Britain, Stalin no longer needed the fortified regions in the depths of Soviet territory.

Hitler faced the same situation, not only on his eastern borders but on the western ones as well. There, in the 1930s, he built the Siegfried Line. Traditionally, since the times of the Franco-Prussian War, a German attack on France was always planned in the north. The Siegfried Line was built to the south of that direction—in other words, on a secondary location—following the principle of attacking the primary and fortifying the secondary location. In 1940, the German army advanced far west, and the Siegfried Line became useless. At that time, Hitler had no idea that in four years he would have to defend his own borders again. The Siegfried Line was abandoned. Its new use was quite unusual—the military constructions were given to farmers for storing potatoes. Some of the military structures had their unbreakable armored doors locked from within; when someone wanted to get in, the keys were nowhere to be found.[20]

We could, of course, call outstanding Soviet and German generals idiots. But stupidity is not the explanation here. Simply put, both sides were aggressors. Both were thinking in terms of attack, and when fortifications could no longer be used for invasion, they tore them down or put them to whatever use they saw fit.

29

Trotsky Murdered, Molotov in Berlin

Hitler will send his main forces west, and Moscow will want to use the advantages of her position.

—L. TROTSKY, JUNE 21, 1939

On August 21, 1940, in Mexico, Leon Trotsky was gruesomely murdered. An agent of the NKVD, Spanish Communist Ramon Mercader (also known as "Jacques Mornar Vandenrein" and "Ramon Ivanovich Lopez") posed as an idealistic Trotskyite and penetrated Trotsky's inner circle. Trotsky liked the essays Mercader wrote and the pleasant young admirer became a fixture at Trotsky's home. On the day of the murder, the two of them were alone in Trotsky's office. Trotsky was bent over his desk reading an article by Mercader when his guest pulled out an ice-pick from inside his trench coat and crushed Trotsky's skull with a monstrous blow.

Mercader was arrested at the scene of the crime; but he refused to testify. The Mexican court sentenced him to twenty years in prison. On May 6, 1960, three months short of completing his term, he was released for good behavior. Mercader returned to the USSR and was awarded the title of Hero of the Soviet Union with the "Golden Star," and the highest governmental award, the Order of Lenin. He was given a position as a researcher at the Marxism-Leninism Institute of the Central Committee of the Soviet Union Communist Party. At that time, people joked that, after becoming a staff fellow at such a respectable academic institution, Mercader was writing a multi-volume dissertation on the topic of "Alternative Uses for Ice-Picks."

Some said that Trotsky's murder had no meaning, that Trotsky had few followers, lived in remote Mexico, and posed no threat. It was said that the murder was Stalin's personal vendetta and a manifestation of his paranoia. But some ambiguities remained. Why was Trotsky in Mexico in the first place?

Trotsky reached the peak of his career in October 1917. Under his leadership, the Bolsheviks engineered the state coup and the takeover of Petrograd (St. Petersburg), the former Russian capital. Trotsky was effectively the founder and leader of the Red Army during the entire Civil War. However, already during the Civil War, he was not the most important man. He shared the top powers with Lenin. Gradually, Trotsky was relegated to secondary roles. His slide from the top accelerated and turned into a rapid fall. By 1923, Trotsky was the head of a leftist opposition within the Communist party, meaning that he was in the minority. By 1927, Trotsky was ousted from all his posts and deprived of all duties and privileges. On November 7, 1927, Trotsky tried to give a speech in front of a column of demonstrators headed for Red Square, but he was pelted with empty bottles and stones. Killing Trotsky was not a challenge. There would have been plenty of volunteers. Why didn't Stalin kill Trotsky then?

In early 1928, Stalin exiled Trotsky to Kazakhstan. A year later, he sent Trotsky to Turkey. Again, we ask: what for? In Kazakhstan, Trotsky was completely isolated and fully monitored by Stalin's secret police. The Soviet Union's borders were hermetically sealed, and running out of the country was extremely difficult. For Trotsky, it would have been completely impossible, since he was under constant surveillance. He could not run away from Stalin. He did not even exhibit any desire to do so. As a political opponent, Trotsky was completely disarmed. He had no power strings, no influence, no money, and no means of communication. No one published anything he wrote. His letters were checked, detained for several months, and in most cases simply disappeared. Trotsky's followers were harshly persecuted. Monstrous beatings of Trotskyites in dark alleys were just the earliest and most modest manifestations of Stalin's aversion. Later on, there were exiles, prisons, torture, public trials, and executions. Millions disassociated themselves from Trotsky. Only a few individuals remained true to him.

Human nature is such that people befriend those who are rich and powerful, but when someone falls from the top to the bottom of the power ladder, the number of his friends and supporters falls drastically. Suddenly volunteers appear to kick yesterday's boss. Stalin exterminated millions whom he considered to be his enemies or potential enemies. Stalin sent his opponents to Siberia, to the Far East, to Kazakhstan, to Sakhalin and Kolyma, or directly to the execution cellars. Only one enemy, Trotsky, the most significant one, Stalin brought out of Kazakhstan and sent to the heavenly islands in Turkey's Sea of Marmara.

If Trotsky had been dangerous, Stalin could have isolated him the same way he isolated Lenin in the last years of his life.[1] Trotsky could have perished on the operating table, like Michael Frunze, who replaced Trotsky as the leader of the Red Army, in 1925. Trotsky could have drowned in a lake, like Efraim Skliansky, Trotsky's deputy commander of the Red Army during the Civil War, in 1925.

Stalin, at that time, had three secretaries: Bazhanov for "daylight operations," Mekhlis for "twilight" ones, and Grigoryi Kanner for "dark" operations. Bazhanov remembered that Michael Frunze had to be placed on the operating table by force; that was how much Stalin cared for the health of his buddy. Frunze was right to put up a fight. Death awaited him on the operating table. He must have guessed this. The arrangements for the operation were handled by Kanner. When the secretary for "daylight operations" Bazhanov heard about this, everything was clear to him.[2] Bazhanov described how he received news of Skliansky's puzzling death: "Mekhlis and I immediately went to Kanner and unanimously said: 'Grisha, it is you who drowned Skliansky.' Mekhlis and I were completely certain that Skliansky was drowned on Stalin's orders, and the "accident" was organized by Kanner and Iagoda."[3] By the way, Kanner was executed by a firing squad in 1937, Iagoda in 1938.

In Kazakhstan, Trotsky could not publish anything. By letting Trotsky go free, Stalin gave him the opportunity to say and write anything he wanted, including the most horrible things about Stalin. Why did Stalin postpone Trotsky's murder for so long? In the 1930s, Stalin accused all his enemies in the country of being Trotskyites. Trotskyites and those who were branded Trotskyites were executed by the thousands or sent to the camps by the thousands. Meanwhile, Trotsky himself was free. He lived on islands of fantastic beauty in Turkey, then in the south of France, in Norway, and finally in Mexico. Then, all of a sudden, the hunt for Trotsky began. There were several assassination attempts until the successful blow with the ice-pick.

Did Stalin's paranoia increase? No. On the eve and at the very beginning of World War II, Trotsky presented a clear and imminent danger not only to Stalin, but to the entire Soviet leadership. Trotsky fanatically supported the World Revolution. Once he realized that it had failed in Germany and throughout the world he warned that Soviet Russia could not survive encircled by capitalist states. The only hope was to turn Soviet Russia into a military camp and use its forces to aid revolutions whenever and wherever an opportunity appeared. Stalin insisted that Trotsky was wrong and the Soviet Union first had to build "Socialism in One Country." The Soviet Union would not export revolution. Then Stalin took more radical measures than Trotsky had proposed to turn the Soviet Union into a military camp. He carried out forced collectivization and industrialization, and built the GULAG camps for forced labor. Under Stalin the Soviet Union became an industrial power and the military base for World Revolution. Summing up, Trotsky loudly called for the World Communist Revolution. Stalin acted to achieve the same goal, but said that Trotsky's slogans were wrong.

Stalin's rhetoric was successful and duped Trotsky, who thought he was exposing Stalin when he declared to the world that Stalin had betrayed the cause of Communism and World Revolution. Trotsky did not understand that criticism was necessary for Stalin and was part of his plan. With his accusations, Trotsky dulled the fears of the West that Stalin would pursue World Revolution. Trotsky claimed that there was no reason to fear Stalin, that Stalin was "the greatest mediocrity in power," and that his regime would implode from within. "Stalin's personal dictatorship clearly nears its sunset," Trotsky said in November 1931.[4] Thus, with Trotsky's dubious endorsement, the West helped Stalin to create a powerful military industry, and to prepare his country and army to crush Western civilization.

Trotsky's opinion had credibility for Western politicians; after all, he had played a key role in the revolution, the Civil War, and the establishment of the Red Army. Trotsky launched the World Revolution, but he lost power. Stalin, if one believed Trotsky, was not instigating revolution but building socialism in one country, the Soviet Union. Stalin let Trotsky leave the Soviet Union and provided him with publicity around the world. Contact with Trotsky was a standard accusation against so called "enemies of the people" at every political trial in Moscow. Stalin could have called his enemies any number of names, but he stubbornly called them Trotskyites, giving Trotsky additional political weight. If Trotsky had asserted the opposite, if he had said that Stalin was preparing for aggression, if he had warned the West of the dangers of Stalin's malice, he would have been murdered as early as 1927.

Gradually, Trotsky sensed Stalin's true intentions. He stopped writing that Stalin had betrayed the cause of the World Revolution and started writing that Hitler had come to power with Stalin's help. "Without Stalin, there would be no Hitler," said Trotsky. "Hitler was preparing for war. . . . The strike against the West in the near or far future could only be realized in the conditions of a military alliance between Fascist Germany and Stalin."[5]

On September 4, 1939, Trotsky reminded the world that "the Kremlin had fed oil to the Italian campaign into Abyssinia," and now it fed oil to Hitler's war against Europe. Trotsky asked why the pact of non-aggression between the Soviet Union and Germany had turned into war. "Is it unclear why Hitler began the advance on Poland immediately after the embraces between Ribbentrop and Molotov? Stalin knew very well what he was doing. For an attack against Poland and a war against England and France, Hitler needed favorable "neutrality" from the USSR, plus Soviet raw materials. The political and economic agreement provides Hitler with one and the other."[6]

At that point Trotsky stopped being useful to Stalin, and Stalin decided to get rid of him. Moreover, Trotsky had become dangerous. He warned Great Britain and France that the root of all evil was not Hitler, but Stalin. Without Stalin's "neutrality" toward Hitler, without Soviet petroleum, chrome, tin, nickel, platinum, iron ore, cotton, grain, manganese, copper, vanadium, molybdenum, and tungsten, Hitler could not have unleashed the war in Europe. But Trotsky warned Hitler as well. Back in June 1939, when very few people in the world had any idea that in a couple of months World War II would start, Trotsky exhibited amazing foresight when he wrote: "Hitler is going to strike to the west with his main forces and Moscow will be eager to fully take advantage of the situation."

Trotsky's predictions began to come true. In May 1940, Hitler invaded Belgium, the Netherlands, and France, and Stalin fully exploited the situation. On November 12, 1940, Soviet foreign minister Molotov arrived in Berlin and presented to Hitler a long list of territorial claims on behalf of the Soviet Union. These demands were repeated on November 25, 1940, when the Soviet Union proposed a peace pact between Germany, Italy, Japan, and the USSR. The Soviet Union demanded:

- from Finland: Pechenga, the only Finnish port on the Barents Sea, and Porkkala-Udd, the strategically located peninsula on the Baltic Sea controlling the entrance to the Gulf of Finland;
- naval bases on the Danish side of the straits of Kattegat and Skagerrak, controlling access to the North Sea and to the Baltic Sea;
- from Yugoslavia: a naval base on the Adriatic Sea;
- from Greece: a naval base in the Greek port of Thessaloniki;
- from Romania: the province of Southern Bukovina , a strategic foothold in the Carpathian Mountains to control access to the Ploești oil fields;
- from Bulgaria: a pact of alliance with the Soviet Union including Bulgaria in the Soviet sphere of influence;
- from Turkey: bases in the Bosporus and Dardanelles straits;
- from Iran: bases in the Persian Gulf;
- the transfer of territories south of the Baku-Batumi line (in eastern Turkey, north of Iraq and Iran) to the Soviet sphere of influence;
- from Japan: the renunciation of its oil concessions in the province of Northern Sakhalin.

Hitler and his officials were dumbfounded by such extraordinary demands and did not respond.

On November 13, 1940, Molotov asked Stalin for instructions "about China, Turkey, and our interests regarding the Persian Gulf and the Arabian Sea."[7] Stalin advised Molotov: "Do not expose our interest in Persia. . . . If the Germans suggest a division of Turkey, you can show our cards."[8] In this correspondence, Stalin "suggested" to Molotov to obtain Germany's consent for another self-serving step to be taken by the Soviet Union. He told Molotov to advise Hitler that the Soviet proposal for an alliance with the Axis powers would "not be possible without a guarantee of our control of Bulgaria and the passage of our troops into Bulgaria."

In November 1940, Germany was in a difficult position. World War II had been going on for more than a year, and no end was in sight. Germany could win only in a quick war. On the evening of November 13, during talks between Hitler and Molotov, the British air force bombed Berlin. The meeting that had started in a luxurious reception room ended in an underground bomb shelter. With the air raid, Churchill showed Hitler and Molotov that Great Britain did not plan to surrender.

For a drawn-out war, Hitler needed tremendous quantities of strategic raw materials, which Stalin could provide. During the meeting, Molotov repeatedly reminded Hitler that without Soviet raw materials German victories in Europe would have been impossible: "The current status would not have been achieved without the influence of the German-Russian agreement [of August 1939] on the great German victories."[9] "As far as Germany is concerned, these [1939] agreements secured a safe rear for Germany and played a major role in the development of a military campaign in the West, including France's defeat."[10] "Germany, not without the help of the pact with the USSR, was able so quickly and with military glory to execute its operations in Norway, Denmark, Belgium, Holland, and France."[11]

Stalin twisted Hitler's arms. Trotsky predicted that Stalin "would want to fully use the advantage of his position." That was precisely what Stalin did. Hitler told Molotov that Germany had conquered so much territory in one year of war that it would need a hundred years to develop it. He offered: if space was needed, Germany and the Soviet Union could both move to the south of their borders. Molotov agreed with the proposal, but added that they had to discuss the issue of the Danish straits Store Baelt and Lille Baelt, as well as the straits between Denmark and Sweden and Norway, Sund, Kattegat, and Skagerrak. For the Germans, these straits were a strategic necessity, since they already occupied Denmark. Why would the Soviet Union need them?

Hitler told Molotov: "While the war is going on, Germany is extremely interested in receiving nickel and timber from Finland." Hitler wanted to know whether the Soviet Union was preparing a war against Finland. If so, could it be postponed to a later date? Molotov answered that Finland was in the Soviet sphere of influence and that Germany had to remove its troops from Finland. Molotov "did not understand why Russia had to postpone the realization of its plans by six months or even a year. After all, the German-Russian pact did not contain any time limits and within their respective spheres of influence neither of the countries had its hands tied."[12]

The Soviet Union had enough oil for both internal consumption and export. The Soviet Union did not need Romanian oil, while Hitler talked about Germany's complete dependency on Romanian petroleum, asserting that Germany would defend the Romanian oil industry at any cost. Hitler hinted that the Soviet Union should move away from Romanian oil. The Soviet Union had already taken over Northern Bukovina. With that invasion, the Soviet Union violated the pact about the division of the spheres of influence. Molotov replied that the Soviet Union did indeed take something from Romania, and did indeed violate the previously reached agreement with Germany. But the Soviet Union would not give up what it got; moreover, Stalin wanted Southern Bukovina and Bulgaria. "The fate of Romania and Hungary also interests the Soviet Union, and under no condition can it ever be indifferent to it."[13]

Hitler reminded Molotov that they had agreed about the division of Europe back in August 1939. Molotov responded that it was time for a new division of Europe that would give an advantage to the Soviet Union. "The USSR considers last year's agreement fulfilled, with the exception of the question of Finland. . . . Now it is time to talk about a broader agreement between the USSR and Germany."[14] Further discussions were in the same tone.

During the course of the talks, Molotov did not raise questions about the security of the Soviet Union. Hitler brought up questions of safety from a Soviet invasion of territory crucial to Germany, but he did not receive any satisfactory reply. On the morning of November 14, 1940, Molotov left for Moscow. On November 25, the German ambassador to Moscow was told that Germany had to withdraw its troops from Finnish territory immediately. In addition, all the claims Molotov had made in his talks with Hitler and Ribbentrop were confirmed, even the demand to create Soviet bases on the Bosporus and Dardanelles straits.[15] On the same day, November 25, 1940, the People's Commissar of Defense of the USSR, Marshal of the Soviet Union S. K. Timoshenko, and the Chief of General Staff of the Red Army, General K. A. Meretskov, wrote a directive to prepare a plan for a new war of aggression against Finland.[16]

Hitler was preparing for a big war against Great Britain when Stalin demanded new territories in Europe—territories on which Germany's economy and armed forces depended completely. If a war against Britain weakened Germany, what would Stalin demand? Hitler found an answer to all of Stalin's demands. "After Molotov's departure, Hitler gathered his most trusted subordinates and clearly let them understand that he planned to invade Russia."[17]

30

Kremlin Games

The use of new means of struggle and new attack tactics has great value for our success. Before the enemy finds a means of countering the advance, the attacker can make use of all the advantages given by the element of surprise.

—General G. K. Zhukov, lecture given at a conference of the High Command of the Red Army, December 26, 1940

A conference of the High Command of the Red Army began on December 23, 1940. It lasted nine days and ended on the evening of December 31. The highest-ranking leaders of the Red Army—274 marshals, generals, and admirals—attended.

The conference was convened in utmost secrecy. The generals arrived in Moscow in closed railroad cars or in military airplanes. They were met in remote places, and in closed cars they were delivered to the inner courtyard of "Hotel Moscow." The generals arriving in Moscow from other places were forbidden to go into the city. The newspapers of military districts continued to print the portraits of their commanders and reports about their daily activities, creating the impression that they were not in Moscow but at their posts. Before the start of the conference, the generals were led into buses in the hotel's inner courtyard and driven to the General Staff building. At the end of the day, they were returned to the hotel in the same fashion. Understandably, the hotel itself was "cleared of outside elements" and placed under special security and surveillance.

Zhukov delivered the first and most important lecture on new tactics of sudden attack. Furthermore, most of the other speakers discussed only that subject. For example, Lieutenant General P. S. Klenov, Chief of Staff of the Baltic special military district, who spoke following Zhukov's lecture, talked about special operations: "These will be operations of the starting phase, when the enemy's armies have not yet completed their concentration and are not prepared for deployment. These are operations of invasion, for carrying out a whole chain of special tasks. . . . This is use of large air and, perhaps, mechanized forces, while the enemy has not yet prepared for decisive action. . . . The mechanized forces will have to be used independently, and they will solve the tasks of invasion into enemy territory."[1]

The title of the second (and very important) lecture was "The Air Force in an Offensive Operation and the Struggle for Air Superiority." The lecturer was Lieutenant General P. V. Rychagov, Chief of the Air Force Main Directorate of the Red Army. Zhukov described the lecture as "very informative."[2] We had to wait another half a century, until the demise of the Soviet Union, for the publication of the conference records. The essence of the "very informative lecture" boiled down to this: "The best means of defeating [an] air force on the ground is a simultaneous strike at a large number of air bases where the enemy's aviation is possibly located."[3]

Colonel General of Tank Troops D. G. Pavlov, commander of the Western special military district, delivered the lecture titled "The use of mechanized units in contemporary offensive operations and breakthrough by mechanized corps." Pavlov said: "Poland has ceased to exist after seventeen days. The operation in Belgium and Holland ended after fifteen days. The operation in France, before France's capitulation, lasted seventeen days. These are three very characteristic numbers, which cannot but force me to accept them as a possible number for our calculations of our offensive operation."[4]

At that time, according to the Soviet Field Statute, the line of defense for a division was eight to twelve kilometers wide. The lecturers at the conference unanimously advocated a widening of that line. That regulation meant a very high density of troops for defense lines. Why put so many troops on the defensive, confining them to sitting without use, when those troops were needed on the offensive? Other possibilities were examined as well, including concentrating all the forces in those locations where the Soviet Union would carry out sudden strikes against Germany, leaving secondary locations defenseless with a completely bare border in those places. This theory was supported by the Chief of Staff of the Leningrad military district, Major General P. G. Ponedelin. When, a month after the conference, Zhukov became the Chief of General Staff of the Red Army he did not forget Ponedelin, who advocated the baring of the front. Zhukov offered Ponedelin a post in a primary location: Ponedelin became commander of the 12th Army in the Lvov-Chernovitsi bulge. Ponedelin acted in the interests of an offensive: all force was concentrated in the "hitting fist" and the border was left bare. In the summer of 1941, Ponedelin's 12th Army, as well as all Soviet troops of the 1st Strategic Echelon, was crushed. Ponedelin himself was taken prisoner. After the war, he was brought to Moscow under guard, tried, and executed.

The lecture titled "The Character of Contemporary Defensive Operations" was given by General of the Army I. V. Tulenev, commander of the Moscow military district. So, the questions dealing with defense were examined after all! Here is what Tulenev had to say in his lecture: "We have no established contemporary defense theory."[5] This was the truth. Until December 1940, Soviet military theory did not work on questions of defense. After December, it did not work on them either. Tulenev said that such a theory was unnecessary. The Soviet Union would defend itself, but only in separate secondary locations. The goal was to conduct grandiose sudden offensive operations on enemy territory, and therefore to amass huge forces in narrow areas. The Soviet Union had to take almost all forces out of secondary locations; it would defend itself in the bare areas. Tulenev expressed the thought that nobody disputed: "Defense will be a part of a general offensive. Defense is an indispensable form of military operations in separate secondary locations, which allows us to save forces for offensive operations and prepare attacks."[6]

In the conclusive speech, the People's Commissar of Defense, Marshal of the Soviet Union Timoshenko reminded his audience to keep in mind "the possibility of the simultaneous conduct of two, maybe even three, offensive operations on different fronts in the theater of war, with the purpose of strategically shaking up the enemy's defense capabilities as widely as possible."[7] Defense at the primary locations was not foreseen, even theoretically. An opinion, which was prevalent in the Red Army from the moment of its founding, was confirmed at that conference: the most important thing was to advance with entire armies, fronts, and groups of fronts; but small formations—regiments or divisions, perhaps even a corps—would sometimes be left for defense in separate locations. Some agreed that if needed, an entire field army could be engaged in defense. . . .We must remember that in June 1941, on the European territory of the USSR, there were twenty-six field armies organized in five fronts, and a group of reserve armies. A situation in which two armies, side by side, could occupy themselves with defense in one location, was considered completely improbable, and was not examined even theoretically.

The conference of the High Command of the Red Army ended at 6 PM on December 31, 1940. Most of the participants were urgently and secretly sent back to their posts. Only the most important generals remained in Moscow. Even before the conference was over, at 11 AM on December 31, a group of forty-nine of the highest-ranking generals received instructions for a strategic staff game on maps. The maps denoted battles between the "Easterners" and "Westerners." The scope and importance of this game was the largest of all the pre-war years.[8] Pavlov, the Commander of the Western special military district, commanded the "Easterners," or the Soviet troops. Zhukov, Commander of the Kiev special military district, led the "Westerners," meaning the German troops.

Pavlov's group had twenty-four generals, one rear-admiral, one navy captain of the first rank, one navy captain of the second rank, and one colonel. Zhukov's group, which played the role of the German command, had twenty generals, admirals, and officers besides Zhukov. The first strategic game began on the morning of January 2, 1941, at the General Staff of the Red Army. The scenario of the future war was being played out. The supervisor of the game was Timoshenko, the People's Commissar of Defense of the USSR. The referees of the game consisted of twelve top commanders of the Red Army, including four Marshals of the Soviet Union. The observers included Joseph Stalin and the entire Politburo.

A colossal battle raged on the giant maps. For the time being just on the maps, the two most powerful armies on the planet clashed. For several days and nights, without rest or sleep, the staffs of the two opposing sides evaluated situations, made decisions, gave orders and directions. For now just on paper, thousands of tanks and airplanes, tens of thousands of guns and mortars, and millions of soldiers were brought into battle. Hundreds of thousands of tons of ammunition, fuel, and engineering and medical equipment were dispatched from the rear. Divisions, corps, and entire armies were going for the breakthrough. Soviet strategists were not working on any defense plans and not making any plans for rebutting a possible German aggression. They were thinking of a way to take Koenigsberg, Warsaw, Prague, Bucharest, Krakow, and Budapest. Soviet preparations for the invasion of Europe neared their final stage.

The game was called "Offensive Operation of the Front with Breaks through the Fortified Regions." The theme was not simply an attack, but an attack on Germany and more precisely on Eastern Prussia, which was defended by a line of fortified regions. The attacker was the Soviet troops on the northwestern front, under Pavlov's leadership. Pavlov delivered the blow to Eastern Prussia, to Koenigsberg, and Zhukov defended it.

The Communist leaders openly said that the war would be conducted only on enemy territory, as the popular Soviet antebellum song said: "And on enemy land we will crush the enemy, shedding little [of our] blood and by a powerful blow." They had in mind a "deep penetration," that is, a blitzkrieg. But this frankness always followed the condition that the enemy would force us into war. The Field Statute clearly stated that if the enemy attacked, the Red Army would transform itself into the most ferocious attacker of any aggressive armies.

It happened that Germany attacked precisely when the Red Army had everything ready to invade it. In November 1939, Stalin concentrated five armies on the Finnish border, got them ready, and then the Finns, as if on command, supposedly fired several cannon shells. Soviet newspapers exploded with rage: "We will repel the Finnish invasion!" "We will respond to the aggressor's blow with a threefold one!" "We will destroy the band of pests!"

Preparations for attacking Germany followed the same rules. Stalin's strategists, with a mysterious smile on their lips, said that if the enemy forced them into war, they would have to retaliate on enemy territory.

The tasks for the strategy game were designed according to that principle:

1. On July 15, 1941, Germany attacks the Soviet Union.
2. German troops force their way 70 to 120 km into Soviet territory, but . . .
3. . . . by August 1, 1941, they are thrown back to their original positions.[9]

The scenarios of how the "Westerners" attacked, how the Soviet army managed to throw them back and get them off Soviet territory, were not played in the game. It was just mentioned that the Germans attacked and then the Red Army drove them back to the state border. The strategic game began precisely then, when there were no enemy troops on the Soviet soil. The "retaliatory actions" of the Red Army in Eastern Prussia began from that point. The German invasion of Soviet territory and the repelling of aggression did not interest Stalin, Zhukov, and the rest. They were interested in the conduct of assault operations from the border. The leadership concluded that "unfolding the main forces of the Red Army in the West and grouping the main forces against Eastern Prussia and in the direction of Warsaw brings about serious fears that the struggle on this front can turn into protracted fighting."[10]

Afterward, they played a second strategic game, but the main idea did not change: the Red Army was still the advancing side. Actually, the game started when the "Easterners" were one hundred kilometers inside the land of the "Westerners."

The actions of German and Soviet generals were almost mirror images of each other. One month earlier, the Germans played the same games. The gap in time between the actions of Soviet and German commanders was slowly decreasing. On November 29, 1940, a large strategic game on maps began in Berlin. The supervisor of the game was Major General Friedrich Paulus, the First *Ober-Kvartirmeister* of the General Staff of the Ground Forces. In Moscow, there had been two games, in Berlin only one, but it was divided into three stages: first, the invasion by German troops of Russian territory, and battles on the border; second, the German advance to the Minsk-Kiev Line; third, the conclusion of the war and destruction of the Red Army's last reserves, if such were found to the east of the Minsk-Kiev Line. The Germans didn't work out how they would reach Kursk, Moscow, and Stalingrad. The generals thought that one blow would bring down the entire Soviet Union and send the Red Army on the run. In Berlin, a debriefing followed each stage of the game. The main debriefing of all stages of the game ended on December 13, 1940. Nineteen days later, the strategic games in Moscow began, the second of which, as we know now, ended on January 11, 1941.

History is written by the victors. The Red Army seized the archives of the *Wehrmacht Heer*, and Soviet historians demonstrated the aggressiveness of German imperialism to the rest of the world, exposing their terrible plans. Meanwhile, Soviet archives were carefully locked. This gave the Communist propagandists and agitators the opportunity to say that Soviet generals, admirals, marshals, and Stalin himself suffered from a chronic love of peace.[11] However, that love of peace was only pretence. The Soviet generals did not sleep. Like their German peers, they prepared an invasion.

Of the two Soviet games, the first one was decisive. "The debriefing of the first one is concluded at the highest political leadership level in the country."[12] The "highest political leadership in the country" meant, of course, Stalin. He carefully followed the course of the first game and became convinced that the army would get bogged down in Eastern Prussia. Therefore, immediately after the first game, Stalin decided that a strike on Europe should be delivered from Ukraine and Moldova, and not from an area north of Polesye.

The second game, which dealt with "retaliatory measures" of the Red Army in Germany, Hungary, and Romania, took place between January 8 and 11, 1941. There were insignificant changes in each group of players. Certain generals were switched from side to side. A number of generals did not participate in the second game at all, others replaced them. But the main opponents remained the same. Only this time, Zhukov commanded the Soviet troops and directed the "retaliatory blow" on enemy territory, whereas Pavlov commanded the German and Romanian troops and tried to repel the Soviet advance. Why did they need to conduct two games?

Polesye—the biggest region of swamplands in Europe, possibly even in the world—lies between the Baltic Sea and the Black Sea. Polesye was unsuitable for the mass movement of troops and the conduct of military operations. The area divided the western theater of operations into two strategic directions. If one tried to be equally strong to the north and to the south of Polesye, then one had to simply divide one's forces in two. However, the main principle of strategy was concentration. The drive to be strong everywhere causes the dissipation of forces and general weakness. Therefore, forces had to be concentrated in one of the two directions to deliver the decisive blow, while in the other direction they delivered just a secondary, auxiliary attack.

The question then was which direction should be considered primary and which secondary. The arguments about this did not end. Both options had their pros and cons. Invasion into Central Europe, north of Polesye, would be a direct blow on Berlin. However, in the attacker's way lay heavily fortified Eastern Prussia and Koenigsberg. A blow to the south, however, was a diversion to the side, a roundabout route. However, it would be a blow to almost unprotected Romania, the oil heart of Germany. On synthetic fuel alone, Germany could not survive. Therefore, it was decided to play two games, compare the results, and make the choice. In the first game, the main attack on Central Europe was carried out north of Polesye, from Belarus and the Baltic.

In the second game, the invasion was carried out from Ukraine and Moldova. If Germany were crushed, the rest of continental Europe would shower Stalin with flowers and his tanks would have an open road right up to the Atlantic Ocean.

In the second game, Zhukov, in command of Soviet troops, attacked Romania and Hungary. He found it easy to advance. First of all, there were no modern fortifications there, like those in Eastern Prussia. Zhukov had indisputable superiority of aviation, tanks, and paratroops. "The second game . . . ended with the 'Eastern' decision being made to attack Budapest." Zhukov commanded the "Eastern" group in the second game, and it was he who made the decisions about breaking through to Lake Balaton and crossing the Danube River near Budapest. The decision so far was only made in the course of a strategy game, but Zhukov himself already said that the games did not have an academic character, but were directly tied to the imminent war. Stalin was not present at the second game and did not conduct its debriefings, because he had already made his choice after seeing the results of the first one. The Soviet invasion of Europe would be conducted south of Polesye.

31

All the Way to Berlin!

The peasant-worker Red Army will be the most aggressive of any attack army that ever existed.

—*Field Statute of the Red Army*, 1939

By sending all his divisions to France, Hitler had turned his back on Stalin. Stalin then feverishly destroyed his defenses and increased the attacking power of the Red Army. The Dnepr military flotilla was one of the many defense systems of the Soviet Union. The great river Dnepr blocked the way into the depth of Soviet territory to aggressors from the west. All the Dnepr bridges were mined before 1939, and they could be demolished in such a way that nothing would be left to restore. In all preceding campaigns, German troops had never had to cross a single water barrier equal to the Dnepr. The pressing of a few buttons, at least in the middle and lower Dnepr regions, could stop German tank units. In the early 1930s, the Dnepr military flotilla was created to prevent the crossing and establishment of temporary bridges across the river. By the beginning of World War II, the flotilla counted 120 warships and motorboats, including eight powerful coastal monitors with cannon up to 130 mm.[1] On top of that, the Dnepr flotilla had its own air force, and shoreline and air-defense batteries. The left bank of the Dnepr was suitable for river warships: it had many islands, bypasses, and backwater hideaways, which allowed warships, including the largest ones, to hide from the enemy and carry out surprise attacks, preventing the enemy from crossing the river.

The Dnepr water barrier—with its bridges primed for demolition and the river flotilla that could act together with field troops, artillery, and aviation—could securely close off the roads to the industrial regions in the south of Ukraine and to the Black Sea bases of the Soviet Navy. The German *blitzkrieg* could be stopped on the Dnepr line, or at least be held up for several months. If that had happened, the entire course of the war would have been different. However, just when Hitler turned his back on Stalin, Stalin ordered the removal of mines from the Dnepr bridges and the disbanding of the military flotilla. The Dnepr flotilla could be used only on the territory of the Soviet Union and only in a defensive war. It was obvious why Stalin believed he did not need it.

Stalin divided the defensive Dnepr flotilla into two: the Danube flotilla and the Pinsk flotilla. In the summer of 1940, Stalin tore Northern Bukovina and Bessarabia from Romania. The Soviet Union received an area of several tens of kilometers on the eastern shore of the Danube River. The Danube flotilla, formed in advance, was immediately transferred to this area. It was not easy to transfer the ships from the Dnepr: small ships were sent by railroad, and large ones sailed in the Black Sea during quiet weather and with special precautions. The Danube military flotilla included sixty-three river warships and motorboats, among them five monitors and twenty-two armored motorboats, plus air force units, and anti-aircraft and shoreline artillery.[2] The location of the flotilla was horrible. The Soviet shore of the Danube was bare and open. Ships were stationed at the banks, while Romanian troops stood nearby, sometimes three hundred meters from the Soviet ships. In the event of a defensive war, the entire Danube flotilla would fall into a trap from the beginning: there was nowhere to retreat from the Danube delta but to the Black Sea, the waves of which could sink the ships built for river. The flotilla had nowhere to maneuver. A surprise attack from the enemy would have meant machine-gun fire at the Soviet ships, not giving them the possibility to lift anchor and detach the mooring lines. Moreover, no enemy would invade the Soviet Union through the Danube delta, since it consisted of hundreds of lakes and impassable swamps. This means that the Danube flotilla was not needed to defend the newly "liberated" lands of Bessarabia.

There was only one possible action for the Danube flotilla: in the course of a general invasion by the troops of the Red Army, the flotilla could carry out operations up the river. If you amassed in the delta of a great river more than sixty river warships, they would have no-where to go except up the stream. There were no other directions. If it sailed up the Danube, the flotilla would have to fight on Romanian, Bulgarian, Yugoslavian, Hungarian, Slovak, Austrian, and German territory.

In a defensive war, the Danube flotilla would be useless, and it would be sentenced to immediate destruction at its open bases on the shores. But in a war of aggression, the Danube flotilla was deadly for Germany: it only had to sail three to four hundred kilometers up the river, and the strategically important bridge at Chernavoda would be within firing range of its cannon, which meant that the petroleum supply from Ploieşti to the port of Constanza would be disrupted. Another hundred kilometers upstream, and the entire German war ma-chine would stop, simply because German tanks, planes, and warships would be out of fuel.

Here is an interesting detail: several mobile shoreline batteries of the Danube flotilla were armed with 130-mm- and 152-mm-caliber cannon. If the Soviet command had truly decided that someone would try to invade the USSR through the Danube delta, the shore-line batteries should immediately have been dug into the ground, and at the first chance reinforced concrete caponiers should have been built. But no one built any caponiers, so the cannon remained mobile. Their mobility could only be used in aggressive operations: the mobile batteries could accompany the flotilla, moving along the shorelines and supporting the warships with fire.

The reaction of the Danube military flotilla's commanders to the beginning of the Soviet-German war was surprising. The word "war" meant to Soviet commanders invasion, not defense. Having learned that the war had begun, the Soviet commanders finished their last preparations for landing operations. The actions of the Soviet flotilla commanders, as well as those of the 14th Rifle Corps, divisions of which were concentrated in the Danube delta region, and of the 79th Border Unit of the NKVD, were planned beforehand and meticulously worked out.

On June 25, 1941, the warships of the Danube flotilla, under cover of fire from the shoreline batteries, landed reconnaissance and sabotage units of the NKVD on the Romanian shores, followed by regiments from the 51st Rifle Division of the 14th Rifle Corps. Soviet soldiers acted decisively, boldly, and quickly. The complicated operation, which involved river ships and aviation, as well as field, shoreline, and ship artillery, units of the Red Army and the NKVD, was worked out with immaculate precision. On the morning of June 26, 1941, a red flag went up above the central church of the Romanian city of Kilia. A key springboard area of seventy kilometers of Romanian territory had fallen into Soviet hands. The Danube flotilla was preparing for further invasion operations up the Danube. To aid the flotilla, the 3rd Paratroops Corps stationed in the Odessa district could be sent out. But all this had to be cancelled, because on other areas of the front the Red Army was retreating; an order to retreat was issued to the Danube flotilla as well. With the Black Sea behind it, the Danube military flotilla found itself cut off from Soviet troops without the possibility of retreat. Most of its ships had to be sunk, while gigantic supplies, stored toward the movement of the flotilla up the river, had to be burned, or simply left behind.

Hitler and Stalin both understood perfectly well what the expression "oil is the blood of war" meant. Colonel General A. Jodl testified that, in an argument with Guderian, Hitler declared: "You want to invade without oil—well, we shall see what comes out of this." As early as 1927, Stalin took seriously the problems of the impending World War II. On December 3, 1927, he said: "It is impossible to fight without oil, and he who has the advantage in terms of oil has the chance of victory in the impending war."[3] In June 1940, when nobody was threatening the Soviet Union, tens of Soviet river military ships appeared in the Danube delta. That step had no defensive value, but was a threat to the unprotected Romanian oil routes and consequently a deadly threat to Germany.

In July 1940, Hitler conducted intensive consultations with his generals and concluded that it was not at all easy to defend Romania: the supply routes extended all over and passed through the mountains. If a huge number of German troops were transferred to defend Romania, western Poland and eastern Germany, including Berlin, would be exposed to a Soviet attack. If a lot of troops were concentrated in Romania and tried to keep it at any cost, it would not help: the territory perhaps would be retained, but oil fields would still burn up from bombings and artillery fire.

In July 1940, Hitler for the first time said that the Soviet Union could be dangerous, especially if German troops left the continent for the British Isles and Africa. On November 13, 1940, in a conversation with Molotov, Hitler indicated the necessity to retain a huge number of German troops in Romania, obviously hinting that the Soviet military posed a threat to Romanian oil.[4] Molotov ignored the hint. After Molotov's departure in December, Hitler issued a directive for the preparation of Operation Barbarossa.

In June 1940, when the German army was fighting in France, Zhukov, on Stalin's orders and without consulting the German allies, brought river warships to the Danube delta. Hitler asked the head of the Soviet government to divert the Soviet threat from the oil heart of Germany. Stalin and Molotov refused.

A fortnight after Hitler's invasion of the USSR, on July 7, 1941, Stalin sent a telegram to the commander of the southern front, General I. V. Tulenev. In the telegram, Stalin demanded that the Soviet Union retain Bessarabia at any cost, "having in mind that we need the Bessarabian territory as a springboard for organizing our invasion."[5] Hitler had already delivered his sudden blow, but Stalin still did not think of defense—his main concern was organizing an invasion from Bessarabia, meaning an attack on the Romanian oil fields.

The invasion of Bessarabia by the Soviet Union and the concentration there of powerful aggressive forces, including the paratroops corps and the Danube flotilla, forced Hitler to look at the strategic situation from a completely different perspective and to take preemptive measures. But it was already too late. Even the sudden attack of the *Wehrmacht Heer* on the Soviet Union could not save Hitler and his empire.

In the memoirs of Marshal of the Soviet Union G. K. Zhukov, there is a map of the location of Soviet naval bases in the first half of 1941. Among these bases, one was in the vicinity of the city of Pinsk, in Belarus.[6] It is at least five hundred kilometers away from the nearest sea. After the disbanding of the purely defensive Dnepr military flotilla, some part of its ships were sent to the Danube delta, and others were sent upstream to the tributary of the Dnepr—the river Pripyat'. Ships were sent up almost to the sources, where the width of the river hardly reached fifty meters. That was where a new base for the flotilla was built.

The Pinsk military flotilla almost rivaled the Danube flotilla in might—it included four 263-ton displacement *Zhelezniakov*-class monitors and five captured Polish monitors, ranging from 130- to 150-ton displacement. Altogether, the Pinsk flotilla had sixty-six river warships and cutters, a squadron of airplanes, a company of marines, and other units.[7] It was difficult to use the Pinsk flotilla for defense: the coastal monitors that came here had their bows turned west, and turning such huge ships around in a narrow river was complicated. If the ships were needed for defense, they should have been left in the Dnepr, because there was nothing for them to do on the quiet forest river Pripyat'. It was unlikely that the enemy would advance through the impassable forests and treacherous swamps.

The purpose of the Pinsk flotilla remains unclear, if one does not think of the Dnepr-Bug Canal.

Immediately after the "liberation" of Western Belarus in 1939, the Red Army started digging a more than 100-km-long canal from Pinsk to Kobrin.[8] The canal was built in the summer and winter. Sapper units of the 4th Army and "construction units of the NKVD"— that is, thousands of inmates from the GULAG—participated in its completion. The fact that the construction was commanded by Colonel (later Marshal of Engineering Troops) Alexey Proshliakov alone spoke of its purely military purpose. The canal was built in truly horrendous conditions. Equipment sank in the swamps, and the only way to complete the canal within the deadline set by Stalin was to do everything by hand. The canal was built. Nobody knows exactly how many human lives it cost. The canal connected the Pripyat' with the river Bug. The only use for the canal could be to let ships reach to the Vistula basin and further west. The canal had no other use. In a defensive war, it would have had to be destroyed to prevent German river ships from passing through the Vistula to the Dnepr. In the defensive war of 1941, all the ships of the Pinsk flotilla had to be blown up and abandoned. At the end of 1943, when the Red Army was rapidly advancing west, a flotilla was once again formed on the Dnepr, and once again it went up the Pripyat' River to the small river Mukhavets, which flowed into the Bug.

Admiral V. Grigoryev, who in 1943 received the new flotilla in the Kiev region, remembered the words of Zhukov: "'Along the Pripyat', you will be able to reach [the] Bug, Narev, and Vistula toward Warsaw, and then transfer to the German rivers. Who knows, perhaps all the way to Berlin!' He made a sharp turn, gave me an intense look, and repeated, stressing each word: 'All the way to Berlin! Ah?'"[9]

In 1945, Admiral Grigoryev reached Berlin with his flotilla.

The Red Army had no marines. For land battles, it was easier and cheaper to use regular infantry, and landing on faraway shores was not yet in the plans. But suddenly Hitler made a thrust to the west, baring his back to Stalin. This careless step by Hitler brought on the most radical structural changes within the Red Army: the remains of defense were obliterated, while the offense was strengthened. The Soviet Marines were born in June 1940, when Hitler crushed France. At that time, there were two ocean fleets and two sea fleets in the Soviet armed forces, as well as two river flotillas: the Amur and the Dnepr. The ocean fleet did not receive any marines. The Pacific and Arctic oceans did not interest Stalin at the time. The Amur flotilla safeguarded the far eastern Soviet borders and also did not receive any marines. The Dnepr flotilla was divided into two attacking flotillas, and the Pinsk one, located in the Belarussian forests, received a company of marines. How interesting: marines not on the oceans, but in the Belarussian swamps. We can infer from these facts where Stalin was preparing for defense and where he was preparing for invasion.

A brigade of marines numbering several thousand men was formed as part of the Baltic fleet, whose only possible enemy could be Germany and its allies. On June 23, 1941, Soviet marines received their "battle baptism" during the defense of the naval base at Liepaja. The base was less than one hundred kilometers away from the German borders, but had no land obstacles and was not at all prepared for defense. According to testimony from Soviet admirals and German trophy documents, the bay of Liepaja was packed with Soviet submarines "like a can of sardines." The official history of the Soviet navy, published by the Academy of Sciences of the USSR, openly acknowledged that Liepaja was being prepared as a frontline base of the Soviet fleet for aggressive warfare on the seas.[10] The marines in Liepaja were situated so close to the German borders that in the first twenty-four hours of the war they had already participated in defensive battles, although, of course, they had been created for a totally different purpose. In a defensive battle, regular infantry was far superior to marines.

The Danube military flotilla had two land-army companies, which officially were not listed as marines. But even before the German invasion, at least two Soviet rifle divisions—the 25th Chapaev and the 51st Perekop from the 14th Rifle Corps—prepared themselves in the Danube region for action as marines, and in the first days of the war they landed on Romanian shores.

The Black Sea fleet had even more powerful forces. Officially it had no marines, but in early June 1941, the 9th Special Rifle Corps under the command of Lieutenant General P. I. Batov was transferred from the Trans-Caucasus to the Crimea. The corps was very unusual in its personnel, arms, and training. On June 18 and 19, 1941, the Black Sea fleet conducted grandiose training exercises of an aggressive nature, during which one of the divisions of the 9th Special Rifle Corps was loaded on warships and performed a landing on "enemy" shores. A landing of an entire division from warships had never before been practiced in the Red Army.

The Kremlin paid special attention to the joint exercises of the fleet and the troops of the 9th Special Rifle Corps. These exercises were observed by high-ranking commanders who had specially arrived from Moscow. One of them, Vice Admiral I. I. Azarov, said that all the participants of the exercises felt that the training was not being conducted without reason, and that soon they would have to use in war what they had learned.[11] If the war began and the Soviet command sent the 9th Special Rifle Corps into action in accordance with its battle profile and designation of its preparations, where could it land? It was unlikely that it would land on Soviet shores, but possibly in Romania, Bulgaria, or Turkey. No matter where the troops landed, they would have to be supplied, which required either additional landing of troops or the advance of other Soviet troops through Romania to connect with the 9th Special Rifle Corps. During those same days, the 3rd Paratroops Corps, also in the Crimea, conducted grandiose training exercises with the landing of corps and brigade staff.

Soviet historians never connected these three events: the training of the 14th Rifle Corps for landing from ships of the Danube flotilla; the 3rd Paratroops Corps exercising in the Crimea (a short flight to the Danube's mouth); the training of the 9th Special Rifle Corps to land from warships of the Black Sea fleet. But these events were linked in time, place, and objective. They were the final stages of preparation for aggression on a grand scale.

32

Mountain Divisions on the Steppes of Ukraine

Airborne assault landings will be effective in mountainous battle areas. Since troops, head-quarters, and support units, which operate in the rear, are particularly reliant on roads, it is possible to use air assaults to capture enemy troops operating in the rear, to attack his communications and roads, commanding heights, ravines, passes, railway junctions, and so on, and this can produce exceptionally important results. In general terms, the dropping of an assault landing force will hardly be expedient outside the framework of an offensive operation.

—VOENNYI VESTNIK [MILITARY HERALD], 1940

In 1941, the Soviet Union was preparing, painstakingly and tirelessly, for war. Each Soviet army had its unique structure, character, and purpose. Each "cover" army was created to deal with a clearly defined task in the forthcoming war of "liberation." Sufficient material has been published to provide for a separate study on each of the thirty Soviet armies that existed in the first half of 1941. If a detailed study were made of the structure, disposition, and direction given to the training of just one Soviet army, the "liberation" tendency inherent to all Soviet preparations would become quite obvious.

Take, for example, the 9th Army. In number and name, it was not different from other Soviet armies, but it was a very unusual army. In 1941, this was the most powerful army in the world. It had six corps, including two mechanized (by June 22, 1941, 799 tanks altogether) and one cavalry corps. In total, on June 21, 1941, the 9th Army counted seventeen divisions, including two aviation, four tank, two motorized rifle, two cavalry, six rifle, and one mountain-rifle division. The rifle, motorized rifle, and cavalry divisions had tanks as well. By June 1, 1941, the Odessa military district, the divisions and corps of which became part of the 9th Army, had 1,114 tanks.[1] Another mechanized corps, the 27th (by June 22, 1941, it had 356 tanks), under the command of Major General I. E. Petrov, was to be added to the 9th Army. The corps was created in the Turkmenistan district and, before completing its formation, was secretly transferred west. After yet another mechanized corps was included, the 9th Army should have had twenty divisions, including six tank divisions.

The Soviet 9th Army was opposed by forces which had no tank divisions at all. The 9th Army was not yet completely manned and equipped, but it was planned to be in the next days and weeks, and by the highest quality weapons.

Colonel General P. Belov (at that time Major General, Commander of the 2nd Cavalry Corps of the 9th Army) testified that even the cavalry of this army was preparing to receive the best tanks in the world, the T-34.[2] At the head of the 9th Army was a colonel general. At that time, this was an extremely high rank. In all the armed forces of the USSR, there were only eight colonel generals; moreover, in the mighty Soviet tank troops there was none, in aviation there was none, and in the NKVD there was none. At the head of thirty Soviet armies were major generals and lieutenant generals. The 9th Army was the only exception among them.

In addition, the most promising officers and generals were gathered in this exceptional army. Three future Marshals of the Soviet Union were among them: Malinovsky, Zakharov, and Krylov, future Marshal of Aviation and three-time Hero of the Soviet Union Pokryshkin, future Marshal of Aviation Pstygo, future Army Generals Petrov, Pavlovsky, and Lashchenko, and many other talented and aggressive commanders who had already proven themselves in battle, like the twenty-eight-year-old Air Force Major General Osipenko. They all expressed hopes, which in most cases were later fulfilled. A caring hand carefully picked the best and most promising and placed them in this army.

But where was this super-army located? Here an amazing discovery awaits us: the 9th Army was not located near the German border. In the first half of June 1941, the Soviet Union was forming the most powerful army in the world on the Romanian border. The 9th Army was created in the fall of 1939, immediately after the signing of the Molotov-Ribbentrop Pact. Its appearance was always an unwelcome sign for the country on whose border it emerged. In the fall of 1939, the 9th Army was deployed on the Finnish border. A week after the completion of its formation and concentration, the 9th Army fought for the bloody "liberation" of Finland. After the Finnish war, the army disappeared. The 9th Army command was disbanded on March 26, 1940. The army suddenly appeared again in June 1940 on the Romanian border. Ahead was a "liberation crusade" into Bessarabia, and Soviet sources indicated that the 9th Army was created especially for the completion of that important task.[3] After another brief "liberation crusade," the 9th Army disappeared again and its command was disbanded on July 10, 1940. In reality, its troops remained on the border, but in order not to alarm the neighbors those troops were not officially called an "army." On June 14, 1941, the 9th Army again "reappeared" on the Romanian border, in the same exact place where a year ago it had completed the "liberation."[4] A new "liberation crusade" of the 9th Army into Romania would have entirely changed the strategic situation in Europe and in the world, since Romania was Germany's main source of oil. A blow to Romania meant death to Germany.

But Hitler did not allow any of that to happen. In the declaration made by the German government to the Soviets at the start of the war, reasons were listed for the German attack against the Soviet Union. Among them was the unjustified concentration of Soviet troops on Romanian borders, which presented a clear danger to Germany.

Let's pay attention to the mountain rifle divisions in the 9th Army. The 9th Army was located on the Romanian border, and its headquarters was in Odessa. There are no mountains in the Odessa military district. The 30th Irkutsk Mountain Rifle Division of the 9th

Army could be used only in Romania. There were plenty of mountains there. It is not at all coincidental that this division (commanded by Major General S. G. Galaktionov) was part of the 48th Rifle Corps of Major General Malinovsky, the most aggressive corps commander on the entire southern front. The 48th Rifle Corps was in the flank of the 9th Army which was closest to the front. If the 9th "Shock" Army moved to Romania, then most of the army would be fighting on flat land, while its right flank would scratch at the mountain chain.[5] For this situation, it was most reasonable to have one mountain-rifle division, and precisely on the rightmost flank, which was exactly what was done.

Let's examine another army, which was a carbon copy of the 9th Army. Formally, it was called just the 12th Army. It had one mechanized and two rifle corps, and other units. It had nine divisions, including two tank divisions and one motorized division. It was indistinguishable in number, name, and composition from other similar invasion armies. It had been set up specifically for the "liberation crusade" of the Red Army into Poland.[6] It then had a tank corps, two cavalry corps, and two rifle divisions. It had little artillery and infantry, because there was no need here to break through a powerful defense. To the contrary, it had mobile troops necessary for a fast advance.[7]

Its subsequent fate was also typical. After the "liberation" campaign in Poland, the army stayed on the German border. Later, the 12th Army underwent the same transformation as all adjacent invasion armies. Its main strike mechanism was no longer called a tank corps, but a mechanized corps, to allay the fears of the leaders of neighboring countries. The deletion of the word "tank" from the corps' name was followed by an increase in the number of tanks in the army. The cavalry was taken away from it. Its capacity for disrupting the enemy's defenses was increased. The number of rifle divisions was tripled, and the amount of artillery in each division was doubled. In addition, one artillery brigade and four separate artillery regiments were added to the army. The capability to counter the enemy's engineering defenses also increased when a separate regiment of engineers was brought into the army.

The unusual feature of the 12th Army was its ethnic composition. When Stalin was preparing to invade Poland in 1939, he filled the 12th Army with Ukrainians, apparently bearing in mind the long-standing animosity between Poles and Ukrainians. The army was formed in Ukraine. Therefore, the reservists were also drawn from there, and they formed a solid majority in the 12th Army. Far-reaching changes had already taken place in 1940. Ethnic Russians were appointed to key posts to mask the army's unusual ethnic composition. The greater part of the army, however, was neither Ukrainian nor Russian. It was Caucasian: there were Georgians, Armenians, and Azeris in other armies, but their presence was particularly strong in the 12th Army. General Zhukov, who commanded the Military District, sought out Colonel I. K. Bagramian, an Armenian who was a longtime friend, from his job as a military academy lecturer, and appointed him Chief of the Operations Branch (War Planning) of the 12th Army. General Agrat Arushunyan, another Armenian, became the army's chief of staff.

Zhukov gathered natives of the Caucasus into the ranks of the 12th Army because it was secretly but steadily changed into a mountain army. Zhukov personally demanded of its commanders that their troops should have a thorough knowledge of the Carpathian passes, not just on paper but from practical experience. In 1940, he ordered that "specially reinforced groups, made up of various combat vehicles and means of transport, should in the autumn be sent through the passes along all more or less passable routes to make sure they could be surmounted in practical conditions by tanks, motor vehicles, tractors, animal-drawn transport, and pack-carrying beasts."[8]

During the same year, German generals were secretly carrying out identical experiments on their western borders in the mountains. Their goal was to prepare a sudden attack against France and its allies. The German generals had to make sure that troops, tanks, artillery tractors, and transport could pass through the Ardennes. The German mountain experiments were successful. The attack on France was unanticipated both in time and place, and it was deadly.

The Soviet commanders were preparing to do the same against Germany. Marshal of the Soviet Union Bagramian, then a colonel responsible for planning the military operations of the 12th Army, said: "When I was studying the operational plans, I was struck by the following fact—our frontier army had neither a deployment nor a border-protection plan." The colonel's words demonstrate that the safe of the operations branch of the 12th Army contained plans. They were complex documents that had to be studied. Yet among those war plans there were none for defense.

Bagramian also described training exercises of the 12th Army attended by General Zhukov. Only offensive tactics were worked on, and on the maps the war took place on German territory. The game began with Soviet troops crossing the border river San. The military game was against a real enemy and it involved top secret intelligence information. Differences arose between Zhukov and the army commander. Commander of the 12th Army General Parusinov insisted: "We must do our best to inflict maximum casualties on the enemy with our first strike." Zhukov understood that these were good intentions, but he wanted a strike on a wide rather than a very narrow front. That was what the argument was about. Shortly after the argument, Parusinov was replaced by General P. G. Ponedelin, Zhukov's old friend. Then, the experiments in how to master the mountain passes continued.

Zhukov wasn't interested in the mountain passes because of defense. If he had wanted to make the passes impassable to the enemy, he would have sent his troops to the mountains, dug up all mountain paths and roads, and built reinforced concrete fortifications near the passes, instead of right alongside the border river. It would have been more economical; the enemy could not have observed the construction work and would have been unable to cross the passes. But would anyone really attack the Soviet Union across mountain ranges when there were plenty of open spaces?

The mountains were exceptionally important to the Soviet command. Germany was separated from her main source of oil by a double barrier of mountains, in Czechoslovakia and Romania. A Soviet strike across the passes in Czechoslovakia or Romania would effectively cut the oil artery. Marshal Zhukov wrote: "Germany's weak spot was oil supply, but it made up for this to some extent by importing oil from Romania."[9] The experiments in the mountains continued. The capabilities of each kind of troops and every type of combat and transport vehicle, operating in the conditions which prevailed in the Carpathian passes, were carefully studied. Standards were established and carefully checked, and guidance was compiled for the troops. The time taken by various types of vehicle to negotiate these mountain passes was carefully recorded and analyzed. The collected information, of course, was crucial for the planning of offensive operations, especially lightning operations. Bagramian was recording time frames to plan on the basis of very specific data.

None of the experiments were needed for defense. If the Carpathian passes had to be defended from the enemy, then speed was not needed: the soldiers simply had to stay where they were and not let the enemy pass.

In the 12th Army, as in all other Soviet armies, things were not called by their real names. In January 1940, the 96th Rifle Division was reorganized into a mountain rifle division. In May 1941, three more rifle divisions (the 44th, 58th, and 60th) were converted into mountain rifle divisions. At the same time, the recently formed 192nd Mountain Rifle Division was also added to the 12th Army. What did one call the 13th Corps, which had two divisions and both were mountain rifle ones? What did one call the 17th Corps, in which three out of four divisions were mountain rifle ones? What did one call an army, which out of its three corps had, in fact, two mountain rifle corps, and in which the mountain rifle divisions were a solid majority? I would call the corps "a mountain rifle corps" and the army "a mountain army." But the Soviet High Command had reasons for not doing this. The corps continued to be called, as before, the 13th and 17th Rifle Corps, while the army was simply called the 12th Army.

The mountain rifle divisions were given their official name on June 1, 1941, while the order was issued on April 23, 1941; the actual transformation of the divisions from "rifle" into "mountain rifle" divisions was going on as early as the autumn of 1940.[10] The 12th Army also influenced adjacent armies. The 72nd Mountain Rifle Division under the command of Major General P. I. Abramidze had been trained in the 12th Army and was transferred to the adjacent 26th army. Lieutenant General I. S. Konev's 19th Army, which was being transferred from the northern Caucasus, was then secretly deployed behind the 12th and 26th armies. It also had mountain rifle divisions, for instance, the 28th Division under the command of Colonel K. I. Novik. It was at this time that deployment of yet another army, the 18th, began in the area between the 12th (mountain) and 9th "super-shock" armies in the eastern Carpathians. There are sufficient documents to infer that the original idea was that the 18th Army would be a carbon copy of the 12th (mountain) Army, although like the 12th it did not bear that name. Any researcher who studies the archives of the 12th and 18th armies will be surprised by their absolute similarity in structure. It is a most unusual example of twin armies.

The mountain rifle divisions were reinforced with specially selected and trained soldiers. These divisions were transferred to a special personnel composition, very different from the regular rifle divisions; they received special weapons and equipment. Just before the war began, a school for mountain training was established in the Caucasus. It trained the best Soviet mountain sportsmen and climbers to be military instructors. Once fully trained, these instructors were sent to the Soviet western frontier, since it was precisely here, and not in the Caucasus or Turkestan, that in June 1941 a great number of mountain rifle troops were concentrated.[11]

It is time to ask: for which mountains? There is only one comparatively small mountain range on the Soviet western frontier. The eastern Carpathians resemble gently sloping hills rather than mountains. There was no point in having a powerful defense in the eastern Carpathians in 1941. First, that area of the Carpathians was dangerous and unfavorable for an aggressor coming from west to east. The enemy would come down from the mountains to the plains, and its army would have to be supplied across the whole of the eastern Carpathian, the Tatry, the Erzgebirge, and the Sudeten mountains. Second, the northern slope of the eastern Carpathians formed a blunt wedge on the enemy's side of the frontier. If many Soviet troops were concentrated there for defensive purposes, even in peacetime, they would be surrounded by the enemy on three sides. By using the plains farther to the south, and especially more to the north of the eastern Carpathians, the enemy could strike at any time at the rest of the troops deployed on the mountains, thereby cutting their supply lines. Third, in 1941, there were too few enemy troops in the Carpathian Mountains to carry out an aggression, and the Soviet High Command was fully aware of this.[12]

The concentration of two Soviet mountain armies in the eastern Carpathians had catastrophic consequences. Nobody attacked these armies in the mountains. The German 1st Tank Group carried out its strike in the plain to the north of the eastern Carpathians, bypassing the mountains and cutting off the Soviet mountain armies from the main forces. The Soviet command confronted a dilemma: should they leave the two mountain armies in the Carpathian Mountains, where they would perish without a supply of ammunition and food, or should they urgently be led out of that mousetrap? They made the second choice. The two mountain armies, unprepared to fight in the plains, having light weapons and a lot of equipment useless in a flat area,[13] fled from the mountains and immediately fell under attack from the German tank units. Having easily destroyed the fleeing Soviet mountain armies, the 1st Tank Group of the German army went ahead full speed and reached the rear of the Soviet 9th Army and defeated it. Once the German troops had dealt with those armies, the road opened to the totally undefended bases of the Soviet navy, to the Don basin, Kharkov, Zaporozhie, and Dnepropetrovsk. These were industrial regions of great importance. Once they were lost to the Germans, the Soviet Union produced only 100,000 tanks for the rest of the war, which was much more than Germany, but without the losses of these regions, the Soviet tank production could have been several times higher. When the Germans broke through to the south of Ukraine, the Soviet troops around Kiev found themselves in a very dangerous position. The Germans had cleared the road to the Caucasus and to Stalingrad—the heart of Soviet oil production.

The two mountain armies in the Carpathians in 1941 were completely unnecessary for defense. They were necessary only for offense. In early 1941, specially trained groups of rock climbers appeared in the mountain rifle divisions. But in the eastern Carpathians, they had nothing to do. Soviet troops had to be moved west by several hundred kilometers. The same factors that made the Carpathians unsuitable for aggression from west to east made them very suitable for aggression from east to west. As the troops moved ahead into the mountains, their supply lines remained on Soviet territory, mainly on very flat terrain. The eastern Carpathians jutted far out into the west and cut the enemy grouping in two. This was a natural springboard which, if heavy forces were built up on it in peacetime, positioned them as if they were in the enemy's rear. They only had to advance, threatening the enemy's rear and thus compelling its troops to withdraw along the whole front.

Only negligible enemy forces were located in the Carpathian Mountains. The Soviet High Command knew this, and that was precisely why they had concentrated two armies there. The only way to use these armies in war was to move them forward. Two mountain ridges spread from the Carpathians: one went west toward Czechoslovakia, the other south toward Romania.

33

Stalin in May

Stalin [has] put before himself a foreign policy goal of tremendous importance, which he hopes to reach through personal efforts.

—Count von der Schulenburg, secret report to
the German government, May 12, 1941

On May 4, 1941, Stalin became chairman of the Soviet government,[1] replacing Molotov who became deputy chairman. At that time, many British and American politicians and diplomats were confused by that turn of events. For the first time in Soviet history, the top party and government leadership was officially concentrated in one man's hands. In 1922, having assumed the position of general secretary of the Communist Party, Stalin refused to take any government positions. Stalin elevated his command post above the government and above the country. Officially, he was responsible for nothing. All successes were attributed to Stalin. All failures were attributed to his enemies, careerists who took advantage of and distorted the orders of Stalin the genius. The "victory of the collectivization" was a creation of Stalin's genius, while millions perished from hunger because of the mistakes of regional level functionaries. Stalin officially had no ties to the Great Purge— Ezhov, the People's Commissar for Interior Affairs, shouldered the whole blame. That period was derogatorily called *Ezhovshchina*.

It wasn't Stalin who signed a pact with Hitler. The treaty entered history as the Molotov-Ribbentrop Pact. In Germany, the responsibility for the pact was borne not so much by Ribbentrop as by Adolf Hitler, the chancellor, though he was not present when the pact was signed. But Stalin, who was present at the signing, had no government position at that moment. On April 13, 1941, a pact was signed with Japan: Stalin was present, but again, did not shoulder any responsibility. Hitler many times invited Stalin to a personal meeting in a friendly atmosphere. But Stalin sent Molotov to meet Hitler.

Then, when the victors were clearly defined, Stalin, of course, personally met with Churchill and Roosevelt. During the course of talks at the highest level, Stalin never said no.

Molotov did it for him. He even received the nickname "Mr. No." All demands came from Molotov, all concessions from Stalin. Simply put, Stalin did good with his hands, and evil with the hands of others. Those who did evil on Stalin's orders carried the responsibility, while Stalin remained clean.

However, in May 1941, Stalin took on the official burden of government responsibility. For Stalin a new title meant not a strengthening of power, but a limiting of it, more precisely self-limiting. From then on, he not only took the most important decisions, but also carried official responsibility for them. Until then, Stalin's power had only been limited by the outside borders of the Soviet Union, and not always even by them. What forced him to voluntarily take on the burden of responsibility for his actions?

Admiral of the Fleet of the Soviet Union N. G. Kuznetsov testified: "When Stalin took on the duties of Chairman of the People's Commissars Council, the system of leadership practically did not change."[2] If practically nothing changed, why did Stalin need the new title? "Meanwhile, all of Stalin's deeds and crimes were focused, logical and calculated."[3]

What was Stalin's logic? "I don't know any problems that could relate to the internal situation in the Soviet Union and be so serious as to elicit such an action from Stalin. I would be more certain in stating that if Stalin decided to take the highest government position, the reasons for his action should be sought in the [realm of] foreign affairs," reported Schulenburg, the German ambassador to Moscow. Soviet marshals said the same thing: Stalin's appointment was tied to foreign affairs.[4]

Let us examine what foreign policy problems Stalin was expected to solve in May 1941. Germany crushed many European countries, so there could be no problems with the governments of those countries. The Soviet Union had friendly relations with France, the large part of which was occupied by Germany. There were no problems with Britain: it retained independence and stretched a hand of friendship to Stalin, exemplified in a letter from Churchill to Stalin dated July 1, 1941. Roosevelt was more than amicable toward Stalin: he warned him of dangers, and American technology flowed into the USSR. There were only two possible enemies. Japan had seen a demonstration of Soviet might at Khalkhin-Gol in August 1939, signed an agreement with the Soviet Union, and looked away from Soviet borders. Therefore, only Germany could have forced Stalin to take the step that seemed inexplicable at first glance.

What could Stalin, using his new official title of head of the government, undertake regarding Germany? There were three possibilities: establish an unshakeable peace with Germany; officially lead an armed struggle against German aggression; or officially lead a sudden attack on Germany.

The first possibility can be ruled out immediately, because Molotov had already signed a peace pact with Germany. Stalin continued to use Molotov for peace talks. It is known that even on June 21, 1941, Molotov tried to meet with German leaders, while Stalin made no such attempts.

The second possibility also doesn't withstand examination. Stalin could not have assumed leadership in anticipation of a German attack, simply because he did not foresee it. In the first day of the war, the head of the government should have addressed the people and told them the terrible news. But Stalin avoided fulfilling his duties, and on June 22 Molotov spoke to the people. Why would Stalin sit in Molotov's chair in May, only to hide behind his back in June? In a defensive war, Stalin used his well-tested method of ruling the country: he took all important decisions, but the responsibility for them was borne by Molotov, Malenkov, Timoshenko, and Zhukov. Only a month later did the members of the Politburo force Stalin to take the official post of People's Commissar for Defense, and on August 8 the post of Supreme Commander in Chief. Would Stalin, "foreseeing a defensive war," have taken a high leadership position, just to shun all responsibility as soon as such a war started?

We are left with the third explanation: Stalin had crushed Europe using Hitler's hands, and was preparing a sudden attack against Germany. Stalin planned to personally lead the "liberation" as the head of the government of the USSR.

The Communist Party prepared the Soviet people and army for the fact that the command to begin a "war of liberation" in Europe would be given personally by Stalin. *Pravda* wrote on August 18, 1940: "And when the Marshal of the Revolution comrade Stalin gives the signal, hundreds of thousands of pilots, navigators, [and] paratroopers will descend upon the enemy's head with all the might of their arms, the arms of socialist justice. The Soviet air force will bring happiness to mankind!" Similar statements filled the pages of *Krasnaya Zvezda* and all other Soviet newspapers and magazines.

Upon entering into office, every head of state declares his agenda. Stalin did so as well. Only Stalin gave his speech, which could be counted as an agenda, in the tight inner circle of the highest Red Army commanders, behind closed doors. On May 5, 1941, the day after his appointment as head of state, Stalin spoke in the Kremlin at a reception in honor of graduates from the military academies. The audience in the convention hall of the Great Kremlyovski Palace, where he gave the speech, consisted of graduates, professors, and teachers from sixteen academies of the Red Army and nine faculties of civilian universities, as well as representatives of the Red Army and the Fleet High Command (including the People's Commissars in both organizations and the Chief of General Staff). Stalin arrived, followed by members, actual and potential, of the Politburo (except for N. S. Khrushchev, who was holding a Central Committee plenary meeting in Kiev). The audience numbered two thousand people. Stalin spoke for forty minutes. Considering Stalin's capability for silence, forty minutes was an extraordinarily long time.

Stalin did not speak before graduates of military academies every year. There were only two such occasions. The first time had been in 1935. The Great Purge was secretly being planned when Stalin told the graduates of military academies that "cadres determine everything." The meaning of Stalin's words was simple: for great feats, the country needed good teams; good commanders would solve all problems, but without them, everything would be lost. It is doubtful that anyone at the time understood the meaning of Stalin's words. But Stalin had in mind nothing less than the complete extermination of almost all of the Communist hierarchy—state, party, military, technical, scientific, cultural, and all others. Stalin planned almost a complete transformation of the leading layer of the country. Almost everyone who listened to Stalin's speech in 1935 in two years landed in torture chambers and execution cellars.

In May 1941, Stalin for the second time spoke before graduates of military academies. Now, a more serious and dark deed was being planned, because this time Stalin's speech was given in secrecy. Stalin spoke about the situation in Europe, the war, and Germany. In his usual manner, Stalin posed questions and then answered them. Was it true that the German army was invincible? This question was repeated in Stalin's speech three times. Stalin's answer was no. Stalin said that Germany fought under the flag of conquering other nations. Under that flag, Germany would not be successful. Stalin asked why Germany lost World War I. Because it fought on two fronts, he answered. This was a very direct hint. Stalin led his audience to a logical conclusion: Germany fought Great Britain, which was backed by the United States. If the Soviet Union opened a second front, Germany would be defeated, just as it was during World War I.

I have in my possession the unpublished memoirs of Major General of the Air Force M. V. Vodopianov, who was the very first Hero of the Soviet Union. According to Vodopianov's memoirs, the listeners correctly understood Stalin's hints, and the room was filled with applause and cheer. The General Secretary of the Comintern, the Bulgarian Communist Georgyi Dimitrov, wrote in his diary that Stalin at that moment was in an extremely good mood. During the banquet that followed his speech, Stalin twice made a toast: the first was to the commanders and the professors from the military academies, the second to the health of artillerymen, tankers, and aviators.[5] A third toast deserved special attention. It was given by Lieutenant General A. K. Sivkov, who toasted Stalin's peaceful foreign policy. Stalin intervened:

> Allow me to make a correction. A peaceful foreign policy secured peace in our country. A peaceful foreign policy is a good thing. For a while, we drew a line of defenses until we re-armed our army [and] supplied it with modern means of combat. Now, when our army has been rebuilt, our technology modernized, [now that we are] strong [enough] for combat, now we must shift from defense to offense. In conducting the defense of our country, we are compelled to act in an aggressive manner. From defense we have to shift to a military policy of offense. It is indispensable that we reform our training, our propaganda, our press to a mindset of offense. The Red Army is a modern army, and the modern army is an army of offense.[6]

On May 5, 1941, Stalin made it perfectly clear to his generals that there would be a war with Germany and that the Soviet Union would be the aggressor. It is interesting to note that a few days after the celebration in the Kremlin, Lieutenant General Sivkov, who made a toast to Stalin's peaceful foreign policy, was discharged.[7]

In March 1939, Stalin publicly accused Great Britain and France of wanting to draw all of Europe into war, while they stayed on the sidelines and would later "enter the scene with fresh forces, fight, of course, 'in the interests of peace,' and dictate their terms to the weakened participants of the war."[8] In the same speech, Stalin for the first time declared that the international arena needed to prepare for "surprises." In August 1939, Stalin presented the first "surprise," which stunned not only the Soviet people, but the entire world, the Molotov-Ribbentrop Pact.

On September 1, 1939, a week after this pact, Germany invaded Poland. On September 17, 1939, the Red Army suddenly attacked the rear of the Polish army. The following day, the Soviet government proclaimed on the radio the cause for the attack: "Poland [has become] a convenient staging ground for any unanticipated events that might create a threat to the USSR. . . . The Soviet government can no longer hold a neutral position towards these facts. . . . In light of such a situation, the Soviet government [has] issued orders to the High

Command of the Red Army to order troops to cross the border and take under their defenses the lives and property of the population."[9]

Here we can see the difference between Stalin and Hitler. They divided Poland and both conducted aggressive war on Polish territory. But Hitler sent his troops to Poland to "expand the living space for Germans," while Stalin sent in the Red Army "to free the Polish people from the evil war, into which they were drawn by foolish governments, and to give the people the opportunity to lead peaceful lives."[10]

Stalin's propaganda could not conceal its joy that Germany was destroying more and more countries, governments, armies, and political parties. The Soviet leadership was ecstatic: *Pravda* declared it "[m]odern warfare in all its terrible glory!"[11] A description of Europe at war read: "a pile of corpses, a pornographic sight, where hyenas eat hyenas."[12] On the same page of *Pravda*, there was a friendly telegram from Stalin to Hitler.

Suddenly, everything changed. May 1941 saw a sharp turn in all Soviet propaganda. Here is *Pravda*'s tone on the day after Stalin's secret speech: "Beyond the borders of our Motherland burns the flame of the Second Imperialist War. All the burden of its countless calamities falls on the shoulders of the workers. The people do not want war. Their eyes are looking toward the land of socialism, which reaps the fruits of peaceful labor. They rightfully see in the armed forces of our Motherland—in the Red Army and Fleet—a reliable bulwark of peace. In the current tumultuous world situation we must be ready for all surprises."[13]

The same tone and the same words were used in September 1939, when the Red Army suddenly attacked the rear of the Polish army and "helped the Polish people to get out of the war."

34

June 13, 1941

Stalin was not one who openly declared his intentions.

—ROBERT CONQUEST, *THE GREAT TERROR*

On May 5, 1941, in the Kremlin, Stalin in essence told the graduates of the military academies to disregard official propaganda and to prepare for war.[1] On June 13, 1941, Moscow radio broadcast a rather unusual announcement of the Soviet Union Telegraph Agency (TASS). It claimed that "Germany was following the conditions of the Soviet-German pact as flawlessly as the Soviet Union," that the rumors of an impending German attack on the USSR "were clumsily fabricated propaganda by the enemies of Germany and the USSR, interested in broadening and prolonging the war." The following day, central Soviet newspapers published that announcement; a week later, Germany invaded the USSR. Everyone knew the author of the TASS announcement. Stalin's characteristic style was recognized by generals in Soviet staffs, inmates in the labor camps, and Western experts.

Both the Soviet and foreign press wrote extensively about the TASS announcement. Many of those who spoke out on the subject laughed at Stalin. The TASS announcement was sometimes described as a sign of nearsightedness. However, the June 13, 1941, TASS announcement was more mysterious and inexplicable than ridiculous. Only its author is clear, while the rest is a puzzle.

The TASS announcement did not at all fit in with Stalin's character. The man most familiar with Stalin, his personal secretary Boris Bazhanov, characterized him in the following way: "Secretive and extremely sly. . . . He possessed an extraordinary ability to remain silent, and in this respect was unique in a country where everyone spoke too much." Following are some more descriptions. A. Avtorkhanov: "He was an implacable enemy of word inflation and excessive talking. Do not say what you are thinking." A. Antonov-Ovseenko: "At critical moments, Stalin's actions came before his words." Robert Conquest, a scholar of the Stalin era, noted Stalin's secretiveness and silence as the strongest points of his personality: "Extremely reserved and secretive. We still have to peer through the darkness of Stalin's exceptional secrecy. . . . Stalin never said what was on his mind, even regarding political goals."

It has been said that the ability to keep silent is much less common among people than any other talent. From that standpoint, Stalin was a genius—he knew how to keep silent. This was not only the strongest point of his character, but his most powerful weapon. With his silence, he disarmed the vigilance of his enemies; Stalin's attacks were always sudden and therefore fatal. Why then did he speak on June 13, 1941, and to a mass audience? Whom did Stalin address? Stalin's empire was highly centralized, and the mechanism of state government, especially after the Great Purge, was so perfected that any order was immediately communicated from the highest ranks to the lowest executors, and was immediately carried out. If in June 1941 Stalin had some concerns that had to be related hastily to millions of executors, why not use the perfect power structure that communicated all orders without distortion or delay? If the TASS announcement of June 13, 1941, was serious, it would have been repeated on all the secret channels. But Marshal of the Soviet Union A. M. Vassilevsky testified that after the announcement was published in print it "was not followed by any directives regarding the armed forces or reexamination of previously adopted policy."[2] He also said that nothing changed in the agendas of the General Staff or the Narkomat (People's Commissariat for Defense), "and nothing was supposed to change. . . . But because no directives followed it, we quickly realized that it was irrelevant both for the armed forces and for the country as a whole."[3]

Not only was the TASS announcement not repeated through secret military channels, but at the same time as the announcement came out, an order was issued to the troops in certain military districts, for example, in the Baltic district, that was in meaning and spirit quite the opposite of the TASS announcement.[4] While the TASS announcement was broadcast on the radio, the military newspapers that were inaccessible to outsiders began to publish radically different ideas. This was reported, for instance, by Vice Admiral I. I. Azarov.[5]

There were five military districts on the Soviet Union's western borders: the First Strategic Echelon of the Red Army. Let's examine what happened around June 13, 1941, in the Kiev special district. There are many records of the events of that day. One of them is kept in the Central Archive of the Defense Ministry of the Russian Federation.[6] This is the "Directive from the People's Commissar for Defense of the USSR and the Chief of General Staff of the Red Army to the Military Council of the Kiev special military district." The document is dated June 13, 1941, and labeled "Top Secret, Special Importance."

The Soviet system of secret classification had four levels of secrecy: "For Official Use Only," "Secret," "Top Secret," and "Top Secret, Special Importance." There was one more level, established by Stalin: "Top Secret, Special File." Documents in this category were produced only in one copy and could not leave the premises of the Kremlin. "Top Secret, Special Importance" was the highest level of secrecy that could have been used beyond the Kremlin. Such a document arrived at the staff headquarters of the Kiev special military district while the radio was broadcasting the strange TASS announcement. The directive ordered the "transfer [of] all deep-rear divisions and corps commands with the corps formations to new camps closer to the state border."

Four armies were camped in the Kiev district; behind them were five rifle corps and four motorized corps. According to the directive of June 13, 1941, all five rifle corps in the Kiev district moved to the border: the 31st, 36th, 37th, 49th, and 55th. A rifle corps three divisions strong had 966 field-guns and mortars, 2,100 machine guns, and more than 2,000 automobiles. A rifle corps had 50,000 soldiers and officers. Five corps made a quarter of a million men. The directive further demanded "to keep the transfer of troops completely secret. March at night and conduct tactical training. Take along with the troops all movable reserves of ammunition and fuel." The document was signed by the People's Commissar for Defense of the USSR, Marshal of the Soviet Union Timoshenko, and the Chief of General Staff Army General Zhukov. "We had to prepare all operational documentation that dealt with moving five rifle and four motorized corps from the positions of permanent location to the border zone," wrote Bagramian (at that time a colonel and chief of operational staff in the Kiev special military district).[7] "They took with them everything necessary for action. The move was conducted at night to secure secrecy."[8] Colonel General I. I. Liudovnikov (at that time a colonel and commander of the 200th Rifle Division in the 31st Corps) was one of those who executed this order: "We were ordered to begin a campaign . . . in full deployment . . . concentrated in the forests 10 to 15 km northeast of the border town Kovel. The move was to be made secretly, only at night, on forested terrain."[9] Marshal of the Soviet Union K. S. Moskalenko (at that time a major general of artillery and commander of the 1st Anti-Tank Brigade) remembered: "New trains kept arriving, with new men and new military equipment."[10] The official history of the Kiev military district stated: "Major General F. F. Aliabushev's 87th Rifle Division on June 14, under pretext of training exercises, was moved to the state border."[11]

The moving of troops to the border under the pretext of training exercises was done on orders from Moscow. Marshal Zhukov said: "The *Narkom* [People's Commissar] for Defense S. K. Timoshenko recommended to the commanders of military districts to conduct tactical exercises in the direction of state borders, with the effect of bringing troops closer to the regions of planned deployment for the purpose of cover." As was previously done prior to the Finnish campaign of 1940, "covering the state borders" was a code expression meaning "preparing to cross the borders." This recommendation was brought into effect by the districts, but with a significant difference: "a significant part of artillery did not take part in the move."[12]

Marshal of the Soviet Union K. K. Rokossovskii (at that time Major General, commander of the 9th Motorized Corps) explains that the artillery had been ordered to the border slightly earlier.[13]

That was a brief description of the events of this day in one of the five border military districts. On the eve of the broadcast of the TASS announcement, the commander of that same Kiev special military district received another directive, with the same signatures and same level of secrecy— "Top Secret, Special Importance." The directive of June 12, 1941, stated:

> During the time period June 15 to July 10, 1941, the 16th army with the following components will arrive on the territory of the Kiev special military district: the command of the army with service personnel, 5th Mechanized Corps (13th and 17th Tank, and 109th Motorized Divisions); 57th Tank Division; 32nd Rifle Corps (46th and 152nd Rifle Divisions, 126th Corps Artillery Regiment). . . . I forbid all open telephone and telegraph communication in connection with the arrival, unloading, and placement of the new troops. Nobody except you, members of the Military Council, and the chief of staff in the district, can know about this. . . . All units arriving to the territory of the district have

been issued false names, listed below. The false name is to be used in all correspondence, including on envelopes of top secret documents.[14]

Four armies and nine separate corps made up the Kiev special military district. In addition, in May 1941 began the intense transfer of troops to the Kiev district from the inner regions of the country and from faraway eastern and southern borders. Bagramian described May in the Kiev district: "On May 25, the command of the 31st Rifle Corps from the Far East arrived in the district. . . . In the second half of May, we received a directive from the General Staff that ordered [us] to receive the command of the 34th Rifle Corps from the North Caucasus district, four 12,000-strong divisions and one mountain rifle division. . . . [At] the end of May, train after train arrived in the district. The Operational Department turned into a train dispatcher bureau and received all information about the incoming troops."[15]

Even before June 13, 1941, troops flowed from the central regions of the Soviet Union to the five border military districts. Just three armies from among these troops required 939 railroad trains—the 22nd Army from the Ural military district, the 21st Army from the Volga military district, and the 16th Army from the Trans-Baikal military district.[16] The 57th Tank Division of the 16th Army came from Mongolia. Preliminary relocation of the armies began in May 1941; other troops were moving as well. The former deputy of the People's Commissar for State Control, I. V. Kovalev, wrote that "in May [and] early June, the transportation system of the USSR had to complete [the] transportation of nearly 800,000 reserve troops. . . . These moves had to be conducted secretly."[17]

The 16th Army consisted of six divisions, among them three tank and one motorized. It had a total of thirty regiments: eleven artillery, seven tank, five motor-rifle, six rifle, and one motorcycle. The army was small in number of divisions and regiments; however it was supreme in technology, especially tanks and artillery. The 5th Mechanized Corps of the 16th Army counted 1,076 tanks.[18] The 57th Separate Tank Division counted 375 tanks, and the two rifle divisions had another thirty-two tanks. In total, the 16th Army had 1,483 tanks and 560 armored cars, among them 397 heavy armored vehicles armed with cannon. The 16th Army was transferred across seven thousand kilometers. Lieutenant General M. F. Lukin commanded the army. The chief of staff of the 16th Army was Colonel M. A. Shalin—the future head of the GRU.

The relocation of the 16th Army from the region beyond Baikal to Ukraine began on May 26, 1941, and was scheduled to end on July 10. Lieutenant General P. A. Kurochkin, commander of the Trans-Baikal military district, personally supervised the dispatching of trains. We can find many testimonials to this massive railroad operation, among them the memoirs of Major General A. A. Lobachev, who at that time was a member of the military council of the 16th Army: "The chief of staff reported that an important cable came in from Moscow, concerning the 16th Army. . . . The order from Moscow proposed to relocate the 16th Army to a new place. M. F. Lukin was to immediately appear before the General Staff to receive directions, and Colonel M. A. Shalin and I were to organize the dispatch of trains."[19]

Only three people—the Commander of the Army General Lukin, Lobachev, and the Chief of Staff of the 16th Army Colonel M. A. Shalin—knew that the 16th Army was being transferred west, but they did not know precisely where. All the other generals of the 16th Army were "secretly" informed that the army was headed for the Iranian border, and that the junior commanders were to be told that the reason for the transfer was training exercises; the wives of the command staff were to be told that the army was leaving for training camps.

I have interviewed hundreds of people from that generation, and they all had forebodings of the war. Where did they come from? They could not have known about Hitler's preparations. They must have seen the preparations of the Red Army and understood that war was unavoidable. General Lobachev described the extraordinary level of secrecy with which the 16th army was transferred: the trains were sent only by night and they did not stop at large and medium stations; the staff of the 16th Army was moved in cargo railroad cars with the doors and windows completely shut; at small stations, where the trains stopped, everyone was forbidden to exit the train. At that time, a passenger train covered the Trans-Siberian route in more than eleven days, while cargo trains were even slower. One could transport soldiers and officers in fully closed cars, but here we are talking about the high-ranking staff of an army. Such level of secrecy was unusual even by Soviet standards. In 1945, a flow of troops going in the opposite direction traveled on the Trans-Siberian railroad, heading for a surprise attack on Japanese troops in Manchuria and China. For the purposes of secrecy, all the generals wore officers' uniforms, with many fewer stars than they had earned, but they still traveled in passenger trains. In 1941, on the other hand, generals were being transported in cargo trains. What for?

There were five military districts in the First Strategic Echelon of the Red Army. We examined what happened in the Kiev special military district on June 13, 1941, and on the days before and after that date. The same went on in the four other military districts. On June 14, the military council of the Odessa military district received an order to create an army headquarters in Tiraspol.[20] This indicated the creation of the 9th Army on the Romanian border. From June 14 to June 19, the military councils of all the western border districts were directed to send out the frontline army commands to their field headquarters by June 22 and 23. Zhukov's June 19 telegram to Kirponos, the commander of the Kiev special military district, stated: "The People's Commissar of Defense has issued the following orders: the command should leave for Ternopol by June 22, 1941, leaving the subordinate district commander in Kiev. . . . The selection and transfer of front command is to be kept top secret, and the district staff personnel should be notified of said secrecy."[21] Zhukov sent out similar telegrams to Kuznetsov, the commander of the Baltic special military district, and Pavlov, the commander of the Western special military district, on the same day. The command of the Northwestern Front, along with its district's commander, should have arrived at Panevezhis on June 22 and 23; the same should have happened on the Western front at Obuz-Lesni. This mass exodus of front and army command units was approved by Stalin on the pretext of conducting joint summer training for commanders and troops.

On June 14, the military council of the Baltic special military district approved a plan for the relocation of a row of divisions and regiments to the border zone.[22] Here are some standard reports from those days. Major General S. Iovlev (at the time commander of the 64th Rifle Division of the 44th Rifle Corps, 13th Army) recounted: "On June 15, 1941, the commander of the Western special military district, General D. G. Pavlov, ordered the divisions of our corps to prepare for relocation in complete formation. . . . We were not told our destination."[23] Colonel General L. M. Sandalov (at that time colonel, chief of staff of the 4th Army of the Western special military district) remembered: "On the southern wing of the 4th Army a new division appeared—the 75th Rifle Division. It advanced from Mosyr and set up well-concealed tent camps in the forests."[24]

Marshal of the Soviet Union K. A. Meretskov (at that time general, and the Deputy People's Commissar of Defense) said: "According to my orders, training exercises of the mechanized corps were conducted. The corps was brought out, as part of the training, to the border zone and left there. Later I told Zakharov that the corps of Major General R. I. Malinovsky was also in the area, and must also be brought to the border zone as part of training exercises."[25] Marshal of the Soviet Union R. I. Malinovsky (at that time major general, commander of the 48th Rifle Corps of the Odessa military district) confirmed that the order was executed: "The corps left the Kirovograd region for Beltsy on June 7, and on June 14 it was in its place. This move was disguised as extensive training exercises."[26] Marshal of the Soviet Union M. V. Zakharov (at the time major general, and chief of staff of the Odessa military district) recounted: "On June 15, the command of the 48th Rifle Corps, the 74th and 30th Rifle Divisions concentrated, under the guise of training, in the forests several kilometers to the east of the city of Beltsy."[27] The marshal noted that the commands of the corps, the units, and the 74th Rifle Division were on high alert. He said that the 16th Tank Division also participated in the "training." Marshal of the Soviet Union A. I. Eremenko (at that time commander of the 1st Army) said: "On June 20, the staff of the 13th Army received an order from the command of the Western military district to relocate from Mogilev to Novogrudok."[28]

Not only armies, corps, and divisions were transferred to the borders. We have hundreds of testimonies of much smaller units being transferred as well. Lieutenant General V. F. Zotov (at the time a major general, and chief of the engineer troops of the Baltic special military district) remembered: "The sapper battalions were mobilized according to wartime regulations . . . ten battalions, which arrived from the Far East, were completely armed."[29] Colonel S. F. Khvaley (at the time deputy commander of the 202nd Motorized Division of the 12th Mechanized Corps of the 8th Army) recounted: "During the night of June 18, 1941, our division left for field training."[30] As the colonel put it, "it so happened" that the units found themselves right at the border before the war began, in the immediate vicinity of the state frontiers.

A small fragment is known from the military order received on that same day by Colonel I. D. Cherniakhovsky, commander of a tank division in that same 12th Mechanized Corps: "Upon the receipt of this order, commander of the 28th Tank Division Colonel Cherniakhovsky is to bring all units to battle condition in accordance with plans of high alert, but without declaring a state of alert. All work is to be conducted quickly, but without noise, without panic and talk; have the necessary norms of portable and transportable reserves needed for life and battle."[31]

Trophy German documents indicate that the Germans' first encounter with the 28th Tank Division occurred near Siauliai. However, as Marshal P. P. Poluboyarov testified, the division was supposed to come out of Riga to the Soviet-German boder.[32] The German invasion found this division, like so many others, still on its way, because it simply did not have enough time to reach the border. The memoirs of Major I. A. Khizenko begin with the chapter "Marching toward the Border."[33] He wrote about the 80th Rifle Division of the 37th Rifle Corps: "In the evening of June 16, General Prokhorov gathered all staff personnel for a conference. He declared an order from the commander of the Kiev special military district to move the divisions to a new region of concentration. . . . There are talks that the impending march will be an unusual one."[34]

This list is endless. Overall, the First Strategic Echelon of the Red Army had 170 tank, motorized, cavalry, and rifle divisions. Fifty-six of them were located right on the border. They could not move any farther ahead. But even of these, everything that could move was moving forward and hiding in the border forests. General I. I. Feduninsky, commander of the 15th Rifle Corps of the Fifth Army, testified that he led four regiments from the 45th and 62nd Rifle Divisions "into the woods, closer to the border."[35] The remaining 114 divisions of the First Strategic Echelon stayed in the deeper territories of the western border districts, and could be moved to the border.

How many of the 114 divisions began to move toward the border in the wake of the reassuring TASS announcement from June 13, 1941? The answer is: all of them! "Between June 12 and June 15, all the western military districts were issued an order to move all deeply located divisions closer to the state borders."[36]

Now, let's look at what was happening on June 13, 1941, in the inner military districts of the Soviet Union, in the far inland Urals, and in the Siberian and Altay provinces. Lieutenant General N. I. Birukov, commander of the 186th Rifle Division of the 62nd Rifle Corps of the Ural military district, recounted: "On June 13, 1941, we received an order of special importance from staff headquarters, which stated that the division had to move to a 'new camp.' The address of the new quarters was not given even to me, the division commander. Only when passing through Moscow did I find out that our division was to concentrate in the forests west of Idritsa."[37]

In peacetime, a division receives "secret," but very rarely "top secret," documents. A document of "special importance" can appear in a division only during wartime and only in extreme cases, when an operation of great importance is prepared. Many Soviet divisions did not receive a single document with this label of top secrecy during the four years of the war. Yet, it was peacetime when the commander of the 186th Rifle Division received a document of such an exceptionally high level of secrecy. The document's contents were ostensibly trivial: send the division to a new camp. General Birukov, however, placed the words "new camp" in quotation marks. He and the superior officials who had sent the document knew perfectly well that they were not talking of a "new camp," but of something much more serious.

All divisions in the Ural military district received similar orders. Official records of the district clearly fixed the date: "The 112th Rifle Division was the first to begin loading. On the morning of June 13, the train left the small railroad station. . . . Other trains followed. Then began the loading of units from the 98th, 153rd, and 186th Rifle Divisions."[38] The 170th and the 174th Rifle Divisions, artillery, sapper, and anti-tank units followed. New administrations were created for operating the Ural divisions, while the old ones were submitted to the command of the staff of the new 22nd Army.

This mass of staffs and troops moved from the Urals toward the Belorussian forests under the cover of the reassuring TASS announcement. The 22nd Army was not alone. General S. M. Shtemenko wrote: "Right before the beginning of the war, under the strictest secrecy, additional forces began to gather in the border forests. Five armies were transferred from the depth of the country toward the borders."[39] General S. P. Ivanov, who in the early 1970s headed a group of experts researching this issue, added: "At the same time, three more armies were preparing for relocation."[40] All these armies would form the Second Strategic Echelon of the Red Army.

Why didn't all eight armies move simultaneously? In February, March, April, and May, a grandiose secret transfer of Soviet troops—from the inner regions to the borders—was conducted. It was concluded in time, but thousands of railroad cars had to return thousands of kilometers back inland. Therefore, on June 13, when the new, giant, secret movement of troops began, there were not enough cars for all the armies. The Second Strategic Echelon contained seventy-seven tank, motorized, and rifle divisions, not counting tens of separate regiments and hundreds of separate battalions. They all began their secret movement toward the western borders of the USSR under the cover of the TASS announcement.[41] To the 114 divisions of the First Strategic Echelon, we must add seventy-seven divisions of the Second Strategic Echelon that began to move toward the western borders from the central regions of the country, from Siberia, and even from the Far East.

Everything that Soviet officers, generals, and marshals wrote about in their memoirs was fully confirmed by reports of German intelligence to their commanders in the spring and early summer of 1941: the Red Army was heading in giant surges toward the western borders. Many independent sources confirm the same fact. The massive Red Army movement toward the western borders was felt even in Soviet prisons. G. Ozerov, one of the deputies of airplane designer A. N. Tupolev, at that time was in prison, together with Tupolev and his entire design bureau. They received an order to create the best dive-bomber in the world. They were told that if they designed the plane, they would be let out of prison. They designed behind bars, but had constant contact with engineers from airplane and automobile factories, and with officials from the People's Commissariat of Aviation Industry. Former inmate Ozerov recounted: "Inhabitants of dachas along the Belorussian and Vindavsk roads complain that they cannot sleep at night [because] trains with tanks and cannon are being herded through!"[42]

Thus, "right before the war, in accordance with orders from the General Staff of the Red Army, certain units of the western special military district began to move to the state border."[43] Having crushed the First Strategic Echelon and broken through its defenses, the first German units suddenly stumbled across new divisions, corps, and armies (for example, the 16th Army near Shepetovka in late June), about whose existence the German commanders had no idea. The plan for the blitzkrieg was built on calculations of lightning-speed destruction of the Soviet troops right along the borders. But having completed this plan, the German army discovered a new wall of armies, which was coming out of the Northern Caucasus, Volga, the Urals, Siberia, Trans-Baikal, and the Far East.

Thousands of railroad cars are needed for the transfer of even one army. They have to be sent to the station of departure, loaded with the army, heavy weapons, and reserves, and then cross thousands of kilometers. If the German troops encountered Siberian, Ural, and Trans-Baikal armies at the end of June, then their transfer to the west had not begun on June 22, but earlier.

The movement of the Soviet navy began at the same time as the movement of ground troops. Before the war, the Soviet Baltic fleet left the eastern part of the Gulf of Finland, heading west.[44] The fleet's objective was to act on the naval communication lines of the enemy.[45]

Simultaneously with the transfer of ground troops and navy, an intensive relocation of aviation was taking place. During the dark early hours of the day, aviation divisions and regiments were transferred in small units to air bases, some of which were less than ten kilometers from the border. In addition to operational air force units, a rigorous transfer of the newest airplanes to these units was under way. Colonel General L. M. Sandalov recounted: "From June 15, we began to receive new combat technology. Kobrinsky and Pruzhansky fighter regiments received the Iak-1 fighters, armed with cannon; the ground attack regiment got the Il-2 plane, the bomber regiments [got] the Pe-2."[46]

Fighter regiments of that time had sixty-two planes each, ground attack regiments had sixty-three, and bomber regiments had sixty. Consequently, a single division (the 10th Mixed Air Force) was awaiting the arrival of 247 new planes. The general reported that the division did in fact begin to receive new technology, but old planes remained in the division. The division turned into a giant combat organism, comprised of several hundred planes. This process occurred everywhere. For example, the nearby 9th Mixed Air Force Division also received 262 new MiG-1s and MiG-3s, as well as several tens of Pe-2s and Il-2s.[47] On the morning of June 22, that same western front got an order to receive 99 MiG-3s at the Orsha airfield.[48] If they were to be received on the morning of June 22, the planes evidently were ready to be shipped out on the evening of June 21. Chief Marshal of Aviation A. A. Novikov reported that on June 21 the Northern Front, where he was commander of the air force, received a trainload of MiG-3 fighters.[49]

Besides the fighter planes, a mighty stream of tanks, artillery, ammunition, and fuel was also flowing in. At dawn on June 22, a trainload of heavy artillery regiments came into the Siauliai station.[50] There were endless rows of trains full of ammunition. The *Krasnaya Zvezda* noted: "On the evening of June 21, 1941, the supervisor of the railroad station at Liepaja was told: 'Receive a special train. It carries ammunition. It must be sent to its destination as a matter of priority.'"[51] Liepaja at that time was very close to the border, but the train was in transit, meaning it was going to the border lines.

Railroad cars on all fronts were full of ammunition, which was usually done in preparation for an offensive of great depth. In a defensive war, it was easier and cheaper to store ammunition in previously prepared storage depots. Having used up all the ammunition from one storage depot, the troops easily retreated to another, where ammunition awaited them, then to a third, and so on. But before an invasion, ammunition was loaded onto mobile transport, which was very risky and expensive. For example, the southwestern front had 1,500 railroad cars of ammunition at the small Kalinovka station alone.[52] Colonel General I. I. Volkotrubenko reported that in 1941, after the German attack, the western front alone lost 4,216 railroad cars of ammunition.[53] There were five fronts, and it is incredible how much ammunition was stored on all fronts. Some of it fell into German hands; some of it was successfully rescued. In the middle of June, that incredible number of troops and ammunition—under the cover of the TASS announcement—was rolling toward the German borders in railroad cars.

Marshal of the Soviet Union S. K. Kurkotkin reported that in the beginning of June the "Soviet government, following a proposal by the General Staff, approved a plan to move 100,000 tons of fuel from the inland regions of the country."[54] In addition, "about 8,500 railroad cisterns with fuel [were] amassed at railroad intersections."[55] If the smallest 20-ton cisterns were being used, this would have meant much more than 100,000 tons. The most frequently used cistern in 1941 was the 62-ton. These 8,500 containers were at the stations waiting to be unloaded in the first days of the war. We also have to take into account all that was destroyed by enemy air raids at the railroad stations in the first minutes and hours of the war. Colonel General I. V. Boldin, deputy commander of the Western Front, related that the 10th Army (the most powerful army on the Western Front) had sufficient supplies of fuel in storage and in railroad containers, but lost everything in the first minutes of the war.[56] On the eve of the war, this mass of cisterns was moving toward the borders, together with troops, military equipment, weapons, and ammunition.

June 13, 1941, marked the beginning of the biggest organized movement of troops, arms, ammunition, and other military supplies in history. Now is the right time to look once again at the TASS announcement of June 13. Many historians for some reason focus their attention on the introduction of this announcement, which speaks of German intentions. But the TASS announcement also speaks of Soviet intentions, and the most interesting information is contained there: "Rumors that the USSR is preparing for war against Germany are false and provocative. . . . The gathering of air forces and reserves of the Red Army and the impending maneuvers have as their objective nothing but [the] training of reserves and [the] testing of railroad functioning; they are conducted, as is known, yearly, so to imagine that these events are hostile to Germany is ridiculous." Comparing the announcement with what occurred in reality, we find a big discrepancy between words and deeds.

The TASS announcement talked about the "testing of railroad functioning." This is questionable. The movement of Soviet troops began in February, in March it intensified, in April and May it reached grandiose proportions, and starting on June 13, 1941, it reached an all-encompassing character. The only divisions that did not participate in the move were those already at the border, those that remained in the Far East, and those that were preparing to invade Iran. The full concentration of Soviet troops along the German border was planned for July 10.[57] For almost half a year, railroad transportation, the main means of transportation in the country, was paralyzed by secret troop transfers. In the first half of 1941, the government plan for industry was only fulfilled for the military requirements. The main reason was that transportation was almost exclusively used for secret military transfers. The second reason was the secret mobilization of the male population to the newly formed armies. The disruption of the government plan could hardly be called "testing."

The TASS announcement described it as "usual training," but Soviet marshals, generals, and admirals contradicted that claim. Major General S. Iovlev said: "The unusual aspect of the gatherings, not foreseen by plans of war readiness, alerted people."[58] Vice Admiral I. I. Azarov remembered: "Usually, training was conducted closer to the fall, but here they were beginning in the middle of the summer."[59] Colonel General I. I. Ludnikov said: "Usually, reserves are called in after the crops have been harvested. . . . In 1941, this rule was broken."[60]

Major General M. I. Kazakov at that time was at the General Staff headquarters. There, he encountered the commander of the 16th Army, Lieutenant General M. F. Lukin, and other generals. Their armies were secretly being transferred by train; the commanders of the armies moved ahead of their troops and arrived in Moscow by airplane. In Moscow, they received their last instructions. General Kazakov said: "It was clear that it was not maneuvers they were going to. It was something else."[61]

Did Stalin have a premonition and concentrate troops along the borders for defense? That explanation is implausible. The massive operation described above couldn't be defensive. Troops preparing for defense dig themselves into the ground. They take over the largest fields that the enemy will have to cross, close off roads, establish barbwire barriers, dig anti-tank trenches, and prepare covers behind the barricades. The Red Army did nothing of the kind. However, Soviet divisions, armies, and corps destroyed all previously constructed defensive structures. Troops were concentrated not behind water barriers, in a fashion convenient for defense, but in front of them, which was convenient for offense. Soviet troops did not take over vast fields that the enemy would need to cross, but hid in the woods, just like the German troops preparing for invasion. Perhaps all this was just a demonstration of might? Of course not—a demonstration has to be visible to the enemy. The Red Army, on the contrary, tried to hide its preparations. The TASS announcement was not written to scare Germany, but to allay its fears.

35

Words and Deeds

When trying to put together a clear picture of Hitler's National Socialism and Stalin's international socialism, we find surprising similarities not only in slogans, songs, and ideologies, but also in events. In the history of German National Socialism there was a moment very similar in spirit and meaning to the TASS Announcement of June 13, 1941. A year before, on May 8, 1940, German radio announced that the talk of two German armies being transferred to the border with Holland was a "ridiculous rumor," being circulated by "British inciters of war." After this, the German armies crushed and occupied Belgium, Holland, Luxemburg, and the greater part of France. The German radio announcement of May 8, 1940, and the TASS announcement of June 13, 1941, match almost word for word. Hitler did not believe Stalin's TASS announcement because he had himself disguised the preparations for a sudden attack using the same exact tricks.

The TASS announcement of June 13, 1941, was meant to stop rumors of imminent war between the USSR and Germany. Stalin decisively fought these rumors. The same problem stood before Hitler at the same time. Preparations for war are difficult to hide. People see them and express all sorts of hypotheses. On April 24, the German naval attaché in Moscow sent a warning report to Berlin, stating that he was combating "obviously ridiculous rumors of an impending German-Soviet war."[1] On May 2, Ambassador Schulenburg reported that he was also fighting rumors, but "everybody who comes to Moscow from Germany brings not just these rumors, but can even support them with evidence."[2] On May 24, the head of the foreign press department of the Ministry of Propaganda in Germany, Karl Bemer, in a drunken state said something undesirable about relations with the Soviet Union. He was arrested immediately. Hitler personally took care of this case and, according to Goebbels, gave this event "too much consideration." On June 13, 1941, on the day of the TASS announcement stating that there would be no war, Karl Bemer stood trial before the People's Court and said that his speech had been a drunken mistake: of course, there would be no war between Germany and the Soviet Union!

Just to make sure no doubts about this remained at home or abroad, on June 15, 1941, Ribbentrop, the German minister of foreign affairs, sent top secret telegrams to his ambassadors: "There are plans [for] important talks with Moscow. [The] Fuehrer is going to sort out relations and raise new demands. Ambassadors must, in complete secrecy, relay this to the governments of the nations in which they are stationed. For example, the German ambassador in Budapest had to relay this piece of information, as a special secret, to the Hungarian president.[3] The German leaders undertook a preplanned program of disinformation toward their own troops, their diplomats, and their military allies. The Soviet high command was doing the exact same thing.

Many people saw the transfer of Soviet troops to the borders. However, every person saw only a part of what was happening. Very few individuals conceived of its true scope. German military intelligence knew that a development of the might of the Red Army was occurring, but it only saw the first strategic echelon, without having any idea that there was a second one. Many Soviet marshals and generals, excluding those who were directly involved in the planning and commanding of the troop movement, also could not conceive of its true scope and, consequently, its meaning. Precisely for this reason, later on many of them freely talked about this transfer of troops. Their lack of knowledge of the whole situation and the true scale of concentration of Soviet troops is not at all coincidental; Stalin undertook draconian measures to keep all this secret. Stalin's TASS announcement was one of those measures. The fact of the transfer itself was impossible to hide, but the most important information—its size and its purpose—Stalin successfully hid from the entire nation, and even from future generations.

Colonel General of the Air Force A. S. Yakovlev (at the time personal advisor to Stalin) testifies that "at the end of May or beginning of June" a conference was held in the Kremlin regarding questions of concealment.[4] Troops were told that they were going to training camps, although the higher command understood that they were not talking of training. In a defensive war or before its start there is no need to fool the troops—officers and soldiers are given a clear and precise objective: here is your line, do not take a single step back! Die here, but do not let the enemy through! If a defensive operation was being prepared, why not tell the troops: yes, comrades, the situation is tense, anything can happen, dig foxholes and sit in them. If troops were indeed being sent to dig foxholes, it would have made no difference whether the objective of their move was told after arrival or upon departure. But Soviet officers were not told so upon arrival or departure. A different task was set before them, which was concealed then and is still concealed now.

In order to understand the level of secrecy of the troop transfers, I will give one example: a district commander and his chief of staff did not know that some other troops were gathering on their territory. Marshal of the Soviet Union M.V. Zakharov tells us:

> In the beginning of June, Colonel P. I. Rumiantsev, the chief of military communications of the Odessa military district, came to me, at that time chief of staff in Odessa, to my cabinet, and secretly reported that during the last few days *Annushkas* had been going through the Znamenka station from the direction of Rostov and were being unloaded in the Cherkassy region. *Annushka* is a term used in military communication to denote a division. Two days later, I received a cable from Cherkassy signed by the deputy commander of the Northern Caucasus military district, M. A. Reiter, in which he asked permission for the temporary use of several barracks of storage space in our district—to place materials arriving from the Northern Caucasus into the district. Because the staff of the Odessa military district was not informed about concentration of troops there, I contacted, using

high-frequency lines, the Operational Directorate of the General Staff.[5] The deputy chief of the directorate, A. F. Anisov, came to the telephone. After telling him about the cable I received from Reiter, I asked for clarification. Anisov replied that Reiter's cable was to be immediately destroyed, that Reiter would receive the necessary orders from the General Staff, while the staff of the district should not get involved in this matter.[6]

The commander of the Odessa district, Colonel General I. T. Cherevichenko also knew nothing of the *Annushkas*.

Some Soviet marshals, including Zhukov, said that twenty-eight rifle divisions were moving out from the deeper inland territories of the country. This is true, but it is not the entire truth. Marshal A. M. Vassilevsky stressed that twenty-eight divisions only "laid the foundation for the execution of the troop gathering plan."[7] Twenty-eight divisions were only the beginning. We know that there was a continuation, which surpassed the beginning, but Marshal Vassilevsky, after having spoken a little, grew silent and did not name concrete figures. If we compile all the data contained in all present-day military history works, we will find out that in May and June of 1941 seven armies were moved from the interior military districts to the western borders.[8] Besides that, several independent corps were on their way west, including the 9th Special Rifle Corps, the 31st Rifle Corps, and the 27th Mechanized Corps. The total number of transferred divisions was seventy-seven, plus there was a huge number of independent combat and auxiliary formations.

On June 13, 1941, Molotov summoned the German ambassador and related to him the text of the TASS announcement.[9] The announcement stated that Germany did not want to attack the USSR, and the USSR did not want to attack Germany, but "enemies of Germany and the USSR interested in unleashing and broadening war" were trying to make them quarrel and were spreading provocations and rumors of imminent war. In the announcement, these "enemy forces" are listed by name: "the British ambassador in Moscow, Mr. Kripps," "London," and "the English press." Our exploration of the day would not be complete if we do not turn to London on June 13, 1941.

It is reasonable to suppose that on June 13 there was a meeting in London between the Soviet ambassador I. M. Maysky and the British foreign minister Anthony Eden. Indeed, the meeting was held, and, surprisingly, in a friendly atmosphere. Discussion revolved around a serious issue: measures Britain would take to aid the Red Army "if in the near future a war between the USSR and Germany begins." Among other specific measures were military operations by the British air force, the transfer of military supplies, and the coordination of command between the two countries.[10]

On June 13, 1941, Stalin's diplomats were laying the foundation of what would soon be called the "Anti-Hitler Coalition." From the British point of view, there was nothing wrong with this picture: at that moment, Britain was involved in a war against Hitler, and had full rights to talk with anyone about joint efforts against him. But the Soviet Union had signed a pact of non-aggression with Germany, and immediately after that an agreement of friendship. If Soviet leadership thought that these documents no longer suited the situation at hand, they should have had them annulled. But Stalin did not do this; he assured Hitler of friendship and in the TASS announcement denounced the British ambassador and press for "wanting to broaden the war." At the same time, talks in London were under way concerning a military alliance with Germany's enemy, and about specific military measures against Germany.

It is surprising that at the talks in London both sides used the phrase "if war begins" instead of "if Germany attacks." In other words, those talking did not exclude the possibility that the war would start not with German aggression, but in some other way. It is interesting that at the talks in London, the USSR was listed first: "if a war between the USSR and Germany occurs." The same words were used in the TASS announcement: "rumors of imminent war between the USSR and Germany." Why not say the opposite, between Germany and the USSR, if one supposes that Germany will be the aggressor?

36

Red Army, Black Gulag Uniforms

Immediately after the partition of Poland in the fall of 1939, a large number of Soviet troops were transferred from their permanent stations to the new borders. But the new territories were not adapted to the permanent deployment of large quantities of troops, especially troops with a lot of military equipment.

The *History of the Second World War* tells us: "The troops in [the] western border districts experienced many difficulties. Everything had to be built and equipped anew: bases and supply points, airfields, systems of roads, lines of communication."[1] The official history of the Byelorussian military district says: "Movement of units from the district to western parts of Byelorussia caused considerable difficulties. . . . The personnel of the 3rd, 10th and 4th armies . . . were busy with repair work and building barracks, storages, [and] camps, [and] furnishing training sites, shooting ranges, and tank depots. The troops were under considerable strain."[2] Colonel General L. M. Sandalov: "The movement of district troops here encountered huge difficulties. The barracks were miserably few. . . . For troops not provided with barracks, dugouts were being built."[3]

But troops kept arriving. General Sandalov says that in order to house all the troops in 1939–40, storages, barracks, and any kind of space was being used. "A large amount of troops concentrated in Brest. . . . Four-tiered bunks were set up on the lower floors of the barracks."[4] Lieutenant General V. N. Kurdumov, the head of the Battle Training Directorate of the Red Army, had said in December 1940 at a meeting of the command staff that, in the new regions, troops often were forced to spend their time doing housework instead of military training.[5] At the same meeting Lieutenant General I. N. Fedorenko, the head of the Automobile-Tank Directorate, said that almost all tank units in 1939–40 changed their positions, sometimes up to three or four times. As a result, "more than half of the units that moved to new places had no training ranges."[6] At the cost of tremendous effort, in 1939 and 1940 the troops of the First Strategic Echelon were set up and quartered. But from February 1941, at first slowly, then faster and faster, the seven armies of the Second Strategic Echelon began pouring into the same areas. At that moment, a change occurred that has not been noticed by historians: Soviet troops stopped caring about how they would spend the coming winter. The troops of the First Strategic Echelon abandoned their dugouts and unfinished barracks and entered the border zone. We are talking of all the troops.[7]

Troops of the Second Strategic Echelon, moving from within the country, did not use the unfinished barracks and camps abandoned by the First Strategic Echelon. The arriving troops were not planning to spend the winter in these locations, and made no preparations for winter. They were not making dugouts or building training facilities and shooting ranges; they were not even digging foxholes.

Many official documents and memoirs of Soviet generals and marshals attest to the fact that now the armies were lodged in tents. In March 1941, the 118th Division of the 16th Rifle Corps of the 11th Army was formed in the Baltic region. In May, reserves arrived. The division put up a temporary summer camp made of tents in the Kozlovo Ruda region (45 to 50 km from the state border). Safe under the cover of the TASS announcement, the division abandoned this camp and headed for the border. Any attempt to find even a hint of preparations for winter is doomed to fail—the division was not preparing to spend the winter here. Right next to it moved the 28th Tank Division, and the picture was the same. In all tank divisions, all newly formed rifle divisions, the attitude toward winter changed—nobody feared winter any longer. Marshal of the Soviet Union K. S. Moskalenko (at the time Major General, commander of the 1st Motorized Artillery Anti-Tank Brigade of the Main Command Reserve) received an assignment from the commander of the 5th Army, Major General M. I. Potapov: "Your brigade began to form here. You will occupy that area of forest [and] set up a camp." A powerful brigade of over six thousand men, with over a hundred heavy guns up to 85 mm in caliber, set up camp in three days. After this, intense battle training began: eight to ten hours a day, not counting night training, homework, maintenance of weapons, and weapon training.[8]

Where were they planning to spend the winter? Staying in tents in the Russian winter? Wasn't Central and Western Europe more comfortable?

Major General A. Zaporozhchenko gives the following description: "The final phase of the strategic deployment was the secret movement of attack groups to staging grounds for invasion. It was carried out during the course of several nights before the attack. The cover of the movement was organized by reinforced battalions that had previously been moved to the border and, before the arrival of the main forces, controlled the areas of the front pre-assigned for the divisions. Transfer of aviation began in the last days of May and ended by June 18. Fighter and ground-attack planes concentrated at air bases up to 40 km from the border, and the bombers were no further than 180 km."[9]

In this description, we can be surprised only by the date of June 18. Soviet aviation did not complete its relocation then; it only started it on June 13 under the cover of the TASS announcement. Why is the general mentioning June 18? The thing is, he is talking not of the Red Army, but of the German *Wehrmacht*, where the same exact thing was occurring—troops were also moving toward the borders at night. Reinforced battalions were sent ahead. Arriving divisions took predesignated areas for attack, or simply put, hid in the forests. The actions of the two armies are mirror images of each other. The only difference is the dates. At first, the Soviet troops were ahead, but then Hitler got two weeks ahead of them—he had fewer troops, and they had less distance to cover. It is interesting that in the beginning of June the German army was in a very unfavorable position: it had troops in railroad trains. Guns were in one train, shells in another. Battalions were unloaded where there were no staffs, staffs where there were no troops. There were no communication lines, since for safety reasons usage of many radio frequencies was banned. German troops also did not prepare dugouts and build training ranges.

But the most important similarity was the huge quantity of supplies, troops, aviation, hospitals, staffs, air bases—all this right on the Soviet borders, and very few people knew the plan of action, which was kept in extreme secrecy. All that we see in the Red Army and discount as stupidity was done, two weeks prior to that, in the German *Wehrmacht*. This is not stupidity, but preparation for invasion.

What was supposed to happen after the gathering of the Second Strategic Echelon of Soviet troops in the western districts of the country? The answer to this question was given long before the beginning of World War II. General V. Sikorsky: "Strategic waiting cannot last after all forces have been mobilized and concentration of troops achieved."[10] This was said by the Chief of the General Staff of the Polish army, in the 1936 book *The Future War*. However, according to a decision of the Soviet General Staff, the book was published in Moscow for Soviet commanders. The book was published because Soviet military science had earlier reached the same conclusion: "In modern conditions the worst idea in the beginning stages of the war is to attempt to use a tactic of waiting."[11]

The advancement of the Second Strategic Echelon was not a reaction to Hitler's actions. The creation of the Second Strategic Echelon began before the massive movements of German troops to the Soviet borders. The movement of the Second Strategic Echelon was a railroad operation that required lengthy preparations and extensive planning. Marshal S. K. Kurkotkin said that the General Staff transferred all necessary documents concerning the troop movements to the People's Commissariat of Transportation on February 21, 1941.[12] But the General Staff also needed time to meticulously prepare those documents; they needed to issue to the railroads precise orders about when, where, and what transport should be supplied, how to conceal loading and transfer, what routes to use, where to prepare areas for unloading the troops. In order to prepare all this, the General Staff had to determine exactly what troops had to appear, and where and at what time. This means that the decision to create the Second Strategic Echelon and the beginning of planning its movement and use for battle must have come sometime earlier.

The process of creating troop formations in inner districts and moving them to western border districts began on August 19, 1939. It originated with a decision by the Politburo; it was never stopped, and slowly gained momentum. Here is just one example: the Ural military district. At the end of August 1939 the 85th Division was formed; in September 1939, the 159th Division was formed. We see the 85th Division on June 21, 1941, right at the German borders in the region of Augustow, where the NKVD is cutting through barbwire. The 159th Division we find right on the border as well, in the Rava-Russkaya region, in the 6th Army. In the same month of September 1939, in the same Ural district, the 125th and 128th Rifle Divisions were created, and each of them we can later find on the German borders. Moreover, according to Soviet sources, the 125th was "on the immediate borders" of East Prussia. The Ural district formed many other regiments and divisions, and all of them quietly crawled closer to the borders.

After the German invasion, the Second Strategic Echelon (as well as the first) was used for defense. But that does not at all mean that it was created for that purpose. General M. I.

Kazakov says of the second echelon: "After the beginning of the war, radical changes to the plans for its use had to be made."[13] Major General V. Zemskov speaks more precisely: "We were forced to use these reserves not for attack, as planned, but for defense."[14] General S. P. Ivanov: "If the troops of the First Strategic Echelon had been successful in . . . transferring the battle action to the enemy's territory before the deployment of the main forces, the Second Strategic Echelon had to fortify the efforts of the first echelon and develop a counterstrike according to the overall strategic plan."[15] The term "counterstrike" should not add confusion. The Red Army always delivered a "counterstrike."

Lieutenant General S. A. Kalinin talks about the mood in the Second Strategic Echelon. Before the beginning of the secret movement west, he prepared the troops of the Siberian military district (later transformed into the 24th Army) for action. During the course of training, the general heard opinions from junior officers: "We probably won't need fortifications either. After all, we are getting ready not for defense, but for invasion, we will hit the enemy on his territory."[16] All armies were prepared to fight "on enemy territory." The commander of the 16th Army of the Second Strategic Echelon, Lieutenant General M. F. Lukin, does not say exactly on what territory he planned to use the 16th Army that was under his command in 1941. But in any case, it was not Soviet territory: "We planned to fight on enemy territory."[17] On the same page of the Soviet military journal where Lukin was quoted, Marshal A. M. Vassilevsky stresses that we should believe Lukin: "[T]here is much harsh truth in his words." Vassilevsky himself was a master at fighting "on enemy territory." It was he who carried out a surprise attack on Japanese troops in Manchuria in 1945, demonstrating the best example of how one has to deliver a sudden treacherous blow to the enemy's rear while he is occupied by war on other fronts.

From experience, as well as from theory, the Soviet High Command knew that not even one division could be left for a winter in the woods, unprepared. A soldier can spend the winter under any conditions—that was not the problem. The problem was that near the western borders there were no shooting ranges, no training camps, no tank depots, and no conditions for battle training. Troops must either immediately enter combat, or inevitable degradation of the level of battle readiness would ensue. The Soviet High Command knew that the culprits would be found, and they knew what the fate of the culprits would be—yet they took practically the entire Red Army into places where there were no conditions for battle training. The Soviet High Command did not fear Stalin's ire, because the move forward did not endanger the troops' combat readiness. Stationing them under such poor conditions was planned for a very short time only, after which the Red Army would attack westward.

Stalin had no choice. He could not turn his armies around. Many armies and corps created in the first half of 1941 had nowhere to turn back to. Another troop transfer would have required many more months, would have paralyzed the entire railroad system, and would have meant economic catastrophe. Moreover, what sense does it make first to spend half a year gathering troops, and then half a year dispersing them? Even if, after a full concentration, an immediate dispersion had begun, even then the process could not have been finished before the arrival of winter. Besides, Stalin kept the process of creation and transfer to the west of the entire Second Strategic Echelon strictly secret. Could he have counted on full secrecy, if he left these armies for several weeks in the border forests?

If the Red Army could not turn back and could not stay in the border regions for long, what was left for it to do? In order to answer this question one needs to bring up the opinion of Stalin: "In the condition when we are surrounded by enemies, a sudden attack from our side, an unanticipated maneuver, quickness, decides everything."[18] In every grandiose process, there is a critical moment, after which events cannot be turned back. For the Soviet Union, this moment came on June 13, 1941. After this day, war for the Soviet Union became inevitable, and it was to be in the summer of 1941, regardless of Hitler's actions.

In the Second Strategic Echelon, which Stalin was secretly transferring to the borders, there were entire divisions, sometimes even corps, of soldiers dressed in old black uniforms. There were enough of these soldiers for the German military intelligence to notice and unofficially dub these divisions and corps "black." One example was the 69th Rifle Corps of the 20th Army. This corps was not the only one. The 63rd Corps of the 21st Army also figures in German documents as the "black corps." The commander of the 63rd Rifle Corps was *Komkor* (Corps Commander) L. G. Petrovsky. During the war *Komkor* Petrovsky fought with dignity and courage, proving his ability as a great strategist in battle. On July 31, 1941, he received the rank of lieutenant general and was promoted to command the 21st Army while the 63rd Rifle Corps, after heavy fighting, was encircled by the enemy. Stalin ordered him to leave the 63rd Corps encircled and to take command of the 21st Army. Petrovsky asked to delay the order of entering his post as army commander for a couple days, and the plane sent for him returned with critically wounded soldiers on board. Petrovsky brought his "black corps" out of encirclement and once again returned to the rear of the enemy, in order to bring another division out of encirclement, the 154th Rifle Division (under the command of Major General. S. Fokanov). During the breakout from encirclement, Petrovsky was fatally wounded. German troops, upon finding and recognizing Petrovsky's body on the battlefield, gave the Soviet general a funeral with all military honors. A huge cross was placed on his tomb, with an inscription in German that read: "Lieutenant General Petrovsky, commander of the 'black corps.'"

The unusual black uniform was noted by the German intelligence in other units of the Second Strategic Echelon as well. When this uniform dominated over the usual green one, then regiments, divisions, and sometimes entire corps received the name "black." The 24th Army of the Second Strategic Echelon, secretly advancing out of Siberia, was no exception. During the fighting, several of its corps and divisions got called "black" by the Germans. By the end of June, the trains of this army stretched across thousands of kilometers. At that time Lieutenant General S. A. Kalinin, the commander of the army, was already in Moscow, working on the problem of how to feed the 24th Army. After the first few battles, the 24th Army found itself in the right hands: Major General of the NKVD Constantin Rakutin took the command. Lieutenant General S. A. Kalinin returned to Siberia. Kalinin, on Stalin's orders, formed ten new divisions. He said: "Units were formed in locations that previously had no military units at all. I began my work by visiting these locations. My first flight was to one of the towns in Siberia. Some years before the war, in the dense forests there, a village of barracks was built for lumberjacks. We used it for housing the units of the forming armies. The village was surrounded almost from all sides by impenetrable taiga."[19] Everything about "barrack villages for lumberjacks" can be found in the three volumes of Alexander Solzhenitsyn's book *The Gulag Archipelago*. The result was that ten new divisions (over 130,000 men) assembled in the Siberian military district not in locations previously established for military units, but in "barrack villages." These people were the Soviet prisoners. That is why the regiments and divisions of this army and other armies of the Second Strategic Echelon were clothed in black:

"lumberjacks" were frequently not even issued military uniforms. That was why Stalin had replaced the commander of the 24th Army with the "chekist" Rakutin.[20]

The armies of the Second Strategic Echelon, which included the "black" divisions and corps, began forming in June 1941. These divisions and corps began their movement west on June 13, 1941. German troops encountered the "black" divisions and corps in early July 1941 Every army of the Second Strategic Echelon was created specifically for the purpose of a surprise arrival at the western borders. Each army was located on a major railroad route. Each was formed in the vicinity of concentration camps: men there were used to order, didn't ask for much, and it was easier to take them out of the camps than out of the villages—all were already gathered in one place, organized into brigades, and, most importantly, it was impossible to take men out of the villages without stirring rumors about mobilization and war. Stalin needed everything to proceed quietly, without rumors. That was why he wrote the TASS announcement. That was why men were in due time taken to concentration camps, trained and disciplined, and then sent to the front without fuss. If in early July the German army met divisions and corps filled with inmates, in the armies coming from the faraway Urals and from the Siberian and Trans-Baikal provinces, it means that Stalin handed weapons to the inmates before June 22, 1941. The main question that German command had to answer was: If we do not attack, what will Stalin do? Take away the weapons from the inmates, return them to the GULAG, or send them home? Or perhaps Stalin had some other options for using the armed inmates that were secretly gathering at the German borders?

37

Military Alignment

Hitler, herded into a corner and full of fear, in June 1941 decided to turn east, and attack the Soviet Union.

—Basil Henry Liddell Hart

In September 1939, as a result of the Red Army's "war of liberation" in Poland, the new western border of the Soviet Union advanced in such a way that the so-called Belostok bulge formed in Byelorussia—a powerful wedge that, like a ship's bow, broke into the territory occupied by Germany. The same thing happened in the Lvov region—there, another powerful wedge of Soviet territory formed. The Belostok and Lvov bulges were like two Soviet peninsulas in the German sea. Basic military logic dictated: if the Red Army intended to defend itself, it could not keep troops in the Belostok and Lvov bulges. Already, in peacetime, enemy troops surrounded the Soviet army on three sides in the bulges. The Soviet flanks were open and vulnerable. A sudden and decisive German attack on the flanks in these bulges would have cut off the best sections of the Red Army from the main forces and supply bases. In the event of an enemy invasion, such an alignment of Soviet troops inevitably and immediately would have led to catastrophe.

That is exactly what happened in 1941. Before the German invasion into the territory of the Kiev military district, the most powerful Soviet front was deployed: the Southwestern Front. The three most powerful armies of that front were in the Lvov bulge. In peacetime, these three armies were already almost surrounded. Hitler only had to shut the trap on them. On June 22, the very weak 1st German Tank Group hit Lutsk, Rovno, and Berdichev, quickly cutting off all three Soviet armies in the Lvov bulge—the 12th (mountain), 6th, and 26th. The 1st Tank Group, faced with open, unprotected operational space, immediately went through the Soviet rear, crushing air bases, staffs, and hospitals. Here, in the rear, they found tremendous quantities of Soviet weapons, fuel, ammunition, foodstuffs, and medical supplies. The Germans seized truly remarkable trophies. The three Soviet armies in the Lvov bulge were left with a problem that had two solutions, both of which were catastrophic: either

228

remain in the trap and wait for the 1st Tank Group to completely lock the encirclement, or run to the east, abandoning everything that cannot be carried. They ran. Soon, they were left without fuel and ammunition. The entire Soviet Southwestern Front crumbled from one rather weak blow. But that was not all: this same blow threatened the entire Southern Front.

Having broken through to open space, the 1st German Tank Group could have freely chosen any direction: all roads were open. It could have struck the rear of the Southern Front. It could have headed to Kiev. If Kiev was being defended it could, instead of engaging in battle, have hit the metal-producing sites of the Ukraine: Dnepropetrovsk, Dneprodzerzhinsk, Zaporozhye. Once there, it could have reached the Crimea. It could have gone to the bases of the Black Sea fleet and taken them. Or it could have taken the largest hydroelectric plant in Europe, DneproGES. It could have crossed the Dnepr and taken Donbass—the largest coal region of the Soviet Union. It was also possible to continue to the North Caucasus toward the main petroleum sources of the Soviet Union. But Hitler was preparing for war in a very strange manner: so many open directions, and he only had one tank group against all of Ukraine, Moldavia, Crimea, Donbass, Don, North Caucasus, and Trans-Caucasus—with only 799 obsolete and worn-out tanks. The First Tank Group fought fierce battles on the western bank of the Dniepr River, then crossed the Dniepr and joined the Second Tank Group. This was how four armies of the Soviets were encircled; 664,000 prisoners were taken, and with them huge quantities of arms and supplies. But the Germans paid for this grandiose bounty by losing the tempo of their attack: it happened in September, so they could not start moving toward Moscow before October, which meant rain, dirt, and mud. No blitzkrieg was possible in the remaining months of 1941.

In Byelorussia, the Red Army had an even worse time. The Western Front had four armies. The main forces of the front were concentrated in the Byelostok bulge. Two German tank groups struck the undefended flanks and linked east of Minsk. The 3rd, 10th, and parts of the 4th and 13th armies, all together almost thirty divisions, found themselves in a pocket. The Western Front collapsed even quicker than the Southwestern and the Southern Fronts. Could it be that before the war General Zhukov did not understand that one cannot herd huge numbers of troops into bulges that become traps?

The answer to this question was given by one of the most brilliant Soviet troop commanders, the deputy commander of the Volkhov front Lieutenant General Andrey Vlassov. On June 22, 1941, he was a major general in command of the 4th Mechanized Corps in the Lvov bulge. In 1942 he was ordered to command the 2nd Shock Army, which found itself in a hopeless position. Vlassov was ordered to complete an operation that he had not prepared, had not started, and that had already failed. The 2nd Shock Army could not be saved. It perished, and Vlassov was taken prisoner. In a protocol from questioning on August 8, 1942, it was recorded: "Regarding the question of whether Stalin had intentions to attack Germany, Vlassov declared that such intentions, undoubtedly, existed. The concentration of troops in the Lvov region points to the fact that a strike against Romania was being planned in the direction of the petroleum sources. . . . The Red Army was not prepared for the German invasion. Despite all the rumors about the operations conducted by Germany, in the Soviet Union nobody believed in such a possibility. During preparations, the Russians meant only their own offensive."[1] There is no other explanation for the concentration of Soviet troops in the Lvov and Byelostok bulges.

Forty-nine years later the same explanation was given by the Deputy Chief of the General Staff of the Soviet Military Forces, General Makhmut Gareev: "A main blow to the flank in the main alignment of the enemy's troops, delivered in the direction of Krakow, would have allowed us to cut Germany off from the Balkans in the very beginning of the war, to deprive her of the Romanian oil, and to separate the allies. On the other hand, carrying out the main blow on the joint flanks of the western and northwestern fronts led to a frontal attack in difficult conditions against heavily fortified defense positions in East Prussia, where the German army could offer fiercer resistance. And totally different conditions, and consequently different objections, could have arisen if the strategic plans were to lead defensive operations to deflect aggression early in the war. In this case, no doubt, it was more advantageous to have main forces in the strip of the western front. But such a course of strategic actions was not planned."[2]

Let's compare the opinions of the two generals. They are saying the same thing: there was no preparation for defense, only offense, moreover, an offensive in the southwestern direction (that is, from the Lvov bulge) with the objective of cutting Germany off from her oil suppliers and main allies. If someone places on the map the Soviet Shock armies, mechanized and airborne corps, air bases, staffs, and Zhukov's generals, he will be forced to acknowledge, even without Vlassov and Gareev's testimonies, that such positioning of troops in the bulges directed toward the enemy could only lead to catastrophe in the event of an invasion by the enemy, while it would lead to a brilliant victory in the event that the Red Army was first to deliver its sudden crushing blow.

Between the Baltic and Black Seas lie the impassible swamps of Polesye. This is the largest area of swamps in Europe. These swamps divided the entire theater of military operations into two regions, two strategic directions. An enemy advancing toward Russia from the west must choose the direction of his main blow: he can go to the north of Polesye, or to the south. Traditionally, conquerors advancing from the west went north of Polesye: Warsaw-Brest-Litovsk-Minsk-Smolensk—this is a direct route to Moscow. The question before Hitler's strategists was: where to plan the primary blow, north of Polesye or south? Hitler's strategists decided that the primary blow was to come to the north, the secondary to the south. In 1941 Hitler had four tank groups. Three of them were designated for action north of Polesye, and one to the south.

Soviet military intelligence knew of the concentration of German troops and knew that three tank groups would act against the Baltic and Byelorussian areas, while only one would go against the Ukraine. What should the Soviet command have done? Since the Germans prepared the primary blow to the north of the swamps, the main forces of the Red Army should also have been placed there—in the western direction. Even if Soviet intelligence had not known anything about Hitler's plans, the main forces should have been kept in the western direction. It is obvious even to the lowest ranking officer that the direct route to Moscow runs through Byelorussia and Smolensk.

Troop alignment is, figuratively speaking, equal to positioning chess figures on the board. The General Staff is the brain of the army. The Chief of the General Staff is the most capable and smartest general in the entire army. Starting in February 1941, Zhukov was chief of the General Staff. Here is the situation we are examining: on June 22, the Germans delivered the primary blow north of Polesye and crushed Soviet armies in the Belostok bulge, from where the German tank groups could head toward Smolensk and Moscow. Meanwhile,

Zhukov's main forces were not there, but south of Polesye. The direction facing the greatest threat was north of the swamps. Conquerors from the west have always advanced to the north, but Zhukov deployed his main alignment to the south.

The consequences of Zhukov's positioning were catastrophic. In order to divert the attack on Moscow, the Red Army had to send, urgently and under heavy enemy bombers' raids, railway trains with divisions, corps, and armies from the Southwestern Front to the Western Front. There, again under heavy bombing, the trains were unloaded and the troops went straight into battle. What happened was that the 16th Army was advanced from the Trans-Baikal region to Ukraine, meaning south of Polesye. The army had just begun to unload when the German invasion happened. They were forced to urgently load the 16th Army back into trains and herd it several hundred kilometers to the north. The staff of the 16th Army arrived at Smolensk from Ukraine and began to unload, but the communications battalion could not be found. Without communications, it is impossible to command troops. An entire army found itself without command. This is what must be called a "headless army." The culprit here is not Stalin, but Zhukov, who in May and early June moved a large part of the armies of the second strategic echelon to the south of Polesye, instead of to the north.

This is just one example, there are plenty more. The 19th Army was secretly moved from the North Caucasus to Ukraine, in other words, south of Polesye. This army also began to unload. It was ordered to get back on the trains and sent to Smolensk. The same thing happened: the artillery was unloaded in one place, while the trains with shells had not yet arrived. Tanks were there, but the repair crews had not arrived. The division staffs were there, but the troops were still far behind. What was General Zhukov thinking about before the German invasion? Why was the strongest Soviet military district before the war not the Western district, which was in the most threatened area, but the Kiev district? If Zhukov had been thinking of defense, he of course would have deployed the most powerful Soviet groupings in the most threatened areas—north of Polesye.

But Zhukov was not thinking of defense, and was not planning for it. There is plenty of testimony that right before the invasion Zhukov, Vatutin, Vasilevsky, and all the generals and officers of the General Staff worked sixteen and seventeen hours a day without weekends or holidays. "The areas for the concentration of primary efforts were not chosen by the Soviet commanders in the interests of strategic defense operations (such an operation was simply not foreseen and not planned), but for entirely different means of action," wrote Gareev.[3]

If we prepare to deliver a sudden all-crushing blow to Germany and her allies, we must also choose the direction of the primary attack: north of Polesye, or south. If we attack to the north, we find ourselves in East Prussia, which is heavily fortified and populated with Germans who will offer resistance. In this area we can only advance from east to west along the shores of the Baltic Sea, so all the rivers and streams would have to be crossed in their lower currents, almost at their mouths. Among those rivers, there are two powerful water barriers: the Vistula and the Oder. In their middle, and especially in their lower currents, they are extremely difficult to cross. However, if we strike south of Polesye the picture changes. In this case, the Red Army would end up in the Krakow region. It is inhabited by Poles who, after two years of German occupation, would have met any other army with flowers and offers of help. Here, on the Polish plains, there are no formidable modern fortifications. Here one does not need to expend efforts to cross rivers. In their upper currents they do not pose serious barriers. If one carries out the attack south of Polesye, then during the advancement his left flank will be defended by the mountains of Slovakia, primarily by the Tatra Mountains which are up to 2,500 meters tall. Advancing troops would only need to worry about securing one flank; the other would be covered.

An attack on Krakow out of Lvov would have divided Hitler's coalition, cutting Germany off from all her eastern allies: Slovakia, Hungary, Romania, and Bulgaria. An attack south of Polesye—and this is the most important point—would have cut Germany off from her primary source of petroleum: Romania. The delivery of just this one strike would have immediately secured the Soviet Union's victory in World War II. Further on from the Krakow region, it was best to turn north. In this case, the Red Army troops could freely advance to the Baltic Sea, cutting the German army off from Berlin and the inner regions of Germany. This would have formed a corridor, in which the Red Army had no threats: to the left, advancing Soviet divisions, corps, and armies would have been covered by the Oder River right up to the sea, and to the right—by the Vistula River. German counterattacks here would have been impossible. This is exactly what Stalin was preparing in the first half of 1941. The plan of such an operation is a picture of diabolical strategic beauty.

38

Churchill's Warning and Stalin's Reaction

Can Churchill be trusted in this matter? He is interested in making us clash with the
Germans as soon as possible. Isn't it so?

—VYACHESLAV MOLOTOV, IN *MOLOTOV: MASTER OF HALF A DOMAIN*

For more than half a century, historians have been saying that Churchill warned Stalin
about the impending German invasion, but Stalin ignored his warnings. Perhaps we
should ask a different question: Why should Stalin have believed Churchill?

Churchill was one of the most powerful political leaders who had understood the
great threat posed by Communism back in 1918. He invested considerable effort in helping
the Russian people get rid of that regime. His efforts turned out to be insufficient but still,
Churchill did more for the destruction of Communism than all other world leaders. Churchill
was an open enemy of the Communists, and never tried to hide that fact. But all of a sudden
in 1941, Churchill rushed to warn Stalin, the most powerful Communist in the world, that
Hitler posed a danger to the Soviet Union.

From the Soviet point of view, Churchill could have had only one political motive:
to deflect the German attack to anywhere other than Britain. Even before World War II
began, on March 10, 1939, at the Eighteenth Congress of the Communist Party, it had been
openly declared that Great Britain wanted to trigger a war between the Soviet Union and
Germany, while it remained on the sidelines of this fight. We do not know whether that was
indeed Churchill's intention, but it was exactly how Stalin interpreted every action of British
leadership and diplomacy. As Admiral N. G. Kuznetsov put it, "Stalin, of course, had more
than enough grounds for thinking that England and America were seeking to have us collide
head-on with Germany."[1] Upon receiving any letter from Churchill, Stalin, without reading
it, could guess its contents.

To understand Stalin's suspicion of Churchill's letters, we must also examine the strategic situation in Europe. The concentration of power against weakness was the main principle
of strategy. Germany was unable to apply this principle in World War I, because it was fight-

ing on two fronts. Attempts to concentrate great efforts on one front automatically led to the weakening of the other front, and the enemy immediately exploited it. As a result, Germany had to renounce a strategy of destruction in favor of the only other alternative, a strategy of attrition. But Germany's resources were limited, in contrast to the resources of its enemies. A war of attrition could only end in catastrophe for Germany.

Both the German General Staff and Hitler himself understood that a war on two fronts would be catastrophic for Germany. Speaking at a meeting with the High Command of the German armed forces on November 23, 1939, Hitler said that a war against the Soviet Union could only begin after the war in the west had ended. In 1939 and 1940, Germany always fought on only one front. The German General Staff was able to apply the concentration principle brilliantly, thrusting the enormous German military power first against one enemy, then against another. The main problem facing German strategy was to prevent war from breaking out on a second front. As long as the Germans were fighting on one front only, they won brilliant victories. Two fronts meant abandoning all strategic principles, regressing from the strategy of crushing to the strategy of attrition. It would spell the end of the blitzkrieg, and would mean catastrophe.

In 1940, in terms of strategy, Churchill could only have dreamt that the war Germany was fighting would transform from a one-front war into a two-front war. It was the only way to save Great Britain. In May 1940, the British army suffered a crushing defeat unprecedented in history. The German tank divisions broke through to La Manche, and trapped forty British, French, and Belgian divisions against the coastline in the region around Dunkirk. The British troops managed to evacuate to Britain from France in early June 1940, but the losses were horrendous. They had left all their military equipment on the French coast, all their tanks, artillery tows, 63,000 automobiles, and more than half a million tons of ammunition and supplies. The human casualties of the British army totaled more than 68,000. After leaving the continent, the British army was left practically without heavy weapons. Fewer than one hundred obsolete tanks were left on the British Isles.[2]

Belgium capitulated on May 28. France fell on June 22, 1940. Hitler's troops reached the shores of the Atlantic Ocean and took over naval bases of tremendous strategic value. From this time, the piracy of German U-boats increased sharply on the sea routes. Britain, an island nation, faced the threat of a naval blockade and the most acute crisis in trade, industry, and finance. Worse still, the German military machine, which at that point seemed invincible, was making intensive preparations to land on the British Isles. It was in this environment that Churchill wrote to Stalin on June 25, 1940. On June 30, the German armed forces captured Guernsey, one of the Channel Islands. In almost a thousand years of British history, this was the first time since 1066, meaning after the Norman conquest of Britain, that an enemy had captured a part of the British Isles. What would follow—a German occupation of mainland Britain? Guernsey was taken without resistance. For how long could Britain resist?

Stalin received Churchill's message the day after Germany had seized Guernsey. What were Churchill's interests? Did he want to save the British Empire or the dictatorship in the Soviet Union? For Stalin, Churchill was not an unbiased observer who, out of friendly sentiments, was warning of danger, but a man who desperately needed help and allies in a conflict against a fearful enemy. Stalin therefore was very suspicious of Churchill's letters.

Японский самолет «Накадзима» Б5Н2. (Вес — 3,8 тонны. Макс. скорость — 378 км/ч. Дальность полета — 2000 км. Боевая нагрузка — 1 торпеда 800 кг).

Советский самолет «Иванов», или СУ-2. (Вес — 4 тонны. Макс. скорость — 486 км/ч, дальность полета 1200 км, бомбовая нагрузка — 600 кг).

The Japanese Nakajima B-5N2. The Japanese used these planes in their surprise attack on Pearl Harbor. By the end of the 1930s the Soviet Union developed the Su-2 (Ivanov). Soviet designers were not aware of the Japanese plane, but in both countries identical planes were developed. Stalin was planning to use the Su-2 against the Germans in the same way the Japanese used the Nakajima against the U.S.

A close-support and anti-tank warplane, the Il-2 was the most produced aircraft in military history. Stalin was prepared to attack first. His focus was not on building interceptors to protect against an enemy strike but on warplanes that could support a first strike.

An 8-inch Howitzer B-4. Each projectile weighed 220 pounds. These guns were needed primarily for an offensive war in order to break hardened enemy defenses or during an assault on cities. By the summer of 1941 the Red Army had concentrated hundreds of them on the German border, each with a supply of six hundred rounds of ammunition. In a defensive war, they proved to be of little use, until 1944 when the Red Army crossed into Germany for the final offensive of the war.

The Red Army was trained to cross rivers, a key element in an offensive war. In a defensive war a retreating army uses its own bridges and then destroys them.

In 1940 Soviet Industry was converted to wartime production. Under Stalin's orders millions of teenagers were mobilized into "Labor Reserves" that provided slave labor for military factories. Defection from the Labor Reserves was punishable by a military court-martial and the death sentence.

In the spring of 1941 the Supreme Soviet commanders spent long weeks on the Soviet Union's western border. People's Commissar of Defense Marshal S. K. Timoshenko and Chief of the General Staff of the Soviet Army, General Georgi Zhukov, on the Romanian border. This is not where Hitler attacked, but an area where the Soviet offensive against Germany was to be launched.

In 1941 the major means of German army transportation was horse-driven wagons and carts, rarely shown in World War II newsreels.

Even heavy artillery was transported by horses.

Soviet attack aircraft massed at airfields close to the western border were vulnerable to Hitler's first strike on June 22 and were destroyed on the ground, wing-tip to wing-tip, in a massive bonfire of aircraft.

In Byelorussia the Red Army abandoned twenty-five thousand railroad cars of artillery ammunition close to the border. Why were they placed there? Why were they on railroad cars? Where were they heading?

T-34 tanks, abandoned by the Red Army in the summer of 1941, fought under the German flag for the rest of World War II.

While the Soviet Union was claiming friendship with Hitler in a deceptive June 13 TASS announcement, Stalin was massing Soviet troops near the western borders. The Germans attacked while the Soviet troops were still moving forward by rail. Once the tracks were destroyed the tanks could not be unloaded and the best ones, the T-34s, were left as a present for Hitler.

Even the best German Panzer divisions were using Soviet T-34 tanks.

Among millions of Soviet prisoners of war was Stalin's son, Yacov Dzhugashvili. A letter from one of his friends, dated June 21, was found in his pocket. It described an upcoming "stroll to Berlin." By striking first Hitler spoiled the stroll.

Soviet troops of the Second Strategic Echelon, drafted from Gulag prisoners, surrender without a fight. Stalin said that if the fire is good even wet logs can burn in the blaze, but if the fire is weak a wet log will not help. If the Soviet first strike had succeeded, the poorly trained and equipped Gulag-drafted soldiers would have fought well. But when the Germans struck first the skeletons from the Gulag were useless.

Released Gulag prisoners had no time to change into new uniforms, and were captured by the Germans in their prison garb at the front. Entire regiments, divisions, and even corps were dressed in the black clothes of prisoners. The Germans called them "Black Divisions." Why would Stalin move his prisoners from the Siberian labor camps to the border and give them weapons, if not to attack Hitler?

Hitler's army was totally unprepared for war in the Soviet Union. The German army was not properly equipped to fight in the frost, snow, and mud of the Russian winter. Even with the most optimistic scenario, Hitler could not have conquered all of the Soviet Union in one summer.

Russian soldiers were wearing sheepskin coats. War could not be fought in Russia without these coats and the Germans did not have them. That is why Stalin did not believe that Hitler would strike first while he was still totally unprepared for a war that would have to last longer than a summer campaign.

Churchill wrote several letters to Stalin. But unfortunately they all reached Stalin at times when Churchill was in dire straits. The best-known letter in this series reached Stalin on April 19, 1941. Churchill wrote this letter on April 3 and requested the British ambassador in Moscow, Sir Stafford Cripps, to immediately hand it to Stalin in person. But neither Stalin nor Molotov would receive the ambassador. Finally, on April 19, Cripps did not hand but transmitted the message, and not to Stalin, but only to Andrei Vyshinsky, Deputy People's Commissar of Foreign Affairs. On April 22, Vyshinsky informed the ambassador that Churchill's message had been handed to Stalin.

By the time Stalin received the letter, the British situation had exacerbated, compared with the time when the letter was written. The German army seized Belgrade on April 13 and headed south, posing threats to British troops in the Balkans. Rommel's tank divisions reached the Egyptian border in the area of Bardia and Es-Sallum on April 12. If they broke through to the Suez Canal, the main artery connecting the British Empire would be cut. Yugoslavia surrendered to Germany on April 17. The road to Greece was open. St. Paul's Cathedral in London was damaged in an air raid on April 16. In April, Greece was on the verge of surrender. On April 18, Korizis, the Greek prime minister, committed suicide. After that, the capitulation talks commenced. On April 23, the Greek armed forces surrendered. British troops there were in a catastrophic position, and the question was whether or not they could be evacuated. In this context, Stalin received the most important of Churchill's letters.

On May 20, 1941, the German armed forces started the most massive airborne operation in German military history to capture Crete. There were 32,000 British and 14,000 Greek troops on the island. Several days later, without having superiority in numbers, German paratroops took control of the island and annihilated the more numerous British and Greek forces. Military experts unanimously concluded that the taking of Crete was an ingenious rehearsal by Hitler's paratroops before landing on the British Isles. On May 24, 1941, the largest ship of the British fleet in the Atlantic, the battle cruiser *Hood*, clashed with the *Bismarck*, Germany's largest battle ship. The battle lasted eight minutes. One direct hit to the British ship caused it to explode and sink in a matter of minutes. Out of the 1,421 crew members, only three survived. In June 1941, German U-boats sank sixty-one British merchant ships, totaling 431,000 tons.[3]

Churchill wrote his first long letter to Stalin on June 25, 1940, when neither Hitler nor the German generals had any intention of invading the Soviet Union. The plan for Operation Barbarossa or any other plan for war against the Soviet Union simply did not exist. Churchill's letters were not based on knowledge of German plans, but on sound calculations. He simply directed Stalin's attention to the situation in Europe: today Britain had problems with Hitler; tomorrow it would inevitably be the Soviet Union's turn. Churchill urged Stalin to unite with him against Hitler, and to lead the Soviet Union into the war on the side of Great Britain and all of vanquished Europe.

The text of Churchill's message received in Moscow on April 19, 1941, can be found in hundreds of Soviet books and articles. Here it is: "I have received reliable information from a trustworthy source that the Germans, after deciding that Yugoslavia had fallen into their clutches on 20 March, began to transfer three armoured divisions, of the five stationed in Romania, into the southern part of Poland. As soon as they learnt of the Serbian revolution, this transfer was cancelled. Your Excellency will easily appreciate the significance of these facts." All Soviet sources publish Churchill's message in this form, insisting and assuring that it was a "warning."

I see no warning here. Churchill was talking about three tank divisions—many by Churchill's standards, but by Stalin's, it was not a great deal. Stalin himself at the time was secretly setting up sixty-three tank divisions, each of which was stronger than a German division both in number and in quality of tanks. Mass production of tanks was already set up in the Soviet Union at that time, and they remained the best in the world throughout the war. Nobody in the world, all through the war, created anything even close to the tanks that Stalin had before the war even began. Having received a report about three German divisions, why should Stalin have guessed that there would be an invasion? If the report about the three tank divisions was sufficient "warning" about preparations of aggression, we should not accuse Hitler of being the aggressor: German intelligence gave Hitler reports about tens of Soviet tank divisions grouping along the German and Romanian borders.

Churchill suggested that Stalin assess "the significance of these facts." How could they be assessed? Poland, historically, has always been the gate through which all aggressors passed from Central Europe to Russia. Hitler wanted to transfer tanks to Poland, but he changed his mind. Compared to Poland, Romania was a very bad springboard for aggression. German troops would be harder to supply there than in Poland. In an attack from Romania, the road to the vital heartland of Russia would be longer and harder for an aggressor, who would have to overcome a multitude of barriers, including the lower reaches of the river Dnepr. Had Stalin been preparing himself for defense, and had he believed Churchill's "warning," he should have breathed a sigh of relief and relaxed his military preparations. In addition, Churchill explained why the German troops were staying in Romania instead of being transferred to Poland: the Germans had problems in Yugoslavia, particularly in Serbia. In other words, Churchill said that the German tank divisions were left in Romania not for aggression eastward against the Soviet Union, but on the contrary, from Romania they were pointed southwest toward Serbia, with their backs to Stalin.

Churchill's letter had tremendous significance, but it absolutely couldn't be regarded as a warning. It was more of an invitation to Stalin: the Germans wanted to transfer their divisions to Poland, but changed their minds; therefore, the Soviet Union had nothing to fear, especially since the German tank divisions in Romania had their backs turned to Stalin. Churchill wanted Stalin to evaluate these facts and act on them.[4] Sir Basil Liddell Hart, the British military historian, made a brilliant analysis of the strategic situation of that time as seen from Hitler's standpoint. According to General Jodl, to whom Liddell Hart referred, Hitler repeatedly told his generals that Britain's only hope was a Soviet invasion of Europe.[5] Churchill himself wrote on April 22, 1941, that "the Soviet government knows full well . . . that we stand in need of its help."[6] The only way Stalin could help Britain was by attacking Germany.

Hitler made one irremediable mistake, but not on July 21, 1940, when he ordered preparations for war against the Soviet Union. The mistake came on August 19, 1939, when he agreed to the Molotov-Ribbentrop Pact. Having agreed to the division of Poland, Hitler had to confront an unavoidable war against the West, having behind him the "neutral" Stalin. Precisely from this moment, Hitler had two fronts. The decision to begin Operation Barbarossa in the east without waiting for victory in the west was not a fatal error, but only an attempt to right the fatal error he had already made. But by then it was too late. Even the capture of Moscow would not have solved Hitler's problem, because beyond Moscow still lay several million square kilometers of unending territory, vast centers of industrial power, and inexhaustible natural and human resources. It is always easy to begin a war with Russia, but not so easy to finish it. It was certainly easy for Hitler to fight in the European part of the Soviet Union: the territory was limited, there were many relatively good roads, and the winters were mild. Was Hitler ready to fight in Siberia, in that limitless expanse, where there were no roads and where the brutality of the cold was only matched by the brutality of Stalin's regime?

Stalin knew that war on two fronts spelled suicide for Hitler. He calculated that Hitler would not commit suicide by starting a war in the east without first finishing the war in the west. Stalin was patiently waiting for the German tank corps to land in Britain. Meanwhile, he did everything possible to convince Hitler of his desire for peace. That was why Soviet anti-aircraft guns were not firing on German aircraft crossing the Soviet borders, and Soviet newspapers and TASS proclaimed that there would be no war between the Soviet Union and Germany. If Stalin had succeeded in convincing Hitler that the Soviet Union was neutral, then the bulk of German forces would have been engaged in fierce battles trying to land on the British Isles and leaving practically all Europe defenseless and ripe to be "liberated" by the Red Army. Poland, Czechoslovakia, Denmark, Norway, Belgium, Holland, Luxembourg, Yugoslavia, France, Greece, and Albania no longer had armies, governments, parliaments, or political parties. Millions of people had been driven into Nazi concentration camps and the whole of Europe was awaiting its liberation.

Stalin had helped Hitler come to power and transformed him, in Stalin's words, into a real "Icebreaker" that would trigger the world revolution in Europe. Stalin pushed along that Icebreaker of the revolution. Stalin demanded from the French and from other Communists that they let the Icebreaker crush Europe. Stalin supplied the Icebreaker with everything needed for a victorious advance. Stalin closed his eyes to all the crimes committed by the Nazis. But Hitler guessed Stalin's design. That was why World War II ended catastrophically for Stalin: he only got half of Europe.

39

A Blitzkrieg against Russia?

The first endless columns of Russian prisoners began to file into Germany. From that moment, the flow did not stop. Endless transports of Russian prisoners moved through roads and railroads all the time. But it was of little use. In the place of each vanquished army, the Russians raised another one. The endless lands of the tsars seemed to have unending human resources. How much longer could Germany stand against such competition? Will there not be a day, when Germany, regardless of the fact that it just achieved yet another victory, will be left without new troops, while the Russian command will again and again move new armies to the front? What will happen then?

—Adolf Hitler, *Mein Kampf*

We are so accustomed to thinking of Hitler and his armies as remarkably superior that we accept without question that Stalin was afraid of Germany. However, why should Stalin have feared Hitler? Everyone, including Hitler himself and his generals, knew that Germany lacked the resources to fight a prolonged war. Hitler's only chance was a lightning war, a blitzkrieg. But a blitzkrieg against the Soviet Union was impossible, because it stretched more than ten thousand kilometers from west to east. If Hitler could seize even one thousand kilometers per month, which was impossible, even then he would have to count on a year of war. In addition, a regular European army could carry out a successful offensive on Soviet territory only four out of the twelve months of the year, from May 15 to September 15 (if there was no rain). Even if it was possible to take over the entire country during these four months, then what would an aggressor do with this territory when fall and winter came? It was easy to enter Russia, but hard to exit. Also, in June 1941 the peacetime Red Army counted 5.5 million soldiers and commanders. If every month Hitler killed and imprisoned one million Soviet soldiers, even then the war would last at least half a year, and the last phase would occur in December. He would have to overcome frost, snow, and blizzards. He would have to prepare for winter.

The challenges for the Germans wouldn't end there. Even in the supercritical conditions of the summer of 1941, the Soviet system of mobilization worked perfectly, and an additional 5.3 million people joined the ranks of the Red Army within one week of the war, before July 1, 1941.[1] After one week of the war, the Red Army consisted of over 10 million people. Even if Hitler continued to destroy a million per month, the war would still last a year. But the Soviet mobilization continued in July, August, September . . . "Our forces are innumerable," Stalin once said. The mobilization resources of the Soviet Union were almost 20 percent of the population, meaning 34.5 million people. This resource was fully used during the war. It was even surpassed. How long would it take to destroy such an army?

Germany was not ready for a war against Russia, and Stalin knew it. In 1940, British aviation already regularly bombed German cities, ports, railroad stations, and factories. Hitler couldn't secure even Berlin's safety from the British bombers. Did he have nothing better to do in these conditions than go conquer new lands in the east? Was Hitler ready to fight on two fronts?

We find some answers in the diary of the Chief of General Staff of Germany's land army, Colonel General F. Halder.

October 7, 1940: "An air war on two fronts is impossible."

November 26, 1940: "Horse-drawn carriages for anti-tank weapons. We have no limbers. . . . We have no capacity to supply our troops in Bulgaria with mountain equipment. . . . We have not a single snow-cleaning machine. . . . It is impossible to maintain a strict control over the large cities of France. . . . The empire's railroads in the future will be unable to work under such strain as today."

November 27, 1940: "Operations to take over the endless Russian spaces will not be successful."

December 3, 1940: "The fuel situation is bad. The tire situation is very bad."

December 4, 1940: "Too little artillery."

December 13, 1940: "Capturing Moscow does not have much significance (in Hitler's opinion). . . . The air forces are facing a war on two fronts."

December 23, 1940: "The situation with rubber is difficult."

January 16, 1941: "Anti-aircraft gun battalions of the land army, forty battalions. The special personnel for them have yet to be prepared. This is feasible only by autumn."

January 28, 1941: "The fuel situation is serious. We can count on fuel supply during the period of concentration and deployment, and two months of operations. . . . Automobile tires. The situation is very serious."[2]

Even though the German command knew that "an air war on two fronts was impossible," they still decided to start a two front air war. Not only Halder but Hitler himself understood that taking Moscow did not mean the end of the war. And yet, Hitler's entire plan boiled down to taking Moscow in the belief that the rest of Russia would crumble. Hitler's generals planned to destroy Russia in three months, but they had only enough fuel for two.

"Operation Barbarossa. The goal of the campaign is unclear. It does not at all affect England. Our economic base does not improve from this. If we are tied down in Russia, the situation will become even more difficult. . . . Operation Barbarossa is extremely risky," Halder wrote.[3] Stalin had iron logic, and when he was warned of a possible German invasion, he asked: "But what for?" Hitler's chief of staff, who planned the war, was wondering exactly the same.

A blitzkrieg is a tank war. On September 1, 1939, Germany only had 2,977 tanks.[4] How did it happen that out of this number almost half (1,445 Pz-I tanks) had no cannon? How come the other half (1,223 Pz-II tanks) had only pathetic 20-mm cannons? How come they only had 98 Pz-III tanks with their useless 37-mm cannon, and only 211 Pz-IVs, which had 75-mm short-barreled cannon, not designed and not useful for war against other tanks?

By June 1941, Hitler had in his invading army 3,332 tanks,[5] all of them light and all of them obsolete—not one single heavy tank. There were medium ones, which were simply light tanks covered with an extra layer of armor plates. Their defenses increased from this, but their mobility decreased: their speed, maneuverability, and ability to pass through rough terrain—all of which were necessary for maneuvers in large open spaces. Hitler didn't have a single amphibious tank, or one with anti-projectile armor, nor one with powerful cannon. Stalin, on the other hand, had 23,925 tanks, including the best models in the world that had the best tank-building innovations of the time: powerful long-barrel cannons, wide caterpillar tracks, anti-tank defenses, diesel motors, and so on. Moreover, Stalin possessed almost endless means for producing these tanks. Stalin had more amphibious tanks than Hitler had tanks in total.

In addition to tanks, an army needed powerful tank formations. In Germany, tank divisions were created. But these divisions, to put it mildly, were inferior. In 1939, Hitler had six tank divisions. Germany entered World War II with six tank divisions! What sort of blitzkrieg could one dream about having only six tank divisions?! And even today some continue to claim that German generals understood the nature of blitzkrieg! In 1940, the number of tank divisions rose to ten, and in 1941 to twenty-one. The increase in the number of tank divisions was attained not by producing tanks, but by reassignment. In practice, the same number of tanks was divided first into six divisions, then ten, then twenty-one.

Liddell Hart commented:

> This doubling in number of armored forces turned out to be sheer illusion, since it was achieved mostly at the expense of reducing the number of tanks in each division. . . . Some of the qualified expert tankers attempted to argue against such a decision, since the result of such measures was to multiply the number of staffs and secondary units in the so-called "tank divisions." . . . Out of 17,000 people in the division, only 2,600 were tankers. But Hitler was stubborn. Seeing before him the vast Russian territory, he wanted to feel that he had more divisions, capable of delivering blows deep into the land, and counted on technological advantage over the Russians to serve as sufficient compensation for the "dilution" of his tank troops. . . . However, cutting the number of tanks in the divisions increased the main disadvantage of the German tank division—the fact that its units and subdivisions mostly consisted of infantry, and could not move on difficult terrain.[6]

Liddell Hart put the term German "tank division" in quotation marks. He explains his point of view: "Tanks could continue an offensive, but they, just like all other track vehicles, made up only a small part of each so-called "tank division.""[7]

Tanks alone do not ensure strength. A lone tank that ventures far ahead is vulnerable. A tank must be supported by infantry. "In 1941, the German army still consisted mostly of plain infantry divisions, which moved on foot, and used animal transport," said German General Guenther Blumentritt.[8] On June 22, Hitler had on the eastern front 750,000 horses.[9] A convoy of 220 horses with carts followed each German tank. Was it on carts that they planned to carry out the blitzkrieg? Out of 153 divisions launched by Hitler against the Soviet Union, only seventeen were tank divisions.[10] There was not a single tank in the thirteen German motorized divisions at the beginning of World War II, while each Soviet rifle division had its own tank battalion of T-26 tanks. We have been taught to laugh at this tank. But the German infantry did not have tanks at all!

The entire German tank force was divided between the four tank groups. The rest of the German army fighting against the Soviet Union didn't have a single tank. It consisted entirely of infantry and 750,000 horses with carts. Colonel General Lotar Rendulic described his 20th Mountain Army: "With the exception of rear transport units, the army consisted entirely of infantry troops—200,000 soldiers and 70,000 horses."[11] The German magazine *Der Spiegel* once published a giant photograph of laughing German soldiers.[12] That one photograph told more truth about the war than the whole article, and many articles like it, and even libraries of books. The photograph showed German soldiers walking on Soviet land in 1941 during the blitzkrieg. All are on foot. They do not have a single submachine gun. Their weapons consist of rifles with bayonets, the 1898 model, and two machine guns. In the background, there are hundreds of carts.

The German army relied heavily on cars and motorized transportation. The plethora of such machinery—more than 500,000 cars in the invading army—played a cruel trick on the Germans. While on the European front, which was heavily road-linked, such an abundance of motorized transportation was more than sufficient, but the German cars on the Russian front (along its so-called roads) often turned into a setback. First, the Germans needed specialized, road-tolerant cars, wheel-track and track-based transport vehicles and tractors. Second, the chronic lack of fuel led to frequent halts in the general mass of automobiles.

Field artillery was the main tool of the Red Army for breaking through enemy defense lines. First were the howitzers. A howitzer, compared to cannon of the same weight, had a slower initial shell speed and a smaller range. But its shells were more powerful and its fire trajectory was curved, which was useful for firing upon an enemy dug into the ground. Marshal Kulik commanded the Red Army artillery for many years. During his leadership, the best artillery systems in the world were created, primarily the howitzers. By June 22, 1941, the Red Army had 15,464 howitzers of all types.[13] The most powerful ammunition factories were created for supplying them. The German army had 10,810 howitzers by June 1, 1941.[14] However, those howitzers had to be divided among several fronts, including the African one. Furthermore, Germany had too few non-ferrous metals to manufacture artillery shells in such quantities as were being produced in the Soviet Union. Finally, the German howitzers were obsolete, developed during World War I or even before it.

Stalin had long-range bombing aviation, which Hitler did not have. In 1940 and 1941, Germany was already being bombed by British strategic aviation. Stalin was ready to add his forces to this effort. Hitler, meanwhile, planned to "bomb Britain out of the war," but that plan failed, because he had no strategic aviation at his disposal. Later on, Hitler decided to take over the European part of the USSR up to the Arkhangelsk-Astrakhan line, and everything east of that line he was going to leave to the bombers. The problem with this plan was that Hitler had almost no long-range bombers.

When he received reports that the German army was preparing to invade, Stalin simply did not believe them. Molotov said before the invasion: "One must be an idiot to attack us." According to Stalin's calculations, an attack on the USSR would have meant suicide for Hitler and his empire. This calculation was entirely confirmed by the results of the war. The question is not whether Stalin was afraid of Hitler or not. Stalin had no reason to be afraid. Stalin considered Hitler and his generals to be reasonable people, and reasonable people would not embark on such an adventure, with Britain on their back. Reasonable people could not plan to crush the Ural and Siberian industrial complexes using long-range bombers, especially when they had no such bombers. Here we must ask a different question: why did Hitler attack the USSR?

Hitler signed Open Directive No. 21 ordering Operation Barbarossa—the attack on the Soviet Union—on December 18, 1940: "The end goal of the operation is the creation of a protective barrier against Asian Russia along the line Volga-Astrakhansk. In this manner, in case of need the last industrial region the Russians have left in the Urals could be paralyzed using aviation." Since Germany invaded the USSR on June 22, it was impossible to reach the Volga line before the autumn rains. German tanks had a short motor operating time, and therefore on the way to Moscow the entire German army inevitably had to stop for two to three weeks for the overall repairs of tanks (replacement of engines, transmissions, pistons, and so forth). If Moscow had been taken in August, they would have had to continue toward the Volga line, and for this another stop would have been needed for the overall repair of tanks and the recovery of the troops' fighting capacity. It would have been impossible to reach the Volga even by September. In October, there would be rain and mud. Even if they could have successfully reached the Volga line in September, it was impossible to bomb the Urals from this position: there were few air bases on the right bank of the Volga. First, they would have to be built, which was hard to do: in October, the area was a bare wet steppe, in November, a bare frozen steppe.

If Hitler had been able to build air bases on the right bank of the Volga River, he still would not have been able to bomb the industry centers of the Urals. The German Do-17, Ju-88, and He-111 bombers were created for completely different tasks. Their missions had been the destruction of small-scale, mostly mobile targets in the area of battle and in the enemy's near rear. These bombers were created for short-range flights, had a small bomb-carrying capacity, and could act only at low and medium altitudes. To reach the Urals and return, the bombers Hitler had in 1941 had to take with them plenty of fuel and no bombs at all. If Hitler's bombers had a sufficient radius of action, even then they could not have bombed the Urals. Germany was running out of fuel. In August 1941, it already had so little fuel that it had to halt large-scale operations.

If there had been enough fuel in October, November, and later on it could not have been delivered to the Volga-area airbases, which were not yet built anyway. Delivery of even one hundred tons of fuel, where there were no roads, across a distance of one thousand kilometers, demanded huge expenditure of fuel and of lubricant materials. Fuel transport had to run on something too. The tractors had to cross the steppes. Even if fuel had been supplied to the non-existing airbases, bombs had to be supplied as well. Thousands of tons of bombs were not enough for such an operation. But the delivery of even 100,000 tons of bombs to the non-existent air bases on the Volga would have required a tremendous amount of fuel.

In December 1940, when Hitler signed the directive for the attack on the Soviet Union, it was perfectly clear that the light single- and dual-engine bombers had too small a radius and too pathetic a bomb load, and were not fit for destroying industrial targets. At the same time, German bombers were flying from the excellent air bases in northern France, across the Channel, and bombing the industrial and military targets of London, Bristol, Coventry, Plymouth, and Southampton. Supplying fuel and ammunition from Germany to the airports of northern France was no problem. The targets were nearby, just across the Channel, and the planes could take less fuel and more bombs. Nonetheless, even in these most favorable circumstances, in nine months of intense bombing raids, from August 12, 1940, to May 12, 1941, all of Germany's aviation was still unable to "bomb British industry out of the war." If the entire German aviation could not in nine months destroy the industry of nearby Britain, how many months did Hitler plan to spend trying to destroy the industry centers of the remote Urals?

To destroy industrial regions situated in the deep rear of the enemy, an aggressor needs long-range bombers with a radius of action of several thousand kilometers and a bomb-carrying capacity of over five tons. The long-range bomber must also be a high-altitude bomber, otherwise it would be vulnerable to the enemy's anti-aircraft artillery. Also, is necessary a minimum of one thousand such bombers. Hitler had none. Even if Hitler had had long-range bombers, it would still have been impossible to use them. A four-engine bomber, carrying five tons of bombs at a multi-kilometer altitude for several thousands of kilometers, was extremely fuel-thirsty. Where would the fuel come from, if there was not enough even for fighters and light bombers?

40

Intelligence Reports and Stalin's Reaction

Stalin had three separate independent espionage services: the First Directorate of the NKGB; the Intelligence Directorate of the General Staff (in 1942 it became Chief Directorate); and Stalin's personal intelligence service, concealed under the name "Special Section of the Central Committee of the Communist Party."

The total power of these agencies was colossal. Sufficient information is available about the penetration into leading German military and political organs by Stalin's espionage services. A group under the code name "Viking" worked in the staff of the OKW (Supreme Command of the Armed Forces); seven high-ranking German officers and generals supplied information straight from Hitler's cabinet to Stalin's agents. In Germany, the Soviet military intelligence managed to gain access to the most secret information from the highest levels of power.[1]

Several networks of agents simultaneously worked for Stalin, completely independent of each other. The lies of one were immediately exposed by information provided by the others. A group under the code name "Alta" worked in the German embassy in Moscow. Its members included Gerhard Kegel and Else Stoebe. The entire embassy was wrapped up in the web of Stalin's espionage. This group of agents "was supplemented by a man who had, in essence, unrestricted access to all [the] state secrets of Germany."[2] The German embassy in Moscow had ties to Goering's staff, to the science and technology organs of the Third Reich, and of course to the Ministry of Foreign Affairs. "Among these agents, there was even one of the closest associates of the foreign affairs minister, Ribbentrop. He was recruited in Poland to work for the British and in his convictions he was an adamant enemy of the Soviet Union."[3] This agent, like many others, thought he was working against Stalin, when in reality he was working for him.

We must remember the friend of Goering's wife, the first-rate Nazi movie star Olga Tschechowa. This woman dazzled Berlin with her blinding beauty and her cruelty, which was inexplicable, unusual, and unseen even for that time. In 1936, on Hitler's orders, Olga Tschechowa was awarded the title People's Actress of Germany. She was often seen next to

Hitler at receptions. Then, in 1945, the popular Third Reich actress was befriended by Stalin and given the highest Soviet marks of distinction.

Stalin's espionage stretched far beyond the borders of the great powers. The Bulgarian Tsar Boris had an advisor, General Konstantin Lukash. Before each meeting with the tsar, the general prepared to answer any question the tsar could ask him. During the course of the preparations, Luben Lukash, the general's brother, played the role of the tsar, and asked the tsar's advisor the trickiest questions. The general had to answer quickly and precisely. As a result, the younger brother was just as informed as the tsar. He worked for the GRU, and asked his brother—the tsar's advisor—questions that interested Stalin.[4]

After World War I, Czechoslovakia was among the ten wealthiest and most developed nations in the world. The Skoda factories produced weapons of the highest world standards, primarily artillery. The daughter of the factory director, Blanca Karlikova, managed to sneak out blueprints of the 210-mm cannon and transfer them to the right person. She worked for the same group of agents that was working against the Bulgarian tsar.[5]

Testimonies about the might of Stalin's espionage abound. For example, Air Force Major General P. M. Stefanovsky recounted, as if it were something utterly insignificant, that in July 1941 he was summoned by Stalin and told: "In three days, the Germans will bomb Moscow."[6] Stefanovsky described the measures that were taken, and in three days the first massive air raid on Moscow was deflected. But we can pause on this seemingly insignificant episode. How could Stalin have known that in precisely three days the Germans would bomb Moscow? The pilots at the air bases did not know what they would be doing the following day. It was always a secret. The success of the upcoming operation, the lives and safety of the pilots, depended on that secret. A very small group of people knew the plans for air war. Commanders of formations and pilots found out the targets they had to bomb only at the last moment. Yet Stalin knew not only what the German pilots would be doing the following day, but also what they would be doing in three days.

Anastas Mikoyan, member of the Politburo, also recounted an instance that demonstrated the extraordinary capabilities of Stalin's intelligence services. On March 27, 1943, at around two o'clock in the morning, Mikoyan was summoned to Stalin's dacha in Volynskoe. Stalin told him what the German command was planning for the summer of 1943.[7] The Battle of Stalingrad had just ended. The Red Army made a thrust forward, but was stopped in the regions around Kharkov, Orel, and Belgorod. A balance of powers set in. Neither one of the sides could advance. Both sides switched to defense, and began intensive preparations for the summer battle that would unfold in these regions in another four months. The Battle of Kursk would be one of the bloodiest battles in human history. It began on July 5, 1943. But German generals began roughly planning the operation on March 13, 1943; on March 27, Stalin announced this fact to Mikoyan and ordered the secret preparation of the strategic reserve of the Steppe military district, consisting of eight armies, including one air and one tank guards army, for a defensive battle and for the following offensive operations. The Steppe military district was deployed behind the main alignment of Soviet troops, and at the critical moment of the battle it was transformed into the Steppe front.

Stalin was constantly peeking at Hitler's cards. During the development of German operations in the Kursk region, all details and all changes in the plan were immediately reported to Stalin. Before the beginning of the operation, German generals, who were the immediate executors of the plans, received the appropriate directives and the final draft of the operation. Stalin had received this draft six days earlier.

Oddly enough, in 1941 Soviet spies reported to Stalin that Hitler was planning to attack, but Stalin did not believe them. Richard Sorge (agency covername—Ramzai) was a spy whom Stalin ordered to return to the USSR "for vacation" on July 29, 1938. He refused to return. In January 1940, he wrote to his Moscow contact: "I am grateful for your greetings and [good] wishes [for] my vacation. However, if I go on vacation, it will immediately reduce the information." In May, he refused for the second time: "It goes without saying that we are postponing the date of our return home because of the present military situation. May we assure you once again that this is not the time to raise this question?" In October, he asked: "May I count on coming home after the end of the war?" It is a strange question. Every secret agent knows that after the war he will be allowed to return home. Moreover, they propose right now that he arrive for vacation. But Sorge refuses. What is going on?

A multitude of books and articles have been written about Sorge in the Soviet Union. Some of them overflow with praise: he was such a great intelligence officer, such a true Communist that he even spent his own money, earned in his difficult work as a journalist, on his illegal work. One of the Soviet weekly magazines[8] published a report that Sorge had very important documents, but was unable to send them to the center, because the center had not sent a courier.

Meanwhile, Yan Berzin, the brilliant chief of Soviet military intelligence who had recruited Sorge, was executed after being horrendously tortured. Solomon Uritsky, another GRU chief who had personally given Sorge his instructions, was also executed. Lev Borovich (agency covername—Rozental), deputy head of the 2nd department of the intelligence headquarters, direct supervisor to Sorge, was shot. Gorev, the Soviet illegal resident who had fixed Sorge's passage from Germany, was in jail.[9] Aino Kuusinen, Sorge's secret collaborator who was the wife of the "president of the Finnish Democratic Republic" and of a future member of the Politburo of the Central Committee of the CPSU, was also in jail. Ekaterina Maksimova, Sorge's wife, had been arrested, admitted to having links with enemies, and died in confinement in 1943. Karl Ramm, the illegal GRU resident in Shanghai and former deputy of Sorge, was summoned back to Moscow "for a vacation" and executed. Sorge received the order to come back for a vacation and refused to travel to the Soviet Union. Undoubtedly, Sorge guessed what was awaiting him in Moscow.

These discrepancies are explained easily: Sorge became a defector. At that time, a more precise term was invented—a malevolent defector. That was why he was paying agents out of his own pocket—the center stopped funding him! Not wishing to return to a hasty trial and certain death, Sorge continued to work for the Communists, but now no longer in the role of a secret agent, but rather as an amateur informer, not for money but for his own satisfaction. Sorge calculated that after the war his superiors would understand that he only told them the truth, and they would pardon him and appreciate his work. The center did not lose contact with him until the end. It accepted his telegrams, but apparently only to urge him: "come home, come home, come home," to which Ramzai replied "too busy, too busy, too busy."

Stalin did not trust Richard Sorge, because he was a defector with a capital sentence hanging over his head. Someone had invented the legend that Richard Sorge supposedly submitted highly important information about the German invasion to the GRU, but nobody believed him. Sorge was a very able intelligence officer, but he told Moscow nothing of significance about the German invasion. What was more, he fell victim to disinformation and fed the GRU false reports. On April 11, 1941, he sent Moscow a telegram: "The representative of the [German] General Staff in Tokyo has stated that war against the Soviet Union will begin immediately after the war in Europe ends."

Hitler prepared the invasion, spreading lies that looked very much like the truth. Hitler knew that it had already become impossible to conceal his preparations to invade the Soviet Union. Therefore, he said in secret, in a way that Stalin could hear, "Yes, I want to attack Stalin . . . after I have finished the war in the west." If Sorge's telegram from April 11 (and other similar telegrams) were to be believed, there was no need to worry: the war against Great Britain was going on with no end in sight.

The GRU did not need Sorge. Based on extensive studies of all the economic, political, and military aspects of the situation, the GRU concluded that Germany could not win a war on two fronts; Hitler would not begin a war in the east without first finishing the war in the west.[10] The first conclusion proved correct; the second did not.

Even before Sorge's "warning," the new head of the GRU Lieutenant General F. I. Golikov submitted a detailed report to Stalin on March 20, 1941, which concluded that "the earliest possible date on which operations against the USSR may begin is the moment following victory over England or after an honorable peace for Germany has been achieved." But Stalin knew this simple truth without Golikov having to tell him. Stalin replied to Churchill's letter from June 25, 1940, that Hitler might begin a war against the Soviet Union in 1941 if Britain had ceased to resist by that time.

But Hitler, whom Stalin had driven into a strategic impasse by the Molotov-Ribbentrop Pact, suddenly realized that he had nothing to lose and that inevitably Germany had two fronts: if he did not attack Stalin, Stalin would stab him in the back. Therefore, Hitler attacked first. Neither Golikov nor Stalin anticipated this. It was a suicidal decision, but Hitler had no choice. Stalin simply could not understand that having found himself in a strategic impasse, Hitler would take such a suicidal step. General Golikov, head of the GRU, had not contemplated that either. Sorge (and several others) simply confirmed this view with the false information in their telegrams.

Some argue that later, on June 15, 1941, Sorge correctly named the date of the German invasion as June 22. But was Richard Sorge to be believed? First, he had said that Hitler would not fight against Stalin without finishing the war against Great Britain, and then, soon after, reported a date for the invasion, June 22, thereby saying that Hitler would invade the Soviet Union after all without ending the war against Britain. Sorge's reports canceled each other out.

Intelligence is the most thankless work in the world. Those who fail and get hanged— like Sorge, for example—become famous. Stalin also had military intelligence officers whose achievements were truly outstanding, but precisely because they were so successful, they remain unknown to us. One Soviet intelligence officer had access to some of Hitler's real secrets. According to Marshal of the Soviet Union A. A. Grechko, "eleven days after Hitler approved the final plan for the war against the Soviet Union (December 18, 1940), this fact and the basic details of the decision taken by the German High Command became known to our intelligence organs."[11]

In December 1940, Lieutenant General F. I. Golikov, chief of the GRU, reported to Stalin that, according to confirmed reports, Hitler had decided to attack the Soviet Union without waiting for the war in the west to end. This highly important document was discussed in early January in a very close circle in the Soviet High Command in Stalin's presence. Stalin did not believe the document, and said that any document could be forged. Stalin demanded of Golikov that he organize Soviet military intelligence so that it would know at any moment whether Hitler was really preparing for war or just bluffing. Golikov reported that he had already done this. The GRU was attentively following a whole range of aspects of German military preparations, and from these the GRU would accurately identify the moment when preparations for invasion would begin. Stalin asked Golikov to explain how he would know this. Golikov answered that he could only tell Stalin personally and not anyone else.

Subsequently, Golikov regularly reported to Stalin personally, and each time he told him that the preparations for invasion had not yet begun. Golikov knew about the massive concentration of German troops on Soviet borders, about the huge ammunition supplies, about the movements of the German air force, about German defectors, and about many other things. He was informed about the numbers of nearly all German divisions, the names of their commanders, and their locations. He knew many important secrets, including the name of Operation Barbarossa and the time of its inception. Even on the eve of the invasion, however, Golikov reported that preparations for invasion had not yet begun, and without these preparations it was not possible for Germany to begin the war.

When the war broke out, Stalin sent Golikov on a trip to Britain and the United States and briefed him personally. Golikov was then put in command of armies and fronts. In 1943, Stalin appointed him to the crucial post of Deputy People's Commissar for Defense, which was deputy to Stalin himself, to deal with cadre matters. Stalin allowed only his most trusted men to handle the delicate task of selecting and placing cadres. Golikov continued to rise in rank after Stalin's death, and eventually became a Marshal of the Soviet Union.

Golikov's impunity for obviously wrong intelligence had been worrying me personally for a long time, until I attended a lecture in the Academy of the GRU. Later, when I was working in the central apparatus of the GRU, I found confirmation to this answer.

Golikov used to report to Stalin that Hitler was not preparing for war against the Soviet Union. It turned out that Golikov was reporting the truth to Stalin, since Hitler was not making such preparations. Golikov knew that Stalin did not trust documents. Golikov did not trust them either. He therefore looked for other indicators which would unerringly signal the moment when Hitler began his preparations for war with the Soviet Union.

All GRU agents in Europe were ordered to infiltrate organizations directly or indirectly connected with sheep farming. Over a few months, intelligence was gathered and carefully processed on the number of sheep in Europe, on the main sheep-breeding centers and slaughterhouses. Golikov was informed twice a day about mutton prices in Europe. In addition, Soviet intelligence began to hunt for dirty cloths and oil-stained pieces of paper left behind by soldiers cleaning their weapons. There were many German troops in Europe. The troops were stationed in field conditions. Each soldier cleaned his weapon at least once a day. Cloths and paper which have been used for weapon cleaning were usually either burned or buried, but of course this rule was not always obeyed. The GRU had ample opportunity to collect an enormous quantity of dirty cloths. A large number of these dirty cloths were sent across the frontier wrapped around various iron implements, so as not to arouse suspicion. Larger-than-usual quantities of kerosene lamps, primus stoves, and lighters were sent across the border, by both legal and illegal means.

Every piece of information was analyzed by hundreds of Soviet experts, and the results reported immediately to Golikov. He immediately informed Stalin that Hitler had not yet begun preparations to invade the Soviet Union, so there was no need to pay attention to every buildup of German troops or German General Staff documents.

Golikov believed, with good reason, that a country needed serious preparation to fight the Soviet Union. One of the vital things Germany would need, if it were to be ready to fight such a war, was sheepskin coats—no fewer than six million of them. As soon as Hitler decided to attack the Soviet Union, his General Staff would have to order industry to begin producing millions of sheepskin coats. This would be reflected immediately on the European markets. In spite of the war, mutton prices would fall because of the simultaneous slaughter of millions of animals, while sheepskin prices would rise sharply.

Golikov also calculated that the German army would have to use a new type of lubricating oil for its weaponry. The usual oil used by Germany would congeal in the frost, component parts would freeze together, and the weapons would not work. Golikov waited for the German army to change the type of oil it used in weapon-cleaning. The Soviet experts' examination of dirty cloths showed that the German army was still using its usual oil, and there were no signs of a change to a new type.

Soviet experts also watched motor fuel. In heavy frost, the normal German fuel broke down into incombustible components. Golikov knew that if Hitler decided to open a second front, he would have to order the mass production of a fuel which would not disintegrate in heavy frost. Soviet intelligence was sending samples of German liquid fuel across the border in lighters and lamps. There were many other indicators, which the GRU followed closely for warning signals.

But Hitler launched Operation Barbarossa without making any preparations. Stalin, therefore, had no reason to punish Golikov. Golikov had done all that was humanly possible to discover German preparations for war. He told Stalin that no preparations were taking place, and this was the truth. There had only been a great buildup of German troops. Golikov gave instructions that not all German divisions had to be targets of attention, but only those that were ready to invade; those were divisions that had 15,000 sheepskin coats in their depots. There were simply no such divisions ready for war in the entire *Wehrmacht*.

The GRU chiefs knew where, what quantities, and what kinds of liquid fuel and lubricating oils were produced in Germany and the occupied territories. The quantities of liquid fuel possessed by Hitler were not at all sufficient to conduct deep offensive operations. But the most attention was paid to the type of fuel they produced. Analysis showed that Germany was not conducting intensive research in the field of creating frost-resistant fuels and oils; German industry was not producing them in any significant quantity; the rear units of the *Wehrmacht Heer* and the *Luftwaffe* were not storing such fuel and oil for a grand-scale war.

The temperature at which pure benzene crystallizes is 5.4 Celsius. In Germany, fuel was obtained by the hydrogenation of low-quality coal. Into this fuel, large quantities of benzol had to be added to raise the levels of octane. Benzol has high anti-detonation qualities. However, it drastically reduces low-temperature qualities. The temperature of crystallization for the main kinds of German fuels ranged between –9.6 and –14.5 Celsius. Only a madman could begin a war with such fuel against a country where in the winter a temperature of −20 Celsius was the norm. Soviet intelligence did not consider the German generals to be madmen, and it concluded that Germany was not preparing for war.

Hitler's soldiers also needed boots, warm underwear, sweaters, special tents, hats, heaters, skis, ski wax, masking robes, oil and lubricants that would not freeze, devices for heating water, frost-resistant car batteries, and winter fuel for tanks, cars, and airplanes. They needed tanks with broad caterpillar tracks, thousands of cars that could drive in poor road conditions, and so on. They had none of these. Their lack of preparedness was total, shameful, and scandalous. The argument was that Hitler did not need coats, because he planned to end the war in three months. However, he still needed to prepare for winter. . . . Hitler's Colonel General H. Hoth, commander of the 3rd Tank Group, wrote: "The objective of destroying the centers of the war industry located farther east was delegated to the air force. These were utopian plans. The radius of action of German bombers then was one thousand kilometers. Even if it had been possible to reach the projected Volga-Arkhangelsk line (which was planned for one campaign, i.e., three to four months), the radius of [the] bombers was not sufficient to disrupt the functioning of industry in the Ural and the Sverdlovsk regions. And even Sverdlovsk is not the end of the world."[12]

Colonel General H. Guderian, commander of the 2nd Tank Group, recounted: "When they unfolded a map of Russia before me, I could not believe my eyes. Everything that I considered impossible I was supposed to make into reality?"[13] Guderian knew that Germany couldn't defeat the Soviet Union. Defeat was impossible not only in three months, but in general.

"Just look at these vast territories," said General Field Marshal Karl von Rundstedt, Commander of Army Group South. "We cannot crush the enemy and occupy all of western Russia from the Baltic to the Black Sea in just a few months."[14]

Stalin and Golikov reasoned in a similar manner. They all expected Hitler and his field marshals to behave reasonably—in other words, to prepare for a prolonged war, including a war in winter. But reasonable actions were not being taken.

41

The War Has Begun

Only now did we realize how well the Russians had been prepared for war.
—ADOLF HITLER, RADIO ADDRESS, OCTOBER 3, 1941

During April, May, and the first half of June 1941, German reconnaissance planes flew "by mistake" over the western regions of the Soviet Union. Stalin ordered not to shoot them down. At the same time, Soviet planes, also "by mistake," flew over territory occupied by German troops.

Both regular pilots and commanders were flying "by mistake" over German territory. Commander of the 43rd Air Force Fighter Division of the Western special military district, Major General G. N. Zakharov, remembered flying in the sky and looking at German troops: "An impression formed that some sort of movement was originating deep within the territories, which was halted only at the edges of the border, and was held by it, as if by an invisible barrier, ready to flow over the edge at any moment."[1] The German pilots flying then over Soviet territory viewed the same picture.

The predicament of General M. F. Lukin demonstrates the full tragedy of the situation. As an army commander, he had already fought in Ukraine in the vicinity of Shepetovka, while the staff of his army still remained in the Trans-Baikal. The trains carrying his army stretched across thousands of kilometers. The worst situation was when a train had to stop in the middle of the fields instead of at a station. A tank battalion is a formidable force, but in a train it is completely defenseless. If the war found a train carrying heavy armor in a place where there were no facilities for unloading, the train either had to be destroyed or abandoned. Those divisions that didn't advance to the border in trains weren't in a better position. A division marching in columns was a great target for air force raids. The entire Red Army presented one great target.

In his memoirs, the German pilot Hans-Ulrich Rudel described the beginning of the war against the Soviet Union. He flew a Ju-87 and completed 2,430 battle missions.

By the evening of the first day I had completed four trips beyond the frontline to the area between Grodno and Vokovysk. We saw huge masses of tanks and trucks here. We mostly saw KV-1, KV-2, and T-34 tanks. We bombed tanks and antiaircraft guns. . . . The next day, we first flew out at 3 AM, and finally returned at 10 PM. One had to forget about normal rest during the night, so we made use of every available minute to fall down on the grass by our airplanes and to sleep. . . . Even on my first mission, I noticed innumerable fortifications built along the borderlines. They stretched for many hundreds of kilometers deep into Russian territory—and yet, they were partly unfinished. We flew over unfinished airbases: in some places, the concrete landing strips were just being constructed. Even at such airbases, however, one could find a few aircraft waiting. We saw, for example, along the road to Vitebsk, which our troops were advancing upon, one such almost-finished airbase with many "Martin" bombers. They either did not have enough fuel or enough crews. While flying over these numerous airbases and fortifications, we all had the same thought in our heads—how lucky we were to have struck first. It seemed that the Soviets were feverishly readying the groundwork for an attack against us. And which other Western country could Russia have attacked? If the Russians had completed their preparations, there would have been almost no hope of stopping them. . . . The highway [from] Smolensk [to] Moscow was the target of many raids; it was packed with huge amounts of Russian military equipment and supplies. Trucks and tanks were lined up one after another almost without any intervals, often in three parallel columns. If all this massive machinery had attacked us. . . . There were no difficulties in attacking so enticing a target. In a few days, the entire road was transformed into piles of rubble.[2]

In the German pilot's description, there is one phrase about the construction of defense structures that might create some confusion. Perhaps the Red Army was preparing defenses? No, it was not. If it had been preparing for defense, the arriving troops would not have been kept in columns along the roads, they would have been sent immediately to the trenches. Rudel also mentioned the "Martin" bombers. Indeed, military supplies from the United States and Great Britain began to arrive in the Soviet Union long before June 22, 1941.

"Strategic defense was born out of necessity during combat, it was not planned ahead of time," says official Soviet military-historical research.[3] The defensive operations of the Red Army in the summer of 1941 were pure improvisation. Before the war, the Red Army neither prepared for defense nor conducted any training in defensive operations. Soviet field manuals don't contain a word about defense on a strategic scale. Not only did the Red Army not have any defense plans, but even in a purely theoretical sense the issues involved in conducting defense operations were never worked out or discussed.

Moreover, the Soviet people and army were not ready for defense, even psychologically. "It is precisely the interests of defending the USSR that will demand the conduct of broad offensive operations on enemy territory, and this does not in any way contradict the character of defensive war," wrote *Pravda* on August 19, 1939. From the first moments of the German invasion, the Red Army tried to go on the offensive, or carry out counterattacks and counteroffensives. But this was also improvisation. Counteroffensives were not worked on at any of the prewar training exercises; they were not even discussed in theory: "The question of counteroffensive . . . was not posed before the Great Patriotic War."[4]

Before the war, the Soviet command prepared neither for defense nor for counterattacks. The Soviet Union planned a different kind of war. Marshal A. M. Vasilevsky reported that during the last year before the war the officers and generals of the General Staff and the staffs of the military districts and fleets worked fifteen to seventeen hours a day without holidays or vacations. Marshals Bagramian and Sokolovsky; Generals Shtemenko, Kurassov, and Malandin; and many others have confirmed that information. General Anissov and General Smorodinov reportedly worked twenty hours a day.

In February 1941, General G. K. Zhukov became the Chief of General Staff of the Red Army. From that time, the General Staff in essence began to operate on a wartime regime. Zhukov himself worked very hard, and did not allow anyone else to relax. The veterans of the General Staff remembered Zhukov's reign as the most frightening period in history, more frightening than the Great Purges. At that time, the General Staff and the other staffs were working with inhuman intensity. Then the Germans invaded. Every commander, starting with regiment level and higher, had in his safe a so-called "Red Packet," which contained the plans for war. The commanders opened their "Red Packets," but they did not find in them anything useful for defense. "Of course we had detailed plans and orders about what was to be done on day "M". . . everything was written to the minute and in great detail. . . . All these plans existed. But, unfortunately, they did not say anything about what was to be done if the enemy suddenly went into attack."[5]

Something else is unclear. If the Red Army entered the war without any plans, then Stalin, upon finding out about this, should have shot the chief of general staff and all those who participated in developing the plans. This did not happen. On the contrary, those who participated in developing Soviet plans—Vassilevsky, Sokolovsky, Vatutin, Malandin, Bagramian, Shtemenko, and Kurassov—began the war as major generals or even lieutenant colonels, and ended it as marshals or at least with the four stars of army generals. During the war, they all proved to be truly great strategists. They were all devoted, even pedantic, staff officers, who could not imagine life without a plan. If Soviet staffs worked very hard and developed war plans before the war, but those were not defense or counteroffensive plans, what kinds of plans could they be?

The Soviet Black Sea fleet had the following military objective before the war: "active military actions against enemy ships and transports near the Bosporus and on the passageways to the enemy's bases, as well as cooperation with land troops during their movement along the Black Sea coast."[6] Admiral S. Gorshkov remembered that the Baltic and Northern fleets, as well as the Black Sea fleet, had purely defensive objectives, but they were to be achieved through aggressive methods. The actions of the Soviet fleet during the first minutes, hours, and days of the war showed with sufficient clarity that they had plans, but these were not plans for defense. On June 22, 1941, Soviet submarines from the Black Sea fleet immediately sailed into the sea toward the shores of Romania, Bulgaria, and Turkey. On that same day, the submarines of the Baltic fleet sailed toward the shores of Germany with the objective of "sinking all enemy ships and vessels according to the rules of unrestricted submarine warfare."[7] The order made no exceptions, not even for medical vessels sailing under the Red Cross flag.

Starting on June 22, the Black Sea naval air force conducted open military actions in the interests of the Danube military flotilla with the objectives of opening the way for it to advance upward along the river. On June 25 and 26, the Black Sea fleet's cruisers appeared in the vicinity of the Romanian port of Constanta and carried out an intensive artillery raid with the goal of landing assault troops on the shores. At the same time, the Danube military flotilla began assault operations in the Danube river delta.

The garrison of the Soviet naval base Hanko, located on Finnish territory, did not switch to a defensive regime after the start of hostilities, but instead began intensive assault operations, taking over nineteen Finnish islands in the course of several days.[8]

On June 25, despite losses suffered by Soviet air forces during the first days of the war, airplanes of the Northern Front carried out a surprise bombing raid. The staff of the Northern Front reported on that morning: "The air force of the front and of the armies started on 6:20 AM to carry out, by bomber formations, the task of exterminating the enemy's air force on his airfields."[9] The enemy's name is spelled out in the report which the staff issued later that same day: "Bombed were all known airfields of the southern part of Finland."[10] The Germans, who happened to have invaded the USSR three days before, are not mentioned in the reports. This means that the USSR, without declaring war and in violation of the peace treaty it signed with Finland just a year earlier, committed an unprovoked act of aggression against its neighbor. Would somebody explain why this crime against peace was not a part of the Nurnberg indictments?

On June 23, the 1st Long-range Bomber Aviation Corps carried out a massive attack against military targets in Koenigsberg and Danzig. This was no improvisation. On the morning of June 22, at 6:44 AM, the Soviet long-range bomber air force received orders to act according to the plans.[11] For several days, it tried to carry out these orders. On June 26, 1941, the 4th Long-Range Bomber Aviation Corps began to bomb the Ploiești oil fields in Romania. After just a few days of raids, the amount of oil obtained in Romania was reduced almost in half. Even when the Soviet air force sustained unimaginable losses at its bases, it had managed to wreak huge damage on the Romanian oil industry. Under any other circumstances, the Soviet air force would have been much more dangerous and could have fully paralyzed the entire German military, industrial, and transportation capacities through its actions against the oil-producing regions. Hitler understood the threat all too well, and saw an invasion of the USSR as his only possible defense. Of course, even that did not save him.

On June 22, 1941, the 41st Rifle Division of the 6th Rifle Corps of the 6th Army, without waiting to hear orders from higher commanders, acted according to prewar plans and crossed the state border in the Rava-Russkaya region. The 102nd Rifle Regiment of this division crossed the border on a front line of eight kilometers and penetrated four to six kilometers into enemy territory. In the morning of June 22, 1941, the commander of the Northwestern Front, Colonel General F. I. Kuznetsov, without awaiting orders from Moscow, issued an order to his troops to attack Tilzit in Eastern Prussia. For the Northwestern Front's staff, for the commanders of the armies and their staffs, this decision was not at all surprising: an attack on Tilzit had been worked out in training exercises just days earlier and "was very familiar to the formations commanders and their staffs."[12] Colonel General Kuznetsov simply put the prewar plans into action. On the evening of that same day, the Soviet high command, not yet knowing about General Kuznetsov's actions, ordered him to do exactly what he had already begun doing: to attack Tilzit in Eastern Prussia.

The High Command also ordered the neighboring Western Front to carry out a powerful attack on the Polish city of Suvalki. This was no surprise to the Western Front commander General D. G. Pavlov. He knew the objectives of his front long before the directives from Moscow arrived, and had already issued the orders to advance on Suvalki. However, because the German air force had not been destroyed in a surprise raid but, on the contrary, the entire Soviet Western Front had lost 738 planes during the first hours of the war, advancing was not at all the best option. The Western Front, its command, staff, the army commanders and the chiefs of their staffs knew long before the war that their primary objective was the encirclement of the German formations in the vicinity of Suvalki. A Soviet attack on Suvalki had been prepared long before the war. The objective had been identified by all Soviet commanders. Of course, the lower-ranking commanders had no right to know the tactical levels of these objectives, but in the higher staffs they were clearly formulated, sealed in secret envelopes and kept in safes in all headquarters, even those of the battalions. For example, the reconnaissance battalion of the 27th Rifle Division, concentrated along the border near the city of Augustow, was getting ready to deploy reconnaissance forces around Suvalki.[13] Its objective was to secure a rapid advance of the entire 27th Rifle Division from Augustow on Suvalki.

Long before the war, huge masses of Soviet troops were gathered in the regions around Augustow. Here, on Soviet territory, the Augustow canal stretched parallel to and right along the border. If the plans had been made for defense, the troops should have been positioned behind the canal, so they could use it as an obstacle, an anti-tank trench. But the Soviet troops were shipped across the canal to its western shores and positioned on a thin strip of land between the canal and the border from which barbwire had already been removed. At dawn on June 22, thousands of Soviet soldiers were killed here by sudden and lethal enemy fire. With the canal behind them, the troops had nowhere to retreat.

The German troops on the other side of the border were also gathered in huge masses right along the border, and had also taken down the barbwire. If the Red Army had attacked a day earlier, the losses on the other side would have been just as great. The positioning of troops right along the border was extremely dangerous if the enemy attacked suddenly. But such a positioning was extremely convenient for carrying out a sudden attack.

Soviet generals never concealed the fact that strictly offensive objectives were set before them. General K. Galitsky, when talking about the concentration of Soviet troops in the Augustow region, stressed that the Soviet command did not believe in the possibility of a German attack, while the Soviet troops were being prepared to conduct an offensive operation.

The Soviet fronts directed against Eastern Prussia and Poland, as well as the fronts positioned against Romania and Hungary, were preparing strictly for an offensive. Major General A. I. Mikhalev acknowledged that the Soviet command did not plan to use the Southern and Southwestern fronts for defensive or counteroffensive actions. "The strategic goals were planned to be attained through the troops' switching to a decisively offensive course of action."[14]

The actions of the Red Army during the first days of the war speak best about Soviet intentions. General Zhukov coordinated the actions of the Southern and Southwestern fronts during the first days of the war, which were aimed at Romania and Hungary. Up until June 30, 1941, Zhukov insisted on advance and demanded that the commanders of the fronts exclusively attack. It was only in July that he and his colleagues concluded that the armies could no longer attack.

It is interesting to look at the Red Army's preparations for war through the eyes of those who were posted right on the border, especially on the Romanian border, because the most significant assault was supposed to take place there. Many books have been written about that time period. In June 1941, Hero of the Soviet Union Major General A.

A. Sviridov commanded the 144th Separate Reconnaissance Battalion of the 164th Rifle Division of the 17th Rifle Corps of the 12th Army posted in the Lvov-Chernovits bulge, on the Romanian border. The 17th Corps was in essence a mountain rifle corps. And the entire 12th Army was, in fact, a mountain army. Sviridov wrote of June 19, 1941: "Our division replaced border guards at the river Prut. Leaving the state border, they handed a fortified shoreline to us." From the Romanian side "we heard the cries from Romanian villages: the peasants were being relocated further away from the borders." "All of us, Soviet warriors were preparing to fight the enemy only on his lands."

Meanwhile, from June 13 to 20, the NKVD troops were relocating by force the population of the border regions from the White Sea to the Black Sea. The Germans relocated people from a strip of land twenty kilometers in width, while the Soviets removed people from land one hundred kilometers wide. The Germans relocated the population. The Soviets relocated some people and sent others to the GULAG. On June 19, the day described by Sviridov, the NKVD operation to clear the front strip entered its bloodiest stage.

After the forced deportation of the population, the border guards dismantled all mines and barbwire obstacles on the Soviet border, and left the borders themselves. On strips tens of kilometers long, in the places where the Soviet assaults were being prepared, the border was opened, and the border guards had left, having handed the borders over to the Red Army. The reconnaissance battalions of the Soviet divisions came out right up to the borders.

Many years before the war in 1941, Shaposhnikov said that the "transfer of armies to wartime positions creates an obvious elevation in their military valiance and their morale." Shaposhnikov warned, however, that an army put on wartime regime and moved to the borders experienced nervous tension that couldn't be contained. Shaposhnikov also cautioned that the army couldn't be kept at the borders for long: it had to be brought into action. Stalin read Shaposhnikov's book with great care, knew it well, and often quoted it. In May 1940, Shaposhnikov was promoted to the rank of Marshal of the Soviet Union. Officially, he was a deputy of the People's Commissar for Defense, but in practice he was Stalin's number one military advisor. By the middle of June 1941, Soviet armies were moved to the borders. The Soviet High Command knew that the commanders and soldiers were eager to enter combat, and that their assault drive couldn't be contained.

The Red Army was not separated from the enemy even by a thin line of NKVD border guards. Neither Zhukov, nor Timoshenko, nor Shaposhnikov had the power to order the guards to leave the borders. The guards were not under their jurisdiction. The guards were subordinate to Beria, the NKVD commissar. But Beria did not have the power to order the army units to replace his people on the borders. Only one man, Stalin, could have ordered the NKVD commissar to remove the border guards and the Defense commissar to move the army divisions to the borders.

Then, the unexpected happened. The German army attacked. Let's examine the consequences of the attack using the example of the 164th Division in which Sviridov served as battalion commander. There are two rivers in this region: the border river Prut, and the river Dniester that runs parallel to it on Soviet territory. If the division had been preparing for defense, there was no reason to move to the land between the two rivers; it would have been logical to dig trenches on the Dniester's eastern shores, using both rivers as water obstacles. Bridges should have been prepared for detonation. There should have been no supplies, hospitals, large army units, and headquarters stationed in the land between the two rivers, only small groups of demolition experts and sappers. But the 164th Division (like all the others) was preparing for an invasion, so it crossed the Dniester, carrying with it hundreds of tons of ammunition, fuel, and supplies, as well as its headquarters, hospitals, and communication units, and stopped at the last border—the river Prut. There were 15,000 soldiers in the division, many cannon, many shells, and many cars. There were other divisions nearby, and all of them were between the two rivers—the Dniester was behind them, and the border river Prut ahead.

The Germans attacked, took over the bridge across the border river—the bridge was not mined—and began to send their units across. They bombed the bridges behind the Soviet divisions. To the north of this strip, the German 1st Tank Group broke through and encircled the Soviet front, cutting the Soviet troops off from their rears. The Soviet divisions were trapped. Masses of people and weapons (the 96th Mountain Rifle Division, 13,000 men strong, was also there) were in this trap. Nobody had prepared defenses, dug trenches or foxholes. Retreat was impossible—the Dniester was behind them, with no remaining bridges. A massacre followed.

Sviridov looked across the river Prut to the border bridge, and saw unending streams of German troops move across it. He remembered: "The bridge! We kept it in order to advance, and now we can't blow it up. . . . All my military training was mostly done under the motto: only advance! Retreat was considered shameful, and we were not taught how to retreat. Now, when we were forced to retreat, we had no experience. We had to learn this art under terrible enemy fire."

During the war, especially in the beginning, the Red Army suffered many defeats. In August and September of 1941, a military catastrophe of historical proportions occurred in the region around Kiev: 665,000 Soviet troops were encircled and captured by the German army. Near Smolensk, 310,000 Soviet soldiers and officers were surrounded. In 1942 on the Crimean front: Soviet troops were encircled near Khar'kov; the 2nd Shock Army, headed by General Vlasov, was surrounded and exterminated.

This kind of information was considered classified. Soviet historians and generals never wrote about these events. But there was an exception to the rule: June 22, 1941. The Soviet propaganda described without mercy everything related to that day, and denounced the Red Army before the entire world. Why was it allowed to talk about the lack of readiness for war?

In the library of the Military-Diplomatic Academy of the Soviet Army, I stumbled across a very small book. It was titled *A Brief Russian-German Military Phrase Book for Soldiers and Junior Commanders*. The booklet was published in Moscow on May 29, 1941, and additionally on June 5 the same booklet was published in Leningrad, Minsk, and Kiev. In total, five million copies were printed. In all Soviet books, including military textbooks, the price was on the last page. The price was not printed only on those books and instructions that related to the conduct of battle. These publications were treated like ammunition, and were handed out to the troops during training exercises, and, when necessary, before and during battle. No price was stamped on the little book I found. It was a battle document; it proved that the USSR was preparing for the war with Germany.

The phrase book was composed very simply and intelligently: a question in Russian, followed by the same question in German written in Russian letters, then in German in Latin letters. The answers were also printed in Russian and German with Latin and Cyrillic letters. It is quite simple to speak according to the booklet—if you do not know how to pronounce the needed German phrase, simply point to the corresponding lines in the book and the Germans can read them themselves. The phrases are very interesting. For example: "Where is the water? Is it drinkable? Drink it first yourself." Imagine the situation: the Soviet soldiers are fighting, defending their motherland, enter a Russian village, take out the phrase book from their packs and read syllable by syllable: "*Trinken Sie zuerst man selbst!*" But they would be taken for Germans in Russia! Here is another example: "What is this station called? Stop the broadcast, or I will shoot you! Bring the conductor! Where is the fuel? Where is the garage? Gather and bring here [so many] horses [farm animals], we will pay!" To communicate with the local populations, it is not a bad idea to know phrases such as: "Where are the German soldiers hiding? Where is the burghermeister? Is there an observation point on the steeple?" But, there was not one burghermeister or steeple in the Soviet Union. Another very important question: "Where are the stores?" The most important phrases are the following: "You do not need to be afraid! The Red Army will come soon!"

A former Soviet diplomat, Nikolai Berezhkov, who accompanied Molotov to Berlin in 1940, wrote in his memoirs *With a Diplomatic Mission in Berlin* that a German printing press worker once brought to the Soviet embassy a German-Russian phrase book of the same kind. For the Soviet embassy, the book was solid proof that the German army was preparing to invade the USSR. But in the USSR they were printing the same exact phrase books.

Soviet soldiers and officers were preparing for a victorious march on Berlin, but the war against Germany in 1941 didn't run according to plan. As a result, when Soviet commanders were captured, the Germans found quite interesting maps and curious orders in their bags. Thousands of soldiers had Russian-German and Russian-Romanian phrase books. Many simply did not think of the necessity to get rid of this compromising evidence.

The commander of the 5th Battery of the 14th Howitzer Regiment of the 14th Tank Division of the 7th Mechanized Corps, Yakov Iosifovich Dzhugashvili, son of Stalin, was no exception. He was taken prisoner, but at first he was not recognized. The senior lieutenant was betrayed by his subordinates. Stalin's son was searched and questioned. A letter was found in his pockets, from a certain junior lieutenant in the reserves named Victor: "I am at the training camps, I would like to be home by fall, but the planned walk to Berlin might hinder this." The letter is dated June 11, 1941. The contents of this letter were reported to Hitler personally; he mentioned it on May 18, 1942.[15] In June 1941, German intelligence officers showed the letter to Yakov Dzhugashvili and asked him to clarify the statement about the "planned walk to Berlin." The questioning protocol recorded Stalin's son's reaction. He read the letter and quietly muttered: "Damn it!"

During questioning, Stalin's son was asked why the Soviet artillery, which had the best cannon and howitzers in the world, and in incredible numbers, fired so poorly. Stalin's son answered: "The maps let the Red Army down, because the war, contrary to expectations, unfolded to the east of the state border."[16] Stalin's son told the truth. In 1941, the Red Army fought without maps. There simply weren't any. But the artillery couldn't fire without maps. Direct aiming and firing was just a small fraction of the work done by artillery in war. Most of the time artillery fired beyond the horizon.

"It turned out that in Soviet Russia a map-making industry was created that surpassed everything that had ever been done before in its size, organization, volume, and quality of work," concluded the Germans about the Soviet topographic services.[17] How do we reconcile the best map-making industry in the world with the complete absence of maps? Lieutenant

General A. I. Lossev explained: "Storages of topographic maps, located unreasonably close to the border, were either seized by the enemy, or destroyed by the enemy during the first bomb raids. As a result, the troops lost 100 million maps."[18]

This is a modern-day evaluation, and the numbers are lowered. Lieutenant General M. K. Kudryavtsev, who under Stalin was director of the topographic services of the Red Army, said that during the first days of the war, and only in the Baltic, Western, and Kiev military districts, the Soviet troops destroyed during retreat over two hundred railcars of their own topographic maps.[19] The smallest cargo railcar in the Soviet Union in 1941 could carry twenty tons. Even if we supposed that the smallest cars were used to store the maps, four thousand tons of maps were destroyed in the three districts. Kudryavtsev said that, on average, every railcar contained 1,033,000 maps. Two hundred cars equaled 200 million maps. Which of the two generals is right? They both are. One talked about what the German troops destroyed, 100 million, and the other added that the Soviets themselves destroyed 200 million maps, so they would not go to the enemy.

If the Soviet army planned to defend Moscow, Kursk, and Stalingrad, it needed maps of those regions. There was no reason to transport these maps to the state border. At the border, the army needed maps of border regions. And, if there was a plan to advance, the army needed maps of the territories that lay ahead. If the Soviet Union planned to take over large territories, it needed the corresponding number of maps to supply a multimillion-strong army. The Red Army did not save its maps in the border regions, because they were useless for defending the country. In 1941, the plans for the "liberation" of Europe crumbled, and the value of the maps that were kept in railcars on the border became zero. Millions of Russian-German and Russian-Romanian phrase books were burned along with the maps.

The Soviet population was expecting a war, but it didn't anticipate a German invasion. Therefore, once the Germans attacked, everyone was shocked. Major General of the KGB O. D. Gotsiridze remembered: "Before July 3, when Stalin made a public appearance, it was completely unclear as to what we were to do. Everyone had thought that the war would be quick and on foreign soil."[20]

"The complete demoralization among our troops occurred because . . . the people had planned to fight on the enemy's territory, and our military commanders were dreaming of a blitzkrieg no less than the Germans were. But everything turned out not quite so happily. . . . The sudden need for defense turned into a total retreat on all fronts for the troops and the people."[21]

42

Stalin's Panic

It is very fortunate for Russia in her agony to have this great rugged war chief at her head. He is a man of massive outstanding personality, suited to the sombre and stormy times in which his life has been cast; a man of inexhaustible courage and will-power and a man direct and even blunt in speech, which, having been brought up in the House of Commons, I do not mind at all, especially when I have something to say of my own. Above all, he is a man with that saving sense of humour which is of high importance to all men and all nations, but particularly to great men and great nations. Stalin also left upon me the impression of a deep, cool wisdom and a complete absence of illusions of any kind

—Winston Churchill, speech in the House of Commons,
September 8, 1942

After Stalin's death, Nikita Khrushchev recounted that in 1941, having found out about the German invasion, Stalin panicked, retreated to his dacha-fortress outside Moscow, completely kept out of all affairs, did not receive anybody, did not ask about developments on the front, and did not answer telephone calls. Stalin was totally apathetic. He isolated himself from all state and party obligations. Stalin was extremely depressed for over a week, and only on July 1 did the members of the Politburo manage to force him to return to the reins of power. This story was accepted and repeated in thousands of books and essays. It served as the main proof of Stalin's lack of readiness for war.

After 1991, the Soviet archives became more accessible, and researchers saw logbooks documenting visitors to Stalin's office from 1927 to 1953. It turned out that Stalin worked extremely hard in the first days of the war. The entry from June 21, 1941, read: "The last [visitors] left at 11 PM." This did not at all mean that Stalin's workday ended. After the last visitors left, he could have worked on the documents himself, talked on the telephone, worked outside of the office, in his Kremlin apartment or at his dacha. Stalin began receiving visitors on June 22, 1941, at 5:45 AM. He worked for eleven hours without breaks. His visitors included Molotov,

Beria, Timoshenko, Mekhlis, Zhukov, Malenkov, Mikoyan, Kaganovich, Voroshilov, Vyshin-skyi, Kuznetsov, Dimitrov, Manuilsky, Shaposhnikov, Vatutin, Kulik, and others.

The following week was one continuous workday for Stalin, with only brief breaks. Reception of visitors began at 3:20 AM (June 23), or at 1 AM (June 25), and ended the following morning. The meetings lasted five, six, twelve hours. Sometimes Stalin's workday lasted twenty-four hours, with short breaks. After this initial week of the war, the logbooks have nothing recorded for two consecutive days, June 29 and 30.

Khrushchev claimed that when the Germans attacked, Stalin got scared and isolated himself. Today, we know that right after the German invasion Stalin worked seven days in a row, as much as humanly possible. During the first moments, Stalin simply did not believe that Hitler had invaded. Stalin had calculated all possible moves, and none of them included an attack by Hitler. During the first week of the war, Stalin herded his troops into an attack. He should have been giving orders for defense, but he resisted. Finally, on June 28, he found out that the Western Front was surrounded, the 4th Army was destroyed, and the 3rd, 10th, and 13th armies were encircled. Only then did Stalin finally understand that his plans for the "liberation" of Europe were over. When he arrived at the People's Commissariat of Defense on June 29, Stalin learned the true dimensions of the utter failure of the Western Front. There, Stalin exploded in anger at Timoshenko and Zhukov, bringing the latter to tears. Anastas Mikoyan recollected: "Stalin was despondent. After leaving the Commissariat, he said: 'Lenin left us a grand legacy, and we, his followers, flushed that legacy down the toilet.' We were shocked by that statement. Was everything lost for good? In the end, we ascribed those words to Stalin's emotionally affected state."[1]

Stalin realized that he could not fix anything. The socialist country was capable of crushing others, but it couldn't compete with other countries in peacetime. From June 22, 1941, the Soviet Union was destined for demise. Sooner or later, it was bound to collapse. It could survive only by consuming everything around it. Otherwise, it was doomed. The Soviet Union could exist only if the Soviet people would have no opportunities to compare their lives with the lives of people in surrounding countries. Therefore, Stalin's main idea was to destroy the capitalism surrounding the Soviet Union. All of Stalin's plans were simple, logical, and understandable: complete victory was only possible on a global scale.

Hitler understood this as well: "The Bolshevized world will be able to hold only if it encompasses everything."[2] On June 22, 1941, Hitler delivered a suicidal but lethal attack on Communism. No matter how events unfolded afterward, Stalin could no longer conquer the whole world, which was the equivalent of his demise. On June 30, 1941, Molotov, Beria, Malenkov, and others entered Stalin's room in his dacha. Anastas Mikoyan, a member of Stalin's Politburo, left a wonderful description of this episode:

> We came to Stalin's dacha. Found him in the small dining room, sitting in his armchair. Upon seeing us, he seemed to shrink into the armchair, then look at us questioningly. Then he asked: 'What did you come for?' He had a wary, strange look on his face—and the question he asked was no less strange. As a matter of fact, he should have summoned us all himself. I had no doubts: he had decided that we had arrived to arrest him. Molotov, speaking for us all, said that power had to be concentrated if the country were to get back on its feet, and that a State Committee of Defense had to be created. 'Who's in charge?'

asked Stalin. When Molotov answered that he, Stalin, was in power, the latter looked at Molotov with surprise, but said nothing. 'Fine,' he eventually pronounced.[3]

The members of the Politburo hadn't come to arrest Stalin. They needed Stalin as a symbol, a flag around which the remnants of a crushed division would rally in battle. They talked of saving the country, but Stalin did not listen to them. Without taking Europe, without expanding the Soviet Union's borders, the USSR would sooner or later crumble. Stalin had lost the country founded by Lenin. In 1941, only Stalin could appreciate the full weight of the German invasion. In 1941, the members of the Politburo could not fully understand that Hitler's invasion meant death for the Soviet Union. The Politburo forced Stalin to resume power, and Stalin, with a careless wave of the hand, returned, fully aware that the cause he had worked for his whole life was dead.

43

If It Weren't for Winter!

Future historians will come to the conclusion that, if one considers the military situation, the invasion of Russia was a political mistake and all military efforts were doomed from the start.

—COLONEL GENERAL HERMANN HOTH, *PANZER OPERATIONS*

Uring the war with the Soviet Union, Goebbels's "Reich Ministry for People's Enlightenment and Propaganda" quickly filled newspaper and magazine pages with thousands of photographs: German automobiles stuck in Russian mud, a horse being flogged because it couldn't pull a cart out of the terrible slush, blizzards covering tanks with a thick layer of snow, and gusts of wind ripping the summer hat off a poor German soldier's head.

The core principle of propaganda is visual appeal. Goebbels showed the shocked Germans back home tons of chronicles: mud, mud, mud, impassable mud, endless fields, plains, snow, and hurricane-strength wind knocking the soldiers off their feet. (The photos were taken on an airfield, where a three-engine J-52's propellers helped the storm, adding wind—and drama—to the situation.) If it were not for winter . . . from German staffs and memoirs of generals were added to Goebbels's propaganda, and featured descriptions of the horrors of the Russian winter, the impassable mud, and the unimaginable lack of roads.

It would seem that Marxist historians should have refuted these claims, so that nobody repeated the conclusions of Hitler's defenders. However, Marxist historians not only did not refute those claims, but they joined the chorus of Nazi voices. Marxist propagandists declared that the Russians were completely unprepared for war, and it wasn't them that defeated Hitler: all the credit should go to the endless Russian plains, the mud, and the fierce winter.

Why did the Communists need to repeat the Nazi lies? The answer was simple: they needed to prove that the Soviet Union could not have invaded Europe. They had to demonstrate weakness. Here is an example: "Artillery, motorcycles, trucks, and even tanks got stuck in the impenetrable mud; airplane wheels got stuck in the ground on air bases. The supply of ammunition, fuel, and produce to the front was drastically reduced. [An] early winter suddenly replaced an unusually rainy autumn. When the ground froze in November, many cannon and vehicles were left right there on the spot, where they had gotten stuck in the mud several weeks earlier."[1]

The combined power of Nazi and Communist propaganda turned out to be so strong that the Hitler legend about the frost and winter, the lack of roads, and the vast open spaces was repeated by people who were wise and far removed from Goebbels's propaganda. It is no surprise that to the question about the reasons for Hitler's defeat, today's German schoolchildren answer in unison: winter, frost, and open spaces.

I will pretend to agree that if it weren't for winter, frost, and vast open spaces, Hitler would have crushed the Red Army and taken the Soviet Union. But if Britain was not an island, and protected by the English Channel from Hitler's tanks, Hitler would have strangled England as well. And if the African desert wasn't hot and full of sand, if there was a tunnel under the Mediterranean Sea to supply German troops with fuel and ammunition, Hitler would have kicked the British out of Libya and Egypt, and taken Africa. And if America was not across the ocean but in Europe, right under Hitler's nose, and if America was a small country, the size of Belgium, Hitler could have crushed America, too. And if the Antarctic had a climate like France, Hitler could have turned it into resorts for his generals, with palm trees and beaches.

When we are told of tanks getting stuck in the mud, we should remember their specific power and their specific pressure on the ground. The best German tank of 1941, the T-IIIA, had a specific pressure of 0.94 kilograms per square centimeter of support surface. Of course it sank in the mud! Its specific power was only 13.9 horsepower per ton of weight. The rest of the German models were even weaker. These tanks were designed by people who simply did not understand the nature of war. These tanks could not compete with the Soviet tanks, and yet we are told that the mud was to blame.

In February 1940, the Red Army broke through the impenetrable Mannerheim Line. At the same time, the German army was simply refusing to fight in France. German generals, by blaming the weather in France, sabotaged orders to invade issued by the High Command. "Here, luckily, nature intervened and forced the postponement of the set date, which between the fall of 1939 and the end of January 1940 changed fifteen times."[2] The order to start the invasion was postponed many times even after January 1940. German generals were unprepared to fight in France even in April.

In 1941, Hitler fought near Moscow. Here there was no Arctic frost like in Finland, no deep snow, no swamps. The topography around Moscow was an invader's dream: there were no rocky rivers and no steep shores. Soviet defenses near Moscow did not compare to the Mannerheim Line. But Hitler got stuck. We are told: the Red Army could not fight, and that is why breaking through the Mannerheim Line took so much time. Nobody remembers the frost, snow, and impassable terrain in Finland. But the German army got stuck at Moscow's gate only because the winter had prevented it.

On August 10, 1941, Colonel General Halder wrote in his journal: "The exhausted German infantry will be unable to oppose with decisive attack measures the enemy's efforts. . . . At the current moment, our troops are heavily exhausted and experience heavy losses."[3] On the following day, Halder wrote: "The troops are exhausted. What we are now undertaking is the last and questionable attempt to avert a transition to a war of attrition.

The command has only very limited resources. . . . We have thrown our last forces into battle."[4] The blitzkrieg was already choking in August. The Germans were running out of strength, and the advance stopped. Hitler's army was so weak and unprepared for war that two months after the start of the war offense was out of the question. On August 22, 1941, Halder wrote: "The Fuehrer's note is full of contradictions. . . . The OKH's position became insufferable due to the Fuehrer's meddling and attacks. No one else but himself can bear the responsibility for the contradictory orders. . . . In the afternoon, our arguments and discussions were interrupted by a telephone conversation with Field Marshal von Bock, who once again stressed that his troops will be unable to defend themselves for long in the positions they took when they counted that an offensive on Moscow was coming."[5] September 5, 1941: "Our units surrendered to the enemy [at] the bend of the frontline near Elnya."[6] In the most strategically significant region of the theater of operations, the Army Group Center was unable to resist the pressure of the Soviet 24th Army and surrendered the staging ground they needed for an attack on Moscow.

Marshal K. K. Rokossovskii remembered: "Upon a realistic evaluation of the situation and a consideration of the coming winter, the enemy was only left with one choice—immediate retreat covering great distance."[7]

Why didn't the Germans retreat? On September 13, 1941, Halder wrote: "At the current moment, we cannot forecast the number of troops that can be freed from the Eastern Front upon arrival of winter, and the number of troops that will be needed for conducting operations in the following year."[8] This entry shows that the blitzkrieg was already over before the snow, before the mud. The war had already turned into a war of attrition—a prolonged war lethal for Germany.

On May 29, 1942, Hitler watched the famous Soviet film *German Defeat near Moscow*. In Henry Piker's *Hitler's Table Conversations*, Hitler's comments are recorded in the entry for that day: "This winter we experienced especially harsh trials, because our soldiers' clothing [and] the level of their motorization and supply did not in any way correspond to the conditions of that winter, when the temperature dropped below 50 [degrees] Celsius."[9] "Then the first German prisoners come, who form hordes without coats, gloves, without winter clothing. They dance from the cold, their hands thrust deep into their pockets, which they take out from time to time to rub their ears and noses! . . . Finally, the frozen German tanks, trucks, and cannon stretch in an endless file; all are abandoned, because the General Staff of land forces did not prepare in time sufficient amounts of frost-resistant fuel and winter clothing."[10]

The following year brought Stalingrad. Moscow in 1941 didn't teach Hitler anything. In Stalingrad, German troops once again were left without warm underwear. The main question is: what conclusions did Hitler and his generals draw from their catastrophic performance in the Russian winter? In 1941, they took no measures to supply their military operations during the winter. What was done to prepare for the following winter? On April 5, 1942, Hitler said: "In the central zone, we must immediately plant all the marshlands and swamps with cane, so that with the coming of the next winter we can stand the horrible Russian frost."[11]

44

A Model War

The victory of socialism in one country does not at one stroke eliminate all wars in general. On the contrary, it presupposes wars.

—Vladimir I. Lenin, *The Military Program of the Proletarian Revolution*

A Soviet historian's account of Japanese-German relations in World War II went as follows: "The German leaders had especially strong expectations from their Japanese allies. They really wanted Japan to be the first to start military action against the USSR. . . . But the Japanese leaders evaded talks with Germany. Only in March 1941 did the Japanese minister of foreign affairs, Iosuke Matsuoka, arrive in Berlin. . . . Matsuoka refused to determine the deadline for Japanese action against the USSR, which led to a strong clash between him and Hitler."[1]

The shortest route between Berlin and Tokyo lay straight through Moscow, and on his return trip from Berlin, the Japanese minister of foreign affairs, Matsuoka, stopped briefly in Moscow. Here, on April 13, 1941, he signed a pact of neutrality between the Soviet Union and Japan. Both countries pledged to "maintain peaceful and friendly relations and mutually respect each other's territorial integrity and independence. . . . In the event that one of the sides becomes the victim of military actions from one or several other nations, the other side of the pact will observe neutrality for the duration of the entire conflict."[2]

The neutrality pact between the USSR and Japan was a remarkable achievement for Stalin's diplomats and a crushing blow to Hitler's plans. Japan was Germany's ally, but it refused to fight against the Soviet Union. Moreover, Japan signed a pact with the Soviet Union instead. "When Matsuoka informed Ribbentrop about the high probability of a Soviet-Japanese pact, the head of German diplomacy stated that one would be wise not to involve oneself too intimately with the Soviet Union, but watch the events in the region."[3] The Japanese government, however, had its own opinion on the matter. On April 14, the day after the signing of the Soviet-Japanese pact, Goebbels wrote in his diary that the agreement caused a great sensation. For Germany, this was quite an unpleasant sensation.[4] "The signing of the Soviet-Japanese neutrality agreement was a great surprise for Germany. Ribbentrop ordered the German ambassador in Tokyo to demand an explanation from the Japanese government."[5] An explanation was provided. Matsuoka told the German ambassador in Tokyo that "if Germany and the Soviet Union were to start fighting, not a single Japanese premier or minister of foreign affairs could keep the nation neutral. Japan will ally with Germany in attacking Russia, whatever the situation. Pacts of neutrality do not matter in this affair."[6] But this intent never materialized. Japan didn't attack the Soviet Union.

On April 13, 1941, right after the signing of the agreement between Japan and the USSR, Matsuoka headed for the train station in Moscow, on his way to Tokyo. According to protocol, many officials accompanied him. Suddenly, the rules of protocol were broken. At the last minute before the train left, Stalin appeared on the platform. He usually never met anyone or saw anyone off. On that day, Stalin was in a remarkably good mood. Obviously, the train departure was delayed. Stalin laughed and joked. He walked with the Japanese minister right to the steps of the railcar, and here he did something entirely uncharacteristic for him—he embraced the Japanese minister and proclaimed that the Soviet Union and Japan would remain friends forever. Among those seeing off the Japanese minister was the German military attaché—Stalin noticed and also embraced him, declaring that Germany and the Soviet Union would also remain friends. Stalin's behavior was very uncommon. He was usually very discreet. He never embraced anyone in the presence of outsiders. Many historians explained this unusual behavior as Stalin's commitment to peace, as proof that he attempted to avoid war with Japan and Germany at any cost.

Exactly ten weeks later, on June 22, 1941, Germany invaded the Soviet Union. Soon, Stalin found himself on the brink of defeat. At this critical moment, the Japanese government kept its word to the Soviets and remained neutral. In that same year, 1941, Japan attacked the U.S. Navy at Pearl Harbor, triggering the war between the United States and Japan. This was advantageous for Stalin, and despite the signed pact, he started secret preparations to attack Japan. "They did not know Stalin well in Tokyo," wrote one observer. "If the Japanese had at least superficially acquainted themselves with the lifestyle and career path of the great follower of Lenin's legacy, they would have noticed that his methods always remained the same: make an alliance with somebody against somebody else, and follow it with a stab in the back to the ally once he becomes useless."[7]

Stalin kept his intentions secret until the right time, but in the beginning of 1943 he told the American president about his decision to attack Japan. Stalin had planned his sudden attack on Japan not for 1943, when America was engaged in a difficult war and needed help, but at the very last moments of the war, when Japan would be already on the verge of defeat. Stalin could have helped the United States much earlier. He had the capacity to drastically quicken Japan's defeat. The United States had a very powerful strategic air force, but they had to fly to Japan across the largest ocean in the world, and then fly back without refueling. Raids on Japan could also be carried out from islands in the Pacific Ocean, but these islands had to be taken first, and therefore it was first necessary to achieve naval domination. And even after taking the islands, the Americans still had to fly several thousand kilometers to their targets and back. Each plane had to carry a large amount of fuel and an insignificant number of bombs. The Soviet Union, on the other hand, was right next to Japan.

"Cordell Hill, the American Secretary of State, tried to obtain from Moscow permission for the American air force to use Soviet military airbases in the Far East."[8] Stalin firmly refused. President Roosevelt sent messages to Stalin on December 30, 1942, and January 8, 1943, urging the Russian leader to allow American air force units to be stationed on bases in the Soviet Far East. Stalin answered the messages with an uncompromising "no."[9]

If Stalin had given the Americans the opportunity to use Soviet air bases, instead of making long flights to Japan from the faraway islands, every plane could have completed several short flights with a large load of bombs. In that case, the American raids on Japanese targets would have been considerably more effective. But it was in Stalin's interest that the war between Japan and the United States be stretched as long as possible.

By the way, Stalin allowed America to use several Soviet air bases in the Poltava region for bombing Germany. American B-17 strategic bombers took off from the airfields at Poltava and flew to bomb Germany. Their takeoffs were covered by Soviet fighters, which accompanied them to the length of their radius of action. At the same time, other waves of American bombers flew out of Britain. Having dropped bombs on German cities and factories, these bombers landed on the airfields at Poltava. They were met by Soviet fighters, which covered them during landing. But Stalin did not give permission to use the air bases in Nakhodka and Petropavlovsk for bombing Japan. Stalin waited for a complete depletion of Japanese forces in a prolonged war, and prepared his own attack. As Japan weakened, Stalin strengthened the preparation for a war against it. Stalin called Japan an aggressor for the first time on November 6, 1944.[10] On April 5, 1945, the USSR leadership cancelled the Soviet-Japanese neutrality pact.

In the summer of 1944, Stalin told Marshal A. M. Vasilevsky that he would be the chief commander of Soviet troops in a war against Japan.[11] The initial figures of the concentration of our troops in the Amur, Pacific Coast, and Trans-Baikal regions were sketched out in the fall of 1944. At the same time, rough calculations of the resources needed for a war in the Far East were made.[12]

Vasilevsky was one of the most talented commanders in the history of the Soviet Union. His talent became apparent during the war. In 1940, he was given the rank of major general. "[As] deputy chief of the Operations branch of the General Staff, he worked on the operational section of planning the strategic deployment of Soviet armed forces on the Northern, Northwestern, and Western Fronts."[13]

A month after the beginning of the German invasion, Stalin appointed Vasilevsky as chief of the General Staff's Operations Directorate. Vasilevsky was responsible now not just for a separate (although the most important) sector of the front, but for all the plans of the war on all fronts. Two months later, Stalin promoted Vasilevsky to lieutenant general. Half a year later, Vasilevsky became colonel general. One month later, Vasilevsky received yet another promotion: Stalin named him chief of the General Staff, the central brain of the Red Army, and entrusted to him the preparations for offensive operations in the Stalingrad region. In October 1942, Colonel General Vasilevsky became Stalin's deputy. According to Vasilevsky's plans, all command and communications posts in the Stalingrad region were moved to the very front lines. He also moved there all air bases, hospitals, huge supplies of shells, cartridges, fuel, and lubricants. Until the very last moment, Soviet troops did not know anything about what they were going to do. By keeping his offensive preparations secret from his own troops, Vasilevsky managed to keep them secret from the enemy as well. And then, a sudden, crushing attack followed. All the so-called "mistakes of 1941," Vasilevsky repeated at Stalingrad, because they were not mistakes at all, but a preparation for sudden attack.

Vasilevsky received the rank of General of the Army for the defeat of the surrounded German formations near Stalingrad. He only carried this title for twenty-nine days; after the Stalingrad operation, Stalin made him a Marshal of the Soviet Union. In the summer of 1944, during the peak of the war with Germany, Stalin not only gave Marshal Vasilevsky the task of planning a sudden attack on Japan, but appointed him to head all Soviet troops in a war against Japan. But Stalin had no intention of landing his troops on the Japanese islands. He had more attractive targets. Korea, Manchuria, the greater part of China, and French Indochina (Vietnam) were all occupied by Japan. Stalin planned to "liberate" them and take them under his control.

Starting in the summer of 1944, Soviet military might in the Far East began to grow, but it could not be observed from outside. There was rearmament and strengthening of divisions, corps, and armies, as well as a storing of the supplies necessary for a sudden and crushing attack. Roads, air bases, bridges, and command and communications posts were being built near the borders with great intensity. Soviet commanders, on orders from Moscow, moved ammunition and fuel storages and hospitals to the borders.

A movement of regiments, brigades, and divisions from the German front to the Far East began in the early spring of 1945. "The most important aspect of the preparations for the operation was the fact that they all had to be done before an official declaration of war on Japan."[14] Exceptional measures of concealment were taken. All sergeants and staff sergeants in the troops transferred to the Far East wore the insignia of privates. Junior officers had sergeant epaulets, and the senior officers wore the insignia of lieutenants and captains. Generals had fewer stars on their epaulets than they had earned. A major general could wear the epaulets of a lieutenant colonel or a major. Marshal Vasilevsky himself arrived in the Far East with the papers for a "Colonel General Vasilyev" and in the appropriate uniform.[15]

In May 1945, the troop transfer took on truly gigantic dimensions. "The mass regrouping of troops began with a transport by railroad from Eastern Prussia of the 5th Army, which had gained rich experience in breaking through fortified regions and operating in forested territories."[16] The 39th Army, also from Eastern Prussia, and the 53rd from Czechoslovakia were simultaneously moved. The 6th Tank Guards Army was to play the decisive role in the defeat of Japanese armies. It was moved from the Prague region. To conceal the movement of the tank army, the tankers not only changed their epaulets, but the insignia on them as well—they temporarily became medics, repairmen, and construction workers. Most importantly, the tanks and the rest of the heavy equipment of the 6th Tank Guards Army were left behind in Czechoslovakia. In Mongolia, near the state border where the tank army was to be relocated, new tanks had been arriving straight from factories in the Urals. They were prepared and carefully concealed well ahead of time.[17] The same exact procedure was performed in the transfer of most artillery, air force, and other formations and regiments. For example, in June and July of 1945, 1,155 war planes of the newest models were sent straight from the factories to the air bases in the Far East.[18] During this time, the pilots and engineer personnel of certain air force regiments, divisions, and corps were transported by railroad, without their equipment. New planes already awaited them in the Far East. On top of all this, the 6th and 7th Bomber Corps and two military-transport air force divisions were moved from air bases in Germany and Poland.[19]

The strategic regrouping of Soviet troops was carried out at a distance of nine thousand to twelve thousand kilometers. A regrouping of troops on such a scale was being performed for only the second time in human history. The first time was in May and June 1941, from the east toward the German borders. In 1945, it was done in the opposite direction. The commands of two fronts, three field armies and one tank army, fifteen rifle, artillery, mechanized, and tank corps—all those were moved to the Far East. The smaller units moved there together with their commands: thirty-six rifle, artillery, and air-defense artillery divisions, fifty-three brigades, and over a hundred separate regiments and battalions were moved there too.[20] In just three months, over 500,000 soldiers and officers were transported from Central Europe to the Far East. To minimize the volume of transports, a large part of the brigades, divisions, corps, and even an entire tank army were transported without their equipment. But some formations still had to be moved with their weapons and military equipment, and the number of arms transported with the troops was enormous: 3,340 tanks and self-propelled guns, 7,500 cannons and howitzers, 3,600 mortars, 1,100 rocket-launching field installations ("Katyusha"), and 1,400 warplanes.[21] It took 135,756 railcars to transport this mass of troops and weapons.[22]

During a surprise offensive operation, it would be necessary to supply a tremendous number of troops, which would be continuously moving forward. The troops immediately would need to receive hundreds of thousands of tons of ammunition, fuel, lubricants, food, and everything else that was indispensable for advancing. The transport of such quantities of cargo over distances of hundreds of kilometers could only be done by railroad. However, the Soviet Union's railroads had a broad gauge, while Manchuria's and China's railroads had a narrow gauge. It was decided to re-weld the railroad gauge there to the Soviet standard. Special brigades of railroad troops with the necessary equipment were prepared for this.

The arriving cargo was unloaded directly onto the ground in each border station's vicinity. Part of the cargo was not unloaded at all. It remained in the railcars, ready to follow the advancing troops across the border. "By the beginning of the operation, there were over 1,500 cisterns with fuel on the railroads of the Far East. . . . This imposed a great strain on the functioning of the railroads."[23]

After the strategic regrouping of the troops was complete, the three Soviet fronts contained eleven field armies, three air defense armies, three air force armies, one tank army, and four separate air force corps.[24] In addition, the Pacific fleet, the Amur flotilla, NKVD troops, and the armed forces of Mongolia were all under the command of the Soviet commander-in-chief in the Far East. The formation of Soviet troops included 1,747,465 men, 29,835 guns and mortars, 5,250 tanks, and 5,171 airplanes.[25] The Pacific fleet had 417 warships, including 78 submarines, and 1,618 airplanes, including 1,312 combat aircraft. The Amur navy flotilla had 126 warships and 68 combat aircraft.[26] Colonel Generals Vasiliev, Morozov, Maksimov, and Zolotov (in reality, Marshals of the Soviet Union A. M. Vasilevsky, R. Y. Malinovsky, K. A. Meretskov, and General of the Army M. V. Zakharov) arrived at the secret command posts ahead of the troops. To maintain secrecy, the "colonel generals" wore plain black jumpsuits over their uniforms, without any insignia, and during their trips to the vicinity of the state border they wore the uniforms of regular NKVD border troops.

A stream of cargo flowed in from the United States at the same time Soviet forces were being transferred out of Central and Eastern Europe. Stalin was the most cunning diplomat of the twentieth century. He demanded that the president of the United States supply food and fuel for all Soviet troop formations. "An agreement was reached with the United States about the concentration of three months' supplies and fuels for our troops in this theater of military operations."[27] The United States also supplied airplanes, armored cars, automobiles, radios, telephone cables, medicines, optical devices, and much more.

Stalin gave instructions to the commander-in-chief in the Far East, Marshal Vasilevsky, and to the other front commanders back in Moscow. There were very few documents about the preparations for a surprise attack on Japan: one notebook with calculations and one map. These documents remained in the Kremlin. Marshals and generals had to remember their objectives without using any papers. Upon arrival in the Far East, the front commanders began detailed planning and calculations. "A strictly limited number of people were allowed to see the drafting of plans for the fronts. Only the commander, the member of the military council, the chief of staff, and the chief of the operations directorate of the front knew the plans in full."[28]

The Trans-Baikal Front was deployed in a territory stretching 2,300 kilometers, and it was supposed to carry out a surprise attack eight hundred kilometers deep into enemy territory. There were 648,000 troops, 2,359 tanks and self-propelled guns, 1,324 warplanes, 9,668 guns and mortars, and 369 salvo-fire field installations ("Katyusha").[29] Four men, without secretaries, draftsmen, or other personnel, did all the planning of military operations for this mass of troops.

The 1st Far Eastern Front had 589,000 troops, 11,430 guns and mortars, 274 salvo-fire field installations, 1,974 tanks and self-propelled guns, and 1,137 combat planes. All the planning on this front was also done by just four men.[30]

The Trans-Baikal and the 1st Far Eastern Fronts were to attack in converging directions. Between these two attack formations there was the relatively weaker 2nd Far Eastern Front, which had 333,000 troops, 5,988 guns and mortars, 72 salvo-fire field installations, 917 tanks and self-propelled guns, and 1,260 combat planes.[31] A classic encirclement operation was being prepared, with a relatively weak middle and two extremely powerful flank formations. The newness lay in the size of the operation. All three fronts were meant to advance simultaneously along the front line of 5,130 kilometers. Such an operation was unprecedented. (Let's hope that it will never again be repeated.)

Stalin issued a special directive, which required the front commanders to define the objectives to the armies verbally, without producing any written documents.[32] After receiving an objective, the army commanders were to commence the planning of the operation. General M. Gareev was at that time a major in the operational staff sector of the 5th Army of the 1st Far Eastern Front: "Near the station Muchnaya, we were shut in a separate, heavily guarded house, [from] which no one was allowed outside. Guards brought in food. We had to work almost around the clock. [33] Exchanging letters with questions regarding the operation preparations was forbidden, even in code. The army commanders described the objectives to the division commanders verbally, using only a map. Radios only received signals. In the artillery units, communication by radio was permitted only after the beginning of artillery softening-up, and in the other units after the beginning of the attack.[34]

The unloading of arriving troops and all troop movements took place during the night. The arriving troops were immediately sent to special areas, where hiding places had been prepared in advance. Before beginning the offensive, the main forces were to be kept back, and part of the artillery was to move closer to the border and be ready to open fire.[35] Special squads of the fortified regions worked in the fields harvesting hay in all the areas visible to the enemy. The officers went to the local resorts and sanatoriums during their leave. The enemy was also confused by the fact that the local population from the border territories was not relocated, and their daily life was not affected by any changes. Training exercises were conducted at the same time as the troop movements, so the local population took everything they saw for regular military drills.[36]

The core principle of strategy is the concentration of force against weakness. The most powerful Soviet formation, the Trans-Baikal Front, was deployed against the weakest area of the Japanese defenses. But even here the forces were not spread out evenly along the entire border. Instead, extremely powerful assault groups gathered. Between these groups remained significant gaps, which were not covered by any troops. For example, on the Trans-Baikal Front, there was a gap of two hundred kilometers between the 17th Army and the 6th Tank Guards Army.[37] Long before World War II, there was a chain of fortified regions erected along the border in the Far East. These regions housed a significant number of troops that were specially trained for conducting long defense operations. But in the summer of 1945, Japan found itself on the verge of defeat. Therefore, the Soviet troops stationed in the forti- fied regions were issued orders to leave their armored concrete fortifications and reinforce the assault formations.[38]

On August 6, 1945, the American air force dropped an atomic bomb over Hiroshima, and on August 9, over Nagasaki. Japan was on its deathbed. And at this moment, on August 9, 1945, the Red Army carried out its sudden and crushing attack against Japanese troops in Manchuria and China. The operations of all the armies were planned according to the principle of surprise attack and overpowering the enemy with the immediate use of gigantic force. Even in secondary locations, the actions immediately took on an active and maneuver- ing character.[39] On August 8, the Soviet government declared: "This kind of action is the only measure capable of speeding up the coming of peace, to save people from further suffering and misery, and give the Japanese people the opportunity to rid themselves of danger and destruction."[40]

In the evening of August 8, 1945, the Japanese ambassador in Moscow was notified of a Soviet statement, which read: "Starting the next day, August 9, the Soviet Union will consider it- self in a state of war with Japan."[41] On August 9, the Soviet armies carried out their surprise attack. One could ask: How was it possible to declare the war on August 8 and to deliver a sudden strike on August 9? The answer is that in Vladivostok the day begins seven hours earlier than in Moscow. Military actions began on August 9 at 12:10 AM Vladivostok time.[42] At that moment in Moscow, it was still 5:10 PM on August 8. No one had yet warned the Japanese ambassador. Then, when night fell in Moscow, the Japanese ambassador was summoned to the People's Commissariat of Foreign Affairs and at 11:50 PM Moscow time, it was announced that a war would begin on the following day. In Moscow, there were still 10 minutes left until the next day, but in the Far East the new day had long since begun. At the time of the announcement, it was already 6:50 AM. War had been going on for over six hours. The most important events had already happened: a sudden Soviet air raid destroyed the Japanese air bases, the border defenses were liquidated, and powerful tank formations entered Manchuria and China, continuing an un- stoppable thrust forward.

The Japanese ambassador in Moscow was told about the beginning of the war, but he still had to reach the embassy and communicate with his government. All the telephone and telegraph lines were not working. Even in normal circumstances, radio connection with Japan, which was almost halfway around the world, was difficult. But here the circumstances were not normal: someone had tampered with the radio stations. In other words, the Japanese government found out that war was declared after a huge delay and through entirely different channels. In military language, this could be called "preparation and carrying out of a sudden initial attack with the opening of a new strategic front."[43] In the language of politics, this was called a "just and humane action by the USSR."[44]

After the first crushing attack, Marshal R. Y. Malinovsky told his troops on August 10, 1945: "The Soviet people cannot live and work in peace while the Japanese imperialists brandish arms at our far-eastern borders and await a convenient moment to attack our motherland."[45] Malinovsky spoke four days after an atomic bomb had been dropped on Hiroshima and one day after an atomic bomb had been dropped on Nagasaki. Those two Japanese cities lay in ruins unseen in human history, and Malinovsky was fully aware of the fact. Did the "Japanese imperialists," after Hiroshima and Nagasaki, really have nothing else to do but "await a convenient moment"?

In March 1939, Stalin had accused Great Britain and France of wanting to draw Europe into war while they remained on the sidelines: "In the politics of non-intervention, there is a desire not to hinder the aggressors while they do their dirty deeds, not to interfere, for example, with Japan involving itself in a war against China . . . the goal is to let all the participants of the conflict become engulfed by the quicksand of war, and let them weaken and exhaust each other. Then, when they are sufficiently weakened, one can enter the scene with fresh forces, act, of course, 'in the interests of peace,' and dictate to the weakened war participants all the terms of peace."[46] Stalin always ascribed his own intentions to his enemies. Stalin did everything that he accused Great Britain and France of doing. Now, Japan was exhausted by the war, and it was time to intervene "in the interests of peace": "The Soviet government, striving for the quickest possible restoration of peace, issued a declaration of war."[47]

The offensive operation by Soviet armies in August 1945 was truly a lightning war. "The forward battalions, accompanied by border guards, silently crossed the border without opening fire, and before the Japanese defenders had time to occupy them, took control of long-term enemy defense structures in a series of locations."[48] In just the first day, the 6th Tank Guards Army completed a thrust of 150 kilometers. The advance took place in extremely difficult conditions. Manchurian summers were extremely rainy, especially in August. Rivers overflowed, and fields and roads turned into impassable swamps. The troops of the 1st and 2nd Far Eastern Fronts had to cross the Amur River, one of the largest rivers on the planet. It stretched 2,850 kilometers in length. In August 1945, the Amur's water levels were four meters higher than usual and flooded thousands of square kilometers. The rivers that flowed into the Amur, among them the Ussuri and the Sungari, also overflowed.

The Trans-Baikal Front faced an entirely different situation—the tank columns advanced through waterless steppes in thick clouds of dust. The temperature was 30 degrees Celsius, sometimes even higher. Ahead, the troops had to overcome the Great Khingan Range, behind which unfolded a territory of rice fields completely unfamiliar to the Soviet soldiers.

It is claimed that the Japanese troops put up weak or no resistance. That is not true. The Japanese soldiers were the most tenacious in the world. They did not yet know about the destruction of Hiroshima and Nagasaki; the Japanese government was in no hurry to tell the troops about the catastrophe. The Japanese resistance stopped only after the troops received orders to capitulate. Before these orders came in, the Japanese fought to the death. But their tenacity was met with maneuvers. The territories fought over were huge, and Soviet troops simply bypassed the points of resistance, without engaging in prolonged combat.

Soviet troops did the impossible. The 6th Tank Guards Army overcame the Great Khingan Range, reached the open areas, and completed an incredible advance toward the Yellow Sea. In eleven days, with battles, its troops covered 810 kilometers. Assault units and paratroops operated ahead of them, taking air bases, bridges, and ferries. Here is a list of just some of the cities around which paratroops were landed successfully: Kharbin, Chongjin, Port-Artur, Mukden, Pyongyang, and Khynnam. The masters of blitzkrieg, German generals, gave high marks to the actions of the 6th Tank Guards Army and other Soviet troops. Major General F. W. von Mellentin recounted: "To illustrate the growing flexibility of the Red Army's military actions and its capacity to successfully conduct broad and decisive tank operations, I want to point to Marshal Malinovsky's sensational advance into Manchuria in August 1945."[49]

Von Mellentin continued to say:

> Other Soviet troops acted just as decisively and successfully. The Soviet navy sank Japanese ships, and landed naval assault forces on Sakhalin, in North Korea, and on the Kuril Islands. After entering the Sungari River, the Amur flotilla supported the advance of the 15th Army right up to the Kharbin Ranges. It constantly received rifle companies on board, and functioned as a sort of vanguard for the main forces of the 15th Army. In ten days of advance, the main forces of the flotilla, together with the troops of the 15th Army, which in part were stationed on the ships and in part advanced along the shorelines of the Sungari, covered over nine hundred kilometers along the Amur and Sungari rivers.[50]

Supplying one and a half million advancing troops was quite a formidable task. "The restoring of railroads, with the changing of the gauge to the Soviet standard, was done on the 1st Far Eastern Front at an average rate of seventy-one kilometers per day. This was achieved through the innovativeness of the railroad workers. They were included in the air assault troops and frontline units, so they were able to take over railroad connections and immediately organize the local population to repair the tracks and change the gauges."[51]

Officially, the Soviet military campaign in the Far East lasted twenty-four days, but battles only took place for twelve days. Not even two weeks had passed before a massive surrender of the Japanese troops began. Japanese losses numbered 84,000 killed and 594,000 taken prisoner. Among the prisoners were 148 Japanese generals. Unbelievable trophies were captured.

The results of the operation were enviable. The United States had fought against Japan for almost four years, and what did it receive? The Soviet Union fought against Japan for twelve days, and all of China, North Korea, and North Vietnam fell under the Soviet Union's control. Vasilevsky happily reported:

> By delivering a crushing blow to the Japanese troops in Korea, the Soviet Army created favorable conditions for the activities of revolutionaries. . . . In the northern section of the country, workers led by Communists began to build the first truly independent, demo-

cratic nation in Korean history. . . . As a result of Japan's defeat, favorable conditions were created in China, North Korea, and North Vietnam for the victory of people's revolutions. . . . The Chinese People's Army of Liberation received huge reserves of trophy arms, military equipment, and supplies. . . . The defeat of Japanese militarism opened the way for national liberation movements throughout Asia. On September 2, when the Japanese foreign affairs minister Sigemitsu and Chief of Staff Umedzu signed the pact of total capitulation, President Ho Chi Minh declared the birth of the Democratic Republic of Vietnam. On October 12, the Laos patriots pronounced the birth of Phatet-Lao.[52]

For many years, Soviet officers have been taught the lightning war of 1945 as an example. That was how one must fight: in two weeks, hundreds of millions of people were under Soviet control. One should be amazed by the assault of the 6th Tank Guards Army, the thrust of the Amur flotilla up the Sungari River, the bold actions of the paratroops. The most amazing was the coordination among the troops. Tankers, pilots, artillerists, sailors, communications men, paratroops, railroad workers, sappers, and the High Command staff in the Far East, the administrations and staffs of the three fronts and one fleet, eighteen armies and one flotilla, tens of corps, divisions, and brigades, hundreds of regiments and thousands of battalions, performed like one symphony orchestra under the direction of the great maestro Vasilevsky.

I reread many times Marshal Vasilevsky's biography, his book, and his articles, before I stumbled across a sentence that made me pause for breath: "Since May 1940, the deputy head of the Operations Directorate of the General Staff worked on the operational part of a plan of strategic deployment of Soviet armed forces in the northern, northwestern, and western directions."[53] In other words, between May 1940 and June 1941—that is, for more than a year—Major General Vasilevsky worked on preparing a plan for war against Germany. He personally prepared war plans for the Northern, Northwestern, and Western Fronts—in other words, for the Soviet troops in the Karelian, Baltic, and Byelorussian regions. These regions were precisely where the Soviet troops were hit the hardest in the summer of 1941. The troops of the Northern Front let the Finnish troops from the north through to Leningrad, and the worst blockade in human history ensued. The formations of the Northwestern Front fell apart, letting German troops through to Leningrad from the south. The troops of the Western Front in Byelorussia were almost instantly surrounded and crushed, leaving the way to Moscow wide open.

Stalin didn't criticize or punish Vasilevsky for such planning. On the contrary, a month after an unprecedented catastrophe for the Red Army, Stalin appointed Vasilevsky to the position of head of the Operations Directorate of the General Staff, entrusting him with drafting all plans on all fronts and in all directions. Vasilevsky walked the path from Major General to Marshal of the Soviet Union faster than anyone else—in just one and a half years. Stalin entrusted him personally with planning the defeat of German troops near Stalingrad, the victory at Kursk, the brilliant operation in Byelorussia, and then the war against Japan.

The selection of other high commanders for the task of the lightning defeat of Japanese troops in 1945 was also surprising. In June 1941, Lieutenant Colonel S. P. Ivanov was the chief of the operations division of the 13th Army headquarters on the Western Front. The significant part of the 13th Army was surrounded and perished on the sixth week of the war with Germany. Ivanov miraculously stayed alive and climbed the peaks of military power. He was first appointed chief of staff of the 38th Army, then chief of staff of the 1st Tank Army, and then of the 1st Guards Army. He successfully fulfilled all these roles. He planned the army operations in the most strategically important locations. In 1942, he became chief of staff of the Southwestern Front, which included the Stalingrad region. Here once again he performed brilliantly. S. P. Ivanov directed a number of staffs on various fronts, and always in the most important locations of the war. In the summer of 1945, he was already a colonel general. Stalin appointed him to be chief of staff of the High Command of Soviet troops in the Far East. Marshal Vasilevsky was the high commander and S. P. Ivanov was the head of the brain center. The lightning-speed defeat of Japanese troops was not only Vasilevsky's accomplishment, but also Ivanov's. S. P. Ivanov was a brilliant staff officer. He never made any mistakes in planning. On the contrary, his plans were examples to be followed by staff officers for many generations. How could it be that in 1941 everything in his plans was completely incorrect?

Until February 1941, General K. A. Meretskov was the chief of general staff of the Red Army. He was personally responsible for all war plans. From February until June 1941, the plans could not have radically changed. Consequently, Meretskov carried the responsibility for the defeat of the Red Army by the Germans in June 1941. But in 1945 Meretskov carried the title of Marshal of the Soviet Union. Stalin entrusted him with the command of the 1st Far Eastern Front.

Lieutenant General M. A. Purkaev in 1941 was the chief of staff of the Kiev special military district, the most powerful of Soviet districts. The district was transformed into the Southwestern Front, which was surrounded and decimated east of Kiev. In 1945, Stalin entrusted General Purkaev with the command of the 2nd Far Eastern Front.

In 1941, Major General R. Ya. Malinovsky commanded the 48th Rifle Corps. The corps was stationed on the Romanian border where there were no German troops. It was preparing for invasion, but it had to retreat. In 1945, Malinovsky was a Marshal of the Soviet Union. Stalin trusted him with the most powerful Trans-Baikal Front and once again placed him where the enemy was most vulnerable.

Generally, Stalin entrusted all the men who had planned the war against Germany with planning and conducting the war against Japan.

I have been taught to search for rules in the actions of enemy troop leaders, to note all moments that repeat themselves. If a general has a propensity to use the same maneuver several times, his conduct in the future can be predicted and his plans can be resisted. I used this method to analyze the battle habits of Soviet generals. I discovered that they had constantly repeated the same preparations: before carrying out the surprise attack against the Japanese 6th Army at Khalkhin-Gol in 1939; before invading Finland in 1939; before the operation to take Bessarabia in 1940; before sending Soviet troops into Iran in August 1941. They did it in all the aggressive operations of World War II, and, finally, before the sudden defeat of Japanese troops in August 1945. In the summer of 1941, they followed the same program.

Understandably, Japanese intelligence was unable to determine the true scope of the Soviet troop transfer, the date of the beginning of the invasion, or the locations chosen for the primary attacks. But still, it saw something, and in the Japanese staffs it was understood that such a troop transfer meant that sooner or later the Red Army would attack. The Japanese had only one way out: to carry out a preemptive strike against the Soviet troops. If the Japanese army had carried out an attack, the disaster of June 1941 would have been repeated in the Far East at the end of July or the beginning of August 1945.

Thousands of Soviet tanks without crews, as well as thousands of airplanes without pilots in the fields, were left right on the borders. The border forests were full of piles of shells, the railroad stations with trains of fuel and ammunition. If the Japanese had attacked, they would have seized all these resources, while the Red Army would have been left without ammunition or fuel. Thousands of soldiers from the railroad troops were ready to change the Japanese tracks to the Soviet standards, but they were not prepared to blow up their own bridges and tunnels. If they had attacked, the Japanese armies could have used Soviet bridges and tunnels. Soviet artillery had advanced right up to the border, but was not protected by infantry. For the purpose of surprise, the tanks and infantry would advance to the border only at the very last moment. If they had attacked, the Japanese could have taken thousands of Soviet cannon and howitzers, millions of shells which were already piled on the ground, and the Red Army would have been left without artillery, just like in 1941. The Red Army's command posts and communication lines were also located right at the borders. In the event of a surprise Japanese attack, the Red Army would have been left without command or communication—in other words, without a head or a nervous system.

On Stalin's orders, the command and staff of the Karelian Front, with Marshal Meretskov in command, was transferred to the Far East. The choice fell on them because the Karelian Front had tremendous experience in breaking through long-term fortified regions. This was exactly the work they were to do in Manchuria. The 5th Army, transferred from Eastern Prussia, was chosen for the same reason. This army also had rich experience in breaking through fortifications. At the same time, Soviet troops designated for the defense of fortified regions left their concrete fortifications and prepared to cross the border. The situation was extremely favorable for a Japanese invasion: the Red Army was preparing for attack, but it was not preparing for defense. It left all its fortified regions without troops. Hundreds of thousands of Red Army soldiers and officers were in trains, not knowing where they were being taken and what they were supposed to do.

Arriving Soviet troops were formed into tight assault formations, which made great targets for the Japanese air force. The bare areas between the attack formations were two hundred kilometers or more. The Japanese would not even have to breach Soviet defenses in these locations, because there were none there. Most importantly, the Soviet troops had no plans for defense in the Far East in the summer of 1945. Invasion plans were relayed to the troops at the very last moment. If the Japanese troops had carried out a surprise attack before August 9, 1945, Soviet troops would have suffered almost the same losses as Soviet troops in the summer of 1941 on the German border. And we would now be laughing at the stupidity of Soviet marshals, who ordered soldiers to harvest the hay in the fortified regions and sent officers to rest homes and sanatoriums. But the Japanese did not attack, since they never planned to attack the USSR, at least not in 1945.

Conclusion
The Aggressor

We will bury you!

—Nikita Khrushchev, at a reception for foreign ambassadors
and journalists in the Kremlin, November 1956

The Soviet Union entered World War II as an aggressor. Poland, Finland, Estonia, Lithuania, Latvia, Romania—all the western neighbors of the Soviet Union—fell victim to the Red Army. During talks in Berlin, Stalin's envoy Molotov demanded strongholds in Yugoslavia, in the Adriatic Sea, in Greece, in the Bosporus and Dardanelles, in the Persian Gulf; he demanded that countries south of the Baku-Batumi line, in the direction of the Persian Gulf, be given over to Soviet control, including eastern Turkey, northern Iran, and Iraq. He also declared the Soviet Union's interest in southern Bukovina.[1] Molotov constantly asked Hitler and Ribbentrop whether Germany had reconsidered its position on the fate of Finland, seeing that the Soviet Union was not going to let that country be independent. Finally, Stalin's major demand at the Berlin talks in November 1940 was for Germany to acquiesce to a Soviet military presence in Bulgaria. Molotov added, in a conversation with Hitler, that "the USSR was ready to support Bulgaria in its desire for an outlet to the Aegean Sea, and considered said desire to be just."[2] Stalin never specified which countries his puppet Bulgaria would have to invade to reach this outlet—Greece, Turkey, or both. In reality, the Germans took Greece and gave the go-ahead for Bulgaria to annex a part of the Greek territory—western Thrace and eastern Macedonia, thus reaching the Aegean Sea. But it was Stalin who wanted to give this go-ahead.

The Soviet Union finished World War II as an aggressor as well. It was the only country that expanded its borders as a result of World War II. Stalin annexed Estonia, Latvia, Lithuania, northern Bukovina, western Ukraine, and western Byelorussia, as well as parts of eastern Prussia with Koenigsberg, Trans-Carpathian Ukraine, the Kuril Islands, South Sakhalin, and Bessarabia.[3] Under the banner of the "great patriotic war," Stalin punished entire peoples and nations. On Stalin's orders, all the Chechens, Ingushes, Crimean Tatars, Volga Germans, and

278

other peoples were transported to empty frozen fields or waterless, lifeless steppes, and abandoned there to die. It is interesting to note that the Kalmyks, who already lived on the steppes, were not relocated further into their depths but into the Siberian taiga. Stalin controlled the fates of entire peoples, not only on the territory of the Soviet Union but also in nearby countries. Stalin relocated millions of Germans from Prussia, Silesia, and Sudet.

When the Nazi leaders went on trial in Nuremberg, Hitler's concentration camps in Buchenwald, Saksenhausen, Mulberg, Furstenwalde, Liebe-Roze, Bautzen, and others were not shut down. These concentration camps were simply taken out of the SS system and incorporated into the system of the GULAG. Thus, for example, the Nazi concentration camp at Buchenwald was transformed into "Special camp #2," which remained operational until 1950. Of the 28,000 people imprisoned there in those five years, seven thousand (25 percent) died. In comparison, from 1937 to 1945, 250,000 people went through the Nazi Buchenwald. Of that number, 50,000 (20 percent) died. The Communist Buchenwald had a higher death rate.

The Red Army came to Central Europe with the supposedly noble goal of liberating it from the Nazis, but it left only after establishing puppet governments in most of those countries. Poland, Czechoslovakia, East Germany, Hungary, Romania, Bulgaria, Yugoslavia, part of Austria, and Albania were forced under Stalin's control, as well as China, North Korea, and Vietnam in Asia. On July 22, 1945, the Soviet delegation suggested that the Soviet Union, the United States, and Great Britain separately or jointly oversee the former Italian colonies in Africa and the Mediterranean.[4] On July 23, Stalin demanded the right to create Soviet military naval bases in the Black Sea region, in the straits of Bosporus and Dardanelles.[5] He also wanted parts of Turkey—the Kars and Ardagan regions—to belong to the Soviet Union.[6] Stalin tried to take control of West Berlin by strangling it through a blockade. Soviet agents appeared in France, Italy, and Greece. The NATO military alliance was formed with the clear goal of preventing Stalin's troops from occupying Greece and Turkey. Stalin declared northern Iran to be a part of Azerbaijan, and right until the end of his life never gave up trying to take control of this province. Stalin set up the People's Democratic Republic of Southern Azerbaijan, and the Kurdish People's Democratic Republic, respectively in northern and western Iran.

In 1945, tens of millions of square kilometers of territory, occupied by millions of people, lay at Stalin's feet. But Stalin at that time did not have the resources to control all his conquests. On June 22, 1941, Hitler dealt a lethal blow to the Soviet Union. The best part of the male population of the Soviet Union perished in the war against Germany. After the war, the USSR was supposed to have conducted a population census and calculated its war losses. But Stalin did not conduct a census. It was only conducted fourteen years after the war, when Stalin was dead. "The decision not to count all the citizens until 1959 was founded on a desire not to draw attention to the huge unjustified human losses during the war period."[7]

During the last year of the war, the Red Army had to recruit underage boys, without saying how many years they would have to serve. They were kept in the army for seven to eight years. Otherwise, there would have been nobody left to serve in the gigantic army, which controlled almost half the globe. Those seven to eight years lasted until Stalin's death. If he had lived longer, these soldiers would have been kept in the army for fifteen years, or even more.

World War II opened unlimited opportunities for Stalin to spread Communism throughout the world, but there was nobody left in the Soviet Union to reap the crops in the fields. Famine broke out in the country in 1946 and 1947. One soldier was quoted as saying: "In this awful regiment, we were awfully hungry. Our rations were very small, plus they somehow managed to rob us."[8] The army, which the government was supposed to feed, starved. The people, whom the government was under no obligation to feed, starved as well. The famine of 1946 and 1947 claimed the lives of about a million people. Stalin had sentenced Europe to death, but he could not carry out the execution.

Hitler, according to Stalin's plans, was supposed to crush Europe, and then Stalin, with a surprise attack, would "liberate" it from Hitler. In the name of that goal, German tankers and pilots were trained in the Soviet Union, and Stalin brought Hitler to power. But Hitler ruined Stalin's plan.

Some people did not even notice that the Soviet Union lost World War II. Where was Stalin's great victorious country? The Soviet Union was created for war and conquest. It was not adapted for peacetime. It could either spread over the entire planet and kill off all normal life, or die. Stalin did not succeed in taking over the world, and this meant another war or the end of the Soviet Union in the near future. The Soviet Union was preparing itself for a new war, World War III. It concentrated all its strength and resources in preparing for a new war, and it was crushed in 1991 by the burden of its military expenditures.

Epilogue

Stalin Was a War Criminal

Stalin was a war criminal who should have been tried at Nuremberg in 1946 along with the German deputy Fuehrer, Rudolf Hess—so argued Hess's defense lawyer, Dr. Alfred Seidl, who opened the defense for Hess on March 22, 1946. Through a secret protocol, Hitler and Stalin had conspired to divide up between them countries conquered by their armies. Hitler was dead, but Stalin, according to the mandate of the Allied Military Tribunal, should have been indicted. The charges against him should have been similar to those against Hess, said Hess's lawyer.

Hess was charged with:

1.   Conspiracy to wage aggressive war
2.   Crimes against peace
3.   War crimes
4.   Crimes against humanity.

Since Hess had flown to England in May of 1941, and had been taken prisoner by the British a month before Hitler attacked the Soviet Union, Dr. Seidl was confident he could gain an acquittal on the charges of war crimes and crimes against humanity. Since Hess was in captivity in England he could have had no part in the atrocities against the Jews. The first two charges would be more difficult to refute since Hess, as Hitler's deputy, had discussed with the Fuehrer the events that led to war, and until May 1941 Hess had agreed with all of Hitler's decisions.

In *Hess: The Man and His Mission* (London: David Bruce and Watson, 1970), the Czech-born journalist, diplomat, and writer J. Bernard Hutton described how Dr. Seidl learned of the secret protocol to the Hitler-Stalin pact signed by Soviet foreign minister Vacheslav Molotov and German foreign minister Joachim von Ribbentrop, which implicated Stalin in war crimes. After a long and frustrating interview with Hess, who insisted he did not want to defend himself with a lawyer, Dr. Seidl was preparing to leave the prison. In the prison yard he overheard *Reichsmarschall* Hermann Goering and Von Ribbentrop talking. Von Ribbentrop offered an astonishing piece of information to Goering. He said that when he visited Moscow in August 1939 to arrange the German-Soviet treaty with Molotov, he had also signed a secret treaty which was not made public. Von Ribbentrop told Goering: "This secret agreement defined spheres of interest in the event of any war."

The two foreign ministers had drawn a line upon a map along the Vistula and the Bug, the two rivers that divide Poland. They had agreed that, should war come, the territory to the west of the two rivers should become a German sphere of interest, and the territory to the east would be under Soviet control. The Soviet sphere included Finland, Estonia, Latvia, Lithuania, the eastern part of Poland, and certain areas of Romania. Von Ribbentrop also told Goering that the Russians had assured him, since his arrest, that it would be made easier for him if he did not talk about this secret agreement in court. Stalin clearly wanted to keep his secret pact with Hitler—to carve up and share Poland and the Baltic states—from being made public at a time when the Russians were part of an international military court passing sentence on war crimes that included conspiracy to wage aggressive war and crimes against peace.

Dr. Seidl realized at once the significance of this secret pact to his client. After the military action of Germany and the Soviet Union against Lithuania, Latvia, and Estonia in June 1940, both Germany and the Soviet Union had denied that any political agreement existed, apart from the German-Soviet treaty concerning boundaries, which was concluded on August 23, 1939. It followed that if Dr. Seidl could prove such a secret plan did exist then Stalin and the Soviet Union were as guilty of waging aggressive war as any of the Nazis in the dock. Dr. Seidl would be able to argue that his client should be found not guilty or else Stalin and other Kremlin men should join him in the dock, explained Hutton.

Dr. Seidl set out to find another witness to the secret protocol signing besides Von Ribbentrop. After a difficult search he managed to come across Dr. Friedrich Gaus, who had been undersecretary of state in the German foreign ministry and had accompanied Von Ribbentrop to Moscow for the treaty signing. "Was there such a secret agreement?" Dr. Seidl asked. "Yes," confirmed Dr. Gaus, "I remember it clearly." When asked where a copy could be found, Gaus said he had no idea since to his knowledge all the important files of the German foreign ministry had been microfilmed and surrendered to American officials.

Dr. Seidl needed documentary evidence to make his case. When his efforts to find the document by going through normal bureaucratic channels failed, he spread the word of his search to all the high-ranking American officers he met socially and told them about the specific document he was looking for.

One evening as he was leaving the court, an American officer, whom he did not know, approached him and asked in German, "Are you Dr. Alfred Seidl?" The lawyer nodded. As Hutton wrote, "The American introduced himself. He then handed Dr. Seidl a plain sealed envelope. 'This is something that may interest you,' he said. Dr. Seidl ripped open the envelope, his fingers trembling as he leafed through the contents. It was a copy of the agreement between Molotov and von Ribbentrop that he was searching for. The American officer discreetly disappeared."

After studying the document Dr. Seidl saw that it was not a photostatic copy and had no official seal. He gave the document to Dr. Gaus, who said it seemed to him to be a true copy of the secret agreement reached between Molotov and von Ribbentrop. Dr. Gaus willingly signed an affidavit:

> About noon on August 23, 1939, the plane in which I was traveling with von Ribbentrop landed in Moscow. I was acting as his legal advisor in regard to certain negotiations between [him] and Stalin. I was not present but there was a counselor from the embassy and Hilger, who acted as interpreter. Also present was Ambassador Count Schulenburg.
>
> The outcome seemed to be satisfactory to Von Ribbentrop, who expressed the opinion that Germany would be successful in her proposals.
>
> In the evening a second discussion took place for the purpose of completing and signing the necessary documents. I had prepared the draft for Herr von Ribbentrop. Ambassador Count Schulenburg and the counselor from the embassy and Hilger were also there. Stalin and Molotov carried on the negotiations for the Russian side assisted by Pavlov, who interpreted.
>
> An agreement was reached regarding the non-aggression pact between Germany and Soviet Russia, but a phrase regarding the friendly shaping of German-Russian relations was objected to by Stalin, who said that the Soviet government could not suddenly publicize a German-Russian friendship after the National Socialist foreign minister had poured "buckets of putrid ditch water" over them for six years. It was necessary for it to be reworded.
>
> Beside the non-aggression pact there were negotiations at some length about a special secret document which in my recollection was called "secret protocol" or "secret additional protocol." This [was] aimed at the delimitation of the mutual spheres of influence in the European territories situated between the two countries. I cannot remember whether the expression "spheres of influence" was used or not. In the document Germany said she was disinterested in Latvia, Estonia, and Finland, but regarded Lithuania as a part of "her sphere of influence." At the same time, Germany wanted to have an interest, but not political, in the Baltic ports which were free from ice. This, of course, was not acceptable to the Russians. Obviously, von Ribbentrop was acting on instructions, as he had booked a telephone call to Hitler, which came through at this time. He was told to accept the Soviet point of view.
>
> For the Polish territory, a demarcation line was fixed. Whether it was marked exactly on a map or described in words in the document I cannot remember. The agreement reached about Poland was to the effect that both powers should settle all questions regarding that country at a final meeting. Regarding the Balkans, it was established that Germany should have only economic interests.
>
> The non-aggression pact and the secret documents were signed at a rather late hour of the same night.
>
> Approximately one month later, at discussions about the second German-Soviet political treaty, the document mentioned above was altered—following a suggestion communicated by the Soviet government to Berlin earlier—to the effect that Lithuania was to be taken out of the "German sphere of interest," except for a "Lappet" [an overhanging piece of land] adjacent to East Prussia. In return, however, the demarcation line in Poland was moved further to the east.
>
> At subsequent negotiations, through diplomatic channels, either at the end of 1940 or the beginning of 1941, this diplomatic "Lappet" was given up by the Germans.

The document not only exposed Stalin and Hitler's political goals, but it was staggering evidence of their willingness to wage war and to share the spoils of war between themselves by dismembering smaller countries.

Dr. Seidl had no illusions as to why he had been given access to the document by an American officer who feared Stalin's intentions in Eastern Europe and a Cold War in Western Europe through the rise of Communist parties in France and Italy. But he was ready to carry out his duty to his client, who sat in the dock reading a novel, appearing to have not the slightest bit of interest in the proceedings.

On March 30, 1946, Dr. Seidl produced his astonishing surprise when he cross-examined Von Ribbentrop about the secret German-Soviet agreement in 1939. Reluctantly, Von Ribbentrop admitted it existed. "If war broke out, occupation of these zones was to be undertaken by Germany and Russia. At that time, I heard expressions—both from Stalin and Hitler—that Polish and other territories thus delineated were regions which both sides had lost in an unfortunate war."

The shocked judges ordered Dr. Seidl to halt his cross-examination. He desisted, but told the court that the secret pact was an essential element in his defense of Hess and if the court did not allow the full details of the secret German-Soviet agreements to be called into evidence he would demand that Molotov, the Soviet foreign minister, be called as a witness. At least one of the prosecuting nations had been involved in the conspiracy that led to World War II, Dr. Seidl charged.

The Soviet prosecutor, General Roman Rudenko, jumped to his feet to protest and urged that the document be suppressed. "The court is investigating the case of the major German criminals. It is not investigating the foreign policy of the allies. This anonymous document . . . can have no value."

The judges conferred and upheld Rudenko's objection to the document being entered as evidence, but decided that Baron von Weizsäcker, a former secretary of state in the German foreign ministry, could be questioned about it. His testimony confirmed the existence of a secret pact and created a sensation when he told the court:

> The secret protocol, of extensive scope, drew a line of demarcation between areas which in certain circumstances would be of interest to the Soviet Union, and those which would belong to the German sphere of interest. In the Soviet sphere were included Finland, Estonia, Latvia, the eastern parts of Poland, and certain parts of Romania. Everything west of that line was left to Germany. Later, in September or October 1939, amendments were agreed upon by which Lithuania, or the greater part of it, was transferred to the Soviet sphere, and the line of demarcation in Poland was moved considerably to the west. Explicitly, or implicitly, the secret agreement was to create a completely new order in Poland. And when it came into operation, this line of demarcation was followed closely.

When the British Lord Justice Lawrence asked Baron von Weizsäcker if he knew whether the secret pact existed in writing, the former foreign office official replied: "I kept a photostatic copy of that pact in my safe and I will have no hesitation in recognizing it if it were put to me." Before Dr. Seidl could present his document to Von Weizsäcker its authenticity was challenged, and Dr. Seidl could only reply that it had been given to him by an unidentified allied army officer. The judges conferred again and ruled that since the origin of the document in the courtroom was unknown, it could not be put before the witness.

Dr. Seidl's efforts bore bitter fruit. He had revealed to the world that a heinous secret pact existed, but the ruling to prevent him from producing the actual document in court prevented him from aiding the defense of his client. Rudolf Hess was not found guilty of crimes against humanity and war crimes, but he was found guilty of conspiracy to wage aggressive war and of crimes against peace. He was sentenced to life imprisonment on October 1, 1946. The Soviet member of the tribunal objected to Hess's sentence, arguing that Hess should have been sentenced to death. Hess spent the rest of his life in prison until he died by suicide at age ninety-two, on August 17, 1987, the last of the convicted Nazi war criminals and the sole occupant of West Berlin's Spandau prison. The Soviet Union rejected all efforts to permit Hess early release.

Had Hess been released, his family and those who urged his release would have been free to draw attention to Stalin's own guilt for crimes against peace and conspiracy to wage aggressive war.

Abbreviations

ACP(b):	All-Union Communist Party (bolsheviks)
CC of RCP(b):	Central Committee of Russian Communist Party (bolsheviks)
CPSU:	Communist Party of the Soviet Union
GRU:	Main Intelligence Directorate of the General Staff of the Soviet Armed Forces
GULAG:	Chief Administration of Collective Labor Camps
NEP:	New Economic Policy
NKVD:	People's Commissariat of Internal Affairs
NSDAP:	National Socialist Workers' Party (Germany)
OKH:	Army High Command (Germany)
OKW:	Supreme Command of the Armed Forces (Germany)

Notes

Author's Note:

Readers may notice that several sources are quoted without full details (city, publisher, page number). My friends and anonymous supporters often send me photocopies of documents without these details. As I live in hiding in the U.K. (the Soviets sentenced me to death for defecting to the West in 1978), getting the original source data is often very difficult. But I do not doubt the veracity of my sources: for the last twenty years my sources have never been challenged by critics, even those who disagree with my conclusions. However, readers who feel that missing source details are absolutely necessary are invited to e-mail their requests to info@suvorov.com. My friends and I will do our best to oblige.

Preface

1. GULAG —*Glavnoe Upravlenie Lagerei* (Main Directorate of Correctional Labor Camps, Labor Settlements and Places of Incarceration), one of the names for the Soviet prison system. It became part of the NKVD—*Narodnyi Commissariat Vnutrennikh Del (People's Commissariat of Internal Affairs)* from 1930, and then became a part of the MVD (Ministry of Internal Affairs) in 1956.

Introduction

1. This name has been used since 1942. Other names were used before, but in this book, only GRU is used.
2. *Soviet Military Encyclopedia* (Moscow: Voyenizdat, 1976), 5:67.

Chapter 1

Epigraph: Lev Davydovich Trotsky, speech during seizure of power, third speech at the Second All-Russian Conference of Soviets, October 26, 1917.

1. Out of an agreed-upon 245 tons of gold, 92 were delivered to Germany, but confiscated from it by victorious France.

Chapter 2

Epigraph: *Zhizn Natzional'nostei*, no. 6 (1918).

1. Vladimir I. Lenin, *Complete Collected Works*, 5th ed. (Moscow: Politizdat, 1977), 41:353.
2. Ibid.
3. V. Ivanov, "Requiem on Victorious Steel Drums, in *Ural*, nos. 2–3 (1994): 242; N. Kakurin and B. Melikov, *Civil War in Russia: War with the White Poles* (Moscow: St. Petersburg, 2002), 670.
4. Kakurin and Melikov, *Civil War in Russia*, 556.
5. *The Comintern and the Idea of the World Revolution: Documents* (Moscow: Nauka, 1998), 186.

6. L. O. Frossard, *De Jaurès à Lénine: notes et souvenirs d'un militant* (Paris: Bibliothèque de documentation sociale, 1930), 137.
7. *Documents and Materials on the History of Soviet-Polish Relations* (Moscow: Voyenizdat, 1964), 3: 221.
8. Kakurin and Melikov, *Civil War in Russia*, 434.
9. Vladimir I. Lenin, Ninth Conference of the Russian Communist Party, September 22, 1920.

Chapter 3

Epigraph: Joseph Stalin, "About the Polish Communist Party" (1926), republished in *Collected Works in 13 Volumes* (Moscow: Gospolitizdat, 1952), 6: 267.
1. Vladimir I. Lenin, "Report on Foreign and Domestic Policy," delivered at the Eighth Congress of Soviets on December 22, 1920, published in *Complete Collected Works*, 143.
2. Lenin, *Complete Collected Works*, 358.
3. Walter Krivitsky, *I Was an Agent of Stalin* (Moscow: Terra, 1991), 97–98.
4. Ibid.
5. Alexander Kolpakidi and Dmitri Prokhorov, *Empire of the GRU: Sketches on the History of Russian Military Intelligence* (Moscow: Olma-Press, 2000), 1: 105–7.
6. *Rodina*, no. 10 (1990): 13.
7. "Politburo of the CC of RCP (b)—ACP (b) [Central Committee of Russian Communist Party (bolsheviks) —All-Union Communist Party (bolsheviks)] and Europe: Decisions of the 'Special Folder,' 1929–1939," in *The Russian Political Encyclopedia* (Moscow, 2001), 21.
8. Ibid., 22–23, and Boris Bazhanov, *Memoirs of a Former Secretary of Stalin* (Paris: The Third Wave, 1980), 68–69. The most important fact is that Bazhanov summarized decisions, made in secret by the Politburo, with absolute certainty. His only mistake is with regard to the date: that session of the Politburo convened on October 4, 1923, not in September of the same year. In 2001 this decision, already unclassified, was made public. The abovementioned session of the Politburo really did consider the question of a specified date for armed insurrection in Germany. A small segment from protocol #38, made on October 4, 1923: "Determined: . . . 3. To agree with the commission with regards to the fixing of the deadline —the 9th of November, this year. 4. To apply all political and organizational efforts so that the appointed deadline may be met. 5. . . . It is to be remembered, that the course of action may lead to the inevitability of ordering the decisive advance ahead of the appointed deadline. . . . 7. To send to Germany comrades Pyatakov, Rudzutak, and Kuibyshev. . . . 11. To let those four [Central Committee members Radek, Pyatakov, Unshlikht, and Vasia Shmidt, NarKom of Labor] decide, upon arrival in Berlin, whether to include comrade Krestinskyi in their work, and, in case of being required to act in a conspiratorial manner, to have comrade Krestinskyi aid the group's activities, allowing him equal voting power in all or some of their meetings. . . . 13. To increase the special fund by 500,000 gold rubles." The decision to include Rudzutak among the four was not carried out due to the latter's illness; instead of Kuibyshev, according to the Politburo decision on October 18, the People's Commissar for Labor, V. V. Schmidt, joined its ranks. Nikolai Krestinskyi was then a plenipotentiary representative of the USSR in Germany. The sum mentioned here is for the deposition of the German government.
9. General Ioakim Vatsetis (1873–1938) was Commander in Chief of Soviet Russia's armed forces in 1918–19.
10. Vyacheslav Menzhinskii (1874–1934) was one of the leaders of Stalin's political police.
11. Meer Trillisser (1883–1940) was one of the heads of political police in the USSR.
12. Genrikh Yagoda (1891–1938) was one of the leaders of Stalin's political police.
13. Gustav Stresemann (1879–1929) was *Reichchancellor* of Germany from 1923, and German minister of foreign affairs from 1923 to 1929.
14. Raymond Poincaré (1860–1934) was premier and minister of foreign affairs in France from 1912, president from 1913 to 1920, and premier once again from 1922 to 1924 and 1926 to 1929.
15. Krivitsky, *I Was an Agent of Stalin*, 49–50.
16. Speech on August 1, 1927, at joint plenum of the Central Committee and Central Control Commission of the Communist Party, quoted in Joseph Stalin, *Collected Works*, 10: 63.
17. Gustav Hilger and Alfred G. Meyer, *Incompatible Allies* (New York: Macmillan, 1953), 267.
18. Krivitsky, *I Was an Agent of Stalin* (Moscow: Sovremennik, 1996), 49-50.

19. Ernst Roehm (d. 1934) was one of the leading figures of the Nazi movement, second only to Hitler himself.

Chapter 4

Epigraph: Adolf Hitler, during a meeting with Lord Halifax, the British foreign minister, November 19, 1937.

Chapter 5

Epigraph: Adolf Hitler, *Mein Kampf* (Russia: T-OKO, 1992), 524.
1. *Voenno-istoricheskiy Zhournal* (*VIZh*) [Military History Journal], no. 4 (1989): 53.
2. *Bulleten Oppozitsii* [Bulletin of Opposition], no. 52–53 (October 1936): 42.
3. Robert Conquest, *The Great Terror*, translated from English into Russian (Florence, Italy: Aurora, 1974).
4. A. Antonov-Ovseenko, *Portrait of a Tyrant* (New York: Khronika, 1980), 296.
5. Joseph Stalin, in *Eighth Congress of the Communist Party: Protocols* (Moscow: Partizdat, 1959), 20.
6. Lenin, *Complete Collected Works*, 41: 353.
7. Hitler, Adolf, *Mein Kampf*, pt. 2, chap. XIII, passim.
8. Rosenberg, Alfred, *Der Zukunftweg einer deutschen Aussenpolitik*, 20.

Chapter 6

Epigraph: Leon Trotsky, "Against National Communism!" *Bulleten Oppozitsii* [Bulletin of Opposition], no. 24 (August 25, 1931).
1. M. I. Meltiukhov, *Stalin's Missed Opportunity: The Soviet Union and the Fight for Europe, 1939–1941* (Moscow: Veche, 2002), 511. As of January 1, 1928, the Red Army had forty-five Ricardo Mk V tanks, six Taylor Mk A tanks, and twenty-eight Renault FT-17 tanks, altogether seventy-nine foreign-made tanks. Mikhail Svirin and Andrei Beskurnikov, "First Soviet Tanks," supplement to *M-Hobby* magazine (Moscow), no. 1 (1995): 43. The domestic production of tanks was launched in the 1928–29 business year. One hundred and twenty-two tanks were produced then: 121 MS-1 (T-18) tanks and one T-12. But only 96 MS-1s were accepted by the state acceptance commission. In 1932, 3,039 tanks and light tanks had already been produced. Overall, in the years of the first Five Year Plan, 3,949 tanks and light tanks were produced altogether. *History of the Second World War, 1939–1945* (Moscow: Voyenizdat, 1973–82), 1: 260. By January 1, 1933, the Red Army had 4,538 tanks. Meltiukhov, *Stalin's Missed Opportunity*, 515.
2. V. S. Shumikhin, *Soviet Military Aviation, 1917–1941* (Moscow: Nauka, 1986), 157.
3. Jacques Rossi, *GULAG Directory* (London: OPI, 1987), 96–97.
4. *GULAG: The Main [Prison] Camp Directorate, 1918–1960: Collection of Documents*, compiled by A. I. Kokurin and M. Petrov (Moscow: International Fund "Democracy," 2000), 753.
5. S. G. Popova, "The World Gold Market and Issues of Gold Export Development in Russia," Ph.D. thesis (Moscow: 1998).
6. V. Z. Rogovin, "Hunger," in *The Power and the Opposition, 1928–1933* (Moscow: Zhurnal Teatr, 1993), chap. XLVIII.
7. *Pravda*, February 2, 1935.
8. Felix Chuev, *Molotov: Master of Half a Domain* (Moscow: Olma-Press, 2002), 458.
9. V. Z. Rogovin, "Hunger," in *The Power and the Opposition, 1928–1933*. Less than 100,000 tons of grain were exported in 1928, but by 1929 that figure had already reached 1.3 million tons; in 1930 it was 4.8 million tons, in 1931 it was 5.2 million tons, in 1932 it was 1.8 million tons, and in 1933 it was 1 million tons.

Chapter 7

Epigraph: G. Zinoviev, member of the Politburo, chairman of the Communist International, in *Collected Works* (Leningrad, 1925), 7: 490.
1. *Pravda*, no. 255, November 6–7, 1927.
2. Stalin, *Collected Works*, 11: 202.

3. Joseph Stalin, speech at the plenary of the Central Committee of the Communist Party, August 1, 1927, published for the first time only twenty-five years later in *Collected Works*, 10: 49.

4. Stalin, *Collected Works*, 7: 72.

5. Stalin, *Collected Works*, 7: 14. This quote is taken from Stalin's speech at the January 1925 plenary of the Central Committee, which discussed, among other things, an increase in military expenditures.

6. Quoted in Joachim Fest, *Hitler: A Biography* (Perm, Russia: Alteya, 1993), 2: 234.

7. Henry Piker, *Hitler's Table Talks* (Smolensk, Russia: Rusich, 1998), entry from May 6, 1942.

8. Stalin, *Collected Works*, 11: 202.

Chapter 8

Epigraph: Alexander Lapchinsky, *The Air Army* (Moscow: Voyenizdat, 1939), 144.

1. P. Stefanovsky, *Three Hundred Unknowns* (Moscow: Voyenizdat, 1968), 83.

2. Shumikhin, *Soviet Military Aviation,* 218.

3. V. B. Shavrov, *The History of Aircraft Design in the USSR, 1939–1950* (Moscow: Mashinostroyenie, 1988), 162.

4. L. Kerber, *TU: Man and Airplane* (Moscow: Sovetskaya Rossia, 1973), 143.

5. L. Kerber, *TU: Man and Airplane*, article in *Trail in the Sky* (Moscow: Politizdat, 1971), 202

6. G. J. Taylor, *Combat Aircraft of the World* (London: Ebury Press, 1969), 592.

7. Vaclav Nemecek, *The History of Soviet Aircraft from 1918* (London: Willow Books, 1986), 134.

8. M. Gallay, *Third Dimension* (Moscow: Sovetski Pisatel, 1973), 330.

9. M. Maslov, "Dreadnought" in *M-Hobby* magazine (Moscow), nos. 5–6 (1997): 9, 11. The order to launch serial production of the TB-7 provided for the plans to produce eight lots of TB-7s, for a total of fifty-one aircraft. However, the order was never signed. Kazan Aircraft Factory #142, which was selected to produce the TB-7, had modern equipment, purchased in the United States and delivered to the factory. Actually, the factory had the capacity to produce up to one hundred TB-7s annually. If necessary, other factories could also have been switched to TB-7 production.

10. The TB-7 was completely unreachable until 1940, when the *Luftwaffe* started to receive mass deliveries of the Bf109 E-3.

11. The operational capabilities of the TB-7 bomber were described in an impartial, comprehensive, and detailed manner by Vladimir Ratkin, "PE-8 Testing by War," in the magazine *Mir Aviatsii* [The World of Aviation], nos. 1 and 2 (1996) and no. 1 (1997), as well as by N. Yakubovich, "The PE-8's Unenviable Fate," in the magazine *Krylia Rodiny* [Wings of the Motherland], no. 11 (1995) and no. 1 (1996); also in *USSR Aircraft Industry, 1917–1945* (Moscow: TSAGI Publications Department, 1994), 2: 68–69.

12. G. Ozerov, *Tupolev's Sharaga* (Frankfurt: Possev, 1971), 47.

13. Vladimir Ratkin, *Mir Aviatsii*, no. 1 (1996), 15. Only four aircraft had the fifth additional engine.

14. *Tupolev's Aircraft ANT-1 —ANT-15* (Moscow: Tupolev ANTK, 1995), 16.

15. E. Riabchikov and A. Magid, *The Becoming* (Moscow: Znanie, 1978), 132.

16. Giulio Douhet, Italian general (1869–1930). In 1910 he theorized that heavy bomber aviation would play a decisive role in the next war.

17. Shumikhin, *Soviet Military Aviation,* 185.

18. A.Yakovlev, *Life's Task* (Moscow: Politizdat, 1973), 168.

19. Ibid., 182.

Chapter 9

Epigraph: Robert Goralski, *World War II Almanac, 1931–1945* (New York: G. P. Putnam's Sons, 1981), 164.

1. *Domestic Armored Vehicles, 1905–1941* (Moscow: Exprint, 2002), 235.

2. *Domestic Armored Vehicles, Twentieth Century,* 121, 127. In April 1938, a prototype of the infantry tank Mark II (A12) Matilda II was built in Britain. In armor thickness, this tank exceeded all other tanks around the world. Its frontal armor was 78 mm, its turret front armor was 75 mm, its side armor was 75 mm, and its aft armor was 55 mm; the T-28 had 30, 20, 20, and 20 mm armor; the T-28E had 50, 80, 40, and 40 mm armor. But the Matilda's weaponry was exceedingly weak: a 40-mm gun and one or two machine guns. There were two engines, 95 horsepower each. Because of the underpowered engines,

this tank —the pride of the British tank industry—could only handle its own weight on level ground or while going down hills. Each armored column of Matildas was escorted by a group of heavy trucks. Their task was to tow each Matilda uphill. The Matilda could only attack the enemy on level ground or roll down at the enemy from the top of a hill. If the reader is interested, I highly recommend the incredible book by D. Fletcher, *The Great Tank Scandal* (London: HMSO, 1990). By the beginning of World War II on September 1, 1939, the British army had only two of those tanks. The tank was slow and had a short range and unsatisfactory open terrain performance and reliability. All of the tank's parameters, with the exception of the armor, did not satisfy battlefield needs.

3. *Encyclopedia of German Tanks of World War Two* (London: AAP, 1978), 89.

4. M. Bariatinsky and M. Pavlov, *Middle Tank T-28* (Moscow: Askold, 1993).

5. A. B. Shirokorad, *The Genius of the Soviet Artillery: The Triumph and Tragedy of V. Grabin* (Moscow: AST, 2002), 141–42.

6. In the summer of 1941, the infantry tank Mark IV (A22) Churchill went into production in Britain. The first production model had the following armor: frontal armor 101 mm, turret frontal armor 89 mm. However, the tank was very weakly armed: a 40-mm gun and two machine guns. The Churchill had a very weak engine and, subsequently, low open-terrain capability and speed. The transmission was unreliable. The tank had an old-fashioned design. The body was assembled on a sub-frame made out of angle beams. Still plates were riveted to the sub-frame, with armor plating attached over them on bolts. Although the armor was very thick, the design lacked rigidity. In the Soviet tanks, the body was a box, welded out of armor plates. This gave the body superb rigidity. This was exactly the method used in the model tanks. Therefore, despite the impressive thickness of the armor, one is looking at a significantly lower technological level in British tank building. Winston Churchill joked that the tank, named after him, had even more shortcomings than he did.

7. Heinz Guderian, *A Soldier's Memoirs* (Moscow: Voyenizdat, 1957), 231.

8. Ibid., 361.

9. *The Wehrmacht's Fateful Decisions* (Moscow: Voyenizdat, 1974), 61.

10. Ibid., 101–2.

11. Heinz Guderian, *Panzer Leader* (London: Futura, 1974), 276.

12. "Second Partial and First Consolidated Report on Russian Medium Tank T-34," Aberdeen Proving Ground, Maryland (archive, 1943), 4.

13. "Military and Numeric Composition of the Armed Forces of the USSR," *Statistical Almanac*, no.1 (June 22, 1941) (Moscow: Military History Institute, Ministry of Defense of the Russian Federation, 1994), 241.

14. I. Shmelev, *The Tank's History, 1916–1996* (Moscow: Tekhnika Molodiozhi, 1996), 145.

15. Starting on September 3, 1939, and through May 8, 1945, Britain produced 25,116 tanks; from 1939 to 1945 Germany produced 24,242 tanks and Japan produced 5,085 tanks. Altogether, this came to 54,443 tanks. In the years of World War II, from the beginning of production in September 1940 and up to September 2, 1945, 54,853 T-34 tanks were manufactured.

16. *Encyclopedia of German Tanks of World War Two* (London: AAP, 1978), 261–62.

17. M. Bariatinsky, *Soviet Armor, 1939–1945* (Moscow: Bronecollectsia, 1998), 13–14.Starting in 1940, there were 33,805 T-34 tanks built, and 21,048 T-34-85 tanks were built from 1944 until the end of the war.

18. 2,644 SU-85 were produced and 2,495 SU 100. Altogether: 5,139. Ibid, pp. 22–23.

19. Guderian, *Panzer Leader*, 283.

20. Steven Zaloga and James Grandsen, *Soviet Tanks and Combat Vehicles of World War Two* (London: Arms and Armour Press, 1984), 175.

21. V. Chalmaev, *Malyshev*, ZhZL series (Moscow: Molodaia Gvardia, 1978), 299. Starting in 1942, in the competition for the quality parameters of the tank guns, the German designers achieved outstanding results. The 75-mm gun KwK 42 (with a 70-caliber barrel length!) that was used on a Panther gun was a designer's masterpiece. The 122-mm gun on the IS-2 and the 75-mm Panther gun had approximately the same effectiveness against the armor. The Panther gun's low caliber meant higher speed. The Panther's load was 79 to 81 rounds, but only 28 on the IS-2. This difference was caused by the lower internal volume of the IS-2 versus the "Panther." Also, the 122-mm gun required bigger and heavier

rounds. The German shell's initial velocity was higher than the Soviet one. Combined with excellent sights and optics, this gave it superiority over the IS-2 in precision. The Panther's armor-busting round weighed 6.8 kg and had an initial velocity of 925 m/s. The sub-caliber shell weighed 4.25 kg and had an initial velocity of 1,120 m/s. The armor-penetrating shell of the IS-2 had a lower initial velocity—790 m/s; however, the weight of the round was monstrous for that time—25 kg. The muzzle energy of the 122-mm gun on the IS-2 was one and a half times higher than the corresponding one on the Royal Tiger, two and a half times higher than the Tiger, and almost three times higher than the Panther. One good shot from the IS-2 redeemed the shortcomings of its gun. In October 1943, during tests at the Kubinka testing grounds near Moscow, an IS-2 with an armor-busting shell broke through the frontal armor of the Panther from a distance of 1,500 meters, then, having excess energy, the round went through the transmission, the armor wall of the weapon section, the engine, and even then, there remained so much energy that the round tore off the back armor wall of the body along the seams and threw it back several meters. The IS-2 tank gun was especially superior when engaging unarmored targets. The high-explosive fragmentation shell of the IS-2 weighed 25 kg against the 7 kg of the Panther shell. In general, what the IS-2 was needed for was not fighting Panthers and Tigers, but for breaking through the enemy's defenses. The main burden of fighting the heavy German tanks was assigned to the tank destroyer SU-100.

22. Colonel Franz Halder, *War Diary, 1939–1942* (Moscow: Voyenizdat, 1971), entry for June 24, 1941.
23. "Military and Numeric Composition of the Armed Forces of the USSR," *Statistical Almanac*, no. 1 (June 22, 1941) (Moscow: Military History Institute, Ministry of Defense of the Russian Federation, 1994), 241.
24. Guderian, *A Soldier's Memoirs*, 121.
25. K. Galitsky, *The Years of Hard Trials* (Moscow: Nauka, 1973), 79.
26. A. I. Rodimtzev, *Motherland, These Are Your Sons* (Kiev: Politizdat, 1982), 291.
27. *World War II Almanac, 1931–1945* (London: Hamish Hamilton, 1981), 164.
28. Steven Zaloga and James Grandsen, *Soviet Heavy Tanks* (London: Osprey, 1981), 12–13.
29. Liddell Hart, ed., *The Soviet Army* (London: Weidenfield and Nicolson, 1956), B.H.122.
30. Zaloga and Grandsen, *Soviet Tanks and Combat Vehicles of World War Two*, 175.
31. Hermann Hoth, *Panzer Operations* (Moscow; Voyenizdat, 1961), 360.

Chapter 10

Epigraph: Adolf Hitler, August 4, 1941, quoted in Guderian, *A Soldier's Memoirs,* 256.
1. *Domestic Armored Vehicles: Twentieth Century*, 1: 17.
2. *Encyclopedia of German Tanks of World War Two*, 261.
3. *Domestic Armored Vehicles: Twentieth Century*, 1: 17. In 1934 the USSR produced 3,556 tanks of all kinds and modifications; in 1935: 2,994; in 1936: 3,905; in 1937: 1,558; in 1938: 2,270; in 1939: 3,034.
4. *Krasnaya Zvezda*, January 17, 1998.
5. *Domestic Armored Vehicles: Twentieth Century*, 1: 17.
6. "Military and Numeric Composition of the Armed Forces of the USSR," 241.
7. *Krasnaya Zvezda*, January 17, 1998.
8. J. F. Milsom, *Russian BT Series* (Surrey, England: Profile Publications, Ltd., 1971).
9. M. Bariatinsky and M. Kolomiets, *Light Tanks BT-2 and BT-5* (Moscow: Modelist-Constructor, 1996), 16; M. Bariatinsky and M. Kolomiets, *Light Tank BT-7* (Moscow: Modelist-Constructor, 1996), 15; M. Pavlov, I. Zheltov, and I. Pavlov, *Domestic Armored Vehicles* (Moscow: Hobby Kniga, 2002), 182.
10. Pavlov, Zheltov, and Pavlov, *Domestic Armored Vehicles*, 182.
11. Meltiukhov, *Stalin's Missed Opportunity*, 525.
12. *Voyna I Revolutsia* [War and Revolution], September-October, 1934.
13. In October 1939, the 6th Armored Brigade (more than 250 BT tanks, commanded by Colonel M. P. Pavelkin) rode from Khalkhin-Gol to Urukhan covering a distance of 670 km. The ride was conducted with tracks removed and the tanks moving on wheels. It took thirty-nine operational hours for the ride to be completed, covering 150 km per 24-hour period on average. The brigade was awarded the Red Banner Order. It shows how impetuous and dangerous BT tanks could have been in breaking through an enemy's territory in case of a sudden blitzkrieg kind of war.

14. *Complete World Encyclopedia of Tanks, 1915–2000* (Minsk: Harvest, 1999), 123–24. For the first time in world history a truly amphibious tank was designed and built by the British firm Vickers-Armstrong in 1931. The vehicle was designated as the Vickers-Carden-Lloyd (A-4) and was considered a progenitor of all the amphibious tanks. It was never added to the British armored forces arsenal. Single units of this tank were sold to China, Japan, the Netherlands, and Thailand. This is another example of how the West did not use the great achievements of its designers, while the Soviet Union was able to appreciate and exploit these products.

15. *British and American Tanks of World War II* (New York: ARCO, 1969), 11.

16. S. Fedoseev, *Japanese Armored Vehicles, 1939–1945* (Moscow: Bronecollectsia, 1995), 20–23.

17. A. V. Karpenko, *Review of National Armor-Tank Technology, 1905–1995* (St. Petersburg: Nevskiy Bastion, 1996), 194.

18. Ibid., 200.

19. "Military and Numerical Composition," 241.

20. Shmelev, *The Tank's History*, 77.

21. Karpenko, *Review of National Armor-Tank Technology*, 189.

Chapter 11

Epigraph: *VIZh*, no. 1 (1969): 62

1. V. N. Shunkov, *Red Army's Weapons* (Minsk: Harvest, 1999), 287–88, 297.

2. A. Kesselring, *Gedanken zum Zweiten Weltkrieg* [Thoughts on World War II] (Bonn: 1956), 78.

3. Shavrov, *The History of Aircraft Design in the USSR, 1938–1950*, 45.

4. N. T. Gordiukov and D. B. Khazanov, *Close-Range Bomber Su-2* (Moscow: Technika-Molodiozhi, 2000), 63–64.

5. Shavrov, *The History of Aircraft Design in the USSR, 1938–1950*, 50.

6. L. M. Kuzmina, *Chief Designer Pavel Sukhoy* (Moscow: Molodaya Gvardia, 1983), 57.

7. D. Horikoshi, M. Okumia, and M. Kaidin, *Zero! Japanese Aviation in the Second World War* (Moscow: AST, 1999), 453.

8. In the spring of 1941, the more powerful Ju-87D-1 went into production. It was equipped with the 1,500-hp motor. Armaments: two wing-mounted machine guns (or two wing 20-mm cannons) plus dual machine guns to defend the rear hemisphere. Bomb payload: nominal—1,000 kg, maximum—1,800 kg.

9. E. Middeldorf, *Tactics in the Russian Campaign* [in Russian], (Moscow: Voyenizdat, 1958), 225.

10. *Krasnaya Zvezda*, December 15, 1992.

Chapter 12

Epigraph: Halder, *War Diary*, entry from July 17, 1941.

1. E. Chernikov, *Armored Ground Attack Aircraft (Shtumovik) IL-2* (Moscow, 1997), 46. Two types of under-wing mount: either 8 RS-82, or 4 RS-82 and 4 RS-132.

2. Ibid., 14.

3. Shavrov, *The History of Aircraft Design in the USSR, 1938–1950*, 263.

4. A. N. Medved and D. B. Khazanov, *Dive Bomber Pe-2* (Moscow: Exprint, 1999), part 1, 16.

5. M. N. Kozhevnikov, *Command and Staff of the Air Forces of the Soviet Army in the Great Patriotic War* (Moscow: Nauka, 1977), 16.

6. *USSR Aircraft Industry, 1917–1945* (Moscow: TSAGI, 1992–1994), 2: 41, 235.

7. *The Great Patriotic War, 1941–1945: Military History Essays* (Moscow: Nauka, 1998), 1: 113; O. Groehler, *Geschichte des Luftkriegs, 1910 bis 1980* [History of Aerial Warfare, 1910–1980] (Berlin, 1981).

8. *Das Deutsche Reich und der Zweite Weltkrieg* [The German Reich and World War II] (Stuttgart: Deutsche Verlags-Anstalt, 1979), 5/1: 555.

9. Groehler, *Geschichte des Luftkriegs*. The majority of historians accept the data provided by German scholar O. Groehler as the most reliable—Hitler deployed against the USSR 3,520 planes, including 945 bombers, 400 dive-bombers and ground attackers (inclusive of sixty ground attack planes from the II.(Sch)/LG2 (formation number), 1,036 single-engine fighters, 93 two-engine fighters, 120 long-range

reconnaissance aircraft integrated into air fleets, 252 transport aircraft, 674 forward-based aircraft (the majority of which were range-reconnaissance aircraft). Hereby, if we would count bombers and fighters of all kinds, we will have 2,474 combat aircraft, that is, aircraft designed to destroy the enemy in air and on land.

10. M. V. Zefirov, *Ground-Attack Aircraft of the Luftwaffe* (Moscow: AST, 2001), 37. The maximum speed of the Hs-123A-1 was 338 km/h.

11. V. R. Kotelnikov, "Flagship of Stalin's Falcons," *Aviatsia i Vremia*, no. 4 (1997). As of June 22, 1941, the Soviet air force had in its ranks 516 TB-3 (Heavy Bomber-3) plus 25 TB-3 within Soviet Naval Aviation, for a total of 541 aircraft.

12. V. B. Shavrov, *The History of Aircraft Design in the USSR before 1938* (Moscow: Mashino-stroyenie, 1985), 488.

13. If one were to compare the Ju-87B-1 with the SB 1941, with M-105P engines.

14. *Luftwaffe's Wings: Combat Aircraft of the Third Reich* (part 4) (Moscow: TsAGI, 1995), 41.

15. Mikhail Maslov, *Fighter I-16* (Moscow: Armada, 1997), 33.

16. A. Price, *World War II Fighter Conflict* (London: Macdonald and Jane's, 1975), 18–21.

17. Maslov, *Fighter I-16*, 77.

18. V. Romanov, *Messerschmitt Bf.109* (Moscow: Exprint, 1994), 29.

19. Maslov, *Fighter I-16*, 40.

20. Maslov, *Fighter I-16*, 33.

21. "The Early Period of the War," *Voyna I Revolutsia*, no. 9 (1929): 19–20.

22. *Posev*, June 17, 1951.

Chapter 13

Epigraph: Colonel A. I. Rodimtsev, speech at the Eighteenth Congress of the Communist Party, 1939.

1. *Voennyi Vestnik* [Military Herald], no. 4 (1940): 76–77.

2. *Field Rules of the Red Army for 1936 (PU-36)*, Article 7.

3. *VIZh*, no. 10 (1982): 75.

4. The Communist Party Archive of the Institute of Party History, Central Committee of the Communist Party of the Ukraine, Fund 7, Index 1, Case 1330, Sheet 32.

5. Deputy Commander of the Air Force Lieutenant General K. Kurochkin, in *VIZh*, no. 8 (1980): 94.

6. *VIZh*, no. 9 (1975): 81.

7. *Moscow Military District* (Moscow: Moskovski Rabochi, 1985), 177.

8. *The Year 1941* (Moscow: International Foundation "Demokratia," 1998), 2: 104–106. Decree of the Central Committee of the ACP (b) and the Council of the People's Commissars "Regarding New Units of the Red Army," no. 1112–459cc, April 23, 1941.

9. *Soviet Air Assault Troops* (Moscow: Voyenizdat, 1986), 51. Here is the structure of the air assault corps at the end of May 1941: 1st Air Assault Corps: Major General M. A. Usenko, brigades 1, 204, 211 (Kiev military district); 2nd Air Assault Corps: Major General F. M. Kharitonov, brigades 2, 3, 4 (Kharkov military district); 3rd Air Assault Corps: Major General V. A. Glazunov, brigades 5, 6, 212 (Odessa); 4th Air Assault Corps: Major General A. S. Zhadov, brigades 7, 8, 214 (Pukhovichi, Byelorussia); 5th Air Assault Corps: Major General I. S. Bezuglyi, brigades 9, 10, 201 (Daugavpils, Latvia); the 202nd Air Assault Brigade remained independent. The corps were fully manned by June 1, 1941.

10. A. I. Rodimtzev, *Motherland, These Are Your Sons* (Kiev: Politizdat, 1982), 162.

11. I. G. Starchak, *From the Sky into the Battle: Memoirs of the Chief of Paratroopers of the Western Front* (Moscow: Voyenizdat, 1965).

12. A. S. Zhadov, *Four Years of War* (Moscow: Voyenizdat, 1978), 14.

13. Here is the structure of these corps in August 1941: 6th Air Assault Corps: Major General A. I. Pastrevich, brigades 11, 12, 13 (Moscow district); 7th Corps: Major General I. I. Gubarevich, brigades 14, 15, 16 (Povolzhie); 8th Corps: Major General V. A. Glazkov, brigades 17, 18, 19 (Moscow district); 9th Corps: Major General M. I. Denissenko, brigades 20, 21, 22 (Ivanov district); 10th Corps: Colonel N. P. Ivanov, brigades 23, 24, 25 (Povolzhie, Gorokhovets camps).

14. *Encyclopedia of Aviation* (Moscow: Bol'shaja Rossijskaja Encyclopedia, 1994), 421.

15. The author of the idea to deploy tanks at the enemy's rear by using gliders' wings was the great American

designer Walter Christie. Back in the early 1930s he designed a draft of this concept. In the late 1930s Oleg Antonov borrowed the American idea and made it a reality. However, Antonov was too late by the time the war began. Besides, the war did not start the way Stalin had planned. A winged tank was flying in 1942, but nobody needed it in a defensive war.

16. *The Year 1941*, 2: 366–67. In 1941: land-based 5-seater gliders: 500; land-based 11-seater gliders: 1,000; 11-seater hydroplanes: 200; land-based 20-seater gliders: 300. Total for 1941: 2,000 units. Total for 1942: 5,500 units.

17. Index mark PS-84—passenger aircraft, factory #84. From September 17, 1942, the aircraft was named the Li-2 in honor of the engineer-in-chief of the factory, B. P. Lisunov.

18. *Aircraft Engineering in the USSR, 1917–1945* (Moscow: 1994), 2: 237.

19. *Aircraft Engineering in the USSR, 1917–1945*, 2: 236; *Aviatsia i Vremia (Aviation and Time)*, no. 1 (1998), 16. Decree of the Central Committee of the VKP(b) and the Council of the People's Commissars from April 23, 1941, Paragraph 4 says: "for the purpose of transportation of the airborne and air-landing troops, the heavy aircraft TB-7 and TB-3 shall be used, as well as the middle-size aircraft DB-3 and Douglas." With appropriate arrangements, the bombers DB-3 and DB-3F could be used to tow A-7 and G-11 gliders and to airdrop up to seven men. In 1939–41, 2,822 bombers of these types were built. By June 22, 1941, in the western regions of the USSR and under long-distance bombing command, 1,332 aircraft were deployed, 1,122 of them DB-3 and DB-3F.

20. Documents of the Red Army High Command, Officers' Conference, December 23–31, 1940.

21. *Airborne Operations*, ed. Philip, St. Croix, (London: Salamander, 1978), 30.

22. Rodimtzev, *Motherland, These Are Your Sons*, 29.

23. Zhadov, *Four Years of War*, 16.

24. The "Guards" designation of military units appeared in the Red Army in September of 1941 as a part of Stalin's overall change from internationalist ideology and rhetoric toward nationalist Russian patriotism, as a means of rallying people towards the defense of their Russian motherland and not the international Communist expansionist movement. "Guards" units in tsarist Russia were the select, privileged, best-trained, and most reliable units prior to 1917.

25. *Krasnaya Zvezda*, September 25, 2002.

26. Yury Nenakhov, *Airborne Troops in the Second World War* (Minsk: Harvest, 1998), 194. The "Guards" designation was awarded to all newly formed air assault rifle divisions in recognition of the feats of their predecessors in the 1941–42 campaigns and as an advance for their future military contribution.

Chapter 14

Epigraph: V. Rapoport, Yu. Alexeyev, *Betrayal of the Motherland: Essays on the History of the Red Army* [in Russian] (London: Overseas Publications Interchange Ltd., 1988).

1. *Questions of Strategy and Operational Art in Soviet Military Works, 1917–1940* (Moscow: Voyenizdat, 1965), 117.

2. M. Tukhachevski, *Selected Works in 2 Volumes* (Moscow: Voyenizdat, 1964).

3. Central Archive of the National Economy of the USSR, Fund 7297, Index 41, Case 9, Sheet 155.

4. *VIZh*, no. 3 (1999).

Chapter 15

1. Walther Schellenberg, *The Labyrinth: Memoirs of a German Intelligence Man* (Moscow: Dom Biruni, 1991).

2. *VIZh*, no. 1 (1993): 60–63.

3. O. F. Suvenirov, *The Tragedy of the RKKA* (Moscow: Terra, 1998).

4. F. W. von Mellentin, *Tank Battles, 1939–1941* (St.Petersburg: Poligon, 1998), 244.

5. G. I. Gerasimov, "The Effective Impact of the 1937–1938 Purges on the Commanding Personnel of the RKKA [Workers' and Peasants' Red Army]," *Russian Historical Journal*, no. 1 (1999).

6. J. Goebbels, *Diaries of 1945,* Smolensk: Rusich, 1998,

Chapter 16

Epigraph: Joseph Stalin, speech at a meeting of the Politburo of the Party Central Committee, August 19, 1939. (HAVAS News Agency, November 28, 1939).

1. M. Vodopianov, *Friends in the Sky* (Moscow: Sovetskaya Rossia, 1971), 147.
2. *Luftwaffe's Wings*, 20.
3. I. M. Maiski, *Spain, 1918–1972: A Historical Sketch* (Moscow: Nauka, 1975), 210.
4. *VIZh*, no. 7 (1986): 85.
5. *Istoricheskiy Arkhiv* [Historical Archive], no. 2 (1962): 172.
6. *VIZh*, no. 7 (1986): 87.
7. Roman Khrapachevskiy, "The Spanish Gold of the Kremlin," *Russkiy Focus*, no. 7 (May 14, 2001). By 1936, Spain's gold reserve was more than six hundred tons. When the military mutiny began, the major part of it was stored in the Bank of Spain cellars in Madrid. After consultations with Soviet representatives, the government of Spain approached Moscow with the request to "accept for storage" the gold of the Republic of Spain. The official reason for this was the threat of the mutineers' takeover of Madrid in October 1936. On October 15, prime minister Francisco Largo Caballero and treasury minister Juan Negrin approached the Soviet Government with the suggestion to "accept for storage" more than five hundred tons of gold. Stalin immediately ordered the evacuation of the Spanish gold reserve. Here is a quote from the minutes of the Politburo of the Central Committee of VKP(b) meeting from October 17, 1936: "Paragraph 56. Comrade Rosenberg's issue. Determination: To authorize Comrade Rosenberg to reply to the Spanish Government that we are ready to accept the gold reserve for storage, and that we approve the evacuation of this gold by our ships returning from [Spanish] ports." After the political decision was made the operation began in full swing: on October 20, the cable with the approval came to Spain, and by October 22–25 it was already loaded on Soviet ships in Cartagena. The total cargo was 510 tons of gold.
8. Ibid, no. 7 (1971): 77.
9. *History of the Second World War, 1939–1945*, 2: 55.
10. Ibid., 54.
11. A. P. Yaremchuk, *Russian Volunteers in Spain, 1936–1939* [in Russian] (San Francisco: Globus, 1983), 12.
12. N. N. Voronov became Chief Marshal of Artillery; F. A. Agaltsov became Marshal of Aviation, commander of long-range aviation, deputy commander of the Air Force; M. I. Nedelin became Chief Marshal of Artillery, deputy minister of defense of the USSR, and, from 1959, head commander of strategic missile forces; P. V. Rychagov became Lieutenant General, head of the Central Command of the Red Army's Air Force, deputy of the People's Commissar for Defense of the USSR; Kh. U. Mamsurov became Colonel General, first deputy of the GRU (Main Intelligence Directorate); P. P. Vechnyi became Lieutenant General, military aide to Stalin; I. I. Proskurov became Lieutenant General of the Air Force, chief of the GRU; P. I. Batov, D. G. Pavlov, V. Y. Kolpakchi, and N. G. Lyachenko became Generals of the Army; A. I. Rodimtzev, G. M. Shtern, M. S. Shumilov, V. A. Yushkevich, and T. T. Khrukin became Colonel Generals; V. A. Alafuzof became Admiral, chief of naval staff; N. E. Bassistyi became Admiral, commander of the Black Sea fleet, first deputy of the minister of the navy; A. G. Golovko became Admiral —during all of World War II he commanded the Northern fleet, after the war he became the chief of naval staff, deputy of the minister of the navy.
13. "National-revolutionary War of the Spanish People," *Voprosy Istorii* [Questions of History], no. 11 (1953): 11.
14. R. Ernest Dupuy and Trevor N. Dupuy, *World History of Wars* (St. Petersburg and Moscow: AST, 1998), 4: 41.
15. N. Voronov, *Serving in the Military* (Moscow: Voyenizdat, 1963), 80.
16. Leon Trotsky, *Bulleten Oppozitsii* [Bulletin of the Opposition] no. 71 (November 1938): 7.
17. Ibid., no. 79–80 (June 21, 1939): 13.
18. S. M. Krivoshein, *Warriors' Stories* (Moscow: Molodaya Gvardia, 1962), 8.

Chapter 17

First Epigraph: Ogonek, no. 30 (1989): 10.
Second Epigraph: A. Avtorkhanov, *Origins of Partocracy (Party-rule)* (Frankfurt: Posev, 1973), 356.
1. *Pravda*, June 1, 1939.
2. Maslov, *Fighter I-16*, 19–20.

3. *Mezhdunarodnaya Zhizn* [International Affairs], no. 3 (1959): 157.
4. *VIZh*, no. 12 (1963): 25.
5. *VIZh*, no. 5 (1989): 35.
6. *VIZh*, no. 6 (1991): 11.
7. Ingeborg Fleischhauer, *The Pact: Hitler, Stalin and the German Diplomatic Initiative, 1938–39* (Moscow: Progress, 1990), 237–38; G. L. Rozanov, *Stalin-Hitler: The Documented Story of the Soviet-German Diplomatic Relationship in 1939–41* (Moscow: Mezhdunarodnyie Otnoshenia, 1991), 84–86. This decision was presented in the form of a telegram, sent by Molotov to the Soviet chargé d'affaires in Germany, Gheorghy Astakhov. He received the message on Saturday, August 12. The same day the telegram's content was conveyed to Hitler, who at that moment was negotiating with the Italian foreign minister Count Ciano. After some deliberation, Hitler told the following to the Italian minister about the telegram in the following way: "The Russians have agreed with the decision to send a German representative to Moscow to conduct political negotiations." Ciano himself left the following entry: "Russian-German contacts are developing very favorably and, specifically, several days ago came the Russian invitation to send a German plenipotentiary representative to Moscow to negotiate a Friendship Pact."
8. On August 19, 1939, Stalin gave an order to the Soviet Trade Mission in Berlin (not a direct one, of course) to immediately sign the Trade and Economic Agreement, which had been ready for a long time. The same day Stalin, via Molotov, told Schulenburg that Ribbentrop might arrive in Moscow on August 26–27. Later, Hitler tearfully begged to move Ribbentrop's visit to Moscow to August 23.
9. Lev Bezymenskiy, *Hitler and Stalin before the Fight* (Moscow: Veche, 2000), 290; A. O. Chubarian, ed., *War and Politics, 1939–1941* (Moscow: Nauka, 1999), 38, 97.
10. Hitler, *Mein Kampf*, pt. 2, chap. XIV.

Chapter 18

Epigraph: Antonov-Ovseenko, *Portrait of a Tyrant*, 296.
1. Yury Felshtinsky, ed., *It Must Be Published: USSR-Germany 1939–1941, Documents and Materials* (Moscow: Moscow Worker, 1991), 90.

Chapter 19

Epigraph: Halder, *War Diary, 1939–1942*, entry from June 23, 1941.
1. *Soviet Military Encyclopedia*, 8: 353.
2. B. Muller-Hillebrand, *Germany's Ground Forces 1933–1945* (Moscow: EKSMO, 2002), 1: 157.
3. *Krasnaya Zvezda*, August 18, 1993.
4. The main strike forces in the breakthrough of the Japanese defense lines in the August 20 offensive were the excellent twin-engine bombers SB, totaling 181 aircraft. Besides these, several squadrons of TB-3 heavy bombers were used. They bombed the Japanese positions from an altitude of 1,500 to 2,000 meters. All together, twenty-three heavy bombers were deployed.
5. Basil Henry Liddell Hart, *Strategy: The Indirect Approach* (Moscow: Innostrannaya Literatura, 1957), 314.

Chapter 20

Epigraph: Boris Shaposhnikov, *The Army's Brain* (Moscow-Leningrad: Voyengiz, 1927–29), 413.
1. *VIZh*, no. 6 (1976). 68.
2. Yakovlev, *Life's Task*, 498.
3. Dmitry F. Ustinov, *In the Name of Victory* (Moscow: Voyenizdat, 1988), 91.
4. G. K. Zhukov, *Memoirs and Reflections* (Moscow: APN, 1969), 296.
5. *VIZh*, no. 2 (1962).
6. K. A. Meretskov, *In Service to the People* (Moscow: Politizdat, 1968), 181.
7. Yakovlev, *Life's Task*, 212.
8. *Pravda* (September 3, 1939). The draft age of eighteen years was established for those who had graduated from high school. Mostly they were drafted into military schools (roughly equivalent to officer training schools)—willing or not.
9. "Operational and total strength of the USSR Armed Forces during the Great Patriotic War (1941–

1945)," *Statistical Digest*, no. 1 (June 22, 1941), (Moscow: Military History Institute, Ministry of Defense of the Russian Federation, 1994),10–12; *50 Years of the Soviet Armed Forces* (Moscow: Voyenizdat, 1968), 201; *History of the Second World War, 1939–1945*, 2: 199–202, 3: 418–19, 4: 18; *The Great Patriotic War, 1941–1945: Military History Essays*, 1: 89; *The Great Patriotic War, 1941–1945: Encyclopedia* (Moscow: Sovetskaya Encyclopedia, 1985), 311; Meltiukhov, *Stalin's Missed Opportunity*, 292–95, 360.

10. The USSR Armed Forces' strength by June 22, 1941, was 5,762,000, including the Red Army—5,081,000, navy—344,000, and interior troops and border guards—337,000. The numerical increase of the Red Army in 1939–41 was not a straightforward process of constant growth. Before Germany attacked the USSR, the Red Army reached its highest numbers not by June 22, 1941, but by September 20, 1939. By September 20, 1939, the Red Army—without the navy, interior troops, and border guards—numbered 5,289,400 men (in comparison to 5,081,000 by June 22, 1941). Here is how it happened: On the night of September 7, 1939, a decision was made to execute a partial mobilization of the Red Army. The troops were given the order to start a "Big Training Call-up" (BUS). Under the People's Commissar Decree No. 2/1/50698 of May 20, 1939, the acronym BUS was a coded signal for the covert mobilization. BUS with an "A" designation meant deployment of individual units with the operational readiness date of up to ten days with their support elements reaching war-level strength. The mobilization was supposed to be executed with the maximum secrecy. All together, at the beginning of the "Big Training Call-up" were involved: headquarters of twenty-two rifle, five cavalry, and three tank corps; ninety-eight rifle and fourteen cavalry divisions; twenty-eight tank and three mechanized rifle/machine-gun; and one airborne brigade, deployed in seven military districts. In total, 2,610,136 men were drafted. Under the Presidium of the Supreme Soviet and People's Commissar of Defense Decree No.177 of September 23, they were declared mobilized until a "special instruction." At the same time, under the Council of People's Commissars of USSR Decree No. 1348-268cc from September 1939, a new military draft was supposed to start from September 5 to reinforce the troops in the Far East region, plus one thousand men for each newly formed division, and from September 15 to reinforce the troops in the rest of the military districts. Besides, under the new law regarding the universal military duty, the call-up period was extended by one year for 190,000 soldiers who were drafted in 1939. As a result, by September 20, 1940, the Red Army's strength reached 5 million men. It was clear evidence of Stalin's insecurity about Great Britain and France's reaction to the Soviet invasion into Poland. Although he did everything possible to make Soviet actions not look like assistance to Hitler, there was a reason to be concerned that, after declaring war on Germany, London and Paris were going to declare war on the USSR as well. Once the intentions of the Western powers became clear, the Red Army began to deflate its swollen ranks, which had been prepared for a big war. A total of 1,613,803 men were retired from the Red Army from September 29 to January 7, 1940. However, when the war with Finland began it required that the Red Army's losses be replenished and its strength boosted. On December 28, 1939, a decision was made to call up to the Red Army 546,400 men to reinforce the troops in the western military districts, as well as fifty thousand reserve officers. In the same time, in the Volga, Ural, and Siberian Military Districts 375,000 young men of five junior conscription ages were drafted. After the war with Finland was over, the Red Army started to decrease its ranks again, and reached its minimum strength by September 1, 1940: 3,423, 499 men. Afterwards, the Red Army's ranks started to increase again.

11. *VIZh*, no. 3 (1999): 10.

Chapter 21

Epigraph: Colonel S. A. Vauphsassov, *At a Troublesome Crossroads: A Chekist's Memoirs* (Moscow: Politizdat, 1971), 203.

1. *VIZh*, no. 7 (1982): 55.

2. Anthony Sutton, *National Suicide: Military Aid to the Soviet Union* (New Rochelle, NY: Arlington House, 1973), 152–53. According to the opinion of the American historian Anthony Sutton, the German delegation transferred to the Soviet Union blueprints of the most successful German submarine designs in June of 1926. The German V-III–class submarine was "the most successful design of all, ever produced." In Sutton's opinion, the Soviet Schuka-class submarine is based exactly on the

German V-III design, and the S-class is based on the German VII-class design. Sergei Gorlov, *Top Secret: The Moscow-Berlin Alliance, 1923–1933* (Moscow: Olma-Press, 2001), 264. In the opinion of the Soviet scientist S. A. Gorlov: "It is, of course, difficult to imagine that Soviet shipbuilding, from which in German professional opinion 'nothing could be learned,' all of a sudden could develop several promising types of submarines. Even though such ship designers as B. M. Malinin, A. N. Krylov, V. P. Kostenko, and others were naturally gifted talents, it is doubtful that they would have ignored such outstanding completed designs and other specific German assistance."

3. A. B. Shirokorad, *Ships and Cutters of the USSR Navy, 1939–1945* (catalog) (Minsk: Harvest, 2002), 241. The following details are of interest: the construction of the ship commenced on January 11, 1937, in Livorno—in other words, at a time when Soviet and Italian "volunteers" were killing each other in Spain. The acceptance act was signed on April 18, 1939, after the unarmed ship, camouflaged as a merchant vessel and manned by an Italian crew, departed for Odessa, where it arrived on May 5, 1939.

4. M. M. Kirian, ed., *Military-Technological Progress and the USSR Armed Forces* (Moscow: Voyenizdat, 1982), 189.

5. *The Great Patriotic War, 1941–1945: Encyclopedia*, 409.

6. *History of the Second World War, 1939–1945*, 2: 190.

7. *VIZh*, no. 5 (1980): 71.

8. N. A. Voznessensky, *War Economics of the USSR during the Period of the Great Patriotic War* (Moscow: Gospolitizdat, 1947), 42.

9. Muller-Hillebrand, *German Ground Forces, 1933–1945*.

10. Ibid., 1: 161.

11. Ibid., 3: 50–51.

12. Several armies that were created for the purpose of attack were officially called "shock" armies from 1942. But the term was unofficially used from the mid-1920s in Soviet military theoretical works. These armies were better equipped than the ordinary ones.

13. Boris V. Sokolov, *The Cost of Victory (Great Patriotic: The Unknown About the Known)* (Moscow: Moskovskiy Rabochiy, 1991), 64–66. The losses of explosives and ammunition production capacities were exceptionally high, one could even say catastrophic. The Soviet Union could not fight Hitler with the remaining 15 percent capacity. That is why, from the beginning of the talks on the Lend-Lease supplies, Stalin and his representatives were asking first of all for the explosives and powder to be sent. From mid-1941 to mid-1945, the production of explosives in the USSR came to 600,000 tons. R. H. Jones, *The Roads to Russia: United States Lend-Lease to the Soviet Union* (Norman, Oklahoma: University of Oklahoma Press, 1969), appendixes. The United States supplied 295,600 tons of explosives. *Soviet Foreign Policy in the Period of the Great Patriotic War* (Moscow: Gospolitizdat, 1946), 145–47. Additionally, Great Britain and Canada delivered 22,300 tons of powder. Therefore, Western deliveries of explosives reached 53 percent of the total volume of Soviet production. Also, the delivery of American equipment for the production of bombs, shells, and ammunition played a tremendous role in the course of the war. Specifically, in June of 1942, the most modern equipment for the daily production of 10 million 7.62-mm rounds (3.5 billion rounds a year) was delivered. Without this truly crucial assistance, the shell and round shortage that struck the Red Army in the fall of 1941 would not have been overcome.

Chapter 22

Epigraph: Jan Gamarnik, Chief of the Political Directorate of the Red Army, in a speech given at a meeting of the National Committee for Defense of the USSR on March 15, 1937.

1. *The Winter War, 1939–1940: A Political History* (Moscow: Nauka, 1998), 1: 118–26.

2. N. L. Volkovski, ed., *Secrets and Lessons of the Winter War, 1939–1940* (St. Petersburg: Poligon, 2000), 141–44; Boris V. Sokolov, *Secrets of the Finnish War* (Moscow: Veche, 2000), 63–70. The 106th Rifles Division was organized in accordance with the October 25, 1939, order of the USSR Defense Commissar. Shortly before the beginning of the war, the division was reorganized as a special corps with the same number, although at that time the Red Army rifle corps were numbered only up to fifty-six. The commander of the corps was Division Commander A. M. Anttila. On November 23, the corps was renamed as the 1st Alpine Rifle Corps of the Finnish People's Army. It was staffed with the Finns

and Karelians that lived in the Leningrad military district. By the beginning of the war Anttila's corps, which consisted of two twin regimental divisions, numbered 13,405 personnel. However, there were not enough Finns and Karelians; therefore many Russians and Ukrainians, especially officers, were entered in the roster as Finns and Karelians. For example, the corps' chief of staff, Brigade Commander F. N. Romanov, was named "Raikas," and the headquarters' political department chief, Regimental Commissar V. P. Tereshkin, was called "Tervonen."

3. Volkovski, *Secrets and Lessons of the Winter War, 1939–1940*, 138. Kuusinen's wife, Aino, was imprisoned in jails and camps from 1938 until 1955.

4. "Diplomatic Note of the USSR Government, handed to the Envoy of Finland, concerning provocative shelling of Soviet troops by Finnish Military Units," *Izvestia* (November 27, 1939.

5. *Soviet Military Encyclopedia*, 7: 419.

6. G. F. Krivosheev, ed., *Russia and the USSR in the Twentieth-Century Wars: Armed Forces Losses (A Statistical Study)* (Moscow: Olma Press, 2001), 213.

7. *The Winter War, 1939–40*, 2: 53.

8. L. Rendulic, *Commanding the Troops* (Moscow: Voyenizdat, 1974), 189.

9. Shunkov, *Red Army's Weapons*, 230–31; *The Great Patriotic War, 1941–1945: Encyclopedia*, 516. The weight of the B-4 type concrete piercing shell from the 1939 203-mm howitzer was 100 kg.

10. In theory, a 203-mm howitzer did have a normal firing speed of one shell per minute, but in the difficult conditions of the Finnish winter, the real firing speed was lower.

11. *The Winter War, 1939–40*, 2: 222.

12. Ibid., 239.

13. *Admissions and Revelations: Nazi Leaders on the Third Reich's War against the USSR: Secret Speeches, Diaries, Memoirs* (Smolensk, Russia: Rusich, 2000), 195–96, 199.

14. Ibid., 195.

15. *The Winter War, 1939–40*, 1: 376.

16. Piker, *Hitler's Table Talks*, 205.

Chapter 23

Epigraph: Halder, *War Diary*, entry for June 30, 1941.

1. Albert Speer, *Memoirs* (Smolensk, Russia: Russich, 1997), 312–13.

2. N. V. Alisov and B. S. Khorev, *Economic and Social Geography of the World* (Moscow: Gardariki, 2001), 448; *History of the Second World War, 1939–1945*, 3: 282. Thirty percent of the German metallurgical industry's demand for iron ore was supplied by Sweden.

3. *The Red Banner Baltic Fleet in the Battle for Leningrad* (Moscow: Nauka, 1973), 8.

4. *VIZh*, no. 3 (1973): 78.

5. F. Ruge, *War on the Sea, 1939–1945* (Moscow: Voyenizdat, 1957), 209.

6. "Testimony of the Admiral of the Soviet Union Fleet, I. S. Isaakov," *Znamia* [Banner], no. 5 (1988): 77.

7. *The Great Patriotic War, 1941–1945: Encyclopedia*, 75.

8. *VIZh*, no. 4 (1962): 34.

9. *The Warpath of the Soviet Navy* (Moscow: Voyenizdat, 1974), 537.

10. Piker, *Hitler's Table Talks*, 348 (entry made on June 5, 1942).

11. *History of the Second World War, 1939–1945*, 4: 329.

12. *The Year 1941*, 1: 418–23.

Chapter 24

Epigraph: Piker, *Hitler's Table Talks*, 303.

1. *History of the Second World War, 1939–1945*, 3: 231–32.

2. Ibid., 10: 17.

3. Piker, *Hitler's Table Talks*, 477 (entry made on June 27, 1942).

4. *The Molotov-Ribbentrop Pact and Its Consequences for Bessarabia: A Collection of Documents* (Chişinău, Moldova: 1991), 51.

5. *Foreign Affairs Documents: 1940–22 June 1941* (Moscow: Mezhdunarodnye Otnoshenia, 1998), 23: 1: 519–20.

6. Ya. T. Eiduss, *Liquid Fuel in War* (Moscow: Akademizdat, 1943), 74–75.
7. Halder, *War Diary*, 2: 534, 536, 574; entries of May 19 and 20, and June 13, 1941.
8. Muller-Hillebrand, *German Ground Forces, 1933–1945*, 3: 67.

Chapter 25

Epigraph: Joseph Stalin, *Pravda*, February 5, 1931.
1. I. G. Starinov, *Mines Await Their Hour* (Moscow: Voyenizdat, 1964), 176.
2. Ibid., 186.
3. One can argue that Hitler's invasion was launched not only from Eastern Prussia and Poland, but from Finland, Hungary, and Romania as well. This is true. However, the USSR and Hungary did not share a common border. It was the Red Army who reached the Hungarian border as a result of the "Liberation March" in September 1939. As a result Hitler was handed an opportunity to attack from that nation's territory, which he did in 1941. Before 1941 there were no major German military units in Romania and Finland. They were deployed there because of Stalin's aggression against these countries. In order to protect themselves against Stalin, the Romanian and Finnish governments allowed German troops to use their territory.
4. Order of National Commissar of Defense no. 400, November 7, 1940. It was published the same day in *Pravda, Krasnaya Zvezda*, and other Soviet newspapers.
5. Stalin's speech at a meeting of the Executive Committee of the Comintern, January 22, 1926, published in *Pravda*, February 18, 1926.
6. Stalin, *Pravda*, September 15, 1927.
7. *Pravda*, March 2, 1936.
8. *Pravda*, May 14, 1939.
9. *Pravda*, August 18, 1940.
10. Krivoshein, *Warriors' Stories*, 8.
11. *Pravda*, January 1, 1941.
12. *Pravda*, March 4, 1941.

Chapter 26

Epigraph: Quoted in Starinov, *Mines Await their Hour*, 179.
1. Ibid., 18.
2. Ibid., 22.
3. Ibid., 175.
4. Meretskov, *In Service to the People*, 184.
5. L. M. Sandalov, *The Bygone* (Moscow: Voyenizdat, 1966), 99.
6. *Krasnaya Zvezda*, September 15, 1984.
7. Zhukov, *Memoirs and Reflections*, 207.
8. *Kievsky Krasnoznamennyii: History of the Krasnoznamennyii Kiev Military District, 1919–1972* (Moscow: Voyenizdat, 1974), 147.
9. Ibid., 143.
10. *Soviet Military Forces* (Moscow: Voyenizdat, 1978), 255.
11. K. S. Moskalenko, *In the Southwestern Direction: A Commander's Memoirs* (Moscow: Nauka, 1969), 24.

Chapter 27

Epigraph: Russian Center for the Archiving and Study of Modern History, Holding 88, Register 1, Dossier 898, Folio 21.
1. V. I. Boyarskiy, *The Guerilla War: A History of Lost Opportunities* (Minsk: Harvest; Moscow: ACT, 2001), 60.
2. Starinov, *Mines Await Their Hour*, 40.
3. P. K. Ponomarenko, *VIZh*, no. 1 (1962).
4. Although he was an ethnic Lithuanian, and in Lithuanian his last name is spelled "Vaupsas," in official documents and historic literature his name was Russified: "Vaupshassov."

5. S. A. Vaupshassov, *At a Troublesome Crossroads: A Chekist's Memoirs* (Moscow: Politizdat, 1971), 203.

Chapter 28

Epigraph: P. G. Grigorenko, *You Only Meet Rats in the Underground* (New York, NY: Detinets, 1981), 140. Grigorenko participated in building the "Stalin Line."

1. *Krasnaya Zvezda*, September 8, 1990.
2. "Red corner": a special room for Communist indoctrination.
3. *Krasnaya Zvezda*, February 25, 1983.
4. Grigorenko, *You Only Meet Rats in the Underground*, 140.
5. R. G. Umanskyi, *On the Threshold of War* (Moscow: Voyenizdat, 1960), 35.
6. A. I. Shebunin, *How Much Ground Have We Covered . . .* (Moscow: Voyenizdat, 1971), 58.
7. *VIZh*, no. 12 (1987): 48.
8. *VIZh*, no. 9 (1961): 120.
9. *VIZh*, no. 7 (1961): 101; *VIZh*, no. 2 (1963): 12.
10. *VIZh*, no. 7 (1961): 101.
11. V. A. Anfilov, *The Immortal Feat of Arms: The Investigation of the Eve of and the First Stage of the Great Patriotic War* (Moscow: Nauka, 1971), 162.
12. Grigorenko, *You Only Meet Rats in the Underground*, 141.
13. Voronov, *Serving in the Military*, 172.
14. *Voprosy Istorii* [Questions of History], no. 5 (1970): 33.
15. L. M. Sandalov, *The First Days of the War* (Moscow: Voyenizdat, 1989), 45.
16. V. F. Zotov, *On the Northwestern Front, 1941–1943: A Collection of Articles by Participants in Military Engagements* (Moscow: Nauka, 1969), 175.
17. *VIZh*, no. 5 (1976): 91.
18. *USSR Border Forces, 1939–June 1941: A Collection of Documents* (Moscow: Nauka, 1970), Documents 287, 344.
19. Zhukov, *Memoirs and Reflections*, 161.
20. K. Mallory and A. Ottar, *Architecture of Aggression* (London: Architectural Press, 1973), 123.

Chapter 29

Epigraph: *Bulleten Oppozitsii* [Bulletin of Opposition], nos. 79–80 (September 1939), 14.

1. Y. Felshtinsky, *Criminal Leaders* (Moscow: Terra, 1999), 290. Lenin spent the last period of his life in isolation, as organized by Stalin. On December 18, 1922, the Central Committee of the Communist Party issued a decree that "charged Comrade Stalin with personal responsibility for the isolation of Vladimir Ilyich from both personal contacts with employees and correspondence." Stalin controlled everything: security, feeding, and medical "treatment." Lenin was allowed to read only what Stalin permitted. Everything that Lenin wrote was given to Stalin. Actually, Stalin's physicians did not allow Lenin to write much because of "concern" for his health.
2. Bazhanov, *Memoirs of a Former Secretary of Stalin*, 141.
3. Ibid., 91.
4. *Bulleten Oppozitsii* [Bulletin of Opposition], nos. 25–26 (November–December, 1931), 11.
5. Ibid., no. 35 (July 1933), 15.
6. Ibid., nos. 79–80 (September 1939).
7. *Foreign Policy Archive of the Russian Federation*, Fund 059, Index 1, Case 2314, Sheets 32–33.
8. Ibid., Storage 059, List 1, File 2315, Sheet 35–35a.
9. *It Must Be Published: USSR-Germany 1939–1941*, 112.
10. *Foreign Affairs Documents: 1940–22 June 1941*, 21: 2: 61–62.
11. *It Must Be Published: USSR-Germany 1939–1941*, 112.
12. Ibid., 115.
13. Ibid., 125.
14. Foreign Policy Archive of the Russian Federation, Fund 059, Index 1, Case 2315, Sheet 35.
15. *Foreign Affairs Documents: 1940–22 June 1941*, 21: 2: 136–37.
16. *The Year 1941*, 1: 418–23.
17. Basil Henry Liddell Hart, *The Second World War* (Moscow: Voyenizdat, 1976), 145.

Chapter 30

Epigraph: General G. K. Zhukov, lecture given at a conference of the High Command of the Red Army, December 26, 1940.

1. *On the Eve of the War: Documents of the Red Army High Command Officers' Conference, December 23–31, 1940,* 153–54
2. Zhukov, *Memoirs and Reflections*, 191.
3. *On the Eve of the War,* 177.
4. Ibid., 255.
5. Ibid., 209–10.
6. Ibid., 210.
7. Ibid., 350.
8. *VIZh*, no. 12 (1986): 41.
9. *On the Eve of War,* 388–89.
10. *VIZh*, no. 2 (1992): 22.
11. *VIZh*, no. 1 (1990): 58.
12. Zolotarev, *Krasnaya Zvezda*, December 27, 1990.

Chapter 31

Epigraph: Field Statute of the Red Army, 1939, article 6.

1. Shirokorad, *Ships and Cutters of the USSR Navy, 1939–1945*, 741–46, 778–82. The most powerful coastal monitors were of the Udarny and Zhelezniakov classes, with 252.5 tons' and 263 tons' displacement and maximum armor of 12 mm and 30 mm, respectively. The Udarny class was armed with two 130-mm B-7 type cannon systems, 2 × 2 45-mm 41K type turrets, and 4 × 4 7.62-mm M-4 machine gun systems. The Zhelezniakov class was armed with: 2 × 1 102/45-mm B-18 type turrets, 2 × 1 45/46-mm 41K type turrets, 1 × 4 7.62-mm M-4 machine guns, and four 7.62-mm M-1 machine guns.
2. Shirokorad, *Ships and Cutters of the USSR Navy, 1939–1945*, 778–88; *The Great Patriotic War, 1941–1945: Encyclopedia*, 255; A. Vakhmut, "First Days of War on the Danube," *VIZh*, no. 9 (1970). The Danube flotilla also included a special rifle company, the 17th Machine Gun Company, the 46th Special Anti-aircraft Artillery Battalion, a Danube shore defense sector consisting of six batteries of different calibers, and the 96th Fighter Squadron.
3. Stalin's political report speech to the Central Committee of VKP 9(b) during the Twenty-fifth Congress of the Communist Party, on December 3, 1927.
4. *The Year 1941*, 1: 377. Hitler expressed himself most clearly and completely in the course of his meeting with Molotov on November 13, 1940.
5. You can find the full text of this document in the book *Russian Archive, Great Patriotic General Headquarters: Documents and Materials, 1941* (Moscow: Terra, 1996), 16: 56–57, "HQ Directive #00226 to the Southern Front Commander, to counterstrike and reinforce defenses on the Prut River." To be precise, it was Directive #00226 from the General Headquarters. Stalin was a member of Headquarters, and General Timoshenko was the chairman. Directive #00226 was signed by Zhukov. Stalin, of course, was the real head of the Headquarters.
6. Zhukov, *Memoirs and Reflections*, 225.
7. Shirokorad, *Ships and Cutters of the USSR Navy, 1939–1945*, 741–56.
8. The construction of the Dnepr-Bug canal started back in 1775. After ten years, this artificial waterway was officially commissioned as the Royal Canal; then it was abandoned. The restoration of the canal started in 1837, with the main work conducted in 1846–48. From 1851, the canal served as the shortest route between Eastern Europe and the Rhine-Atlantic waterway system. In 1918 and 1920, it was completely abandoned once again. In 1940, the canal was restored and rebuilt: its dimensions were brought to a level acceptable to the river-sea class combined navigation vessels. The total length of the canal was combined from the channeled part of the Pina River (74 km), the canal waterway (58 km), and the channeled part of the Mukhavets River (64 km).
9. *VIZh*, no. 7 (1984): 68.
10. A. V. Basov, *The Navy in the Great Patriotic War, 1941–1945* (Moscow: Nauka, 1980), 138.
11. I. I. Azarov, *Odessa under Siege* (Moscow: Voyenizdat, 1962), 3–8.

Chapter 32

Epigraph: *Voennyi Vestnik*, no. 4 (1940): 76–77.

1. Meltiukhov, *Stalin's Missed Opportunity*, 535.
2. *VIZh.*
3. *VIZh*, no. 10 (1972): 83.
4. Meltiukhov, *Stalin's Missed Opportunity*.
5. In accordance with Soviet military theory, a special designation was assigned to the armies that were re-inforced and intended for rapid advance in the main strategic direction. This designation only appeared in Soviet military nomenclature in 1930 and was internal. In 1941, the designation became open and was used in identifying armies. Although the 9th Army was not officially called "Shock," it was equally equipped, staffed, and trained to qualify as a "shock" army. See note for chapter 21.
6. On September 16, 1939, the Cavalry Army Group of the Kiev Special Military District (under the command of II-degree *Komandarm* I. V. Tiulenev) was renamed the Kamenets-Podolsk Group; on September 20 it was rechristened as the Southern Group, and starting September 24 it became the 12th Army.
7. *Soviet Military Encyclopedia*, 8: 181.
8. Marshal I. Bagramian, *VIZh*, no. 1 (1967): 54.
9. Zhukov, *Memoirs and Reflections*, 224.
10. *The Year 1941*, 2: 104–6. The Central Committee of the VKP (b) and the Council of People's Commissars Decree, "Regarding creation of new units of the Red Army # 1112-459cc" of April 23, 1941, Paragraph 2-B: "Convert 10 Rifle Divisions into Mountain Rifle Divisions."
11. *Krasnaya Zvezda*, November 1, 1986.
12. See for example Lieutenant-General Bagrat Arushunyan, *VIZh*, no. 6 (1973): 61.
13. *VIZh*, no. 1 (1976): 55.

Chapter 33

Epigraph: *Soviet-Nazi Relations, 1939: Documents and Materials on the Soviet-German Relations in April–September 1939* (Paris and New York: Tretia Volna, 1983), 326.

1. *Stalin's Politburo in the 1930s: A Collection of Documents* (Moscow: AIRO-XX, 1995), Document #17; *Izvestia*, May 7, 1941. Until recently it was widely assumed that it happened on May 6, when the Presidium of the Supreme Soviet of the USSR issued a decree regarding the appointment of Joseph I. Stalin as the Chairman of the People's Commissars Council. However, the appropriate decision of the Politburo of the Central Committee of the VKP (b) was made on May 4. Stalin's appointment as the Chief of Government was justified in this top-secret decision by the "tense present-day international situation." In the non-classified section of the Supreme Soviet of the USSR Decree concerning Stalin's appointment there was no justification for it—Stalin simply filled a vacant position. According to the Presidium's Decree, Molotov was relieved of his duty as chairman of the People's Commissars Council because he repeatedly complained about the difficulty of combining two positions—that of the Chief of Government and the Foreign Affairs People's Commissar.
2. *VIZh*, no. 9 (1965): 66.
3. A. Avtorkhanov, *The Mystery of Stalin's Death* (Frankfurt: Possev, 1976), 132.
4. I. Bagramian, *This Is How the War Began* (Moscow: Voyenizdat, 1971), 62. The explanation offered by Marshal of the Soviet Union Ivan Bagramian completely matches the opinion of Soviet historians: "In May the international situation remained tense. The Soviet Union was preparing to rebut. This is exactly how we in the military district HQ had interpreted Stalin's appointment as the Chairman of the People's Commissars Council.
5. *Pravda*, May 6, 1941.
6. Russian Center for Storing and Studying Documents of Recent History, Fund 558, Index 1, Document 3808, Sheet 12.
7. Eduard Muratov, *Six Hours with Stalin at a Reception in the Kremlin* (St. Petersburg: Neva), no. 7 (1993): 285.
8. Stalin, report from March 10, 1939, at the Eighteenth Communist Party Congress.
9. *Pravda*, September 18, 1939.

10. *Pravda*, September 18, 1939.
11. *Pravda*, August 19, 1940.
12. *Pravda*, December 25, 1939.
13. *Pravda*, May 6, 1941, front-page article.

Chapter 34

Epigraph: Conquest, *The Great Terror*, 129.

1. *VIZh*, no. 6 (1995): 6.
2. Central Archive of the Defense Ministry of the Russian Federation, Fund 16, Index 2951, Case 261, Sheets 20–21.
3. Bagramian, *This Is How the War Began*, 64.
4. Ibid., 77.
5. I. I. Liudovnikov, *Across Storms: An Autobiographical Sketch* (Donetsk, Ukraine: Donbass, 1973), 24.
6. Moskalenko, *In the Southwestern Direction*, 19.
7. *Kievsky Krasnoznamennyii: History of the Krasnoznamennyii Kiev Military District, 1919–1972*, 162.
8. Zhukov, *Memoirs and Reflections*, 242.
9. K. K. Rokossovsky, *A Soldier's Duty* (Moscow: Voyenizdat, 1997), 8.
10. Central Archive of the Defense Ministry of the Russian Federation, Fund 16, Index 2951, Case 261, Sheets 20–21.
11. *VIZh*, no. 1 (1967): 62.
12. Central Archive of the Defense Ministry of the Russian Federation, Fund 16, Index 2951, Case 406, Sheets 109–19.
13. *Transport in the Great Patriotic War, 1941–45* (Moscow: Nauka, 1981), 41.
14. Central Archive of the Defense Ministry of the Russian Federation, Fund 208, Index 2511, Case 20, Sheet 128.
15. A. A. Lobachev, *Arduous Roads* (Moscow: Voyenizdat, 1960), 123.
16. *VIZh*, no. 4 (1978): 86.
17. Central Archive of the Defense Ministry of the Russian Federation, Fund 48, Index 3408, Case 14, Sheets 442–44.
18. *Soviet Military Encyclopedia*, 6: 517.
19. *VIZh*, no. 9 (1960): 56.
20. Sandalov, *The Bygone*, 71.
21. Meretskov, *In Service to the People*, 204.
22. *VIZh*, no. 6 (1961): 6.
23. *Voprosy Istorii* [Questions of History], no. 5 (1970): 45.
24. A. I. Eremenko, *In the Beginning of War* (Moscow: Nauka, 1964), 109.
25. V. F. Zotov, in *On the Northwestern Front, 1941–1943*, ed. P. A. Zhilin (Moscow: Nauka, 1969), 172.
26. S. F. Khvaley, in *On the Northwestern Front, 1941–1943*, 310.
27. *VIZh*, no. 6 (1986): 75
28. P. P. Poluboyarov, in *On the Northwestern Front, 1941–1943*, 114.
29. I. A. Khizenko, *The Pages that Came Alive: Diary of a Political Officer of the 80th Lenin Rifle Division* (Moscow: Voyenizdat, 1963), 5.
30. Major General Vasilyi Ivanovich Prokhorov was commander of the 80th Rifle Division of the 37th Rifle Regiment.
31. I. I. Fediuninskiy, *Called up to Alarm* (Moscow: Voyenizdat, 1964), 12.
32. A. Grylev, V. Khvostov, *Communist*, no. 12 (1968): 68.
33. *VIZh*, no. 4 (1961): 80.
34. *Krasnoznamennyi Uralsky: History of the Ural Military District* (Moscow: Voyenizdat, 1983), 104.
35. Serghei M. Shtemenko, *The Soviet General Staff at War, 1941–1945* (Moscow: Voyenizdat, 1968), 30.
36. S. P. Ivanov, *The Early Stage of the War* (Moscow: Voyenizdat, 1974), 211.
37. G. D. Plaskov, *Artillery Thunder* (Moscow: Voyenizdat, 1974), 125.
38. Ozerov, *Tupolev's Sharaga*, 90.
39. *Krasnoznamennyi Byelorussian Military District* (Minsk: Belorus, 1973), 88.

40. *Estonian People in the Great Patriotic War of the Soviet Union, 1941–1945* (Tallinn: Eesti raamat, 1973), 1: 43.

41. Ibid.

42. L. M. Sandalov, *On the Moscow Direction* (Moscow: Nauka, 1970), 63.

43. V. A. Anfilov, *The Path that Led to the Tragedy of 1941* (Moscow: Akopov, 1997), 219–20.

44. *Command and HQ of the Soviet Army in the Great Patriotic War, 1941–1945*, ed. M.N. Kozhevnikov, (Moscow: Nauka, 1977), 41.

45. *VIZh*, no. 1 (1969): 61.

46. *Battle for Leningrad, 1941–1944* (Moscow: Voyenizdat, 1964), 22.

47. *Krasnaya Zvezda*, April 28, 1985.

48. G. A. Kumanev, *Soviet Railroad Personnel during the Years of the Great Patriotic War, 1941–1945* (Moscow: AN SSSR, 1963), 36.

49. *VIZh*, no. 5 (1980): 71.

50. *The Rear of the Soviet Armed Forces in the Great Patriotic War, 1941–1945* (Moscow: Voyenizdat, 1977), 59.

51. Ibid., 173.

52. I. V. Boldin, *The Pages of My Life* (Moscow: Voyenizdat, 1961), 92.

53. S.P. Ivanov, *The Early Stage of the War*, 211.

54. *VIZh*, no. 9 (1960): 56.

55. *VIZh*, no. 6 (1962): 77.

56. *VIZh*, no. 9 (1966): 66.

57. M. I. Kazakov, *Reflections over Maps of Former Battlefields* (Moscow: Voyenizdat, 1971), 64.

Chapter 35

1. *The Year 1941*, 2: 112.

2. Ibid., 2: 151.

3. *It Must Be Published*, 167.

4. Yakovlev, *Life's Task*, 252.

5. "High-frequency lines": Encoded communication equipment.

6. *Voprosy Istorii* [Questions of History], no. 5 (1970): 42.

7. Vassilevsky, *Life's Mission*, 119.

8. These seven armies were (RC is rifle corps, MC is mechanized corps, RD is rifle division, TD is tank division): the 16th Army (32nd RC, 5th MC, 57th TD), the 19th Army (25th and 34th RC—the latter had five divisions, 26th MC, 38th RD), the 20th Army (61st and 69th RC, 7th MC, 18th RD), the 21st Army (63rd and 66th RC, 25th MC), the 22nd Army (51st and 62nd RC), the 24th Army (52nd and 53rd RC, 23rd MC), and the 28th Army (30th and 33rd RC, 69th MC).

9. V. Khvostov and Major General A. Grylov, *Communist*, no. 12 (1968): 68.

10. *History of the Second World War, 1939–1945*, 3: 352.

Chapter 36

1. *History of the Second World War, 1939–1945*, 4: 27.

2. *Krasnoznamennyi Byelorussian Military District* (Minsk: Belorus:, 1973), 84.

3. Sandalov, *On Moscow Direction*, 41.

4. Ibid.

5. "On the Eve of the War: Documents of the Conference of the Supreme Command of the Red Army, December 23–31, 1940," in *The Russian Archive: the Great Patriotic War* (Moscow: Terra, 1993), 12: 1: 34.

6. Ibid., 12: 1: 40–41.

7. I. Bagramian, *VIZh*, no. 1 (1976): 62.

8. Moskalenko, *In the Southwestern Direction*, 18.

9. *VIZh*, no. 4 (1984): 42.

10. V. Sikorsky, *The Future War* (Moscow: Voyenizdat, 1936), 240.

11. *Voyna I Revolutsia* [War and Revolution], no. 8 (1931): 11.
12. *The Rear of the Soviet Armed Forces in the Great Patriotic War, 1941–1945*, 33.
13. *VIZh*, no. 12 (1972): 46
14. *VIZh*, no. 10 (1971): 13.
15. Ivanov, *The Early Stage of the War*, 206.
16. S. A. Kalinin, *Reflections on the Past* (Moscow: Voyenizdat, 1963), 124.
17. *VIZh*, no. 7 (1979): 43.
18. Stalin, *Collected Works*, 5: 225.
19. F. A. Kalinin, *Thoughts about the Past* (Moscow: Voyenizdat, 1963), 182.
20. The ChK (*Chrezvychainaia Comissia*, or Extraordinary Commission) was a precursor of the NKVD. "Chekist" to this day means a member of the political police.

Chapter 37

Epigraph: Liddell Hart, *Strategy: The Indirect Approach*, 336.
1. *Krasnaya Zvezda*, October 27, 1992.
2. Makhmut Gareev, in the collection of articles titled *Courage* (Moscow, 1991), 253.
3. *Krasnaya Zvezda*, July 27, 1991.

Chapter 38

Epigraph: F. Chuev, *Molotov*, 48.
1. Nikolai G. Kuznetsov, *On the Eve of . . .* (Moscow: Voyenizdat, 1966), 321.
2. Peter Chamberlain and Chris Ellis, *British and American Tanks of World War II* (New York: ARCO, 1969), 66.
3. Winston Churchill, *The Second World War* (Moscow: Terra, 1998), 3: 80. The losses of the British merchant and navy fleets (in imperial tons, where 1 imperial ton is equal to 1.016 metric ton) were as follows: January—320,000, February—402,000, March —537,000, April—654,000, May—500,000, June—431,000.
4. *Foreign Affairs Documents, 1940–22 June 1941*, 21: 2: 739. A warning about a possible German attack came from the British government only on June 16, 1941. British ambassador Cripps was not in Moscow and the warning about the possible German invasion was handed to the Soviet ambassador in London, Maisky, who immediately transmitted the message to Molotov in Moscow. Here is the beginning of this quite long message: "Today, Cadogan, upon Eden's directive, provided me with more detailed information about the concentration of German troops at the Soviet border. . . . Total number of German troops presently concentrated at the Soviet borders, according to British General Headquarters data, is eighty divisions in Poland, thirty in Romania, and five in Finland and northern Norway, total 115 divisions, not counting the mobilized Romanian army." Further on, there was a detailed description of which German troops were at the border, and when and where they went. One notices the outstanding work of British intelligence, which reported absolutely precise data about the German invasion army. Now we know that by June 22, 1941, 125 divisions and two brigades were deployed in the first strategic echelon of the German invading army, in other words, along the Soviet borders. By mid-June, most likely, there were 115 divisions, as the message reported. Stalin did not believe this message, since all previous messages gave him reasons for doubt. Most importantly, however, Stalin, at that time, had his own plans for Germany.
5. Liddell Hart, *The Second World War*, 151.
6. L. Woodward, *British Foreign Policy in the Second World War* (London: HMSO, 1971–76), 611.

Chapter 39

Epigraph: Adolf Hitler, *Mein Kampf*, part 1, chapter VII, 164.
1. *Soviet Military Encyclopedia*, 5: 343.
2. Halder, War Diary, 2.
3. Ibid.
4. Muller-Hillebrand, *German Ground Forces*, 1933–1945, 2: 144.

5. Ibid., 267.
6. Liddell Hart, *The Second World War,* 152–53.
7. Ibid., 158.
8. *The Wehrmacht's Fateful Decisions,* 328.
9. Robert Goralski, *World War II Almanac* (New York: G. P. Putnam's Sons, 1981), 164.
10. *History of the Second World War, 1939–1945,* 3: 328.
11. Rendulic, *Commanding the Troops,* 60.
12. *Der Spiegel,* no. 6 (1996): 100–101.
13. Shirokorad, *The Genius of the Soviet Artillery,* 169–70.
14. Ibid., 169.

Chapter 40

1. *Krasnaya Zvezda,* December 23, 1989.
2. *Krasnaya Zvezda,* October 1, 1987.
3. *VIZh,* no. 4 (1992): 30.
4. *Krasnaya Zvezda,* August 21, 1986.
5. Ibid.
6. P. Stefanovsky, *Three Hundred Unknowns* (Moscow: Voyenizdat, 1968), 206.
7. *VIZh,* no. 6 (1976): 62.
8. *Ogonek,* no. 17 (1965).
9. *Comsomol'skaya Pravda,* October 8, 1968.
10. *The Year 1941,* 1: 780.
11. *VIZh,* no. 6 (1966): 8.
12. Hermann Hoth, *Tank Operations* (Smolensk, Russia: Rusich, 1999), 34.
13. Guderian, *A Soldier's Memoirs,* 191.
14. Blumentritt, *The Wehrmacht's Fateful Decisions,* 76.

Chapter 41

Epigraph: Hitler's radio address on the occasion of launching the Winter Assistance campaign on October 3, 1941.
1. G. N. Zakharov, *The Fighters' Story* (Moscow: DOSAAF, 1977), 43.
2. Hans-Ulrich Rudel, "Stuka Pilot," in *Bombs Away!* (Moscow: AST, 2002), 30, 35.
3. Anfilov, *The Immortal Feat of Arms,* 517.
4. *History of the Great Patriotic War of the Soviet Union, 1941–1945* (Moscow: Voyenizdat, 1960–65), 1: 441.
5. Major General M. Gretsov, *VIZh,* no. 9 (1965): 84.
6. Basov, *The Navy in the Great Patriotic War, 1941–1945,* 117.
7. Order of the commander of the Baltic fleet, from June 22, 1941.
8. *Soviet Military Encyclopedia,* 8: 356.
9. M. Solonin, *June 25: Stupidity or Aggression?* (Moscow: Yauza-EXMO, 2008), 442.
10. Ibid., 443.
11. A. B. Shirokorad, *Russia's Northern Wars* (Moscow: AST; Minsk: Harvest, 2001), 702.
12. *The Battle for the Soviet Baltic* (Tallinn, Estonia: Eesti raamat, 1980), 67.
13. Central Archive of the Defense Ministry of the Russian Federation, Fund 181, Index 1631, Case 1, Sheet 128.
14. *VIZh,* no. 5 (1986): 49.
15. Piker, *Hitler's Table Talks,* 303.
16. *Otechestvennaya Istoria* [History of the Motherland], no. 4 (1993): 26.
17. *Petermanns geographischen Mitteilungen* (Germany, 1943), vols. 9, 10.
18. *VIZh,* no. 10 (1992): 82.
19. *VIZh,* no. 12 (1970): 22.
20. *Literaturnaya Gazeta* [Literary Gazette], August 20, 2002.
21. A. B. Zubov, *Continent,* no. 84 (1995).

Chapter 42

Epigraph: Winston Churchill, Parliamentory Debates, House of Commons Official Report, September 8, 1942.

1. Anastas I. Mikoyan, *The Way It Was: Reflections on the Past* (Moscow: Vagrius, 1999), 380.
2. Hitler, *Mein Kampf*, Part 2, Ch. XIII, 542.
3. Mikoyan, *The Way It Was*, 391.

Chapter 43

Epigraph: Hoth, *Panzer Operations*, 163.

1. *Novoe Russkoe Slovo* [New Russian Word], May 20, 1990.
2. Ibid., 95.
3. Halder, *War Diary,* 3: 259–60.
4. Ibid., 263.
5. Ibid., 297–98.
6. Ibid., 328.
7. *VIZh*, no. 7 (1991): 9
8. Halder, *War Diary*, 3: 344.
9. Piker, *Hitler's Table Talks*, 331.
10. Ibid., 332.
11. Ibid., 173.

Chapter 44

Epigraph: Vladimir I. Lenin, *The Military Program of the Proletarian Revolution* (Zurich: Jugend-Internationale, 1917), vols. 9, 10.

1. G. A. Deborin, *The Second World War* (Moscow: Voyenizdat, 1958), 108.
2. *International Policy of the USSR: A Compilation of Documents*, 4: 550.
3. *History of the Second World War, 1939–1945*, 3: 274.
4. *Admissions and Revelations*, 266.
5. *History of the Great Patriotic War of the Soviet Union, 1941–1945*, 1: 400.
6. *History of the Second World War, 1939–1945*, 3: 355.
7. Y. Gal'perin, "The Third Front," *Vesti*, June 19, 1997.
8. Ibid.
9. *Correspondence of the Chairman of Council of Ministers of the USSR with the President of the USA and the Prime Minister of Great Britain during the Great Patriotic War, 1941–1945* (Moscow: Politizdat, 1989), 2: 49.
10. Joseph V. Stalin, *On the Great Patriotic War of the Soviet Union* (Moscow: Politizdat, 1947), 166.
11. *VIZh*, no. 10 (1975): 60; Vassilevsky, *Life's Mission*, 499.
12. Vassilevsky, *Life's Mission*, 502.
13. *Soviet Military Encyclopedia*, 2: 27.
14. *Krasnaya Zvezda*, March 16, 2000.
15. Vassilevsky, *Life's Mission*, 502.
16. Central Archive of the Defense Ministry of the Russian Federation, Fund 326, Index 5047, Case 701, Sheets 1–99.
17. Ibid., Fund 14-A, Index 272, Case 19, Sheets 5–20.
18. Ibid., Fund 35, Index 11287, Case 1417, Sheet 134.
19. Ibid., Fund 6 BAC (Bomber Aviation Corps, Index 541971, Case 1, Sheets 1–4; Fund 7 BAC, Index 555981, Case 1, Sheets 1–3.
20. *VIZh*, no. 8 (1985): 16.
21. *The USSR's Victory in the War with Militarist Japan and Post-war Development of Eastern and South-Eastern Asia* (Moscow: Nauka, 1977), 47.
22. *VIZh*, no. 38 (1985): 43.
23. Ibid., 44.
24. Vassilevsky, *Life's Mission*, 507.

25. *History of the Second World War, 1939–1945*, 11: 197.

26. Ibid., 11: 196.

27. *Krasnaya Zvezda*, September 26, 2000.

28. *VIZh*, no. 8 (1985): 16.

29. *History of the Second World War, 1939–1945*, 11: 195.

30. Ibid.

31. Ibid., 196.

32. Central Archive of the Defense Ministry of the Russian Federation, Fund 210, Index 3116, Case 294, Sheet 70.

33. *Krasnaya Zvezda*, August 5, 1995.

34. *VIZh*, no. 6 (1986): 18.

35. *Krasnaya Zvezda*, September 1, 2000.

36. *Suddenness in Offensive Operations of the Great Patriotic War* (Moscow: Nauka, 1986), 51.

37. *VIZh*, no. 8 (1975): 19.

38. *VIZh*, no. 8 (1971): 68.

39. *Krasnaya Zvezda,* September 26, 2000.

40. Declaration of the Soviet leadership on August 8, 1945.

41. General I. Tretyak, *VIZh*, no. 8 (1985): 12.

42. *Krasnaya Zvezda*, September 26, 2000.

43. Ivanov, *The Beginning Period of the War*, 281.

44. Colonel A. S. Savin, *VIZh*, no. 8 (1985): 56.

45. *Communist*, no. 12 (1985): 85

46. Joseph Stalin, speech at the Eighteenth Communist Party Congress, March 10, 1939.

47. *Soviet Tank Troops, 1941–1945* (Moscow: Voyenizdat, 1973), 308.

48. *Krasnaya Zvezda*, August 5, 1995.

49. Von Mellentin, *Tank Battles, 1939–1945* (St. Petersburg: Poligon, 1998), 249.

50. *VIZh*, no. 8 (1975): 25.

51. *VIZh*, no. 38 (1985): 45.

52. *VIZh*, no. 10 (1975): 70, 73.

53. *Soviet Military Encyclopedia*, 2: 27.

Conclusion

Epigraph: Nikita Khrushchev, at a Kremlin reception for foreign diplomats and journalists, November 1956.

1. *The Year 1941*, 1: 377.

2. Ibid., 383.

3. Formally, besides the USSR, two more countries expanded their borders as a result of World War II: Yugoslavia and Poland. Yugoslavia got a significant chunk of land—practically the whole Istri (with the exception of Trieste), and Zadar (Zara). Poland's borders moved westward, while a wide swath of Polish territory in the east was seized by the USSR. The size of the territory Poland acquired in the west is quite comparable to that lost in the east. On the other hand, in 1945 both Poland and Yugoslavia were loyal satellites of the Soviet Union. It was expected that in the near future both nations would become a part of the USSR. Thus, one way or another, in terms of territorial expansion, Stalin benefited from World War II.

4. *The Soviet Union on the International Conferences during the Great Patriotic War 1941–1945*, vol. 6, "Berlin (Potsdam) Conference of the Three Leaders of the Allied Powers—USSR, USA, and Great Britain (July 17–August 2, 1945)" (Moscow: Politizdat, 1984), 131–34, 310–11.

5. Ibid., 149.

6. Ibid.

7. *Krasnaya Zvezda*, April 27, 2002.

8. *Krasnaya Zvezda*, December 22, 1999.

Bibliography

50 Years of the Soviet Armed Forces. Moscow: Voyenizdat, 1968.

Admissions and Revelations: Nazi Leaders on the Third Reich's War against the USSR: Secret Speeches, Diaries, Memoirs. Smolensk, Russia: Rusich, 2000.

Aircraft Engineering in the USSR, 1917–1945. Moscow: Tsagi, 1994.

Alisov, N. V., and B. S. Khorev. *Economic and Social Geography of the World.* Moscow: Gardariki, 2001.

Anfilov, V. A. *The Immortal Feat of Arms.* Moscow: Nauka, 1971.

———. *The Path that Led to the Tragedy of 1941.* Moscow: Akopov, 1997.

Antonov-Ovseenko, A. V. *Portrait of a Tyrant* [in Russian]. New York: Khronika, 1980.

Aviatsia i Vremia [Aviation and Time] (periodical)

Avtorkhanov, A. *The Mystery of Stalin's Death* [in Russian]. Frankfurt: Posev, 1976.

———. *Origins of Partocracy (Party-rule)* [in Russian]. Frankfurt: Posev, 1973.

Azarov, I. I. *Odessa under Siege.* Moscow: Voyenizdat, 1962.

Bagramian, I. *This is How the War Began.* Moscow: Voyenizdat, 1971.

Bariatinsky, M. *Soviet Armor, 1939–1945.* Moscow: Bronecollectsia, 1998.

Bariatinsky, M. *Light Tanks BT-2 and BT-5.* Moscow: Modelist-Constructor, 1996.

———, and M. Kolomiets. *Light Tank BT-7.* Moscow: Modelist-Constructor, 1996.

———, and M. Pavlov. *Middle Tank T-28.* Moscow: Askold, 1993.

Basov, A. V. *The Navy in the Great Patriotic War, 1941–1945.* Moscow: Nauka, 1980.

Battle for Leningrad, 1941–1944. Moscow: Voyenizdat, 1964.

The Battle for the Soviet Baltic. Tallinn, Estonia: Eesti raamat, 1980.

Bazhanov, Boris. *Memoirs of a Former Secretary of Stalin* [in Russian]. Paris: The Third Wave, 1980.

Bezymenskiy, Lev, *Hitler and Stalin before the Fight.* Moscow: Veche, 2000.

Boldin, I. V. *The Pages of My Life.* Moscow: Voyenizdat, 1961.

Boyarskiy, V. I. *The Guerilla War: A History of Lost Opportunities.* Minsk: Harvest; Moscow: AST (co-production), 2001

Brickhill, P. *The Dam Busters.* London: Evans Brothers, 1951.

British and American Tanks of World War II. New York: ARCO, 1984.

Bulleten Oppozitsii [Bulletin of Opposition] (periodical)

Chalmaev, V. *Malyshev.* Moscow: Molodaya Gvardia, 1978.

Chernikov, M. *Armored Ground Attack Aircraft (Shturmovik) IL-2.* Moscow: Armada, 1997.

Chubarian, A. O., ed. *War and Politics, 1939–1941.* Moscow: Nauka, 1999.

Chuev, Felix. *Molotov: Master of Half a Domain,* Moscow: Olma-Press, 2002.

Churchill, Winston. *The Second World War.* Moscow: Terra, 1998.

Combat Aircraft of the World. London: Ebury Press, 1969.

The Comintern and the Idea of the World Revolution: Documents. Moscow: Nauka, 1998.

Communist (periodical)

Complete World Aviation Encyclopedia. Samara, Russia: Korporatsia Fedorova, 1997.

Complete World Encyclopedia of Tanks, 1915–2000. Minsk: Harvest, 1999.

Comsomol'skaya Pravda (periodical)

Conquest, Robert. *The Great Terror* [in Russian]. Florence, Italy: Aurora, 1974.

Continent (periodical)

Correspondence of the Chairman of Council of Ministers of the USSR with the Presidents of USA and Prime Ministers of Great Britain during the Great Patriotic War, 1941–1945. Moscow: Politizdat, 1989.

Courage, collection of articles, Moscow, 1991.

Das Deutsche Reich und der Zweite Weltkrieg. Stuttgart: Deutsche Verlags-Anstalt, 1979.

Deborin, G. A. *The Second World War.* Moscow: Voyenizdat, 1958.

Der Spiegel (periodical)

Documents and Materials on the History of Soviet-Polish Relations. Moscow: Voyenizdat, 1964.

Domestic Armored Vehicles: Twentieth Century. Moscow: Exprint, 2002–5.

Drogovoz, I. G. *The Armored Sword of the USSR.* Moscow: Pedestal, 2001.

Dupuy, R. Ernest, and N. Trevor Dupuy. *World History of Wars,* 3 vols. St. Petersburg: Poligon, and Moscow: AST (co-production), 1997–98.

Eiduss, Ya. T. *Liquid Fuel in War.* Moscow: Akademizdat, 1943.

Eighth Congress of the Communist Party: Protocols. Moscow: Partizdat, 1959.

Encyclopedia of Aviation. Moscow: Bol'shaja Rossijskaja Encyclopedia, 1994.

Eremenko, A. I. *In the Beginning of War.* Moscow: Nauka, 1964.

Estonian People in the Great Patriotic War of the Soviet Union, 1941–1945, 2 vols. Tallinn: Eesti raamat, 1973–80.

Fediuninskiy, I. I. *Called up to Alarm.* Moscow: Voyenizdat, 1964.

Fedoseev, S. *Japanese Armored Vehicles, 1939–1945.* Moscow: Bronecollectsia, 1995.

Felshtinsky, Yu. *Criminal Leaders.* Moscow: Terra, 1999.

———, ed. *It Must Be Published: USSR–Germany 1939–1945, Documents and Materials.* Moscow: Moscow Worker, 1991.

Fest, Joachim. *Hitler: A Biography.* Perm, Russia: Alteya, 1993.

Fleischhauer, Ingeborg. *The Pact: Hitler, Stalin, and the German Diplomatic Initiative, 1938–39.* Moscow: Progress, 1990.

Foreign Affairs Documents: 1940–22 June 1941. Moscow: Mezhdunarodnye Otnoshenia, 1998.

Frossard, L.-O. *De Jaurès à Lénine: notes et souvenirs d'un militant.* Paris: Bibliothèque de documentation sociale, 1930.

Galitsky, K. *The Years of Hard Trials.* Moscow: Nauka, 1973.

Gallay, M. *Third Dimension.* Moscow: Sovetsky Pisatel, 1973.

Goralski, Robert. *World War II Almanac, 1931–1945.* New York: G. P. Putnam's Sons, 1981.

Gordiukov, N. T., and D. B. Khazanov. *Close-Range Bomber Su-2.* Moscow: Technika-Molodiozhi, 2000.

Gorlov, Sergei. *Top Secret: The Moscow-Berlin Alliance, 1923–1933.* Moscow: Olma-Press, 2001.

The Great Patriotic War, 1941–1945: Encyclopedia. Moscow: Sovetskaya Encyclopedia, 1985.

The Great Patriotic War, 1941–1945: Military History Essays, 2 vols. Moscow: Nauka, 1998.

Grigorenko, P. G. *You Only Meet Rats in the Underground* [in Russian]. New York: Detinets, 1981.

Groehler, O. *Geschichte des Luftkriegs 1910 bis 1980* [History of Aerial Warfare]. Berlin, 1981.

Guderian, Heinz. *Panzer Leader.* London: Futura, 1974.

———. *A Soldier's Memoirs.* Moscow: Voyenizdat, 1957.

Halder, Franz. *War Diary, 1939–1942,* 3 vols. Moscow: Voyenizdat, 1971.

History of Aircraft Design in the USSR (1938–1950). Moscow: Mashinostroyenie, 1988.

History of the Great Patriotic War of the Soviet Union, 1941–1945, 6 vols. Moscow: Voyenizdat, 1960–65.

History of the Second World War, 1939–1945, 12 vols. Moscow: Voyenizdat, 1973–82.

Hitler, Adolf. *Mein Kampf.* Russia (city not mentioned): T-OKO, 1992.

Horikoshi, D., M. Okumia, and M. Kaidin. *Zero! Japanese Aviation in the Second World War.* Moscow: AST, 1999.

Hoth, Hermann. *Tank Operations.* Smolensk, Russia: Rusich, 1999.

Innostrannaya Literatura [Foreign Literature] (periodical)

Interfax (periodical)

The Issues of Strategy and Operational Doctrine in Soviet Military Science, 1917–1940. Moscow: Voyenizdat, 1965.

Istoricheskiy Arkhiv [Historical Archive] (periodical)

Ivanov, S. P. *The Early Stage of the War.* Moscow: Voyenizdat, 1974.

Izvestia (periodical)

Jones, R. H. *The Roads to Russia: United States Lend-Lease to the Soviet Union.* Norman, Oklahoma: University of Oklahoma Press, 1969.

Kakurin, N., and B. Melikov. *Civil War in Russia: War with the White Poles.* Moscow: AST, 2002.

Kalinin, S. A. *Reflections on the Past.* Moscow: Voyenizdat, 1963.

Karpenko, A. V. *Review of National Armor-Tank Technology, 1905–1995.* St. Petersburg: Nevskiy Bastion, 1996.

Kazakov, M. I. *Reflections over Maps of Former Battlefields.* Moscow: Voyenizdat, 1971.

Kerber, L. *TU—Man and Airplane.* Moscow: Sovetskaya Rossia, 1973.

Kesselring, A. *Gedanken zum Zweiten Weltkrieg* [Recollections from World War II]. Bonn: 1955.

Khizenko, I. A. *The Pages that Came Alive: Diary of a Political Officer of the 80th Lenin Rifle Division.* Moscow: Voyenizdat, 1963.

Khrapachevskiy, Roman. "The Spanish Gold of Kremlin," *Russkiy Focus,* no. 7 (May 14, 2001).

Kievsky Krasnoznamennyi: History of the Kiev Military District, 1919–1972. Moscow: Voyenizdat, 1974.

Kirian, M. M., ed. *Military-Technological Progress and the USSR Armed Forces.* Moscow: Voyenizdat, 1982.

Kokurin, A., and M. Petrov, compilers. *GULAG: The Main [Prison] Camp Directorate. 1918–1960, Collection of Documents.* Moscow: International Fund "Democracy," 2000.

Kolpakidi, Alexander, and Dmitri Prokhorov. *Empire of the GRU: Sketches on the History of Russian Military Intelligence, Book One.* Moscow: Olma-Press, 2000.

Kosminkov, K, and D. Griniuk. *Stalin's Falcons.* St. Petersburg: Aeromuzei, 1992.

Kozhevnikov, M. N. *Command and Staff of the Air Forces of the Soviet Army in the Great Patriotic War* Moscow: Nauka, 1977.

Krasnaya Zvezda [Red Star] (periodical)

Krasnoznamennyi Byelorussian Military District. Minsk: Belorus, 1973.

Krasnoznamennyi Uralsky: History of the Ural Military District. Moscow: Voyenizdat, 1983.

Krivitsky, Walter. *I Was an Agent of Stalin.* Moscow: Terra, 1991.

Krivoshein, S. M. *Warrior's Stories.* Moscow: Molodaya Gvardia, 1962.

Krylia Rodiny [Wings of the Motherland] (periodical)

Kumanev, G. A. *Soviet Railroad Personnel during the Years of the Great Patriotic War, 1941–1945.* Moscow: AN SSSR, 1963.

Kuzmina. L. M. *Chief Designer Pavel Sukhoy.* Moscow: Molodaya Gvardia, 1983.

Kuznetsov, N. G. *On the Eve of . . .* Moscow: Voyenizdat, 1966.

Lapchinsky, Alexander. *The Air Army.* Moscow: Voyenizdat, 1939.

Lenin, Vladimir I. *Complete Collected Works.* Moscow: Politizdat, 1977.

Liddell Hart, Basil Henry. *The Second World War.* Moscow: Voyenizdat, 1976.

———. *Strategy: The Indirect Approach.* Moscow: Inostrannaya Literatura, 1957.

Literaturnaya Gazeta [Literary Gazette] (periodical)

Liudnikov, I. I. *Across Storms: An Autobiographical Sketch.* Donetsk: Donbass, 1973.

Lobachev, A. A. *Arduous Roads.* Moscow: Voyenizdat, 1960.

Luftwaffe's Wings: Combat Aircraft of the Third Reich. Moscow: TsAGI, 1995.

Maiski, I. M., ed. *Spain, 1918–1972: A Historical Sketch.* Moscow: Nauka. 1975.

Mallory, K., and A. Ottar. *Architecture of Aggression.* London: Architectural Press, 1973.

Maslov, M. *Fighter I-16.* Moscow: Armada, 1997.

Medved, A. N., and D. B. Khazanov. *Dive Bomber Pe-2.* Moscow: Exprint, 1999.

Meltiukhov, Mikhail. *Stalin's Missed Opportunity: The Soviet Union and the Fight for Europe, 1939–1941.* Moscow: Veche, 2002.

Mellentin, F. W. von. *Tank Battles, 1939–1941.* St.Petersburg: Poligon, 1998.

Meretskov, K. A. *In Service to the People.* Moscow: Politizdat, 1968.

Mezhdunarodnaya Zhizn [International Life] (periodical)

Mezhdunarodnye Otnosheniya [International Relations] (periodical)

Middeldorf, E. *Tactics in the Russian Campaign.* Moscow: Voyenizdat, 1958.

Mikoyan, Anastas. *The Way It Was: Reflections on the Past.* Moscow: Vagrius, 1999.

"Military and Numeric Composition of the Armed Forces of the USSR," *Statistical Almanac,* no. 1 (June 22, 1941). Moscow: Military History Institute of the Russian Federation Ministry of Defense, 1994.

Military Engagements. Moscow: Nauka, 1969.

Milsom, J. F. *Russian BT Series.* Surrey, England: Profile Publications Ltd., 1971.

Mir Aviatsii [The World of Aviation] (periodical)

The Molotov-Ribbentrop Pact and Its Consequences for Bessarabia: A Collection of Documents. Chişinău, Moldova, 1991.

Moscow Military District. Moscow: Moskovski Rabochi, 1985.

Moskalenko, K.S. *In the Southwestern Direction: A Commander's Memoirs.* Moscow: Nauka, 1969.

Muller-Hillebrand, B. *Germany's Ground Forces, 1933–1945.* Moscow: EKSMO, 2002.

Nemecek, Vaclav. *The History of Soviet Aircraft from 1918.* London: Willow Books, 1986.

Nenakhov, Yury. *Airborne Troops in the Second World War.* Minsk: Harvest, 1998.

Neva (periodical)

Novoe Russkoe Slovo [New Russian Word] (periodical)

Ogonek (periodical)

On the Eve of the War: Documents of the Red Army High Command Officers' Conference, December 23–31, 1940—The Russian Archive. Moscow: Terra, 1993.

Otechestvennaya Istoria [History of the Motherland] (periodical)

Ozerov, G. *Tupolev's Sharaga* [in Russian]. Frankfurt: Possev, 1971.

Patriotic War. Moscow: Nauka, 1977.

Pavlov, M., I. Zheltov, and I. Pavlov. *Domestic Armored Vehicles.* Moscow: Hobby Kniga, 2002.

Piker, Henry. *Hitler's Table Talks.* Smolensk (Russia): Rusich, 1998.

Plaskov, G. D. *Artillery Thunder.* Moscow: Voyenizdat, 1974.

Popova, S. G. "The World Gold Market and Issues of Gold Export Development in Russia." PhD diss., Russian Academy of International Trade, 1998.

Posev (periodical)

Pravda (periodical)

Price, A. *World War II Fighter Conflict.* London: Macdonald and Jane's, 1975.

The Rear of Soviet Armed Forces in the Great Patriotic War 1941–1945. Moscow: Voyenizdat, 1977.

The Red Banner Baltic Fleet in the Battle for Leningrad. Moscow: Nauka, 1973.

Rendulic, L. *Commanding the Troops.* Moscow: Voyenizdat, 1974.

Riabchikov, E., and A. Magid. *The Becoming.* Moscow: Znanie, 1978.

Rodimtzev, A. I. *Motherland, These Are Your Sons.* Kiev: Politizdat, 1982.

Rogovin, V. Z. *The Power and the Opposition (1928–1933).* Moscow: Zhurnal Teatr, 1993.

Rokossovsky, K. K. *Soldier's Duty.* Moscow: Voyenizdat, 1997.

Romanov, V. *Messerschmitt Bf.109.* Moscow: Exprint, 1994.

Rosenberg, Alfred. *Der Zukunftweg einer deutschen Aussenpolitik* [The Future of German Foreign Policy]. Munich, 1927.

Rossi, Jacques. *GULAG Directory.* London: OPI, 1987.

Rozanov, G. L. *Stalin-Hitler: The Documented Story of the Soviet-German Diplomatic Relationship in 1939–41.* Moscow: Mezhdunarodnyie Otnoshenia, 1991.

Ruge, F. *War on the Sea, 1939–1945.* Moscow: Voyenizdat, 1957.

Russia and the USSR in the Twentieth-Century Wars: Armed Forces Losses (A Statistical Study). Moscow: Olma-Press, 2001.

Russian Archive. Great Patriotic. General Headquarters. Documents and Materials. 1941. Moscow: Terra, 1996.

Russkiy Focus (periodical)

Sandalov, L. M. *The Bygone.* Moscow: Voyenizdat, 1966.

————. *The First Days of the War.* Moscow: Voyenizdat, 1989.

————. *On the Moscow Direction.* Moscow: Nauka, 1970.

Second Partial and First Consolidated Report on Russian Medium Tank T.34. Maryland: Aberdeen Proving Ground (archive), 1943.

Shaposhnikov, Boris. *The Army's Brain.* Moscow: Voyengiz, 1927.

Shavrov, V. B. *The History of Aircraft Design in the USSR before 1938.* Moscow: Mashinostroyenie, 1985.

————. *The History of Aircraft Design in the USSR, 1938–1950.* Moscow: Mashinostroyenie, 1988.

Shebunin, A. I. *How Much Ground Have We Covered . . .* Moscow: Voyenizdat, 1971.

Shirokorad, A. B. *The Genius of the Soviet Artillery: Grabin's Triumph and Tragedy.* Moscow: AST, 2002.

————. *Russia's Northern Wars.* Moscow: AST, and Minsk: Harvest, 2001 (co-production).

————. *Ships and Cutters of the USSR Navy, 1939–1945* (catalog). Minsk: Harvest, 2002.

Shmelev, I. *The Tank's History (1916–1996).* Moscow: Tekhnika Molodiozhi, 1996.

Shtemenko, S. M. *The Soviet General Staff at War, 1941–1945.* Moscow: Voyenizdat, 1968.

Shumikhin, V. S. *Soviet Military Aviation: 1917–1941.* Moscow: Nauka, 1986.

Shunkov, V. N. *Red Army's Weapons.* Minsk: Harvest, 1999.

Sikorsky, V. *The Future War.* Moscow: Voyenizdat, 1936.

Sokolov, Boris V. *The Cost of Victory (Great Patriotic: The Unknown About the Known).* Moscow: Moskovskiy Rabochiy, 1991.

————. *Secrets of the Finnish War.* Moscow: Veche, 2000.

Solonin, M. *June 25: Stupidity or Aggression?* Moscow: Yauza-EKSMO, 2008.

Soviet Air Assault Troops. Moscow: Voyenizdat, 1986.

The Soviet Army, ed. Liddell Hart, B. H. London: Weidenfield and Nicolson, 1956.

Soviet Foreign Policy in the Period of the Great Patriotic War. Moscow: Gospolitizdat, 1944–47.

Soviet Military Encyclopedia. Moscow: Voyenizdat, 1976.

Soviet Military Forces. Moscow: Voyenizdat, 1978.

Soviet Tank Troops, 1941–1945. Moscow: Voyenizdat, 1973.

The Soviet Union on the International Conferences during the Great Patriotic War 1941–1945, Volume VI, "Berlin (Potsdam) Conference of the Three Leaders of the Allied Powers—USSR, USA, and Great Britain (July 17–August 2, 1945)." Moscow: Politizdat, 1984.

Speer, Albert. *Memoirs.* Smolensk, Russia: Russich, 1997.

Stalin, Joseph. *Collected Works in 13 Volumes.* Moscow: Gospolitizdat, 1946.

————. *On the Great Patriotic War of the Soviet Union.* Moscow: Politizdat, 1947.

Starchak, I. G. *From the Sky into the Battle: Memoirs of the Chief of Paratroopers of the Western Front.* Moscow: Voyenizdat, 1965.

Starinov, I. G. *Mines Await Their Hour.* Moscow: Voyenizdat, 1964.

Stefanovsky, P. *Three Hundred Unknowns.* Moscow: Voyenizdat, 1968.

Suddenness in Offensive Operations of the Great Patriotic War. Moscow: Nauka, 1986.

Sutton, Anthony. *National Suicide: Military Aid to the Soviet Union.* New Rochelle, NY: Arlington House, 1973.

Trail in the Sky (Collected volume). Moscow: Politizdat, 1971.

Transport in the Great Patriotic War, 1941–45. Moscow: Nauka, 1981.

Tukhachevski, M. *Selected Works in 2 Volumes.* Moscow: Voyenizdat, 1964.

Tupolev's Aircraft ANT-1—ANT-15. Moscow: Tupolev ANTK, 1995.

Umansky, R. G. *On the Threshold of War.* Moscow: Voyenizdat, 1960.

Ural (periodical)

USSR Aircraft Industry, 1917–1945. Moscow: TSAGI, 1992–94.

USSR Border Forces, 1939—June 1941, a collection of documents. Moscow: Nauka, 1970.

The USSR's Victory in the War with Militarist Japan and Post-war Development of Eastern and South-Eastern Asia. Moscow: Nauka, 1977.

Ustinov, D. F. *In the Name of Victory.* Moscow: Voyenizdat, 1988.

Vassilevsky, A. M. *Life's Mission.* Moscow: Politizdat, 1973.

Vaupshassov, S. A. *At a Troublesome Crossroads: A Chekist's Memoirs.* Moscow: Politizdat, 1971.

Vesti (periodical)

Vodopianov, M. *Friends in the Sky*. Moscow: Sovetskaya Rossia, 1971.

Voenno-istoricheskiy Zhournal (VIZh) [Military History Journal] (periodical)

Voennyi Vestnik [Military Herald] (periodical)

Volkovski, N. L., ed. *Secrets and Lessons of the Winter War, 1939–1940*. St. Petersburg: Poligon, 2000.

Voprosy Istorii [Questions of History] (periodical)

Voronov, N. N. *Serving in the Military*. Moscow: Voyenizdat, 1963.

Voyna I Revolutsia [War and Revolution] (periodical)

Voznessensky, N. A. *War Economics of the USSR during the Period of the Great Patriotic War*. Moscow: Gospolitizdat, 1947.

The Warpath of the Soviet Navy. Moscow: Voyenizdat, 1974.

The Wehrmacht's Fateful Decisions. Moscow: Voyenizdat, 1974; Rostov-on-Don, Russia: Phenix, 1999.

The Winter War, 1939–40: A Political History. Moscow: Nauka, 1999.

Woodward, L. *British Foreign Policy in the Second World War*, 5 vols. London: HMSO (Her Majesty's Stationery Office), 1971–76.

World War II Almanac, 1931–1945. London: Hamish Hamilton, 1981.

World War II Warplanes, 1939–1945. Moscow: Libri, 1995.

Yakovlev, A. S. *Life's Task*. Moscow: Politizdat, 1973.

Yaremchuk, A. P. *Russian Volunteers in Spain, 1936–1939* [in Russian]. San Francisco: Globus, 1983.

The Year 1941, 2 vols. Moscow: International Foundation "Democracy," 1998.

Zakharov, G. N. *The Fighters' Story*. Moscow: DOSAAF, 1977.

Zaloga, Steven, and James Grandsen. *Soviet Heavy Tanks*. London: Osprey, 1981.

———. *Soviet Tanks and Combat Vehicles of World War Two*. London: Arms and Armour Press, 1984.

Zefirov, M.V. *Ground-Attack Aircraft of the Luftwaffe*. Moscow: AST, 2001.

Zhadov, A. S. *Four Years of War*. Moscow: Voyenizdat, 1978.

Zhukov, G. K. *Memoirs and Reflections*. Moscow: APN, 1969.

Znamia [Banner] (periodical)

Index

About the Author

Viktor Suvorov is the pen name of Vladimir Rezun, 61, who was born in the USSR. Suvorov is the author of eighteen books, including three works of fiction. His books have been published in more than thirty languages. In Russia and Poland they have sold more than a million copies. Suvorov was a Soviet Army officer who served in military intelligence (GRU). In 1978, when stationed in Geneva under cover as a Soviet diplomat, he defected with his wife and two young children to the United Kingdom, where he worked as an intelligence analyst and lecturer. He lives in hiding in England because he was sentenced to death by a Soviet military court, and today's Russia has refused to pardon him.